Chinese Culture of Intelligence

Keping Wang

Chinese Culture of Intelligence

Keping Wang
Chinese Academy of Social Sciences
Beijing, China

ISBN 978-981-13-3172-5   ISBN 978-981-13-3173-2 (eBook)
https://doi.org/10.1007/978-981-13-3173-2

Jointly published with Foreign Language Teaching and Research Publishing Co., Ltd., Beijing, China

The edition is not for sale in the mainland of China. Customers from the mainland of China please order the print book from: Foreign Language Teaching and Research Publishing Co., Ltd.

Library of Congress Control Number: 2018962907

© Foreign Language Teaching and Research Publishing Co., Ltd. This international edition is exclusively licensed to Springer Nature Singapore Pte Ltd. for worldwide distribution outside of China 2019
This work is subject to copyright. All rights are solely and exclusively licensed by the Publisher, whether the whole or part of the material is concerned, specifically the rights of translation, reprinting, reuse of illustrations, recitation, broadcasting, reproduction on microfilms or in any other physical way, and transmission or information storage and retrieval, electronic adaptation, computer software, or by similar or dissimilar methodology now known or hereafter developed.
The use of general descriptive names, registered names, trademarks, service marks, etc. in this publication does not imply, even in the absence of a specific statement, that such names are exempt from the relevant protective laws and regulations and therefore free for general use.
The publisher, the authors and the editors are safe to assume that the advice and information in this book are believed to be true and accurate at the date of publication. Neither the publisher nor the authors or the editors give a warranty, express or implied, with respect to the material contained herein or for any errors or omissions that may have been made. The publisher remains neutral with regard to jurisdictional claims in published maps and institutional affiliations.

Cover credit: Marina Lohrbach_shutterstock.com

This Palgrave Macmillan imprint is published by the registered company Springer Nature Singapore Pte Ltd.
The registered company address is: 152 Beach Road, #21-01/04 Gateway East, Singapore 189721, Singapore

Preface

The new millennium witnesses the rejuvenation or renaissance of China with her increasing impact in more areas across the world. Accordingly, there arise a number of such assumptions as China model, China erection, China collapse, and China threat. Observed and articulated from different angles for different purposes, they are all set out to be somewhat eye-catching, thought-provoking, anxiety-hatching, or fear-raising. In order to render these disputable and paradoxical scenarios more substantial and justifiable rather than sensational and confusing, a variety of approaches are called for to find out what really matters behind the Chinese way of thinking and doing from the past to the present. One of them, in my view, seems to be more fruitful than any others in a cognitive sense. It is based on Chinese culture of intelligence as is reasonably verified by virtue of my working contact with many colleagues from the West, and my teaching experience in some universities overseas. The core substance of such culture consists in Chinese ideals and philosophical ponderings, all preoccupied with the Way (*Dao*) of heaven and human, the expectation of ecumenism via harmonism, the virtue of sageliness within and kingliness without, the *telos* of keeping the country in peace and its people at ease, the humane governance through wise leadership, the rationale of appropriate inheritance and innovation, the theorem of character building through education, the approach to aesthetic contemplation, and so forth. This book is intended to have a second reflection on them with due consideration of their historical relevance to the human condition and the global issues at large.

Incidentally, what is noteworthy is the notion of *wen hua qua* culture in Chinese tradition. It is the shortened form of *ren wen jiao hua*. Originally it means to enlighten, cultivate, and moralize persons by means of education in rites and music (*li yue*) apart from the classics by ancient thinkers. As noted in early history, rites (*li*) used to stand for legal rules, social institutions, ceremonial rituals, and codes of conduct, which were designed and regulated to impose on personal cultivation and citizenship from without. Music was then a trinity of arts as it was integrated with poetry and dance. It would be performed in accord with rites and their specific requirements, and deployed to facilitate character building and human fulfillment from within. Naturally it was supposed to realize these teleological aims through joy-conscious recreation and appreciation as well.

This being the case, what Chinese culture (*wen hua*) implies is more corresponding to its Hellenic counterpart (*paideia*). It is by nature multi-dimensional and multi-functional. Say, it is related not only to the continuing evolution of philosophical, pedagogical, and artistic thoughts, but also to the historical sedimentation of social ethos, spiritual pursuit, and national mentality. All this is, explicitly and implicitly, embodied in the political, economic, ideological, ethical, and other practical domains. As discerned in these domains ever since the New Culture Movement (i.e., the Westernization) launched in the early twentieth century, the positive aspects would provide Chinese citizens with an inexhaustible fountainhead of initiative and spirituality and motivate them to work hard toward the long-term goals and dreams for a just society, a prosperous state, and a good life altogether. Instead, the negative aspects would lead them to pin down the endogenous shortcomings, shrug off the redundant components, and hanker after other alternatives with particular reference to the Western counterpart. It thus helps promote the pragmatic conception of transformational creation or transformational creation among the Chinese practitioners at confrontation with modernity in the past century or so.

In brief, this volume is schemed to reconsider some cultural ideals along with some leading thinkers ranging from antiquity to modernity in China. The reconsideration is to be carried out from a transcultural perspective against the background of both globalization and glocalization at home and abroad. As widely acknowledged in the recent period, transcultural approach is comparative and interactive in essence. It is hereby employed to explore the cardinal features, including differences and similarities, of more than two target cultures in striking contrast. Very often than not, it tends to take up the other culture (s) as a mirror to show up the merits and demerits of the endogenous heritage. Further on, it is claimed to attain an in-depth understanding of the chosen objects through comparative analysis and draw out complementary possibilities for the sake of transformational creation via selective innovation.

Conducted as a thematic inquiry, this book will look specifically into such conceptual entities and thinking strategies as heaven-human oneness, the meeting of East and West, harmonization without being patternized, all under heaven as a genre of ecumenism through harmonism, cultivating wisdom for a good life, ancient quarrel over music, gentle and kind character building by poetry education, poetic wisdom in Zen enlightenment, moralistic poetics in Neo-Confucianism, the poetic state *par excellence*, transcultural pursuit of the Overman, pragmatic reason in view of anthropo-historical ontology, emotional root of aesthetic metaphysics, sublime poetics of *Māratic* type, experience of appreciating landscape, art as sedimentation in a trifold linkage, and so forth. During the process, it will expose some theoretical hypotheses with reference to the interaction and synthesis between Chinese and Western doctrines. In a word, what is to be discussed herein attempts to rediscover the old in order to perceive the new in light of the historical union of the past, the present, and the future.

These discussions comprise 17 essays in all. Some are written recently for international symposiums. Others are partly reproduced out of the papers I have contributed to the journals and books over the past decade, which are published by such bodies as Ashgate, Blackwell, China Social Sciences, Fudan University, Rodopi, Springer, University of Sydney, University of Hawaii, and so on. Most of them were initially presented at international conferences organized by universities or societies across Europe, America, Australia, Asia, and Africa. Afterward they were further developed and formulated as a result of the comments and queries collected on those rewarding roundtable and panel sessions. When fitted into this volume, they are all subject to further clarifications, modifications, and additions regarding certain arguments in question.

I would like hereby tender my tremendous appreciation to Ms. Wang Lin, editor from Foreign Language Teaching and Research Press, who has kindly helped me contact with the renowned Palgrave Macmillan under Springer. Moreover, I am feeling very much obliged to express my sincere thanks to Ms. Sara Crowley-Vigneau, the editor from the publisher, for her professional and impressive patience that has made this publication possible within such a short span of time. It goes without saying that I am personably responsible for any deficits left in this work.

Beijing, China   Keping Wang

ACKNOWLEDGEMENTS

I would first of all like to express my great appreciation to all the colleagues at home and abroad who have encouraged me to write more in English about Chinese thoughts related to the theoretical and practical spheres from a transcultural perspective. An offhanded list of them includes, for instance, Li Zehou, Ru Xin, and Yao Jiehou from China, Roger Aims, Rick Benitez, Nicholas Bunnin, David Cooper, Stephen Halliwell, Richard Lynn, Karl-Heinz Pohl, Joseph Margolis, Wolfgang Welsch, Robert Wilkinson, late Professor Herbert Mainusch, and Dr. Sonja Servomaa, among many others from overseas. Meanwhile, I am feeling so grateful to their advices and observations from which I have gained so much.

I would also like to extend my gratitude to the postgraduates and other participants in the seminars and presentations I have offered at Beijing International Studies University, Graduate School of Chinese Academy of Social Sciences, the Bureau of Foreign Languages on behalf of the Publicity Office of the State Council, University of Sydney, Sciences Politiques Bordeaux et al. Some of the participants are either government officials or professional journalists from many countries over Asia, Africa and, Europe and South America. Their active engagement and critical reflection have motivated me to make more efforts to reconsider some topics as part of my research.

Finally, my deepest thanks go to my wife, Professor Li Zhongze, and my daughter, Lindsey, for their devoted support and timely help. They have managed to let me concentrate on the project alone in an amiable and rewarding atmosphere. Our free discussions and their cross-questioning inquiries at the dinner table have always inspired me to think over what is concerned about during my working process.

Praise for *Chinese Culture of Intelligence*

"Since the days of Lin Yutang and his wonderful books *My Country and My People* and *The Importance of Living* (1935 and 1937), there seems to be a lack of comprehensive interpretations of Chinese culture for the Westerner. Keping Wang's *Chinese Culture of Intelligence* can be seen as an attempt to fill this lacuna. His inspiring book highlights some Chinese cultural ideals and their relevance to the human condition from a modern transcultural perspective. It reconsiders such fundamentals as the human-nature relationship, the ideal of harmony, character cultivation, the role of poetry and music, Zen Buddhist views and many more of the intriguing aspects of Chinese culture that have not lost their relevance today. Keping Wang's book provides insights into what really matters behind the Chinese mode of thinking and doing from the past to the present. And so we discover that Chinese culture, yet so little understood in the West, still can teach us a lot—as way of life."
—Karl-Heinz Pohl, *Professor, Sinology Department, Trier University, Germany*

"This marvelous book considers the dramatic, complex renaissance of China in the 21st century and offers a deeply humane and ecumenical perspective. Beginning from the most basic Heaven-human relations, Professor Wang describes the place of the human being in the world, and a response to our situation that emphasizes cultivation of wisdom. The vision of self-cultivation is then extended in such a way that the practical

application of poetics, with all its far-reaching capabilities, holds out an elegant, if subtle, hope for the future. The outlook is both intimately Chinese and eminently transcultural at the same time, a testament to Professor Wang's wide experience in history, philosophy and aesthetics."
—Rick Benitez, *Professor, Department of Philosophy, University of Sydney, Australia*

Contents

1	**A Rediscovery of Heaven-Human Oneness**	1
	1.1 The Threefold Significance	2
	1.2 The Two-Dimensional Orientation	13
	1.3 A Pragmatic Alternative	20
2	**What Matters Behind Ecumenism?**	25
	2.1 "All Under Heaven" and Its Historical Implementation	26
	2.2 Ecumenism as an Alternative	29
	2.3 Harmonism as the Key Drive	35
3	**Harmonization Without Being Patternized**	47
	3.1 The Meeting of East and West	48
	3.2 Harmony Versus Uniformity	52
	3.3 The Need of a New Philosophos Poiesis	59
4	**The *Dao* of Human Existence**	65
	4.1 Frame of Reference: The Dao of Man, Heaven, and the Sage	67
	4.2 Pursuit of Sageliness: Practical and Sagely Wisdom	72
	4.3 Path to Freedom: Attitudes Toward Life and Death	79

5	A Symbolic Way of Thinking Through Fables	85
	5.1 The Peng *and Happy Excursion to the Infinite*	87
	5.2 *The Butterfly and Self-Emancipation*	100
6	Two Models of Cultivating Wisdom for a Good Life	107
	6.1 *The Beauty Ladder*	108
	6.2 *The Mind-Heart Excursion*	115
	6.3 *Comparative Models of Cultivation*	124
7	Poetic Wisdom in Zen Enlightenment	135
	7.1 *Revelation from Natural Scenes*	136
	7.2 *Natural Spontaneity as a Psychical Path*	140
	7.3 *A Poetic Way of Zen Enlightenment*	147
	7.4 *The Realm of* Śūnyatā *as Beauty*	157
8	A New Ideal and Transcultural Pursuit	163
	8.1 *The Cultural Ideal and the Pagoda Allegory*	163
	8.2 *The Transcultural Pursuit and the Transformed Overman*	168
	8.3 *A Second Reflection and a Threefold Process Strategy*	173
9	A Transformational Creation of Pragmatic Reason	183
	9.1 *The First Argument*	185
	9.2 *The Second Argument*	192
	9.3 *A Philosophical Alternative*	199
	9.4 *Li's Sui Generis World-Picture*	211
10	A Manifold Expectation of Poetry	217
	10.1 *Poetry as a Special Social Discourse*	218
	10.2 *Poetry as a Unique Aesthetic Discourse*	221
	10.3 *Poetry as a Particular Moral Discourse*	230
11	A Debate on the Function of Music	235
	11.1 *Against Music: Mozi's Negative Utilitarianism*	237
	11.2 *For Music: Xunzi's Positive Utilitarianism*	242
	11.3 *A Reconsideration of the Opposing Views*	248

12 A Critical Illumination of Poetic Styles — 253
12.1 *The Literary Development: Form and Style* — 255
12.2 *Artistic Creation: Proper Inclusiveness and Holistic Vision* — 262
12.3 *Stylistic Paradigms: Naturalness, Gracefulness, and Elegance* — 269

13 A Moralistic View of Poetry — 277
13.1 *Conformity to the Moral Principle a Priori* — 278
13.2 *A Bi-polarized Treatment of the* Guofeng — 285
13.3 *Second Reflection on "Having no Depraved Thoughts"* — 294

14 Between Chinese and Western Aesthetics — 303
14.1 *Fragmentary Elaboration of Western Aesthetics* — 306
14.2 *Systematic Construction of Aesthetics as a Discipline* — 309
14.3 *Theoretical Incorporation Through East-West Interaction* — 311
14.4 *Cross-Disciplinary and Comprehensive Practice of Art Education* — 314
14.5 *Transcultural Pondering in View of Cultural Origins* — 317

15 Aesthetic Criticism of Transculturality — 323
15.1 *Beyond East and West: A Transcultural Transformation* — 324
15.2 *Aesthetic Education as a Critical Necessity* (Meiyu Shuo) — 329
15.3 *Art as a Refuge from Suffering* (Jietuo Shuo) — 335
15.4 *Art as Aesthetic Play for Freedom* (Youxi Shuo) — 340
15.5 *The Artist as Creative Genius* (Tiancai Shuo) — 342
15.6 *The Refined as the Second Form* (Gu-ya Shuo) — 345
15.7 *The Theory of Poetic State* par Excellence (Jingjie Shuo) — 349

16 A Sublime Poetics of *Māratic* Type — 361
16.1 *Historical Significance in Perspective* — 362
16.2 *The* Māratic *School and the* Māra *Allegory* — 367
16.3 *Dismantling the Old While Establishing the New* — 374
16.4 *A Tentative Observation* — 390

17	**An Escalated Experience of Appreciating Nature**	393
	17.1 Three Levels of Aesthetic Experience	394
	17.2 Aesthetic Effects of Heaven-Human Oneness	399
18	**Art as Sedimentation**	405
	18.1 Art as Sedimentation	406
	18.2 A Critical Pondering	411
	18.3 A Methodological Reflection	418

Chinese Materials — 425

Author Index — 437

Subject Index — 443

List of Figures

Fig. 8.1 The pagoda allegory   165
Fig. 8.2 The blueprint   174

CHAPTER 1

A Rediscovery of Heaven-Human Oneness

> Man is fallen; nature is erect, and serves as a differential thermometer, detecting the presence or absence of the divine sentiment in man. (Ralph Waldo Emerson)

It is chiefly due to the eco-environmental pressure that people tend to be more concerned with the interaction between nature and humankind. The history of Chinese intelligence witnesses a constant probe into the chiasmic encounters between heaven (*tian*) and human (*ren*), which is conducive to a core conception of heaven-human oneness (*tian ren he yi*) as the general *ethos* of Chinese philosophy. The polysemy of the conception is extended along with the passage of time according to the sociocultural context. At the present-day stage, the tendency to rediscover the relevance of heaven-human oneness is conducted by reading new and even modern messages into the old conception as such. It has consequently become an open-ended activity, inviting a second reflection on its hidden universality for the common good.

This discussion attempts to expose the essential bearings and relevance of heaven-human oneness by tracing back to its historical line of thought with reference to updated reinterpretations. The whole argument is intended to cover the following three sub-topics: the threefold significance, the two-dimensional orientation, and a pragmatic alternative.

1.1 The Threefold Significance

Chinese culture was originated from a nomadic tradition followed by an agricultural counterpart. This being the case, heaven was worshiped because it was seen to be both a dominant force and a dependent means in terms of food production and human survival. According to the antiquities, heaven is above, and earth is below, thus making up the universe or Nature as a whole, in which all things or beings are begotten and conserved. Hence, the tri-party interaction has been the focus of consideration in Chinese thought from ancient to present. Confucianism, for instance, is preoccupied with *san cai* as "three basic substances" that involve *tian* as heaven, *di* as earth, and *ren* as human; and Daoism is concerned with *si da* as "four great parts" that comprise *tian, di, ren,* and *dao* (*tao*). It is owing to shamanistic or magic heritage that *tian* is regarded as embodiment of a divine mandate and thus conceptualized for the Lord of Heaven. Yet, the Lord of Heaven stays and communicates with humans, things, tribes, or societies through magic force. It is neither beyond the empirical domain nor personified into a transcendental power like the Christian God. This is why *tian* as heaven and *ren* as human are interacted with each other so closely that the conception of oneness between the two came into shape in pre-Qin period. Speaking generally, the conception itself can be dated back to Mencius (c. 372–289 B.C.) and Zhuangzi (c. 369–286 B.C.), further developed by Dong Zhongshu (179–104 B.C.), and metaphysically moralized by Neo-Confucianism in the Song Dynasty especially from eleventh to thirteenth centuries A.D. Along with the passage of time, the idea of *tian* is extended into a cluster of concepts, such as *tiandi* (Heaven and Earth), *tianming* (the mandate of Heaven), *tianyi* (the will of Heaven), *tiandao* (the way of Heaven), *xianxia* (the land under Heaven), and among many others. I hereby look into three of them that I think are more important and relevant to the general concern of humankind nowadays. They are *tiandi* as Nature, *tiandao* as the Heavenly Way, and *tianxia* as all under heaven, thus consisting of the threefold significance in the Chinese notion of heaven-human oneness.

1.1.1 Tiandi *and Its Naturalistic Aspects*

The literal translation of *tiandi* is "heaven and earth" that make up the universe or Nature as a whole. The use of the term is of high frequency in many Chinese classics, and almost always set in a context where Nature and humankind are interrelated.

In the book of Zhuangzi (Chuang-tzu), for instance, we read the following: "Heaven and Earth and I came into existence together, and the myriad things with me are one."[1] "Heaven and Earth have great beauty but remain in silence.... The myriad things have perfect principles but say nothing of them. The sage is a person who is in pursuit of the great beauty and the perfect principles."[2] Heaven and Earth are the producer of the myriad things (*wanwu*). The myriad things take shelter in Heaven and Earth. They all gather together to form up the entirety of Nature that is then synthesized with humankind into oneness. By such oneness, Zhuangzi tries to equalize all things and justify his principle of making no distinction, for he believes that the cosmic order or harmony is to be attained in no other way than this. In many cases, he advises those who attempt to pursue the Dao of absolute freedom and independent personality to follow the course of Nature. This is not simply because Nature operates characteristically in spontaneity or naturalness (*zi ran er ran*), but because Nature also has great beauty and virtuous silence. Under such circumstances, Nature is not only the place to live and act, but also the object for aesthetic appreciation. Accordingly, the sage as the idealized personality in Daoism is not merely part of Nature, but the discoverer of natural beauty as well. As is discerned in *The Happy Excursion* and other chapters, Zhuangzi tenders much credit to the aesthetic value of natural beauty owing to its nourishment of spiritual freedom. He is in fact ready to embrace the natural but reject the artificial. Thus, on many occasions he bestows the natural with joyous charm whereas the artificial with evil distortion, for instance, the bull tamed by man for plowing. All this leads to his philosophizing of aesthetic naturalism.

When it comes to Dong Zhongshu's *Rich Dews in Spring and Autumn* (*Chunqiu fanlu*), the natural beauty is said to embody the harmony of Heaven and Earth, and anyone who has a peaceful mind

---

[1] Cf. Zhuangzi, "On the Equality of Things," in *A Taoist Classic: Chuang-tzu* (trans. Fung Yu-lan, Beijing: Foreign Languages Press, 1989), p. 49.

[2] Cf. Zhuangzi, *Zhi bei you* [Intelligence Traveling Northward], in Chen Guying (ed.), *Zhuangzi jinzhu jinyi* [Zhuangzi Newly Annotated and Paraphrased] (Beijing: Zhonghua shuju, 1983), p. 563.

and right conduct is able to nourish his body by means of this beauty.³ In a rather affectionate tone, Dong assumes that Nature is the "grandfather of man," making man as man as it bears the virtue of humaneness or benevolence (*ren*).⁴ It follows that Nature and man share a strong resemblance. For example, Nature has the sun and the moon, man has the left and right eye; Nature has four seasons, and man has four limbs; and Nature has four kinds of emotional power such as joy revealed in spring, happiness in summer, anger in autumn, sorrow in winter, and so is the case with man. Nature and man are therefore one in a classificatory sense. Accordingly, there arises a harmonious order when man identifies himself with Nature. There arises terrible disorder when man separates himself from Nature.⁵ The above comparison is ostensibly far-fetched and logically ridiculous. But, it aims to remind humankind of their dependent position and inborn connection with Nature. The emphasis on the strong resemblance between Nature and man is not meaningless at all since it serves at least to let man attend to Nature as much as he attends to himself. This is hopefully conducive to necessary respect and emotional caring for Nature. Historically, Dong is the first to coin the concept of heaven-human oneness that is seen as a milestone regarding the relations between Nature and humankind in Chinese thought. Somewhat like Zhuangzi, Dong acknowledges the natural beauty underlined by the principle of proper harmony. But, he finds such beauty beneficial in a number of ways. It is not merely aesthetically satisfying, but physically rewarding and morally generating. In other words, it satisfies aesthetic needs, nurtures the body, and facilitates the becoming of man as man by its rich resources and varied functions. However, Dong's preoccupation like this represents a mystical naturalism. For his approach to the oneness is essentially based on the school of Yin and Yang, his personification of Heaven exemplifies a kind of mystification instead of divination, and likewise, his contemplation of natural beauty reveals some mystical rapture.

---

³ Dong Zhongshu, *Xun tian zhi dao* [Act Upon the *Dao* of Heaven], in *Chunqiu fanlu* [Exuberant Dew of the Spring and Autumn] (Shanghai: Shanghai Guji Press, 1989), pp. 91–93.

⁴ Dong Zhongshu, *Wei ren zhe tian* [Heaven Serves Man], and *Wangdao tong san* [The Kingly Way], in *Chunqiu fanlu*, pp. 64, 67.

⁵ Dong Zhongshu, *Yin Yang yi* [The Meaning of Yin and Yang], in *Chunqiu fanlu*, p. 71.

Mencius is one of the early Chinese thinkers who promote the notion of heaven-human oneness. He perceives the above notion mainly in view of Confucianism. He therefore seeks to maintain a balance by exposing the reciprocal interaction between the two sides. From a cognitive perspective, Mencius claims that "One who has exhausted his mental constitution knows his own nature. Knowing his own nature, he knows Heaven. To preserve his mental constitution, and nourish his own nature, is the way to serve Heaven."[6] This argument shows how man and heaven interact with each other. On the part of man in particular, it requires a sense of mission and more initiative not only to develop one's cognitive power and cultivate one's character, but also to do one's utmost for Heaven. As is detected in this context, Heaven implies abstractly an inborn destiny (*tian ming*) and substantially the myriad things (*wan wu*). What is meant by "to serve Heaven" is related to fulfilling the inborn destiny and looking after the myriad things. Then, from a pragmatic viewpoint, Mencius proposes the ideal of "loving people and treasuring things" (*ren min er ai wu*).[7] "Loving people" (*ren min*) is the result of extending affection from one's parents to others in general. "Treasuring things" (*ai wu*) signifies the caretaking of all things or beings according to the law of reciprocity. For instance, "If the farming seasons be not interfered with, the grain will be more than can be eaten. If close nets are not allowed to enter the pools and ponds, the fishes and turtles will be more than can be consumed. If the axes and bills enter the hills and forests only at the proper time, the wood and timber would be more than can be used."[8] Consequently, things are protected and multiplied at the same time, and people are, in turn, enabled to enjoy sufficient means and live a reasonably good life. Otherwise, it would bring about a detrimental outcome of abusing the natural resources and depriving Nature of generative capacity. This is often metaphorically described in Chinese as though a greed-trodden farmer kills the hen for its eggs.

Among the three thinkers mentioned above, Nature is perceived to be good and beautiful a priori. Distinguished from Zhuangzi's preoccupation with aesthetic naturalism and Dong Zhongshu's concern with

---

[6] Mencius, *The Book of Mencius*, in *The Four Books* (trans. James Legge, Changsha: Hunan Press, 1992), 13.1.
[7] Ibid., 13.45.
[8] Ibid., 1.4.

mystical naturalism, Mencius seems to be in favor of pragmatic naturalism. Relatively, the aesthetic naturalism tends to exaggerate the perfect beauty of Nature while ignoring the active role of humankind; the mystical naturalism tends to reinforce the heaven-human resemblance in order to project human affection into Nature; and the pragmatic naturalism tends to stress the mutual independence and reciprocal interaction between Nature and humankind so as to secure a balanced development for the sake of human existence as its ultimate *telos*.

The 1990s witnessed the revival of the rationale of heaven-human oneness. It occurred against the background of eco-environmental pressure in China and the world over. Quite some thinkers reexamine the rationale in order to build up a great awareness of the problematic relations between human and Nature. They regard Nature as an organic whole of the cosmic scheme and propose a new operation of heaven-human oneness for eco-environmental protection in terms of "sustainable development." In their minds, the organic whole ought to be taken care of because no part of it is a separated island, and everyone is accountable for its protection. As for the general objective of sustainable development, it is not merely economy-based, but morality-based because it is also intended for the welfare of later generations of human race in its entirety.

1.1.2 Tiandao *and Its Moralistic Expectations*

The Chinese conception of *tiandao* means the "Heavenly Way" concretized through its counterpart of *rendao* as the "Human Way." The former poses a higher frame of reference for the latter as is directed toward moral development. This idea can be traced back to *The Book of Changes* (*Yi jing* or *I Ching*) in the following statement: "The great man is someone whose virtue is constant with Heaven and Earth, his brightness with the sun and the moon, his orderly procedure with the four seasons.... When he precedes Heaven, Heaven will not act in opposition to him; and when he follows Heaven, he obeys the timing of its motion."[9] What is emphasized here appears to be the interactive oneness between Heaven

---

[9] Cf. *Book of Changes* (trans. James Legge, Changsha: Hunan Press, 1993), *Qian* (The Creative), p. 15. Also see *The Classic of Changes* (trans. Richard John Lynn, New York: Columbia University Press, 1994), Hexagram 1: *Qian*, p. 138. The citation is modified herein.

and Humankind. In reality, the key message is hidden in the human virtue and consistency with Heaven and Earth. As noticed in the commentary on the first two hexagrams—the symbol of Heaven (*qian*) and the symbol of Earth (*kun*)—the human virtue is expected to assimilate the counterpart of both Heaven and Earth. It says in the *Great Symbolism*, "The action of Heaven is strong and dynamic. In the same manner, the noble man never ceases to strengthen himself."[10] "The disposition of Earth bears sustaining power. The noble man, in accordance with this, supports all beings with his generous virtue."[11] Observably, the dynamic action of Heaven is demonstrated through the ceaseless cycle of the four seasons, and the sustaining power of Earth through the carrying capacity of mountains, waters, and all other beings. Such doings suggest respective virtues of Heaven and Earth (*tian di zhi de*). These virtues come together to form as the Way of Heaven and Earth (*tian di zhi dao*), which is shortened into the Heavenly Way (*tiandao*). The nobleman as an idealized personality becomes what he is by learning from the Heavenly Way. He strives to develop himself persistently like Heaven, and similarly like Earth, he tries to achieve the generous virtue to help all other beings grow properly. His deed of this kind works to establish *rendao* as the Human Way for moral accomplishment.

This line of thought has been extended throughout the Chinese history of ideas. Mencius, for instance, pushes it further as a moral requirement on character training. "Wherever the noble man passes through," as he says, "transformation of others follows; wherever he abides, his instructive influence is too subtle and great to be measured; his virtuous achievement flows above and beneath, like that of Heaven and Earth."[12] The Human Way is embodied in what the nobleman does, and the Heavenly Way represented by "that of Heaven and Earth." The former is supposed to reach the corresponding level of the latter. It is on this point that the heaven-human oneness is accomplished, and so is the idealized personality of the nobleman. The similar idea is also found in *The Doctrine of the Mean (Zhong yong)*. The nobleman is assumed to be a person with the most complete sincerity that exists under Heaven. When

---

[10] Cf. *Book of Changes* (trans. James Legge), *Qian* (The Creative). Also see *The Classic of Changes* (trans. Richard John Lynn), Hexagram 1: *Qian*, p. 130.

[11] Ibid., *Book of Changes* (trans. James Legge), *Kun* (The Receptive). Also see *The Classic of Changes* (trans. Richard John Lynn), Hexagram 2: *Kun*, p. 144.

[12] Mencius, *The Book of Mencius* (trans. James Legge), 13.12.

he can give its full development to his own nature, he can do the same to the nature of other men. When he can give its full development to the nature of other men, he can give their full development to the nature of animals and things. When he can do this job, he can help the transforming and nourishing powers of Heaven and Earth. When he can help this way, he may with Heaven and Earth form a ternion.[13] The process demonstrates a hypothesized sequence about how the Human Way mingles with the Heavenly Way. It commences with the virtue of sincerity that is capable of transforming oneself and others for the better; it goes through a number of stages by virtue of applying altruism to other men, animals, and things, etc. Finally, it arrives at the highest possible state of forming a ternion. The ternion in this context involves the union among the three components, that is, Heaven, Earth, and Mankind. Actually, it indicates again the heaven-human oneness and a sense of mission on the part of human as human. In order to fulfill this oneness and mission, it calls for a gradual transcendence and self-development from low to high.

Confucianism pays more attention to the reciprocal interaction between the Heavenly Way and the Human Way. This tradition has been carried onward by Confucianists from the past to the present. Among the Neo-Confucianists in the Song Dynasty, there is a general agreement on canceling out the distinction between the Heavenly Way and the Human Way. That is to say, they tend to identify the former with the latter and ascertain the oneness between the two. For example, Zhang Zai (1020–1077 A.D.) argues that the Heavenly Way and the Human Way seem to be different in size, but remain the same in essence because it is through human to know and experience Heaven.[14] Cheng Hao (1032–1085 A.D.) simply refuses to distinguish one from another. For he thinks that Heaven and humankind are originally not two but one, it is therefore needless to ponder over their synthesis at all.[15] Cheng Yi (1033–1107 A.D.) goes even further to define the relationship in such concise terms as follows: The Way (*dao*) is freed from any distinction between

---

[13] Cf. *The Doctrine of the Mean*, in *The Four Books* (trans. James Legge), p. 22.

[14] Wang Fuzhi, *Zhangzi zhengmeng zhu* [Commentary on Zhang Zai's Works] (Beijing: Zhonghua Book Company, 1975), p. 94.

[15] Cheng Hao and Cheng Yi, *Yu lu* [Collected Sayings], Vols. 2, 11, in Institute of Philosophy of Chinese Academy of Social Sciences (ed.), *Zhongguo zhexueshi ziliao xuanji* [Selected Sources of the History of Chinese Philosophy: Part 1 of Song, Yuan and Ming Dynasties] (Beijing: Zhonghua Book Company, 1982), p. 220.

Heaven and human. Yet, it is called the Heavenly Way when it is with Heaven, the Earthly Way when it is with Earth, and the Human Way when it is with human. The Way is one only. It is shared by Heaven, Earth, and humankind altogether.[16]

In recent decades, modern Confucianists attempt to revive the thoughtway of Neo-Confucianism for the sake of moral reconstruction. Mou Zongsan (1909–1995), for example, has made tremendous endeavors to reinterpret the moral expectation of heaven-human oneness. He places much emphasis on integrating the virtue of Heaven with its human counterpart. In his mind, the individual life ought to be completely in conciliation with the cosmic life. He thus affirms that the attainment of this conciliation leads to the accomplishment not merely of moral being but also inward sageliness. In order to fulfill this *telos*, one must follow the Heavenly Way and model his own nature upon it. How is that possible then? Mou's illustration gives rise to a circle of development. The circle is consisted of four components. Down below is the becoming of individual life filled with possibilities. High above is the working of the Heavenly Way that is both religiously "transcendent" (*chaoyue*) and morally "immanent" (*neizai*). On the right-hand side stands the process of moral praxis relating to the virtues of humaneness and truth. On the left-hand side stands the mandate of Heaven in constant movement. It is reckoned that the process of moral praxis and the movement of the mandate make possible the transformational interaction between the individual life and the Heavenly Way. On this occasion, the individual life will rise up to combine itself with the Heavenly Way as a result of praxis of the virtues of humaneness and truth. It has nourished a moral mind and transformed itself into a "real life," "real subject," or "real self." Meanwhile, the Heavenly Way has turned itself into a "metaphysical substance" and penetrated into the human nature, thus breaking the estrangement and causing the conciliation between the individual life and the Heavenly Way.[17] In plain language, the individual life of humankind below will ascend upward to meet the Heavenly Way through moral praxis, whereas the Heavenly Way will descend downward to meet the individual life of humankind through constant movement. They create the conciliation or heaven-human oneness in which the Heavenly Way

---

[16] Ibid., Vols. 2, 18.

[17] Mou Zongsan, *Zhongguo zhexue de tezhi* [The Characteristics of Chinese Philosophy] (Shanghai: Shanghai Guji Press, 1997), pp. 20–32, 74–81, 114–117.

will transform itself into a "metaphysical reality" while the individual life into a moral being or "real self." The key to this idealized outcome lies in sincere and persistent praxis of such virtues as humaneness and truth. Otherwise, there is no chance for the Heavenly Way to become a "metaphysical reality" but to remain as an abstract vision hanging in the air, and similarly, the individual life will not be able to become a moral person but to remain as a physical being down to the earth.

In the final analysis, the Confucianists of whatever type do use such terms as the Heavenly Way (*tiandao*) and the Human Way (*rendao*) in discourse. But, very often they identify them with one another by illustrating the Heavenly Way in light of the Human Way for a moral purpose. As a matter of fact, this line of thought is derived from a learning strategy recommended by Confucius. When talking about himself with Zi Gong, Confucius confesses, "I do not complain against Heaven, nor do I grumble against Man. My learning start from what is down below and get through to what is up above. If I am understood at all, it is perhaps by Heaven."[18] This confession reflects Confucius' learning attitude, strategy, and objective altogether. He concentrates on what he is learning and what progress he is making disregarding what others may say about him. The most important message of the remark is *xiaxue er shangda*, say, "My learning start from what is down below and get through to what is up above." Here by "what is down below" is meant human affairs or social commitment, and by "what is up above" is meant such virtues as humaneness and righteousness (*ren yi*). According to Confucius, learning is both a cognitive and practical process. It begins with knowing human affairs and social deeds, but its penetration must rise high; it thus continues to facilitate the attainment and praxis of "what is up above" in terms of the virtues aforementioned. Eventually, the learning process comes up with a transformation of what is learned into the virtues expected. Such virtues as humaneness and righteousness are all symbolized in the Heavenly Way and practically exercised by human beings. A synthesis to be made in this regard exemplifies the highest form of achievement of which human as human is capable in one sense, and in the other, it advises people to be realistic in pragmatic learning but idealistic in moral cultivation. This, of course, calls for a pursuit of moral transcendence as an elementary part of character building.

---

[18] Confucius, *The Analects* (trans. D. C. Lau, London: Penguin Books, 1979), pp. XIV, 35. Also see Confucius, *The Confucian Analects*, in *The Four Books* (trans. James Legge), p. 14.35.

1.1.3   Tianxia *and Its Cosmopolitan Ideal*

Both Daoism and Confucianism show deep concern for all under heaven (*tianxia*) as a political rather than a geographical notion. In a narrow sense, it is referred to China as it was once divided into many states; and in a broad sense, it is intended to signify the world in its entirety. As highly celebrated by Chinese literati, the conception itself is more than necessary for peaceful coexistence and reciprocal collaboration. Hence, it is deeply rooted in their mentality as a cosmopolitan ideal and ultimate goal of their lifetime mission. The mission itself is composed of four segments abbreviated as *xiu qi zhi ping*, which means four major tasks such as "cultivating the personality," "regulating the family," "governing well the state," and "keeping the world in peace." The whole idea is elaborated in a Confucian classic of *The Great Learning* (*Da xue*):

> The Dao of great learning is to manifest the illustrious virtue, renovate the people, and to achieve the highest excellence.... The ancients who manifested the illustrious virtue to the world first governed well their states. Wishing to govern well their states, they first regulated their families. Wishing to regulate their families, they first cultivated their personalities. Wishing to cultivate their personalities, they first rectified their minds. Wishing to rectify their minds, they first sought to be sincere in their thoughts. Wishing to be sincere in their thoughts, they first extended to the utmost their knowledge. Such extension of knowledge lay in the investigation of things. Things being investigated, knowledge was extended. Their knowledge being extended, their thoughts were sincere. Their thoughts being sincere, their minds were then rectified. Their minds being rectified, their personalities were cultivated. Their personalities being cultivated, their families were rightly regulated. Their families being regulated, their states were well governed. Their states being governed, the whole world was kept in peace. From the son of Heaven [emperor] down to the mass of the people, all must consider the cultivation of the personality the root of everything besides.[19]

---

[19] *The Great Learning*, in *The Four Books* (trans. James Legge), p. 1. The English version is offered here with some minor modifications according to the original text. For instance, James Legge rendered *tianxia* in "empire," and I changed it into "the world." He translated *tianxia ping* into "the whole empire was made tranquil and happy," and I revised it as "the world was kept in peace." Some translators prefer to say "the whole world was brought into peace."

As observed in this picture of great learning, there are eight major steps ranging from near to far or rising from low to high in a logical sequence. The first step is the investigation of things (*ge wu*); the second is the extension of knowledge (*zhi zhi*); the third is the sincerity of the thoughts (*cheng yi*); the fourth is the rectification of the mind (*zheng xin*); the fifth is the cultivation of the personality (*xiu shen*); the sixth is the regulation of the family (*qi jia*); the seventh is the proper governance of the state (*zhi guo*); and the eighth is keeping the world in peace (*ping tianxia*). All these eight steps form a progressive process sustained by the law of cause and effect. Among them, the first step is where the learning process begins with a cognitive motivation as the cause and then leads to the second step as the effect. In the similar manner, it gets through the rest of other steps before ending up with the ultimate objective. This means all the other seven steps or tasks serve as premises for "keeping the world in peace." In order to keep the world in peace, the most determinate of all the premises is "the cultivation of the personality" as the root of everything besides. For the personality thus cultivated is not only an able and learned person, but a moral and rectified one as well. Without such kind of personality, the family cannot be regulated, the state cannot be well governed, and accordingly, the world cannot be brought into peace. In practice, the entire process of great learning also demonstrates the Confucianist scheme of sageliness within and kingliness without. Comparatively, the first five steps contribute to the nurture of sageliness within (*neisheng*) that embodies the personality characterized with the highest excellence of humaneness and righteousness, and the last three steps contribute to the development of kingliness without (*waiwang*) that is verified through proper treatment of family, state, and world affairs altogether.

It is assumed that one may read the old text and understand the new situation better. This is only possible by means of extending the implications of the text in view of the status quo. Regarding what is discussed above, the most appealing of all is not the learning process itself but the conventional ideal of "keeping the world in peace." Looking into the extended meaning of all under heaven (*tianxia*), we are inclined to compare it with the widespread and over-treasured notion of state in modern politics. Geographically and ideologically, the notion of state is as a rule nationality-based and largely confined to the marked borderline or national territory. If it is by any chance produced no radical nationalism or did less harm to other nations for the sake of national identity, it would be utilized to justify a kind of egoist patriotism at least. It is usually in the name of state interests, national volition, and blind patriotism that some unreasonable destruction and even war crimes are committed along with unnecessary cost of human lives and other resources. In contrast, the ideal of "all under heaven" is world-oriented and thus features a cosmopolitan horizon. As idealistic as it may be, it appears more constructive and reciprocal *par excellence* in the realm of international relations. After all, it could be employed to encourage a world outlook and high awareness of cosmopolitanism. It was actually tried and pertained to positive consequence when it came to the long-term conflict between the Han Dynasty and the Huns (Xiongnu) in ancient China. The historic import of this case is authentically brought up in light of ecumenism by Arnold Toynbee and Eric Voegelin as is shown in the subsequent chapter.

Now, with respect of the three derived aspects of heaven-human oneness explicated above, the theory of Heaven and Earth (Nature) connotes a cosmic scheme of appropriate praxis for humankind to act according to the law of reciprocity; the doctrine of the Heavenly Way implies a moral scheme of spiritual cultivation for humankind to pursue self-perfection; and the conception of all under heaven indicates a political scheme of cosmopolitan consciousness for humankind to develop a broader vision. This line of thought is said to function as a keystone in the formation of the cultural mentality among the educated in particular. It always stays open to be rediscovered and reinterpreted with the passage of time, however.

1.2   The Two-Dimensional Orientation

It is worth mentioning that, after the founding in 1949 of the New China as it so-called, the rationale of heaven-human oneness was brought under attack by the official ideology. The mainstream ideology went so far as to declare a kind of "civil war" against Heaven or Nature. As a consequence, the separation of heaven and human was politically imposed and reinforced. This situation lasted for a decade or so when China paid a heavy price during the rash period of the "Great Leap Forward" in the late 1950s and suffered a nationwide catastrophe resulted from "man-made natural disasters" in the early 1960s.

It is not until early 1980s that the academics in the mainland of China resumed the reconsideration of heaven-human oneness. But this time, the methodology manifests a two-dimensional orientation by means of the "pragmatic reason" (*shiyong lixing*), and in this regard, Li Zehou's observation stands out for its philosophical insights. The two-dimensional orientation involves the humanization of Nature (*ziran renhua*) and the naturalization of humankind (*ren ziranhua*).

1.2.1 The Humanization of Nature

According to Li Zehou, Nature could be classified conceptually into two modes: the external and the internal. The external Nature stands for the living surroundings of humankind, while the internal Nature for the physical faculties of humankind. In 1999, he makes a metaphorical use of such binary terms as "hardware" and "software" to illustrate the humanization of both the external and internal Nature.

Regarding the humanization of the external Nature, the analogy of "hardware" refers to the recreation or reformation of the natural environment in which humankind live. It is reflected, for instance, in the man-made reservoirs, canals, artificial lakes, husbandry and agriculture, etc. Nowadays, this form of practice continues, for instance, in the field of transforming the biological genes of plants and vegetables with the help of modern technology. Then, the analogy of "software" points to the crucial changes that have occurred to the interrelationship between Nature and Humankind. As a result of the development of the "hardware" mentioned above, human fear and worship for natural elements, things, and phenomena are gradually vanished in the course of civilization, and replaced by an aesthetic affinity and other utilitarian expectations. Hence, the beauty of natural landscape is discovered and appreciated. It is on this point that Li Zehou grounds his argument on a historical ontology. As he stresses, it is historical development that has altered the heaven-human relations and also made possible the humanization of Nature. In this sense, "humanization" is not something merely conceptual or subjective, but essentially anthropo-ontological. Say, the objective relationship between Nature and Humankind has been changed historically, thus making Nature as part of human existence. Eventually, Nature was turned from a fearful object in itself into an object for itself that is approachable with human affinity. All this is the fundamental and objective basis of the humanization of Nature in the subjective consciousness of humankind.[20] As read in *The Four Lectures on Aesthetics* (*Meixue si jiang*), Li Zehou utilizes a broad and narrow vision to formulate his observation as follows:

> The "Humanization of Nature" in its broad sense is a philosophical concept. The sky, oceans, deserts, wild forests and so on are not directly reformed by humankind, but perceived as the outcome of the "humanization of Nature." For such humanization indicates the historical measure of human conquest of Nature, and the developmental stage of the entire society. In effect, there arises a fundamental change in the interrelationship between humankind and Nature. This abandons the sheer conception of Nature in its narrow sense, and refuses to take it as a reformed object via labor only. Then, the "humanization of Nature" in its narrow sense is evinced in the natural objects recreated by humankind, for example, the cultivated flowers and grass that appear beautiful indeed. Yet, as social development goes further ahead, human beings become more and more interested in contemplating such landscapes as thunderstorms and wild deserts that remain untouched by human hands.... For these things are already freed from any harmful or hostile content, and their sensuous forms turn out to be more appealing to human attention. During the contemplation of these natural forms that seem to revolt against humankind in appearance, one is most likely to experience an aesthetic pleasure of a sublime kind.[21]

The humanization of Nature is by principle a process that goes hand in hand with the progression of human civilization or culture. It involves the historical relationship between human praxis and Nature, and transforms, directly or indirectly, natural things into aesthetic objects. In this respect, the humanization of Nature in its narrow sense that is operated through human labor and technological recreation provides the basis (if not direct basis) for the humanization of Nature in its broad sense, that is, it is the basic cause of changing the Nature-and-human relations. In other words, "the humanization of Nature in its broad sense could

---

[20] Li Zehou, *Shuo ziran renhua* [On the Humanization of Nature], in Li Zehou, *Lishi bentilun/Jimao wushuo* [Historical Ontology/Five Essays from 1999] (Beijing: Sanlian Bookshop, 2003), pp. 242–243.

[21] Li Zehou, *Meixue sijiang* [Four Lectures on Aesthetics] (Beijing: Sanlian Bookshop, 1989), pp. 88–89. The English translation is based on the Chinese text. The English version of the whole book did not come out in print in late 2006. See Li Zehou and Jane Cauvel, *Four Essays on Aesthetics* (Lanham, Oxford: Lexington Books, 2006), pp. 90–94.

take place only when the humanization of Nature in its narrow sense has developed to a certain historical stage."[22] The primitives, for instance, could hardly appreciate such natural scenes as mountains, waters, flowers, and birds simply because they used to live under the fearfulness of Nature that was not humanized either in its broad or narrow sense.

In the case of the humanization of the internal Nature, Li Zehou again offers an analogical analysis. By the analogy of "hardware," he means the transformation of physical faculties and DNA structures, etc. It involves a deliberated human control and recreation of the natural faculties and their functions. As a result, the five faculties or senses, for example, are humanized or enculturated, and we humans therefore can enjoy a musical ear for music, an artistic hand for painting, and literary eye for poetry, etc. This implies that the instinctive utility of the faculties is gradually decreased and in turn modified by non-utilitarian functions, including aesthetic sensibility and taste. The analogy of software in this context refers mainly to the humanization of desires and eros. The historical process of enculturation differentiates humans from animals even though they share something in common. Specifically speaking, the long history of making and using tools along with social group organization has helped the psychical organisms and functions become different from that of animals. The difference lies chiefly in the mixture of animal-ness with cultural-ness. This leads to the cultural-psychological formation (*wenhua xinli jiegou*) in which the animal mentality and the cultural achievement are sedimented (*jidian*), and so are the sociality (rationality and cultural-ness) and the individuality (sensibility and animal-ness). Among many others, an offhanded example could be the virtue of human love originated from sheer sex. This shows the fact that the humanization of the internal Nature has made human as human from a moral perspective.

On this point, human ethics or practical reason is identified with the kernel of the "humanization of the internal Nature,"[23] and connected with it is human taste or new sensibility from an aesthetic perspective.[24] This is because "Both humanization of the external Nature and that of the internal Nature are the historical products of human society as a

---

[22] Li Zehou, *Meixue sijiang* [Four Lectures on Aesthetics], p. 91.

[23] Li Zehou, *Shuo ziran renhua* [On the Humanization of Nature], in Li Zehou, *Lishi bentilun/Jimao wushuo* [Historical Ontology/Five Essays from 1999], pp. 248–259.

[24] Li Zehou, *Meixue sijiang* [Four Lectures on Aesthetics], pp. 110–125.

whole. Aesthetically, the former turns the objective world into beautiful reality, and bears the essential cause of the beautiful, while the latter helps the subjective mentality experience aesthetic feeling, and reveals the essential cause of the aesthetic feeling. They are all attained through the entire history of social praxis."[25] With other arguments alike, this one expresses the primary aspect of Li's hypothesis of historical sedimentation that is challenged and reexamined by other philosophers at home and abroad in recent decades. The limited length of this reflection only allows for a brief description rather than a critical analysis.

1.2.2 The Naturalization of Humanity

If the humanization of Nature is borrowed from Karl Marx and extended from a historico- and anthropo-ontological viewpoint, the "naturalization of humanity" (*ren zi ran hua*) is chiefly inspired by the Chinese thoughtway of heaven-human oneness. According to Li Zehou, the naturalization of humanity serves as the counterpart of the humanization of Nature, which represents two dimensions of the historical process of human culture. Above all, the naturalization of humanity aims at the human fulfillment or the wholeness of human nature. It is historically preconditioned by the humanization of Nature and pointed to the individual development in particular.

Correspondingly, the naturalization of humanity is assumed to contain at least two aspects. One of them is composed of three kinds of activity as follows: firstly, establish a coexistent and harmonized interaction between Humankind and Nature, and perceive Nature as a shelter to live and rest in; secondly, return to Nature for aesthetic contemplation of its beautiful landscapes and help things grow properly by taking care of flora and fauna; and thirdly, learn how to breathe naturally (e.g., through appropriate practice of *qigong* or yoga) in order to conciliate the rhythm of human body and heart with that of Nature and reach the heaven-human oneness.[26] All of them are associated with a certain kind of aesthetic feeling or state of mind in which the rational is fused with the emotional, the subject identified with the object, and the social consciousness accompanied with the individual freedom. In a word, by virtue of naturalization of humanity, one could possibly turn back to Nature for "dwelling poetically" in

---

[25] Li Zehou, *Meixue sijiang* [Four Lectures on Aesthetics], pp. 112–113.
[26] Ibid., pp. 95–96.

the world as he may free himself from control by instrumental rationality, from the alienation by material fetishism, and from the enslavement by the system of power, knowledge, and language, etc.

The other of the two aspects lies in an aesthetic issue. It is found in the free enjoyment that is stemmed from the cultural-psychological formation of the person who returns to Nature with a humanized as well as socialized mentality. Compared with the service of the humanized faculties and emotions, the naturalization of humanity enables man to dwell poetically in the world and exposes him to free enjoyment in an aesthetic and spiritual sense. That is why Li Zehou asserts the superiority of the aesthetic to both the cognitive and the ethical. For the aesthetic is neither the internalization of reason (the cognitive) nor the condensation of reason (the ethical), but the sedimentation of both reason and sense, or rationality and sensation. This being the case, it works to facilitate "the rectification of seven human emotions, including joy, anger, sorrow, fear, love, hate and desire" (*qiqing zheng*) and "the delight in heaven-human oneness" (*tianren le*). In other words, the aesthetic of "free enjoyment" is neither the ethical in which rationality dominates sensibility, nor the cognitive in which rationality shapes sensibility. It is fully open and individual creativity in which rationality and a variety of psychical factors (e.g., perception, imagination, desire, emotion, and unconscious) are penetrating into and interweaving with each other. This creativity is significant to both the cognitive and the ethical because it serves to "illuminate the true with the beautiful" (*yimei qizhen*) and "enhance the good through the beautiful" (*yimei chushan*).[27] In this context, the true leads to the discovery of real knowledge and wisdom, and the good to the cultivation of moral personality.

Metaphorically, the humanization of Nature and the naturalization of humanity seem to be two wheels of a moving cart symbolic of the historical development of human culture. A human person is up there riding the cart toward a destination of self-fulfillment or wholeness. During this process, humankind as a super-biological species stirs up not only the "humanization of the external Nature" (*waizai ziran de renhua*), but also the "humanization of the internal Nature," which then opens

---

[27] Li Zehou, *Shuo ziran renhua* [On the Humanization of Nature], in Li Zehou, *Lishi bentilun/Jimao wushuo* [Historical Ontology/Five Essays from 1999], pp. 263–264.

up both the cognitive realm (free intuition) and the ethical realm (free will). All this is extended further and blended with the "naturalization of humanity," thus underlying the aesthetic realm (free enjoyment) per se. As a result, there arises the cultural-psychological formation with the help of historical sedimentation, and it is from this perspective of historical ontology and philosophical psychology that the new implications of heaven-human oneness are proposed.[28]

I personally think more implications can be proposed in accordance with what is in need of. As we know, the human expression of ideas and feelings in art can be broadly categorized into three basic genres in the course of history. At the very beginning, there were no pictures and words. People therefore expressed themselves through sounds and gestures. Then, there arose the audio expression in the genre of music-dance. Later on, people started to learn how to draw pictures and signs in order to keep records or express themselves. Then, there arose the visual expression in the genre of drawing or painting in particular. Eventually, words were invented and came into use. Then, there arose the verbal expression in the genre of literature and poetry, for instance. In recent centuries, humankind tends to be verbally trapped or yoked by language of any conceivable kind. The situation is worsened to the extent that a person does not speak words but instead words speak the person. This is often the case with those who are reluctant to think on their own but ready to parrot back what is said by others. Moreover, the situation as such is conducive to the retrogression of audio and visual capacities. Some people attribute it to the over-humanization of the faculties and senses as modern city dwellers are imprisoned in high-rises and contact Nature merely by peeping out at the moon or the sun in the sky through windows, for example. Under such circumstances, the "naturalization of humanity" becomes indispensable in that it will be apt to revive human sensibility in an aesthetic sense. That is, the audio and visual sensibilities will be enhanced as one is exposed to natural sounds and scenes upon his return to Nature. All this can be seen as a favorable effect of heaven-human oneness to some extent.

---

[28] Ibid., pp. 266–267.

1.3 A Pragmatic Alternative

As is explicated above, the threefold significance and the two-dimensional orientation are all leagued with the rationale of heaven-human oneness. Hypothesized from all this is the highest form of achievement that human as human pursues. It is called "heaven-and-earth realm" or "cosmic realm of being" (*tiandi jingjie*), symbolizing the cultivation of a superior personality with a universal view and cosmopolitan mind. By principle, "the cosmic realm of being" is preoccupied with the excellence of heaven-human oneness. Accordingly, the cosmic personality is capable of serving not only the society and humankind, but also the universe and all things. He is therefore willing to do whatever possible so as to retain all beings or things in their most proper positions. What he heads for is, in Mencius' terms, the becoming of "heavenly citizen" (*tianmin*).[29] Such citizenship is expected to transcend the conventional limits of ethnic race, nationality, state territory, or political borderlines altogether.

In brief, the cosmic realm of being is based on a sense of mission to "serve heaven" (*shi tian*) by doing the utmost to help all things grow properly in the universe. Those who are in favor of this realm of being will see themselves not merely as social beings, but also as universal beings, claiming personal commitment to both society and universe at the same time. Being in this case, they enjoy a thorough understanding of human nature, and of the interrelationship between humankind and the universe. And in a spiritual sense, they seem to have moved from the finite "I" into the infinite "I," and thereby live in freedom instead of necessity.

As is detected, the cosmic realm of being sounds as much idealistic as abstract. But, it can be made somewhat accessible when specified in terms of loving people and treasuring things. If it is properly applied in this regard, it will come out to be in favor of both cosmopolitan consciousness and eco-environmental protection to a certain degree. For this

---

[29] Hierarchically according to Fung Yu-lan's comparison, "the cosmic realm of being" is above the other three categories, including "the moral realm of being" (*daode jingjie*) preoccupied with the values of humanity and righteousness, "the utilitarian realm of being" (*gongli jinngjie*) preoccupied with the gaining of merits and profits, and "the instinctive realm of being" (*ziran jingjie*) preoccupied with the satisfaction of desires and wants. Cf. Fung Yu-lan, *Xin yuan ren* [On the Meaning of Human Life], in Fung Yu-lan, *Zhenyuan liushu* [Consistency and Fundamentality: Six Books] (Shanghai: Huadong Norman University Press, 1996), Vol. 2, pp. 568–649.

reason, it could be recommended as a pragmatic alternative to confront with the eco-environmental problems according to the law of reciprocity between Nature and Humankind.

In my perception, the applicability of this alternative is preconditioned by the motivation to know natural law *(tian li)* and develop humane mind *(ren xin)*. Here, natural law also stands for the universal principle while humane mind for the altruist love. The knowledge of natural law helps one take rational actions when making use of natural resources, and the development of humane mind guides one to treat people and things alike with equal affinity. Relatively speaking, the former requires great-mindedness and insightfulness into the principles of all things through investigation, whereas the latter requires humaneness and adherence to the virtue of sincerity. Both of them involve a sense of mission and an awareness of reciprocal relationship. This is because we human beings are part of Nature. We are susceptible to the impact from other species and things in the world, and in return, we have impact on them as well by what we do in general.

Mostly, the mind is acknowledged to play a vital role in conducting the virtue of loving people and treasuring things either for sociocultural or eco-environmental enterprises. Just imagine, if the mind is merely confined to human welfare proper, it will be too narrow and self-centered to take into due consideration the welfare of those other than *homo sapiens*. Such narrow-mindedness or anthropocentrism is inclined to meet human needs by overexploiting other things like natural and maritime recourses. Then, the eco-development might be thrown out of balance and the eco-environment be put into jeopardy. An offhanded case in North China is the environmental crisis relating both to the desertification of the grassland due to excessive husbandry[30] and to the increase of sandstorms due to the wide-spreading desertification. Facing this vicious cycle, we predict a decisive breakthrough to be made by looking into the cultivation of the mind per se.

Then, there arises the question about how to cultivate the mind to the fullest extent as is expected. As far I could see, this involves a process of which there are at least three essential stages. First and foremost, it

---

[30] According to official statistics, the proportion of excessive animal husbandry in China is up to 36.1% of the total area in Inner Mongolia, Ningxia, Gansu, Tibet, Xinjiang regions, and Qinghai Province.

is expected to do what Zhang Zai advices: Man ought to "broaden the mind to accommodate the whole universe" (*da qi xin, yi ti tianxia zhi wu*). The will to "broaden the mind" represents a transcendent pursuit as is schemed to turn the small "I" into the big "We." Accordingly, it is conducive to the mind-universe relationship that is by nature spiritual rather than physical, and mental rather than spatial. Then, what is it for in this regard? It is intended to enable humans to "experience and understand the real condition of all under heaven." "The real condition" as such embodies the living and environmental *status quo* that affects directly or indirectly the human condition. "To experience and understand the real condition" is not possible unless we have relevant knowledge and empathy at least. In this case, the knowledge comes from investigating the connections among all things and the empathy from projecting feelings into the surroundings. With this state of mind, humans will be ready to transposition themselves into "all things in the whole universe" and naturally develop a conscience of treasuring them in all. It is noteworthy that Zhang Zai's notion also implies something negative. He calls on people to broaden the mind simply because it usually remains small, confining itself to the narrow domain of personal gains and losses only. Such small-mindedness is conducive to either egoism or anthropocentrism, say, the self-claimed privilege that man is the measure of all things. Hence, the cultivation of broad-mindedness is indispensable in this regard.

Subsequently, efforts must be redoubled to exercise the second strategy. That is, human race ought to "empty the mind to receive and appreciate all the good in the world" (*xu qi xin, yi shou tianxia zhi shan*). By emptying the mind is meant freeing it from any egoism or self-interestedness. The good of this kind stands for the good conscience and serves for the common good of all beings. It is derived from the altruist aspects of human individuals, social events, and natural existents at large. It needs therefore to learn the merits and virtues from others in order to do right things for all. Meanwhile, it needs to appreciate the benefits offered by others and then do them a favor in return. The whole idea seems to be that a good turn deserves another from a reciprocal perspective. It is common sense, for instance, that no one can survive without breathing in the oxygen largely produced by the plants. It is therefore the same to take care of the plants as to take care of the breathers themselves. Otherwise, it will be as harmful as to lift up a stone and then drop it on the toes of the lifter himself.

Last but not the least, it is of practical value to follow the third strategy. That is, humankind ought to "complete the mind to plan and conduct all the world affairs" (*jin qi xin, yi mou tianxia zhi shi*). As a matter of fact, the action to "complete the mind" means to engage oneself in three things at least, say, to rediscover the original mind (*benxin*), to nurture the good mind (*liangxin*), and to do the utmost through the mind (*jinxin*) by taking right actions. Confucianism believes that the mind is originally good, but might be covered up with human desires; its original good can be regained if the desires are reduced and eliminated. This asks for a cultivating process with moral sincerity. What is to be emphasized on this point is bilateral regarding the service of the mind. The service as such should be good-natured and best deployed to "plan and conduct all the world affairs." In order to fulfill this mission it is necessary not merely to make the most of the mind, but follow the logical order by making the mind broad to experience and understand all the things in the universe, by making the mind empty to receive and appreciate all the good in the world, and above all, by making the mind humane to love people and treasure things altogether.

In sum, the cosmic realm of being for humankind features loving people and treasuring things in view of heaven-human oneness. As a hypothesis, it can be creatively developed into a pragmatic alternative frame for human fulfillment and eco-environmental protection as well. Practically and ultimately, it is intended to upgrade the quality of life for humankind as a whole providing we humans become more cosmopolitan and more conscious of Heaven or Nature as part of our own being, so to speak.

CHAPTER 2

What Matters Behind Ecumenism?

Literally derived from the Hellenic idea of *Oikoumenē* (ecumene) meaning "the inhabited world," ecumenism—the word and the notion—refers today to the pursuit of peaceful cooperation between all nations and coexistence of all humans on this planet. With regard to its cardinal and teleological meanings, it broadly corresponds to the signification of the Chinese notion *tian-xia*—all under heaven,[1] which is positively revisited and recommended by some historians and thinkers from time to time.

Arnold J. Toynbee dated the first recorded use of the notion back to the regime of Liu Bang (Han Supreme Emperor 202–195 B.C.) during the early Han Dynasty and discerned that ecumenism was equated with pioneering success in international interactions and therefore proposed as remarkable means to facilitate global peace and order for the good of humankind viewed as a whole.

Today, ecumenism is once again reconsidered in a global context, for it remains relevant in social, political, economic, and cultural fields. Its relevance is deemed to apply quite extensively to world governance and global collaboration in particular. For instance, it not merely underlies the contemporary mission of "building a community of shared destiny

---

[1]The Chinese notion of *tian-xia* is rendered in English by all under heaven, all below heaven, all-under-heaven, or all-under-sky, etc.

for humankind," but also illuminates the thematic focus on "Creating a Shared Future in a Fractured World" during the 2018 Davos Forum.

This chapter looks into the rediscovery of ecumenism by Toynbee and others, revisits the idealistic uses and the historical facts related to ecumenism, and specifies the sense of compassion, the virtue of humaneness, and the teleology of harmony. Moreover, it perceives harmony as being essential to what made ecumenical policies possible in the past, and still makes them possible at the present.

2.1 "All Under Heaven" and Its Historical Implementation

The Chinese notion of *"tian-xia"*—all under heaven—can be traced back to the ancient times around the eleventh century B.C. It is now reappraised across the world and rejuvenated as a catchphrase in the political culture. According to Sebastian Harnisch, for example, it is supposed not to "depict a geographical, but a cultural community, whose boundaries are determined by knowledge and practices of China's Confucian philosophical and moral traditions."[2] I partly agree with this stimulating explanation. Yet, when probing from a historical perspective, I find the notion shows three interconnected meanings. That is to say, when used in a geographical sense, it means the entire territory of China in ancient time; when used in a political sense, it refers to the governance or regime of the whole region; and finally, when used in a cosmopolitan sense, it denotes international interactions and collaborations.

As depicted in *The Historical Records* (*Shiji*),[3] "Jia Yi concludes that '*tian-xia*' made it possible to enjoy peaceful collaboration for more than two decades during the regime of Liu Heng (Han Emperor of Wen)."[4] "*Tian-xia*" here is one of the typical justifications of the three aforementioned meanings of the term. Historically, "peaceful collaboration" was actually the consequence of Liu Bang's decision: He took the risk to make a truce agreement with his rival Empire of Huns

---

[2] Sebastian Harnisch, "China's Historical Self and Its International Role," in S. Harnisch and J.-C. Gottwald (eds.), *China's International Roles: Challenging or Supporting International Order?* (New York and London: Routledge, 2016), pp. 39–40.

[3] *The Historical Records* (*Shiji*) by Sima Qian is also rendered as *The Records of the Historian in the Han*.

[4] Sima Qian, "Qu Yuan and Jia Yi," in *The Historical Records*.

headed by Modun, after an unsuccessful confrontation at Pingcheng (modern Datong of Shanxi Province) in 200 B.C., and ever since then, this agreement has defined a national policy that was carried onward until about 127 B.C. by his successors to the throne, including Liu Heng (Han Emperor of Wen 180–157 B.C.), Liu Qi (Han Emperor of Jing 157–141 B.C.), and Liu Che (Han Emperor of Wu 141–87 B.C.).

Why did this policy keep working so well? It was largely because the Han Dynasty was established after years of domestic and foreign warfare. The new regime had a strong army that had vanquished the forces which opposed it, and united the fractured China not long ago; but politically, it could not afford to get involved in another war against the nomadic Huns and their rising power, while its priority was to secure postwar order out of a rampant chaos. In addition, it faced economic bankruptcy and had to tackle not merely a short supply of daily necessities (its agricultural basis had suffered great damage during the war years), but also a changing situation across the country: More and more people grew thirsty for peace and resentful of war. In this situation, the central government decided to embrace the Daoist (Taoist) philosophy of inaction and serenity, placed stress on the worth of tranquility for social stability, and retained the truce agreement with the aggressive Huns. All this created a long period of peace between both sides; the Han could recover from the economic difficulties and hardships during that span of time.

Under such circumstances, the Han Court was enabled to do what should be done in a sequence of critical necessity and expectation. Say, in order to primarily restore the agricultural production, it issued a disarmament program and sent veterans back home to reclaim wasteland; at the same time, it encouraged people to reactivate business markets and develop commercial enterprises, reformed many rigorous laws in order to keep its subjects safe from panic-ridden pressure and brutal punishment for wrongdoings, implemented a top-down policy of frugality in order to accumulate more savings, and improved the livelihood of its people to win their support and loyalty—and so on and so forth. According to historically authentic sources, the Han Dynasty successfully managed to attain social order and economic prosperity within decades. Sima Qian reveals a part of the picture:

> The seven decades or so witnessed a peaceful period ever since the founding of the Han Dynasty. People across the country lived a self-sufficient life all these years except for some disturbances caused by draughts and

floods. Fully saturated with grain or money were the official barns and treasuries at all levels. For example, the capital treasury was reported to store up billions of coins, and the capital barn to have an abundant amount of grain. Both of them were far beyond either the fiscal or consumption demands.[5]

As the old Chinese saying claims, "The sight of a fallen leave can help to perceive the coming autumn." That means: to see the whole through a part. Take grain, for example. When it was in short supply at the beginning of the Han Dynasty around 200 B.C., it used to cost 5000 *wen* (a unit of net value for money) per *dan* (a unit of dry measure for grain). These conditions implied a great deal of social tension and other issues. As a result of the peaceful environment that made a steady development possible for two decades—or so—during the reign of Liu Heng (Han Emperor of Wen), agricultural productivity was restored and increased because of the extensive use of iron farm tools; a tremendous output of grain ensured full supply all over the country, while its price dropped down to a little more than 10 *wen* per *dan*, nearly 500 times cheaper in fact. Ample evidences of this achievement are procured by recent archeological findings and historical studies: They are linked to actual remains of large-sized barns of the Han period.[6] Let us have an incidental remark: It is quite crucial for the state government to ensure food supply for its people because it is the most important institution in Chinese political culture throughout China's history. The people count most for the ruler, whereas the food counts most for the people. The people are most liable to take the risk to create endless troubles and to challenge the authority of their leadership that failed to make their ends meet. As luck would have it, the Han rulers succeeded in getting out of the crisis and other related problems by doing the right thing for the right reason at the right time; and by the same token, they built up a solid foundation for the subsequent advancement of national economy and strength.

---

[5] Sima Qian, "Peace and Development Documents," in *The Historical Records*.

[6] Shan'xi Institute of Archeology, *Xi Han jingshi cang* [The Capital Barns of the Western Han Dynasty] (Beijing: Cultural Relics Press, 1990). Also see Zhang Kaisheng, "Han dai liangcang chu tan" [An Initial Inquiry into the Barns of the Han Dynasty], in *Zhongyuan Wenwu* [Journal of Cultural Relics in Central China], No. 1, 1986.

2.2 Ecumenism as an Alternative

Quite interestingly, Toynbee pays a special heed to the operation aforementioned and treats it as a poster example of *tian-xia* governance pertaining to a primordial and applicable paradigm of ecumenism per se. In order to defend his observation as such, he sets out to formulate his historical approach to the unity of the past, the present, and the future, more or less in the same way as Karl Jaspers did in his historical hypothesis of "the axial period." Ostensibly, Toynbee holds this position in order to review the past and consequently to obtain a better understanding of the present, in compliance with the relevance of the lessons of history. The following lines express Toynbee's views:

> The future does not yet exist; the past has ceased to exist, and therefore, in so far as a record of the past survives, the recorded events are immutable. However, this immutable past does not present the same appearance always and everywhere. It looks different at different times and places, and either an increase or a decrease in our information may also change the picture. Our view of the relations of past events to each other, of their relative importance, and of their significance, changes constantly in consequence of the constant change of the fugitive present. The same past viewed in the same country by the same person, first in 1897 and then in 1973, presents two very different pictures; and no doubt the self-same past will look still more different when viewed in China in 2073 and even more different again when viewed in Nigeria in 2173.[7]

Noticeably, Toynbee is highly aware of past's signification—the past can mean different things at different times and places for different reasons and purposes. By virtue of a comparative study in view of the human condition, he proceeds to expose not only a disparity between Man's technological progression and his social performance, but also the "morality gap" between Man's physical power to do evil and his spiritual capacity to cope with this power. He thus arrives at the conclusion that during the last 5000 years, the gap has yawned as wide open as the mystical jaws of Hell and caused mankind to inflict on itself grievous disasters. Accordingly, Man's spiritual inadequacy has set a limit to his social

---

[7] Arnold Toynbee, *Mankind and Mother Earth: A Narrative History of the World* (Oxford: Oxford University Press, 1976), p. 589.

progress and therefore to his technological progress too.[8] This imbalance between human immaturity and technological achievements will create more problems in the field of morality than benefits in the field of economy. As a consequence, "the present-day global set of local sovereign states is not capable of keeping the peace, and it is also not capable of saving the biosphere from man-made pollution or of conserving the biosphere's non-replaceable natural resources. This ecumenical anarchy on the political plane cannot continue for much longer in an *Oikoumenē* that has already become a unity on the technological and economic planes."[9]

Then, what could be done to help humankind to get out of this plight? Toynbee looks into the past for a working alternative, focuses his attention on the Chinese outlook of *tian-xia*, understood as all under heaven, and connects the latter's feasibility to a special kind of civil service. Toynbee affirms as follows:

> The Chinese Imperial civil service had been the best of any in the Oikoumenē; it had held together a larger number of human beings in peace and order for a greater number of years than any other civil service anywhere. Yet, time after time, the Chinese civil servants had betrayed their trust and had brought China to grief by abusing their power for their own personal advantage. China's leaders have taken steps to prevent this from happening again. Whether they will be more successful than earlier Chinese reformers remains to be seen, but at least the vigour of their current action is a good augury. If the Chinese take to heart the lesson of past Chinese errors, and if they succeed in saving themselves from repeating these errors, they may do a great service, not only to their own country, but to the whole of mankind at a critical stage in mankind's enigmatic course.[10]

Obviously, Toynbee is a humanistic historian. He thereby displays a strong sense of mission when coming to reflecting upon the prospect and destiny of humankind in a global setting. His sense of mission manifests itself not merely in the above argument, but also through his dialogue with Daisaku Ikeda, the Japanese thinker—this dialogue is to

---

[8] Ibid., pp. 591–592.
[9] Ibid., p. 593.
[10] Ibid., p. 595.

be read in the *Choose Life*.[11] This book title is in fact borrowed from a divine logos in the *Bible*, that is, "I call Heaven and earth to witness against you today that I have set before you life and death, blessings and curses. **Choose life** so that you and your descendants may live."[12]

It is noteworthy that Toynbee advises humankind to choose life as a vital action to salvage human destiny by virtue of a revolution in thinking and morality. He conjectures it is a rather crucial choice because of this hard fact: Humans today are pursuing their course toward self-defeat and self-destruction. Since the survival of the human race is threatened by the imbalance between human immaturity and technological achievements, he attempts to look for a human-made cure to harness the dramatic increase in human-made evils here and across the world. Being a humanistic and insightful historian, Toynbee proposes a double check of what the Chinese civil service did in the Han Dynasty. He thereby celebrates the Chinese experimentation of *tian-xia* as a paradigm of ecumenism due to its distinct sense of compassion, peacefulness, inclusiveness, and cooperativeness in the fields of international politics, economy, and culture in particular. In accord with his discovery and comparative analysis, he places much hope on the way of governance and the form of ecumenism exercised by Liu Bang, the first Emperor of the Han Dynasty. He regards Liu as a historical example to unify all under heaven with a specific reference to the global unification that should enable us to prevent global conflicts. To Toynbee's mind, Liu Bang has learned the bitter lessons from the past events in Chinese history, abandoned the war-like ethos as well as punish-oriented rule, and introduced the *tian-xia* policy to handling international relations. For this reason, Toynbee gives much recognition to the civil service of the Han Dynasty. He does so mainly because it implemented ecumenical principles in the region. Such principles call for a humanistic stance—we should treat all humans as fellow beings in one sense, and in the other sense, we should promote an unconditional acceptance of a universal humanity, at any rate. This kind of capacity is presumed to lie in such virtues as peace-loving spirit, dynamic engagement, diligent work, persistent courage, and practical wisdom, among others.

---

[11] Arnold Toynbee and Daisaku Ikeda, *Choose Life: A Dialogue* (Oxford: Oxford University Press, 1977).

[12] *Holy Bible* (Nanking: National TSPM & CCC, 2000), Deuteronomy 30.19.

To my understanding, "the Chinese errors" herein may vary from time to time, but mainly take the form of social disorder or chaos within China as a consequence of political corruption and misleading governance. For in many cases, such disorder would weaken the institutions and undercut the social structures, and worse still, cause civil wars or foreign invasions that would turn the entire kingdom into an horrible catastrophe and split states (*guo*).

In this respect, Eric Voegelin has made a meaningful distinction between the *tian-xia* and the *guo* as a result of his comparative analysis of the Chinese ecumenism and its Western counterpart. According to his observations, the Chinese *tian-xia* is neither the cosmos nor the earth as a territorial expanse under heaven, but the earth as the carrier of human society. It is no other than the exact equivalent of the Greek *oikoumenē* in the cultural sense.[13] Moreover, Chinese ecumenism receives its peculiar coloration from the unbroken consciousness of the identity of China with humankind.[14] Eric Voegelin therefore claims:

> The tian-xia is organized as a manifold of guo, while the guo recognize themselves as part of the ecumene... there are guo that try to overthrow and replace the dynasty; but there are no guo that pretend to form a rival ecumene. The Chinese kinship over 'all below Heaven,' though it is definitely a position of power, acquired and held by force, is singularly devoid of associations with imperial conquest. The extant documents let tian-xia and guo exist in a pre-established harmony.[15]

Voegelin goes further and takes a closer look at the primordial correlation between *tian-xia* as an ecumene of states and *guo* as the states of the ecumene. He finds that this correlation forms the nucleus of layers of meaning of *tian-xia*, with a stress upon the ritual and cultural aspects of the *tian-xia* rule: These aspects are essentially in opposition to the competitive and dominant features of the *guo* administration. The *tian-xia* is hereby associated with *wen*. The *wen* is cultural in essence. Originally, it symbolizes the meaning of a pattern; subsequently, it was bestowed with further meanings—characters, ideograms, and decoration—that were

---

[13] Eric Voegelin, *The Ecumenical Age* (ed. Michael Franz, Columbia: University of Missouri Press, 2000), p. 352.

[14] Eric Voegelin, *The Ecumenical Age*, p. 354.

[15] Ibid., p. 361.

generally referred to the ornamental aspects of human life. Finally, it was associated with the arts of peace, such as dancing, music, and literature, as opposed to those of war that are designated as *wu*. The *wen* and the *wu* are mutually antagonistic because of their respective operational powers: The former operates through the attraction of its virtuous prestige (*dé*), and the latter through its armed force (*li*). At the institutional level, further ramifications of meaning arise with regard to the ruling types of *wang* and *ba*. The *wang* is the ruler of the ecumene who tends to govern through the virtuous prestige of culture for peaceful coexistence. In contrast, the *ba* stands for a hegemonic leader who tends to govern through the armed forces for war-oriented conquests. In the aggregate outcome of distinct governmental strategies, two sets of symbols have developed: The series of *guo, wu, li, ba* corresponds to the series of *tian-xia, wen, dé, wang*.[16]

Apparently, what is stated above helps rounding out the essential features of the *tian-xia* or ecumenical rule through soft power and leads to play down those of the *guo* or hegemonic rule through hard power, even though the antagonistic link between *tian-xia* and *guo* is not neglected. This observation is teleologically close to what Toynbee stresses. I do share much sympathy with all these efforts to rediscover the constructive merits of *tian-xia* policy that was pursued during the early Han Dynasty, and paid due consideration to the *status quo* of the human condition and to the global reality. In this regard, *tian-xia* can be seen as the kernel of ecumenism related to our present-day preoccupations about a possible better world order for humankind in its entirety. Apart from being something spiritual and sentimental, the idea itself can be seen as a transcultural concept because it transgresses the borders of all cultures or civilizations in the world. Moreover, it can be employed as an international asset to call for the collaboration of all the nations, which live on the same planet. Accordingly, *tian-xia* can be deployed as a co-relational concept because it commands the harmonization of human relations among all human beings who tend to embrace the sense of compassion for all fellow human beings.

However, we should point to the hidden tendency to idealize the political arena of the historical period that is referred to. According to what I could find in the historical documents, the collaboration between

[16] Ibid., pp. 361–362.

the Han and the Huns was not always smooth or peaceful. It was actually bumpy, twisty, and rather costly, because the Huns not merely asked for more compensations or tributes (living materials such as cotton cloth, silk fabrics, food and drink, rare luxuries, and forced brides) each year, but also launched sporadic incursions into North China (Daijun, Shangjun et al.) with brutal slaughtering and plundering. Moreover, the long-term compromise on the side of the Han regime conduced to the dominant power of the Huns: They conquered over 20 kingdoms in the region, including Donghu, Wusun, Hujie, and so forth, meanwhile they drove Rouzhi or Kucina Kingdom out of its homeland. All this led to the hegemony of the Huns' nomadic Empire and fast occupation of five million square kilometers, about twice more than the territory of the Han Empire itself. Such strengths and gains stretched aggressive Huns' power and encouraged them to invade frequently North China. Consequently, the Han Court had to pay *high sums* to the Huns in order to avoid conflicts and war confrontations. I am therefore inclined to perceive the practice of ecumenism at that stage as unbalanced and to stress that it benefited more to the Huns than to the Han in one sense, and in the other sense, other small and adjacent kingdoms around the Huns became the latter's preys.[17] From a geopolitical perspective, this kind of situation was likely to break the regional stability and to cause endless clashes. In other words, it would trigger the excessive exercise of the jungle law at the cost of the smaller states.

As the Chinese old saying remarks, "Anything that goes to extremes will be bound to reverse." During the regime of Liu Che (Han Emperor of Wu), a new policy was adopted to confront with the Huns. The initial confrontations were difficult and not successful, but the later campaigns turned out highly victorious. After six tough battles, the Han army eventually banished the Huns away from their headquarters close to China's borderline and chased them down to the far north of Mongolia. It was under such circumstances that the Han Dynasty reduced the heavy pressure of invasion, secured the national safety along the Northern section of the Great Wall, and restored its entire sovereignty in the proper sense of this term. By so doing, Liu Che developed a balanced mode of ecumenism that helped to open up the Silk Road for trade and cultural interactions with many countries. The Silk Road was paved through 36

---

[17] Sima Qian, "The Huns," in *The Historical Records*.

kingdoms west of China and extended first as far as to the Middle East and after to Rome.

In actuality, the application of the *tian-xia* policy to the relations between the Han and the Huns was international per se, and conducive to the first success in Chinese history of political culture. The application as such was maintained for decades; it facilitated and strengthened a bilateral peace for long periods of time. Due to geopolitical and national reasons, the unbalanced mode of ecumenism that characterized Han and Huns relation could not last forever. It was substituted by the balanced mode that helped to open up the Silk Road and to connect more countries and make them benefiting from many trades, economic interactions, cultural exchanges, international collaborations, and so on. Ever since then, China has been in the position to view the *tian-xia* policy as an important element of its ideology when handling nation-to-nation relationships, and could put it into practice extensively. However, China will be able to retain this policy when it is strong and open enough. It would fail to do so, should it be plunged into domestic chaos and drastic decline. The *tian-xia* policy would become no more than a kind of political rhetoric or verbal service. Some phases of China's long history and its ups and downs can exemplify this rhetoric and verbal service. Let us refer to the periods of the Tang, Song, Yuan, Ming, and Qing Dynasties ranging from the seventh century to early twentieth century.

2.3 Harmonism as the Key Drive

At this point, a question arises: What does really matter behind ecumenism? In other words, what could be the key drive to facilitate and propel the maneuver of ecumenism? As far as I could see, Toynbee tends to relate this drive to "a sense of compassion"—a human being is expected to love and serve all his fellow beings with an impartial devotion. In his opinion, the worldview of *tian-xia* is based on the "sense of compassion"; the latter unite "love inspired by personal acquaintance and love for all fellow human beings simply in virtue of a common humanity."[18]

As we can learn from Chinese thought, this "sense of compassion" can be identified with the concept of *ce-yin* in Mencius—the latter concept originated from the cardinal virtue of *ren* (*jen*) in Confucius.

---

[18] Arnold Toynbee, *Mankind and Mother Earth: A Narrative History of the World*, pp. 594–595.

That *ce-yin* is usually conceived as the beginning of *ren*. In classical Confucianism, *ren* means human love (*ren-ai*), often rendered as humaneness, human-heartedness, benevolence, kindness, and love above all. The doctrine of *ren* and its association with virtuous conduct is largely grounded on a double rationale: It is sustained by benevolent reason and stemmed from the emotional root. Because of the affectionate engagements it commands, it hankers after universal love (*fan-ai*) that implies to be cultivated in a processual way. First, it is directed to family members, afterward, extended to other human individuals, and finally, motivated by the desire to treasure all things in the end.

More specifically, the Chinese character *ren* (仁) itself shows a pictographic structure: It is composed of two parts, with "human" on the left side and "two" on the right side; the denotation is clear: The character involves an intimate interaction between two human individuals at least. It leads naturally to the reciprocal principle that is in line with the common interest, which the involved individuals share to a full extent. In order to act upon the virtue of *ren*, the benevolent reason is required to guide the conduct and secure the goodwill. Being deeply rooted in the synthesis of emotionality and reasonability, the exercise of *ren* consequently discloses emotion and reason as inseparable. It resorts to the benevolent reason that is inclined to work through affectionate engagement, because any form of rational action with no consideration of emotional expectation could be lopsided, discouraging, and even fruitless in many cases. Human nature shows two dimensions that are innate and binary: emotional and rational.

The developing process of the universal love sets out from who is near and reaches for what is far. Say, it starts with the love of family members and close relatives within the kinship, moves toward the love of neighbors and peoples from other nations, and ends by treasuring all things on the Earth. It undoubtedly illustrates the fundamental pivot of Chinese tradition: Family is respected as the core of affectionate relationship and social network. The family love radiates from this core to all other fellow beings, living near and afar. Such being the case, the universal love, the highest state of humaneness, or kindness in Confucianism, can be attained only when the family love goes beyond its limit and dedicates itself to all fellow human beings through altruistic cultivation and spiritual sublimation. The universal love is naturally linked to the act of treasuring all things under heaven. Nowadays, this type of love is often interpreted in terms of modern ecumenism and eco-environmental protection: It owes to its universality and inclusiveness, the convergence of the human being with nature, and so forth.

Nevertheless, the sense of compassion in connection with the virtue of humaneness is of critical necessity with regard to harmonizing human relations and facilitating social cohesion in any case. Quite distinctively, the notion of universal love seems to be more idealistic rather than realistic. In contrast, the notion of *hé* qua harmony goes the other way round in human practice. It can be therefore presumed to be the key drive to the *tian-xia* policy and its practical implementation either in the past or at the present. I hold this position with regard to the inherent logic and teleological pursuit of ecumenism proper. Actually, the Chinese word *hé* contains a gradation of meanings encompassing harmony, harmonization, concordance, and peaceful collaboration. It originally emerged in the ancient culture of rites and music (*li yue wen hua*), and was firstly employed as a musical term not merely to synthesize a variety of sounds, which were produced by diverse musical instruments, into a concordant whole, but also to ally music and dance into a harmonious union. The latter aiming at an art education to refine primitive folklores and edify homo sapiens in antiquity. Subsequently, *hé* was transformed into a doctrine of harmony, and its application extended to political, social, and moral areas. For instance, it was primarily due to the high frequency of conflicts and wars among the large and small states that harmony was sublimated up to one of Chinese political ideals for the sake of social order and human existence. Since then, it has been promoted forever and nurtured a kind of harmony-conscious heritage that led to harmonism. In this regard, harmonism is nothing else than a way to think that involves, adjusts, and coordinates different components in order to trigger practical collaboration between the shareholders from all walks of life in a community or all nation-states in the global village. In most cases, harmonism as a way of thinking and doing things together reveals such primary tendencies as follows: Distinct characteristics contribute to mutual service for mutual accomplishment; mutual opposition and assistance search for the common ground for the common good while letting differences remain differences; and because it harmonizes without being submitted to any pattern it can tackle contradictions or conflicts. From a pragmatic point of view, it puts in place a strategy that harmonizes human relations—the latter are to be understood in a sociological sense. From a teleological point of view, it is thought to be the underlying rationale of ecumenism and ultimately striving to "keep the country in peace and the people at ease" (*guo tai min an*). These characterizations of *hé* show that the latter supports a sociopolitical aspiration that has been pursued in China from the past to the present.

All in all, the concept of harmony represents not only the finality of humane governance in the Confucian teleology, but also the essential stratum of "harmonism" in Chinese mentality. As stressed repeatedly in Confucianism, harmony-consciousness is a critical component of political ideology throughout Chinese history. It is essentially peace-loving on the basis of attending to bilateral interests, mutual concerns, and cooperative interactions. Ever since the Han Dynasty in particular, it remains preoccupied with the permanent pursuit of social stability at home and international peace abroad. It therefore serves in line with an inter-beneficial rationale that tends to use ecumenism as a possible means to set up peaceful coexistence and cooperation in international relationships. Moreover, it is attributed largely to pragmatic reason[19] and concerned with responding to utilitarian demands. Accordingly, it invites to a coordinating praxis via equal-footed dialogues and consultative negotiations in order to ensure what is mutually constructive and acceptable. Its impact still remains alive: It is deeply rooted in Chinese ideology linked to sociopolitical matters in particular. And theoretically, its core substance is exemplified in certain modes of harmony with distinct and yet interactive features.[20] We hereby examine four of the latter because they are of particular relevance to ecumenism, namely the paradigmatic, the dialectic, the synthetic, and the receptive.

First and foremost, the paradigmatic mode of harmony puts much emphasis on the ideological significance of harmonization for humane governance, in light of the rites-music culture. The conception of harmony (*hé*) does not work as a guideline alone. For it requires such auxiliaries as rites that are a synthetic whole of legal codes, authorized regulations, institutional systems, mores or codes of conduct, and so forth. It was in Confucianism that the notion of harmony had been recognized as the highest form of achievement in Chinese political culture. In principle, it is intended to ensure and actualize order and peace, and to allow to assume that further social development should be possible:

---

[19] Wang Keping, "Humane Governance and Pragmatic Reason," in Wang Keping (ed.), *Rediscovery of Sino-Hellenic Ideas* (Beijing: Foreign Languages Press, 2016), pp. 159–165.

[20] Wang Keping, "Reconsidering Harmonism in China Today," in Wang Keping (ed.), *Rediscovery of Sino-Hellenic Ideas*, pp. 111–112, 119–134.

Every member of the society, from the old to the young and from the able to the disabled, should live a good and just life. This ideal is allegorically depicted in *The Confucian Analects*:

> In the process of conducting the rites, seeking harmony is the most valuable principle (*lǐ zhī yòng, hé wéi guì*). Of the ways prescribed and cherished by the ancient sage-rulers, this is the most beautiful and therefore followed alike in dealing with matters great and small. Yet, if harmony is sought merely for its own sake without having it regulated by the rites, the principle will not work in fact.[21]

Why is it so? As recorded in the historical documents, the rites in ancient China happened to be employed as a kind of performing art on many occasions including ancestral sacrifices and divinity worship. The performance incorporated not only ceremonial proprieties or rituals, but also music and dance. In its actual process, harmony is the premium goal to be attained in terms of unity in variety. Its charm and appropriateness are determined by the implementation of proper rites, the choice of suitable music and instruments, and the right number of dancers and rows. However, the artistic effect of harmony should go beyond aesthetic appreciation and be symbolically extended to the social utility of harmony in political praxis—humane leadership and efficient teamwork are linked to harmony.

In Confucius, harmony forms the keystone of good and humane leadership, and operates as it does in music. It radiates upward to the superiors and downwards to the subordinates, thus facilitating concord and cohesion among people from all walks of life. This is the chief reason why the ancient sage-rulers prescribed and cherished the principle of harmony. In order to maintain its function, they also regulated it by means

---

[21] The English translation is modified with a particular reference to that of the same passage in these two versions: (1) "Of the things brought about by the rites, harmony is the most valuable. Of the ways of the Former Kings, this is the most beautiful, and is followed alike in matters great and small, yet this will not always work: to aim always at harmony without regulating it by the rites simply because one knows only about harmony will not, in fact, work." See Confucius, *The Analects* (trans. D. C. Lau, London: Penguin Books, 1979), 1:12. (2) "In practicing the rules of propriety, appropriateness is to be prized. In the ways prescribed by the ancient kings, this is the excellent quality, and in things small and great we follow them. Yet it is not to be observed in all cases. If one, knowing how such appropriateness should be prized, manifests it, without regulating it by the rules of propriety, this likewise is not to be done." See Confucius, *The Confucian Analects*, in *The Four Books* (trans. James Legge, Changsha: Hunan Press, 1995), 1:12.

of rites in specific situations. All this suggests that a really rational and appropriate assessment of harmony lies not merely in viewing the rites as institutional regulations and codes of conduct, but also in considering the principle of correctness that works according to specific situations. Otherwise, harmony is to be vain when it is attained for its own sake by means of a mechanical patternization or uniformity of all the differences.

At this point of our argumentation, there arise at least two questions: Why such an importance is recognized to harmony? Why is it necessary to distinguish between harmony and uniformity or harmonization and patternization. To answer the first question, let us turn to the dialectic mode of harmony. This mode requests a wise treatment of the interactive connection of opposites within forms of things: It complies with the principle of harmonizing or conciliating the conflict caused by the opposition. That has been proposed by Zhang Zai, a later Confucian thinker in the Song Dynasty:

> As there are forms or aspects of things, there are their opposites within (*yŏu xiang si yŏu dui*). These opposites will likely stand in opposition to what they do (*dui bi făn qi wei*). Opposition leads to conflict (*yŏu fan si yŏu chou*). Conflict is then to be harmonized and resolved (*chou bi hé er jie*).[22]

This hypothesis bears a dialectic methodology. Its line of thought obeys to this logical sequence: Wherever are forms of things (*xiang*) of any conceivable kind, there is inevitably the objective existence of opposites (*dui*) within them. These opposites are not merely interdependent, but also interactive as regards their respective functions. As a consequence, they will lead to their coexistence in an ontological sense, and meanwhile, to their reciprocal opposition (*făn*) in a kinetic sense. When the power of their opposition grows to a certain extent, it gives rise to the tension of conflict (*chou*).

According to Zhang Zai, the tension of conflict will be removed or reduced if the opposites are brought to unity or concord by virtue of harmonization or reconciliation (*hé*). In this case, the emphasis on harmonization or reconciliation corresponds to the conventional focus on the value of union or convergence of opposites or differences in the

---

[22] Wang Fuzhi, *Zhangzi zhengmeng zhu* [Commentary on Zhang Zai's Works] (Beijing: Zhonghua Book Company, 1975), p. 25. The English rendering is slightly modified with a particular reference to Wing-tsit Chan's translation. Cf. Wing-tsit Chan, *A Source Book in Chinese Philosophy* (New Jersey: Princeton University Press, 1973), p. 506.

Chinese mode of thought. It consequently claims that the final solution to the tension of conflict is hidden in the power of harmony. Noticeably, this logic is less applicable to the natural world in spite of artificial interferences from without. In contrast, it is more applicable to many realms of the human world where the pursuit of varied desires and wants may lead to possible conflicts between persons, families, communities, companies, races, nations, and countries. Due to this practical applicability, the substance of harmonism is often viewed as the philosophical ground for the win-win approach to address any conflict or strife that happen.

Now, let us look at the second question about the distinction between harmony and uniformity. It is recognized that the notion of harmony tends to accommodate and reconcile differences for the sake of a common ground, while that of uniformity tends to reject any difference as it attempts to uniform all differences by applying one pattern. At this point, we shall shift to the synthetic mode of harmony and its distinct but correlated characteristics. The synthetic mode not merely stresses the distinction between harmony and uniformity, but also calls for a proportionate synthesis of varied elements engaged in a common pursuit. It is exemplified by the soup allegory that Yan Ying uses to illustrate the categories of harmony and uniformity.[23]

---

[23] Zuo Qiuming, *Zuozhuan* (Zuo's Commentaries on the Spring and Autumn Annals, ed. Wang Shouqian et al. Guizhou: Guizhou Renmin Press, 1992), p. 1303. The translation is mine. "Harmony (*hé*) is different from uniformity (*tong*). Seeking harmony is like making a soup. One uses water, fire, vinegar, soy source and prunes all together to stew with fish and meat. The chef mélanges harmoniously all the ingredients for a tasteful soup. In the process of making, he adds something more into it when finding its taste a bit too light; and he reduces something less when finding its taste a bit too heavy. The gentleman enjoys such a soup because it keeps one's mind in peace. The interrelationship between the ruler and his courtier should be correspondingly similar in this case. When observing what the ruler thinks right contains something wrong, the courtier points out the wrong aspects and meanwhile reinforces the right aspects. When observing what the ruler thinks wrong contains something right, the courtier points out the right factors and meanwhile rules out the wrong factors. By so doing, the governance is retained in peace and harmony without violating the rites such that the masses are freed from the mind of competitiveness and contentiousness.... The ancient sage-rulers used to adjust the five flavors (sweet, sour, bitter, spicy, salty) for soup and harmonize the five sounds (*gong, shang, jue, zhi, yu* that parallel to the five-note scale of 1, 2, 3, 5, 6) for music in a metaphorical sense that they did this in order to ensure the calmness of their minds and accomplish their conduct of state affairs.... But there arises a problem if what the ruler thinks right or wrong is readily and repeatedly considered right or wrong by the courtier called *Ju*. This is just like making a soup with water only. It will be tasteless and no one would like to have it. It is also like playing the same note by the musical instrument of *qin-se*. It will be boring and no one would like to listen to it. The same is true of the idea of uniformity (*tong*)."

As it is claimed in the given allegory, no one can make a nice soup out of a single ingredient. Nor can one compose a fine piece of music with a single sound. The soup that is cooked out of a diversity of ingredients becomes more tasteful and appealing. It features an appropriate mixture of the five flavors, including sweet, sour, bitter, spicy, and salty, say each flavor preserves its individuality but at the same time merges with other flavors, making all of them much richer and pleasant in a comprehensive manner. The same is true of music with the integrated melody of the five sounds comprising *gong, shang, jue, zhi,* and *yu* that are correspondingly parallel to the five-note scale of 1, 2, 3, 5, 6. Hence, it is advantageous to have some more ingredients involved because they produce better results when brought into function by the principle of harmony in a metaphorical sense. Likewise, the category of harmony suggests more than it appears in this case.

Above all, harmony embodies a complementary relationship within which all the components are organically interactive and mutually beneficial. This is not merely observable in the making of soup and music, but also in conducting state affairs as the cooperation between the ruling and the ruled shows. Even though two sides do have opposite views and different judgments, they should consider things from each other's standpoints according to the principle of harmony. As the positive aspects are properly combined and the negative ones tentatively suspended in the search for the common good, harmony serves to decrease the wrong actions and to increase the right ones in the praxis of governance and the process of decision making. That's why harmony is always cherished as the highest strategy in the art of leadership or political philosophy in China. Contrarily, if the courtier follows the ruler blindly, the two sides seem to have bilateral agreement or false harmony, which may well be named uniformity in the pure sense of this term. Then, what would be decided could be lopsided and misleading, if it is viewed from the perspective of the de facto situation. Such features of uniformity obviously go against those of real harmony in effect.

Undeniably, this kind of synthetic tactic connotes a dynamic process of transformational creation. During this process, all the involved elements undergo a transformational synthesis: they change and collaborate while maintaining their individual identity, just as depicted in the soup, the salt is dissolved while its taste persists. Moreover, it is mixed up with other ingredients like vinegar or sugar to produce something more special and tasteful. This process is, by itself, creative in the true sense of this term.

It draws upon diversity in a harmonized form rather than upon uniformity and its patternizing effect. As a rule, diversity in a harmonized form shows the compatibility of different elements that are treated as necessary and indispensable. The harmonized form is therefore able to constitute an organic whole in which different elements are transformed, interact and reveal a new vitality, thus conducing to newborn things in a reconstructive and recurring system. This process pertains to chain reaction and sustainable development as well. Quite reversely, uniformity in a patternized mode rejects any difference and accepts similarities only. Hence, it is characterized by a mechanical multiplication of the same identities. Such sameness has no catalyst and produces no chemical change or combination. Just as the soup analogy shows, one single ingredient makes nothing rich and appealing. Such being the case, uniformity in a patternized mode is assumed to be static and short-lived, whereas diversity in a harmonized form is thought to be dynamic and long-lived (*hé neng sheng wu, tong ze bu ji*).

Linked with the synthetic mode is the receptive mode of harmony that depends upon the principle of harmonization without being patternized or of harmony with no uniformity. This kind of principle contains a moral message related to the discrepancy between the gentleman (*junzi*) and the petty man (*xiaoren*) according to what Confucius asserts:

> The gentleman harmonizes his relationship with others but never follow them blindly (*hé er bu tong*). The petty man just follows others blindly disregarding any principle of harmony (*tong er bu hé*).[24]

As we can read in this statement, the gentleman acts according to the principle of harmonization without being "patternized," while the petty man acts according the rule of "patternization" without being harmonized. The rationale of harmonization with no patternization is by nature inclusive and tolerant because it is receptive and open to different but constructive components. It consequently hankers after unity in diversity and revolts against any hegemonic dominance of the one over the many. Conversely, the rule of patternization without harmonization is factually exclusive and intolerant because it tends to be non-receptive

---

[24] The English rendering of the original Chinese expression is rephrased with reference to the above two versions apart from a bilingual one by Cai Xiqin and Lai Bo. Cf. Confucius, *Analects of Confucius* (trans. Cai Xiqin and Lai Bo, Beijing: Sinolingua, 1994), 13:23.

and closed to elements that are not absolutely similar. It therefore refuses to draw similarity from discrepancy, but clings to singular similarities alone. The one who "follows others blindly" is meant to adopt the same pattern of behavior as these others have, because they share beliefs, hobbies, identifications, interests, or value system without reasonable consideration and thus tend to form a clique or group that disregards the nature of harmonization and the virtue of justice altogether. In contrast, the gentleman is alleged never to do so because he tends to put himself in other's position and to search the common good, whereas the petty man is different—he cares more about personal interests than anything else. He ignores public ethics, readily mingles with his so-called group or gang members of an exclusive kind, and does not think of doing justice to others and society viewed as a whole. In other words, selfish and narrow-minded as he is, the petty man embraces the idea of patternization merely as the model of being similar to others within a group, complying with what they share in order to secure the same identification and exclusive interests; they disregard any commitment to the common good. He and his like will in no way appreciate and even understand real harmony as a moral imperative that is based on such cardinal virtues as human-heartedness, righteousness, and reciprocal kindness. Instead, they distort harmony and shape it into uniformity. We could therefore conclude that the rationale of harmony or harmonization without being patternized will lead to inclusive harmonism in a positive manner, whereas the rule of uniformity or patternization without being harmonized leads toward exclusive groupism in a negative manner.

In addition, the two categories of harmony and uniformity indicate two different moral codes. The former is oriented toward the community's good and grounded on the virtues of *ren* (reciprocal benevolence, human-heartedness, kindness, and love) and *yi* (righteousness or justice). Harmony is possible only when personal cultivation develops into the supreme level of "gentlemanship" that allows to go beyond one's own interest-pursuit. Uniformity is directed toward the individual good and determined by one's own desires and profits. It is confined to selfishness and working at the cost of others' welfare. Moreover, either harmony or uniformity suggests a kind of means preconditioned by value judgment, say harmony is intended to integrate and reconcile organically certain things and orient them toward a higher *telos* related to the collective-conscious many, whereas uniformity is intended to impose patterns to anything and a lower *telos* related to the self-centered few.

Accordingly, the gentleman as a moral being is prone to persuade and convince people on a reasonable basis: He considers things in all possible aspects and in the most adequate and appropriate fashion. He is so capable and trustworthy that he will win support, respect, cooperation, and even submission from others. The petty man—as an egoist—always readily clings to his own interests of various kinds by imposing his will upon others or is prone to patternize cliques' or gangs' mental and behavioral modes by force. Should he be unable to impose his will, he will go off the track and turn into a yes-man, pleasing people around just for the sake of a pretentious and fake harmonized relationship, at the expense of justice or righteousness. Such a relationship is definitely false and short-lived as it disguises petty man's real intention to serve his personal purposes and to meet his practical needs. This type of personality is therefore accused to be *xiangyuan* (a person who appears honest and cautious, but is actually pretentious as a name-dropper or a deceiver is). This kind of man is by nature "a thief of morality" (*de zhi zei ye*) who will ruin all the virtues.[25]

From the above comments, we can conclude that the four modes of harmony trigger the collaboration to confront with differences, contradictions, and even conflicts. They are therefore considered to be underlying principles in the application of ecumenism. As we have shown, they constitute the main part of harmonism, which is often conceived as an indispensible prerequisite or fundamental drive of ecumenism. Relatively speaking, the paradigmatic and dialectic modes are sociopolitical by nature, for they are intended to approach the ultimate goal of harmonized human relations and social order by means of humane governance. The synthetic and the receptive modes are methodological in practice, for they are designed to integrate different but constructive components and to foster unity within diversity, while evading the arbitrary One over the symphonic Many. Let's have examples. If we lived in a fractured world with a low index of happiness, we could turn to the paradigmatic mode and join our efforts to build up a harmonized world for all. If we had to confront with a high frequency of conflicts and clashes, we could take up the dialectic mode as a possible solution to reduce, if not to eradicate, this awesome frequency and have a more inhabitable world. Running into so many discrepancies and oppositions in this domain, we

---

[25] Confucius, *Analects of Confucius*, 17:13.

could proceed to reconsider the synthetic mode in order to create something transcendent and more agreeable. Should we have to respond to transient misunderstandings and moderate biases in social and even international encounters, we could think over the receptive mode and utilize it to enhance intercultural communication and trigger empathic reactions. Sure enough, more should be done in all these fields in order to ameliorate our problematic ecumene and the human condition as well.

In the final analysis, the operation of ecumenism is culturally determined in general. It relies on harmonism in a large proportion. As for Toynbee's assessment of ecumenism as an alternative to peace and order, we should view it as being of much relevance for global governance today. Yet, the promotion of ecumenism is by no means an easy enterprise. As early Daoism proposed, a working approach to the most difficult task lies in dealing first with the easiest part of it. Accordingly, we should first begin by fostering a conceptual perception of ecumenism for a shared future. And second, we should take specific actions to facilitate multilateral dialogues, political consensus, practical guidelines, institutional mechanisms, and other engagements we may be in need of. All these actions will be gradually processed, rather than equated with dramatic changes.

CHAPTER 3

Harmonization Without Being Patternized

The new millennium has been expected to be a promising era for peace and development. Contrary to all these expectations, its very outset is shrouded in terror, fear, hatred, tension, conflict, and war, among many other forms of frictions and disputes. Hence, there arise questions in this regard. For instance, what is wrong with this world and humankind in practice? And what is the possible origin of such agonies now and then?

As noted in the conventional ideology of China, Buddhism tends to conceive life as the fountainhead of all miseries and sufferings due to insatiable desires and passions amid *homo sapiens*. Likewise, Daoism (Taoism) share more or less a similar view by taking life as a tumor and death as the breaking of the tumor. These ideas seem to be somewhat relevant to human nature in a negative sense, but irrelevant to the de facto human condition because they appear as special types of "black humor," making people feel closer to tears rather than laughter.

With respect to the status quo today, one of the most destructive and blind forces is assumed to lie in misunderstanding or lack of mutual understanding across cultures and values concerned. This leads naturally to the advent of radical faith in either violence or the law of the jungle. History has proved that any radical faith of such a kind is liable to render the situation worse apart from conducing to dehumanized actions and disastrous consequences. To handle this core problem is no easy matter at all. To say the least, it calls for adequate attention to the enhancement of mutual understanding via intercultural communication and transformational creation as well. All this may firstly require seeking after certain universal guidelines or working strategies as a starting point. In this regard, some observations are offered hereby for further discussion. They start with a particular reference to F. S. C. Northrop's comparative philosophy first and then look into the Confucianist notion of harmony without uniformity (*he er bu tong*) that can be also translated as harmonization without being patternized. It is to me as one of the multicultural strategies or philosophical principles thus deployed to meet with the chaotic times relating to global or glocal tendencies at present stage.

3.1   The Meeting of East and West

Mass media witnesses a voluminous publicity of globalization and its aftermath today. It is one of the most imposing culturescapes we encounter here and there in many areas. Globalization as a worldwide phenomenon is often described in such metaphorical terms as "global village" either for good or bad. It has its undeniable impact on us moderns to the extent that we think of its effects, positive or negative, in various ways. Talking about the status quo of the "global village," its "potential villagers" across the world can hardly see eye to eye with each other on this point. Some of them assume it as an actual reality; some regard it as a seeming possibility; some view it as an idealistic fantasy; some hold it as a form of discourse power intended to allure a weak culture to model itself on its strong counterpart; some even go on to condemn it as a hidden monster to promote "the law of the jungle" via sugarcoated promises, serving as a driving force of post-colonialism; and others simply take actions, radical or moderate, to freeze it by forcing it back into "Pandora's Box". Different attitudes and positions represent different values, judgments, and interests alike. Quite naturally, it gives rise to endless disputing about it.

Yet, the conception of the so-called global village is seen grounded on a rolling pebble of hypothesis, for such a village is nowhere to be found in fact and its blueprint still remains as a dream-like image. Self-evidently, the world as a whole is still divided culturally and geographically into two major hemispheres, East and West. These two parts used to be depicted by Joseph R. Kipling as follows:

> East is East, West is West,
> And never the twain shall meet.[1]

Of course, outdated is this arbitrary argument about the traditional boundary between East and West, because there have been a great deal of global changes due to the international and intercultural interactions that have been carried on for so long a time ever since the Industrial Revolution. Moreover, a considerable number of scholars throughout the world have made tremendous endeavors to remove such boundary by proposing a variety of necessary and constructive syntheses. Among many others, F. S. C. Northrop is relatively forward-looking as a result of his early initiative to stir up an intellectual pondering on the possibility of intercultural transformation. As is signified in his book of *The Meeting of East and West* (1945), he attempts to break up Kipling's dogma. This counterargument could be, as it occurs to me, generalized into two lines in contrast with Kipling's:

> East is East, West is West,
> And why not the twain shall meet.

Having lived through the two wars, Northrop sharply spots out the ideological conflicts demonstrated by the two allies in the 1940s known as the traditional democracies and the communist Russia, and stays therefore aware of the eve of the forthcoming Cold War. But, as an idealist and pacifist, he seemingly fails to see through the entire nature of political power and its dominant force. Instead, he pursues his ideals by advocating the primary importance and critical necessity of mutual understanding, intercultural communication, and complimentary interaction between East and West. He is considerably observant and optimistic for the time then. Accordingly, he voices such a viewpoint with straightforward clarity in the "Preface":

> The time has come when these ideological conflicts must be faced and if possible resolved. Otherwise, the social policies, moral ideals and religious aspirations of men, because of their incompatibility one with another, will continue to generate misunderstanding and war instead of mutual

---

[1] F. S. C. Northrop, *The Meeting of East and West* (New York: Macmillan Company, 1946, rep. 1960), p. 454.

understanding and peace.... It is hardly likely that these sources of conflicts can be faced and removed in practice within the halls of parliaments and the heated actions of the market place, where slogans are carelessly bandied about, special interests are at work, and passions are easily aroused, unless the problems raised are first traced to their roots and then resolved in theory within the calmness of the study where the meaning of words like "democracy" and "communism" can be carefully determined and the issues which they define can be looked at more objectively. It is with this timely, important and difficult undertaking that this book is concerned, as its sub-title indicates.[2]

"This book" mentioned here is no other than *The Meeting of East and West*, and its subtitle is *An Inquiry Concerning World Understanding*. As read in the passage cited, Northrop is deeply concerned and even worried about the destructive force of misunderstanding stemmed from ideological conflicts as a hidden cause of war. At the same time, he is highly conscious of the service of mutual understanding and its possibility of peace. For this reason, he makes a crying demand for filling up the gap between East and West and goes on to distinguish between practice and theory regarding the effect of such work. Owing to his skepticism in view of the practical operation, he places more stress on the theoretical aspect. He claims the credits of the calmness of the study and the significance of exploring the roots or spirit of both Oriental and Occidental cultures. His hypothesis lies in that a world understanding can be reached by virtue of sufficient knowledge and complimentary synthesis of the two cultures in the main. All this implies a hidden form of dialogue among civilizations and cultures as it seems to me.

As a consequence of his exploration of the two broad cultures in pursuit of world understanding, he eventually arrives at a two-term-based relation of epistemic correlation. The relation is supposed to take place between two components: aesthetic and theoretical. The former symbolizes the spirit of the Eastern culture, while the latter the spirit of the Western culture. One is accounted, according to Northrop, for the emotional, aesthetically intuitive, and ineffably spiritual nature of man and the universe, and the other for the scientific methods of hypothesis, deduction, logic analysis, and experimental confirmation. Henceforth, one is conducive to the development of art and the becoming of artist,

---

[2] F. S. C. Northrop, *The Meeting of East and West*, pp. ix–x.

while the other to the development of economy and the becoming of scientist. Eventually, there arises a reconciliation of practical wisdom. In other words, just like art and economy, artist and scientist, the aesthetic component and the theoretical component work to foster a complimentary relationship. As is affirmed in Northrop's terminology, the two components

> supplement each other in society in a remarkable manner ... so that the equally real and important differences between men do not lead them to their mutual destruction, it should eventually be possible to achieve a society for mankind generally in which the higher standard of living of the most scientifically advanced and theoretically guided Western nations is combined with the compassion, the universal sensibility to the beautiful and the abiding equanimity and calm joy of the spirit which characterize the sages and many of the humblest people of the Orient.[3]

In spite of Northrop's oversimplification and overgeneralization of the Oriental culture in terms of Chinese and Indian cultures at large, and his pompous announcement of a science-technology myth, his intention to bridge between East and West should be acknowledged and recommended for its good-natured and creative features. For he believes that such bridging between East and West can secure a peaceful world, a benefiting society, and profound human freedom, a kind of freedom that is based on the fulfillment of material needs by means of economy, and of spiritual needs by means of art. All this serves as the philosophical foundation of a decent or happy life, so to speak.

Nevertheless, what to be heeded is his lopsided judgment of the two-term-based relation which in turn contains an implicit Occident- or Euro-centrism, even though he tries hard to approach other cultures for nourishing a cosmopolitanism of his own. Such centrism is later on merged with some traces of American-centrism as is revealed in his book, *The Taming of Nations: A Study of the Cultural Bases of International Policy* (Macmillan 1953). In its last chapter, he champions a centrist notion that the American city of Philadelphia can move toward a world state. It is therefore attacked by Nakamura Moto, a Japanese thinker, because of its liability to put the reader under a strong impression of

---

[3] Ibid., pp. 495–496.

Americanized cultural imperialism.[4] Even so, no one denies Northrop's constructive efforts to promote a desirable consideration and understanding of heterogeneous cultures in favor of achieving world understanding. His mission is left undone, thus calling for a reconsideration of an alternative strategy in the current context. It is undoubtedly an urgent task because we are now living in greater jeopardy than ever at the confrontation with omnipresent shadows of terrors and clashes the world over.

3.2 Harmony Versus Uniformity

The attention Northrop pays to the Oriental heritages induces to his conclusion of the aesthetic component as the cultural spirit of the East. This is basically valid with regard to the way of intuitive thinking and artistic creation in particular. Yet, it is just one episode of the whole story. In the case of Confucianism as the cornerstone of Chinese culture, it is characterized with a strong pragmatist reason as is reflected in its ethical and political doctrines.

This pragmatist reason is both evinced and demonstrated in the ultimate goal of Confucianism that is no other than the social ideal of harmony (*hé*).[5] Compared with this ideal, the most cardinal virtue of humaneness (*ren*) as the kernel of Confucianist ethics turns out to be secondary due to its instrumental role by nature. The same is true of other Confucianist doctrines like the golden mean (*zhong yong*) as a principle of correctness and the rites-music culture (*liyue wenhua*) for moral cultivation and personality development.

The sociopolitical philosophy of Confucianism is a pragmatist one in principle. Its highest achievement is identified with the ideal of harmony that is to ensure social order and corresponding development in the meantime; its final telos is to enable every member, from old to young and from male to female, to live a good and just life. The ideal is institutionally facilitated by a system that is consisted in two leading disciplines

---

[4] Nakamura Moto, *Bijiao sixiang lun* [A Comparative Study of Ideas] (trans. Wu Zhen, Hangzhou: Zhejiang Renmin Press, 1987), p. 140.

[5] The argument is also shared by other Confucian scholars like Luo Chenglie. Cf. Luo Chenglie, "*Kongzi de sixiang hexin—hé*" [Harmony as the Kernel of Confucius' Thought], in Fudan Daxue Lishixi (ed.), *Rujia sixiang yu weilai shehui* [Confucianist Ideas and the Future Society] (Shanghai: Shanghai Renmin Press, 1991), pp. 315–326.

known as rites (*li*) and music (*yue*). The former is designed to moralize one's conduct, and the latter to humanize one's heart. In addition, the two disciplines aim to help one complete his personality through self-control and self-cultivation in one sense and to nourish the virtue of humaneness and harmonize human relations (*ren lun*) in the other sense. The essence of rites *par excellence* is distinction pointed to social stratification. The essence of music is unification with attempt to unite people of different social ranks in concord. "Once the two essentials are united organically, it is expected that they will have a restraining and moderating effect on one another, enabling society to reach a state of perfect order … which nevertheless maintain contact, join forces, and cooperate. This is the societal ideal of Confucianism."[6] That is to say, so long as people embrace and foster the virtue of humaneness and become self-conscious of harmonizing human relations, the ideal of harmony is supposed to be fulfilled and actualized in the pure sense of this term. It reveals the Confucianist logic that is determined by the pragmatist reason instead of the aesthetic intuition in this case.

Historically, the notion of harmony can be dated back to *The Book of Changes* (*Yi jing* or *I Ching*). It is in the *Xiang* commentary (*Xiang zhuan*) on the *qian* hexagram (*qian gua*) that the idea of "great harmony" (*tai he*) is touched upon for the first time. "It explains that all beings find the ultimate and proper purpose of their existence by virtue of the transformations of the *qian* path: the hard and the soft are reconciled and united, thus producing the perfect harmony by which all beings are created and on which they thrive, and then bringing a state of ultimate peace to the world."[7]

However, it is Confucius who develops the ideal of harmony in light of his political philosophy and ethics apart from his poetics. As read in *The Confucian Analects* (*Lun yü*), the concept of harmony is repeated and stressed as many as eight times on different occasions. Among many others, two expressions are most fundamental. In the first place, Confucius speaks of the merit of harmony through the voice of his contemporary Youzi as they share the same viewpoint:

---

[6] Yu Dunkang, "The Concept of 'Great Harmony' in *The Book of Changes*," in Silke Krieger & Rolf Trauzettel (eds.), *Confucianism and the Modernization of China* (Mainz: v. Hase & Koehler Verlag, 1991), p. 51.

[7] Ibid., p. 53.

> In the process of conducting the rites, seeking harmony is the most valuable principle (li zhi yong, hé wei gui). Of the ways prescribed and cherished by the ancient sage-rulers, this is the most beautiful and therefore followed alike in dealing with matters great and small. Yet, if harmony is sought merely for its own sake without having it regulated by the rites, the principle will not work in fact. (1:12)[8]

Why harmony is so important then? As known in ancient China, the rites would be constituted by legal rules, social norms, ceremonial rituals, codes of conduct, and so forth. They would be employed comprehensively as a kind of performing art to some extent. Their performance would involve not only a variety of proprieties, but also the arrangement of music and dance all together. In its actual process of organic cooperation and integration, harmony is the ultimate goal in view of unity in variety. Its charm and appropriateness are all dependent upon the proper implementation of proprieties, the suitable choice of music and its instruments, and the right number of dancers and even dancing rows, etc. However, the significance of harmony is not simply confined to the artistic performing of the rites for the sake of aesthetic contemplation and appreciation. It is analogically extended to the domain of politics and governance. Therein harmony as the keystone of good leadership radiates upward to the superiors, and downward to the subordinates, thus facilitating a concord and cohesion among the people from all walks of life in the society. This is the chief reason why the ancient sage-rulers prescribed and cherished the principle of harmony at any rate. In order to retain its function, they would also regulate it by means of the rites in accord with specific situations. Otherwise, it will end up in vain when harmony is attained for harmony's sake by patternizing all the dynamic differences within.

Aside from the political dimension, harmony as a principle is also applied to human relations. Hence, there arises another interesting argument in *The Confucian Analects*. When talking about the key discrepancy between the gentleman (*junzi*) and the petty man (*xiaoren*), Confucius

---

[8] The English translation is modified with a particular reference to these two versions: Confucius, *The Analects* (trans. D. C. Lau, London: Penguin Books, 1979), p. 61; *The Confucian Analects*. In *The Four Books* (trans. James Legge, Changsha: Hunan Press, 1995), p. 69.

utilizes the same principle in a sense of harmonizing human relations with others instead of forming a clique without any principle. As he asserts,

> The gentleman harmonizes his relationship with others but never follow them blindly (hé er bu tong). The petty man just follows others blindly disregarding any principle (tong er bu hé). (13:23)[9]

Right in this context, by "follows others blindly" is meant to form a clique disregarding not merely the nature of harmony among human relations, but also the principle of justice for all the human beings alike. A gentleman is claimed never to do so because he tends to put himself in other's position and be preoccupied with the common good. In striking contrast, the petty man is different in that he cares more about personal interests than anything else. He ignores public ethics and readily mingles himself with his so-called mates of the similar caliber in pursuit of the similar ends without thinking of doing justice to others and society as a whole. In other words, selfish and narrow-minded as he is, the petty man takes the idea of harmony merely as a vulgarized means of being uniformed within an informal group for the sake of its own purposes, regardless of any commitment to the common good or community interests. He and his like in no way appreciate and even understand the real harmony as a moral law that is based on the virtues of humaneness and righteousness. Instead, they distort harmony and shape it into uniformity instead.

Characteristically, the two categories of harmony (*hé*) and uniformity (*tong*) indicate two different ideals. The former is oriented toward the community good and grounded on the virtues of *ren* (reciprocal benevolence, humaneness, kindness, and love) and *yi* (righteousness or justice). It would be possible only when one's personal cultivation develops into the high state of gentlemanship and enables one to go beyond one's own interests. The latter is directed toward the individual good and determined by one's own desires (*yu*) and profits (*li*). It is confined to selfishness and therefore working at the cost of others' welfare. Moreover, either harmony or uniformity suggests a kind of means preconditioned by personal values. The former is intended to integrate

---

[9]The English rendering is rephrased with reference to the above two versions by D. C. Lau and James Legge apart from a bilingual one by Cai Xiqin and Lai Bo. See *Analects of Confucius* (Beijing: Sinolingua, 1994), p. 244.

and reconcile organically certain things for a higher objective related to the collective-based many, whereas the latter is intended to patternize imposingly all things for a lower objective related to the self-centered few. Accordingly, the gentleman as a moral being is prone to persuade and convince people with reasonability as he considers things most duly and appropriately in all possible aspects. He is so capable and trustworthy that he will win support, respect, cooperation, and even submission from others. The petty man as an egoist is always ready to attain his own interests of various kinds by imposing his will upon others, or to patternize mental and behavioral mode within a clique or gang by force. If not, he would go off the track and turn into a yes-man, pleasing people around for the sake of a pretentiously harmonized relationship at the expense of the preconditions or principles concerned. Such a relationship he caters for is definitely false and short-lived as it disguises his real intention to fulfill his personal purposes and practical interests. This type of personality is therefore accused to be *xiangyuan* (a person who appears honest and cautious but is actually pretentious as a name-dropper or deceiver). It is by nature "a thief of morality" (*de zhi zei ye*)[10] who will ruin all the virtues.

As discerned from above, Confucius' consideration of harmony and uniformity is generally moralized and directed to the undertakings of human relations, personal cultivation, and state governance. When traced back to its original source, more of its significance can be rediscovered. It is derived from what Yan Ying says allegorically about the categories of harmony and uniformity:

> Harmony (hé) is different from uniformity (tong). Seeking harmony is like making a soup. One uses water, fire, vinegar, soy source and prunes all together to stew with fish and meat. The chef mélanges harmoniously all the ingredients so as to make a tasteful soup. In the process of making, he adds something more into it when finding its taste a bit too light; and he reduces something less when finding its taste a bit too heavy. The gentleman enjoys such a soup because it keeps one's mind in peace. The interrelationship between the ruler and his courtier should be correspondingly similar in this case. When observing what the ruler thinks right contains something wrong, the courtier points out the wrong aspects and meanwhile reinforces the right aspects. When observing what the ruler thinks

---

[10] *The Confucian Analects* (trans. James Legge), 17:13.

wrong contains something right, the courtier points out the right factors and meanwhile rules out the wrong factors. By so doing, the governance is retained in peace and harmony without violating the rites such that the masses are freed from the mind of competitiveness and contentiousness.... The ancient sage-rulers used to adjust the five flavors (sweet, sour, bitter, spicy, salty) for soup and harmonize the five sounds (gong, shang, jue, zhi, yu that parallel to the five-note scale of 1, 2, 3, 5, 6) for music in a metaphorical sense that they did this in order to ensure the calmness of their minds and accomplish their conduct of state affairs.... But there arises a problem if what the ruler thinks right or wrong is readily and repeatedly considered right or wrong by the courtier called Ju. This is just like making a soup with water only. It will be tasteless and no one would like to have it. It is also like playing the same note by the musical instrument of qin-se. It will be boring and no one would like to listen to it. The same is true of the idea of uniformity (tong).[11]

As noted in the allegory, no one can make a nice soup out of a single ingredient such as water only. Nor can one compose a fine piece of music with a single sound. In striking contrast, the soup that is so cooked out of a variety of ingredients becomes more tasteful. It features an organic mixture of the five flavors; that is to say, each flavor keeps its identity but at the same time merges with other flavors, making all of them richer and more appetizing. The same is true of music with the integrated melody of the five sounds. Hence, it is advantageous to have more ingredients involved because they produce better results when brought into function by the principle of harmony. Likewise, harmony as a category denotes much more as follows.

Fore and foremost, it embodies a complementary relationship within which all the components are interactive and mutually beneficial. This is not merely observable in the making of soup and music, but also in the conducting of state affairs as is shown in the cooperation between the ruler and the courtier. Even though both sides do have opposite views and different judgments, they would consider things from each other's standpoints according to the principle of harmony. When the positive aspects are properly combined while the negative ones are tentatively suspended in pursuit of the common good, it serves to decrease the wrong actions but increase the right actions in the praxis of governance and the

---

[11] The passage is quoted from *Zuo zhuan* [Zuo Qiuming's Commentary on the *Spring and Autumn Annals*], Zhaogong XX, 522 B.C.

process of decision making. Hence, harmony is always cherished as the highest strategy in the art of leadership or political philosophy in China. Contrarily, if the courtier follows the ruler blindly, the two sides seem to pose a gesture of bilateral agreement or false harmony, which may well be called "uniformity". Then, what they decide on could be lopsided and misleading from the perspective of the de facto situation. Such characteristics of uniformity self-evidently go against those of real harmony in effect.

Secondly, the strategy as such connotes a dynamic process of transformational creation. During the process, all the elements involved undergo a transformational synthesis, thus changing and collaborating with one another yet meanwhile maintaining their individual identity. Just as is savored in the soup, the salt is dissolved but its taste remains inside. Moreover, it is mixed up with other ingredients like vinegar to produce something more distinctive and tasteful. The process as such is creative and productive in its true sense. It draws upon diversity in a harmonized form rather than uniformity in a patternized mode. As a rule, diversity in a harmonized form features compatibility with different elements that are treated as something necessary and indispensable. It is therefore able to constitute an organic whole in which different elements are transformed and interacting with new vitality, thus conducing to newborn things in a reconstructive and recurring system. This gives rise to chain reaction and sustainable development as well. Quite reversely, uniformity in a patternized mode rejects different elements but accepts what is alike only. Hence, it is characterized with a mechanical multiplication of the same substance or a one-plus-one connection. Such sameness has no catalyst and produces no chemical change or combination. Just as the soup analogy shows, one single ingredient makes nothing rich and appealing. Such being the case, uniformity in a patternized mode is assumed to be static and short-lived, whereas diversity in a harmonized form to be dynamic and long-lived.

Last but not least, the category of harmony also suggests a dialectic state. United therein are the opposites. This makes possible further development and all the other services aforementioned. Yet, it must be pointed out that Yan Ying's description of harmony as a principle focuses on the positive aspects of unity in opposites only. His knowledge of the dialectic relations revealed by means of harmony is so limited that he fails to detect the intrinsic struggle or conflict among the opposites. In a word, the soup he proposes is a collected soup in harmonious proportion. Likewise, his understanding of unity remains at the level of reconciliation. His philosophy of this kind is obviously intended to supply a theoretical foundation of his political reformism. Such reformism is to my mind worthwhile if compared with any blood-shedding revolution or inter-civilization clashes in whatever rhetoric or propaganda.

3.3 The Need of a New *Philosophos Poiesis*

As noticed from above, the first part of this argument revisits the Northropian cosmopolitanism with regard to the meeting of East and West. The second part exposes a rediscovery of the Confucianist ideal of harmony in contrast with uniformity. At this point, a kind of relevance can be drawn from what is presented foregoingly with reference to the sociocultural background.

It is no secret that globalization haunts almost every corner of the earth. Its key service is often likened to a double-edged sword under certain circumstances. That is to say, it can be utilized diplomatically either as an intruding force to patternize values worldwide or as a defensive impetus to stir up glocalization here and there in many countries. Encountered with such a paradoxical situation, we need to nurture a new *philosophos poiesis* in praxis. What is literally meant by *philosophos* (φιλοσοφος) is the love of wisdom, by *poiesis* (ποιησις) is the act of making or creating, and by *philosophos poiesis* is no other than the search for wisdom-oriented creation. Accordingly, this new *philosophos poiesis* is claimed to stay open to transcultural reconsideration above all. It is thus intended to foster and procure intercultural sensibility, cosmopolitan outlook, and transformational creation for the sake of "world understanding".

More specifically, the new *philosophos poiesis* is cultural in essence. It is deployed to help one revalue the beaten track, transcend the conventional mentality, and broaden the constrained horizon. As formulated by anthropologists on many occasions, culture amounts to a way of life in a broad sense. It is constituted by such major dimensions as material, linguistic, institutional, and conceptual. It is historically evolved and sedimented in a dynamic and organic progression. As observed in reality, those who share the same way of life in the same community tend to be accustomed to it and take it for granted. They would adhere and prefer to it instead of any other way at any cost. No matter how they are advised or encouraged to be receptive to another culture discrepant from theirs, they may try it occasionally out of curiosity, shrink back from it sooner or later, and turn back to their habitualized routine. As seen in an extreme case, they would most likely uphold a centeristic worship of their own culture and stay closed to other cultures, which indicates a kind of exclusive appreciation with prejudice against others. Naturally, they are subject to a mindset filled with national sentiment, historical pride, superiority complex, and so forth. Their preference and selection seem to be so plausible that there is little to complain about it. However, it would be good for a change under certain circumstances and conditions. For instance, when they have more encounters with peoples from other communities, they are supposed to learn more about the different aspects of heterogeneous cultures involved. Quite probably, they would grow more tolerant with others and more apt to adopt a liberal attitude to different cultures. Say, they embrace their own heritage as usual, but meanwhile retain an open attitude toward other heritages. This will conduce to what is called the respective appreciation of cultures without bothering each other. So far so good. For it produces cultural co-existence, motivates reasonable interaction, paves the way for two-way communication, and upgrades transcultural awareness. Further on in the globalizational context, the increasing frequency of social encounters and cultural exchanges elicits peoples from diversified backgrounds to become more and more empathetic with one another due to mutual familiarity and active collaboration. They all can manage to pin down the merits and demerits of the cultures examined and adapt themselves to varied situations with vicarious apprehension. This represents a type of reciprocal appreciation with multilateral communication of high efficiency. At such a stage, they are well in a position to work self-consciously for higher achievements. For example, they are able to obtain a deeper insight into their homogenous culture by taking a heterogeneous counterpart as the frame of reference and facilitate the necessity of transformational creation or synthesis in terms of the complementary elements from other sources. The finality of the reciprocal appreciation embodies a teleological principle of cultural pluralism, because it purports multilateral sensibility, transcultural empathy, dialogical spirit, cosmopolitan outlook, and "world understanding" at its best.

Then, how is it possible to approach this finality of reciprocal appreciation? My personal perception in this scope ends up in a multicultural strategy as is proposed foregoingly. It is inspired by the meeting of East and West and grounded on the virtue of harmonization without being patternized. Since globalization dominated by strong culture(s) works in a way to patternize rather than harmonize other cultures or whatsoever, I would treat the strategy as a constructive alternative. This strategy runs parallel to unity in diversity, featuring a one-and-many interrelationship. It is therefore in favor of transformational creation, because it enables different components to interact and complement with each other within an organically harmonized whole. It is receptive and inclusive to the extent that it absorbs other sources into its own and thus secures a long-standing continuity or vital power for mutual motivation and sustainable innovation in accord with the common good per se

Deployed as a multicultural strategy, harmonization without being patterned is also expected to offer its service in such areas as practical morality, human relations, cultural conflicts, and international affairs, etc. Regarding the cultural conflicts that often put the world into jeopardy, for example, the strategy itself signifies a dialectical approach to the interaction between opposites. This is noticeable in Zhang Zai's hypothesis: As there are forms, there are their opposites within. These opposites necessarily stand in opposition to what they do. Opposition leads to conflict. Conflict will necessarily be harmonized and resolved.[12]

Just imagine what if the conflict remains unharmonized and unresolved. It will go on to be intensified and thus conduce to other forms of clash or warfare. Originally, the hypothesis is made with reference to all things or beings in the universe, say, how they are produced, changed, and reconciled and made co-existent by the *qi* as vital energy or material force. The *qi* is of paramount importance and serving as a hidden mover as is further explained by Wang Fuzhi as follows,

> Viewed from the transforming capacity of the qi, or material force, the Yin and the Yang bring forth respective forms in polar pairs. Hard and gentle, cold and warm, birth and death are opposite and in conflict, for instance. They help accomplish each other, free from any reason for ever-lasting and enemy-like conflict, however. Eventually, they will disperse and return to the universe of Ultimate Void (taixu). Viewed from the human nature, human beings are born to be opposite to the external things. To preserve

---

[12] Zhang Zai, "Taihe pian" [On Great Harmony], in Wang Fuzhi, *Zhangzi zhengmeng zhu* [Commentary on Zhang Zai's Works] (Beijing: Zhonghua Book Company, 1975), p. 25. The English rendering is slightly modified with a particular reference to Wing-tsit Chan's translation. Cf. Wing-tsit Chan, *A Source Book in Chinese Philosophy* (New Jersey: Princeton University Press, 1973), p. 506.

things at the expense of humans or vice versa gives rise to opposition. Opposition as such leads to conflict. However, humans cannot but make use of things to benefit themselves. This is done by means of reconciling and resolving the conflict. Hence, the key to the problem of conflict is similar in light of human nature and material force.[13]

Detected in the hypothesis is a dialectic feature. It exposes the natural existence of the opposites among things or beings and the interdependent relationship between the opposites as such. As a result of the interaction between the opposites, there arises opposition and then conflict. However, conflict will be removed as the two sides within the opposites develop into unity by virtue of harmonization or reconciliation. Harmonization (*hé*) in this context is distinctively different from patternization (*tong*). The former is ready to accommodate and reconcile differences in pursuit of a common ground, while the latter rejects any differences and attempts to uniform all by one frame of reference as if it is exclusively single-tuned or single-tracked. The emphasis on harmonization or reconciliation in this regard corresponds to the conventional focus on the value of unity in ancient Chinese thought and thus bears an important message in many fields of human practice.

Take political culture for example. The principle of harmonization without being patternized is prone to commend an organic synthesis between rule of law and rule by virtue according to the specific social setting and cultural legacy. It reserves the differences but seeks a common ground among them. By so doing would it be possible to set up a complementary interrelationship. The principle is highly conditional in that it is designed to integrate what is positive and constructive while keeping aside what is negative and destructive. However, it has no intention to deny or cover up the existence of opposition and potential conflict. Rather, it lets them interact to the extent of complementing and benefiting each other instead of turning them into a big chaos or going out of control in a *laissez-faire* manner. In addition, it takes into due consideration the suitability of cultural soil. As has been proved historically, rule of law grows well in one cultural soil, but it does not in another cultural soil due to unfavorable conditions. If transplanted by

---

[13] The English rendering is slightly modified with a particular reference to Wing-tsit Chan's translation.

force disregarding the specific circumstances, it is liable to wither or get distorted. This reminds us of a fable that reads:

> In China, the River Huai marks a borderline for different geographical features. As is usually assumed, when an orange tree is planted to its south, it bears edible fruits. When it is transplanted to its north, it turns into a tangerine tree and bears non-edible fruits. The leaves of the two trees look alike, but the fruits taste very different.[14]

To what extent are they "different" in this case? Say, one is sweet and nutritious whereas the other bitter and poisonous. Then, what is the reason behind this? It is the difference in natural environment and climate. Metaphorically speaking, if a political culture is thus transplanted in spite of the local conditions, the outcome will be much more than a bitter and poisonous kind of fruit. Hence, a creative mode of transcultural transformation is desirable and so is the due consideration of cultural differences concerned. In this case, what really counts as one of the guidelines lies in the philosophic foundation of harmonization without being patternized, for harmonization recommends transcultural transformation and reconciles cultural differences. It is in contrast with patternization that tends to worship might as right and exercise the law of the jungle in order to wipe out all differences since they are considered obstacles on the path to absolute uniformity. This does not mean that patternization never effects in handling conflict caused by cultural differences. When sustained by a strong power, it can help remove conflict such as that between cultures or civilizations in some cases. However, the conflict thus removed by force may be like burnt grass. When spring arrives, it will shoot out and flourish again. Besides, patternization by force may conduce to more problems. It may function as a sharp sword to kill a nine-headed monster. Whenever one head is chopped off, two or more would come out afterward. Regarding the delicate situation today, it is not too difficult for us to predict if such a conflict in cultures is treated by means of radical patternization, it may keep rolling like a snowball, and therefore lead to either Crusade or *Jihad* of all conceivable kinds. None of them we need because of their destructive and tragic costs.

---

[14]The fable is cited from *Yanzi chunqiu* (Historical Anecdotes of Yanzi). See K. L. Kiu (ed. & tr.), *100 Ancient Chinese Fables* (Hong Kong: Commercial Press Limited, 1991), p. 145.

To conclude, what makes the meeting of East and West possible is reckoned hereby with particular reference to the principle of harmonization without being patternized. The principle as such is proposed as a multicultural strategy in a practical sense. Its relevant application to the exchange of ideas and interaction between cultures serves to make any fancy of pure east or pure west groundless to a reasonably extensive degree. Nowadays, it is the undeniable fact that it is no longer difficult to come across some Western elements in the Eastern culture or way of life, and vice versa. In fact, the exchange and interaction as such have inspired many new findings and transcultural creations. Take John Dewey for example. His philosophy of pragmatism is surely labeled as an American type. Yet, he claimed that he got much of his inspiration from his experience and observation during his stay in China from 1919 to 1921, where he learnt not only from Chinese books but also from local life, society, and culture as a whole. Just as Jane Dewey, his daughter, proved that his experience in China is so crucial that it helps revive his intellectual and cognitive enthusiasm again. He therefore takes China as a country like his own that is closest to his soul.[15] This recollection is quoted not to justify what China matters to John Dewey and his philosophical development. Instead, it is intended to manifest the mutual benefits and fruitfulness of the contributions that all cultures can possibly make to human wisdom in one sense, and in the other, such wisdom is like a sponge always ready to take in various ingredients from all the sources available in order to get more enriched. On this account, we need to keep in mind and reflect upon the new *philosophos poiesis* with particular reference to both Kipling's division and Northrop's integration of East and West. It could be tentatively sketched in these four lines:

> East is not all East, West is not all West,
> And why not the twain shall meet.
> Let the world be in order with diversity
> Or be in harmony without uniformity.

---

[15] Jane Dewy, "Biography of John Dewey," in P. A. Schilpp (ed.), *The Philosophy of John Dewey* (New York: Tudor, 1951), p. 42. Also see Richard Shusterman, "Preface to the Chinese Version," in his *Pragmatist Aesthetics* (trans. Peng Feng, Beijing: The Commercial Press, 2002), pp. 2–3. Note: The Chinese version is translated from the English original. Cf. Richard Shusterman, *Pragmatist Aesthetics: Living Beauty, Rethinking Art* (Rowman & Littlefield Publishers, 2000).

CHAPTER 4

The *Dao* of Human Existence

It is for decades so far that China repeatedly claims itself to be one of the developing countries with the largest population in the world. Its government has therefore launched its ambitious anti-poverty program to help millions of people ameliorate their living condition. Now tremendous progress has been made year by year, but the quality of life across the entire country is still left behind if compared with that in the advanced nations all over the world. Nevertheless, the life expectancy in China has climbed up to 75 years on average according to 2017 statistics, and grown even much higher (80 years or so) in megacities like Shanghai and Beijing, among others. It turns out to be a kind of miracle in this sphere.

How come does it get up to such a point? What is the secret behind it? Noticeably, there are a number of key reasons involved in this domain, for instance, a long-term social stability, successive advancement of productivity, steady amelioration of welfare, nation-wide improvement of medical care, and gradual reinforcement of anti-pollution campaign, so on and so forth. Notwithstanding all this, I personally assume that one of the hidden reasons is associated with the practical wisdom in Chinese Daoism (Taoism), the wisdom that lies in the Dao of human existence per se. It is actually evinced in a popular saying as follows: "Most of Chinese nationals, the educated in particular, would know much less about how to live well for preserving life without reading the classics by early Daoists (Taoists)." It seems to me in this realm, the *Dao De Jing* (*Tao Te Cing*) is the most typical of all the classics concerned, and Laozi, the author, is the most pioneering of all the thinkers then.

As denoted in some historical documents, Laozi is allegedly an older contemporary of Confucius (551–479 B.C.) and acclaimed as the first Chinese thinker to coin the special concept of the *Dao* (Tao) that is treated as the keystone of Daoism (Taoism).[1] He is preoccupied with the concept in his philosophy, which progresses by way of elucidating this concept. The Chinese term *Dao* literally means "way" or "road." Based on this primary meaning, it assumes a metaphorical sense and is usually identified with "the way of man," signifying human morality, code of conduct, etc. But with respect to Laozi's thinking mode at large, the meaning of the *Dao* transcends the ethical and social domains. It is then found to have certain extended implications related to the origin of the universe, the root of all things, the law of natural change and social development, the principle of political and military affairs, and above all, the truth of human existence.

In a word, the *Dao* can be conceived of as the constellation of Laozi's philosophizing as a whole. The most complicated but fascinating of all its aspects is that its connotations vary with the different contexts in which it is used. This is chiefly because the *Dao De Jing* itself has a unique and poetic form of expression encompassing allegories, similes, metaphors, aphorisms, and apothegms along with inspiring insights into the ways of human world. Consequently, his speculative expression is more suggestive than articulate, his insightful observation is more thought provocative than dogmatic, and naturally his intellectual wisdom turns out to be one of a poetic type due to the reasons above mentioned. Hence, his line of thought must be closely followed in order to spot out and experience what message it implies in its subtle and even imaginative mode. This of course does not play down at all the textual scrutiny and contextual analysis as they also work to help one approach this poetic thinker and his preoccupation with an abstruse conception of the *Dao*.

---

[1] A distinction is made between Daoism as a philosophy (*Daojia* or *Daoxue*) and Daoism as a religion (*Daojiao*) according to the traditional Chinese philosophy. Cf. Fung Yu-lan, *A Short History of Chinese Philosophy*, in *Selected Philosophical Writings of Fung Yu-lan* (Beijing: Foreign Languages Press, 1991), pp. 193–198; also see Wang Ming, *Daojia yu Daojiao sixiang yanjiu* [Studies of Daoism as a Philosophy and a Religion] (Beijing: China Social Sciences Press, 1987).

Elsewhere, I have attempted to expound on Laozi's doctrine of the *Dao* from eight dimensions as follows: the *Dao* of the Universe, the *Dao* of the dialectic, the *Dao* of human life, the *Dao* of Heaven and man, the *Dao* of personal cultivation, the *Dao* of governance, the *Dao* of warfare, and the *Dao* of peace.[2] The consideration to be presented hereinafter will focus more on the *Dao* of human existence, with a particular reference to the three categories of wisdom on the one hand, and to the *status quo* of the human condition on the other.

4.1 Frame of Reference: The *Dao* of Man, Heaven, and the Sage

In China today, people are confronted with a paradoxical situation as a result of the rapid economic development and the dilemmas this poses as regards traditional ethics and moral civilization. With the implementation of the "open-door policy," most Chinese citizens have ventured to free themselves from the spiritual yokes of chimerical ideals and to peep out of the window at the outside world. The result is that they are shocked to discover the hard fact that they have been left far behind in the aspect of material civilization, and accordingly, they are feeling profoundly regretted that they used to live in ideological fantasies for too long a time. Then, during the process of reform launched in the late 1970s, economic wonders have been created and living standards obviously improved. But many sociocultural problems arise. As in the West, the idea of competition has been embraced in China as the key to getting rich, strong, and prosperous. No one denies the fact that competition as a rule does work effectively to promote economic growth, from which people benefit a great deal. However, it is carried out to extremes in some cases and unjustly in others, thus turning out to be a fountainhead of such problems as obnoxious competitiveness, acquisitiveness, selfishness, inequality, injustice, frustration, and anxiety. So haunted by these troubles, people seem to have no sooner shaken off the spiritual yokes mentioned above than they find themselves burdened with new shackles. As we reflect on this situation, it easily reminds us of what Laozi thinks of as "the *Dao* of man" (*ren zhi dao*) that is in principle characterized

---

[2] Wang Keping, "Laozi's Doctrine of the *Dao* in Multi-dimensions," in *The Classic of the Dao: A New Investigation* (Beijing: Foreign Languages Press, 1998), pp. 1–21.

by competitiveness, acquisitiveness, selfishness, inequality, and injustice. Specifically in his terminology employed in the *Dao De Jing*, the *Dao* of man "reduces the insufficient and offers more to the excessive."[3] The *Dao* of man as such is identified with sheer exploitation and even robbery in practice. It can be traced back to the historical background of the Spring and Autumn Period (722–481 B.C.) in ancient China. During that period, conflicts and clashes were of frequent occurrence, being stirred up by acquisitive and possessive desires for more land, power, and property. Laozi excoriates the negative aspects of the *Dao* of man as a social norm and moral code widely exercised to such a degree that it is somewhat similar to the "law of the jungle" in modern terms.

According to Laozi, the *Dao* of man itself is often taken for granted in human society. It will, if made the norm of conduct, excite insatiable greed or desire for more possession. This is inevitably conducive to the exploitation of man by man and class discrimination, and then to interpersonal struggle, and eventually to societal disorder and suffering.… In a word, it will bring about a vicious circle in both the social and moral orders.

Because of the negative aspects of the *Dao* of man, Laozi recommends the "*Dao* of Heaven" (*tian zhi dao*) as its antidote. In Chapter 77, he expounds on the *Dao* of Heaven:

> The Dao of Heaven resembles the drawing of a bow.
> When its string is taut, press it down.
> When it is low, raise it up.
> When it is excessive, reduce it.
> When it is insufficient, supplement it.
> The Dao of Heaven reduces whatever is excessive
> And supplements whatever is insufficient.…
> The Dao of Heaven benefits all things and causes no harm.…[4]

Basically inferred from his intuitive and empirical observation of natural phenomena, such as transition and change, motion and replacement, growth and decline, and the progress of time, space and all beings in the world, Laozi reaches the conviction that there exists the *Dao* of Heaven.

---

[3] Laozi, *Dao De Jing* (trans. Wang Keping, Beijing: Foreign Languages Press, 2008), p. 128.
[4] Laozi, *Dao De Jing* (trans. Wang Keping), Ch. 77, p. 128.

The *Dao* of Heaven as the law of Nature lets everything be what it can be or become without imposing, dominating or taking any blind action. Thus, it is reckoned to function as the heart of the universe that benefits all things. It is worth mentioning in passing that the *Dao* of Heaven is also reflected in Laozi's statement that "Heaven and Earth unite to drop sweet dew that falls evenly over all things without being forced." All this can be seen as the conceptual source of the egalitarianism or equal division of property, which is deeply rooted in the mentality of the Chinese people. When its merits are appreciated in view of its possible contribution to social stability, its demerits should not be neglected in view of its potential to block economic development.

As is noted in the *Dao De Jing*, a sharp distinction is made between the *Dao* of Heaven and the *Dao* of man. The former demonstrates itself as a symbol of naturalness, selflessness, and equality in a virtuous sense, whereas the latter, as a negative product of human civilization, is the very opposite. It might be concluded from the context involved that the *Dao* of Heaven is promoted not only as a rebuff to the practitioners of the *Dao* of man, but also as an ultimate measurement or flame of reference. That is to say, the *Dao* of Heaven is idealized as a model to be imitated, followed and acted upon by man. Laozi advocates this as a result of his deep concern and sympathy for the people of his time who were exposed to frequent suffering from all sorts of calamities. That is why Laozi further emphasizes that "the *Dao* of Heaven has no preference. It is constantly with the good man."[5] As a consequence, there arises the *Dao* of the sage (*shengren zhi dao*) in striking contrast to the *Dao* of man (*ren zhi dao*). According to Laozi, it "acts for others but never competes with them."[6] I personally think that the *Dao* of the sage is the fruit on the tree rooted in the *Dao* of Heaven but planted by man, that is, the "good man" or the "virtuous man," and not the "non-virtuous man" in Laozi's terms. Incidentally, the sage here refers to the sage of the Daoist type. He is "the only one who has got the *Dao*" (i.e., the *Dao* of Heaven) and he possesses such virtues as universal love and generosity typical of an absolute giver. In fact, the *Dao* of the sage is the realization of the *Dao* of Heaven extended to human praxis. All men alike are encouraged not simply to admire the virtues of the Daoist sage, but to model themselves

---

[5] Ibid., Ch. 79, p. 131.
[6] Ibid., Ch. 81, p. 134.

upon him via self-cultivation. Only by so doing, according to Laozi, can people enjoy harmonious relations and the society be in peace.

What is more, the *Dao* of the sage can be seen, if we borrow Fung Yu-lan's phrase, as "the highest form of achievement of which man as a man is capable." All this tends to result in and from the state of "oneness between Heaven and man." This notion itself can be also rendered as "Heaven-human oneness" or "nature-man oneness" in accordance with the word order of the Chinese notion *tian ren he yi*. This key concept threads through the development of Chinese intellectual history. Its origin is more often than not dated back to Mencius (c. 372–289 B.C.)[7] or Dong Zhongshu (179–104 B.C.).[8] I personally think that it can be dated back to Laozi, or even further back to the *Yi Jing* (i.e., *I Ching* or *The Book of Changes*).[9] In Chapter 25 of the *Dao De Jing*, Laozi lists "four great things in the universe," including *Dao*, Heaven, Earth, and Man. As a rule, it runs,

> Man follows the way of Earth.
> Earth follows the way of Heaven.
> Heaven follows the way of Dao.
> And Dao follows the way of spontaneity.[10]

In this context, the *Dao* that is signified by the way of spontaneity or naturalness is the highest but hidden principle beyond perception; Heaven and Earth as a whole mean nature or the universe. Man gets integrated with nature (i.e., Heaven and Earth) by acting upon the *Dao*. In more straightforward language, Laozi expounds in Chapter 23 that[11]

---

[7] Mencius, *Jin xin shang* [Chapter 7A], in *Meng Zi* [The Book of Mencius] (Beijing: Zhonghua Book Company, 1988).

[8] Dong Zhongshu, *Yin Yang yi* [The Meaning of Yin and Yang], in *Chunqiu fanlu* [Exuberant Dew of the Spring and Autumn] (Shanghai: Shanghai Guji Press, 1990).

[9] Liu Shuxian, *You tianren heyi xinshi kan ren yu ziran zhi guanxi* [The Relations Between Man and Nature in View of the Newly Interpreted Heaven-Human Oneness], in *Rujia sixiang yu xiandaihua* [Ideas of Confucianism and Modernization] (Beijing: Zhongguuo Guangbo Dianshi Press, 1993).

[10] Laozi, *Dao De Jing* (trans. Wang Keping), Ch. 25, p. 49.

[11] Gu Di & Zhou Ying, *Laozi tong* [Complete Studies of Laozi's *Dao De Jing*] (Changchun: Jilin RenminPress, 1991), Vol. 2, pp. 85–92; also see Gao Heng, *Laozi zhenggu* [A Revised Annotation of Laozi's *Dao De Jing*] (Beijing: Zhonghua Book Company, 1988), pp. 56–58.

> He who seeks the Dao is identified with the Dao;
> He who seeks Heaven is identified with Heaven;
> He who is identified with the Dao is also happy to have him;
> He who is identified with Heaven,
> Heaven is also happy to have him.[12]

In this case, "He who seeks…" apparently refers to man, and "Heaven" stands for nature or the universe. The identification of man with Heaven and with the *Dao* as well is surely a happy situation due to mutual receptivity and reciprocity. The doctrine of Heaven-man oneness is all the more important to the Chinese people since their culture is essentially a non-religious one. Thus, their pursuit of super-moral values is mostly inspired and guided by their pursuit of the state of Heaven-man oneness as an ideal form of spiritual life. The doctrine itself has been carried on and further developed as exemplified in Neo-Daoism, Neo-Confucianism and modern schools of thought in the course of Chinese history. As far as I understand it, the doctrine of Heaven-man or nature-man oneness can be rediscovered and more rewardingly approached nowadays from at least four dimensions, that is, spiritual, aesthetic, social, and environmental. The notion of "nature-man oneness" functions as a bay where the anchor of the "lifeboat" can be dropped. In other words, it is chiefly concerned with the cultivation and sublimation of human life in an ethical sense, and with the pursuit and location of man's destination in a spiritual sense. To my mind, this idea in Daoism emphasizes self-identification with nature, unconditioned pursuit of spontaneity and absolute freedom from social ambitions. Secondly, in respect of "nature-man oneness" from an aesthetic viewpoint, it primarily refers to the inspiring interaction between the limited stream of personal life and the unlimited flow of universal change, which usually takes place in one's emotional world or at the time when one contemplates external objects. Interaction of this kind can facilitate a bilateral projection, reinforcement, and sublimation in a vital sense. Thirdly, in a social sense, the notion of "nature-man oneness" basically means the adaptation of individuals to the community as a group. It is supposed to

---

[12] Laozi, *Dao De Jing* (trans. Wang Keping), Ch. 23, p. 46.

underline the development of harmonious human relations, and meanwhile the improvement of teamwork in the entire society. This is actually equivalent to the realization of "unity" or "harmony" in human relations. Finally, with regard to the doctrine of "nature-man oneness" from an environmental perspective, it directs man to reconsider his place in Nature. It thereby consolidates his consciousness of environmental protection, and in turn ameliorates the quality of his life in general.[13]

In the final analysis, the *Dao* of the sage is essentially characterized by the will to eschew competition. This "virtue of non-competition" is, according to Laozi, equal to "the supreme principle of matching Heaven,"[14] say, matching the *Dao* of Heaven. Consequently, "in order to be above the people," the sage with the *Dao* "must place himself below them in his words. In order to be ahead of the people, he must place himself behind them in his person. In this way, he is above the people, but they do not feel his weight. He is ahead of the people, but they do not feel his hindrance. Therefore, the whole world delights in praising him and never gets tired of him. Just because he does not compete with others, nobody under the sky can compete with him,"[15] and moreover, "he is free from any fault."[16]

After all, Laozi's advocacy of the *Dao* of the sage seems, however good-natured it may be, to be a kind of wishful thinking in front of harsh reality. But, this does not necessarily mean that his wish has no instructive message at all as regards the keenly competitive and frustratingly problematic society in which we live nowadays.

4.2 Pursuit of Sageliness: Practical and Sagely Wisdom

From Laozi's preoccupation with the three categories of the *Dao* discussed above, it may be discerned that there arise correspondingly three forms of wisdom, namely, divine wisdom, practical wisdom, and sagely

---

[13] Wang Keping, *Shehui fazhan yu tianren heyi shuo chonggu* [On Social the Development and the Rediscovery of the Doctrine of Heaven-Human Oneness], in *The Journal of Beijing Second Foreign Languages Institute*, No. 2, April 1995. Note: The article is based on a paper delivered at the 1994 Bering International Symposium on "Social Development and Oriental Culture."

[14] Laozi, *Dao De Jing* (trans. Wang Keping), Ch. 68, p. 118.

[15] Ibid., Ch. 66, p. 116.

[16] Ibid., Ch. 8, p. 23.

wisdom. To be more specific, the *Dao* of Heaven reflects a kind of mysteriously divine wisdom, the *Dao* of man a kind of secularly practical wisdom, and the *Dao* of the sage a kind of transcendentally sagely wisdom. As has been observed, the first is, as it were, an idealized frame of reference based on a personified characterization of natural phenomena and can therefore be suspended in our discussion here; rather, the second is of high frequency in social praxis and daily life against the background of human civilization; and the third serves as the highest possible goal of achievement that a Daoist sage strives for.

By "practical wisdom" is generally meant the wisdom of instructive significance and instrumental usage related to human activities with obviously pragmatic purposes, say, in the aspects of self-achievement, self-development, self-interest, human relations, etc. Such wisdom can be easily identified in many of Laozi's sayings. In respect of self-achievement, for instance, Laozi says in Chapter 63,

> It is a rule in the world
> that the most difficult things begin with the easy,
> and the largest things arise from the minute.
> Hence, tackle the difficult while it is still easy;
> and achieve the large while it is still minute.[17]

In respect of self-development, Laozi advises metaphorically in Chapter 64 that one should

> Deal with things before their occurrences.
> Put them in order before disorder arises.
> A tree as huge as one's embrace grows from a tiny shoot.
> A tower of nine-stories rises up from a heap of earth.
> A journey of a thousand miles starts from the first step.
> People often fail when they are about to succeed in their conduct of affairs.
> If they stay as careful at the end as at the beginning,
> they will never suffer failure.[18]

---

[17] Laozi, *Dao De Jing* (trans. Wang Keping), Ch. 63, p. 113.
[18] Ibid., Ch. 64, p. 114.

In coping with human relations, Laozi warns in Chapters 63 and 33 that

> He who makes promises too readily surely lacks credibility.
> He who takes things too easily will surely encounter difficulty.[19]
> ....
> He who knows others is knowledgeable,
> but he who knows himself is wise.
> He who conquers others is physically strong,
> but he who conquers himself is mighty.[20]

In respect of self-interest, diplomatic strategies can be detected in condensed form in Chapter 36, as follows:

> In order to contract it,
> it is necessary to expand it first.
> In order to weaken it,
> it is necessary to strengthen it first.
> In order to destroy it,
> it is necessary to promote it first.
> In order to grasp it,
> it is necessary to offer it first.
> This is called Subtle Light (wei ming).[21]

These cited lines are well-known among the Chinese people in general and politicians in particular. The ideas presented are often considered, if taken literally, as conspiratorial tactics applied to gain self-interest or play power games. This may involve a purposeful and conventional misreading that naturally leads to a misconception. And accordingly, Laozi himself is often labeled a political conspirator. This is understandable to the extent that each reader is liable to form his own image of Laozi by reading modern ideas and personal feelings into his book. This well explains why Laozi's thought can be renewed and revived from time to time. We tend to maintain that Laozi describes the interactions between all those categories simply in order to justify his conception of the inexorable transformation between opposites. According to Gao Heng, Chen Guying and many other Laozi scholars, Laozi is here talking about the

---

[19] Ibid., Ch. 63, p. 113.
[20] Ibid., Ch. 33, p. 60.
[21] Laozi, *Dao De Jing* (trans. Wang Keping), Ch. 36, p. 63.

Dao of Heaven or the natural law. Hence, it is groundless to accuse him of being a conspirator.[22]

In fact, Laozi consistently holds on to his observation that everything has two sides, which seem to be in a state of continuous opposition and mutual transformation. That is to say, when one of the two sides involved develops to its extreme or acme, it will inevitably move over toward its opposite. A flower, for example, will naturally wither or close up (contraction) when it is in full blossom (expansion). Thus, the latter can be viewed as a sign of the former. Conversely, an inchworm draws itself together when it wants to stretch out. Dragons and snakes hibernate in order to preserve life. It is therefore concluded that "Contraction and expansion act upon each other; hereby arises that which furthers." In other words, "it is by the impact upon each other of this contraction and expansion that the advantages (of different conditions) are produced." Correspondingly, "when loopers coil themselves up, they thereby straighten themselves again; when worms move into the state of hibernation, they thereby keep themselves alive."[23] This dialectical speculation is illustrated in Laozi's description of the interrelations and interactions between contraction and expansion, weakening and strengthening, destruction and promotion, taking and giving, etc. His analysis of the development of these matters and phenomena ultimately leads to his generalization that "Reversion is the movement of the *Dao*."[24]

It is noteworthy that "reversion" (*fan*) is a dynamic term. It refers to the interrelation between opposites in one sense, and the return to the root known as the unity or union of opposites in another. The former reveals the state of being opposite while the latter the state of transformation or change. A situation of this kind may be symbolized by the traditional sign of *Taiji* ("Supreme Ultimate" in literal translation) where the two forces known as Yin and Yang are always on the move, interdependent, and interacting at the same time. Laozi was incredibly observant with regard to the changes that take place between and within

---

[22] Gao Heng, *Laozi zhenggu* [A Revised Annotation of Laozi's *Dao De Jing*] (Beijing: Zhonghua Book Company, 1988), p. 81; also see Chen Guying, *Laozi zhuyi ji pingjie* [An Annotated and Paraphrased Version of Laozi's *Dao De Jing* with Commentary] (Beijing: Zhonghua Book Company, 1992), pp. 205–207.

[23] *Yi jing xi ci* [The Great Treatise], in *Book of Changes* (trans. James Legge, Changsha: Hunan Press, 1993), p. 325.

[24] Laozi, *Dao De Jing* (trans. Wang Keping), Ch. 40, p. 72.

things themselves, indicating that things are inclined to reverse to their opposite in any changing process. It is noticeable in both Nature and human society that everything is doomed to roll downhill once it reaches the summit. Things that are too lofty fall down easily; things that are too white stain easily; songs that are too pretentious have few listeners; and reputations that are too high fall short of reality. All these vicissitudes seem to be in conformity with the Chinese conception of "inevitable reversal of the extreme (*wu ji bi fan*)." In addition, it is worth emphasizing that Laozi himself recognizes the objective existence of two extremes in the developmental process of a thing. However, he advises people not to cling to one side only because of the inevitable "movement" toward its opposite. Under such circumstances, one has to take into account both ends and keep an eye on the dynamic change that occurs on the verge or border district of interactions between the opposites. It is right there that one may grasp the chance and stay in an advantageous position.

A relevant and profound understanding of the principle that "Reversion is the movement of the *Dao*" is believed to be the key to the sagely wisdom mentioned above. This wisdom can be looked upon as the highest form of wisdom if the realization of sageliness is taken as the highest form of achievement of man. It provides enlightenment and guidance, visibly and invisibly, to human existence as well as spiritual nourishment. In view of pleasure-seeking, for example, the sagely wisdom sheds its light on the fact that "The five colors make one's eyes blind. The five tones make one's ears deaf. The five flavors cause one's palate to go stale. Racing and hunting cause one's mind to go mad...."[25] The negative and even destructive outcome is a moral lesson for those who indulge in sensuous enjoyment or hedonistic way of life.

Then, in view of fame-oriented love and wealth-directed acquisitiveness, the sagely wisdom tenders a significant message that "An excessive love of fame is bound to bring about an extravagant expense. A rich hoard of wealth is bound to suffer a heavy loss. Therefore, he who is contented will encounter no disgrace" in one sense, and "be always contented," "rich," or happy in another.[26] As often detected in human society, what people desire and seek after are chiefly fame and wealth.

---

[25] Ibid., Ch. 12, p. 27.
[26] Laozi, *Dao De Jing* (trans. Wang Keping), Chs. 33, 44, 46, pp. 60, 78, 81.

They may go so far as to be alienated or enslaved by "the reins of fame and the shackles of wealth" (*ming jiang li suo*) as is metaphorically stated in the Chinese aphorism. Hence, Laozi advises people to be contented with what they have, and at the same time warns the avaricious rich and fame-thirsty people not to go to extremes. Thus, the concept of contentment with what one has comprises part of the traditional Chinese attitude toward material possessions.

Subsequently, in view of the development of any thing or situation as is depicted in Chapters 76 and 78, the sagely wisdom maintains that

> The hard and stiff are the companions of death,
> whereas the soft and tender are the companions of life....[27]
> Therefore, the soft can overcome the hard,
> and the weak can overcome the strong.[28]

This potentiality is dialectically asserted by Laozi in the notion that "Weakness is the function of the *Dao*."[29] He therefore recommends people to "keep to the tender and weak" because these are assumed to develop and surely conquer "the firm and the strong" in the end. To justify this assertion, he makes constant use of "water" as a simile when illustrating the potential and overwhelming power of "the tender and weak." At this point, nevertheless, one must be highly conscious of the problematic facet of his tendency to absolutize the function of "weakness" by cutting it off from actual and varying conditions. Yet, this does not negate the enlightenment contained therein.

Furthermore, in view of the true and the beautiful social discourse interactions, the sagely wisdom tells us in Chapter 81 that

> True words are not beautiful;
> beautiful words are not true.[30]

This implies an intention to encourage people to become good listeners by distinguishing between the real and the false. Otherwise, they will run the risk of being swallowed up in a sea of "beautiful words" that

---

[27] Ibid., Ch. 76, p. 126.
[28] Ibid., Ch. 78, p. 130.
[29] Ibid., Ch. 40, p. 72.
[30] Ibid., Ch. 81, p. 134.

is more easily available in a society or community less democratic and with less freedom of speech. Next, as regards fortune and misfortune, the sagely wisdom demonstrates a dialectical interrelationship between the two opposites in Chapter 58. That is,

> Misfortune is that beside which fortune lies.
> Fortune is that beneath which misfortune lurks.[31]

As is known to all, fortune as the symbol of gain is what people like to embrace while misfortune as the symbol of loss is what people try to avoid. Yet, people hardly realize that the two opposites go hand in hand like twins. This again reveals the potential change or transformation to the antithesis at a certain point. The thought itself is naturally corresponding to Laozi's generalization that "Reversion is the movement of the *Dao*."

Finally, with regard to codes of social conduct, the sagely wisdom is exemplified through "the three treasures" championed by Laozi: "The first is 'kindness,' the second is 'frugality,' and the third is 'to dare not be ahead of the world'." It is proclaimed in Chapter 67 that

> With kindness one can become courageous;
> with frugality one can become generous;
> and with not daring to be ahead of the world
> one can become the leader of the world.[32]

The whole idea is largely based on the viewpoint of "retreat" that seems to be somewhat defensive and passive. But, Laozi assures that only the ability to fall back is bravery, the ability to shrink is to stretch, and that avoiding prominence and precedence makes one the first. He is convinced that any breach of these three rules of wisdom will bring about complete failure. That is why "the three treasures" are also proposed as possible solutions to such social problems as harsh human relations, insatiable desires and keen competition among the people in general, and among the rich and powerful in particular.

In short, practical wisdom and sagely wisdom work on different levels and have different orientations. They help people gratify their needs and

---

[31] Laozi, *Dao De Jing* (trans. Wang Keping), Ch. 38, p. 102.
[32] Ibid., Ch. 67, p. 117.

fulfill their purposes. The pursuit of either of them tends to be influenced by at least two major factors: one is the predetermined objective linked with one's value system, and the other is the understanding of the principle that "Reversion is the movement of the *Dao*." Needless to say, this understanding varies in degree from person to person. As regards, those who prefer to seek instrumental benefits more than anything else. They will only scratch the surface and focus on the pragmatic dimension of wisdom. Conversely, those who prefer to pursue possible self-transcendence can reach into its depth and concentrate on the sagely dimension of wisdom. I presume to argue that the experience and practice of the sagely wisdom turns out to be a process of artistizing the way of life that in turn leads to absolute spiritual freedom and an independent personality. Yet, as far as I can see, the accomplishment of the process is not attainable, so to speak, unless a proper attitude toward life and death is derived from the Daoist viewpoint.

4.3 Path to Freedom: Attitudes Toward Life and Death

According to his observation and experience, Bertrand Russell once acknowledged that the Chinese people in general seemed to know well how to enjoy life even though they were immersed in poverty-stricken conditions mostly intolerable to most Westerners. Hence, the longer you stayed with them, the more you began to like and appreciate them and their culture as a whole. There are many reasons for this. Yet, the most important reason lies, I believe, in their philosophically matter-of-fact attitude toward life itself. This attitude is usually expressed in plain language but in a poetic form: One lives through his life in the same way as the grass goes through autumn (*ren sheng yi shi, cao mu yi qiu*), implying that, like grass, life itself is a natural process, flourishing in spring (youth) and then withering in autumn (ageing). As an aphorism widely accepted and frequently mouthed by Chinese people, it contains a moral value to indicate not only the commonplace trip from life to death, but also a hidden advice to those who are liable to fall victims to the cares and worries encountered in the life to which they cling. Such a notion is deeply rooted in the psychology of most Chinese people and stays influential because of its subtle enlightenment. It originated, as far as I understand, in early Daoism as a philosophy associated with Laozi and Zhuangzi in particular.

As we know, the conceptions of both life and death are crucially important to all human beings alike. Almost all living beings are afraid to die, and especially so for human beings. The love of life and fear of death seem to be connected with the natural instinct or the life-and-death emotional complex in the case of humankind. These emotions hinder human beings from attaining true spiritual freedom. Accordingly, almost all philosophers, East or West, were and are preoccupied in one way or another with various outlooks on life and death. Laozi, as the founder of Daoism, asserts that both life and death are as natural as anything else in the world. Zhuangzi, who continues this thoughtway, holds that they are neither to be welcomed nor to be rejected. Therefore, these two thinkers view life and death as nothing but natural phenomena to the extent that the former is not to be overvalued and the latter not to be dreaded. Chapter 50 expounds on this theme as follows:

> Man comes alive into the world
> And goes dead into the earth.
> Three out of ten will live longer.
> Three out of ten will live shorter.
> And three out of ten will strive for long life
> but meet premature death.
> And for what reason?
> It is because of excessive preservation of life.
> Only those who don't value their lives are wiser
> Than those who overvalue their lives.
> I have heard that those who are good at preserving life
> Will not meet rhinoceroses or tigers when traveling the byways,
> Nor will be wounded or killed when fighting battles.
> Rhinoceroses cannot butt their horns against them.
> Tigers cannot fasten their claws upon them.
> And weapons cannot thrust their blades into them.
> And for what reason?
> Because they are out of the range of death.[33]

This chapter discloses a message that both life and death are nothing more than natural phenomena, apart from the implicit criticism of the matter-corrupted rich and nobility. The "excessive preservation of life" that will be most likely to end in premature death can be well attested

---

[33] Laozi, *Dao De Jing* (trans. Wang Keping), Ch. 50, pp. 86–87.

by the exposure of the destructive effects related to the "five colors" that cause blindness, the "five tones" that cause deafness, the "five flavors" that cause loss of taste, and "racing and hunting" that cause madness.[34] Observant and critical as he was, Laozi could do nothing to alter or improve the situation. He therefore stuck to his philosophy of plainness and simplicity by advising people to live in accordance with the principle of the *Dao*. Under such circumstances, the best way to preserve life is, according to Laozi, to live through one's natural life free from cares and worries by going beyond "the range of death."

"Man comes alive into the world and goes dead in the earth." This statement is noticeably a manifestation of Laozi's attitude toward life and death. Its implied message aims to remind one of three things at least:

1. To live one's life as naturally as possible so as to enjoy it to the full;
2. Not to be oppressed by a tragic sense of death that befalls all men alike;
3. Not to overvalue life because it is in vain to strive for excessive preservation of life.

In Zhuangzi's philosophy, there is frequent explication of the naturalness of both life and death. Once he even goes so far as to proclaim that life is a tumor and death as the breaking of the tumor. Elsewhere, Zhuangzi concludes that all living beings in the world are evolved from *qi*, or the vital force. Thus, one comes to be alive when this vital force becomes compact, and one dies when this vital force disperses. Zhuangzi continues to remark that the earth offers one a paradigm of prime; he then toils throughout his life; he lives an easy life when old and retired; and he finally enjoys rest after death. Describing life and death as such a cycle, Zhuangzi tells people not to welcome life when it comes along, and not to struggle against death when it befalls you. That thinking is vividly illustrated by the story of Zhuangzi beating a drum and singing following the death of his beloved wife.

The Daoist position on death is that one can possibly achieve freedom in the pure sense of this term only when he sees through the essence of death as a natural and inevitable phenomenon. This argument is, of course, open to criticism and counterargument as well. It is, on the

---

[34] Ibid., Ch. 12, p. 27.

one hand, somewhat shrouded in obscurity and paradox; thus it could be viewed as something pessimistically negative, leading one to be psychologically crushed by such a dark and tragic sense of death. The result might be the reduction of a person into a passive being due to the consciousness of the inevitability of death. In other words, he would set no aims but muddle through life simply because death is like a sword hanging overhead, ready to fall upon him at any minute. In short, he may have no drive to take any action, but simply wait for the coming of death. Such being the case, whether to be or not to be is no longer the question, because this kind of life is more or less similar to death in essence. This easily reminds us of the Chinese saying, "The suffering of misery is no worse than the death of the heart (i.e., loss of hope)."

On the other hand, this argument about death could possibly lead to a positive stance toward life itself. That is to say, with a high awareness of the inevitability of death, one may first of all work a meaning or a purpose into life as a natural passage from birth to death. Thus, he may make the most out of it because he treasures every minute of the process. He knows well that time is on the wing and can never be recaptured once it passes by. We therefore have an old saying that "He who is with high aspirations tends to sigh with a feeling that time is always too short." Hence, he would be ready to adopt a sense of mission or social commitment. Consequently, he contributes and constructs more in his life and work. He expects that what he has achieved may extend the significance of his existence into society and history as well. Secondly, since he recognizes death for what it is, he will be able to make light of whatever hardships, difficulties, miseries, and sufferings—all the negative experiences—he confronts throughout his life. This may be expressed in Nietzsche's phrase: He may be in a position to "laugh at all tragedies." Thirdly, since he recognizes death for what it is, he may devote or sacrifice his life to a cause or causes in case of need. For instance, revolutionaries, religious martyrs, etc., choose to die a hero's death for their ideals. Confucianism recommends that a *junzi* (superior man) should give up his body for the advancement of humanity. This spirit of devotion obviously demands a positive conception of death as a natural phenomenon.

In a word, when we argue that one can be possibly free in the real sense of the term only by seeing through the nature of death, we are encouraged to face death without fear. Thus, we have no reason to be either panicked or enslaved by death to the degree that we have to crawl under its imagined claws. We should accordingly be masters of our own fate and of death as well. In that case, we could be able to improve our quality of existence in its spiritual dimension and have access to absolute freedom in the pure sense of this term.

To wrap up this discussion, there are three more statements to be added herein. First, we tend to read the modern into the old when rediscovering such classics as the *Dao De Jing*. This is understandable due to the fact that the texts concerned are poetically more suggestive than articulate on the one hand, and on the other, they remain open to new interpretations so long as the latter are justifiable in the textual and historical contexts. Second, the *Dao* of human existence is likely to swing or slant toward either the *Dao* of man or the *Dao* of the sage. The former appears more closely leagued with practical wisdom, whereas the latter consorts with sagely wisdom. Last but not least, as regards Laozi's *Dao* of human existence, it is oriented toward the *Dao* of the sage and associated with sagely wisdom when it is applied to living experience. The possible attitudes toward it can be broadly categorized into three types exclaimed by Laozi in Chapter 41:

> When the highest type of shi (i.e. literati) hear of the Dao,
> They diligently practice it.
> When the average type of shi hear of the Dao,
> They half-believe it.
> When the lowest type of shi hear of the Dao,
> They laugh heartily at it.
> If they did not laugh at it.
> It would not be the Dao.[35]

---

[35] Laozi, *Dao De Jing* (trans. Wang Keping), Ch. 41, p. 74.

CHAPTER 5

A Symbolic Way of Thinking Through Fables

The Chinese mode of thought is inclined to perform through emblematic symbols or suggestive images. It is usually exemplified in literary writings and philosophical ponderings, among other genres of discourse. This is mainly because Chinese written characters are originated from a picture-writing system. Simplified and abstracted as they are in their modern forms, some of them, for instance, *ri* (日) as sun, *yue* (月) as moon, *shan* (山) as mountain, and *chuan* (川) as river can still be traced back to the hidden outlooks of the natural objects concerned. Moreover, ancient Chinese thinkers would play down the role of langue and parole owing to their limited expressiveness, but play up the usage of symbols and images because of their extensive expressiveness and rich significance. To their mind, "The written characters (langue) are not the full exponent of speech (parole), and speech is not the full expression of ideas…The sages therefore made their emblematic symbols to set forth fully their ideas."[1] As a result in antiquity, the eight hexagrams came into being as the most abstract and representative of emblematic symbols associated with all things in the cosmos and all deeds of human race.

---

[1] *Book of Changes* (trans. James Legge, Changsha: Hunan Press, 1993), p. 313.

They appear to be rather enigmatic, mystical, and profound as are illustrated in the *Book of Changes* (*Yi jing*).

With the passage of time, such symbols and images are created in a diversified manner. For example, they are chiefly presented through verbal pictures in poems, and deliberately drawn from thought-provoking fables, legendary stories, and so forth. Among all the Chinese thinkers in history, Zhuangzi (c. 369–286 B.C.) proceeds along Laozi's line of thought and prefers to using fables to explicate his ideas in a symbolic way. His writing style is metaphorically engaging and suggestive but shrouded in considerable ambiguity. Hence, it often leads to a variety of interpretations. A serious reader of *The Book of Zhuangzi* tends to be inspired each time when scrutinizing it, and consequently comes out with new findings in accordance with one's life experience, individual perspective, and ever deepened understanding of human existence per se.

No matter what semantic variances people may encounter when reading the book, they are able to get hold of the primary message provided they explore along Zhuangzi's path of thought. This path winds through all his writings and reflects his constant preoccupation with the *Dao* (Tao, Way) of attaining spirited emancipation and independent personality. These two aspects of the *Dao* can be identified with the two sides of the same coin termed as absolute freedom. The freedom as such is assumed to facilitate human fulfillment that is conceived of as the ultimate *telos* for life. All this is largely grounded on a sincere and suprautilitarian attitude toward the pursuit of spiritual transcendence. Keeping this keynote in mind, one will find it less perplexing when trying to pinpoint what Zhuangzi claims as "a happy and boundless excursion" by searching through his philosophizing saturated with thought-provoking fables.

Let us look into two fables among many others. Although the narrative structure of each appears unidentical, the hidden scheme stays interrelated such that it encourages a doublefold freedom from both inward and outward confinements. This does not necessarily mean to deny their respective focus and locus in the process of speculation concerning the human condition in general, and personal cultivation in particular.

5.1 THE *PENG* AND HAPPY EXCURSION TO THE INFINITE

Regarding the complete works of Zhuangzi, the "Inner Chapters" (*Neipian*) are considered to be the most authentic in terms of his authorship.[2] Of the seven entries in the Inner Chapters, what stands out first is the discourse on *xiao yao you*. The title is made up of three Chinese characters that signify the main theme of the entire argument in question. Here, *xiao* implies the abolishing of all confinements and constraints imposed from both within and without; *yao* refers to the boundlessly remote, and *you* to the act of excursion as a special genre of roaming or wandering. They are brought together to indicate literally a free and joyful travel to a far-reaching place. Employed as a compound by Zhuangzi, *xiao yao you* connotes more than its literal and separate meanings. This is noticeable in an annotation as follows: By the term *you* is meant nothing but a free excursion between the sky and the earth. It is self-enjoyment in everything. It ignores the distinction between the great and the small. It is freed from any practical purpose and dependent of nothing at all. Say, it does not rely on anything, any enterprise, or any action in order to establish oneself, make social achievement, and gain worldly fame. It serves to equalize the great and the small, apart from abiding with the Dao as the principle of all principles. It is therefore an experience of *xiao* and *yao*. Terminologically, *xiao* indicates not only the terminating of all the confrontations in action, but also the forgetting of all the matters on mind; *yao* suggests not merely going beyond the surroundings into the boundlessly remote, but also liberating oneself from the bondage to knowledge and opinion. By so doing, all things would be equalized. Accordingly, life is to be cultivated, body is to be forgotten, virtue is to be fulfilled, the

---

[2] The complete works of Zhuangzi comprises 33 chapters in total. Judging from the lexical choice, style, and structure, Chinese scholars mostly agree to the division between the *Neipian* [Inner Chapters], the *Waipian* [Outer Chapters] and the *Zapian* [Miscellaneous Chapters]. The first part is made up of seven chapters, the second part of 15 chapters and the third part of 11 chapters. The *Neipian* are said to be written by Zhuangzi because of the sufficiently shared vocabulary, style, and thought in a complete unity. The *Waipian* or Outer Chapters and the *Zapian* are assumed to be written by the followers of Zhuangzi and completed in the late years of the Warring States Period before 225 B.C. Cf. Wang Fuzhi. *Zhuangzi jie* [Zhuangzai's Works Interpreted] (Beijing: Zhonghua Book Company, 1976); Chen Guying, *Zhuangzi jinzhu jinyi* [The Book of Zhuangzi Newly Annotated and Paraphrased] (Beijing: Zhonghua Book Company, 1983); especially Liu Xiaogan, *Classifying the Zhuangzi Chapters* (trans. William E. Savage, Michigan: The University of Michigan Press, 1994).

human world is to be lived through without harm, the sage-ruler is to be responded with the country governed in peace, and all beings are to be identified with the Dao as the principle of all principles. Hence life and death alike are to be put out of mind. Under such circumstances, excursion (*you*) occurs to all, and all is but excursion.[3]

As a matter of fact, Zhuangzi invented this concept to denote a pursuit of absolute freedom or a search for "perfect happiness" (*zhi le*) according to his own claims. It is a kind of spirited excursion characteristic of being independent of all bounds in one way, and in the other, being enlightened with insights into the *Dao* of taking-no-action, making no distinction, self-forgetfulness, and above all, oneness with the universe. For the sake of convenience in expression, a relatively economical, even though far-fetched, English rendering could be "the happy and boundless excursion."[4] This may well capture more of what it means in the context concerned.

As is read in the first chapter "Xiao Yao You," the notion of "happy and boundless excursion" (*xiao yao*) turns up as many as six times. Contextually, it is used three times to celebrate the happiness and boundlessness in terms of "taking-no-action" (*wu wei*), and another three times to embrace the happiness and boundlessness in the transcendent way of life. They both imply self-adaptation to and self-identification with all things under the sky. However, they all commence with a grotesque image of "happy excursion" emerged from a *mythos* as follows:

> In the Northern Ocean there is a fish, by the name of Kun, which is many thousand miles in size. This fish metamorphoses into a bird by the name of Peng, whose back is many thousand miles in breadth. When the bird rouses itself and flies, its wings obscure the sky like clouds.... When the Peng is moving to the Southern Ocean (Nanhai), it flaps along the water for 3,000 miles. Then, it ascends on a whirlwind up to a height of 90,000 miles, for a flight of six months' duration. There is the wandering air; there are the motes; there are living things that blow one against another with their breath. We do not know whether the blueness of the sky is its original color, or is simply caused by its infinite height. When the Peng sees the earth from above, just as we see the sky from below.... Without sufficient

---

[3] Wang Fuzhi, *Zhuangzi jie* [Zhuang Zai's Works Interpreted], 1976, Ch. 1.

[4] There exist several English renderings for *Xiao Yao You*. For instance, Fung Yu-lan translated it as "The Happy Excursion," and Burton Waston put it into "The Free and Easy Wandering."

density, the wind would not be able to support the large wings. Therefore, when the Peng ascends to the height of 90,000 miles, the wind is all beneath it. Then, with the blue sky above, and no obstacle on the way, it mounts upon the wind and starts for the south. A cicada and a young dove laugh at the Peng, saying: 'When we make an effort, we fly up to the trees. Sometimes, not able to reach, we fall to the ground midway. What is the use of going up 90,000 miles in order to fly toward the south?' (He who goes to the grassy suburbs, taking enough food for three meals with him, comes back with his stomach as full as when he started. But, he who travels a 100 miles must grind flours enough for a night's halt. And he who travels a 1,000 miles must supply with provisions for three months. Small knowledge is neither to be compared with great knowledge, nor a short life to a long one....) A quail also laughs at it, saying: 'Where is that bird going? I spring up with a bound, and when I have reached no more than a few yards I come down again. I just fly about among the brushwood and the bushes. It is also perfect flying....' There is the difference between the great and the small.[5]

What the story suggests is ambiguous and polysemous. In one sense, the enormous discrepancy between the great and the small is observable in their respective qualities and pursuits. The *Peng* has large wings and flies that high and far. The cicada or quail has tiny wings and flies that low and short. It is ostensibly impossible to make the *Peng* follow the cicada and its like to fly low and short among trees or grassy suburbs. Likewise, it is out of the question to make the cicada and its like follow the *Peng* to fly that high and afar to the remote Southern Ocean. Accordingly, what the great experiences and achieves is not the same with what the small does. This is also true of what they need and enjoy each. If they all go against nature by imitating each other in either lifestyle or flying mode, they will invite distress and frustration for certain. Therefore, self-enjoyment arises in due and relative degrees because of inborn capacity, respective momentum, and conditioned circumstance as well.

In the other sense, the great and the small are discerned to be different by nature. They move and live in distinctive ways simply because they just comply with their own nature and behave in accord with their inborn power. They both indulge in what they are doing and enjoy themselves to their fullest extent. Such self-enjoyment on either side

---

[5] Fung Yu-lan (trans.), *The Taoist Classic: Chuang-tzu* (Beijing: Foreign Languages Press, 1989), pp. 25–29.

can be equated in value if no distinction is made between superior and inferior. Accordingly, their experience of self-contentment is of similar intensity in the measurement of their own feeling. It is just like two equally pleased guests to a royal banquet. It makes no difference in their enjoyment even though one differs from the other in the size of appetite and the amount of food and wine taken in. In actuality, Zhuangzi often advocates the notion of "equalizing" (*qi*) as the fundamental principle of his philosophy.[6] He argues that people like to make distinctions between such things as "this" (*ci*) and "that" (*bi*) merely due to their opinions. They stick to the distinctions as much as they hold fast to their opinions. Hence, they are so single-minded as to distinguish between great and small, high and low, long and short, right and wrong, true and false, good and bad, superior and inferior, and so on. With these distinctions, the *Dao* becomes obscured and people grow confused such that they argue ceaselessly with one another, and even slip into the mire of conflicts. The distinctions thus made are consequences of overlooking the fact that all is on the constant move or in the eternal flux of change. To solve this problem, we have no other choice but recourse to the *Dao*. That is, all things and opinions ought to be equated with the *Dao*.

Then, what exactly is the *Dao* in his mind? It is, in short, the way of making no distinction. Just as Zhuangzi himself affirms, "That the 'that' and the 'this' cease to be opposites is the essence of the *Dao*. Only the essence, an axis as it were, is the center of the circle responding to the endless changes. The right is on endless change. The wrong is also on endless change. Therefore, it is said that nothing is better than using the light of reason (*yi ming*)."[7] In the final analysis, the way or *Dao* of making no distinction is a synonym for the Supreme One (*tai yi*), serving as the ultimate unity or fusion of all in the universe. Its service is as dramatic as "the magic sack" in Chinese mythology: When set to use by its master, it is automatically enlarged to swallow up the enemy's weapons in all and deprive them of their entire functions.

Although the two respects of the story are plausible in general, a cluster of implications and associations are to be further explored. First of all, the great and the small are set shoulder by shoulder in striking contrast. The great is represented by the *Peng*, and the small by the cicada,

---

[6] Zhuangzi, "On the Equality of Things and Opinions," in Fung Yu-lan (trans.), *The Taoist Classic: Chuang-tzu*, pp. 39–55.

[7] Ibid., p. 44.

dove, and quail. Regarding "the happy and boundless excursion," neither of them fulfills it to its fullest extent. Practically, both of them are engaged in a kind of lopsided excursion. The *Peng* is self-pleased with an excursion from the north to the south. However, the excursion is remote enough but not free enough because the flight relies so much on the wind. However powerful the *Peng* may be, it could not fly up into the sky without the wind to support its wings. This confinement to the wind not only reduces the degree of freedom and happiness, but also deconstructs the possibility of boundlessness. Instead, the cicada and its like are self-pleased with an excursion from one tree to another, which is easygoing enough but not remote at all. Representing the small, they call what they do "the perfection of flight" according to their living circumstances. In fact, they never bother about their flying distance and height. They are so ready to tie themselves up to their natural capability and living situation, with no slightest attempt to alter or derail their beaten track. Instead, they deride the *Peng* who attempts to turn into a "new leaf" by venturing out of its birthplace in the Northern Ocean and heading for a new destination in the Southern Ocean. The geographical description is contextually meaningful on this occasion. For the Northern Ocean is allegedly more gloomy while the Southern Ocean more bright. That is why Zhuangzi terms the Southern Ocean as the Heavenly Lake (*tian chi*) to symbolize an imagined paradise. All this may help justify the endeavor and the will to pursue both brightness and happiness as are demonstrated by the *Peng*. It is therefore inferred from their opposing attitudes and actions that life without a change is not worth living in the case of the *Peng*, but in the case of the cicada and its like life is an easy comfort and meager satisfaction. Consequently, the *Peng* is in the process of becoming what it wants to become in the direction of the great and active, whereas the cicada and its like remain to be what they are in the direction of the small and passive.

Secondly, both sides are ignorant of their own limitations but disdain for one another. As is noted in the story, what enables the *Peng* to ascend out of the Northern Ocean and up into the sky is the whirlwind produced when the ocean moves. Even when it is flying at the height of 90,000 miles with the wind beneath it, "the blue sky" is still above the cock-sure monster. The blueness of the sky is caused by its infinite height. It signifies infinity or boundlessness, so to speak. All this manifests that the *Peng* performs at its best a limited transcendence since it still stays trapped within the finite. In addition, when it sees the earth from above, it is just like we see the sky from below. Neither can obtain a clear sight owing to "the wandering air," "the motes" and the distance involved. Yet, the giant bird is feeling so pleased and conceited that it looks down upon anything else below itself. Around it, there flows the air of hidden pride and unexpressed contempt pointed to other creatures. On the contrary, the cicada and its like are pleasure-seeking and comfort-oriented among trees or grassy suburbs. They play safe and cling to their immediate circumstance, never giving a thought about going beyond their natural limits. Nothing should be blamed if they were only self-contented with their *status quo*. But, their self-contentment inflates so much as to put on an air of self-importance. This is shown through their mockery at the *Peng* and their arrogant remarks, which turn up as self-defensive bias and self-centered comparison. In the final analysis, both the great and the small birds appear to bestow themselves with a privilege to over-stretch their own standards to measure the conduct of all other beings. This in turn intensifies their egoism in different manifestations and widens their rift in value judgment as well.

Thirdly, both the big and small birds cynically laugh at one another as a result of lopsided judgment in their own favor. However, they are hardly aware of the fact that they themselves are all laughable if viewed from the *Dao* of happy and boundless excursion. It is surely an ironic parody. Just as is detected in the story, the *Peng* embodies the great. It looks down upon the cicada and its like from above. Conversely, the cicada exemplifies the small. It sneers at the *Peng* from below. This is apparently due to their perception of "the perfection of flying" in terms of their natural capacity and living circumstance each. They both hold fast to the difference between the great and the small because they maintain their faith in *xiaozhi buji dazhi*. This phrase of Zhuangzi is not as straightforward as it is thought to be. Its literal translation, such as "the small knowledge is not to be compared with the great knowledge" for example, is rather misleading. It tends, contextually, to mean that the small cannot understand the great. For what the small knows and experiences is almost always discrepant from what the great knows and experiences. This is the same with what they can do and expect with reference to self-adaptation and self-enjoyment. That is why Zhuangzi makes such a comment following the quail's mockery of the *Peng*. It runs,

> There are some people whose knowledge is sufficient for the duties of some office. There are some people whose conduct will secure unity in

some district. There are some people whose virtue befits him for a ruler. There are some people whose ability wins credit in the country. In their opinion of themselves, they are just like what is mentioned above.[8]

What is most noteworthy here is the analogy drawn between the birds and human beings. It suggests that all come out to be succumbing to the principle of relativity. Just like the birds of either small or great size, they enjoy themselves each in their own scope. They are self-satisfied with what they can manage according to their individual ability. The situation as such sounds so natural and reasonable as though no more argument about it would be needed. Yet, there comes up Song Rongzi who gives them no credit but mocks at them both. Acting as a mouthpiece of the so-called worthy men (*xian ren*), he discards all the social norms and lives a life in considerable peace, free from any disturbances and ambitions. Just as Zhuangzi portrays,

> He [Song Rongzi] would not be encouraged thereby if the entire world should praise him. He would not be discouraged thereby if the entire world should condemn him. He pinpoints but never bothers the discrimination between the internal and the external. He knows but transcends the boundary between honor and disgrace. This is the best of him. In the world such a man is rare, yet, there is still something which he fails to establish himself.[9]

In this context, what is meant by "the internal" is the inward self, and what is meant by "the external" is the outward things or outside world. Song Rongzi is highly conscious of the difference between them but deliberately keep it out of his mind in order to secure a spiritual tranquility. Furthermore, he crosses the borderline between honor and disgrace, treating them alike under any circumstances. By so doing, he has no intention to gain anything and hence has no fear of losing anything, either. This is chiefly an exercise of the Daoist philosophy of "No gains therefore no losses," which is usually applied to self-preservation or self-protection. This notwithstanding, he stops progressing ahead and retains a distance away from the sphere of happy and boundless

---

[8] Zhuangzi, "The Happy Excursion," in Fung Yu-lan (trans.), *The Taoist Classic: Chuang-tzu*, p. 29.
[9] Ibid.

excursion. Probably he does not realize the discrepancy and his limitation, but stands still with self-appreciation while lavishing contempt to others. He turns himself into a laughing stock just as the cicada does. Actually Song Rongzi's situation reveals no more happy and boundless excursion than that of Liezi, another cited character in the story as is described in the following:

> Liezi can ride upon the wind and pursue his way far ahead, in a refreshing and good manner, returning after fifteen days. Among those who attained happiness, such a man is rare. Yet, he is still dependent upon something (youdai) even though he is able to dispense walking.[10]

Like the monstrous *Peng*, the supernatural Liezi appears to be free and able to fly afar. But both of them rely on the wind, without which they fall down for sure. In addition, the *Peng* has its "light of six months' duration" and Liezi has his of "fifteen days." All this evinces their limited capacity and relative freedom because they are both hindered by the external factor of wind. In a word, they are both dependent beings after all.

Now how can the happy and boundless excursion be possible in any case? We have Zhuangzi's hypothesis:

> Suppose there is one who chariots on the normality of the universe, rides upon the change of the six elements, and thus makes excursion in the infinite, what has he to depend upon? Therefore, it is said that the perfect man has no self; the spiritual man has no achievement; and the true sage has no name.[11]

The conditions are clarified at two levels. Objectively, one must possess a good command of "the normality of the universe," which means to follow the *Dao* or the nature of all things. At the same time, one must be able to control "the change of the six elements," which means to make most of the potential power of such natural elements as "the Yin, Yang, wind, rain, dark and bright."[12] If able to do all this, one is sure

---

[10] Ibid.

[11] Ibid., p. 30.

[12] This is based on Sima Biao's interpretation. Cf. Chen Guying, *Zhuangzi jinzhu jinyi* [The Book of Zhuangzi Newly Annotated and Paraphrased] (Beijing: Zhonghua Book Company, 1983), p. 17.

to employ at one's disposal whatever he encounters to fulfill personal purposes. On this point, one is well in the position to rid himself of the external constraints as a whole and no longer depends upon anything at all for free motion. This renders possible the happy and boundless excursion with regard to the outer conditions. Subjectively, one must act upon the supreme principle of taking-no-action and making no distinction so as to achieve the *Dao* for complete enlightenment. Such personality is virtually idealized by Zhuangzi in a tripartite model. It is ascribed to "the perfect man without self" (*zhiren wuji*), "the spiritual man without achievement" (*shenren wugong*), and "the true sage without name" (*shengren wuming*). The perfect man without self-indicates that one has purified oneself of all selfishness, desires, and egoism to the degree that he makes no more distinction between his self and its other. The spiritual man without achievement denotes that one has thrown away all his ambitions and has no intention to go in for any social establishment or take up any commitment. He regards them as nothing but self-invited bounds and fetters detrimental to personal freedom. The true sage without name signifies that one has liberated oneself from all the this-worldly values and therefore ignores any form of fame, honor, social status, or ranking, because such things foster a rather self-defensive psychology or mental tension. That is to say, he who hankers after all this social capital in various forms will come across at least two possibilities: failure or success. It is self-evident that failure is most conducive to a negative experience of frustration while success is most conducive to a positive feeling of delight. Yet, it is liable that he has no sooner enjoyed such delight than he grows worried about what to do in order not to lose what has been gained. On many occasions, a winner this time fears to be a loser next time, especially in the case of personal fame and status. He would be most apt to fall a victim into the abyss of care and anxiety. Life as such is no fun for certain. Comparatively, "the perfect man" who has achieved thorough enlightenment by virtue of the *Dao* tends to abandon his own self, makes no personal achievement, and ignores any fame. He equalizes whatever differences in this regard. All this ends up with a complete detachment (*wudai*) from the secular values or the mundane affairs. It is at this stage that he transforms himself from a dependent being into an independent one, that is, from the state of self-confinement into the state of self-emancipation. Correspondingly, he moves out of the finite sphere and then steps into the infinite sphere. He thereby sets his feet on the road for the happy and boundless excursion. The significance of being independent in this respect is exposed and fortified by the comment that reads:

> If one has to depend upon something, one cannot be happy and free, unless one gets hold of the thing which one depends upon. Although Liezi could pursue his way in such a fine manner, he still had to depend upon the wind, and the Peng was even more dependent. Only he who ignores the distinction between things and follows the great evolution can he be really independent and always free.... The independent man has no self, achievement or name. He therefore unites the great and the small as he makes no distinction between them. He embraces life and death alike as he equalizes them.... Consequently he who makes excursion in the non-distinction of the great and the small has no limitation. He who ignores the distinction between life and death has no terminal. Those whose happiness is attached within the finite sphere will certainly have limitation. Though they are allowed to make excursion, they are unable to be independent.[13]

In other words, they have no way to enjoy the happy and boundless excursion. This situation is further formulated by another observation:

> If things enjoy themselves only in their finite spheres, their enjoyment must be finite. For instance, if one enjoys only in life, he would suffer in death. If one enjoys only in power, he would suffer at the loss of it. The 'independent man' transcends the finite. He 'hides the universe in the universe,' as mentioned by Zhuangzi in the chapter Da Zongshi (The Great Vulnerable Teacher). He thus becomes infinite, and so is his happiness. 'The perfect man has no self' because he has transcended the finite and identified himself with the universe. 'The spiritual man has no achievement' because he follows the nature of things and lets everything enjoy itself. 'The true sage has no name' because his virtue is perfect; every name is a determination as well as a limitation.[14]

Finally, the anecdotic narrative is utilized to exemplify Zhuangzi's notion of the happy and boundless excursion. But, its symbolism signifies more than that. As its descriptive structure shifts from the fish *Kun* to the bird *Peng*, then from the cicada and its like to human beings of different

---

[13] Guo Xiang, *Zhuangzi jishi* [Collected Commentary on the Book of Zhuangzi], see Fung Yu-lan (trans.), *The Taoist Classic: Chuang-tzu*, pp. 30–31.

[14] Ibid., p. 31.

types, we find a meaningful incarnation of the spirit of life along with a deep concern with the possible development of personality. The whole process features three general phases, namely, body transformation, dynamic transformation, and spiritual transformation.

The first phase is attributed to a dramatic body transformation, which is embodied in the metamorphosis of the *Kun* into the *Peng*. The *Kun* is originally a small fish. But, Zhuangzi makes it into a giant one. It naturally metamorphoses into a great bird, preparing to get out of the Northern Ocean and cover a long distance to the Southern Ocean known as the Heavenly Lake. Such a transformation is necessary for three reasons. (1) The bird of enormous size finds the current habitat a confinement for its free movement. (2) It wants to have a change for better conditions. (3) It wishes to adventure out for a happy and boundless excursion. In the case of human race, all persons are supposed to be born free, but bounded in one way or another through acculturation or socialization. As one grows from childhood into adulthood, one comes across more constraints, pressures, and cares of any conceivable kind. More often than not, one's lifestyle is so routinized that one can hardly get off the beaten track. This fashion of life is, in the eyes of Zhuangzi, not merely pathetic and intolerable, but also not worth living at all. Hence along his line of thought, an analogy can be drawn between the *Peng* and a type of person who strives for self-emancipation. The story is deliberately dramatized. It seems to characterize the great bird into a model for human beings, encouraging those who are keen on freedom and independence to display an adventurous spirit and start off for a happy and boundless excursion. A human cannot transform into a bird in a physical sense. But in imagination, everything is possible. All this depends on an individual initiative.

Subsequently, there comes the dynamic transformation. It is at this stage that the *Peng* as the transformed figure makes tremendous endeavors when enfolding its wings and flying up to the sky. It thus demonstrates its monstrous size and power and consequently creates such a grotesque image. It flaps along the waters of the Northern Ocean for 3000 miles. With a back as huge as the Mount Tai, and wings like clouds across the sky, it rides on a whirlwind and ascends up to a height of 90,000 miles, for a flight of six months' duration toward the Southern Ocean, the Heavenly Lake (*tian chi*). The greatness or sublimity is revealed fully in all aspects: strength, speed, size, manner, and height…. The dynamic element is prevailing through its intended remote excursion and intensified by its spatial movement. The expectation is justified by its craving for a change accompanied with adventures. The resolution is shining through its persistency of going along its own way even when it is misunderstood and derided by such species as cicada, quail, and its like. In this organic context, the Heavenly Lake as its destination stands out as a paradise with Utopian fantasy. The whole ambiance under Zhuangzi's pen is filled with excitement, stimulation, and temptation. Its hidden message is strikingly brought forth to motivate people to lift up their spirit for self-emancipation and sublimation altogether. It is inspiring to those who crave for happy and boundless excursion. Yet, it is not enough for what Zhuangzi acclaims as the happy and boundless excursion. In his mind, those who have succeeded in reaching this stage are expected to push forward for further transcendence. For the freedom undergone so far is still limited within the finite sphere, just like the *Peng* that is soaring high over others but still below the blue sky itself. In addition, such freedom is still dependent upon people's control of thought about social values, and upon their initiative to break free from the values in all. It is just like the *Peng* that is also dependent upon the wind to sustain its large wings. Hence, a spiritual transformation is advisable at this point.

Spiritual transformation *par excellence* is presupposed by both body and dynamic transformation. It is chiefly meant to facilitate an ultimate development of personal cultivation, which then leads to a complete enlightenment and happy excursion of infinity. To fulfill this requirement proposed by Zhuangzi, people will treat all values alike as they make no distinction, view all things alike as they take them as one, and be free from any confinement as they follow the nature of all. Like "the perfect man without self," they lose themselves as they discard their body and learned knowledge. Like "the spiritual man without achievement," they have no sense of self-establishment as they ignore any form of gains or losses. Like "the true sage without name," they are neither encouraged by honor nor discouraged by disgrace as they embrace the two things alike. They simply identify themselves with the universe. They hereby enjoy their happy and boundless excursion by "charioting on the normality of the universe" and "riding on the change of the six elements" as is expressed in Zhuangzi's hyperbole. That is to say, people of this type are ontologically free beings with independent personality. Specifically, they are free to the extent that they live in oneness with the myriad things by equalizing them all in one sense, and in the other, they are independent to the extent that they ride over whatever they meet with and therefore have nothing to depend upon. In a word, they are living and reposing within the *Dao* and vice versa.

As a result of his thought that deviates from the mainstream, Zhuangzi is labeled in a number of ways by the reader of different times. Xunzi,[15] for instance, criticized him for "being obsessed with the law of nature without knowledge of mankind" (*bi yu tian er bu zhi ren*). Under his influence, some approach Zhuangzi as a naturalist rather than a humanist. This critique could be only valid if it were meant to relate it to Zhuangzi's advice of "abandoning knowledge" (*qu zhi*) after "having knowledge" (*you zhi*). The knowledge here referred to is the knowledge about human affairs (*ren shi*) in close connection with social norms and this-worldly values. It is true that Zhuangzi regards such knowledge as troublesome because it tends to get one entangled in social bound. Additionally, it works to plunge one into a restless and dilemmatic mentality of desiring to gain while fearing to lose. In actuality, Zhuangzi has insights into the human condition as such and explores the human world philosophically as a humanist. His philosophy as a whole contains a deep concern with the human condition and quality of life. Quite obviously, he feels pity for the burdensome human existence that bears the cross of social commitment, and even stays all along resentful against such social norms as reflected in personal achievement, status, name, or honor, etc. He calls them as "external things" (*wai wu*) since they mean little to living a truly happy life. Instead, they function much to enslave or alienate people. He therefore advocates the way of happy and boundless excursion to counterbalance social alienation and confinement all together.

Since Zhuangzi maintains a sarcastic attitude toward the role of human knowledge and civilization in life, some others crown Zhuangzi as a skeptic. But, this viewpoint is not amply holding because he publicly negates and repeatedly derides the social norms in general and the Confucian values in particular. Meanwhile, he is so sure about his value system that he offers a generous wholesale in a preaching tone. This is quite prominent in the foregoing discussion.

Moreover, some others cynically point out that Zhuangzi proposes his way of so-called happy and boundless excursion as an escapist. Despaired

---

[15] Xunzi (c. 298–238 B.C.) has been considered mainly a Confucianist thinker during the Warring States Period.

with the hopeless society and harsh environment, he turns a blind eye to all and purposefully retreats into his inner world as a refuge for spiritual detachment, which is rhetorically called "happy and boundless excursion." Such excursion embodies absolute spiritual freedom and can be only accessible to the independent personality like "the perfect man" (*zhiren*). "The perfect man is," says Zhuangzi, "spiritually mysterious. He would not feel hot were the great forests burned up. He would not feel cold were the great rivers frozen hard. He would not be frightened were the mountains being shaken with thunder or the seas being thrown into waves by a storm. Being such, he would mount upon the clouds up in the sky and ride on the sun and moon, and would thus ramble at ease beyond the four oceans (i.e., the world). Neither life nor death can affect him (as he treats them alike); how much less can bother him the consideration of what is beneficial and what is harmful?"[16]

Hence, Sima Qian[17] concludes that Zhuangzi "exaggerates his ideas in boasting and pompous terms for the sake of self-enjoyment." I would hereby reckon that, so long as what he says does have the service for self-enjoyment, either poetically or philosophically, it is still of value and relevance especially to those who happen to take it amusingly or seriously. As to whether they would go into the happy and boundless excursion, it is rather a question of individual experience, if not wishful thinking, about which there is of far less need to bother too much.

5.2 THE BUTTERFLY AND SELF-EMANCIPATION

As has been detected in the discourse "On the Equality of Things and Opinions" (*Qi Wu Lun*), Zhuangzi constantly emphasizes the principle of Oneness (*yi*) as the unity of opposites and differences. This Oneness is the ideal outcome of the act of equalizing (*qi*) things and opinions.

On one occasion, Zhuangzi analogizes that "the universe is a finger (*yi zhi*); all things are a horse (*yi ma*)."[18] By this generalization, it is meant that the *Dao* makes no distinctions and all things are thereby united into the One. The One can be incarnated in either a finger or a horse. Hence, he claims that "only the truly wise knows the oneness of things (*zhi tong wei yi*). They therefore do not make distinctions,

---

[16] Fung Yu-lan (trans.), *The Taoist Classic: Chuang-tzu*, p. 52.
[17] Sima Qian (145–86 B.C.), author of *Shi ji* [Historical Records].
[18] Fung Yu-lan (trans.), *The Taoist Classic: Chuang-tzu*, p. 45.

but follow the common and ordinary. The common and ordinary are the natural functions of all things, which express the common nature of the whole. Following the common nature of the whole, they are happy. Being happy, they are near perfection. Such perfection is for them to take no action. When they take no action, they even do not know they take no action. This is the *Dao*."[19]

Ironically, some people who prefer to make distinctions dispute with one another all the time. They often wear out their mind and intelligence to seek an agreement out of disagreements but go nowhere. It is simply because they do not know things are by nature united into the *Dao* as the One. With regard to the discrimination of right and wrong, for instance, they behave more or less like the monkeys when it comes to the arrangement of acorn rations, so to speak in Zhuangzi's terms. The monkeys are very angry when their keeper let them have "three [acorns] in the morning and four [acorns] in the evening" (*zhao san er mu si*). But, they are very pleased when allowed to have "four [acorns] in the morning and three [acorns] in the evening" (*zhao si er mu san*). They react so differently even though the actual number of acorns all together remains the same. Therefore, the sage harmonizes the systems of right and wrong and rests in the evolution of nature. That is, they just do what is most proper in accordance with the specific situation by leaving the different opinions alone. Furthermore, they have no intention to rule out the different opinions but just go beyond them. This is called, according to Zhuangzi, "following the two courses at once."[20]

On the other occasion, Zhuangzi stresses the idea of Oneness (*yi*) by claiming that "Heaven and Earth and I came into existence together, and all things with me are one."[21] To justify this argument, he uses as many as five fables in succession. Among them, the first is about ten suns that are said to come out together once upon a time and illuminate all things alike without any preference. This is apparently excelled by the power of virtue. Such virtue suggests the comprehensiveness of the *Dao*. It makes no discrimination and embraces all things alike, only to let everything follow its own course and enjoy its own nature.

The second fable tells of a factual absence of any common standard or taste of judging things in the world. For instance, "Men eat meat;

[19] Ibid., p. 46.
[20] Ibid., p. 46.
[21] Ibid., p. 49.

deer feed on grass. Centipedes enjoy snakes; owls and crows delight in mice.... Mao Qiang and Li Ji were admired by men as the most beautiful of women, but at the sight of them fish dived deep in the water, birds scored up in the air, and deer hurried away in fear."[22] Hence, it is better to wipe out any form or egoism and leave all things alone in their own place.

The third tale exposes the dream quality of human life and describes the spiritual realm of the Daoist sage. The sage asserts that life is nothing but a dream. He has no interest in seeking such gains as self, achievement or name, and detaches himself from the world affairs. He even does not purposely adhere to the *Dao* of making no distinction. Therefore, he not simply roams beyond the limits of the dusty world of immediate reality, but holds the universe in his arms. In order to do so, he blends the myriad things into a harmonious whole, rejects the confusion of distinctions, ignores the differences of social rank, and remains innocently naive, purely simple and without knowledge. In the end, he finds enjoyment in the realm of infinite, and settles down with tranquility.

The next story is concerned with the dramatic movement of the Shadow. The Shadow seems to be dependent upon something or attachedness (*youdai*) in appearance. But, it affirms its actual independence or complete detachedness (*wudai*) because it never bothers about its identity in any sense. It just becomes spontaneously what it is without asking why it is so and not otherwise.

The last fable is about the butterfly and self-transformation. Compared with all the other ones, the butterfly image is the most influential but ambiguous as well. It reads,

> Once upon a time, Zhuang Zhou (Zhuangzi) dreamed that he was a butterfly. The butterfly was flying about and enjoying itself. It did not know it was Zhuang Zhou. Suddenly he awoke, and veritably was Zhuang Zhou again. We do know whether it was Zhuang Zhou dreaming that he was a butterfly, or whether it was the butterfly dreaming that it was Zhuang Zhou. Between Zhuang Zhou and the butterfly there must be some distinction. This is a case of what is called the transformation of things.[23]

---

[22] Ibid., p. 51.
[23] Ibid., pp. 54–55.

The key to this passage is basically doublefold. It is, on the one hand, related to the last statement about "the transformation of things" (*wu hua*), because the myth itself is deployed for the exemplification of this abstract conception. On the other hand, it is hidden in the interaction between dreaming and awakening. According to Guo Xiang, "the transformation of things" is "delightful" (*ke le*) to the extent that life and death are natural phenomena determined by the principle of change. Like all the other things, they are involved in the process of transformation, thus coming and going as suddenly as the interplay between dreaming and awakening. One should therefore be happy by not making any distinction between life as a cause of possible joy and death as a cause of plain misery. In other word, one should emancipate oneself from the unnecessary cares and worries that stem from the love for life and fear of death. The discrimination between dreaming and awakening is, as it were, identical to that between life and death. They can all be discriminated. But, if one treats them alike and remains happy to accept them as such, there is no much difference between their discrimination and non-discrimination.[24]

Many other interpretations exist for this notion. As Wang Fuzhi puts it, "'The transformation of things' is pointed to the change of things. For instance, the *Kun* transforms into the *Peng*, the dung beetle into the cicada and the eagle into the vulture.... The great transforms into the great while the small into the small. As for the mutual transformation between Zhuang Zhou and the butterfly, it implies that all is transformable in the world (via dream). One must keep in mind that, although distinctions come into being when transformation of things takes place, it is by nature the same in the respect that they all follow their own course each."[25]

Regarding the story as a whole, Fung Yu-lan deems that "This shows that, although in ordinary appearance there are differences between things, in delusions or in dreams one thing can also be another. 'The transformation of things' proves that the differences among things are not absolute."[26] Chen Guying even goes further to affirm that "what 'the transformation of things' really means is that the distinction between

---

[24] Guo Xiang, *Zhuangzi jishi* [Collected Commentary on the Book of Zhuangzi], Vol. 2, p. 39.

[25] Wang Fuzhi, *Zhuangzi jie* [Zhuang Zai's Works Interpreted], p. 29.

[26] Fung Yu-lan (trans.), *The Taoist Classic: Chuang-tzu*, p. 55.

the self (subject) and its other (object) is swept out and all things are fused into one."[27]

In my mind, "the transformation of things" should be placed in the context of Zhuangzi's philosophizing as a whole, and meanwhile approached from his primary preoccupation with self-emancipation or spiritual freedom. His conception of such "transformation" refers to all things, including human beings. It metaphorically denotes the process of self-transformation from a bounded self into an unbounded self, say, from confinement to freedom in plain language. This freedom is two dimensional: It is not merely from the externally imposed constraints related to social values, but also from the internally added hindrances based on personal wants. In respect to the distinction between dreaming and awakening, it is similar to the distinction between Zhuang Zhou and the butterfly. Here, distinctions are made in either case. Otherwise, it is no point of talking about "the transformation of things." But, such distinctions mean only too little against the *Dao* of making no distinction as Zhuangzi thinks. It is equally true of it if viewed from the recommended self-transformation for the sake of spiritual freedom. It can be therefore affirmed that the literal distinctions between dreaming and awakening will cancel each other out due to the effect of "the transformation of things." Correspondingly, the borderline between Zhang Zhou and the butterfly will get blurred and eventually removed by the underlying principle. This principle is a priori and predetermined. Just as it is aforementioned at the outset of this section, it is coupled with the correlation between the idea of Oneness (*yi*) as the unity of all opposites and differences and the act of equalizing (*qi*) all things and opinions.

After all, Zhuang Zhou, the dreamer, is self-satisfied with the butterfly image and feels all the way happy about his experience of self-transformation. This is self-evident and stirs up more associations. His experience, for instance, has two aspects: aesthetic and spiritual. The aesthetic aspect is associated with the beautiful image of the butterfly due to its glamorous form and color. In fact, the butterfly is a wonder of natural creation and serves as a symbol of the beautiful. The employment of the butterfly as a metaphor is by no means a coincidence because the little creature has been traditionally leagued with the idea of beauty, charm, and grace alike in terms of its sense image. The idea of beauty carries much value with it.

---

[27] Chen Guying, *Zhuangzi jinzhu jinyi* [The Book of Zhuangzi Newly Annotated and Paraphrased], p. 92.

It transfuses so much significance into the butterfly image that its effect captures the Chinese mentality and evokes their aesthetic ideal of appreciation. On the other hand, the spiritual aspect is proportionately originated from the self-transformation as the threshold of self-emancipation or spiritual freedom. The self-transformation is from the old into the new in identity; likewise, the self-emancipation is from the confined into the unconfined in spirit. They both are incarnated through the butterfly image. Here in the context, the butterfly is not simply a symbol of metamorphosis from a caterpillar, but also as a symbol of freedom reflected in its easy and playful flying manners. When Zhuang Zhou dreamed he was a butterfly and did not know he was Zhuang Zhou, the self-transformation was thus accomplished allegorically. When he was happy to see himself flying around freely as a butterfly, the self-emancipation was thus fulfilled spiritually. Judging from an objective perspective, one argues that such a process is false and all in fantasy. But, this plausible argument will lose its target in question and its logic as well so long as the dreamer himself adopts the Dao of making no distinction and bends his mind to his self-inventive way of seeking spiritual freedom. Obviously, this experience as a whole is neither scientific nor mysterious, but rather esoteric in close connection with one's self-cultivation and spiritual nourishment, so to speak according to Zhuangzi's philosophy of life.

Incidentally, it is ever since Zhuangzi that the butterfly dream has been highly influential and significant in the Chinese literary heritage. Perceived as an archetypal symbol of beauty, freedom, and even love, the butterfly image frequents many poems and dramas. The Chinese tragedy of the *Liang-Zhu*, the shortened form for the romance of the *Liang Shanbo and Zhu Yingtai* that is often likened to the *Romeo and Juliet*, makes a sensational use of the butterfly image at its climax. To cut the long story short, once there were two lovers who were prevented by feudal conventions from meeting and marrying each other. After a harsh separation and fruitless struggle for being together, the hero died in deep sorrow and was buried underground outside his hometown village. Upon hearing about his death, the heroine came all the way to mourn his beloved at the graveside. She was so sad and heartbroken when cherishing the memory of their good off days. Her grief and tragedy moved the Heaven. All of a sudden, a mighty thunder struck the grave apart, and right at this sight she threw herself into it for a reunion. Soon afterward, a couple of beautiful butterflies ascended out of the tomb, flying together so happily and freely into the blue sky. Thus, incorporated into the butterfly image are the ideas of togetherness, love, and devotion, apart from beauty and freedom.

All in all, when illustrating his notions of self-transformation and self-emancipation, Zhuangzi deploys two most prominent metaphors. One is the *Peng*, an ambitious and powerful monster. The other is the butterfly (*die*), a delicate and graceful creature. The *Peng* is great, sublime, dependent and engaged in its journey to an intended destination, and the transformation it goes through is incomplete and therefore finite. In striking contrast, the butterfly is little, beautiful but independent and free from any intended destination. Consequently, its transformation is complete and therefore infinite, symbolizing the closest to the ideal of happy excursion to the boundless remote. Moreover, the butterfly as a twofold symbol of beauty and freedom well embodies the integration of the aesthetic and spiritual aspects. It is because of such integration that the highest form of the spiritual freedom is both corresponding to and identified with the intellectual enlightenment and aesthetic *Erlebnis* in Chinese aesthetic culture and psychology.

CHAPTER 6

Two Models of Cultivating Wisdom for a Good Life

Pascal once says: "I blame equally those who choose to praise man, those who choose to blame him, and those who choose to amuse themselves; and I can only approve of those who seek with lamentation."[1] What he suggests above strikes me as encouraging people not to take up negative engagement in self-praise, self-contempt, or self-amusement, but to hanker after an alternative conception of a good life as its finality.

This chapter attempts to expose two alternatives in this regard. One is Plato's analogy of the beauty ladder, which implies a process of cognitive development ranging from the cultivation of wisdom to the pursuit of ultimate truth, and the other is Zhuangzi's (Chuang-tse's) analogy of the mind-heart excursion, which features a process of spiritual cultivation comprising a series of mental enlightenment in search for the supreme Dao. Even though the two alternatives represent two distinct modes of thinking, they share the common goal of cultivating wisdom for the sake of a good life. Coincidentally, Plato (427–347 B.C.) and Zhuangzi

---

[1] Psacal, *Pensées* (Paris: Librairie Générals Française, rep. 1962), p. 333. The original statement follows: "Je blâme également, et ceux qui prennent de parti de louer l'homme, et ceux qui le prennent de le blamer, et ceux qui le prennent de se divertir; et je ne puis approuver que ceux qui cherchent en gémissant." The English rendering is cited from Pascal, *Pensées* (trans. W. F. Trotter, New York: E. P. Dutton, 1904).

(c. 369–286 B.C.) were two historical thinkers and approximate contemporaries living in the "axial period."[2] The former was the founder of the Academie in Athens of Greece, and the latter was intellectually related to the Jixia Literati Palace in Linzi (modern Zibo) of China.[3]

As is presented below, the discussion examines the two analogies in detail before considering their similarities and differences. It finds out four general ways in which these two models of a good life are similar, namely in their teleological focus; their promotion of progressive methods of cultivation; their detachment from political involvement; and the tranquility associated with the respective final stages when considered from the perspectives of Hellenic Quietism and Chinese *Dao*ism (Taoism). Finally, the two models provide us with alternative pictures of a good life and how that might be approached, as well as some ways in which elements of each may be integrated in practice.

6.1 The Beauty Ladder

In Plato's *Symposium*, the ladder analogy is used to indicate a process of cognitive development that ranges from the cultivation of wisdom to the pursuit of ultimate truth by means of approaching varied forms of beauty. Climbing the ladder itself can be construed as a kind of pilgrimage that is love-driven and beauty-oriented, setting out from a natural erotic disposition directed to a beautiful body and eventually arriving at a noetic enlightenment infused with a metaphysical insight into the absolute archē. The pilgrimage is outlined as follows:

> A lover who goes about the love-matters correctly must begin in his youth to devote himself to beautiful bodies…This is what is to go aright, or be led by another correctly, into the mystery of Love: one begins from beautiful things, and goes always upwards for the sake of that highest beauty. He climbs aloft as on the rungs of a ladder (*epanabathmois*), from the beauty of one particular body to that of two bodies in cognate relationship, and from the beauty of two bodies to that of all bodies; from the

---

[2] Karl Jaspers, *The Origin and Goal of History* (London: Routledge, 1953), pp. 1–2.

[3] The Academie in Athens was founded in 387 B.C. and closed in 629. The Jixia Literati Palace (Jixia Xuegong) was founded during the period from 374 B.C. to 357 B.C., reached its prime time during the period from 319 B.C. to 301 B.C., and declined gradually to its end from 264 B.C. to 221 B.C.

personal beauty of souls he proceeds to the beauty in people's observances and laws, and then up to the beauty of knowledge or science; and at last from the beauty of knowledge to that particular study which is concerned with the beauty in itself and that alone; so that in the end he comes to know the very essence of the beautiful (*tou kalou mathēma*). In that state of life (*entautha tou biou*) above all others, a man finds it truly worthwhile to live, as he contemplates essential beauty.[4]

The rungs of the beauty ladder are demarcated by seven classes of beauty extending from the physical to the metaphysical, from the empirical to the transcendental, as well as from the particular to the universal or absolute. The ladder represents a hierarchical formation with each rung denoting an up-going increase in difficulty. The analogy here gives rise to at least three basic questions: What brings the lover to step on to the ladder? How is it possible for him to climb up to the top? And what does each class of beauty mean in connection with others during the whole process?

The answer to the first question is "the power and courage of Love" (*tēn dynamin kai andreian tou Erōtos*).[5] Love works to instill into animals the desire to beget. They become amorously disposed, first to have union one with another and next to find food for their young. In order to fulfill this purpose, they are prepared to fight, even the weakest against the strongest, ready to sacrifice their lives or tolerate starvation. As for men, they have similar natural feelings, but act on the promptings of calculation.[6] Love is potent because of his erotic disposition, which stems from his Spirit-Like genesis. Love was born to the demi-goddess Poverty and the demi-god Resource. Begotten during a birthday feast in honor of Aphrodite and staying attendant to the beautiful Goddess, he is a lover bent on beauty.[7] With a mixed parentage, he inherits a paradoxical disposition that is partly resourceful and partly poverty-stricken. His resourceful dimension is embodied in his infinite longing for all kinds of beauty, and his poverty-stricken counterpart is reflected in his lack of satisfaction with what he has possessed. Consequently, he lives in an incomplete state

---

[4] Plato, *Symposium*, 210a–211d (trans. A. Nehamas and Paul Woodruff, W. R. M. Lamb). The citation is here given with minor modifications.
[5] Ibid., 212c.
[6] Ibid., 207a–b.
[7] Ibid., 203b–c.

but claims an inexhaustible enthusiasm. This enthusiasm is conveyed to human beings. Once he has gained sight of beauty, a person is inclined, like Love, to be active and courageous. Driven by such a powerful force, the lover has no desire to prevent himself from ascending the beauty ladder that exposes him to a variety of charms at different levels.

With respect to the second question—how it is possible for the lover to get up to the top of the ladder—the answer is again linked to Love. As "the best helper (*synergou ameinō*) our human nature (*tē anthrōpeia physei*) can hope to find,"[8] Love is not denied his Spirit-Like genesis, but is intimately aligned with human nature. Being spiritual, Love is in a position to permeate human nature, even though the two are not identical. Nevertheless, being "the best helper," Love plays an important role in leading humans to discover the path to beauty, because "Love is a love for the beautiful" (*Erōs d' estin erōs peri to kalon*).

Moreover, "Love is a lover of wisdom" (*Erōta philosophon einai*) even though his state is between "wise and ignorant (*sophou kai amathous*)."[9] Why is it so? Having a share of wisdom, Love is supposed to know or wants to know all the beauties rather than some of them. Having a share of ignorance, he is ready to learn more and explore the unknown. This philosophic nature of Love is directed to the inquiry about both the beautiful and the good because the acquisition of them would secure happiness in the pure sense of this term: Love makes "men love what is simply and solely good" (*allo estin ou erōsin anthrōpoi ē tou agathou*), and the necessary condition to be truly wise lies in the understanding of the good.[10] Thus, Plato regards Love as "the leader" who "leads aright" at the very beginning of the ladder analogy.

What is noteworthy therein is Plato's emphasis on the word *orthōs* ("correctly")—which is used three times in connection with love-matters (*ta erotica*)[11] and twice in connection with the Greek practice of boy-loving (*to paiderastein*).[12] It seems as though Plato applies a principle of correctness to all kinds of love-matters. Such a principle demands that the act of loving beauty takes place in light of wisdom, with the expectation that the act as such should take into due consideration appropriate

[8] Ibid., 212b–c.
[9] Ibid., 204b–c.
[10] Ibid., 205a–e.
[11] Ibid., 210a.
[12] Ibid., 211b.

moderation and self-control. Otherwise, the entire enterprise with love-matters will be spoiled for certain. This is noticeably a moral judgment and an empirical one at the same time.

Third, what does each class of beauty mean in connection with others during the process of ascent? The answer is embodied in a low-to-high progression during which one class of beauty is prerequisite to another. The progression is like a pilgrimage, setting out with the love of beautiful bodies (*ta kala sōmata*) that involves three elementary steps.[13]

Initially, one gets up to the first rung and falls in love of the beauty of one particular body. To my mind, this love is primarily engendered by two forms of agency: the erotic and the philikos. The erotic agency tends to focus more on somatic love, whereas the philikos agency on friendship. When they are well balanced, there arises *humanus amore* or human love that is moderate and prosperous. If the erotic agency becomes dominant over all, it will give birth to *ferinus amore* or animal love.[14] If this happens, the love of one particular body could become one-sided, inclined toward confrontation, anxiety, and frustration. It is usually the case that filial love tends toward humane sentiment, while erotic love toward voluptuous enjoyment. The former can be constructive and rational, while the latter destructive and irrational. On the other hand, if the erotic agency happens to be lacking, normal couples may produce no offspring and may find the philikos agency shared between them insufficient to maintain their marriage in certain cases. When the balanced love aforementioned is evoked by the philikos agency proper, it will be deepened and consolidated to a great extent. In view of Plato's principle of correctness, such love stays reciprocal and interactive between the lover and the beloved. It is accordingly sustained by the art of love that depends upon mutual contribution to the amorous relationship. What comes out of this mutuality resembles the third category of what Plato and Aristotle have said about true friendship (*philia*), friendship that mirrors the virtuous concerns and moral personalities enjoyed

---

[13] Ibid., 210a–b.

[14] Marsilius Ficinus, *De Amore: Commentarium in Convivium Platonis* (trans. Liang Zhonghe and Li Yang, Shanghai: East China Normal University Press, 2012), 6:8, pp. 168–169 (Chinese version). Ficinus talks about five kinds of love in this section. I think three kinds of them relevant to the Platonic love of beauty in the analogy of the beauty ladder. They include the humanus amore that is essentially active, the ferinus amore that is voluptuous, and the divinus amore that is contemplative.

and appreciated among friends or lovers. Definitely, it goes beyond not merely the first category of friendship based on shared pleasures and hobbies, but also the second category based on interpersonal utility or practical interests.

The second step upward to the love of bodies involves appreciation of the beauty of two bodies. By means of comparing one with another, the lover observes the similarity between them according to beautiful form (*eidei kalon*). In a third step, the lover attends to the beauty in all bodies (*tois sōmasi kallos*). This movement widens the horizon from the beautiful imagery for the eye to the formal commonality of all beautiful bodies as is appreciated by the human capacity for aesthetic experience. As a matter of fact, the commonality supplies a master key to all beautiful bodies in one sense, and in the other sense, it provides a hidden link between the one (principle) and the many (particulars) exemplified formally in all the beautiful bodies.

The three basic classes of beauty involve one body, two bodies, and all bodies. They are conducive to a genre of somatic aesthetics. This aesthetics in turn nurtures a refined taste for the appreciation of the beautiful bodies. The taste begins with the perception of amorous sensuousness directed to a particular body beloved and proceeds to recognize the formal cognateness of two bodies. Then, it goes further to abstract the formal commonality from all bodies. It is an exercise that procures aesthetic wisdom and enables one to enjoy an aesthetic life wherein the love of somatic beauty interacts with a creative initiative. As recorded in the history of ancient Greeks, they were equipped with high aesthetic sensibility and especially fond of beautiful bodies. They would resort to regular gymnastic training in order to build up fair and masculine bodies of their own. At the same time, they would develop themselves into *kalokagathia* as the synthesis of physical beauty and good character.

When stepping up to the fourth class, the lover sets a higher value on the beauty of souls (*tais psychais kallos*) than on the "beauty of bodies."[15] What is meant by beauty (*kallos*) herein is actually goodness (agathos) for certain. Accordingly, the beauty of souls is more cherished than that of bodies, because it is more appealing to spiritual loveliness and conducive to the building of a noble nature.[16] Sure enough, it is revealed through

---

[15] Plato, *Symposium*, 210b–c.
[16] Ibid.

what is virtuous in practice. At this stage, the love of such beauty involves moral judgment through a psychic agency that cultivates the inner world, furthering moral wisdom as part of the philosophic nature of Love (Eros), which will in turn elicit good conduct, expose the lover to a moral life, and prevent him from any possible ills and wrongs.

Moving onward up to the fifth step, the lover discovers the beauty contained in observances and laws (*tois epitēdeumasi kai tois nomois kalon*).[17] At the sight of this more valuable category, the beauty of bodies turns out to be a slight affair. Here, the lover sees goodness, righteousness, and justice in the daily habituation of legal compliance and the validity of laws in both written and unwritten forms. This kind of beauty is drawn from ethical judgment and sustained by noble and virtuous doings. It is grounded on a *nomophylaktic* agency that calls for the spirit of law-abiding action. When it is well established, it contributes to constructing a political community that will secure the good life for its citizens. The capability of perceiving this beauty requires political wisdom that not only facilitates sound judgment in the regime, but generates justice and temperance in the citizens. Accordingly, both social commitment and qualified citizenship are exercised and developed. All this is deployed to procure a lawful or just life that is both approachable and agreeable at the same time.

Higher up on the sixth rung of the ladder is the "beauty of knowledge" (*epistēmōn kallos*) that stands for the truth of knowledge (*epistēmōn alētheia*) in essence. It is the great fruit born from the branches of knowledge (*tas epistēmas*).[18] In my observation, these branches foreshadow the disciplines in the curricula of the *Republic* and *Laws*, encompassing art and literature (*mousikē*), mathematics, geometry, astronomy, harmonics, and philosophy. Arriving at this stage, the climber encounters "the great ocean of the beautiful" (*to polu pelagos tou kalon*) and engages in contemplating the multiple splendors of fair and magnificent discourses as well as theories (*pollous kai kalous logous kai megaloprepeis*), from which he harvests a rich crop of plentiful thoughts in philosophy (*dianoēmata en philosophia aphthonō*),[19] broadens his horizon, and frees himself from the mean and meticulous slavery of a single

---

[17] Ibid., 210c.
[18] Ibid., 210c.
[19] Ibid., 210c d.

example to which he used to be attached. In other words, he is no longer small-minded or confined to the beauty of a particular person or observance. Rather, he is driven by an epistemic agency that is always in search of real knowledge, and well prepared to explore further for the knowledge of the very essence of beauty that in turn enhances and upgrades his theoretical wisdom.

Now, with this wisdom as his guide, he enters the realm of philosophy comprehensive of "various branches of knowledge or sciences" and lives a most contemplative life that is intellect-based above all. At this point, there arises the divine or extraordinary love oriented toward the most concentrated study of philosophy as love of wisdom, truth, and virtue altogether. It is always in search for perfection. According to Ficino, this *divinus amore* guides the lover toward a contemplative life that lifts him from the sense of sight (*aspectus*) to the power of thought (*mentem*). In striking contrast, the *humanus amore* directs the lover to an active life that focuses on sight, while the *ferinus amore* focuses on a voluptuous life and the sense of touch (*tactum*).[20]

The climber who advances to the top of the ladder gets engrossed in the wondrous vision of "the beautiful in its nature" (*tēn physin kalon*) as the final *telos* after all the preceding toils. He is persistently motivated by a noetic agency that is centered on insightful reasoning, and thus empowered to go through such an arduous travail in order to gain this metaphysical insight into beauty in itself. He seems to have sublimated the contemplative life to the acme. Suddenly, he discovers eternality, completeness, absoluteness, and purity of beauty in itself and understands that all the multitude of beautiful things become what they are only because they partake of this essential entity per se. He thereby obtains a command of "the beautiful learning [great profundity]" (*ta kala mathēmata*)[21] and comes to realize the ultimate cause of what is beautiful. The cause as such can be considered to be either the absolute archē of all or the universal in contrast to the particular, which exhibits a distinctive relationship totally discrepant from the foregoing ones at lower planes. In addition, the noetic agency not only helps the lover to accomplish his ascent, but leads him to develop a kind of divine wisdom as the outcome of the *divinus amore*. Such wisdom enables him to descry "the divinely beautiful itself (*to theion kalon*)," contact with absolute

---

[20] Marsilius Ficinus, *De Amore: Commentarium in Convivium Platonis*, 6:8.

[21] Plato, *Symposium*, 211c.

truth, beget "a real virtue" (*aretēn alēthē*), rear it up to win "the divine friendship" (*theophilei*), and eventually "hold himself immortal in that way."²² Quite distinctively, all this creates "that state of life" above all others in which "a man finds it truly worthwhile to live while contemplating the beauty in itself."²³ And such life that is "truly worthwhile to live" can be seen as the good life at its best in the Platonic sense.

6.2 The Mind-Heart Excursion

The analogy of the mind-heart excursion appears in *The Great Venerable Master* (*Da zong shi*), a chapter of a text written by Zhuangzi (c. 369–286 BCE). Discussions in this text are often formulated in analogies, fables, myths, or legendary stories. The mind-heart excursion (*you xin*) is an analogy employed to indicate a process of spiritual cultivation in order to attain the *Dao* (*wen dao*). In the text, the *Dao* may refer to a liberated self that lives a life of freedom. It is described as follows:

> Nanbo Zikui meets Ru Yu who is old but still looks like a child, and asks him the reason about it. Ru replies that he has acquired the Dao (*wen dao*). Nanbo wonders if he can learn the Dao. Ru answers and explains: "No, you can't. You're not the right kind of person. Bu Liangyi has the talent of a sage, but doesn't have the Dao of a sage; I have the Dao of a sage, but don't have the talent of a sage. I wanted to teach him about it so that he might be s true sage. In any case, it should have been easier to teach the Dao of a sage to a man with the talent of a sage. So, with a concentrated mind, I began to enlighten (*shou*) him. When three days passed, he was able to go beyond the human world (*wai tianxia*). I went on to enlighten him. When seven days passed, he was able to go beyond external things (*wai wu*). I again went on to enlighten him. When nine days passed, he was able to go beyond his life (*wai sheng*). Then he was able to have a clean mind as fresh as dawn (*zhao che*). Afterwards he was able to discern the Independent (*jian du*). Subsequently he was able to obscure the distinction between the past and the present (*wu gu jin*). Eventually he was able to ignore life and death (*bu sheng bu si*). From this point onward he will live in a realm of 'tranquility amid turmoil' (*ying ning*)."²⁴

---

²² Ibid., 211e.
²³ Ibid., 211d–212a.
²⁴ Zhuangzi, *The Zhuangzi* (trans. Wang Rongpei, Beijing: Foreign Languages Press, 1999), Ch. 6, pp. 97–99. The citation is condensed and modified in accord with the Chinese original.

Ostensibly, what astonishes and impresses Nanbo is no other than Ru's fresh complexion that appears so incredible and appealing. The portrayal of Ru's physical appearance assures his ruddy state of being like a golden boy. It indicates that he himself enjoys longevity without deliberate life preservation and remains in his prime condition beyond any expectation. Actually, Ru's given name Yu means "walk alone," symbolizing his personhood of walking or living alone with the Dao itself. This being the case, he looks energetic and healthy for his old age, as his face glows with youth and fairness, and his child-like image embodies how the *Dao* keeps himself in the best possible condition. The magic effect of this kind comes out as a result of spiritual cultivation that frees himself from cares and worries, exhibits the good life in the Daoist conception, and appeals to those who are obsessed in the pursuit of the Dao itself. The pursuit as such is exemplified by the mind-heart excursion that involves seven stages in all, each of which has its own specific characteristics. The number of days for the first three stages of enlightenment is more notional than functional. It is set up only to mean a span of time required for relevant cultivation. It is actually not specific due to the different times taken by individuals; hence, the reference to time is dropped in the later stages. The description of the entire experience covers such four dimensions as the prerequisite of learning the *Dao*, the approach to the *Dao*, the progression of acquiring the *Dao*, and the outcome of having acquired it.

The prerequisite is twofold in principle. The first relates to the capabilities of a sage, while the second to the *Dao* of the sage. The two are each necessary for the other: While the former serves as the basis, the latter is the guidance. As illuminated in the case of Bu Liangyi, he who has the capabilities of a sage can learn the *Dao*; yet, whether or not he can acquire it relies on the condition that he is correctly instructed and enlightened by someone who has the *Dao* of a sage. Noticeably, Ru Yu has the *Dao* of a sage, but doesn't have the talent of a sage; yet, he proclaims his ability to help Bu obtain the *Dao*.

According to Cheng Xuanying's annotation, the capabilities of a sage (*sheng ren zhi cai*) refer to a capacity for understanding and sensibility, while the *Dao* of a sage (*sheng ren zhi dao*) refers to the characteristic of emptiness and detachment resulting from the highest level of cultivation.[25]

---

[25] Guo Xiang and Cheng Xuanying (eds.), *Zhuangzi zhu shu* [The Works of Zhuangzi Annotated and Explained] (Beijing: Zhonghua Shuju, rep. 2013), p. 139.

This means that neither of the two aspects is perfect, because each slants toward one side only. However, the capabilities of a sage are secondary when compared with the *Dao* of a sage in light of value judgment; the former applies to the handling of external matters in social and political realms, and the latter facilitates and guides the "inner" attainment of spiritual enlightenment and mental purification. One is helpful but dependent, whereas the other fundamental and independent; consequently, one follows from the other in principle; that is why, Ru is the instructor of Bu in this matter. All this follows a presupposed logic that is peculiar to Zhuangzi's conception of ultimate knowledge (*zhi zhi*), true knowledge (*zhen zhi*), and the true person (*zhen ren*).

To Zhuangzi's mind, the ultimate knowledge to be obtained by humanity is to understand the respective scope of what heaven and man can do in their utmost. Such understanding equals the acme of human knowledge and remains rather elusive by nature.[26] Moreover, human life is limited, but all knowledge is limitless. It will only be in vain when a person attempts to pursue the limitless with the limited[27]: As human life is confined to a limited span, it is in vain for a person to strive for the ultimate knowledge that is unlimited. The task is bound for failure. Therefore, it would be better for a person to strive for true knowledge rather than the ultimate knowledge. True knowledge is found nowhere but in the true person himself or herself (*qie you zhen ren er hou you zhen zhi*). The true person knows neither the joy of life nor the sorrow of death. Here, the text projects a timeless view of birth and death: The true person is not elated when he was born; he is not reluctant when he dies. Casually he goes to another world; casually he comes back into this world. He doesn't forget the origin of his life; he doesn't explore the destiny of his life. He is pleased to accept whatever occurs to him. Such a person has an empty mind, a calm countenance, and a broad forehead. He is as austere as autumn and as warm as spring. His joy and anger substitute one another as naturally as the succession of the four seasons. He is in conformity with everything in the world, but he stays fathomless to all. That is why all these may only be achieved by someone whose knowledge has approached the *Dao*.[28]

---

[26] Zhuangzi, *The Zhuangzi* (trans. Wang Rongpei, Beijing: Foreign Languages Press, 1999), Ch. 6, p. 89.
[27] Ibid., Ch. 3, p. 43.
[28] Ibid., Ch. 6, pp. 89–90.

Observably, what the true person knows represents the true knowledge, and what the true person does embodies the *Dao* itself. It is on this account that the true person can be seen as the master of the true knowledge and the embodiment of the *Dao*. This being the case, when you are learning to become the true person, you are learning to attain the *Dao*, and correspondingly, you are learning to acquire true knowledge. Upon becoming the true person, you have attained the *Dao*, and naturally you have acquired the true knowledge, the knowledge that is about the virtue of the true person and the operation of the Dao per se.

The approach to the Dao is reflected in the act of enlightening (*shou*) in accord with the *Dao* itself. It is repeatedly emphasized during the entire progression of the mind-heart excursion. Other passages in the *Zhuangzi* also refer to this action. For instance, to enlighten through the *Dao* is to leave things to themselves while aligning with the Origin (*shou qi zong ye*).[29] As one aligns with the Origin, she also keeps to the One (*wo shou qi yi*) and lives in harmony with it.[30] She sees clearly the nature of everything because she embraces the Root of everything (*neng shou qi ben*).[31] "The Origin" (*zong*), "the One" (*yi*), and "the Root" (*ben*) are all different names for the *Dao* itself. The act of aligning with the *Dao* is neither cognitive nor analytical by nature, for it involves neither the apprehension of an object of the known nor that of the unknown. Instead, it seems to me as if it indicates an intuitive perception of the *Dao* itself simultaneously with a self-conscious internalization of it at the same time. Such perception and internalization are surely part of spiritual cultivation and enlightenment.

In the *Zhuangzi* story, the progression of acquiring the *Dao* involves seven successive stages, which I describe in turn. In the first stage, a person moves beyond the concerns of this world; the phrase *"wai tian xia"* means literally to forget about or ignore all under the sky. It is used here to denote detachment from prevailing social norms or customs, including entanglement the tensions within that environment. This stands in distinct contrast to the Confucian view and represents one of the key tensions between Confucian and Daoist thought in Chinese intellectual history. The Confucian tradition encourages social engagement and advocates a practical approach to social ills, calling for necessary action

---

[29] Ibid., Ch. 5, p. 73.
[30] Ibid., Ch. 11, p. 163.
[31] Ibid., Ch. 13, p. 217.

to bring order to the world (*ping tian xia*).³² By contrast, *Dao*ism seems pessimistic about worldly matters, purporting to favor a more quietist life.

The second stage moves beyond external things (*wai wu*). The *Zhuangzi* holds that the human condition is drastically problematic because humans are enslaved by external things (*ren wei wu yi*). Such external things can be divided into the intangible and the non-intangible. The intangible refers to material wealth, profit, and the like while the non-intangible to fame, social status, and the like. For Daoist, philosophy holds that such pursuits will spur human wants and ambitions that will in turn render the human mind restless and calculating all the time. It is for this reason that one needs to free himself from this plight by going beyond these pursuits altogether. More specifically, one does so by turning off the active power of such faculties as ears, eyes, mouth, nose, and heart which are born to be sensitive to the external things on the one hand and conducive to related desires on the other hand. He is then in a position to secure an undisturbed mentality that renders purification possible, say he enters the realm of tranquility that facilitates his further progression of the mind-heart excursion engaged.

The third stage involves transcending a particular conception of life (*wai sheng* 外生): Human life is physical by nature such that it requires bodily preservation. Bodily preservation can be potentially risky if one pursues longevity for its own sake. Hence, the *Zhuangzi* regards this view of life as the tumor of sufferings or the fountainhead of all cares and worries, and death as cutting off the tumor.³³ Going beyond this conception of life means to have freedom from this troublesome burden in one sense and in the other sense, to make no distinction between life and death that are conceived of as a recurrent cycle, with neither beginning nor ending. The placing of this stage is indicative of the level of difficulty encountered here. After transcending the human world and the external things therein, one needs to recheck his view on the personal life that is so vital to himself.

---

³² *The Great Learning* (*Da xue*), one of the Confucian classics, advocates a sense of mission to do whatever possible for actualizing this sociopolitical objective. This sense of mission is condensed into four Chinese notions that stand for four cardinal tasks: personal cultivation (*xiu shen*), regulating the family (*qi jia*), governing the state well (*zhi guo*), and bringing order to the world (*ping tian xia*). Wing-Tsit Chan (trans.), *The Great Learning*, in *A Source Book in Chinese Philosophy* (New Jersey: Princeton University Press, 1973), p. 86.

³³ Zhuangzi, *The Zhuangzi*, Ch. 6, p. 105.

The fourth stage, to "have a clear mind" (*zhao che*), can be literally rendered as "having a thorough or complete enlightenment at the daybreak." This stage is more spontaneous than protracted, as though one gets a glimpse of the morning light in supreme brightness and clarity. In the *Zhuangzi*'s view, this clear-mindedness involves the purification of the mind as it is emptied of wants, desires, ambitions, cares, worries, and so on. It therefore resembles "the fasting of the mind" (*xin zhai*) in principle. In Chapter 4 of the *Zhuangzi*, the "*Ways of the Human World*," the fasting of the mind features a special type of emptiness (*xu*) identified with the natural flow of vital energy (*qi* 气) that moves freely in the cosmos and embraces everything alike while expecting nothing from them at all. Only when a person is empty in this way can he be responsive to and well comprehend the reality of everything. As to a person who has not fasted the mind, he remains conscious of himself.[34] Therefore, he is most liable to be enslaved by the external things qua tantalizing attractions or temptations. Conversely, a person who has successfully fasted his mind is on the way of becoming a true person who is free from not merely egoism, but all other forms of bothering and disturbance derived from the problematic human world as such.[35]

Having a clear, pure, and empty mind, a person has mental space to accommodate something different: He is now able to "see the Independent" (*jian du*) at the fifth stage. The "Independent" herein refers to a set of characteristics of the *Dao*, say its self-independence, self-sufficiency, and self-immortality. One who sees it enters a new realm of experiencing the unique *Dao* and has access to a fascinating vision of the origin of all. Apart from that, he becomes so broad-minded and enlightened. He is well in a position "to neither show distain for anything nor question for right and wrong while seeking communication with the infinity of the Heaven and the Earth."[36]

---

[34] Zhuangzi, *The Zhuangzi*, Ch. 4, p. 55.

[35] Zhuangzi's notion of "having a clear mind" seems to share something with the Schopenhauerian idea of "the pure subject of knowledge" in spite of the discrepancy that the former is oriented toward the *Dao* whereas the latter toward the idea. Neither of them could be actualized without serene contemplation in distinct mode each due to the different philosophical backgrounds involved. Cf. Arthur Schopenhauer, *The World as Will and Idea* (trans. R. B. Haldane and J. Kemp, London: Kegan Paul, 1909), Third Book, pp. 231–233.

[36] Zhuangzi, *The Zhuangzi*, Ch. 33, p. 603.

By so doing does he then progress to the sixth stage of "obscuring the distinction between the past and the present" (*wu gu jin*). The *Dao* is not only the origin of all in the process of creation, but the oldest of all in the current of time. Meanwhile, it is omnipresent as it exists in everything and conditions what they are. Thus, the past and the present are unified in the Oneness of the *Dao*. Unified with the *Dao* as such, a person has awareness neither of the past nor the present. He seems to get into a timeless state where he perceives the broad sweep of a long history merely by a glimpse of the moon overhead (*yi zhao feng yue, wan gu chang kong*).

Eventually, she is able to "ignore life and death" (*bu sheng bu si*) at the seventh stage. "To ignore life and death" is to see through the real nature of life and death. It is only by so doing that one can become absolutely and spiritually free. In addition, the Dao comes from its own source and grows from its own root. It exists since time immemorial before the Heaven and the Earth came into being. It has neither beginning nor end and celebrates neither life nor death. When the person in search for the Dao has entered the realm of going beyond life and dearth as it is, one is actually identified oneself with the Dao per se.

Yet, there arises a question about the reason why the concern with life is stressed twice during the excursion? In my observation, most human individuals are life-conscious by nature. It is usually difficult for them to act upon the advice to "go beyond life" or "ignore life" for the sake of approaching the *Dao*. In other words, it is easier said than done when it comes to the critical moment of ending life and embracing death. For life-consciousness is persistent in almost all humans and deeply rooted in their instinct and mentality altogether. It is common sense that one can live once for all after being "thrown" into this world. He is in most cases inclined to live but reluctant to die even though his living condition is saturated with frustrations, anxieties, and other problems. If possible, he tends to face such matters and look forward to some improvement for the better. Zhuangzi is highly aware of the workings of human nature. He therefore advises the pursuer of the *Dao* to make double effort to emancipate himself from either the entangled bridle of life preservation or the haunting fear of mortality destiny. Accordingly, he ascribes both life and death to vital energy (*qi* 气) and promotes the following argument: Life comes along when the vital energy assembles; death occurs when vital energy disperses. The true person understands life and death in light of the *Dao*; he therefore leaves things to themselves and settles down in a realm where he is no longer bothered by either. Moreover, he is neither elated with the joy of life nor sad with the sorrow of death. Under such circumstances, so casually he goes to another world and returns to this world again. In a word, he is ready to accept whatever comes to himself, for he stays in conformity with everything but fathomless to all.[37] Furthermore, Zhuangzi recommends such a natural and taking-for-granted stance toward life and death that is based on his personal outlook: "The great earth endows me with a physical form to dwell myself in, makes me toil to sustain my life, gives me ease to idle away my old age, and offers me a resting place when I die. Therefore, to live is something good and to die is also something good."[38] This evinces Zhuangzi's way of living a life at ease by idealizing death itself. He thus tends to advise people to embrace the conviction that a miserable life is far more inferior to a happy death. It is on this account that Zhuangzi is said to be singing and beating time on a basin over his dear wife departed. When criticized by his friend for such an abnormal and pitiless act, he explains that he was weeping sadly upon her death, but stopped to conduct a different ritual of mourning like this, simply because he has realized that his wife has now gone through another transformation, and returned to the air-like vital energy that is lying peacefully between the heaven and the earth.[39]

The most immediate result of having acquired the *Dao* is no other than pure tranquility or serene contemplation. As Zhuangzi describes,

> The Dao begets life and finishes life, but it was never born and it will never die. The Dao exists in everything in the world. There is nothing it does not send off and nothing it does not welcome; there is nothing it does not destroy and nothing it does not complete. This is called 'tranquility amid turmoil', that is to say, it is a turmoil that has brought tranquility to perfection.[40]

The idea of bringing tranquility to perfection through turmoil appears paradoxical in logic. Normally, tranquility is opposite to turmoil. Yet, dialectically, the former comes into being because of the latter.

---

[37] Zhuangzi, *The Zhuangzi*, Ch. 22, p. 363; Ch. 6, p. 91; Ch. 19, pp. 297–301.
[38] Ibid., Ch. 6, p. 95.
[39] Ibid., Ch. 18, p. 289.
[40] Zhuangzi, *The Zhuangzi*, Ch. 6, p. 99.

In practice, the merits of tranquility are rounded out by the demerits of turmoil. A person who perceives and experiences both of them will typically tend to treasure the former while evading the latter. It is by so doing that he develops tranquility further and retains it in its best possible condition. This reminds us of what Laozi, a figure in the early Daoist tradition, says about the interaction between the muddy and the clear or between the still and the alive. That is, "He was merged and indifferent like muddy water. Who could make the muddy gradually clear via tranquility? Who could make the still gradually come to life via activity? (It was nobody else but him.)"[41] It is assumed that he who can do this has attained *Dao*. Now, he lives in serenity without being disturbed by anything external to the self. He must be happy with his true self in absolute spiritual freedom and independent personality.

In brief, the mind-heart excursion is meditation-based and pertains to spiritual experience and cultivation alike. It is conducive to the Daoist

---

[41] Laozi, *Dao De Jing* (trans. Wang Keping, Beijing: Foreign Languages Press, 2008), Ch. 15, pp. 32–33. Comparatively speaking, these two rhetorical questions contain a crucial and instructive message. "The muddy" has rich connotations. On one level, it means "muddy water," but metaphorically it signifies a muddy mind, turbid situation, chaotic order, confused environment, decadent morality, etc. All this is the opposite of "the clear" as its antithetical counterpart. Likewise, "the still" is regarded as denoting "the dead," "the static," "the inert," "the inactive," etc. All this is antithetical to the qualities of "the alive" or "the dynamic." As regards, these two pairs of opposite categories—the muddy and the clear, the still and the alive—a vehicle of transformation is highly desirable. The vehicle itself seems to be made up of such essential but contradictory elements as "tranquility" and "activity." As has often been observed in practice and experience, it is through concentration and tranquility that one is able to get out of the mire of muddiness and confusion on the one hand, and eventually become clear-minded and remain at ease on the other. This is often true of the natural process during which muddy water becomes clear through tranquility or freedom from disturbance. However, in terms of psychology and development, the involvement in tranquility and peace for too long a time can turn into a state of stillness, during which one may grow slack, inert or indolent. At this stage, activity is required as a stimulus. When activated and motivated, one becomes renewed, energetic, and creative again. This can be seen as an exposition of the reason why stillness (static state) taken to its extreme degree will turn into activity (dynamic state) and *vice versa* in the existence of all beings. The dialectical form of their transformation is actually extended from the general principle that "Reversion is the movement of the *Dao*." It is said that Martin Heidegger (1889–1976) was deeply impressed by the two rhetoric questions. He had them written on a wall scroll and hung it in his study for contemplation. We guess that the German philosopher may have had a profound reason to do so, because he himself was at the time preoccupied with seeking the possibility of "clarity." Cf. Wang Keping, *The Classic of the Dao: A New Investigation* (Beijing: Foreign Languages Press, 2011), pp. 193–194.

wisdom of the good life proper. Such wisdom is intended to make one live a really worthwhile life in absolute freedom from all cares and help one develop an independent personality without any enslavement to external things. It is by nature intuitive instead of epistemological, often representing something between gradual apprehension and sudden enlightenment. Under this circumstance, gradual apprehension is progressive as it ranges from the outward to the inward at large, and sudden enlightenment is momentary as it focuses on the freedom of varied levels in particular. They are working interactively and complementarily to lead one up to the attainment of the *Dao* as the most important foundation stone of the Daoist wisdom at its best.

6.3 Comparative Models of Cultivation

Plato's and Zhuangzi's models of cultivation differ from each other in their respective modes of thinking as well as articulation. When viewed as two alternatives and applied to the good life, they would appeal to different practitioners and work in characteristically distinct ways. The ascension of the beauty ladder as a process of cognitive development through philosophical learning, for example, has epistemological overtones with nous-based enlightenment. As a rule, it escorts a feeling of joy with the increase in learning about know-how. Such feeling varies from person to person because it depends upon how high one can move up to the ladder, that is, how much he knows about the classes of beauty involved. It could be transformed into a feeling of ecstasy the moment one manages to gain an insight into the essence of beauty in itself. The essence of this kind serves as a master key (One) to all other types of beauty (Many), for it connotes the universal nature of all other beautiful particulars. This being true, the ladder analogy apparently features an epistemological framework. The classes of beauty represent a hierarchy of truth-content with relevant values. The higher one goes up on the ladder, the more truth-content one gathers in, and accordingly, the more felicity he experiences. Eventually, he is enabled to enter the kingdom of immortality as the final teleological pursuit. In Plato's view, immortality is not merely referred to the characteristic property of gods, but also stands for the all-round perfection of becoming divine.

As noted in the *Symposium*, Plato's idea of becoming divine or godlike is embodied in his formulation of the beauty ladder. Hereby, the ladder is deployed to lead people to go upward, ranging from the sensational experience to its intellectual counterpart. It appears as though it ascends from the earth to the heaven, from the physical to the spiritual, from the visible to the invisible, and from the finite to the infinite. In order to escalate people up to the top of the ladder, Plato employs beauty (*kallos*) as a comprehensive term to cover the aesthetic significance of beautiful bodies, the moral meaning of good conduct and law compliance, and the intellectual value of wisdom and truth. The mounting process begins with the actual life and ends up in the metaphysical idea, between which there is the love as the intermediate or a symbolic bridge. As the subject matter of the *Symposium* unfolds, according to Stanley Rosen, the power of beauty is retained in the flux of being and serves as the eternal cause of human existence. It thus seems to embody the immediate presence of divinity in both humanity and the universe. Thereby beauty in itself shines on its own and meanwhile enlightens others. What it means in this context is probably equal to god.[42] Plato eventually divinizes the process when expounding over the ultimate knowledge of the essential beauty in terms of immortality. In other words, he lays bare his hidden concern with the possibility of becoming divine of the human.

On several occasions elsewhere in other dialogues, Plato shows his intention to advocate the possibility of becoming divine of the human. He thus affirms that man is given by god a divine gift of reason, and advices that man as man is to become god-like by taking up the upward way in his lifetime. The upward way is no other than the philosophical way. To become god-like is no other than to become a real philosopher in the Platonic sense. Hence, anyone who studies philosophy sanely by "holding ever to the upward way" (*tēs anō hodou aei hexometha*) is assured to "fare well and live well" (*eu prattōmen*) as reconfirmed at the end of the myth of Er.[43]

Moreover, a real philosopher portrayed in the *Phaedrus* is promised to benefit even more. He is said to possess the first category of soul on the one hand and apt to grow wings again that will help him fly back to the heaven. Evidently, Plato deploys the beauty ladder to denote the upward way and applies it to training god-like philosophers who are expected to

---

[42] Stanley Rosen, *Plato's Symposium* (New Haven: Yale University Press, 1987), Ch. 7. Also see the simplified Chinese version (trans. Yang Junjie, Shanghai: East China Normal University Press, 2011), p. 239.

[43] Plato, *Republic* (trans. Paul Shorey), 621c–d.

be intellectually wise and truly virtuous. Such philosophers are models not only for the perfect citizens themselves who can fulfill their social commitments, but for the qualified guardians of the *kallipolis* who can take good care of human matters. Interestingly, the beauty ladder commences with a discussion of somatic beauty or somatic aesthetics that is fairly physical and by no means mystical. Yet, as it extends skyward to its top rung, the description of the beauty in itself is obviously metaphysical and somewhat mystical as it is underlined by the immortal or divine dimension.

Quite conversely, the mind-heart excursion is a process of spiritual cultivation through serene contemplation in the Daoist sense. It essentially features intuitive perception and spiritual experience rather than cognitive reasoning or epistemological exploration. This is chiefly due to the three leading determinants. The first one can be traced back to the Daoist logic that the true person as the embodiment of the *Dao* comes before the true knowledge. Moreover, the true knowledge herein "has nothing to do with the common sense of knowledge associated with the outer world because of its dominant tendency of mysticism and nihilism."[44] The matter of fact is that it attempts to have no-knowledge of this kind, for it is directed to the enlightenment of the inner world and the subjective conversion to the *Dao*.

The second factor is the palpable teleological considerations in cultivation. In this respect, the mind-heart excursion is the pursuit of the Dao rather than any acquisition of knowledge. It is largely due to the tendency that the early Daoists, Laozi and Zhuangzi alike, take up a negative approach to knowledge. They maintain that the Dao instead of knowledge is the root of wisdom for the good life. This takes them apart from Plato and Platonists who hold on a positive approach to knowledge and firmly believe that one who knows more is most prone to obtain more wisdom for the good life. What leads to this difference can be further illustrated by what Laozi claims: "the pursuit of learning is to increase day after day," as it will lead to the acquisition of more conventionally bound knowledge of the world and recharge the "learned" with such things as more capability, ambition, and desire. In clear-cut

---

[44]Yang Anlun, *Zhongguo gudai jingshen xiangxiangxue--Zhuangzi sixiang yu zhongguo yishu* [The Phenomenology of Spirit in Ancient China: Zhuangzi's Thought and Chinese Art] (Changchun: Northeast Normal University Press, 1993), pp. 152–153.

contrast, "the pursuit of the *Dao* is to decrease day after day. It deceases and decreases again until one gets to the point of take-no-action. He takes no action, and yet nothing is left undone."[45] Naturally, Zhuangzi proceeds along with this line of thought. He resolutely sheds knowledge while emphasizing the *Dao* for its incomparable power of subtlety, creativity, inexhaustibility, and attainability. To his mind, the *Dao* is a reality that has its substance, remaining inert and formless. It can be transmitted and acquired by the heart, but it cannot be taught by the words of mouth or seen by the eyes. It comes from its own source and grows from its own root, existing since time immemorial before the heaven and the earth came into existence. It gives birth to demons and gods, and begets the heaven and the earth. It is above the zenith but does not seem high; it is beneath the nadir but does not seem low; it came into being before the universe but does not seem long ago; it was there before the time immemorial but does not seem old.[46] Herein detectable are the seemingly metaphysical, theological, and cosmological features of the *Dao*. They turn out to be some kind of rhetorical hyperbole, mystical and incomprehensible all the way through. Yet, if you shift your conventional mode of thought to that of Daoism, you may find it no other than a mental state based on intuition-bound subjectivity and spirituality as is confined to the inner world alone. The inner world is not merely indispensable to the becoming of the real self, but also capable of comprising the outer world providing it is completely emptied (*xu* 虚) in the pure sense of the Daoist term. All this is pointed to the attraction, apprehension, and attainment of the *Dao* as its ultimate *telos*.

The third element comes from the underlying preoccupation with the highest realm of human living proper. Such a realm is largely determined by spiritual cultivation through empirical artistry and acuity rather than cognitive power through epistemological development. In the *Zhuangzi*, spiritual cultivation is always first priority. It is aimed at the attainment of the *Dao* in one sense and in the other sense, at "a complete self-conscientiousness of the original nature of humankind. It is thus embodied in the in-depth experience of the oneness of the true self with the heaven, the earth and all things, which will conduce to a mental concentration to converge the self with the cosmos. At this point,

---

[45] Laozi, *Dao De Jing*, Ch. 48, p. 83.
[46] Zhuangzi, *The Zhuangzi*, Ch. 6, pp. 95–97.

one is engaged in a free play with the spirit or the vital energy of the cosmos without being attached to external things. He is then exposed to a spiritual feeling of being broad-minded and free wandering."[47] Consequently, he is provided with easy access to absolute freedom and independent personality at a time when he is living with the *Dao*, in Zhuangzi's expectation.

Being identified with the *Dao* as such, the true person is by nature invented as a metaphorical or symbolic figure, mainly deployed to appeal to those who happen to be curious but prepared to seek after what the true knowledge of the *Dao* could be. It is noteworthy in Zhuangzi's characterization that the true person appears to be primarily wise and mystical. This may be overconclusive. In my opinion, one aspect of this personality turns out to be more accessible than commonly assumed. For instance, "the true person in ancient times did not dream when he slept; he did not worry when he was awake; he did not mind his food when he ate; he inhaled deeply when he breathed. His breath rose from the heels while the breath of ordinary men rises from the throat."[48] The true person enjoys such mental serenity that he is freed from any disturbances and worries. He lives so simply, happily, and naturally as he wholeheartedly concentrates on *Dao* itself. Some people are most liable to see the way of his breath as something strange or peculiar, but those who are engaged in the exercise of breathing system (*qi gong*) tend to take it as a normal form of practice in daily life.

Is there any room to accommodate the aspects in which the two models of cultivation, in spite of their differences, may complement each other? The answer is positive, in the ways I describe below. First and foremost, it cannot be denied that both of them are empirically inspired by the physical beauty of a particular body or fresh complexion, and teleologically preoccupied with the pursuit of true wisdom for the good life, notwithstanding the fact that they are motivated by differing conceptions and approaches in this regard. Quite coincidentally and similarly, the beauty ladder covers seven steps to reach the greatest insight and so does the mind-heart excursion to achieve the ultimate *Dao*; in order to arrive at the final destination of self-sublimation, both of them are schemed to guide the person from the outer world into the inner world of his own

---

[47] Cui Dahua, *Zhuang xue yan jiu* [A Study of Zhuangzi's Thought] (Beijing: Renmin Press, 1992), p. 302.

[48] Zhuangzi, *The Zhuangzi*, Ch. 6, p. 89.

through either cognitive development or spiritual cultivation by virtue of discrepant paths. The number "seven" shared therein implies at least two things: a gradual process and a preset logic. The distinct features of the gradual process in each case are already exposed foregoingly, and here is no need of repetition. As for the preset logic, it denotes a sequential order of deduction that preconditions the step-by-step progression from low to high or from superficial to profound. However, in Plato it is directed to knowing what is unknown, while in Zhuangzi it is pertained to forgetting what ought to be forgotten. In other words, the former is pointed to knowledge-oriented learning via rational contemplation, whereas the latter on "sitting in self-forgetfulness" (*zuo wang*) through intuitive meditation. Consequently, the former leads to an increasing amount of know-how and meta-cognition, but the latter ends up with self-erasement and empty-mindedness. More specifically, the ladder allegory takes beauty as the object of knowledge, but categorizes it into hierarchical levels. Its inherent logic lies in the upgoing journey from cultivating wisdom and goodness to pursuing absolute truth through contemplating varied forms of beauty. The mind-heart excursion is the same with the experience of inward enlightenment and moves through a sequence of different stages. Its effective approach to the Dao works as follows: Treat "sitting in self-forgetfulness" as the most crucial strategy, a strategy that is employed not only to empty and fast the mind, but also to fulfill the utmost of human nature (*qiong li jinx in*) in the Daoist sense. All this sets up the premise only from which one can go forward to "cast off one's limb and trunk, give up one's hearing and sight, leave one's physical form, deprive oneself of learned knowledge, and identify oneself with the Dao itself."[49]

By contrast, the beauty ladder calls for a kind of purification due to the hierarchical but conditional movement. Say, it is logically possible to move up to enjoy the higher class of beauty only when the love of the lower and preceding class of beauty is purified or sublimated. The assent to the summit for the beauty in itself is motivated and encouraged, but seems to leave a room to pause somewhere during the entire process. As regards the progression of the mind-heart excursion, Zhuangzi appears to be somewhat arbitrary or single-minded due to his rigid logic. Thus, he sets up a closed circuit and leaves it as it is to the *Dao* pursuer.

[49] Ibid., Ch. 6, p. 111.

That is, if and only if one succeeds in going through all the seven stages, he is enabled to attain the *Dao* and live the good life of complete purification and absolute freedom in the Daoist sense. If by any chance he fails at any stage during the progressive process, he is most likely to live an uneasy life because he will expose himself to inevitable disturbances and temptations from the outside world. As the two paths to the good life are juxtaposed, we may find that the difference between them does really count to some degree. For instance, when a Platonic lover of beauty could not go any further during his adventure of exploring the unknown field, he could have his own reason to hold up somewhere and try to "sit in self-forgetfulness" from the perspective of Daoism. Then, if a Zhuangzi's pursuer of the *Dao* could not manage to "sit in self-forgetfulness," he could persuade himself into reflecting upon what ought to know from the viewpoint of Platonism. In a word, everyone happens to possess an innate free will, which serves to let him choose a lifestyle more appropriate to himself from the two alternative frames proposed. Undoubtedly, the choice of a lifestyle means the becoming of a kind of personality or personhood. It is therefore a matter of anthropological ontology in this case. As for the teleological pursuit in the ultimate sense of this term, however, the model of ladder analogy encourages the real lover of beauty to climb up to the top and become god-like in terms of a Platonic philosopher. The model of mind-heart excursion expects the genuine learner of the Dao to roam above all at ease and become Dao-conscious in terms of a Daoist quietist.

Moreover, Plato's tale hints an attitude related to the tradition of Hellenic Quietism, and Zhuangzi's tale exposes an attitude leagued with the heritage of Chinese *Dao*ism. The two attitudes are in accord with their shared preference to the contemplative life instead of the political life. Historically, Plato himself demonstrates his quietist tendency by rejecting the invitation to join the Thirty for the governance of Athens. Zhuangzi does the same when he is invited to be a prime minister of a state during the Warring States period. He even goes so far as to ridicule the envoy by pointing to a free mudlump and saying that he would become this little creature in freedom rather than a high official in confinement. Actually, both Plato and Zhuangzi have their sharp observations on political affairs, but abstain from any direct involvement because of their high awareness of the constant and unjust in-fights or power games in the arena. Notwithstanding such common aspects, the discrepancy between Quietism and Daoism is worth reconsidering from a complementary standpoint. As usual, Quietism is mainly preoccupied with real knowledge of all. In order to acquire it, it tends to favor tranquil contemplation, prefer a philosophical life, and withdraw from the political arena shrouded in troublesome human affairs. Simply put, it so does in order to know more in the areas probed. As to Daoism, it is chiefly concerned with the *Dao* itself. Even though it shares with its Hellenic counterpart a similar stance toward certain things, it sticks to another strategy to accomplish its purpose. That is, it acknowledges a sequence of three distinguishing stages in the entire course of human development. The sequence consists of having no-knowledge (*wu zhi*) as being born ignorant during the infancy, having knowledge (*you zhi*) as becoming learned through study during the period of maturity, and shedding knowledge (*qu zhi*) as striving to forget what ought to be forgotten during the period of spiritual cultivation for the sake of the *Dao*. Generally speaking, it is difficult for a person to transit from having no-knowledge to having knowledge, because it demands a great deal of hard work; it is even more difficult for a person to shift from having knowledge to shedding knowledge, because it involves not only the psychological reluctance to forget it, but also the cognitive resistance to erase it from memory. Given the three stages, the first is fairly easy to figure out because it is a universal phenomenon. The third is rendered intelligible through a relevant formulation as is shown in the mind-heart excursion. Unfortunately, the second remains rather obscure and scarcely discussed in Daoism because of the negative approach to knowledge abovementioned. It is in this domain that Quietism has much to offer. An off-handed example can be drawn from the ladder analogy with reference to "the beauty of knowledge" elaborated here and there in Plato's dialogues, the *Republic* and the *Laws* in particular.

Furthermore, the contemplative life in the Platonic notion is thought to be attainable with help of philosophical training and epistemological improvement. It meanwhile needs mental tranquility and serene contemplation under such circumstances. It is mostly explicated by virtue of logos-based reasoning or rational thinking, which is in turn characterized with *philologos* as love of word, and discursive clarity in either theoretical argumentation or analytical classification. Similarly, what the mind-heart excursion attempts to furnish is no other than mental tranquility and serene contemplation, which can be extended one way or another into relevant contributors to the contemplative life after all. Nevertheless, it is almost always described by means of experience-oriented conclusion and intuitive assumption, which usually features *philopraxis* as love of action, and mystical obscurity in either practical generalization or imposing solution. With respect to the alternatives in question, *philologos* without *hilopraxis* could be ineffective, and *philopraxis* without *philologos* could be misleading. Either of them fails to meet the standard of appropriate measure as it oversteps the mesos of never too much and never too little. By this account, it violates the rule that "overdone is as bad as underdone." It is for this reason that they are expected to work interactively so as to bring forth and even consolidate their respective potential of illumination or enlightenment on one another.

As luck would have it, this complementary assumption can be well reinforced by a particular reference to Nietzsche. As read in the *Twilight*, Nietzsche advises the Europeans to turn to China so as to adjust themselves to the Chinese way of thinking and living, and infuse into the blood of the instable Europe a bit of Asian-type tranquility, contemplative spirit, and persistence.[50] Noticeably, these Asian-type virtues are exemplified in the Daoist way of thinking, among others. They should be applied not merely to the Europeans, but also to the Asians as well, especially at the time of the confrontation with the similar issues due to cultural and economic globalization today. On the other hand, it is also necessary to infuse into the blood of the stable Asians a bit of European-type rationality, pioneering spirit, and creativity at least. All this calls for an intercultural interaction and transformational creation in these areas.

Presumably at last, if what is proposed above could be acceptable by any chance, the two alternatives might be pragmatically utilized to create a synthetic frame of reference in a modified manner. This may sound to some like holding a "forced marriage" and to others like cooking a "collected soup." Yet, it would be better to give a try in spite of running the risk of being torn apart in between. For such a frame of reference is intended to help those who would love a variety of beauty or a series of

---

[50] Friedrich Nietzsche, *Aurore* (Paris: Gallimard, 1980), p. 162. The statement referred to in this passage follows: "Puet-être ira-t-on alors chercher des Chinois: et ceux-ci apporteraient la façon de penser et de vivre qui convient à des fourmis travailleuses. Oui, dan l'ensemble ils pourraient contribuer à infuser dans le sang de l'Europe instable qui s'exténue elle-même un peu de la tranquilité et de l'esprit contemplative de l'Asie et--ce qui est bien le plus nécessaire--un peu de la ténacité asiatique."

meditation in order to nurture types of desirable wisdom for the good life of any attainable kind. By the way, in contrast to "those who seek with lamentation" approved by Pascal as is mentioned at the outset of this discussion, we hereby recommend all those who seek with pleasure. Such "pleasure" signifies not simply a joyful state of mind, but a great feeling of enlightenment.

CHAPTER 7

Poetic Wisdom in Zen Enlightenment

The introduction of Buddhism into China from India can be dated back to about first century B.C. It has enriched the Chinese culture of intelligence at large and been preserved in its entirety when it is later found abolished in its birthplace. Interestingly, it has spread far and wide all over China, inspired the Chinese to create Daoism as a religion (*Dao Jiao*) on the basis of Daoism as a philosophy (*Dao Xue*), and then developed into more than a dozen of sects with respective characteristics. Comparatively speaking, the Zen (Chan) Sect is most special in terms of its way of meditation and most popular among its practitioners at home and abroad.

The genesis of Zen is depicted in a legendary story, where Siddhartha Sākyamuni (c. 565–486 B.C.) referred silently to *dharma* nature by showing a flower to his disciples on Mount Sumeru, the imagined paradise of Buddhist believers. The flower is symbolic of beauty in silence, characteristically similar to the fundamental aspect of *dharma* nature. Therein, the Buddha got no response from others except a knowing smile from Mahakasyapa, his favorite disciple who got the message as was so subtly indicated in such a metaphorical manner. Ever since then, the Zen Buddhism formed a unique mode of expressing its enlightenment via a poetic genre of *gatha* that was mostly composed of special images or symbolisms relating to either a budding flower or a natural scene.

Coincidently, the Sudden School (*dunwu zong*) was also allegedly developed from a poetic genre of *gatha* improvised by Hui Neng, the Sixth Patriarch of Zen Buddhism. Allegorically, the *gatha* itself has created some images out of a Bodhi-tree and a mirror to be discussed later. It is due to such a background that the understanding of Zen is very often identified thereafter with the appreciation of poetic images, symbolisms, and natural scenes. It goes so far as to the extent that the perceiving of the *dhyāna* (Zen) message is just like contemplating the beautiful in either nature or poetry through intuition and sensibility. Accordingly, what is considered as *prajñā* may well be compared to poetic wisdom. It is appealing and delicate, like the moon in a lake or the flower in a mirror; it is vague and elusive, like a passing cloud in the sky or mist rising after a rainfall; it is easygoing but far-reaching, like the wind shaking huge pines or the sound of bells from a remote temple. On the surface, this kind of wisdom seems meaningless and useless to those who are preoccupied with practical profits and benefits, but turns out to be useful in the form of *prajñā pāramitā* (wisdom in perfection) to those who live freely beyond any utilitarian purpose or attachment.

The cultivation of *dhyāna* and Buddha-hood alike depends on the chance of causality. Whenever we put aside our worldly cares and crafty minds, move out of our extravagant abodes and busy streets into the countryside, and look up at the streaming clouds overhead or gaze upon the fresh flora around, we are most apt to rediscover our real selves and share a special affinity with the beautiful in nature. All this is conducive to the nourishment and awareness of *dhyāna*, through which we can realize and further approach an ontological understanding of human life. Such wisdom is peculiar to Zen perception and experience. In order to expose its basic features and alternatives, we set off to reflect on the revelation from natural scenes and then proceed to reconsider the psychical path to Zen enlightenment, and the poetic enhancement of *śūnyatā* (emptiness or void) *qua* beauty, freedom and happiness altogether.

7.1 Revelation from Natural Scenes

The entire process of Chinese history witnesses a continuing investigation of the nexus between heaven and humankind. Now, this nexus is slightly modified and has generally replaced the interaction between man and nature. According to Chinese thinkers, all things can be appreciated through serene contemplation, and beautiful scenes from nature are easily found. To some Western philosophers, nature can enchant humans into a transcendent feeling or aesthetic ecstasy by means of an offhanded demonstration of its magic power. It can endow them not merely with what they need materially and physically, but also with what they need spiritually and intellectually, owing to the light it sheds on existential insight and the human condition. Just as is exemplified in Emerson's *Nature*, "Only as far as the masters of the world have called in nature to their aid, can they reach the height of magnificence. This is the meaning of their hanging-gardens, villas, to back their faulty personality with these strong accessories.... These bribe and invite; not kings, not palaces, not men, not women, but these tender and poetic stars, eloquent of secret promises."[1]

It must be pointed out, however, that the Zen Sect of Buddhism holds a similar attitude toward nature as Daoism (Taoism) does. In most cases, the Daoists (Taoists) advocate the way of "following the spontaneity in nature" (*shunying ziran*) because they believe that nature as a whole has the virtue of great beauty in silence. Corresponding to Daoism in this respect is Zen Buddhism, which finds inspiration from nature and takes all natural phenomena as symbols of, or gates to, *dhyāna* apprehension. Thus, regarding Zen insightfulness, what should inspire and illuminate us are not Buddhist sutras, not religious doctrines, not logos, not rituals, but hidden revelations from natural scenes. Those who are observant and sincere enough about the experience of *Dao* or *dhyāna* will see clearly what is meant thereby. That is, so long as they are sensitive to natural scenes, they are most likely to feel the oneness between man and nature. Quite possibly they will "come to realize the true essence of human life even in calm breeze and velvet ripples, and to know the real origin of mental state even in tasteless drinks and still surroundings. They are not startled by either grace or disgrace, but obsessed with the blooming or falling flowers in the courtyard; they are so relaxed and at ease, wandering off along with the free movement of clouds overhead. As a result, they are able to enjoy the most fascinating melody while listening to the echoes among pines and streams flowing across pebbles, and to discover the most brilliant patterns in the cosmos when contemplating leisurely the moonlight over the boundless prairie

---

[1] Ralph Waldo Emerson, *Nature*, in *Emerson: Essays* (Tianjin: Tianjin Education Press, 2004), p. 171.

and the shadowy clouds down in the transparent lakes."[2] As is noticed from the above description, such elements as breeze, ripples, flowers, clouds, wind among pines, springs flowing across stones, moonlight over the grassland, and images reflected in lakes, all gather together to compose scenic vistas, so picturesque and musical, conducive to the aesthetic pleasure and poetic feelings that are accessible only to those who are carefree and non-competitive, broad-minded and tolerant, receptive and sensitive. Here, the depiction as such reveals the picturesque realm and literary mind in one sense and in the other sense, enjoyable leisure and spiritual freedom derived from the poetic ambience and *dhyāna* mentality. All this plainly expresses the psychical state of internal tranquility and the *dhyāna* perception of metaphysical subtlety as well. No matter what it signifies under such circumstances, we cannot deny its implicit insights into the cosmic order and human condition aside from its poetic wisdom and revelation serving to coordinate harmonious interrelationship between man and nature.

This type of poetic wisdom is uniquely represented not only in the *Works of Zhuangzi* (*Zhuangzi*), the *Sutra of Hui Neng* (*Tan jing*), and the *Tending the Roots of Wisdom* (*Caigen tan*), but also in the *Walden* and many others. Henry Thoreau, for example, speaks in a tone of a poet-philosopher and advises people to count the flowers on the trees instead of calculating the fallen leaves on the ground when going out for a morning walk. As is known to all, blooming flowers are symbolic of beauty, brilliance, and hope, whereas fallen leaves are a sign of death, decay, and loss. Rather, one is delighted by counting flowers and concentrating on a positive aspect with an optimistic outlook. On the contrary, you will feel depressed while calculating the fallen leaves, your attention

---

[2] Hong Yingming, *Caigen tan* [*Tending the Roots of Wisdom*]. The translation given here is mine. The readers can also see the English version provided by Paul White. It is cited here for reference: "In the course of your career, keep inured to the fact that you are in favour or out of favour with your superior; watch the flowers as they bloom and droop outside your door. Pay no heed to whether you remain in or are removed from office; calmly gaze at the clouds on the horizon, as they gather and disperse.... In utter repose, hearing the tune of waving pine branches, or the tinkling of a brook over pebbles on sense that these are the murmurings of Nature. With an undisturbed mind, gazing at the delicate wisps of smoke flickering on the horizon of the boundless prairie or the reflections of clouds in a still lake, one can perceive the exquisitely beautiful pattern of Nature." Cf. Hong Yingming, *Tending the Roots of Wisdom* (trans. Paul White, Beijing: New World Press, 2001), pp. 289, 295.

drawn to a negative dimension and a pessimistic vision. Apparently, in this case, an attitude can be determinant in that it transforms the situation involved, say a positive attitude will end up in a positive response, while a negative one results in negativity—even though the entire setting is the same. Furthermore, whenever you are confronted with a difficult situation, what you should do is adjust your mentality; you can choose to look at either "blooming flowers" or "fallen leaves." It is for this reason that many philosophers keep endorsing us to learn from nature by nurturing our interest in things and our wisdom in regard to life. In fact, nature becomes beautiful because of human existence, and humankind becomes wise because of natural beauty. Those who can perceive the beauty of great nature will be able to ride up to the highest sphere of human life filled with excellence, spirituality, and divinity, so to speak.

Up to this point, one may wonder whether a Zen Buddhism with such a poetic character is a religion or a philosophy. It is actually both *par excellence*. The Chinese concept of *zhexue* came from Japan. It was first coined by Nishi Amane (1829–1897), a Japanese scholar who once studied in Europe. Actually, *zhexue* was a creative translation of philosophy that can be traced back to the Greek notion of *philosophia* (φιλοσοφια), a compound word made up of *philo* (φιλο as love) and *sophia* (σοφια as wisdom), meaning "love of wisdom." Among ancient Greeks, *sophia qua* wisdom is characterized with emphasis on both thinking and action in a reasonable way. It is therefore subdivided into its two most fundamental aspects: One is *theoria* (θεωρια) based on intelligence and contemplation, and the other is praxis (πραχις) operated through doing and techne (τεχνη). Both of them aim teleologically to seek *aletheia* (αληθεια) as truth and to explore the everlasting principle of real knowledge (επιστημη). After all, it is intended to guide us through the journey of life. Now, it extends into two domains: One is referred to theoretical wisdom and the other to practical wisdom.

With respect to Chinese philosophy and religion, it cannot do without reference to Zen Buddhism. As for its position and function in Chinese ideology, Zen Buddhism straddles two provinces; it is both a religion and a philosophy. Under certain circumstances, it is a philosophy rather than a religion, owing to its being a study of the wisdom of human existence. Such wisdom is usually contained in poetic imagery or allegorical symbolisms. It is essentially oriented toward spiritual emancipation or liberation. It is exercised through such approaches as self-control, self-concentration, and self enlightenment, thus helping people awaken and transcend the formidable chasm between reality and ideality on the one hand and on the other, leading people to face anxieties and frustrations with ease. It pertains to a psychological balance and joy out of the so-called bitter sea of boundlessness (*ku hai wu bian*). Eventually, it enables people to enter into the kingdom of Zen or *dhyāna* delight, where the human mind is assumed to be intrinsically purified, peacefully settled, and genuinely pleased.

It is noteworthy that Zen Buddhism as a special form of wisdom stresses mainly these two factors: apprehension and action. The former is achieved via deep contemplation and high awareness, and the latter is actualized through personal engagement and praxis. All of this is somewhat approximating the Greek conception of *sophia* as wisdom in the theoretical and practical sense aforementioned. However, it is in striking contrast to any religious cults that favor *philo-logos*, a love of words rather than *philo-praxis*, a love of action. This being the case, anyone who is serious about the cultivation of *dhyāna* or Zen enlightenment is not supposed to be a chatterbox, ready to recite doctrines from scriptures or canons. Instead, he devotes himself to insightful understanding and constant praxis so as to stay carefree and transcendent in the mentality of absolute freedom.

Then, what suggestions does Zen Buddhism usually offer as to how to "apprehend" or "act" in light of *dhyāna* and *prajñā*? This question is open to many possible answers. What I attempt to do next is to cut through the mist of various interpretations and propose the most significant ones in accordance with a common methodology for self-directed practice in Zen or *dhyāna*. They are to be discussed subsequently under the subheadings of "natural spontaneity as a psychical path" and "poetic way of Zen enlightenment."

7.2 Natural Spontaneity as a Psychical Path

When the laymen happen to chat about Zen, they tend to believe in a stereotyped image of a practitioner sitting on a *zafu* (cattail cushion) while doing *zazen* (meditation) in a *zendo* (hall for Zen cultivation). This is often taken for granted as the one and only *dharma* gate to Zen enlightenment. As a matter of fact, *zazen* is no more than a form of meditation. In other words, it is nothing but an external means to mind-purification and wisdom-awakening for the ultimate purpose of Zen enlightenment. It follows that a person may well link all his daily activities and even routines up to Zen praxis, provided he is self-conscious of his *dhyāna* cultivation. Accordingly, he can feel mental serenity when walking so long as he is carefree. Conversely, he may be tied up with anxiety when doing meditation so long as he is burdened by cares. In its final analysis, Zen apprehension or enlightenment does not lie in the adherence to formal procedures, but in the capacity of self-awakening. If what is said above is too abstract, let us try to clarify it more specifically by virtue of a typical case in modern art.

Modern art in the West is largely sustained by the avant-garde. The year 1917 witnessed a particular event in art history when Michel Duchamp, a French artist, submitted to the New York Armoury Show a ready-made urinal picked up from among refuse. He labeled it with the title of "*La Fontaine*" and presented it as a work of art. Actually, it was a product by the Mutt Company and whose practical use was in men's washroom. Now, it was through Duchamp's hand deviated from its original application, lying there upside down like a motionless turtle. The moment when the viewers saw it, they are naturally reminded of the familiar sight of someone pissing, as unpleasant or disgusting as it were. Such a "work of art" was flatly rejected by the organization panel, but Duchamp as its "author" made a big story about it by using the panel to give a justifiable explication. This event stirred up a heated debate over such issues as "What is art?" and "Is this the end of art?" The whole process brought tremendous benefit and fame to Duchamp in that a number of curious customers queued up to order this "masterpiece." Among them were at least two well-known art galleries. Surely enough, Duchamp made a lot of money with a deal of eight identical pieces in all. He purchased them first from the Mutt and then signed his autograph on each; afterward, he sold them out at a much higher price. It is not surprising that Duchamp did his business in a way as if he was issuing a set of pictures printed from an etched plate of copper.[3]

From 1960s to 1980s, Arthur Danto made use of Duchamp's "*La Fontaine*" together with Warhol's "Brillo Box" and Rauschenberg's "Bed" when reflecting on the question about how ready-mades become found art or artworks. On those occasions, he reconsidered the end as well as death of art in comparison and introduced the notion of the "artworld"

---

[3] Arthur C. Danto, *After the End of Art: Contemporary Art and the Pale of History* (Princeton: Princeton University Press, 1997). Also see Stephen David Ross (ed.), *Art and Its Significance* (Albany: State University of New York Press, 1994), pp. 470–481.

to acknowledge that a work of art could be culture-specific; that is, what would be a work of art in one cultural context would not be a work in another. He also probed into the relationship between art and theory in determining whether something is a work of art in a special atmosphere or situation.[4] He discovered that such ready-mades and practical objects as toilets, supermarkets, or bedrooms transfigured into works of art when displayed in other places by the artists concerned. The magic power of this transfiguration of the commonplace is said to stem from the "artworld" that consists in certain necessary conditions. In Arthur's terminology, "To see something as art requires something the eye cannot decry—an atmosphere of artistic theory, a knowledge of the history of art: an artworld."[5] According to this, one sees something as art just because he bases his judgment on the "artistic identifications" supplied by the "artworld." Otherwise, he would never regard that something as art, for he would act no differently than a child who holds a matter-of-fact attitude, who only believes what he sees with his own eyes. It follows that the ready-mades could not turn out to be found art without art theories and histories comprising the so-called artworld.

Interestingly, Danto made a particular reference to a famous Zen *ko-an* as he intended to reinforce his argument and specify how ready-mades are altered into found artworks. The *ko-an* itself implies a sort of wisdom of silent argumentation as it follows:

> Before I had studied Zen for thirty years, I saw mountains as mountains and waters as waters. When I arrived at a more intimate knowledge, I came to the point where I saw that mountains are not mountains, and waters are not waters. But now that I have got the very substance I am at rest. For it is just that I see mountains once again as mountains, and waters once again as waters.[6]

---

[4] Arthur C. Danto, "The Artworld," in *The Journal of Philosophy* (1964), pp. 571–584. Also see his other writings, including *The Transfiguration of the Commonplace*, *The Philosophical Disenfranchisement of Art*, *The State of the Art*, and *After the End of Art*, etc.

[5] Arthur C. Danto, "The Artworld," in Stephen David Ross (ed.), *Art and Its Significance*, p. 477.

[6] Ibid. According to a footnote given by Dabney Townsend, Danto identifies this passage elsewhere as coming from one of the more radical forms of Zen, the Diamond Sutra. See Dabney Townsend (ed.), *Aesthetics: Classical Readings from Western Tradition*, Wadsworth, 2001, p. 332. Actually, it comes from another source book instead of the Diamond Sutra, for its original version in Chinese, see Pu Ji (ed.), *Wu deng hui yuan* [A Collection of Ko-an in Zen Buddhism] (Beijing: Zhonghua Book Company, 2002), Vol. 3, p. 1135.

Enigmatic as it is, it verifies a personal experience of Zen learning and enlightenment in the name of Qing Yuan Weixin, an old Chinese monk who lived during the Song Dynasty more than a thousand years ago. Right after the above citation, Qing Yuan continued, "Learned practitioners, do you see the differences and similarities between these three opinions? If some of you think of them in black and white terms, I would suggest that you come to me for a vis-à-vis conversation."[7] A rough reading of the entire passage will indicate three levels of perception relating to the interaction between the subject and the object. At the initial stage, there is a sharp subject-object dichotomy, and external things are conceived to be independent of the subject proper. Therefore, the old monk saw mountains as mountains and waters as waters. When it came to the intermediate stage, the subject expanded to the extent that it encompassed all the external things within its self-centered imagination, and consequently, he came to the point where he saw that mountains were not mountains, and waters were not waters. At the final stage, the subject projected all himself into the outside world and thus overcame the dichotomy by integrating all into a synthetic whole. The external things were thus imbued with vital and even spiritual energy, and accordingly, mountains were seen once again as mountains and waters once again as waters. On this occasion, the monk became enlightened so completely that he would see things for what they really were without making any artificial distinction on the one hand, and on the other hand, he could naturally discern a *dhyāna* message from all his surroundings.

Apparently, attitude counts a great deal in this peculiar logic of affirmation, negation, and re-affirmation of the same objects. The images of mountains and waters are altered along with the attitude shaped by the progression of Zen apprehension. Metaphorically speaking, the Zen practitioner could be compared to the audience, and the mountains and waters could be taken as ready-mades, then in this case, the recognition of the ready-mades as found artworks would be largely determined by the audience's attitude toward their "artistic identifications" or artistic status. The audience might also go through a process of confirming, denying, and reconfirming these "ready-mades" in view of their "artistic identifications." Hence, Danto deliberately extended this implication by asserting that one's "identification of what he has made is logically

---

[7] Pu Ji (ed.), *Wu deng hui yuan* [A Collection of Ko-an in Zen Buddhism], p. 1135.

dependent upon the theories and history he rejects."[8] Conversely, one's identification of what he has made or contemplated is also logically dependent upon the theories and history he accepts. For his rejecting or accepting of art theories and history will cause corresponding changes in cognitive stance and identification consciousness. Under such circumstances, what are looked upon as ready-mades before will be transfigured into works of art, and likewise, what is conceived of as art will be turned back into ready-mades. This could be the case with Duchamp's work: a urinal transformed into "*La fontaine*" in the context of avant-garde theories, and then "*La fontaine*" into a urinal or something else in the atmosphere of some other forms of theories and whatsoever. As is detected at this point, Danto at his best has partly resolved the issue about the transformation of ready-mades into artworks from the perspective of artistic identifications. "*La fontaine*," for instance, seems to have hereby obtained its artistic status in a classificatory sense. But, whether or not it is a good work of art in an evaluative sense will remain another matter.

Incidentally, "*La fontaine*" is a typical example employed to manifest the changing process of audience attitudes and artistic identifications. If we go further to apply the Zen *ko-an* to identifying the true wisdom in human perception and understanding, what else can we draw from it? To my mind, the first perception of mountains as mountains and waters as waters is based on common sense, which classifies things according to what they appear to be. The subsequent perception of mountains not as mountains and waters not as waters features a seeming attainment of *samadhi*, the quintessence of *prajna* as wisdom. The person in this situation is self-opinionated about his Zen cultivation and considers himself capable of looking at things from a Zen perspective. With an intention to testify and show his Zen experience, he imagines that he gets hold of the subtle images and *dhyāna* messages from what he beholds. He then sticks to "perceiving things from an egoist vision" (*yi wo guan wu*) and presumes to have the objects distorted in his eyes. However, he seems complacent about such a perceptual deception as he ventures to render mountains and waters mystified and obscured. He even feels himself intellectually wiser than and spiritually superior to other people. The third perception of mountains once again as mountains and waters once

---

[8] Arthur C. Danto, "The Artworld," in Stephen David Ross (ed.), *Art and Its Significance*, p. 477.

again as waters denotes a crucial turn as an outcome of real enlightenment. It seems to be a kind of return to the objective world, but it in fact reveals a high cognition of "natural spontaneity" (*ziran er ran*). This cognition is the principle to "contemplate things in view of what they are" (*yi wu guan wu*), and exemplifies the following fact: The Zen practitioner has abandoned mechanical doctrines (purposive mindfulness and self-opinionated superiority) since he has eventually comprehended the essence of *dhyāna* on his return to his real self. Being free, plain, and at ease, he cultivates natural spontaneity and takes things as they are without coloring them with his personal preferences or emotions. He lives an ordinary life as he used to, but he shares an insight into the true nature and value of life, as well as all things in the universe. With his mind purified and emptied, he enjoys serene contemplation of mountains and waters, while making no more distinctions in this regard.

It is worth mentioning that the way of natural spontaneity signifies at least two main dimensions: One is just like "the grass that grows freshly green on the arrival of springtime," because it follows the cycle of four seasons, and the other symbolizes the *dhyāna* of "Thus Come One" (*rulai chan*), claiming to "speak out the truth" (*rushi daolai*) and "be after self-awakening Buddha-hood" (*zijue foxing*). "Thus Come One"[9] stands for one of the ten titles of the Buddha and originally meant to "speak out the truth" the realization of complete Buddha-hood. Along with this line of thought, it is certain that mountains thus come as mountains and waters thus come as waters through the eyes of "Thus Come One."

In brief, the attitude toward the way of natural spontaneity is by nature a free and purified state of mind. This state of mind is not to be searched for outside, but to be introspected from within, largely dependent upon the self-awakening of the soul, and the subtle apprehending of Zen. It is somewhat similar to what a Chinese nun in the Song Dynasty writes in the poem:

> I had traveled thousands of miles to look for spring but in vain,
> My shoes were wearing out the clouds across the mountain tops;
> On return home I happened to pick up a plum flower to smell,
> And found spring already there upon the tree in full blossom.

---

[9]Burton Wasten (tr.), *The Lotus Sutra* (New York: Columbia University Press, 1993), p. 14, etc. Another title that is frequently used for Buddha is "The World Honored One" (*Shizun*).

Just imagine, the hard search for spring scene allegorical to *dhyāna* from outside tells about nothing but the persistence and sincerity of the Zen practitioner who came back bare-handed. When she approached, consciously or unconsciously, the blooming plum and smelled its fragrance, she became enlightened instantly as she observed the spring scene, already waiting for her to appreciate. The spring scene and the blooming plum alike are symbols of *dhyāna, samadhi, prajna,* and *paramita* all together. It shows that there is no way to gain them outwardly, because they are right there in her home, in her heart, or in her Buddha-nature. Thus, the pursuit of Zen from outside is no less than "riding a donkey to search for the donkey" (*qilü zhaolü*). By this, it is meant to be seen as a mere obstacle working against Zen cultivation and apprehension in all cases, because it is a search for reality outside of the phenomenal.

It is worthwhile to mention in passing that the Zen perception of mountains and waters resembles another Zen *ko-an* known as "rising a further step over the top of the hundred-foot bamboo" (*baichi gantou, gengjin yibu*). The top of the bamboo in this context symbolizes the climax of attained enlightenment, and "rising a further step" signifies that the Buddhist sage still has something to do after his attainment of enlightenment. What he has to do, however, is no more than the ordinary things of daily life. As Nan-chuan said, "after coming to understand the other side, you come back and live on this side."[10] Even though the sage continues living on this side, his understanding of the other side is not in vain at all. Even though what he does is just what everybody else does, it bears a different significance to him after all. Even though what he does is no different from what he used to do before, it is only that he himself is not the same as he was, for his life outlook has changed, his sphere of spirituality is sublimated, and his mind is freed from all defilements and afflictions. He is thus enabled to tend things with ease, treat people with tolerance, and stay above worldly considerations or contentions. This being the case, he follows the way of natural spontaneity in that whatever thus comes is not welcomed, and whatever thus goes is not declined. It can be said that he "lives poetically on earth" just like Tao Yuanming, who secured his tranquility within the chaos of a city by means of his insightfulness, cheerfulness, and detachment as is depicted in the poem:

---

[10] Fung Yu-lan, *A Short History of Chinese Philosophy*, in Fung Yulan, *Selected Philosophical Writings of Fung Yu-lan* (Beijing: Foreign Languages Press, 1991), p. 482.

> I built my hut in a zone of human habitation,
> Yet near me there sounds no noise of horse or coach,
> Would you know how that is possible?
> A heart that is distant creates a wilderness round it.
> I pluck chrysanthemums under the eastern hedge,
> Then gaze long at the distant summer hills.
> The mountain air is fresh at the dusk of day,
> The flying birds two by two return.
> In these things there lies a deep meaning;
> Yet when we would express it, words suddenly fail us.[11]

This poetic depiction suggests the liberation of body and the freedom of mind. As is noticed in the line that "A heart that is distant creates a wilderness round it," the hustles and bustles and noises produced by human habitation are all thus reduced to quietude and even solitude. It is somewhat similar to the old saying that "A heart that is calm naturally creates coolness within it" (*xin jing zi ran liang*). It seems to serve as a kind of expedient means for *dhyāna*. "Then gaze long at the distant summer hills" demonstrates an aesthetic obsession in a disinterested contemplation of the beautiful in the surroundings which include blooming chrysanthemums, summer hills, mountain air, the waning of the day, and birds flying together, from which one can also feel the joy of nature and the pleasure of Zen. It is more or less corresponding to what Cheng Hao experiences in his "Autumn Days":

> All creatures run their course in true content,
> As I calmly contemplate.
> The pleasure of each season through the year,
> I enjoy with others.

7.3 A Poetic Way of Zen Enlightenment

As is mentioned briefly, the original cause of Zen Buddhism in China bears poetic features and aesthetic qualities owing to the metaphorical components embodied in a flower, a smile, and other things. It can be observed from a legend as follows:

---

[11] Ibid., p. 217. It is translated by Arthur Waley.

Once the Buddha (the World Honored One) showed a flower to his disciples at an assembly near the Mount Sumeru. All of them made no response except Mahakasypa who gave a smile. The Buddha remarked: "I have the observant eye of prajna, the wonderful mind of nirvana, the true wisdom of pāramitā, and the delicate door of dharma. Yet, I will write no word about it and leave it to Mahakasypa to disseminate in a different manner."[12]

The story means a lot as it gives rise to the Zen methodology. Apart from the fundamental characteristics of Buddhism in general, it employs the Buddha as the mouthpiece to express two important principles: One is the deconstructive stance toward the Buddhist sutras, and the other is the legitimacy of discriminating the Zen Sect from the rest of others. Ever since then, the most frequent catchphrase and the supreme doctrine of Zen Buddhism are represented in these four expressions: "Write no word about it, disseminate it in a different manner, awaken human mind straight away, and become Buddha while seeing Buddha-nature," all of which have evolved from what the Buddha says above.

Relatively speaking, the most poetic touch in this story is exemplified by showing a flower and giving a smile through which the Buddha conveyed the essence of Zen to Mahakasyapa. It is right at that moment that "the wonderful mind of *nirvana*" and "the true wisdom of *pāramitā*" were imparted from one to another because of "the observant eye of *prajna*" as "the delicate door of *dharma*." Then, the Master and his disciple turn into one, say they become each other cognitively in so far as the Zen enlightenment is concerned. This demonstrates "a heart to heart communication" that can be implicitly sensed but not verbally explained, and thus opens the path to "non-verbal impartation" and "sudden enlightenment" that are highly championed by the Zen School in South China (*nan chan*). Moreover, the "flower and smile" legend was further extended in accordance with its poetic wisdom. Practically, it was substituted by *gatha*, a poetic form used to express one's understanding and nurturing of Zen message or Buddha-nature. In the long tradition of Zen Buddhism from Bodhidharma onward, the patriarch would hand down the cassock and bowl to his favorite disciple who could write a piece of most impressive *gatha* to the master's satisfaction.

---

[12] Pu Ji (ed.), *Wu deng hui yuna* [A Collection of Ko-an in Zen Buddhism], p. 10. The translation is mine.

It was no exception when Hong Ren, the Fifth Patriarch, was intended to select his exponent to inherit the position. By then, he had two outstanding but competitive disciples, Shen Xiu (c. 606–706) and Hui Neng (638–713). In order to decide on who would be the new patriarch, he asked them to compose a piece of *gatha*, each to express their achievement in Zen cultivation. As Shen Xiu practiced Zen with preference for the step-by-step approach, the *gatha* he created justified it and then led him to establish the Gradual School in North China (*bei zong*) later on. On the contrary, since Hui Neng favored the sudden approach to Zen apprehension, the *gatha* he composed emphasized this and thus led him to set up the Sudden School in South China (*nan chan*).

7.3.1 Gradual Enlightenment

Shen Xiu was in fact the premier disciple of Hong Ren, the Fifth Patriarch. When his Master tried to test out his level of Zen cultivation and asked him to describe it in a piece of *gatha*, he was so self-confident that he accomplished the task by virtue of his personal experience. As he wrote,

> The body is the Bodhi-tree,
> And the mind a mirror bright.
> Carefully we wipe them hour by hour,
> And let no dust alight.[13]

"The Bodhi-tree" is allegedly the locus where Sākyamuni attained his great awakening and became Buddha, and "Bodhi" in Sanskrit means enlightenment. Such a tree is therefore symbolic of the accomplishment of enlightenment or Buddha-hood. That Shen Xiu likened metaphorically "body" to it not merely indicates his certainty of following the Buddha's example and achieving Buddha-hood, but also his self-consciousness of nourishing Zen as well as his inborn Buddha-nature. According to Zen Buddhism, everyone is supposed to have Buddha-nature and will become Buddha himself (i.e., self-enlightened). But, many people are rarely self-conscious of this innate virtue. They need to be reminded and awakened to the degree that they realize and concentrate on it. As is read in the third line, the mirror

---

[13] Huang Maolin (tr.), *The Sutra of Hui Neng* (Changsha: Hunan Press, 1996), p. 13.

analogy implies a state of mind purified with insight and wisdom, and meanwhile, it signifies the character of Buddha-hood itself. Coincidently, mirror is also used analogically in both Daoism and Confucianism. Zhuangzi, for instance, asserts that the sage "makes use of the mind as a mirror" (*yong xin ruo jing*). By this, analogy is meant that the sage purifies his mind and identifies himself with the *Dao* just by following the way of natural spontaneity and having no recourse to any manmade device. Mencius once considers human mind to be like a mirror. When the mirror is clean and bright, one will accordingly stay innocent and good-natured, able to tell right from wrong, approach good, and undo evil. If by any chance the mirror is covered with dust and rendered blurred, one is liable to lose his mind and nature and fall into an alienated self. To my mind, the mirror allegory Shen Xiu introduced to confirm his method of Zen somewhat corresponds in a hidden sense to its counterpart in both Daoism and Confucianism. On the surface, he applies a dualist notion of body and mind, and whereby, he takes symbolically the body as an external condition and the mind as an internal factor for the awakening of Buddha-nature and the realization of Buddha-hood. But in practice the distinction between body and mind is rather vague and almost impossible in view of Zen cultivation from both inside and outside. The two are actually one and vice versa as a result of their strong affinity.

Quite ostensibly, the first two lines of Shen Xiu's *gatha* are rather figurative, whereas the last two lines are more practical. Both a methodological means and a teleological end are thus specified in that "Carefully we wipe them hour by hour, and let no dust alight." This can be viewed from either a positive or negative standpoint. Positively, the action of "careful wiping hour by hour" implies advice and encouragement to the Zen practitioner in general. It calls on him to be persistent and constant in what he himself engages. As he continuously reduces his desires and keeps himself away from disturbances from without, he will be able to keep his mind calm and pure, clear and bright as a mirror free from any dust or worldly defilement. Spiritually, he will be transcendent, going beyond all secular cares and worries. As perceived herein, the way he acts like this hints upon a hidden warning that the human world is filled with dust or defilement, and no one can escape from it because it is ubiquitous and permeates every opening. He who is too slack and reluctant to do the careful wiping in a duly successive mode will leave the mirror dusty for sure. Then, he will become "blind," ignorant, and even confused with the outflow of afflictions and wants, and eventually lose his originally innocent and good nature. According to the Mahayana outlook, all external things are "phenomenal" (*dharma* or *se*), real reality is "empty" (*sūnyatā* or *kong*), and the world is derived from the everlasting, all-knowing and omnipotent "suchness" (*tathata* or *zhenru*). As a derivative, it turns up in varied appearances that are changing, confusing, and appealing to human beings. Similar to a victim trapped in infatuation, one will be plunged into a world of dust or a mire of defilement. He will then be exposed to the suffering of endless *klesa* (afflictions) contaminations and vexations. It is for this reason that he ought to keep the mirror of his mind clean by careful wiping away the dust.

Above all, the careful wiping hour by hour denotes the way of gradual enlightenment. Since everyone has the Buddha-nature and encounters so much interference from the dusty world, he must resist it again and again and persist in continuous cultivation. Only by so doing will he apprehend bit by bit the dharma-nature and gain more access to the realm of Buddha-hood. Throughout the process of this gradual enlightenment, he should be determined to adhere to a threefold mode in order to enhance his personal cultivation and ensure his ultimate awakening. This threefold mode consists in *sila*, *dhyana*, and *prajna*. In this context, *sila* involves certain precepts or disciplinary rules, working to prevent people from hankering after material wealth, sexual lust, extravagant food, and exaggerated discourse. *Dhyana* here refers to meditation, requiring the Zen practitioner to "be at ease and eradicate all the desires" by focusing on the notion of nothingness or emptiness. This is the way to have his mind purified and emptied of any desires and defilements. *Prajna* that stands for true wisdom here is the final harvest of the proceeding praxis and nourishment. It is equivalent to great awakening and profound enlightenment. On this occasion, one has extinguished all the cares and worries from within, and accomplished the highest virtue of transcendence in the mental state of *nirvana*. As it is noted in the threefold mode, it performs obviously an organic whole of three interconnected stages of Zen praxis. All this is poetically presented and cleverly condensed by Shen Xiu in a short *gatha* of 20 Chinese words, so plain in language and so suggestive in expression. As luck would have it, Shen Xiu submitted this *gatha* to Hong Ren, the Master, and won his appreciation, but his competitor Hui Neng went even much further in this contest.

7.3.2 Sudden Enlightenment

Hui Neng is said to have been an illiterate woodsman who was once inspired and illuminated when hearing someone recite the *Diamond Sutra* (*Vajracchedika*).[14] Then, he was a disciple to Hong Ren, the Fifth Patriarch, and later succeeded his Master as the Sixth Patriarch, renowned in the history of Zen Buddhism. Since he promoted the principle of "realizing Buddha-nature and fulfilling Buddha-hood at the same time" (*jianxing chengfo*), he branched off from the mainstream and went on to found the Sudden School of Zen Sect in South China (*nanchan dunwupai* or *nanchan* as its shortened name). The whole event began with a *gatha* composed by Hui Neng himself:

> Fundamentally there is no Bodhi-tree,
> Nor stand of a mirror bright.
> Since originally there was nothing,
> Whereon can the dust fall?[15]

This *gatha* turns out to be like a pendulum, swinging to the other side in striking contrast to the previous one composed by Shen Xiu. It claims that there are no such things as the Bodhi-tree and the mirror, and accordingly, there is no such distinction between body and mind. According to the conception of *śūnyatā*, "all is void from the beginning," or in other words, all phenomena bear no reality at all. It thus terminates the logic of gradual enlightenment and takes as shear

---

[14] For this, we can find some hint in *The Sutra of Hui Neng* regarding the practice and attainment of *prajna*. "When Mahayanists and the followers of the highest school hear about the *Diamond Sutra* (*Vajracchedika*), their minds become enlightened; they know that *prajna* is immanent in their Essence of Mind and that they need not rely on scriptural authority or logos (*bu jia wen zi*), since they can make use of their own wisdom by constant practice and contemplation and observation. The *prajna* immanent in the Essence of Mind of every one may be likened to a rainfall. Rain does not come from the sky but is produced by the miracle of the Naga. The moisture of which refreshes every living thing, trees and plants as well as sentient beings. When rivers and streams reach the sea, the water carried by them merges into on body. This is another analogy." Cf. "On Prajna," in *The Sutra of Hui Neng*, pp. 47–49.

[15] Huang Maolin (tr.), *The Sutra of Hui Neng*, p. 19. The last two lines of this *gatha* are modified in accordance with its original Chinese version (*ben lai wu yi wu, he chu ruo chen ai*). In Huang's translation, the last two lines are rendered as such "Since all is void from the beginning/Where can the dust alight?"

redundancy the step-by-step approach to Zen cultivation. For Hui Neng believes that everyone has the Buddha-nature and carries to the extreme the notion of "realizing Buddha-nature and fulfilling Buddha-hood at the same time." In his opinion, everyone has Buddha-nature within himself, and what one needs to do is to awaken it and fulfill it oneself straight away. This is because all is empty (*śūnyatā*) and your Buddha-nature is all, say nothing outside it can be imagined or invented to be either an obstacle against it or a vehicle for Zen apprehension and enlightenment. Furthermore, there is nowhere the dust can alight. One can obtain sudden enlightenment and realizes Buddha-hood as soon as he attends directly to his Buddha-nature, and makes no distinction between Buddha and himself. Hence, Hui Neng complacently recalls that "When the Fifth Patriarch preached to me I became enlightened immediately after he had spoken, and spontaneously realized the real nature of *tathata* (suchness or *zhenru*). For this reason it is my particular task to propagate the teaching of this Sudden School, so that learners may find Bodhi at once and realize their true nature by introspection of mind."[16] Yet for Shen Xiu, all things in the world are defiled and chaotic, ready to confuse the human mind and corrupt human nature. It is therefore a must for all Zen practitioners to act upon the threefold mode of *sila*, *dhyana*, and *prajna*, which can possibly secure the process of gradual cultivation, enlightenment, and even fulfillment of Buddha-hood.

In contrast, the method of sudden enlightenment proposed by Hui Neng does not simply discard the primary stage of passive *sila qua* precepts, but also the intermediate stage of gradual *dhyana qua* meditation. Instead, it points directly to the final stage of complete *prajna qua* wisdom. This being the case, all kinds of formal rituals for Zen cultivation are no longer necessary, and all the Buddhist teachings are no longer valid, and all the rules, requirements, and auxiliaries for Zen apprehension are reduced into illusions and vanish like vapors. Now, one avoids all detours and looks into the real nature of *dharma*—highly conscious of his mind as the original mind, leading to immanent *prajna*, and of his nature as the Buddha-nature due to the absoluteness of its void. Just as Hui Neng assures,

> Prajna does not vary with different persons; what makes the difference is whether one's mind is enlightened or deluded. He who does not know his own Essence of Mind, and is under the delusion that Buddha-hood can

[16] Ibid., pp. 51–53.

attained by outward religious rites is called the slow-witted. He who knows the teaching of the Sudden School and attaches no importance to rituals, and whose mind functions always under right views, so that he is absolutely free from defilements or contaminations, is said to have known his Essence of Mind (jianxing).[17]

Then, how is it possible to "know the Essence of Mind" (*jian xing*)? It is of course conditional rather than *laissez-faire* at this point. According to Hui Neng, the mind should be first of all liberated (*ziyou*) and remain detached (*wu'ai*). It should be framed in such a way that it will be independent of external or internal objects, free to come and go, and thoroughly enlightened without the least befuddlement. He who is able to do this is of the same standard required by the *Sutra of the Prajna School*. Second, he should not resort to extraneous help (*bujia waiqiu*). Because it is by our own innate wisdom that we enlighten ourselves (*ziwu*), and any extraneous help and instructions from a learned friend would be of no use if we were deluded by false doctrines and erroneous opinions. Should we introspect our mind with real *prajna*, all erroneous opinions would be vanquished in a moment, and as soon as we know the Essence of Mind we arrive immediately at the Buddha realm. Third, it should be illuminated within and without (*neiwai mingche*). In this case, we are in a position to know our own mind and to obtain fundamental liberation (*jietuo*), which then helps us to attain the *samadhi* of *prajna*, characteristic of thoughtlessness (*wu nian*) as the way of great awakening.[18] The idea of thoughtlessness is more or less equal to the way of natural spontaneity. And the approach to sudden enlightenment is, as it were, suitable to the pragmatic reason at the core of Chinese thought in its long cultural heritage. Pragmatic reasoning of this kind always stresses the value of immediate effect in a manner as "cutting vegetables with a sharp chop" (*daoxia jiancai*). It also goes without saying that the act of contemplation is not caused by innate wisdom but guided by the original mind. That is why the Sixth Patriarch affirms that "If we knew our mind and nature, all of us would attain Buddha-hood. As the *Vimalakirti Nirdesa Sutra* says, 'At once we become enlightened and regain our original mind'."[19]

[17] Ibid., pp. 49–51.
[18] Ibid., pp. 49–53.
[19] Ibid., p. 51.

As for this original mind (*benxin*) in view of Zen Buddhism, it is seen as an idealistic entity and the cause of all things in the phenomenal world. When it focuses on Buddha-nature and realizes the *tathata*, it has a broadened scope to accommodate and even transform all things as though they were no longer existent outside it. Taken this for granted, Hui Neng pronounces that the capacity of the mind is as great as that of cosmos. It is infinite, neither round nor square, neither huge nor small, neither long nor short, neither first nor last. It works just like the absolute void of the universe capable of holding myriad things of various shapes and forms, such as the sun, moon, stars, mountains, rivers, worlds, springs, rivulets, bushes, woods, good men, bad men, *dharmas* pertaining to goodness or badness, Deva places, hells, great oceans, and all the mountains of the Sumeru. We say that the Essence of Mind is great because it embraces all things and all things are within the mind. When we see the goodness or the badness of other people, we are neither attracted by it nor attached to it, so that our mind remains as void as the cosmos. Therefore, we call it "*maha*" (great and broad).[20] The mind allegory in terms of the absolute void of the universe signifies its accommodating capacity. Nevertheless, such capacity differs from a possessing capacity. When the mind assumes nothing from outside, it retains nothing inside either. This shows the peculiar logic of Zen that is intended to secure *prajna* and *tathata* by vanquishing all things in a second according to its attitude toward *sūnyatā*. It therefore takes all things alike and makes no distinctions because it bases its perception on the ultimate principle of nothingness and emptiness with regard to the phenomenal and transient world all around. In addition, it reveals an essential feature of sudden enlightenment as is ensured by the awareness of the infinite and absolute void. Once you have arrived at this stage in light of Zen logic, all gone is the discrepancy between all things and entities, including appearance and essence, substance and emptiness, subject and object, commonness and sageliness, I and the Buddha, apart from any form of value judgments mentioned above. What is more, the sense of time in sudden enlightenment is by nature immediate, and the sense of space is the zero distance between I and Buddha. Such sense of time and space seems to be not easily obtainable as it comes along very much in the same manner as the poem describes,

[20] Ibid., pp. 39–41.

> Looking anxiously for the beloved here and there,
> But I found no sign of her at all.
> When I suddenly turned my head around
> I saw her standing right there below a waning light.

Surely enough, the process of searching is accompanied with anxiety, eagerness, persistence, and even confusion because it is so difficult and frustrating. Then, a pleasant surprise comes up at the moment of success to compensate all. It is just like what the French motto says, "*Tout va bien qui finit bien.*"

It is worth noticing that the identification of "I" with Buddha is the due outcome of sudden enlightenment. He who seeks after this identification will fall into confusion if he dedicates all his attention in an erroneous direction. It is allegorically similar to the fact that he plans to go to the south but drives his chariot toward the north; the faster he goes, the farther away he moves away from his destination. Hence, the attainment of Zen and *prajna* is not merely dependent upon the immediacy of enlightenment, but also upon the ability of "self-awakening and self-liberating of his original nature" (*zi xing zi du*). This nature is actually Buddha-nature immanent in himself. It should be realized and then fulfilled by detaching himself from all outer objects of a *dharma*-ridden kind and purifying his mind of depravations, cares, ignorance, stubbornness, prejudice, and so on. Above all, the pure mind is most crucial because the Buddha land is simultaneously pure when the mind is pure, and accordingly, the Buddha-nature is simultaneously awakened when the original nature is liberated. In order to achieve all this, Hui Neng advises people to deal with *dharma* while keeping inner peace in *Samadhi* (*waichan neiding*). He even proclaims in terms of *The Bodhisattva Sila Sutra* that "Our Essence of Mind is intrinsically pure," and encourages us to realize this for ourselves at all times, practice it by ourselves, and attain Buddha-hood by our own effort.[21] This effort is not supposed to be applied to religious rites conducted in temples, but to such daily activities as collecting firewood, fetching water, and walking around in the courtyard.

Up to this stage, we may find Zen logic a bit absurd and self-contradictive. As is read in the *gatha* by Hui Neng, for example, he explicitly denies the existence of all things by assuring that "originally there was

---

[21] Ibid., pp. 91–93.

nothing" in terms of the Mahayana principle of *sūnyatā*. Then, why does he repeat again and again that the existence of myriad outer objects in deliberate contrast to the pure mind, the original nature, and even the Buddha himself? We therefore assume that his denial is no more than an expedient means for the sake of Zen apprehension, and his logic as such is pragmatically serving only within his defined scope. Besides, the above distinction between gradual enlightenment and its sudden counterpart is not that striking and permanent so long as the mind is purified, the Buddha-nature is awakened, and the Buddha-hood is realized. For this reason, there is some relevance in this statement: "In orthodox Buddhism the distinction between the Sudden School and the Gradual School does not really exist. The only difference recognized is that by nature some men are quick-witted, while others are dull in understanding. Those who are enlightened realize the truth in a flash, while those who are under delusion have to train themselves gradually. But such a difference will disappear when we know our own mind and realize our own nature. Therefore these terms, gradual and sudden, are more apparent than real."[22]

7.4 The Realm of *Sūnyatā* as Beauty

As is inferred from above, both the Gradual School and the Sudden School belong to Zen Buddhism, and their division is merely apparent in that they introduce two approaches to *dhyāna* practice. In the final analysis, they are no more than two roads leading to one destination, that is, the attainment of *prajna* and the enlightenment of Buddha-hood. For they are grounded on the Mahayana theory of *sūnyatā*, claiming that "all around in the four directions to be empty and void by nature" (*sida jiekong*).[23] In the Zen experience, when you are enlightened to the extent that you perceive all things in view of absolute emptiness or voidness, you are thought to have reached the realm of *sūnyatā*, attained the truth of *prajna*, and fulfilled the nature of Buddha-hood. Hence, what is more crucial and determinant to either Zen monks or Zen poets is the realization and expression of *sūnyatā* as the most appealing and beautiful of all.

---

[22] Ibid., p. 83.

[23] The four directions (*sida*) here stand for east and west, south and north. They are often used to indicate the universe.

The realm of *sūnyatā* is highly recommended in Zen Buddhism and often expressed poetically by means of three scenes. The first scene follows,

> Everywhere the wild hills are covered with fallen leaves,
> Where can I find a trodden trail to walk out?

The couplet indicates metaphorically a persistent search for Zen in a *dhyāna* exercise. The practitioner here was looking up and down for a shortcut to Zen apprehension, but was wandering around in eagerness and confusion as he failed to get anywhere, simply because he pursued from without. As is indicated in the question "where could I find a trodden trail to walk out?" his introspective cultivation still remains at the initial stage where he cannot purify his own mind and awaken his own nature. Then, there follows the second scene,

> In the wild hills there are no persons,
> But flowing waters and blooming flowers.

Tranquil and empty as the hills are, but there are vitality and charm hidden in running waters and beautiful flowers. All things are as natural as can be in this environment, implying an intermediate stage of Zen cultivation at which the state of *nirvana* is not completed yet, and the realm of *sūnyatā* is still some distance away because one can still recognize the outside objects with reference to the *dharma*-ridden law. Some people tend to assume that the Zen practitioner at this point has already entered into tranquility, and apprehended the true meaning of Zen only in part so far. It is somewhat like "something that was grasped in hand but then slipped through the fingers." Finally, there emerges the third scene as such,

> The broad sky is of eternal existence,
> The entire landscape turns out in one morning.

By this, it is meant that the eternal being of the universe is conceived of in a moment and so is the long history of natural and human evolution. There is no discrepancy between the momentary and the eternal with respect to time, but just oneness between all things with respect to space. Taken as the highest awareness of Zen, it is associated not merely with a sudden mystical and subtle enlightenment, but also with an intuitive perception and *sūnyatā* experience. It is right at the moment that the practitioner has regained real liberation and absolute freedom. Thereupon, he projects himself into harmonious and serene Nature, and makes no distinction between mountains and waters, the sun and the moon, the sky and the earth, the phenomenal and the real, and even the day and the night, etc. He feels as if this moment "had seemingly transcended time and space, cause and effect, and as if the past, present and future were seemingly fused together such that any division became rather impossible." Actually, he has no intention to make any division in this regard as he is no longer conscious of either where he is or where he is from. All this, of course, goes beyond the man-made boundary between oneself and other things, and leads him to identify himself with the outside world and thus become integrated into everlasting oneness.[24] However, the moment is an indispensable factor, without which eternity cannot be in and of itself despite the equivalence between them, in terms of the Zen sense of time. The *sūnyatā* experience may justify that all is empty or void, but at the same time it may mean the enlightened does not bother about such emptiness or voidness. He lives his life naturally as he used to, but in reality he has transformed himself into a greatly awakened sage with insights into *prajna* and Buddha-nature. In other words, he has the feeling that he is Buddha himself at a time when he is experiencing something eternal in a moment.

Such an experience is typical both of sudden apprehension through which you enter into the *sūnyatā* realm, the highest state of being in Zen Buddhism. The realm itself is not only retained in the absolute voidness, serenity and profundity, but also in subtlety, inspiration and transcendence. Now, it has transformed the finite I into the infinite I, the ordinary into the extraordinary, the depressed into the delighted, the necessary into the natural, and above all, brought forth the oneness between Brahma and I (*fan wo he yi*) or between heaven and human (*tian ren he yi*). In a word, it has eventually rendered human existence spiritually free and aesthetically artistic. Hence, the process of Zen cultivation is thought of as the process of artistizing human life, the outcome of Zen

---

[24]Li Zehou, "Chan yi ang ran" [The Meaning of Zen], in *Zou wo ziji de lu* [Along My Own Path] (Beijing: Sanlian Bookshop, 1986), pp. 392–393. Also see Li Zehou, *Zhongguo gudai sixiang shilun* [Essays on Traditional Chinese Thoughts] (Beijing: Renmin Press, 1985), pp. 207–210.

apprehension as the outcome of such artistization, and the essence of Zen wisdom as the essence of life wisdom. This kind of wisdom calls for the purification of your own mind and the return to nature where you may well apprehend Zen's message in the beautiful and mystical scenery, or perceive the poetic appeal in the plain and familiar things around. For Zen, momentum and its silent delight are embodied in nowhere but in the everyday routines and surroundings as is so depicted in the poems:

> In spring days that come along a bit warm or cool,
> Peach flowers bloom red and misty willows turn green,
> The Zen delight arises in singing birds and dancing butterflies,
> And the wisdom of prajna is just in front of your own eyes.

> There are myriad flowers in spring and full moon in autumn;
> There are cool breezes in summer and snowfalls in winter.
> So long as you are freed from all cares and worries,
> You enjoy every minute of human life in the four seasons.

As is observed from the above exposition, Zen Buddhism is a kind of life philosophy saturated with poetic wisdom. Regardless of any formal rites or rituals concerning *dhyāna*, an aesthetic contemplation of such landscapes as mountains and waters opens up a main entrance to spiritual revelation and Zen apprehension connected with *prajñā pāramitā*. This is sustained by the way of natural spontaneity as one of the principal paradigms on the one hand, and on the other hand, it is characterized by either gradual or sudden enlightenment in the process of Zen cultivation or practice. The ultimate purpose in this context is, as it were, to explore and pursue the realm of *śūnyatā* as absolute beauty and freedom. In order to facilitate such a perception and experience of highest *prajñā pāramitā* as wisdom in perfection, it requires at least an artistic vision and literary mind with emotionally and intellectually tinged percipience, in addition to a Zen heart and poetic sensibility with an insightful understanding of *śūnyatā*. The former can be looked upon as the primary potential for Zen nurturing, whereas the latter as the dharma-door to Zen *Erlebnis*. By means of the former, we can appreciate the beautiful and the picturesque in cosmic creations and changes; by means of the latter, we can feel ourselves the realm of *śūnyatā* in all natural scenes. We are thereby in a position to draw aesthetic pleasure from the act of appreciation, and attain spiritual freedom from the realm of *śūnyatā*.

It is in this sense we may well conceive the message in what Wittgenstein asserts: Philosophy should produce more poem-like writings. Zen Buddhism is to my mind poetic philosophy, for it is concerned with the way of being and the quality of life at the same time. Anyone who is fond of such poetic philosophy and life wisdom alike is most likely to become more sensitive and percipient to the beautiful and the meaningful in the natural surroundings altogether, I believe.

CHAPTER 8

A New Ideal and Transcultural Pursuit

Ever since the New Culture Movement that took place in China in early 1920s, most of the Chinese thinkers tend to reflect on the possibility of reconstructing the indigenous heritage upon the model of its Western counterpart. They have been preoccupied with this aspiration to rebuild the country and national identity as well. In this arena, what has turned out to be most influential could be the tempting contribution made by the modern Confucianists. Among them, Thomé Fang (Fang Dongmei 1899–1977) stands out in that he attempts to contemplate this task via a transformational experimentation. This then leads him to philosophize in view of cosmopolitan harmonism characterized by his cultural ideal and transcultural pursuit. A second reflection on what he ponders over in this regard attempts to expose some hidden aspects of his theoretical hypothesis in question and also to reconsider the possible alternative to transcultural interaction and transformational synthesis with reference to a threefold process strategy.

8.1 The Cultural Ideal and the Pagoda Allegory

Fang's conception of cultural ideal is based on a general theme running through almost all his writings. It can be termed, in my opinion, *ren-wenhuacheng*, or humane enculturation. By humane enculturation, it is meant in Chinese tradition the activity of enlightenment by culture and the process of accomplishing a fine personality. In fact, Fang deliberately links culture up with education, which I personally understand in light of Greek *paideia* (παιδεια) in its original sense. That is, *paideia* is a kind of pedagogical activity that enables a person to grow and develop in order to nurture the becoming of a whole being. Coincidentally, it involves an interwoven connection between culture and education, and therefore indicates the essential function of both culture and education according to its specific context in modern Greek. As is noticed in Fang's explications, culture and education seem to be two sides of the same medal, closely interrelated to the extent that they walk hand in hand as twins in his thinking space.

As read in Fang's essay on "Education and Culture," for instance, he starts with an argument cited from Alfred Whitehead about the primary objective of university education as follows: "During the school period the student has been mentally bending over his desk; at the University he should stand up and look around."[1] By so doing, the student will be able to apprehend that such education is intended to facilitate real intellectual development, nourish human virtues within, and bring forth into full play his natural gifts or potential talents. Consequently, he will be capable of creating wonders in scholarship and contributing more to his nation, the world, and humankind altogether. If university has really fulfilled this mission, it can be considered the education for human, and accordingly, the educated will be freed from many problems in pedagogical, social, and psychical domains. But in Fang's eyes, the practice of education nowadays is often confronted with the issue of problematic man particularly in the case of the youth.[2] This issue is mostly stemmed from the expansion of irrational desires liable to transform the problematic man into the irrational beast according to the Freudian depth-psychology. For this reason, Fang cries out for the development of height-psychology in order to enhance moral science and overcome the lopsided development of physical science. He himself draws a blueprint of cultural ideal in anthropological terms. This blueprint is morally based

---

[1] Alfred North Whitehead, *The Aims of Education*, p. 37.
[2] Thomé Fang, "Jiaoyu yu wenhua" [Education and Culture], in Jiang Guobao and Zhou Yazhou (eds.), *Fang Dongmei xinruxue lunzhu jiyao* [Thomé Fang's Selected Writings on Modern Confucianism] (Beijing: Zhongguo Guangbo Dianshi Press, 1993), pp. 12ff.

8 A NEW IDEAL AND TRANSCULTURAL PURSUIT   165

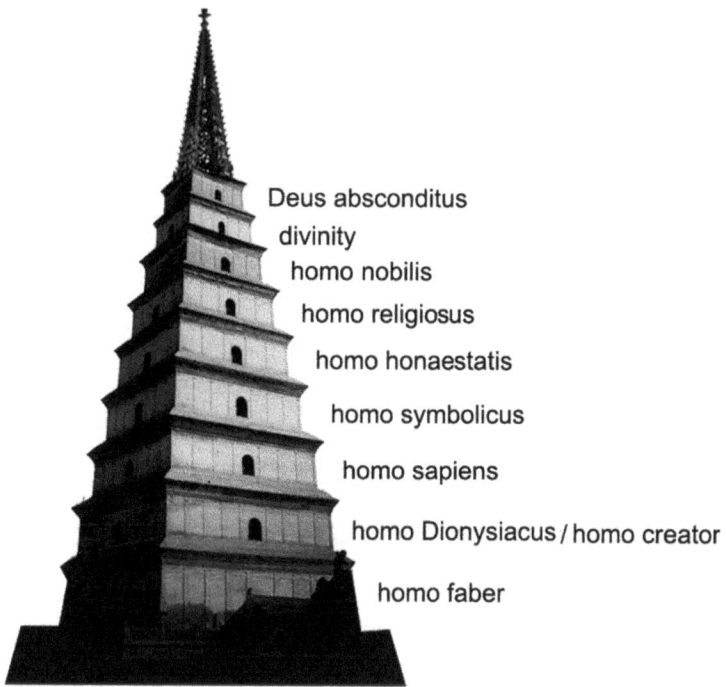

Fig. 8.1 The pagoda allegory

and spiritually oriented in light of humane enculturation by and large. It consists of nine realms that correspond metaphorically to a nine-storied pagoda with a Gothic steeple overhead. It can be visually illustrated like this (Fig. 8.1).

The pagoda allegory is hierarchical by nature, but structurally organic and interactive due to its step-by-step uplifting of the soul or the progressive cultivation of personality.[3] It begins with the *Homo Faber* who

---

[3] Thomé Fang, "Zhongguo zhexue dui weilai shijie de yingxiang" [The Impact of Chinese Philosophy on the Future World], in Jiang Guobao and Zhou Yazhou (eds.), *Fang Dongmei xinruxue lunzhu jiyao* [Thomé Fang's Selected Writings on Modern Confucianism], pp. 615ff. Also see Thomé Fang's English essays, such as "A Philosophical Glimpse of Man and Nature in Chinese Culture" and "The Alienation of Man in Religion, Philosophy and Philosophical Anthropology."

basically acts at a natural level and lives in the sphere of physical existence. What comes next as a better substitute is the *Homo Dionysiacus* who tends to act in a manic way and put his life in destructive jeopardy. Therefore, it should be enculturated into the *Homo Creator* who usually acts creatively and looks forward to a higher realm of meaning. In Fang's terminology, the *Homo Dionysiacus* is mingled with the *Homo Creator* and thus produces the *Homo Sapiens* with sound learning and wisdom. By contrast, the *Homo Faber* remains in the sphere of physical existence, the combination of *Homo Dionysiacus* with *Homo Creator* enters into the sphere of humane life, and the *Homo Sapiens* settles down in the sphere of intellectual life. At this stage, the *Homo Sapiens* emphasizes the performance of reason or rationality by virtue of which he works to formulate varied systems of knowledge. Whence he frees himself from all instinctive drive and blind deed, and approaches the truth world with rational consideration and guidance. In other words, he will base his life upon the truth world.[4] Relatively speaking, these three realms comprise a kind of Natural Personality (*ziran ren*) who is assumed to feature healthy body, vital energy and rich knowledge, capable of building up a natural world sustained by scientific culture of universality so eulogized here and there in the twentieth century. Nevertheless, the natural world as such is only one-sided owing to its being obsessed with scientific culture while neglecting philosophical culture.[5]

In order to secure a balance in this scope, Thomé Fang proposes a scheme of exalting the Natural Personality into the Transcendent Personality (*xing shang ren*). Herein, the former is attributed to the natural world of physical existence guided by social progression, whereas the latter to the Spiritual World of transcendent life based on cultural sublimation. On this point, Fang borrows a term from Ernst Cassirer and claims that the *Homo Sapiens* needs to be cultivated into the

---

[4] Thomé Fang, "Zhongguo zhexue dui weilai shijie de yingxiang" [The Impact of Chinese Philosophy on the Future World], in Jiang Guobao and Zhou Yazhou (eds.), *Fang Dongmei xinruxue lunzhu jiyao* [Thomé Fang's Selected Writings on Modern Confucianism], p. 615. Also see Thomé Fang's English essays, such as "A Philosophical Glimpse of Man and Nature in Chinese Culture" and "The Alienation of Man in Religion, Philosophy and Philosophical Anthropology."

[5] Thomé Fang, "Zhongguo zhexue dui weilai shijie de yingxiang" [The Impact of Chinese Philosophy on the Future World], in Jiang Guobao and Zhou Yazhou (eds.), *Fang Dongmei xinruxue lunzhu jiyao* [Thomé Fang's Selected Writings on Modern Confucianism], p. 615.

Homo Symbolicus, the man as the operator of symbols who is able to discover and experience the mysteries in the artistic realm. This realm is by no means a representation of the perfect as it lies in the expression of both the beautiful and the ugly on the one hand, and subjects itself to individual sentimentality as well as volition. It therefore follows that the *Homo Symbolicus* calls for a higher enculturation in order to exalt himself into the *Homo Honaestatis*, the man of fine virtue or morality who transcends the artistic realm and nurtures the ethical realm along with "sage-like characteristics" (*shengzhe qixiang*). This facilitates the becoming of *quanren*, or the perfect and perfected man, who integrates the natural, artistic, and moral aspects of personality into a complete whole. Being such a perfected man, his life is fulfilled and expanded to the extent that it can accommodate and influence the entire world, and his ability is displayed as outstanding and omnipotent. When his perfection is spiritually sublimated into the Divine World, it will give rise to the *Homo Religiosus* who is regarded as the God-man, or the co-creator with the divine. Right in this sense, it can be said that "To be human is to be divine." Analogously speaking, the *Homo Religiosus* is equal to the *Homo Nobilis* standing on the top of the pagoda and often compared to the Confucianist ideal of the Sagely Man, the Taoist ideal of the Perfected Man, and the Buddhist ideal of the Enlightened Buddha.

Up till then, the structure of the pagoda seems completed. But there is still a coping stone overhead. Above the stone stands the Gothic steeple turning upwards to the invisible height of Heaven and signifying the infinity of the cosmic truth and the endless cultivation of the perfected personality. It leads further to the possible becoming of the *Divinity* and the highest realm of mysteriously mysterious experience of the *Deus Absconditus*. These last two realms of spiritualization are overlapped to a noticeable degree. They are, in their essence, symbolic of the supreme power and mysterious mystery of religious divineness, which can be merely imagined and thought a priori. The deployment of them on this occasion is of "importance, value, and ideal beyond the actual" just as what Alfred Whitehead conceives Deity to be "that factor in the universe" for his necessary presence as such. For "it is by reference of the spatial immediacies to the ideals of Deity that the sense of worth beyond ourselves arises. The unity of a transcendent universe, and the multiplicity of realized actualities, both enter into our experience by this sense of Deity. Apart from this sense of transcendent worth, the otherness of reality would not enter into our consciousness. There must be value beyond ourselves. Otherwise, everything experienced would be merely a barren detail in our own solipsist mode of existence. We owe to the sense of Deity the obviousness of the many actualities of the world, and the obviousness of the unity of the world for the preservation of the values realized and for the transition to ideals beyond realized fact."[6] This argument proves the fact that man cannot live by bread alone. In spite of its religious tint, it seems to me more convincing and significant than any other rhetoric preaching of a personified God. Its emphasis on the sense of Deity will possibly elicit an awareness of transcendent worth beyond the actual and the finite in human existence.

8.2 The Transcultural Pursuit and the Transformed Overman

Then, a question arises regarding the cultural ideal mentioned above. That is, among all the existent cultures, is there anything approximate to this ideal? To Fang's mind, there is nothing ready-made in this case, but there are desirable components available in three cultural patterns, including ancient Greek, modern European, and traditional Chinese. These patterns are represented respectively in the domains of religion, philosophy, and art, for it is in these domains that the permanent ethos and main current of each culture are embodied and sedimented from a historical point of view.

Take philosophy for example. It is derived from its investigation of the causal interactions between feeling and reason (*qingli*), attempting to expose the possible origin, truth, and subtlety alike and leading to the development of insightful wisdom. According to Fang's observation, the Greeks would employ *nous* (reason and intellect) to illuminate *aletheia* (truth and reality) and thus develop the truth-directed wisdom; the Europeans would use practical means to meet varied occasions and thus develop the convenience-oriented technology; and the Chinese would utilize subtle intuition to see through the secret of transformation, and thus develop the parallel-featured wisdom by complying the truth-directed wisdom and operating the convenience-oriented technology. Accordingly, the seed of Greek wisdom came out of naming objects

---

[6] Alfred N. Whitehead, *Modes of Thought* (Cambridge: Cambridge University Press, 1956), p. 140.

in *logos* and thinking over *aletheia*; the seed of European wisdom came out of seeking power for industrial interest and increasing capacity of mighty performance; the seed of Chinese wisdom came out of loving to assist all things grow and striving for an intuitively subtle enlightenment.[7] By contrast, the Greek wisdom evolved into a reason-worshiped culture with focus on the justification of *aletheia* through *nous*, the European wisdom into a capacity-worshiped culture with focus on driving sentiment into grotesque imagination, and the Chinese wisdom into a subtlety-directed culture with focus on returning to primordial harmony via poetic intuition. Hence, in more specific terms, the life of the Greeks could be characteristically represented through three types of spirit, including the Dionysian in favor of passion, the Apollonian in favor of reason, and the Olympian as a result of belittled reason and decreased passion. Among these three, the Apollonian is granted the leading role. When it comes to the life of the Europeans, it is chiefly manifested through three types of spirit, including the Renaissance, the Baroque, and the Rococo. The Renaissance reveals the appealing power of artistic enthusiasm, the Baroque the profound reasoning via science, and the Rococo the ambivalence between reason and feeling. What brings these three into an integrated one is the Faustian spirit. As for the life of the Chinese people, it is expressed in the thoughts of Laozi, Confucius, and Mozi altogether. The thought of Laozi explicates the subtle function of the primordial Dao (*yuan dao*), the thought of Confucius formulates the principle of reciprocal love (*renli*), and the thought of Mozi elaborates the value of extensive love (*jian'ai*). Thus correspondingly, the formation of the Greek psychology is consisted in a tripartite model of three elements. They are the rational, the spirited, and the appetite among which the rational is encouraged to take the lead for the fostering of temperance, and the spirited is auxiliary for the controlling of the appetite. Hence, an ideal personality is dependent on the harmonization of the three parts. Then, the formation of the European psychology bears some features of double character typified by the Faustian pursuit and the Mephistophelian temptation. Even though these two dimensions remain internally contradictive, they are dynamically interactive, transformational, and non-exhaustive. As for

---

[7] Thomé Fang, "Zhexue san hui" [The Three Forms of Wisdom in Greek, European and Chinese Philosophies], in Jiang Guobao and Zhou Yazhou (eds.), *Fang Dongmei xinruxue lunzhu jiyao* [Thomé Fang's Selected Writings on Modern Confucianism], p. 87.

the formation of Chinese mentality, it is composed of a ternion among human, Heaven, and Earth as three shareholders of the universe. In order to form this ternion in a constructive sense, one is expected to enculturate his soul, fulfill his nature, pursue the *Dao* of sageliness within and kingliness without (*neisheng waiwang*), help all things transform and grow, and approach the state of being in heaven-human oneness. All this is assumingly conducive to self-perfection along with supreme morality.[8]

Nevertheless, everything has two sides, and similarly, each of the three cultural paradigms has its own merits and demerits. Speaking in general terms, the Greek culture is reason-based, truth-worshiped, and justice-oriented; therefore, the Greeks are enabled to perceive the knowledge of the minute, understand the order of the universe, appreciate the beauty of the sublime, and pursue ontologically the Being of all beings. In a word, they are concerned not merely with what a thing is, but with how and why it is. They have thus embraced radical intellectualism and gone to extremes by using knowledge as the one and only measurement to judge cosmic reality, analyze social structure, and calculate human virtue. This has then brought forth the overexpansion of reason but the decline of feeling. Since reason keeps running about without being preserved and sustained by feeling, it has become split up and gradually shrunk into a withering entity. Eventually, Greek culture has discontinued, its philosophy declined, and its polis collapsed.[9]

As regards the modern European culture, it is convenience-centered, and for this reason, it worships power, might and right. Its belief in knowledge as power is reflected in the Faustian dissatisfaction. Hence, the Europeans tend to be so engrossed in their endless pursuit of knowledge, seeming to be lost in it and never to return. They probe into the bottom of things, dig up the most possible depth for the really real reality, and even play a game with knowledge by mere logos or boundless imagination. This being the case, the European philosophy turns out to be more analytical but less integrative, apart from being mixed up with dichotomy, skepticism, and even nihilism which will in turn cause more problems with hyper-rationalization, internal contradiction, and spiritual illusion.

---

[8] Ibid., pp. 90–93.
[9] Ibid., pp. 94–96.

By contrast, the Chinese culture is morality-based and humanity-centered. It therefore feels a strong affinity for a fair balance between reason and feeling, righteousness and profit, and at the same time, it values the oneness between Heaven and human or the Heavenly Dao and the Human Dao. It pays more attention to the importance of such matters as human life (*shengming*), reciprocal love (*ren'ai*), transformational and generating energy (*huayu*), return to the primordial harmony (*yuanshitonghui*), mean-directed harmonization (*zhong hé*) and analogical approach to understanding the entire category through a single example (*pangtong*), etc. But owing to the long tradition of the centralized social structure, Chinese scholarship culture is usually confined to the bureaucratic control and the powerful few. This prevents its pragmatic wisdom from spreading afar and obstructs the successive advancement and wider application of its inventions. On certain occasions in this social setting, the truth is regulated by the authority, the mind is corrupted by vanity and name-dropping, the freedom is governed by the ruling class, and the creative thinking is strangled by the politically imposed ideology. In order to evade this tension and retain the intellectual joy, most Chinese philosophers tend to attach their ideas to artistic fantasy as well as moral cultivation for the sake of their own appreciative contemplation and body–soul preservation. Worse still, they would tread on the beaten track of their teachers or predecessors, and conform themselves to the old habits and doctrines at the cost of their initiative to seek after the new and the true. Their discourse would be rather conventional instead of individual, implicit instead of explicit, suggestive instead of straightforward, and even absurdly obscure to the extent that the real arguments are covered up in the midst of poetic images or hidden allusions from classical texts. All this leaves an impression that they lack the courage to explore the truth, hesitate to get to the bottom of the things concerned, and fail to examine both the beginning and the end in a more logical system.[10]

According to Thomé Fang, the three cultures aforementioned are complementary to one another in at least two modes, say redemption by self (*zijiu*) and help by other (*tazhu*). In the former case, the Greeks may go ahead to clarify *aletheia* with *nous* and *logos* as they usually do, but they should not make light of human life; the Europeans may confront with all the chances by their convenience-oriented craftiness as they often

---

[10] Ibid., pp. 99–103.

do, but they should not plunge themselves into absurdity or fantasy; the Chinese may hanker after the knowledge of transformational powers with subtle apprehension, but they should not slip into superficiality. Then, in the latter case, the Greek way of abandoning the world so rashly may help modify the European way of living in craftiness and fantasy; the European way of using power for varied purposes may help modify the Chinese way of treasuring and preserving life alone to an excessive degree; in return, the Chinese way of appreciating superficially the empty or imagined state of being may help modify the Greek way of worshiping substantial appropriateness and the European way of applying craftiness in all aspects.

In brief, Fang tries to read a new message into the Nietzschean idea of the Overman (*Übermensch*). Therein, he attempts to strip the Overman off its empty and queer transfiguration, and reconstruct it into an ideal personality by introducing a transcultural transformation. That is, he attempts to remold it by means of three rich forms of wisdom in Greek, modern European, and Chinese cultures. In Fang's terminology, one who will be able to get over the Greek weaknesses will become an outstanding European or Chinese; one who will be able to overcome the European weaknesses will become a fine Chinese or Greek; and one who will be able to transcend the Chinese weaknesses will become an excellent Greek or European. That is to say, one who will be able to synthesize all the virtues of the Greek, European, and Chinese will be likely to become the Overman of an ideal type.[11] All this shows a harmonious synthesis (*hehe*) of transcultural transformation. Ostensibly, such a synthesis is conducted in a meaningful selection of complimentary ingredients from different sources. The methodological implication it carries is deeply rooted in the mentality of Chinese thinkers. Additionally, the solution Fang proposes is good-natured in that it contains a considerable relevance to cosmopolitan harmonism. This harmonism calls for a deconstruction of cultural boundaries since it relies on transcultural integration proper. It features a global concern along with a Chinese vision. Actually, in Fang's transcultural preoccupation, what is taken into due account is the common good for humankind as a whole. But, this is not supposed to weaken his sensibility to the fact that the Chinese culture needs to be reconstructed with reference to its Greek and European counterparts so

---

[11] Ibid., pp. 105–106.

long as it is intended to advance anew and contribute more to the nation and the human race alike. Only by so doing, in his belief, such a noble *telos* could be fulfilled. What else is worth taking heed of could be Fang's super-cultural ambition. It is discernible in that he passionately advices his fellow citizens to go beyond the regional and traditional constraints, and redouble their efforts for a transcultural transformation in a creative mode. In order to spur their confidence and enthusiasm, he makes a particular reference to ancient Athens, "the school of Hellas," as a historical model. Even though it was geographically small and limited, it became culturally large and unlimited with respect to its influence.[12]

8.3　A Second Reflection and a Threefold Process Strategy

If we make a second reflection on the pagoda allegory with reference to Fang's blueprint of human and cosmos in an ideal culture (Fig. 8.2), we will find several points to be noteworthy. First and foremost, the allegory implies an ontological hypothesis. The six kinds of personality ranging from the *Homo Faber* up to the *Homo Religiosus* represent six realms of being. As is depicted in Fang's words, the *Homo Faber* corresponds to the sphere of physical existence (*wuzhi shijie*), the *Homo Dionysiacus-Creator* to the sphere of life (*shengming shijie*), the *Homo Sapiens* to the sphere of the soul (*xinling shijie*), the *Homo Symbolicus* to the artistic realm (*yishu shijie*), the *Homo Honestatis* to the moral realm (*daode shijie*), and the *Homo Religiosus* to the religious realm (*zongjiao shijie*). In comparative language, the former three spheres are within the natural world of universality largely based on scientific culture, whereas the latter three realms are within the Spiritual World of transcendence mainly based on philosophical culture. In a separate sense, each of them suggests a state of being and a quality of life. In an integrative sense,

---

[12]Thomé Fang, "Zhongguo zhexue dui weilai shijie de yingxiang" [The Impact of Chinese Philosophy on the Future World], in Jiang Guobao and Zhou Yazhou (eds.), *Fang Dongmei xinruxue lunzhu jiyao* [Thomé Fang's Selected Writings on Modern Confucianism], p. 634. His statement is translated as follows: "We have a population of over ten million living on the Island of Taiwan. We can do what the ancient Greeks had done before in order to develop a small *polis* with a small population into a culturally great state. This being the case, we can do our best to build up a centre of spiritual culture hereupon so long as we attain a high awareness, set up a truth standard, bring forth a value ideal, and work altogether to upgrade the meaning and worth of life step by step."

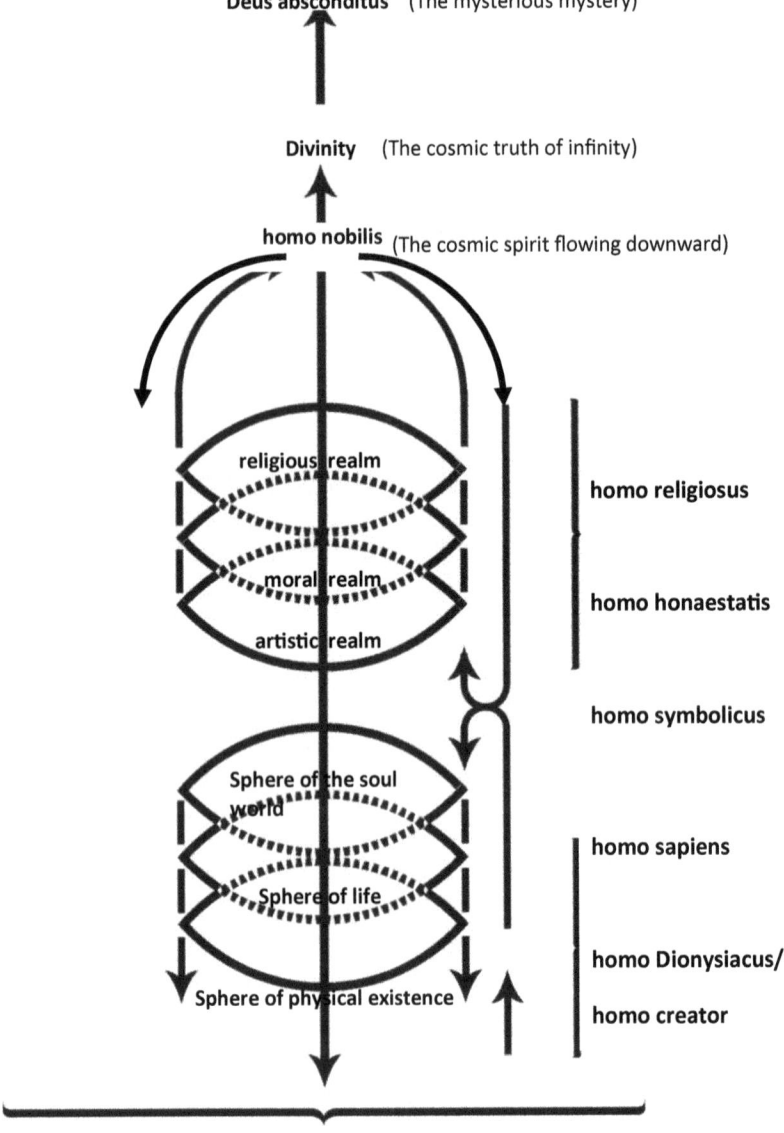

Fig. 8.2 The blueprint

they manifest a hierarchy of levels or alternatives among which one can choose on his own for personal development. What one can become and what life one expects to live all depend on the choice and endeavors he makes.

Second, the *Homo Nobilis* serves as a special bridge between the human and the divine. Downward it is appealing to the humane enculturation, while upward it is motivating the continuous sublimation of the soul from the finite to the infinite. It will then procure a spiritual pursuit of absolute freedom and independent personality. It can be perceived as a cosmic state of being similar to the experience of heaven-human oneness. Up here in a metaphorical sense, one will be well in the position to "drive on the cloud and air, ride upon the sun and moon, and roam about freely beyond the four oceans" according to Zhuangzi's assumption.[13] This may pave the path for the *Homo Nobilis* to climb up ultimately to the *Divinity* and the *Deus Absconditus*.

Third, the blueprint involves a two-way orientation: On the one hand, it ascends to the realm of mysteriously mysterious experience via the organic process of humane enculturation, and on the other, it descends to the sphere of physical existence through the generating power of infinite cosmic spirit. When engaged in this two-way activity, the mere man moves upward to mingle with the cosmic spirit, whereas the cosmic spirit comes downward to transfuse itself into the mere man. Under such circumstances, the "constitution of man" will be filled with the "constitution of divine," and the natural being will be transformed into a religious or spiritual being. That is to say, the person will be qualified not only to act as much as what the *Homo Sapiens* does, but also to act as much as the *Divinity* do. The purpose of his action is not simply to improve personal cultivation, but upgrade the value of the entire world. As an artist, for example, he is "in the capacity not merely of man but in the capacity of the cosmic creator." He can create a great artwork of first rate and "come in ingress into the world as a whole." The beauty of this artwork is just like that of a blooming flower due to its receptiveness to the mystified power of sunlight or "the universal presence of the Spirit in the natural world." It is for this reason that man can experience and feel inwardly the sacred significance hidden mysteriously in all things around

---

[13] Zhuangzi, *Qi wu lun* [Making All Things Equal] or (On the Uniformity of All Things), in *Zhuangzi* (trans. Wang Rongpei, Beijing: Foreign Languages Press, 1999), Vol. 1, p. 35.

us. In addition, it justifies somewhat the qualification of the superior man who is in a Confucianist sense possessed of the most complete sincerity and also facilitates a full development of human nature and the natures of all things alike (*jinxing*). Hence, the man of this kind can assist the transforming and nourishing powers of Heaven and Earth (*huayu*), and may eventually form a ternion with Heaven and Earth (*yu tiandi can*).[14]

Last but not least, Fang argues that the cosmic spirit sounds abstract, but bears concrete effect when it is transfused into any living creatures or existents. It is more or less equal to the neo-Platonist notion of the Great One as the highest *nous* of the universe permeating into the hierarchical forms of life or states of being. It is like a giant water gate as it were. When it is opened, it flows into every field and downward to the lowest place. Its power comes from above.[15] But in my personal observation, this is no more than a poetic depiction. For any downward flow (*xiaguan*) of the cosmic spirit is subjective assumption rather than objective justification. This is also true of Fang's claim of the two-way orientation. In practice, it is merely through the cognitive faculty and humane enculturation that the upward movement (*shangda*) from the lower realm to its higher counterpart is rendered possible in the case of spiritual nourishment and personality development. As for the cosmic spirit itself, it is akin to the Chinese imagination of *tiandao*, or Heavenly Dao, which is meant to be a kind of super-moral guiding rope to uplift the human soul from low to high. It is therefore deployed as the spiritual pillar of human condition and the determinant force of human destiny. Just as is stated in *The Doctrine of the Mean*, "What Heaven (*tian*) has conferred to human is called natural temperament (*xing*); all that is acting in accord with this temperament is called the Way (*dao*); the approach to helping one know the Way is called education (*jiao*)."[16] In many cases, those who recommend the downward flow assumption

---

[14] *Zhong yong* (*The Doctrine of the Mean*, 22), in *The Four Books* (trans. James Legge, Changsha: Hunan Press, 1992), p. 22.

[15] Thomé Fang, "Zhongguo zhexue dui weilai shijie de yingxiang" [The Impact of Chinese Philosophy on the Future World], in Jiang Guobao and Zhou Yazhou (eds.), *Fang Dongmei xinruxue lunzhu jiyao* [Thomé Fang's Selected Writings on Modern Confucianism], p. 632.

[16] The translation is mine. Also see *The Doctrine of the Mean (Zhong yong)*, in *The Four Books* (trans. James Legge), 1, p. 25. Legge's translation follows: "What Heaven has conferred is called the Nature; an accordance with this nature is called the Path of duty; the regulation of this path is called Instruction."

tend to find from this statement some kind of walking stick to support their argument. Yet, when looking closely into the logical order of the four categories, including heaven, natural temperament, Way, and teaching, we may discover that the Way (*dao*) as the medium is most important of all. That is why it is said "not to be left for an instant. Otherwise, it would not be the Way anymore."[17] Then, the knowing of the Way depends on education which is intended to awaken through human culture the good conscience within the individual self. On this point, one will be able to act in accord with the Way and follows the natural temperament as his nature of purity and simplicity allegedly conferred by Heaven. The practical sequence in this process is then corresponding to what Mencius argues, i.e., "He who has exhausted all his mental constitution knows his nature. Knowing his nature, he knows Heaven. To preserve one's mental constitution, and nourish one's nature, is the way to serve Heaven. When neither a premature death nor long life causes a man any double-mindedness, but he waits in the cultivation of his personal character in whatever issue, this is the way in which he establishes his Heaven-ordained being."[18] Quite naturally, "the mental constitution" is most determinant and fundamental. It is enculturated and developed to the extent that it becomes what it could be, coming to know one's nature and Heaven, and eventually able to serve Heaven and locate his Heaven-ordained being. This explicates the fact that *xin* as mental constitution is guided and nurtured by virtue of education and enculturation such that it moves upward to meet Heaven. As is so proved in the Confucian tradition, *xin* also suggests good conscience within, and *zhi* as knowledge is a special kind possessed by the sage. It is through *xin* that the purity and innocence of *xing* as human nature are enlightened and realized; it is through *zhi* that *tiandao*, or Heavenly Way, and *tiande*, or Heavenly Virtue, are apprehended and approached; and thus, it is through *renxin* as human good conscience that *tianxin* as Cosmic Spirit is established. Therefore, the so-called Heavenly Way and Heavenly Virtue are actually embodied in the human way and human virtue, and for this reason, the downward flow of the Cosmic spirit ought to be reversed because it is practically facilitated and exerted via the upward

---

[17] *The Doctrine of the Mean (Zhongyong)*, in *The Four Books* (trans. James Legge), 1, p. 25. Legge's translation follows: "The path may not be left for an instant. If it could be left, it would not be the path."

[18] Mencius, *The Works of Mencius*, in *The Four Books* (trans. James Legge), 13.1, p. 513.

movement of human good conscience involving a continuous process of personal cultivation or moral enhancement. This can also be detected in some of Qian Mu's writings. For instance, what he repeatedly stresses is one of the arguments as follows: As usual in human life, one's heart–mind can communicate not only with that of other contemporaries, but also with that of the other ancients, and moreover, with that of the subsequent generations. It will be divine to enable it to communicate with Heaven and Earth. Yet, it is not every human individual who can manage it. It is the heart–mind of humankind that can fulfill it. At this point, it becomes divine as well as sagely. In China, all the indigenous religions have no Personal God but Supreme Lord instead, the Lord that is identified with Heaven and Ancestry. Their teachings of spirituality go so deep into the human heart–mind and link it closely with Heaven and Ancestry in the meantime. They thus assure human beings to succeed in great enterprises without suffering unexpected loss. All this leads human beings to grow into sages with profound knowledge, knowledge that helps one interact with the heavenly heart–mind, reach the Heavenly Virtue, and obtain an insight into integrity and sincerity that make up the essential substance of the Human Way (Dao).[19]

Apart from what is mentioned above, we need to move further and reflect upon Fang's exposition of the three cultures and their leading features. In my observation, his exposition as such strikes upon the keynote by all means, but turns out to be rather overgeneralized and oversimplified in certain cases. His perception of the Greek paradigm, for instance, is mainly derived from a Platonic view, his notion of the modern European paradigm is chiefly inferred from an industrial and pragmatic position, and his observation on the Chinese paradigm is largely stemmed from Confucianism. As a matter of fact, the Hellenic naturalism and sophism, the continental idealism and rationalism, the American pioneering spirit and creative thinking, and the Chinese Taoism and Buddhism all count respectively a great deal regarding the complex features and rich formations of the three cultures concerned. If these elements were neglected or marginalized, any abstraction or summary of

---

[19] Qian Mu, *Xiandai zhongguo xueshu lunheng* [Essays on Modern Chinese Scholarship] (Beijing: Sanlian Bookshop, 2006), pp. 2, 11; also see Qian Mu, *Zhongguo sixiang tongsu jianghua* [Lectures on Chinese Thought] (Beijing: Sanlian Bookshop, 2006), p. 4; and Qian Mu, *Kongzi yu lunyu* [Confucius and the Analects] (Taipei: Lianjing Publishing Company, 1985), p. 198.

the three cultures in terms of their merits and demerits would hardly be holistic in a justifiable sense. Similarly, along this line of thought, Fang's hypothetical model of the Overman is inspiring as it is, but again it is conceptually idealized and mechanized.

Apparently, the Overman of this type is a resemblance of the ideal personality in the pagoda analogy, and an outcome of transcultural transformation involving the three forms of wisdom in Greek, European, and Chinese cultures. According to Thomé Fang, such a transformation is associated with three alternatives termed as learning (*wen*), thinking (*si*), and practicing (*xiu*), which consist of a hierarchical approach to accomplishment and denote three levels of enlightenment, so to speak at least. Likened to a river in most cases, the wisdom attained through learning would be shallow as if it stays at its surface, the wisdom achieved through thinking would be intermediate as if it hangs around the middle, and the wisdom accomplished through practicing would be profound as if it enters the depth. Contrarily, the wisdom nourished through learning, thinking, and practicing altogether in a creative manner would be full and complete in degree, for the three methods are organically interactive and interdependent by nature. One will obtain a little if he engages himself in practicing without thinking and learning; one will get nowhere if he engages himself in thinking without learning and practicing; and one will go astray if he engages himself in learning without thinking and practicing.[20]

In my observation after all, the transcultural transformation in this regard is no easy enterprise at all. I therefore assume that, apart from a combined application of the three alternatives, a threefold process strategy will be desirable. It commences with the comparative phase of transcultural cognition. In this regard, there will be a mélange of self-driven motivation, observant perception, authentic experience, and modeling behavior with a cognitive initiative and reflective conscientiousness. What proceeds then is a transcultural comparison by identifying via evaluative judgment of the essential differences, similarities, advantages, and disadvantages in order to frame a potentially complimentary interrelationship. More often than not, for instance, we Chinese who have been to the West tend to feel so strongly about their impressive performance

---

[20] Thomé Fang, "Zhexue san hui" [The Three Forms of Wisdom in Greek, European and Chinese Philosophies], in Jiang Guobao and Zhou Yazhou (eds.), *Fang Dongmei xinruxue lunzhu jiyao* [Thomé Fang's Selected Writings on Modern Confucianism], p. 86.

of public ethics (*gong de*) and high awareness of social environment. Personally, I find it culturally complimentary to the Chinese conduct of private morality (*si de*) within the family network. Subsequently, when time is ripe, it comes to the empathetic phase of transcultural transpection. At this stage, the person is quite at home with not only his native culture as much as the target culture and even goes so far as to put himself in the mind of someone else from a heterogenic-cultural community. Thus empathetically, he is able to feel, think, speak, and even act correspondingly in the same manner like the other. However, he is conscious of his own cultural identity and remains more adaptable himself on various occasions. Naturally, his actions and reactions will be emotionally reasonable or rationally sensible, and meanwhile justifiable with a moderate balance between feeling and reasoning. In other words, what appeals to the empathy or transpection is not merely determined by personal satisfaction, but also by the common good. All this endows him with more insights into the merits and demerits of both his indigenous culture and its heterogenic counterpart. He will then, with a sense of mission, push on and step forward into the creative phase of transcultural transformation. Right in this phase, he will be able to pinpoint the complimentary fundamentals from both cultures and ponder over a possible solution to any transcultural transformation. It goes without saying that this transformation is a selective and synthetic process largely based on the stem of the home culture, say it is not a complete substitution of one with the other at all. Its accomplishment is rendered possible by means of such factors as theoretical hypothesis, gradual internalization, constructive gradation, and even necessary elimination. This is by no means a business deal for quick profit. Instead, it is a long and creative process of interactive experimentation. For example, the improvement of any democratic movement originated from the Western tradition is rather time- and energy-consuming with respect to its localization in culturally different regions or its transplantation in politically authoritarian soils.

In a word, the threefold process is correlative and interdependent, all serving in principle to demolish the cultural boundaries, break the homoculture-centerism of any kind, and promote the transformational creation *par excellence* in a cosmopolitan sense. In addition, it bears a hidden link with the Whitehead's notion of "organic process" that is "proceeding from phase to phase, each phase being the real basis from which its successor proceeds towards the completion of the thing in question."[21] Incidentally, such completion may be conducive not only to the Whitehead's conception of Beauty as "the mutual adaptation of several factors in an occasion of experience,"[22] but also to the creative Beauty of transcultural harmonization in favor of both the community good and the cosmopolitan good.

---

[21] Alfred N. Whitehead, *Process and Reality* (Cambridge: Cambridge University Press, 1929), p. 305.
[22] Alfred N. Whitehead, *Adventures of Ideas* (New York: Mentor Books, 1932), p. 251.

CHAPTER 9

A Transformational Creation of Pragmatic Reason

For more than 2500 years ever since its advent, Confucianism remains as the keystone of the ideological mainstream in China. In spite of the ups and downs it has undergone in history, its impact remains persistent, and its development stays alive with the passage of time. When reinterpreted in light of Western ideology in recent decades, Confucianism is considered to be characterized with a kind of pragmatic reason as the underlying component of its thoughtway. As distinguished from the Kantian concept of practical reason, the notion of pragmatic reason is initially coined in 1980s by Li Zehou who employs it to bring forth the practical wisdom and primary features of classical Confucianism in particular. Moreover, he attempts to make the most of it when reconsidering the possibility of addressing other social and philosophical issues from a transcultural perspective and world outlook.

As revealed in many of his writings, Li Zehou has been preoccupied with the China reality in particular and the human condition in general. The China reality is mainly concerned about what to do to develop material productivity and secure necessary provisions in order to feed the large population that used to live at a starvation budget. Thanks to the reform and open-door policy in the past three decades or so, the majority of Chinese citizens have now benefited a great deal from the socioeconomic achievements and enjoyed a tremendous improvement of their living standards. Nevertheless, there are still 70 million people struggling under the poverty line at present stage. Just imagine. What contribution would China, with a population that occupies a fifth of the world total, make at a time when the problem with food supply is completely resolved by self-reliance. As for the human condition in Li's consideration, it is related to the process of human evolution, the state of human living, the possibility of human becoming, and fulfillment at large. In search of possible solutions to the formidable tasks aforementioned, Li's philosophizing features a close interaction between practical expectation and theoretical hypothesis, and a rediscovery of classical Confucianism in comparison with Western ideas. By so doing has he worked out an alternative solution to the sociocultural issues and human concerns in both Chinese and global contexts.

All this is chiefly reflected in Li's view of pragmatic reason (*shiyong lixing*) per se. His view as such evolves through two primary stages and can be perceived as the first argument and the second one due to their respective but complementary components. The first argument is largely drawn from Confucianism by looking into the typical aspects of pragmatic reason including usefulness (*youyong xing*), ethicalness (*lunli xing*), emotio-reasonable inseparableness (*qingli bufen*), historical consciousness (*lishi yishi*), quasi-religiousness (*zhunzongjiao xing*), and openness (*kaifang xing*) to the necessity of transformational creation.

The second argument demonstrates Li's individual observation and changes the pragmatic reason of Chinese tradition into that of historical ontology. At this point, he lays down a theoretical keystone that consists of three leading assumptions: history constitutes rationality (*lishi jian lixing*), the empirical changes into the transcendental (*jingyan bian xianyan*), and psychology turns into substratum (*xinli cheng benti*).[1] Along

---

[1] This compound word *benti* can be divided into *ben* and *ti*. Etymologically and semantically, *ben* means root and fundamental source that can be taken as a rationale in an abstract sense, and *ti* means body and organic power that can be seen as the basis upon which property and function rely. As regards Li Zehou's conception of *benti*, it is used to suggest something fundamental, primary, and most important in light of his anthropologico-historical ontology (*renleixue lishi bentilun*) that is often shortened into historical ontology (*lishi bentilun*). It is therefore rendered as substratum or root according to the specific terms used in specific contexts in my observation. Incidentally, it is fore and foremost distinct from the Kantian term *noumenon* that is referred to the unknowable "thing in itself." Then, it is different from the notion of substance used in the Western intellectual history to mean *ousia* in Aristotle, God in Descartes or the absolute in Hegel. Moreover, it is deviated from the usage of *benti* in Neo-Confucianism where it would be employed to indicate such

this line of thought, he goes on to propose the notions of appropriate measure (*du*) and emotional root (*qing benti*).[2]

The discussion hereby is intended to cover four parts as follows: the first argument in 1990s, the second argument in the new millennia, Li's philosophical alternative in view of pragmatic reason, and a tentative remark on Li's world-picture in comparison with Albert Einstein's *weltbild*.

9.1 The First Argument

Li's first consideration of pragmatic reason can be dated back to his essay on China's wisdom in 1985,[3] and a more specific interpretation in 1993.[4] As he asserts thereby, pragmatic reason played a crucial role in shaping the Chinese tradition with regard to the mode of thought and the ideas about human living. Moreover, it gave rise to the joy-conscious

---

things as the primary essence of the ultimate void without form, the fundamental source of the heavenly principle of naturalness, and the knowledge of good conscience in human mind, etc. Recent discussions can be seen in the following: Qian Shangang, *Benti zhi si yu ren de cunzai: Li Zehou sixiang yanjiu* [Thinking of Substance and Human Existence: A Study of Li Zehou's Thoughts] (Hefei: Anhui University Press, 2011), pp. 5–6; Han Fengming, "'Tianren heyi' shi benti zhengming" [The Justification of Substance in View of "Heaven-Human Oneness"], in *Zhexue yanjiu* [The Journal of Philosophical Researches], No. 6, 2013, p. 46.

[2] Li Zehou uses this term somewhat metaphorically to mean "fundamental root" (*bengen*) that contains generative power or growing potential. For the emotion of humankind is so vital to human living that it is correlated with the emergence of the human Dao (*ren dao*), the origin of psychological substratum (*xinli benbti*), the mode of joy-conscious culture (*legan wenhua*), and the basis of aesthetic metaphysics (*shenmei xingershangxue*), among others. I hereby translate it into "emotional root" instead of "emotional substance" owing to the account given in the first footnote.

[3] Li Zehou, "Shitan Zhonguo de zhihui" [Some Tentative Remarks on China's Wisdom], in *Zhongguo gudai sixiangshi lun* [On Traditional Chinese Intellectual History] (Beijing: Renmin Press, 1985), pp. 299–322. Also see Li Zehou, *Xinban Zhongguo gudai sixiangshi lun* [On Traditional Chinese Intellectual History, repr.] (Tianjin: Tianjin Academy of Social Sciences Press, 2008), pp. 234–255. Its selected passages in English translation are made available in M. E. Sharpe (trans.), "Contemporary Chinese Thought: Li Zehou," *Translation and Studies*, Winter 1999–2000, Vol. 31, No. 2, 2000, pp. 44–65.

[4] Li Zehou, "Guanyu 'shiyong lixing'" [About 'Pragmatic Reason'] (1993), in *Shiyong lixing yu legan wenhua* [Pragmatic Reason and a Culture of Optimism] (Beijing: Sanlian Bookshop, 2005), pp. 325–332.

culture (*legan wenhua*)⁵ in striking contrast to the sin-conscious culture (*zuigan wenhua*) underlined by Western Christianity. The joy-conscious culture contains "an ontological meaning in Chinese philosophy" in an optimistic and aesthetic tone whereas its sin-conscious counterpart implies the original sin and hidden pessimism in search of transcendent self-redemption.

In respect to Chinese pragmatic reason according to Li's viewpoint, it can be conceived as "a creative principle in a dynamic or living process"⁶ of historical accumulation, cultural formation and psychological sedimentation from which certain "absolute values or moral norms of objective and universal necessity could be developed."⁷ It was endogenously fostered in early Confucianism but stays open to further modification with the passage of time. In brief, it displays such six key aspects as ethicalness, usefulness, emotive-cum-reasonable inseparableness, historical awareness, quasi-religiousness, and openness to the future reconstruction.

In the first place, the ethicalness (*lunli xing*) or moral sense (*daode gan*) as a crucial dimension of Chinese pragmatic reason has been all along stressed in Confucianism. It shares something common with Kant's advocate of "categorical imperative" grounded on practical reason. For both of them emphasize the necessity of moral perfection and ethical conduct for both personal cultivation and final happiness. On the account of this similarity, Li brings forth the notion of pragmatic reason in order to distinguish it from Kant's expectation of practical reason. For Li deploys it to deny the existence of reason a priori as well as transcendental comprehensive judgment, because what pragmatic reason pursues has little to do with the Kantian metaphysics and theo-ethics. As a rule,

---

⁵ Li Zehou himself offers his English rendering of *legan wenhua* as a culture of optimism. However, he once brought forth this notion in contrast to *zuigan wenhua* as sin-conscious culture with regard to the Western tradition that is Christianized by the deep-set conception of original sin. In addition, he is aware of the fact that *legan wenhua* is tridimensional in Chinese heritage of which the interpretation is to be given later. I therefore tend to translate *legan wenhua* into "joy-conscious culture" according to the Chinese tradition proper even though it is characteristic of some kind of optimism as regards its hidden and positive stance towards varied possibilities of human living.

⁶ Li Zehou, *Zhongguo gudai sixiangshi lun* [On Traditional Chinese Intellectual History], p. 329.

⁷ Li Zehou, *Li Zehou jinnian dawenlu* [Interviews with Li Zehou from 2004 to 2006] (Tianjin: Tianjin Academy of Social Sciences, 2006), p. 205.

it refuses to keep reason in the supreme position but uses it as an instrument to serve for human existence or living as its highest purpose. It has no transcendental quality and never disconnects it from experience and history at all. In a word, it is derived from a philosophical generalization of empirical reasonableness in the historical process. With focus on the possibility of human becoming, it advises one to be morally cultivated to the extent that he behaves well within the private space and the public space. That is, he must be responsible for the family by fulfilling such requirements as being pious to the old, kind to the young, and loyal to the spouse when married. And meanwhile, he must be observing the public codes of conduct, trustworthy to the friends, and reciprocally considerate of the neighbors in the community. Such moral obligations are prone to grow extensive and demanding. According to Confucianism, they are up to five constant virtues including humaneness (*ren*), righteousness (*yi*), rites (*li*), wisdom (*zhi*), and trustworthiness (*xin*), in addition to five character traits of being temperate (*wen*), kind (*liang*), courteous (*gong*), restrained (*jian*), and magnanimous (*rang*). These two sets of virtues aim to develop a person into a fine personality of all gentrice or nobility (*junzi renge*).

Secondly, the usefulness (*youyong xing*) as a primary aspect of Chinese pragmatic reason is somewhat identical to its counterpart in American pragmatism. For both of them apply a similar criterion to measuring truth and its value, and accordingly maintain that truth should be practically useful or functional in the pure sense of this term. Mutually they are more concerned with taking effective and right actions instead of abstract or metaphysical theories in the domain of living experiences. Yet, Chinese pragmatic reason differs from Dewey's pragmatism in that the former stresses and even believes in the adaptation to an objective principle or ordination. This principle lies in the heavenly Dao or destiny independent of human thinking. However, it cannot be separated from the human Dao because the latter should follow the former such that they are one in two or two in one in a dialectic link. In actuality, the usefulness of this kind can conduce to a down-to-earth stance, a stance that is well denoted in such a popular allegory, say "A good cat, no matter whether it is black or white, is the one that catches the mouse." This cat allegory implies that the external distinction between the apparently discrepant means is not as valuable or valid as the actual attainment of the final end. As discerned in their quotidian acts, for instance, many Chinese people would hardly confine themselves to any stereotyped or conventionalized track when handling varied matters. Instead, they would take a working choice out of all the means available according to their pragmatic judgment. It is in this case that they would make their choice disregarding whether it is traditional or modern, national or global, endogenous or exotic. For they pay more attention to the fulfillment of the end rather than the type of the means.

Thirdly, preoccupied with the equilibrium of human becoming, Chinese pragmatic reason tends to interlink the two indispensable elements of human nature: emotion and reason. It is therefore characterized with a form of emotio-reasonable inseparableness (*qingli bufen*), almost always attempting to procure a balance between them, a balance that is acclaimed to do things and treat humans altogether in a fair manner by gratifying both emotional and reasonable needs in order to sustain the quality of life. Emotional needs are principally guided to assuring an equitable and reciprocal enhancement of human relationships, whereas reasonable needs are chiefly oriented to doing justice to the human activities according to the established rules and regulations in both written and unwritten genres. They are to be harnessed properly and cooperatively rather than rigidly and separately, because they are supposed to go hand in hand on most occasions. Very often they are adjusted or moderated by virtue of the golden mean (*zhong yong*) as the rule of timely correctness (*shi zhong*). Any act of slanting to the extremes would be thought of as being out of balance, eventually failing to meet the ideal of being emotively and reasonably satisfying at a simultaneous level. As noticed in either artistic expression of artworks or individual conduct in social encounters, what is reasonable tends to penetrate into what is emotive and vise versa. Thus there arises a hidden control of excessive passions and inflexible reasoning in both domains as the principle of suitability and moderation is always commended for the sake of moral and aesthetic exaltation. Nevertheless, the pursuit of this balance would entail a kind of tension between the legal verdict and the affectionate mentality in many cases, which would produce some negative impact upon the all-round implementation of rule of law in spite of the social changes that have taken place ever since the modernization of China from late nineteenth century onward.

Fourthly, Chinese pragmatic reason is intimately leagued with historical consciousness (*lishi yishi*) aside from its certain materialistic inclinations. Such awareness is deeply rooted in Chinese ideology itself. It is keen on "the objective investigation, consideration, and calculation of things and events from a long-term, systematic perspective, and is less interested in the transient gains and losses, successes and failures of the present."[8] It thus differs from other forms of instrumental or speculative reason. Inclined to get the gist of historical lessons in order to serve the specific interests of social life, it bears no hindrance to prevent people from learning new and exotic things so long as they are needed and relevant to practical objectives. Moreover, it helps elevate historical awareness up to the level of a worldview that embraces the trinity of the past, the present, and the future, and meanwhile stresses the oneness between heaven and humankind. Being peculiar to Chinese cultural heritage, pragmatic reason works "to fuse the philosophy of nature and the philosophy of history so that the view of history, epistemology, ethics, and dialectics are emerged, leading to the rise of a kind of historical reason imbued with emotion and feeling. (The focus on history reflects the concern with experience, and the emotional dimension reflects the concern with human relationships.)"[9] Noticeable as it is, the spirit of pragmatic reason is mostly derived from classical Confucianism, and conducive to a kind of paradigmatic character and a mode of thought, all of which remold the Chinese mentality that tends to avoid extremes by striking the mean in their living experiences or everyday routines. By "striking the mean" is referred to the doctrine of "Excess like inadequacy" (*guo you bu ji*), because neither of them is up to the golden mean as the rule of correctness. Embracing the mean, one is inclined to be more cool-minded and warmhearted, nonviolent, but have less fantasy or novelty. They may value "higher insight but make light of logic; they are fond of history in order to make it serve live in the present; they aim at the preservation of harmony and stability in the existing organic system, have a high regard for human relationships, reject risk-taking, and do not have a high regard for innovation.... All these factors bring many strong points as well as short-comings to science, culture, ideology, patterns of conduct of the Chinese people. On the road of adapting to the modern and

---

[8] Li Zehou, "Some Tentative Remarks on China's Wisdom" (excerpts); M. E. Sharpe (trans.), "Contemporary Chinese Thought: Li Zehou," *Translations and Studies*, p. 49. Also see the original text of "Shitan zhongguo de zhihui" [Some Tentative Remarks on China's Wisdom]; and Li Zehou, *Zhongguo gudai sixiang shilun* [Essays on Traditional ChineseThoughts], pp. 305–306.

[9] Li Zehou, "Some Tentative Remarks on China's Wisdom" (excerpts); M. E. Sharpe (trans.), "Contemporary Chinese Thought: Li Zehou," *Translations and Studies*, p. 50.

contemporary life of rapid change and scientific advancements, China seems to walk haltingly and with difficulty."[10]

Fifthly, the quasi-religiousness (*zhun zongjiao xing*) of Chinese pragmatic reason is distinct from any other cultures in existence. It inherited some of the intrinsic and problematic tendencies from Confucianism in which religion and philosophy would operate in synthesis. This being true, Confucianism could be seen either a quasi-religion or a quasi-philosophy. In spite of the absence of such a religion as Christianity, for instance, Confucian ethics is still bestowed with certain religious characteristics that are to be exercised in a secular society of this-worldly matters. As a result, it would lead to the Chinese type of "unification of the state and the church" by which ethics was identified with politics and vise versa. Once a new movement or revolution was launched, it would spur up a type of quasi-religious faith sustained by a quasi-religious enthusiasm. In certain historical events such as the New Culture Movement in early 1920s and the Cultural Revolution from 1960s to 1970s, there arose the problem with too much fanaticism but too less cool-minded reasoning. Accordingly, it did much more harm than good in many realms.

Last but not least, Chinese pragmatic reason features openness (*kaifang xing*) to the future and calls for timely modifications in accord with the circumstances in flux. This is due to its being no closed or immutable concept itself. Alike "cultural-psychological formation," it is not referred to a rigid mode, but to a dynamic progression. It is always in the process of continuous development, reconstructing, and sedimentating in the historical process. It lays emphasis on change, expansion, innovation, and advancement, creates no roadblock to obstruct the modernization of China proper, and asks for a solid research and transformational creation. Hence it must retain and carry forward a calm, rational, and realistic stance toward empirical, historical, and actual effects in order to obtain a clear distinction between morality and politics on the one hand, and on the other, it must keep and enhance the optimistic and tenacious attitude toward life so as to rebuild the psychical plane for the ethics of inward sublimation. By so doing may we break through the conventional unification of the state and the church being extended until

---

[10] Li Zehou, "Some Tentative Remarks on China's Wisdom" (excerpts); M. E. Sharpe (trans.), "Contemporary Chinese Thought: Li Zehou," *Translations and Studies*, p. 50.

today, and overcome the worsening tendency of moral decline and faith crisis at the present.[11]

When exposing the basic features of Chinese pragmatic reason, Li makes a relevant use of otherness to shed light on the understanding of them all. Here by otherness is meant other culture, other tradition, other philosophy, or other thinker. For instance, he looks into the aspect of ethicalness or moral sense with reference to Kant's consideration of practical reason and categorical imperative, into the aspect of usefulness with reference to Dewey's conception of truth and utility, and into the aspect of quasi-religiousness with reference to the Christian tradition and so forth.

Quite observantly, Li himself never neglects the demerits of Chinese pragmatic reason. As he points out, it is due to its shadowy influence in Chinese ideology that human emotion is confined to the boundaries of human relationships, and human reason can hardly go beyond the limits of the empirical field. This being true, "Chinese philosophy and culture were generally not directed to the type of investigation that is based on rigorous reasoning and abstract theorizing. Rather, they were preferable to and even content with vague, holistic reasoning and intuitive understanding in their pursuit of truth and enlightenment through a kind of analysis that is not purely logical, intellectual or formal."[12] There are of course many other weaknesses as are revealed in the Chinese mode of thought and the Chinese way of life. As observed in the exercise of theoretical exploration, it is very often motivated by practical drives. Say, it is dependent upon problem-solving intentions rather than curiosity-oriented gratifications. Hence the theoretical thinking is apt to be carried on during the progression of seeking for a solution to the problem, and it is likely to be suspended as a result of having the problem removed. All this tends to beget an obstacle for the development of scientific probing and the maturity of theoretical speculation in certain realms.

To tackle the negative factors, both an open stance and a transcultural approach are to be introduced. As Li argues, while attempting to retain the good things of Chinese culture, one faces an enormous and difficult task of finding out how he can seriously investigate and assimilate

---

[11] Li Zehou, "Guanyu 'shiyong lixing'" [About "Pragmatic Reason"] (1993), in *Shiyong lixing yu legan wenhua* [Pragmatic Reason and a Culture of Optimism], pp. 331–332.

[12] Li Zehou, "Some Tentative Remarks on China's Wisdom" (excerpts); M. E. Sharpe (trans.), "Contemporary Chinese Thought: Li Zehou," *Translations and Studies*, p. 50.

the strong points of other cultures, such as "the astonishing profundity and power of German abstract thought, the spirit of sobriety and clarity in the tradition of Anglo-American empiricism, the melancholic and profound transcendent needs of the Russian people…in such a way that Chinese pragmatic reason can take a big stride and re-establish itself on a higher level. This will also be a historical process."[13] Apart from the merits of the three sources above mentioned, what should be added is the pioneering spirit and scientific creativity of the American way as it seems to me. Needless to say, this is an arduous and complicated project for Chinese philosophers to accomplish in the present-day context of glocalization.

9.2 The Second Argument

The first decade of the new millennium witnessed what Li has done for the transformational creation of pragmatic reason. His endeavors and achievements in this regard are mainly displayed in his treatises published in 2002 and 2005.[14] All this ends up with the second argument of a renewed mode of pragmatic reason.

In brief, the second argument comprises a new framework in contrast to the first one. This does not necessarily mean that one cuts off its hidden link with the other. For both of them are exposed and formulated from a historical and empirical viewpoint. Nevertheless, the second argument differs from the first one in that it is largely grounded on a theoretical keystone from Li's historical ontology. The keystone is made up of at least three leading hypotheses.

The first is that "history constitutes rationality". According to Li, rationality is secondary if compared with the priority of human living, say, the former is valuable and meaningful only when it is employed as a tool for the latter. It is evolved in history and originated from reasonableness due to instrumental functions. According to Li's conclusion,

---

[13] Li Zehou, "Shitan zhongguo de zhihui" [Some Tentative Remarks on China's Wisdom], in *Zhongguo gudai sixiang shilun* [Essays on Traditional Chinese Thoughts], p. 243. The translation is cited from M. E. Sharpe (trans.), "Contemporary Chinese Thought: Li Zehou," *Translations and Studies*, p. 51.

[14] Li Zehou, *Lishi bentilun* [Historical Ontology] (Beijing: Sanlian Bookshop, 2002), and *Shiyong lixing yu legan wenhua* [Pragmatic Reason and a Culture of Optimism] (Beijing: Sanlian Bookshop, 2005).

pragmatic reason is just a philosophical generalization of reasonableness as it negates any form of speculative reasoning a priori. It emphasizes relativity, uncertainty, and non-objectivity, but it is not relativism at all. For it is after all determined by the absolute norm of "human living" or "philosophy of eating." Moreover, it upholds that "objective sociality" qua "universal necessity" is established and complied by human beings during the process of historical accumulation. To repeat once again: Pragmatic reason in Chinese tradition is not a priori, fixed, and absolute at all. It is close to reasonableness that is historically constructed and empirically attested. "It can be termed as a historical reason because it is attached to human history (i.e., the temporal process of the actual existence, living, and life of humankind as a whole), and thus comes into being and grows along with it. It is so alterable and adaptable that it is molded into appropriate measure (*du*)."[15]

The second is that "the empirical changes into the transcendental." As noticed in the moral scope, what is compulsory to an individual comes from within. It helps one self-consciously curb his desires and wants ranging from food, sex to varied "private interests," and renders his conduct, consciously or unconsciously, fitting into the norms. Such working leads to "the solidification of reason" (*lixing ningju*) in terms of human psychology and will power (free will). In Li's phrase, "the solidification of reason" is consequently the outcome of the self-conscientious manipulation of sensational faculty by its rational counterpart. As each person becomes a member of the human group through a long-time education and training via rational faculty, his moral sense is psychologically the fruit of the solidification attributed to humankind alone. The solidification of this kind is so powerful as to dominate the sensational aspect of human existence. It is therefore named as "categorical imperative" by Kant, "heavenly principle" by Zhu Xi, and "good conscience" by Wang Yangming, all of which bear universality and absoluteness as much as what are divined into either "heavenly Dao" of everlasting permanence or "historical necessity" of omnipresent applicability. In effect, "categorical imperative," "heavenly principle," and "good conscience" lead humans to acknowledge the meanings, values, and responsibilities of life as though they drop an anchor to locate a floating boat for the sake of stability. These moral rules are there to regulate and normalize

---

[15] Li Zehou, *Lishi bentilun* [Historical Ontology] (Beijing: Sanlian Bookshop, 2002, repr. 2006), p. 43.

human conduct from inward without any mental resistance or cognitive disputability. They are overriding and rational as well, but they demand empirical feelings, faiths, piousness, and fear to support its actual performance.[16] All this reveals the probability that moral rules like "categorical imperative," "heavenly principle," and "good conscience" are formed by the empirical in the historical process of human praxis and civilization. They are then developed into what is transcendental or divinely supreme in guiding human behaviors from within as they are self-consciously chosen by the power of free will.

The third is that "psychology turns into substratum." It is in a way elicited from Heidegger's) philosophy of *Dasein*, a philosophy that is shrouded in a veil of such haunting feelings as "care" and "fear" evoked by the capricious uncertainty of death. These feelings are associated not only with empirical psychology and human self-consciousness, but with the existential status quo of us moderns. They are of "ontological" quality that nurtures the process of human living haunted by "care" and "fear." Talking about his historical ontology, Li affirms that "he proposes it by formulating two type of rationale with due modifications: one is technico-social substratum (*gongju benti*) connected with Marx, and the other psychological substratum (*xinli benti*) linked with Heidegger). When combined with Chinese tradition, the former is conducive to pragmatic reason while the latter to joy-conscious culture. Both of them take history as what is most fundamental, and therefore become integrated in the historical being of humankind (*renlei de lishi cunzai*)."[17] Such kind of "historical being" is hereby underlined by the crucial role of historical ontology concerning human living and human becoming altogether.

It is noteworthy that Li keeps reemphasizes the fundamentality of historical ontology from time to time. He even goes so far as to round it out by juxtaposing it with other sources. For instance, he says, "Historical ontology comes from Marx, Kant and Chinese tradition, but deviates from them to quite some extent. More specifically, it differs from Marx who merely heeds the social aspect of *homo sapiens* but ignores the psychical dimension of the individual. It differs from Kant who ascribes the psychological form to the super-human reason but

---

[16] Li Zehou, *Lishi bentilun* [Historical Ontology], pp. 49–51.

[17] Ibid., p. 92. In the 2006 edition of the book, the Chinese expression "*renlei lishi de benti*" should be "*renlei de lishi cunzai*" according to the context concerned.

neglects its origin of historical living in actuality. It differs from Chinese tradition that lays an excessive stress on usefulness but makes light of the vital importance of abstract speculation. However, historical ontology as such absorbs and integrates them all. It generally brings forth its key arguments via the concepts of pragmatic reason and joy-conscious culture, and intends to deal with the issues of psychological constitution concerning an all-round realization of personal potentials in modern life."[18] To my mind, Li is obliged to upgrade his philosophy of historical ontology as he is deeply concerned with the primacy of human living and the possibility of human becoming in the post-modern era. For he finds human race confronted with a lot of challenges and problems related to human culture and psychology during this historical phase. He does not hesitate to prescribe his remedy to which we will turn back later.

Here let us look at the logic of the pragmatic reason as an integral part of the second argument in accord with historical ontology. Closely leagued with the empirical reasonableness as the kernel of pragmatic reason, the logic in question is indicated in the notion of appropriate measure. This measure is dependent upon technico-social substratum in principle, but it possesses a root-like character (*zhutixing*) such that it is considered to be "the first category of anthropologico-historical ontology."[19] It is present in the praxis of human production rather than in the existing objects or consciousness alone. Its root-like character functions as a fundamental source related not only to man-made (subjective) invention but also to natural (objective) discovery. In this regard, human praxis is elementary whereas the subject–object dichotomy secondary in view of appropriate measure.[20] In plain words, the measure itself implies a good command of the most proper measurement and proportion for humans to handle all matters encountered. It means technical correctness, suitability, and effectiveness as though it is approximate to what ancient Greeks thought of as *pan metron ariston* or the best measure for all. As usual, it is actualized and objectified

---

[18] Li Zehou, *Shiyong lixing yu legan wenhua* [Pragmatic Reason and a Culture of Optimism], p. 108.

[19] Li Zehou, *Lishi benti lun* [Historical Ontology], p 10. Li Zehou keeps this book of his in a very important position. He sometimes substitutes the book title with *Renleixue benti lun* [Anthropological Ontology], and sometimes with *Renleixue lishi benti lun* [Anthropological and Historical Ontology].

[20] Li Zehou, *Lishi bentilun* [Historical Ontology], p. 13.

in what ancient Chinese conceived as the mean (*zhong*) or harmony (*he*) and applied to all domains ranging from the art of music, art of war, art of politics, and the like. In this sense, it can be somewhat identified with the principle of ultimate appropriateness and best proportion in both qualitative and quantitative considerations against the changing situation or specific time-space involved. It is not easy to be commanded at its best, but remains so crucial and desirable that without it, humans couldn't preserve their existence, species, and even personal life. For this reason, Li treats appropriate measure as the first category in contrast to Hegel's classification of quality as the first category, quantity as the second category, and measure as the third category. Such distinction is set out between Li's concern with how human living is possible in view of historical ontology and Hegel's concern with defining what things are in terms of metaphysical ontology.

In my observation, the concept of appropriate measure is assumed to operate at three major planes. First and foremost, it works at the plane of material and symbolic operations that engages physical and spiritual praxes, such as productive activities, language communications, artistic creations, scientific explorations, and religious prayers, and so forth. All this is pointed to "the solidification of reason" and "the internalization of reason" as a consequence of human engagement with intellectual power and constant labor. Then, it serves at the plane of dialectic wisdom as it goes through the operational field to the existential counterpart. It is mirrored, for example, in the Chinese notion of "complementary interaction between Ying and Yang," the Greek theory of "unity in diversity," and the Western doctrine of "unity of opposites." Subsequently, it performs at the plane of unique creation. It is herein characteristic of best appropriateness that is neither too much nor too less. It is employed to create what is artistically beautiful so as to foster the sense of beauty among those who are contemplating the beautiful. On this account, it is utilized to procure beauty (*mei*)[21] throughout human activities encompassing material productions, living behaviors, and so on. It delivers a pleasant feeling of mental freedom as the origin

---

[21] The Chinese notion of *mei* is semantically closer to the Greek idea of *kallos* as it is tridimensional. That is, it is firstly referred to something beautiful in terms of its fair shape or appearance, secondly referred to some moral conduct that is judged in terms of goodness or righteousness, and thirdly referred to some virtuous and higher personality ascribed to a kind of nobility.

of the sense of beauty itself. Meanwhile, it serves as the foundational stone of the beautiful instead of beauty in itself. Accordingly, beauty represents the free operation of appropriate measure and the sufficient manifestation of human capacity. However, the measure itself is still "skill" (*ji*), and the beauty is "art" (*yi*). "Art" is above "skill" owing to its free and creative use of "skill."22 In the final analysis, the concept of appropriate measure contains a root-like trait in its causality-based operation as is shown in the foregoing formulation of the three planes.

Incidentally, the exposure of the second argument is not complete without referring to the joy-conscious culture. In Li's thought, this kind of culture and the appropriate measure are typical of Chinese tradition, complementary in effect when it comes to coping with the current issues of the human condition. As explicated in the *Historical Ontology*, the joy-conscious culture in Chinese context has a trifold implication. It firstly signals "a culture of worldly happiness" that embodies the basic tendency of Chinese tradition, a culture that centers around human living and material life directed to worldly happiness and relational harmony. It subsequently signifies "a culture of optimism" as it focuses on the general theme of "human living" and probes its possibility from a humanistic and optimistic viewpoint. It keeps veritable confidence in human power and initiative in spite of the historical progression through tragic events and maintains that the bright prospect will come along and the situation of the human condition can be ameliorated so long as humans pluck up their courage and retain their perseverance in their struggle against the hardships and challenges on the way. It thirdly indicates "a culture of music and aesthetics" because the Chinese word *le* is also pronounced as *yue*. Literally the former means joy while the latter music. In Chinese heritage, such joy (*le*) is symbolic of the essence and function of music (*yue*), both of which are regarded as integral parts of human nature in light of teleological pursuit of final joyfulness or happiness. It is accordingly reckoned that such culture helps facilitate the final accomplishment of human nature by virtue of musical appreciation and aesthetic sensibility at its best.23

Noticeably, the joy-conscious culture finds its kernel in nowhere but the emotional root, the root that is in fact a sustaining part of

---

22 Li Zehou, *Shiyong lixing yu legan wenhua* [Pragmatic Reason and a Culture of Optimism], p. 42.

23 Li Zehou, *Lishi benti lun* [Historical Ontology], p. 408.

psychological substratum or cultural-psychological formation proper. Such culture is prone to work against the theory of identifying moral order with cosmic order, against the principle of taking the moral state of being for the highest realm in human life, and against the notion of ruling all by the so-called supreme rationality itself. Instead, it asserts that human as human ought to return to his natural but free state of being in a spiritual sense. It proceeds to treat human as the final purpose and grounds human upon the emotional root instead of the mere appetite-based root (for animals) or the pure rational root (for divinities).[24]

To mention in passing, the notion of emotion (*qing*) in Confucianism denotes essentially the enculturated love of humans, the love that is stemmed from an instinctive *eros* of animals, enculturated to an innate compassion (*ceyin*), nurtured to an affection for relatives (*qinqin*), extended to loving people (*renmin*) and treasuring things (*aiwu*), and eventually exalted to the universal love of all beings in the world (*fan aizhong*). In Li's opinion, *qing* as emotion is no longer restricted to the old scope of such natural feelings as pleasure, anger, sorrow, joy, shock, fear, and grief (*xi nu ai le jing kong bei*). It is so renewed as to cover seven types of affection for relatives (*qinqing*), friends (*youqing*), lovers (*aiqing*), human relations (*renji guanxi qing*), home lands (*xiangtu jiayuan qing*), collective endeavors for the common good (*jiti fenjin qing*), and science as well as art (*kexue yishu qing*). These seven types are humanized and permeated by social rationality.[25]

In this special setting, emotional root is metaphorically used for the fundamental source of generative power and growing potential that is correlated with the emergence of the human Dao (*rendao*), the basis of aesthetic metaphysics (*shenmei xing er shang xue*), and the mode of joy-conscious culture, among others. It is therefore the primary cause of growth or change in the process of human becoming.[26] As noted in the Guodian text in ancient China, the Dao is said to be generated from emotion (*dao you qing sheng*), suggesting that the human Dao came from human emotion even though it attempts to tame human emotion to the due degree by virtue of its intrinsic interaction with moral codes or

---

[24] Li Zehou, *Shiyong lixing yu legan wenhua* [Pragmatic Reason and a Culture of Optimism], pp. 71–72.

[25] Li Zehou, *Lishi benti lun* [Historical Ontology], p. 108.

[26] Li Zehou, *Shiyong lixing yu legan wenhua* [Pragmatic Reason and a Culture of Optimism], p. 55.

social norms. On this account, Li assumes that the root of humanity is not what is rational but what is aesthetic owing to the mutual fusion of the emotional and the rational aspects. He therefore plays up emotional root while playing down "the fundamentality of human nature" (*xing benti*) and "the fundamentality of heavenly principle" (*li benti*) in Neo-Confucianism. He even goes so far as to promote a new shift from moral metaphysics to aesthetic metaphysics for the sake of human living today. Repeatedly as he proclaims, emotion involves an allocation and integration of varied proportions of human nature (morals) and human appetite (instincts). It can never constitute some type of fixed framework, system, or "substance" (in terms of either outward or inward transcendence).[27] In his view, emotional root is more decisive to human race as it is deeply set in "the sedimentation of reason" (*lixing jidian*) in its narrow sense rather than "the solidification of reason" in its ethical sense. This is in a way justified by the hard fact that man comes first from Nature, and then goes beyond Nature when he has grown into a cultural-moral being. However, he cannot stay all the time within the state of going beyond Nature, because he is physically a natural being, and eventually returns to Nature after all.[28] Hence humans are exposed to two historical events: the humanization of nature and the naturalization of the human.[29]

9.3 A Philosophical Alternative

The two arguments above disclose Li's reconsideration of pragmatic reason in Chinese tradition and his transformational creation from a transcultural horizon. They in fact contribute a significant part to his practical philosophy of humanism that is based on the teleological rationale of his anthropologico-historical ontology. As a thinker with deep humanistic concern, he treats philosophy as an exploration of the spectrum of human fate and constantly looks into the status quo of the human condition in general and the possibility of human becoming in particular. Like Kant, he is highly aware of that a cognition is called practical as opposed

---

[27] Li Zehou, "Zhexue tanxun lu (1994)" [An Inquiry into Philosophy in 1994], in *Shiyong lixing yu legan wenhua* [Pragmatic Reason and a Culture of Optimism], p. 187.

[28] Li Zehou, *Shiyong lixing yu legan wenhua* [Pragmatic Reason and a Culture of Optimism], p. 70.

[29] Li Zehou, "Shuo ren de ziranhua" [About the Naturalization of the Human], in *Lishi benti lun* [Historical Ontology].

to theoretical, for practical cognition is directed to the act of doing while theoretical cognition to the nature of being. He confesses that he himself enjoys both forms of cognition, but prefers to the practical tactics because of his engagement with how to address the issues or challenges in human living under current circumstances.

With respect to Li's humanism as an alternative frame, it is often found distinct from the mainstream as it proclaims its inquiry into a "philosophy of eating" (*chifan zhexue*). Starting with Engels' emphasis on the food supply as the primary prerequisite of human practice, it utilizes this "sarcastic" term as a counterargument to challenge those who are indulging themselves in the elusive and speculative theorizing while sneering at the down-to-earth mode of thought. Li paves up a path along which he walks on his own, neglecting any contemptuous mockeries or criticisms. Quite deliberately he deploys "philosophy of eating" not merely as a seemingly non-philosophical notion to ridicule himself and other self-important critics alike, but also as a rhetorical device to arouse public attention to his philosophical enterprise, humanistic concern and teleological pursuit. Examining his thoughts holistically, one may discover that his approach to philosophizing hankers after a moderate equilibrium between practical cognition and its theoretical counterpart.

As regards his transformation of pragmatic reason, he strives to promote a synthetic whole by combing the practical aspect with its theoretical counterpart. Yet, he thereby applies to enriching the rationale of pragmatic reason two distinct notions: One is pragmatic character (*shiyong xingge*) related to Chinese pragmatism in particular, and the other is abstract speculation (*chouxiang sibian*) linked with German idealism. He does so in order to upgrade its usefulness and increase its profundity. As he pronounces,

> pragmatic reason takes its service for human existence as the final objective. It neither resorts to anything transcendental nor separates itself from experience and history. It worked to facilitate the advancement of technique in ancient China, but failed to produce such axiomatic systems of mathematics and abstract speculations of philosophy as those in Hellenic Greece. It therefore encounters with big challenges in modern area. However, its pragmatic character enables Chinese people to acknowledge their cultural weaknesses, and at the same time, to redouble their efforts to receive and incorporate the elements of abstract speculation and

scientific systems from other cultures that they find beneficial to human beings altogether.[30]

What Li is meant by "human existence as the final objective" is synonymic of human living (*ren huo zhe*). It is of most critical necessity if compared with other concerns. Noticeably to Li's mind, the hard fact of human living is decisive to the possibility of either human becoming or human fulfillment. It usually involves a trifold challenge, say, it encounters firstly with the existent miseries of birth, aging, disease, and death, secondly with the omnipresent manipulation of socio-discourse power, productive pattern, and human interaction, and thirdly with the difficulties in adapting oneself to the antimony of advancing history and declining morality during the dynamic span of social change.[31] In order to upgrade the quality of human living, what needs to do is more than making the ends meet. For human living as such consists in at least four cardinal dimensions, such as the material, the epistemological, the ethical, and the aesthetic. More specifically, the material dimension deals with what to live on (*yihe huo*) in terms of fair satisfaction of basic needs, the epistemological dimension with why to live (*weihe huo*) in terms of sound knowledge of what life and death really mean, the ethical dimension with how to live (*ruhe huo*) in terms of observant compliance with public and private morals, and the aesthetic dimension with how well to live (*huo de zenyang*) in terms of a self-conscious motive for human fulfillment or perfection through the free intuition (knowing) of the world (*ziyou zhiguan*) and the free appreciating of beauty (*ziyou shenmei*). What is to be explicated subsequently will focus more on the material and aesthetic dimensions in order to manifest the useful and speculative worth of pragmatic reason.

Naturally as it does, Li's "philosophy of eating" stands out as it looks for a feasible solution to secure the material dimension of human living. Such concretization ostensibly relies upon the ample supply of daily necessities that turns out to be the precondition of addressing other dimensions of human living. It follows that the actualization of the material dimension is the overriding task of his practical philosophy. It is to

---

[30] Li Zehou, "Ke xuwu yi zeyou" [The Autobiography of Li Zehou], in *Shiyong lixing yu legan wenhua* [Pragmatic Reason and a Culture of Optimism], p. 364.

[31] Li Zehou, *Lishi benti lun* [Historical Ontology], p. 125.

be reified by human labor that proceeds to using and making tools while procuring appropriate measure in historical process of civilization.

Notwithstanding all this, the actualization therein is not individual but social matter for it is sought after by all humans or communities. Hence Li himself keeps an eye on the situation of China in this respect and gives much attention to the social development and reform process from a pragmatic perspective. With a historical and reflective judgment on empirical reasonableness, he advocates his proposal on the progression of China reform. His proposal is composed of such four successive steps as "economic development (*jingji fazhan*), individual freedom (*geren ziyou*), social justice (*shehui zhengyi*) and political democracy (*zhengzhi minzhu*)." He labels them as the theory of four-item sequence (*si shunxu shuo*)[32] and defends it when it is criticized by those who objects it. As he argues,

> The four items in the sequence are permeating into each other rather than being sharply divided into separate phases. They are so ordered in accord with their respective levels of importance and urgency. Nevertheless, they are to be treated as a whole instead of a mechanical and rigid regulation. They are characteristic of flexibility and changeability in the course of specific events and situations. This being the case, it remains crucial to manipulate the complicated interconnections among them when it comes to different periods and different issues. It is thus related to my emphasis on the art of appropriate measure (*du de yishu*).[33]

Quite persistently, he continues to champion this sequence ever since 1995 when he initially proposed it. For he is conscious of the fact that how to feed the large population through economic growth is prior to all other affairs in one sense, and in the other sense, any reform that leaves the populace hungry or starving is bound to rebuff or end up in chaos. Moreover, any radical reform that runs the risk of putting individual liberty and political democracy into first priority under immature conditions could be more destructive than constructive as it violates the social reality in China for the time being. It is evinced by the bitter experiences in the history of China, and in some other countries across the

---

[32] Li Zehou, *Lunli xue gang yao* [Ethics] (Beijing: Renmin Press, 2010), p. 189.
[33] Li Zehou, "Shuo lishi beiju" [About the Tragedy of History], in *Lishi bentilun* [Historical Ontology], p. 234.

planet. Notwithstanding this, Li's proposal is sharply attacked by those who claim themselves to be either new liberalists or populists. He is derided as being either conservative for his old age or cowardly because of his losing courage. Nevertheless, he beats on and goes so far as to declare that "harmony is above justice" (*hexie gao yu zhengyi*). I personally have sympathy with him on the point of positing "economic development" in the first priority, but I could hardly agree with him on the point of leaving "political democracy" behind "individual freedom" and "social justice" even though he has accounted for their inter-permeating relationship in his statement cited above. For in practice, the sequence could be adopted, its relationship suspended, and the art of appropriate measure neglected. Hence I grow a bit skeptical of it as I think how "individual freedom" and "social justice" could be possible and authentic without relevant institutionalization of "political democracy." I firmly believe that "political democracy" can be secured and sustained only by rule of law instead of rule by law, and it is the same case with "individual freedom" and "social justice." This seems to be the working logic as is justified by historical experiences time and again. As for his advocate of "harmony above justice," it involves the similar problem on one hand, and on the other, it is already proved as more costly and less feasible by the recent experimentation of "building a harmonious society" (*goujian hexie shehui*) via "maintaining social stability" (*weihu shehui wending*) in China. As exposed in this dangling experimentation, judicial procedure would fall into jeopardy of being weakened or abused for the sake of so-called social harmony and stability alone. Bitter lessons of this kind were easily available all over China in the past decade or so when fine-sounding political catchphrases were rampant, certain civil lawsuits harshly treated, and some civil rights legally violated. That is factually one of the chief reasons why the new government in China has waged a campaign of reinforcing the full-scaled rule of law in such a high pitch at the current stage.

Now let us turn to Li's approach to the aesthetic dimension of human living. Since this dimension is mainly concerned about "how well can humans live," its possible fulfillment lies in the insight into the human condition and its relevant improvement via aesthetic sublimation. As detected in each affluent society nowadays, the leading problems with the human condition are shifting to those with the cultural-psychological formation. They are predicted to cause mental ills and morbid acts like anxiety, autism, *mal de siècle*, and suicide, among others.

The cultural-psychological formation is trifold at least. Say, it is human at large in terms of human species; it is cultural from an environmental viewpoint; and it is individual in an elementary sense due to the process of psycho-cultural sedimentation.

In Li's opinion, all the cultural-psychological issues can be properly treated through aesthetic sublimation owing to the dynamic organism of his practical aesthetics as the first philosophy. In this regard, the free appreciating of the beautiful is considered to be the final destination in the system of subjectality (*zhutixing*), for it works together with free intuition as a process of rational sedimentation for the acme of humanity formation. More specifically, the beautiful as such is created out of the organic synthesis of both lawfulness and purposefulness and therefore perceived as the glory of both the true and the good in essence. And the free appreciating of the beautiful corresponds to the highest realm of human living allegorical to heaven-human oneness (*tianren heyi*). This oneness arises out of the material reality via the humanized nature that is involved in the remold of both the outer and the inner world. It is due to the productive power of the techno-social instruments rather than the individual spirit itself, the instruments that provide the foundation for such three things as the development of humankind and individual, the existence and advancement of social structure, and the individual psychological formation.[34]

According to Li, the Chinese conception of contemplating the beautiful (*shenmei*) differs from the Western notion of aesthetic involvement. It stays above the religious vision for at least two momentums: the first lies in a hidden, substantial, and super-moral state of being, which will lead to the possibility of moral realization beyond life, death, and any kind of interestedness; the second is characteristic of the intrinsic mélange between the collective and the individual, in which the historical, psychological, social, personal, rational, and perceptual aspects become united in the threefold mechanism of psychology, individuality, and sensibility. All this then slants to the consequence of rational sedimentation wherein the potential of individuality (*gexing qianneng*) in general gets fully nurtured and manifested.[35] In my view, the free act of contemplating the beautiful performs a crucial part in the pursuit of

---

[34] Li Zehou, "Guanyu bentixing de buchong shuoming (1983)" [A Supplementary Explication of Subjectivity in 1983], in *Shiyong lixing yu legan wenhua* [Pragmatic Reason and a Culture of Optimism], p. 231.

[35] Ibid., pp. 230–231.

inward sublimation that depends on moral cultivation from within rather than religious redemption from without. As observed in Chinese tradition, inward sublimation and heaven-human oneness enhance and facilitate one another to the extent that both of them aim to go beyond any interest-ridden concerns and obligations. With the help of the rational sedimentation and personality potential, what the free act hankers after could generate a positive ambiance for human fulfillment or perfection at its best.

As noticed in the second argument, Li's articulation of the appropriate measure parallels to that of "illuminating the true through the beautiful" (*yi mei qi zhen*), both of which are directed to the special role of his practical aesthetics. Correspondingly, his formulation of emotional root accompanies that of "accumulating the good through the beautiful" (*yi mei chu shan*), both of which are oriented toward the internal value of his practical aesthetics. All this is due to Li's conviction that the beautiful be symbolic of both the true and the good. The aesthetic illumination in this case serves as a kind of enlightenment that enables the contemplator of the beautiful to gain insights into the epistemological worth of the true and to raise the moral consciousness of the good.

To my mind, what underlies the agency of appropriate measure can be perceived as three interrelated principles operating in three domains. One is the principle of suitableness with focus on functional effectiveness and productiveness. It is intended to do the work according to appropriate measure (*yi du lao zuo*). When applied to both physical and spiritual operations aforementioned, it is more helpful and fruitful to preserve human living and tackle the problems with the "philosophy of eating." The other is the principle of correctness with emphasis on the relevance of cognition and the soundness of judgment. It is schemed to attain the dialectic wisdom according to the measure (*yi du huo zhi*). For such wisdom is decisive to sort out the delicate and confusing phenomena in the human world and is attainable only by so doing in accord with the changing time and space. It is no easy matter at any rate. It requires constant trial and testing in living experiences. The third is the principle of creativeness with stress on the power of imagination and the exercise of free intuition. It is designed to create the beautiful by means of the measure (*yi du li mei*). It demands a good mastery of skill (*ji*) and a fine sensibility of art (*yi*). Then, only by free application of the skill can the beautiful be produced and appreciated. However, this is not enough, because the beautiful is to be used for a higher purpose. That is, it is employed to illuminate the true, embodying the "logical" nucleus of pragmatic reason that delivers no specific methodology at all.[36] All this is naturally pointed to the subsequent these.

Fore and foremost, what is to be kept in mind is what is meant by "illuminating the true through the beautiful." It is no other than gaining real knowledge of a new type of thing in itself that is identified with the "coexistence of humankind with the cosmos" (*ren yu yuzhou de gongzai*) in Li's view. This is a metaphysical assumption without which aesthetic experience would have no origin, and the sense of form would find nowhere. The existence of the cosmos is like an unknown object a priori, whereas the creative and cognitive power of man-made operational-symbolic system is like the subject a priori. Both of them are unified on the basis of human praxis from the outlook of historical ontology. With the help of "illuminating the true through the beautiful," *homo sapiens* manage to peep into the mysteries of the cosmos and to secure a position for human existence therein. It is via such an active life full of contingency and spontaneity that the communication between human and the cosmos is rendered possible. It is therefore a must to have a metaphysical assumption of such a thing in itself in the name of the physical concordance and coexistence of humankind with the cosmos, because it will shift into an indispensable premise that makes it possible for humans to bestow kinds of order to the cosmos or nature.[37]

As for the effect of emotional root, it is as subtle and desirable as it is. I suppose that it can be perceived in three ways at least with regard to its leading functions. First, it encourages humans to treat things with emotion (*yi qing dai wu*). By so dong, it may enable them to extend their affection for family members to neighbors, and further up to all peoples and all things alike in a way of the Confucian notion of "universal love for all" (*fan ai zhong*). Secondly, it advices humans to nourish morality with emotion (*yi qing yu de*). In this case, emotion itself is humanized, enculturated, and duly moderated by moral codes or social norms. Eventually, it helps them become moral or cultural beings in a teleological sense. Thirdly, it leads humans to contemplate the beautiful with emotion (*yi qing shen mei*). At this stage, it elicits them to make the most of their sense of beauty as is booming the aesthetic experience pleasant to the ear

---

[36] Li Zehou, *Shiyong lixing yu legan wenhua* [Pragmatic Reason and a Culture of Optimism], p. 45.

[37] Ibid., pp. 53–54.

and the eye (*yue er yue mu*), guides them to go beyond this level and move up to the aesthetic feeling pleasant to mind and mood (*yue xin yue yi*), and enlightens them to the aesthetic exaltation of intellectual intuition and spiritual freedom (*yue zhi yue shen*).

Coincidently, Li orients the emotional root toward his practical aesthetics as the first philosophy. Just as he does with the appropriate measure, he bestows such aesthetics with a primary credit so as to resolve the critical issues related to the cultural-psychological formation of modern humans. In his belief, such aesthetics has more to do with anthropological ontology in one sense, and with psychology a priori in the other, thus helping embrace human fulfillment as the final *telos*.

Then, how is it possible to attain the *telos*? According to Li's alternative, it is to illuminate the true through the beautiful with the help of the appropriate measure, and meanwhile to accumulate the good through the beautiful with the help of emotional root. At this point, what is to do in the first case is related to the hypothesis of the thing in itself as a logical premise for humans to obtain more knowledge of the cosmos; what is to do in the second case is related to the assumption of the thing in itself as a sufficient condition for humans to choose to emotion and faith.[38] The thing in itself is in its new form of human coexistence with the cosmos that resembles the Chinese conception of heaven-human oneness. As reconfirmed in his analysis, the two modes of action here are relevant to the cultivation of sound emotions that will help foster both the genuine growth of human soul and the cultural development of human nature. They are all apt to facilitate and lift human fulfillment by harmonizing such four parts as the individual, the personal, the natural, and the social into an organic whole. There is hardly any other alternative as effective and reliable as this one in question. It is often evinced in history that human enculturation or character building cannot be carried forth merely by means of outward imperatives, religious regulations, or revolutionary isms. For human, individuals differ from one to another. Say, some of them may be prone to fall into the victims of decadent tramps without even minimum morality when the ethical demands happen to have collapsed or thrown away.[39] An offhanded example can be found in most of "the red guards" during the Cultural Revolution in China.

[38] Li Zehou, *Shiyong lixing yu legan wenhua* [Pragmatic Reason and a Culture of Optimism], p. 111.

[39] Li Zehou, *Lishi benti lun* [Historical Ontology], p. 123.

Quite naturally, I assume that Li's approach to practical aesthetics as the first philosophy results in his recommendation of aesthetic metaphysics, an aesthetic metaphysics that is schemed to enhance inward sublimation through aesthetic wisdom. This sublimation can be thought of as the outcome of higher spiritual or moral cultivation. It is alleged not only to help humans become what they are in empirical time-space by exercising other-worldly values in this-worldly life, but also to help them upgrade human capacity so as to face this-worldly cares and fears with free intuition and contemplative serenity. Accordingly, the aesthetic wisdom can be granted as the substratum of such intuition, serenity, and sensibility altogether.

In order to justify the intrinsic logic in this regard, Li reconsiders the possibility of human becoming with particular reference to human nature and human capacity in terms of his anthropologico-historical ontology. He therefore asserts that human nature is the interwoven synthesis of divine nature and animal nature owing to the fact that humans rely upon certain physical needs to preserve their corporeal existence, and meanwhile, they apply their acquired ability to manipulating such needs and guiding them to noble purposes. What underlines human nature is human capacity. This capacity is mainly referred to the moral psychology that distinguishes human race from other animal species. More specifically, it is supposed to comprise three key elements, namely, "the solidification of reason" in terms of human moral psychology and will power (free will), "the internalization of reason" (*lixing neihua*) in view of human cognitive faculty for logic, mathematics, and dialectic concepts, and "the melting of reason" (*lixing ronghua*) in accordance with the dynamic condition of aesthetic sedimentation (*shenmei jidian*) as is characterized with aesthetic competence.[40]

More specifically, the psychological ground of the solidification of reason might be an auxiliary for establishing a special channel between the cognition-thinking area and its emotion-will counterpart in the central nervous system (CNS) evolved in the long process of practice (by human race as a whole) and education (received by individual beings). Li identifies this process with "the cultural-psychological formation" (*wenhua xinli jiegou*) or "the sedimentational form of human capacity" (*renxing*

---

[40] Li Zehou, "Of Human Nature and Aesthetic Metaphysics," in Wang Keping (ed.), *Diversity and Universality in Aesthetics*, in *IAA International Yearbook of Aesthetics*, Vol. 14, 2010, pp. 4–5.

nengli de jidian xingshi). Therein, the internalization of reason and the melting of reason resemble each other to certain extent. "The long process of practice" parallels with that of history. They are interwoven in that human practice involves historical progression originated from the using-making tools whereas human history goes along with human evolution through human practice. As regards human capacity and human nature of each individual, they are interconnected in one's own cognitive, moral, and aesthetic competence as a result of practical and historical interaction. In most cases, human individuals tend to become what they are due to different kinds of innate gifts, upbringing habituations, educational performances, and so forth.

Particularly on this account, Li moves on to promote his aesthetic metaphysics in which he pushes forwards the Kantian idea of "purposiveness without purpose" that targets at the wholeness of humanity and involves "illuminating the true through the beautiful," "accumulating the good through the beautiful, and "making life worth living through the beautiful" (*yi mei li ming*). Nevertheless, Li differentiates his thinking from the Kantian in that he develops his aesthetic metaphysics for the most possible attainment of human fulfillment in a complete sense (*renxing wanquan shixian*) by means of integrating the rational with the emotional via universal love. He does so from the viewpoint of historical ontology with reference to natural law and pragmatic reason, whereas Kant goes ahead from aesthetic judgment to teleological judgment according to which he advocates his position of the highest good (i.e., the maximal possible human happiness as the product of human virtue that is seen as the ultimate end of nature) from the perspective of theo-ethics with reference to moral law and speculative reason. In contrast, Li is more concerned about the becoming of man as a whole being in view of the synthesis of the rational and the emotional dichotomy. Kant is more concerned about the cultivation of man as a moral being in view of his practical reason interacting with his theo-ethical awareness of the highest good and the categorical imperative.

Moreover, Li's theory of practical aesthetics retains its stress on the generative potency of emotional root to balance the dominance of rational power in general and the excess of instrumental rationality in particular. In this case, emotional root is working with humane love that has *eros* and *agape* intertwined in a complicate and interactive manner. Since any conceptual vision of the other world is absent in Confucianism, the necessity of aesthetic metaphysics is proposed to address the sociocultural ills today, the ills that exert much negative influence upon human mentality and human living at the same time. According to this aesthetic metaphysics, aesthetic engagement is meant to go beyond mere pleasures and animal desires, and strives for "detachment and emancipation" (*chaoyue*) in a spiritual scope. "It is intended to pursue a super-biological state as a higher realm of life. However, it is not a pure spiritual scope because man cannot abandon the physical body, just like what ascetic monks did in the Dark Ages. On the contrary, man can only look for any detachment and emancipation within the physical body itself. This could be felt in the mysterious experience of heaven-human oneness as an outcome of the correspondence between the body–mind cultivation and nature-cosmos rhythm in the "naturalization of the human."[41]

In actuality, the emotional root implies a kind of "cherishment" or inclination to cherish humans, changes, events, occasions, and incidents in time, only to usher them into the realm of *Dasein*. Under such circumstances, "If one wants to grasp the infinity and reality in his limited span of life equated to his incidental and finite physical existence, 'cherishing' becomes a necessary and sufficient condition. Instead of seeking any homogenized mind, reason or vital energy (*qi*), 'emotional root' only admits all occasional things and events in this short span of life alone, because man as man 'cherishes' the short and contingent life, events and things encountered. Every individual owns a poetic sense of existence that enables him to expperience the eternity of temporality in the 'emotional root' of 'cherishing' in spite of his being a passing traveler 'in time.'"[42] Granted, a momentary cherishing could repeat itself so often as though it were escorted by an eternal return. This peculiar experience and perception make a hell of difference to human living and becoming.

Further more, man is self-awakening in his own way. He accepts his accidental and temporal existence, and struggles to survive without blaming God or others. He tries to learn from the bottom and then moves up to the top. This statement metaphorically means to seek spiritual freedom through personal cultivation.... Therefore, the ideas about "what is man?" and "man as the end" will eventually realized in the human creation of the fully fledged "aesthetic double helix," in the emotional root of temporality and in the pursuit of aesthetic metaphysics.[43]

[41] Ibid., p. 8.
[42] Ibid., pp. 11–12.
[43] Ibid., p. 13.

As it seems to me after all, Li's aesthetic thinking is transcultural or intercultural in principle. It integrates Chinese tradition with its Western counterpart while deviating from both of them as a result of transformational creation. His conception of aesthetic metaphysics finds its ontological basis in the hypothesis of the "coexistence of humankind with the cosmos" that bears the hidden idea of heaven-human oneness. Such coexistence involves the process of both human becoming and human fulfillment by virtue of external and internal constitution. The external constitution is largely determined by the appropriate measure and the technico-social substratum stemmed from the practical substance and embodied in the dynamic interaction between the two main domains of human activities known as the humanization of nature and the naturalization of humanity. Then, the internal constitution is essentially shrouded in the cultural-psychological formation and reflected in the complementary exercise of either "illuminating the true through the beautiful" or "accumulating the good through the beautiful." The former is expected to obtain a balanced development of humanity in concord with the entire cosmos, and the latter to facilitate the inward sublimation via aesthetic wisdom grounded on the emotional root. All this is schemed to resist the rampant excess of both anthropocentrism and instrumental rationality.

Well, it is noteworthy that Li's theory of aesthetic metaphysics appears rather ambitious with its aim to reduce the cultural-psychological problems for the sake of human fulfillment via inward sublimation. It provokes either skeptical or critical rethinking. That is, it strikes some as an aesthetic utopia for its being unable to remove the problems in all, whereas it occurs to others as a practical alternative for its being helpful to subdue the issues one way or another. In any case, it is there to be cross-questioned and testified in the time to come.

9.4 Li's Sui Generis World-Picture

A panoramic view of Li's writings proves the fact that his philosophizing runs through the ideas of Kant, Hegel, Marx, Dewey, Piaget, Freud, Nietzsche, Max Weber, M. Heidegger, F. Hayek, J. Rawls, Chinese Confucianism, Daoism, Zen Buddhism, and postmodernism, among many others. He rethinks and selects the relevant ones to build up his structure of thought from the angle of pragmatic reason. He does so by means of both critical reflection and transformational creation in light of transcultural investigations and reconstructive motives.

As noted in his autobiography in 2003,[44] he lists some of his leading ideas as he agrees with G. Delouse on the point that philosophy is the fabrication of concepts to ponder over the world. The concepts Li has fabricated on the incomplete list given by himself are up to 14 in number among which we see "humanization of nature" (*ziran de renhua*), "sedimentation" (*jidian*), "cultural-psychological formation" (*wenhua xinli jiegou*), "naturalization of the human" (*ren de ziranhua*), "pragmatic reason" (*shiyong licing*), "joy-conscious culture" (*legan wenhua*), "emotional root" (*qing benti*), and "appropriate measure as the first category" (*du zuowei diyi fanchou*), and so on. We may hereby extend the list by adding such key concepts as "subjectality" (*zhutixing*), "techno-social substratum" (*gongju benti*), "psychological substratum" (*xinli benti*), "aesthetic metaphysics" (*shenmei xingershangxue*), and "historical ontology" (*lishi bentilun*) so as to compose a sketch of his philosophy concerning human living and human becoming. It is by this sketch that Li tries to sum up the fruit of his most evocative thoughts. Just as he declares, he intends to "provide a philosophical perspective when probing into the status quo of the world and China altogether," and hopes that such a large and populated China with a long history will find her own modernity during the process of "transformational creation in culture."[45]

It seems to me that Li's philosophical sketch highlights his sui generis world-picture in outline. He portrays it by virtue of conceptual guidelines instead of articulate details. This accords with his preference of the "grand narration" of core arguments instead of "trivial professionalization" (*suoxi de zhuanyehua*)[46] that relies upon elaborate and minute proofs. Incidentally, Nietzsche once gave a warning about excessive professionalization because of its harmful consequence that was most liable to take a special kind of knowledge as the end rather than the means. Li shares sympathy with Nietzsche at this point, for both of them are individual thinkers instead of presumptuous specialists in a narrow area. In actuality, Li himself attempts to stimulate his reader to think and rethink critically what he says and writes. It is for this reason that he works as a midwife

---

[44] Li Zehou, "Ke xuwu yi ze you" [An autobiography of Li Zehou], in *Shiyong lixing yu legan wenhua* [Pragmatic Reason and a Culture of Optimism], p. 371.

[45] Ibid., p. 371.

[46] Ibid., p. 357.

of thought rather than a transmitter of information, for he avows that any information of whatever kinds can be easily accessible via computer database nowadays. Actually since 1980s he has been both an intellectual tutor and an inspiring source to several generations in China who happen to be interested in either aesthetics or philosophy, thus serving to emancipate them from the shackles of rigid ideology and inert thinking.

Above all, Li devotes all his energy and time to look for a possible remedy to the issues derived from the social reality across China and the world. As being aged, he often claims a sense of mission to work for humankind at large. His world-picture is somewhat allegorical to Albert Einstein's *weltbild* in my eyes As luck would have it, Li makes a particular reference to Einstein's statement as follows:

> Man tries to make for himself in the fashion that suits him best a simplified and intelligible world-picture; he then tries to some extent to substitute this cosmos of his for the world of experience, and thus to overcome it. This is what the painter, the poet, the speculative philosopher, and the natural scientist do, each in his own fashion. Each makes this cosmos and its construction the pivot of his emotional life, in order to find in this way the peace and security which he cannot find in the narrow whirlpool of personal experience.[47]

This is the *weltbild* that Einstein recommends in his address delivered at a symposium in honor of Max Plank's 60th birthday in 1918. Ostensibly, Li appreciates it so much that he first places the statement at the front page of his *Historical Ontology* and quotes it again to support his argumentation later amid the text.[48] In Einstein's opinion, such a world-picture denotes a positive motive in distinct contrast to the negative one that leads men to art and science as Schopenhauer advocates. It is designed to keep aloof from everyday life with its painful crudity and hopeless dreariness, and from the fetters of one's own ever shifting

---

[47] Albert Einstein, "Principles of Research," in Carl Seelig (ed.), *Ideas and Opinions* (trans. Sonja Barmann, New York: WINGS Books, 1954), p. 225. It is the address delivered at a celebration of Max Planck's 60th birthday (1918) before the Physical Society in Berlin, and first published in *Mein Weltbild*, Amsterdam: Querido Verlag, 1934. Max Planck (1858–1947) was for many years professor of theoretical physics at the University of Berlin. By fare the most outstanding of his contributions to physics is his quantum theory, which he advanced in 1900 and which has provided the basis for the whole development of modern atomic physics.

[48] Li Zehou, *Lishi benti lun* [*Historical Ontology*]. Also see Li Zehou, *Lishi benti lun & Jimao wu shuo* [Historical Ontology & Five Essays from 1999] (Beijing: Sanlian Bookshop, 2003, repr. 2006), front page, p. 111.

desires. It "may be compared with the townsman's irresistible longing to escape from his noisy, cramped surroundings into the silence of high mountains, where the eye ranges freely through the still, pure air and fondly traces out the restful contours apparently built for eternity."[49]

As observed in Einstein, his *weltbild* is somewhat paradigmatic as it is offered to advice the physicist that "he must content himself with describing the most simple events which can be brought within the domain of our experience; all events of a more complex order are beyond the power of the human intellect to reconstruct with the subtle accuracy and logical perfection which the theoretical physicist demands. Supreme purity, clarity, and certainty at the cost of completeness."[50]

On the account of the key characteristics of Einstein's *weltbild*, Li seems to pursue his own goal. What he does is to draw out a similar kind of *weltbild* so as to suit humankind at best in one sense and sets up "the pivot of his emotional life" in the other sense. He hereby breaks through the "narrow whirlpool of personal experience" about the picture of China proper and embraces the mission to offer his "simplified and intelligible world-picture" symbolic of his cosmopolitan mentality as a consequence of his stay in the USA for more than two decades. From his seventies onward, he repeatedly proclaims himself to work for humankind in its entirety. His writing style and thoughtway in his output all justify "the simplified and intelligible" aspects of the *weltbild* in question.

The world-picture he provides features his lifelong preoccupation with the possibility of human becoming in terms of the natural law. But the natural law is of a new type due to its pragmatic orientation. Traditionally, the natural law of morality is identified mainly with human nature and free will. But to Li's mind the natural law itself is of a cultural character. That is, he associates human nature with human culture, but considers human nature to be no product of personal free choice alone. Instead, he treats the cultivation of human nature as the consequence of developing human capacity through human culture in the dynamic process of human practice and historical progression. This being the case, it must be taken into due consideration the function and evolution of

---

[49] Albert Einstein, "Principles of Research," *Ideas and Opinions*, p. 225.
[50] Ibid.

human brain in the context of cultural pluralism. For human race as a whole has not been living on an island, but in a global village ever since the advent of transcultural interaction in history. This fact will surely affect the growth of human brain as is connected with human capacity and human nature altogether. As noticed in the development of brain science at the present-day stage, the discovery of the double-helix phenomenon provides an impressive justification in this regard. We hope that more discoveries in this field are to be made in the time to come, and by then we will be able to gain some insights into the unknown mystery in question. I really expect so even though it is no easy matter at all.

CHAPTER 10

A Manifold Expectation of Poetry

The development of modern education in China today is put into the first priority because it is more crucial and important than any other enterprises. But it encounters one of the biggest challenges that concerns with the nourishment of cultural literacy and constitution on the part of the students as a whole. In order to deal with this mater, a particular reference is made to a seemingly working remedy chiefly based on the Western conception of general education. No one would have objection to borrowing any positive ideas or possible alternatives from whatever sources and experiences available. Yet, if we embrace the pragmatic view that every road leads to Rome, we are not supposed to take an unnecessary detour when we can get something just offhandedly beside us. This being the case, it is desirable for us to look into the indigenous tradition of Confucianism. By so doing, we need to rediscover Confucius' philosophy of education that largely consists in the learning and praxis of the six arts and the six classics. The six arts involve rites, music, archery chariot-driving, reading, and arithmetic, which are required as six genres of *teche* for basic schooling; and the six classics include *The Book of Poetry*, *The Book of History*, *The Book of Rites*, *The Book of Music*, *The Book of Changes*, and *The Spring and Autumn Annals*, which are offered as six compulsory subjects for higher learning. In this section, I will reconsider Confucius' expectation of poetry *sui generis* in terms of its potential outcomes associated with cultural literacy and constitution as part of character building.

As is observed in *The Analects* (*Lun yü*), Confucius (551–479 B.C.) places equal emphasis on poetry, rites, and music in terms of personal cultivation (*xiu shen*). As is known from history, poetry used to be extremely popular in ancient China for its social, aesthetic, and moral import. Its popularity was, so to speak, largely due to the fact that it would serve as a threefold form of social, aesthetic, and moral discourse. It is therefore assumed that Confucius' curriculum for poetry education was generally grounded on the considerations of this trinity with regard to the principle of "gentle and kind" character building (*wen rou dun hou*).

10.1 Poetry as a Special Social Discourse

In ancient China, poetry (i.e., songs, lyrics, odes, epics, and hymns in general) was widely employed on such important occasions as feasting and sacrifices, and in many other realms of social interaction. It was then sung and performed to a musical accompaniment. Evidence can be found in the *Zuo zhuan* (*Zuo's Commentaries on the Spring and Autumn Annals*) to show that poetry was used by scholars in general as a primary medium for exchanging opinions, expressing values, in daily conversations or in diplomatic relationships. This was apart from its use in essay writing and cultural entertainments.

The diplomatic usage of poetry, for example, can be well illustrated by events recorded in the *Zuo zhuan*, which dates back to 526 B.C. when Confucius was about 25 years old. For instance, once the six ministers of the Zheng State gave a farewell banquet in the honor of Xuan Zi, an envoy from a neighboring state.[1] Xuan Zi asked his hosts to sing some songs of their own, hoping to determine their views, in general about their way of life and in particular their political attitudes toward neighboring states. They each took turns to sing songs that were collected in the *Shi jing* (*The Book of Poetry*). After each of the three delightful love songs titled "The Creeping Grass" (*Ye you man cao*), "Officer in the Lambs Fleece" (*Gao qiu*), and "Lift up Your Robe" (*Qian shang*), Xuan Zi made comments to show his understanding and appreciation.

---

[1] *Zuo zhuan*, [Zuo's Commentaries on the Spring and Autumn Annals], Vol. 13, in *Sishu wujing* [The Four Books and Five Classics] (Tianjin: Guji Bookshop, 1990), Vol. 3, p. 451.

The singing continued throughout the feast. One guest sang "Wind and Rain" (*Feng yu*) which describes the joy of a lonely wife on seeing her husband return home in dreadful weather. As soon as it was over, another went on to sing "Lady Jiang" (*You nü tong che*) which lauds the beauty of a newlywed woman. Right afterward, another picked up the tone and sang "Sing Together" (*Tuo xi*) which describes a songstress asking her companions to sing and dance together like drifting leaves after harvest. The atmosphere was so engaging that Xuan Zi, as a guest of the state, recognized their good and friendly intentions as suggested by the songs performed. In addition to expressing his delight and gratitude with positive remarks on the choice of the songs suitable to the diplomatic occasion, Xuan Zi presented them all with horses as a sign of friendship. He also sang "King Wen's Sacrificial Hymn" (*Wo jiang*) as a subtle and grateful reply to his hosts:

> I offer a sacrifice
> Of ram and bull so nice
> May Heaven bless my state!
> I observe King Wen's statues great;
> I'll pacify the land....

As a natural consequence of this appropriate form of singing and behavior, a harmonious ambiance was gradually built up and a mutual understanding obtained. Their mutual appreciation and friendship deepened, and a consensus was reached in relation to forging and maintaining peace. These activities recorded in the *Zuo zhuan* justify the following observation made by Chen Jingpan (Joseph C. P. Chen): "It was of supreme importance that those songs should be suitable to the situations. They should be able to express the desires of those who chose them, and at the same time they should not hurt the feelings of others. Very often owing to inability to select songs, or to select the right and appropriate ones, serious national disgrace and calamity resulted."[2] It is noteworthy here that poetry as a social discourse *sui generis* was encouraged in various ways, either diplomatic or conversational, writing or singing, public or private, friendly or formal. In spite of this, it was most often recommended as a way of inferring ideas or principles from the songs or lyrics concerned and then applying them to specific situations.

---

[2] Chen Jingpan, *Confucius as a Teacher* (Beijing, 1990), p. 329.

Those ideas, often idiosyncratically expressed, could be a long way from the original intentions of the composers. However, if the lyrics could be suggestively applied to certain forms of social interaction, they would be cited or chanted for the occasions involved. In a number of cases, Confucius himself explained poetry in such an inferential way. For example, Zi Xia once asked about the meaning of these lines from the poem "Duchess Zhuang Jiang" (*Shuo ren*):

> Ah! dark on white her speaking eyes,
> Her cheeks with smiles and dimples glow
> Like flowers painted on a plain background.

Confucius answered, "It is only after the white background is prepared that any painting is possible." "In that case," replied Zi Xia, "can we say that the rites can only base themselves on humanity?" "That is it," joyfully replied Confucius, "since you have thrown some new light on this verse, now I can begin to discuss *The Book of Poetry* with you."[3] Confucius also made the same remark to encourage Zi Gong once he found his student able to "tell what may happen in the future when he is told about the past" by virtue of reading poetry between the lines. It is undeniable that the Confucian approach to interpreting poetry seems far-fetched at first sight. Yet, if the Confucian concept of beauty is identified with its essence, consisting of inborn grace and simplicity without artificial adornment, the extended version above could be naturally understood in terms of his intrinsic logic. To be precise, the "plain background" in the poem is symbolic of the lady's inward charm that is essential to her outward beauty. Likewise, the "white background" in a material sense is basic to any painting upon it, and thus analogous to the fact that one's sense of humanity or human-heartedness cultivated from within is fundamental to any rites performed from without. The internal aspect is accentuated rather than the external aspect, notwithstanding the fact that Confucius persistently advocates the balanced development of both aspects in an ideal personality.

---

[3] Confucius, *The Confucian Analects*, in *The Four Books* (trans. James Legge, Changsha: Hunan Press, 1992), 3:8, p. 81; also see Confucius, *The Analects* (trans. D. C. Lau, London: Penguin Books, 1979), III:8, p. 68; All the English citations in this discussion are slightly modified according to the contexts involved.

Highly conscious of the values of poetry as a form of social discourse, Confucius resolutely advises his immediate disciples to study *The Book of Poetry* (*Shi jing*) with the ultimate aim, on the one hand, of enabling them to appropriate the songs for the right occasions or social interactions, and on the other, of refining their taste and art of speech. These are associated with two further aims: One lies in the recommended way of using poetry by inferring certain ideas, suggested or projected, from the verses and then applying them in certain verbal interactions or on diplomatic occasions; the other is related to Confucius' educational curriculum. Since most of his students were trained to be statesmen, their knowledge of poetry and its proper use was important and indispensable qualifications at that time. His advice was also rigidly applied to his son, Kong Li, who once recalled for a guest one of his personal encounters with his father: "One day my father (Confucius) was standing in the courtyard and I quickened my steps to pass through. He stopped me and asked, 'Have you studied *The Book of Poetry*?' I answered, 'Not yet.' He then said, 'You will not know how to speak properly unless you study it.' After that I began to study the book."[4] But this is only the first step if compared to the full use of poetry in diverse and appropriate ways advocated. Just as Confucius proclaims, "If a man is able to recite the three hundred pieces of *The Book of Poetry*, but fails when given governmental responsibilities; and if he fails to act according to circumstances and to deal with affairs independently when sent on diplomatic missions, what is the use of so much learning?"[5] This reveals the Confucian concept that what is acquired should be put into practice for the good of individual development and the interests of the community.

10.2 Poetry as a Unique Aesthetic Discourse

The Book of Poetry (*Shi jing*) available today is alleged to have been selectively edited by Confucius himself on the basis of a wide range of information dating from remote antiquity. This anthology comprises of several genres as follows: *guo feng* (songs or lyrics), *xiao ya* (odes), *da ya* (epics), and *song* (hymns). Here, *The Book of Poetry* is subdivided into four major sections: the "Chapter of Songs," which reflects mainly the everyday lives

---

[4] Confucius, *The Confucian Analects* (trans. James Legge), 16:13, p. 223; also see Confucius, *The Analects* (trans. D. C. Lau), XVI:13, p. 141.

[5] Ibid., 13:5, p. 179; also see Confucius, *The Analects* (trans. D. C. Lau), XIII:5, p. 119.

of people in general; the "Chapter of Odes," reflecting the lives of the nobility; the "Chapter of Epics," recording historical deeds and reflecting the life of the rulers; and finally, the "Chapter of Hymns," intended to glorify the ancestors of the rulers and inspire their descendants to worship them as gods (i.e., political models). In the time before Confucius, poems were considered and used as historical, political, and religious records and not merely as works of art. In Confucius' era, poetry straddled the two provinces of intellectual learning and aesthetic education. That is to say, it began to be looked upon not merely as a source of knowledge related to politics, ethics, and history, but as a form of art directed toward the cultivation of the mind and the person as a whole.

Because of its aesthetic values, poetry plays an indispensable part in the personal cultivation required to facilitate the becoming of a gentleman or superior man (*jun zi*), one of the highest ideals of individual life. This notion is emphasized by Confucius in his remark: "Personal cultivation [of a gentleman] is inspired by poetry, made firm by rites, and completed by music."[6] For poetry is generally believed to be expressive of feelings and affections through its descriptions of both inner and outer experiences. It can be read, recited, and appreciated so that one may get to the bottom of the moral message implied in the work concerned. The reader is prone to be deeply impressed and moved by such human values as a love for the good, a hatred of the evil, and sympathy for the miserable, etc. That is to say, poetry *par excellence* may serve as a potent guide, stimulating and helping the reader in his or her moral development through aesthetic experience, setting his will on the right path and, above all, determining his personal cultivation or character formation.

Considering the aesthetic and artistic functions of poetry, Confucius so sincerely reminds his disciples:

> Why don't you study The Book of Poetry? Poetry can serve to inspire (xing), to reflect (guan), to communicate (qun) and to admonish (yuan). On one hand, the teachings presented in The Book of Poetry can help serve one's parents well; on the other hand, the knowledge and methods provided in it can help serve one's lord well. Moreover, one can learn a lot of names of birds, beasts, plants and trees.[7]

---

[6] Confucius, *The Confucian Analects* (trans. James Legge), 8:8, p. 129; also see Confucius, *The Analects* (trans. D. C. Lau), VIII:8, p. 93.

[7] Ibid., 17:9, p. 231; also see Confucius, *The Analects* (trans. D. C. Lau), XVII:9, p. 145.

The Confucian view of poetry is largely derived from this comment. It is apparently intended to teach the disciples how to study poetry as a form of aesthetic discourse; but in praxis it turns out to be an overall guideline or relatively systematic theory oriented to poetic composition in particular and literary creation in general. Li Zhi (1527–1602), for example, asserts that legends can also perform the functions of *xing, guan, qun,* and *yuan*.[8]

As is observed, the entire argument aforementioned reveals at least six functions of poetry as the key aspects of Confucius' program of art education. First and foremost, poetry is inspiring in that it can evoke and exalt sentiments, thoughts, and intentions through vividly suggestive and associative imagery, in addition to its faculty enriching the imagination. Secondly, poetry allows reflection on the human condition and way of life so that insightful judgments can be made through contemplation, in addition to enhancing the powers of observation. Thirdly, the communicative dimension of poetry can be used to smooth and harmonize human relations through two-way communication and remold ideas by virtue of the values expressed. Fourthly, the admonitory tendency in poetry can provoke regret, complaints, and critique of the social environment, in addition to helping one master the art of satire in relation to human problems. Fifthly, the moral dimension of poetry helps cultivate a sense of piety toward one's parents as a natural result of the moral teachings drawn from such poetry. Subsequently, the political dimension of poetry helps to develop a sense of mission, and the diplomatic tactics necessary to serve one's ruler, because of the cultural heritage and historical significance of *The Book of Poetry*, and the possibility of extrapolating from poetry to other situations or occasions and vice versa. Finally, the cognitive dimension of poetry helps identify the names or species of fauna and flora.

At this point, it is desirable to explain what is implied by these statements in relation to such paramount functions of poetry as *xing* (to inspire), *guan* (to reflect), *qun* (to communicate), and *yuan* (to admonish), the four major elements comprising an aesthetic discourse in Confucius' poetics.

---

[8] Peking University Philosophy Department (ed.), *Zhongguo meixueshi ziliao xuanbian* [Selected Materials of Chinese Aesthetic History] (Beijing: Zhonghua Book Company, 1981), Vol. 2, p. 130.

10.2.1 Poetic Xing

The Chinese notion of *xing* (to inspire) carries at least two meanings that can be broadly defined as follows: the ability of an education in poetry to "move and evoke the will and spirit"[9] for good (virtue), and a rhetorical technique for poetic composition that is often generalized as "a way of symbolizing through the imagery of things,"[10] or to draw an extended meaning from a relevant image (or analogy) via (poetic) association.

The former helps to purify the mind and lift the spirit, aiming at the cultivation of a gentleman through aesthetic experience. This experience usually features some sort of catharsis and results in exalted activities designed to attain the highest possible form of life. During this process, such factors as understanding, imagination, and contemplation all work together. This idea can be seen in the "Chapter of Hymns" (*song*) which serves to glorify the ancestors of the sage-rulers and inspire their offspring to worship them as divine models. In "King Cheng's Inaugural Address" (*Lie wen*), written to commemorate Cheng's accession to the throne in 1109 B.C., we read:

> O princes bright and brave
> Favored by former kings!
> The boundless blessings we have
> Will pass to our offspring.
> Do not sin against your state
> And you will be honored as before.
> Think of your service great
> You may enlarge still more.
> Try to employ wise men,
> Your influence will spread from land to land....

The singer or reader would be inspired, if vicariously, to model himself on the former kings in terms of individual devotion to the service of the state, and the development of personal virtue. Kong Anguo's

---

[9] "Gan fa zhi yi." Cf. Zhu Xi, *Lun yü ji zhu* [The Confucian Analects Annotated], in *Si shu wu jing* [The Four Books and Five Classics] (Tianjin: Guji Bookshop, 1990), Vol. 1, p. 74.

[10] "Tuo shi yu wu." Cf. Hu Jingzhi (ed.), *Zhongguo gudian meixue congbian* [Selected Writings of Chinese Classic Aesthetics] (Beijing: Zhonghua Book Company, 1988), Vol. 1, p. 282.

concept of *xing* is "the employment of analogy and the practice of association,"¹¹ while for Zhu Xi it denotes to "first describing something else by evoking images in order to illustrate the actual theme."¹² As a procedure, *xing* involves depicting a particular image of a particular object in a poetic style. When such poetry is contemplated, the imagination is stirred and so is the understanding of contextual suggestiveness to purify the mind and sublimate the spirit by arousing feelings and emotions, by influencing the inner world for good, and by teaching the reader to refine his mind and conduct. This is analogous to the use of *xing* as a poetic device to describe a scene or thing that has sparked off ideas or sentiments in the poet. An example is provided by "The Large Rat" (*Shuo shu*), a song from the ancient State of Wei (modern Shanxi):

> Large rat, large rat,
> Eat no more millet we grow!
> Three years you have grown fat;
> No care for us you show.
> We'll leave you now, I swear,
> For a happier land,
> A happier land where
> We may have a free hand....

As often noted, this "large rat" is seen as a symbol for the corrupted official or wealthy landlords who have exploited the laborers or ordinary farmhands. The "happier land" is perceived as an allegory for an imaginary Utopia. Naturally, this leads to criticism of the exploiter and sympathy for the exploited. This poem is thus a subtle satire related to political criticism and moral teaching.

Another widely noted case could be "The Newlywed" (*Tao yao*), a song from south of the capital of the Zhou Dynasty:

> The peach tree beams so red;
> How brilliant are its flowers!
> The maiden's getting wed,
> Good for the nuptial bowers.

---

[11] "Yin pi lian lei." Cf. Peking University Philosophy Department (ed.), *Zhongguo meixueshi ziliao xuanbian* [Selected Materials of Chinese Aesthetic History], Vol. 2, p. 214.

[12] "Xian yan ta wu yi yin qi suo youg zhi ci ye." Cf. Hu Jingzhi (ed.), *Zhongguo gudian meixue congbian* [Selected Writings of Chinese Classic Aesthetics], Vol. 1, p. 281.

It was customary in the Zhou Dynasty for young people to marry in spring when the peach trees were in full bloom. There is no direct portrayal of the newlywed bride in this lyric, and the emphasis appears to fall on the vivid image of the peach tree, indicative of the golden time for the marriage of the young couple. The beauty of the bride is implicitly likened to that of the peach blossoms. The inspiration of poetry is assumed to "originate from the experience touched off by contemplating things,"[13] and "the source of the inspiring aspect of poetry lies in the description of birds, plants and trees."[14] In addition, "the fact that the central theme is brought into play by the descriptive context confirms the notion of the inspirational dimension (*xing*),"[15] These concepts are validated by the foregoing examples.

10.2.2 Poetic Guan

The Chinese term *guan* in one sense means to look at or contemplate, and in another to manifest or reflect. In a poetic context, according to Zheng Xuan, it is chiefly intended to "reflect or represent the rise and fall of social customs" during historical periods.[16] That is to say, in poetic creation, it involves the exploration and observation of the social environment and the human condition and is used to expose the moral climate and the mentality of the people as social beings. In the "Chapter of Songs," for example, the first and second sections (i.e., the *Zhou nan*, *Shao nan*) are mainly reflecting the family life of the ancient Chinese, and the seventh and twelfth sections (i.e., *Zheng feng* and *Chen feng*) are mostly love songs expressing the emotions of the people in general. The lives of the nobles and the rulers are reflected in the "Chapter of Odes" (*Xiao ya*) and the "Chapter of Epics" (*Da ya*).

In the ode "Revelry" (*Bin zhi chu yan*) we read:

---

[13] "Guan wu you gan yan, ze you xing." Cf. Hu Jingzhi (ed.), *Zhongguo gudian meixue congbian* [Selected Writings of Chinese Classic Aesthetics], Vol. 2, p. 326.

[14] "Niao shou cao mu nai fa xing zhi ben." Cf. Hu Jingzhi (ed.), *Zhongguo gudian meixue congbian* [Selected Writings of Chinese Classic Aesthetics], Vol. 2, p. 214.

[15] "Qi yiju jiu jing zhong xuanchu zhe, keyi xing ye." Cf. Note 4, p. 214.

[16] "Guan feng su zhi sheng shuai." Cf. Peking University Philosophy Department (ed.), *Zhongguo meixueshi ziliao xuanbian* [Selected Materials of Chinese Aesthetic History], Vol. 2, p. 214.

> The guests come with delight
> And take places left and right....
> They dance to music sweet
> Of flute and the drumbeat....
> When they' ve drunk their cups dry,
> They shout out, brawl and cry.
> They put plates upside down;
> They dance like funny columns.
> When they have drunk wine strong,
> They know not right from wrong.
> With their caps on one side,
> They dance and slip and slide....

This ode features a satirical touch, thus picturing sensationally the licentiousness of the time of King You in the late Zhou Dynasty, which was then at the point of collapse. The depiction is vivid and detailed, the message hidden and suggestive, ostensibly directed against drunkenness, but in essence against corruption.

The "Chapter of Epics" chiefly reflects historical deeds and the life of the rulers in connection with the rise and fall of the Zhou Dynasty, from "The Three Kings of Zhou" to "King You's Time." The former praises the first rulers of the Zhou Dynasty for their great virtues and achievements, whereas the latter censures on King You of the late Zhou Dynasty for his vices and wrongdoings. The epics thus serve as a mirror of that historical period, from which instructive lessons can be drawn by scrutinized reading. This obviously corresponds to Zhu Xi's definition of the poetic *guan* as "the investigation and demonstration of gains and losses" in history.[17]

Nevertheless, the Chinese concept of *guan* cannot be fully interpreted without referring to its aesthetic aspect. It surely involves a taste judgment or aesthetic contemplation when used in poetry or any other forms of art. Conventionally, *guan* is usually applied to evaluating and appreciating artworks, landscapes, and personalities, etc., from an aesthetic as well as a moral perspective. The idea that "poetry can serve to reflect" (*guan*) is supposed to denote that the poet himself would contemplate and judge his subject matter, both aesthetically and critically, during the

---

[17] "Kao jian de shi." Cf. Zhu Xi, *Lun yü ji zhu* [The Confucian Analects Annotated], in *Si shu wu jing* [The Four Books and Five Classics], Vol. 1, p. 74.

process of the poetic reflection. This is also true for the reader when he examines the experience or event presented in poetry so long as he has adequate awareness and sensibility. In this sense, the idea that "poetry can serve to reflect" can be also understood to mean that poetry is a form of art to be aesthetically contemplated and relished. Its function is thus closely associated with art education since it assists the reader to satisfy his aesthetic needs, improve his taste, and mold his temperament all at the same time.

10.2.3 Poetic Qun

The Chinese word *qun* means social grouping or gathering, but the poetic *qun* has broader connotations. It implies, according to Kong Anguo, "the exercise of two-way communication during social interactions."[18] For Zhu Xi, it means "maintaining harmony and unity without dispersion."[19] In plain language, this aspect of poetry helps facilitate a two-way communication process on a range of social occasions (i.e., at feasts and diplomatic meetings, etc.), to promote a friendly atmosphere, and eventually to harmonize human relations in all. This function can be seen in the examples mentioned above.

As has been often detected, poetic communication (*qun*) thus performs a similar role to music in the Confucian mind. It can create an engagingly harmonious climate, arousing human emotions in an attempt to awaken mutual understanding, and then bring concord to human relations. Like music, this kind of *qun* is inseparably linked to the concept of "humanity" (*ren*), since it denies any tendency to form cliques in order to suppress or win the upper hand over other people. Rather, it is intended to trigger and foster a sense of humanity or benevolence on the part of individuals, which, in turn, leads people to come together and create a peaceful social environment. In addition, the notion of *qun* indicates a sense of responsibility, mission, commitment, and above all cooperation with one's fellow men. These concepts have been rewarding, since in general the Chinese people take pleasure from and delight in social harmony, affinity, and cooperation. This demonstrates the

---

[18] "Qun ju xiang qie cuo." Cf. Peking University Philosophy Department (ed.), *Zhongguo meixueshi ziliao xuanbian* [Selected Materials of Chinese Aesthetic History], Vol. 2, p. 214.

[19] "He er bu liu." Cf. Zhu Xi, *Lun yü ji zhu* [The Confucian Analects Annotated], in *Si shu wu jing* [The Four Books and Five Classics], Vol. 1, p. 74.

imperceptible influence of poetry or poetic experience on people's thinking, character, and relationships with others.

10.2.4 Poetic Yuan

According to Kong Anguo, the Chinese concept *yuan* signifies a "critique of bad politics and inadequate government."[20] This is obviously a one-sided interpretation. The truth of the matter is that the poetic *yuan* can be classified into two broad categories known as sociopolitical and psycho-sentimental. The former often included references to social problems that violated the fundamental principle of humanity (*ren*). These social problems could be subdivided into moral weaknesses, such as evil-doings of an individual, and injustice in community, political scandals, in-fighting or corruption among the ruling class, harsh suppression of the populace, the failures of the government related to tight control, and serious exploitation of the ordinary citizens. The frustration that is involved in trying to promote a humanitarian government worthy of a gentlemanly status also comes into this category. The poetic *yuan* is self-evident, for instance, in the criticisms of the luxurious life of the nobility, the unqualified King You, the prevailing tyranny and misery in the reign of King Li, and of the Ji Family's violation of rites by getting eight rows of dancers to perform in their private courtyard.

The psycho-sentimental category refers to the exposure of emotions in romantic and other types of relationships. These emotions involve a wide variety of moods, including frustration, anxiety, depression, discordance, sorrow, and despair. They can be easily discerned in the sentimental interactions between men and women recorded in "Chapter of Songs." However, the critical aspect of poetry, according to Confucius, must be based on the principle of humanity or human-heartedness, and work for the good of society and the people. This demands authenticity and sincerity of expression on the one hand, and purity and moral perfection on the other. Otherwise, poetry would become a mere verbal exercise, only discouraging the exaltation of the human spirit and hence losing its value for aesthetic education. This explicates the reason why Confucius detests pretentiousness in both word and deed. He thus proclaims that those who speak with

---

[20] "Yuan ci shang zheng." Cf. Peking University Philosophy Department (ed.), *Zhongguo meixueshi ziliao xuanbian* [Selected Materials of Chinese Aesthetic History], Vol. 2, p. 214.

honeyed words and pretend to be kind cannot be humane or benevolent, nor can those who try to subvert the state with clever terms.

The respective functions and interrelationships between the poetic *xing*, *guan*, *qun*, and *yuan*, which make up the four basic components of aesthetic discourse, are described by Wang Fuzhi in his comments on poetry: "What is inspiring (*xing*) can be reflected (*guan*), thus making *xing* more profound; what is reflected (*guan*) can be inspiring (*xing*), thus making *guan* more manifest; what is communicated (*qun*) leads to admonition (*yuan*), thus making *yuan* more unforgettable; what is admonished (*yuan*) leads to communication (*qun*), thus making *qun* more sincere and authentic.... There arises a natural flow of emotions and feelings. The poet expresses his thought or message with consistency whereas the reader undergoes an individual experience of diversity due to his own emotions or mood."[21] The four qualities of poetry must therefore be approached and exercised as an interrelated whole. However, the poetic *xing* appears to be the most essential of all because it is integral to art and artistic effect. To be sure, if poetry is not appealing enough to inspire or move the reader emotionally, it cannot evoke a reaction nor an aesthetic response, and quite naturally the other functions also go off the track. Poetic *xing* and *yuan* tend more toward inspiring and expressing the emotions and thoughts of individuals, while poetic *guan* and *qun* are used to obtain social and moral effects through an aesthetic contemplation that imperceptibly influences and cultivates the thinking and character of individuals. All these functions may lead, as they were expected to do, to the development of one's ability to serve one's father (i.e., parents) and lord (i.e., sovereign) in both a moral and a social sense. This notion reveals the Confucian ideal of "efficient government and harmonious human relations" (*zheng tong ren he*).

10.3 Poetry as a Particular Moral Discourse

Confucius is renowned for his preoccupation with the development of the ideal gentleman (*jun zi*). The personality of such a gentleman requires maintaining a balance between two qualities termed *wen* and *zhi*. "One would seem uncouth with more *zhi* than *wen*, and seem superficial with more *wen* than *zhi*. Only then these two qualities are well-balanced can

---

[21] Peking University Philosophy Department (ed.), *Zhongguo meixueshi ziliao xuanbian* [Selected Materials of Chinese Aesthetic History], Vol. 2, pp. 292–293.

one become a gentleman." (*Lun yü*, 6:18) The Chinese notion *wen* symbolizes outward cultivation characterized by refinement, scholarship, proper conduct, and good manners while *zhi* inward cultivation characterized by simplicity, sincerity, honesty, and virtuousness. The former is assumed to be primarily achieved through extensive study of classics and the frequent practice of rites, while the latter involves an ethical education and sincere actions based on the principle of humanity. During the process of becoming a gentleman, *The Book of Poetry* plays a cardinal role. This is precisely because poetry also serves as a special form of moral discourse in addition to its social and aesthetic role.

As has been mentioned previously, Confucius himself lays much stress on both the social and aesthetic effects of poetry, since it works in a diplomatic sense to bring people together, as well as imperceptibly influencing the ideas and the temperament of individuals. Yet he never fails to recognize the moral impact of poetry on the reader or user, and the ability of poetry to make imposed codes of conduct into internalized necessities. Eventually, this is conducive to the harmony between members of a community and the community itself, and to order and stability of society as a whole.

In the eyes of Confucius, poetry performs multiple services toward the achievement of the end. Poetry, as a historical record, helps one identify the rites of the Zhou Dynasty and extend one's knowledge; as social discourse it helps one refine his manners and improve his art of speech as well; as an aesthetic discourse it helped to cultivate the spirit and will through aesthetic experience; and above all, as a moral discourse it helps one cleanse his mind of depraved thoughts because "The theme of the 300 pieces in *The Book of Poetry* can be summed up in one phrase—having no depraved thoughts" (*si wu xie*).[22] This phrase is in fact quoted from the hymn "Horses" (*Jiong*) in *The Hymns of Lu* (*Lu song*) in the last section of *The Book of Poetry*. It is one of the lines of an ode praising Duke Xi of Lu (658–626 B.C.) for his admirable thoughtfulness, rightful judgment, and great foresight. It is used by Confucius to encapsulate the significance of *The Book of Poetry* as a whole. According to Fung Yu-lan, it serves as a principle "simply applied

---

[22] Confucius, *The Confucian Analects* (trans. James Legge), 2:2, p. 71; also see Confucius, *The Analects* (trans. D. C. Lau), II:2, p. 63.

to measuring the literary values by political standards."[23] As far as what can be discerned from the text concerned, the expression itself is seemingly employed to denote the pure and unadulterated tone, in an ethical sense, which runs through all the poems allegedly compiled by Confucius in the anthology. This implies that Confucius be inclined to use moral rather than political standards to measure literary or poetic value. If this were the case, Confucius would have preferred to link the poems to moral problems, even though the former originally had got little to do with the latter. For the same reason, poetry was then rendered to occupy a prime position in Confucius' curriculum of art education.

As a result, poetry as a moral discourse needs to remain in accord with the principle of moderation set by Confucius himself. That is, poetry should be "expressive of enjoyment without being licentious, and expressive of sadness without grieving."[24] According to Confucius, the lyric "Wooing and wedding" (*Guan ju*) is a perfect example. It depicts a love story which carefully avoids excessive expression. In the first stanza, it suggests a young man falling in love with a beautiful maiden in spring when turtledoves are cooing. In the second stanza, he woos her in summer as cress floats on the water, and in the subsequent stanza, he restlessly yearns for her day and night. As is described in the fourth stanza, both of them become engaged in the autumn when the cress is gathered, and eventually in the last stanza, they marry in winter when the cress is cooked. The representation of emotion is tactfully measured, and there is no opportunity to be swept away by vulgar desires and passions. The expression of the seemingly one-sided love extends only to this degree:

> His yearning grows so strong,
> He cannot fall asleep,
> But tosses all night long,
> So deep in love, so deep!

This intensity of pathos and anxiety expresses "sadness," but it is moderate rather than excessive as there is no sense of intense grief. The happiness of the wedding is likewise expressed with moderation:

---

[23] Fung Yu-lan, *Zhongguo zhexueshi xinbian* [New Edition of the History of Chinese Philosophy] (Beijing: Renmin Press, 1992), Vol. 1, p. 160.

[24] Confucius, *The Confucian Analects* (trans. James Legge), 3:20, p. 83; also see Confucius, *The Analects* (trans. D. C. Lau), III:20, p. 70.

Feast friends at left and right
On cress cooked so tender!
O bells and drums, delight
The bride so sweet and slender!

"Bells and drums" here indicate the performance of rites and music to celebrate the wedding ceremony. The poet thus creates a delightful ambiance and eulogizes the beauty of the bride. Nevertheless, the delight in this kind of "enjoyment," so inviting but well-measured, precludes any licentiousness of temptation. The poem "Wooing and Wedding" (*Guan ju*) does not simply serve as an encapsulation of the principle of poetry as a moral discourse, but also incorporates the philosophy of governing by the state and public education in relation to rites and music. One can perhaps understand at this point why the poem "Wooing and Wedding" is placed at the very beginning of *The Book of Poetry*.

It is noteworthy that Confucius stresses the principle of moderation with regard to the expression of emotions in poetry. He decries excessiveness while highly recommending moderation in all cases. This is because he appears highly conscious of the necessity to temper sentimental expression in both poetry and music. Otherwise, it would go to extremes, either encouraging licentious hedonism or provoking gross sentimentality. All this must be avoided in poetry due to its being harmful to human life and dignity in one sense, and in the other, detrimental to the normal and rational of a virtuous character. Actually, "it is as a result of this notion that the expression of emotions in Chinese art is reasonably controlled in most cases, and poetry rarely becomes simply an outlet of base and callous desires, or mysterious and fanatical impulses."[25] It is generally agreed that this concept originated from the application of the "Doctrine of the Mean" (*zhong yong zhi dao*) to the emotional expression in poetic composition. The "Mean" of his kind requires the combination of opposites (i.e., sensuous pleasure and moral requirements, instinctive drives and rational pursuits, emotional expression and moral restraint) to be represented in artworks in order to attain a balanced and harmonized development of the personality which is the ultimate objective of art education. Under such circumstances, the concept of the golden mean is emphasized in plain language as such: "To go

---

[25] Li Zehou and Liu Gangji (ed.), *Zhongguo meixueshi* [A History of Chinese Aesthetics] (Beijing: China Social Science Press, 1984), Vol. 1, p. 150.

beyond is as wrong as to fall short" (*guo you bu ji*).²⁶ In other words as it implies in practice, what is overdone is as bad as what is underdone. Likewise, Zhu Xi's interpretation of the poetic *yuan* as "expressing complaint without being angry"²⁷ may be inferred from the same doctrine, although it's more overt intention is to maintain social stability and established order.

It is obvious that the Confucian principle of non-excessiveness gives rise to a paradox with respect to art creation. That is to say, it imposes a yoke on the poet since the excessive expression of emotions, such as pleasure and sadness, is considered as undesirable as their inadequate expression. This will possibly make it a formidable task for any artist to achieve the moderation of expression. However, this paradox seems commendable and may be used as a positive frame of reference in face of the modern trend toward transforming poetry into a form of absurdly violent discourse (e.g., "To murder a man is to pick a lotus flower/When murdered, hold it in hand which cannot be replaced"), or one that is sensual and erotic (e.g., "With two legs apart, practicing marshal art").

In conclusion, Confucius attempts to infuse into poetry a cluster of social, political, aesthetic, cognitive, and moral functions, as he often does with rites and music, in accordance with his preoccupation with the formation of a gentleman (*jun zi*) as the ideal personality. This ideal personality is characterized with the well-balanced inner and outer development, which is assumed to be achieved at least in part by poetry as a special form of social, aesthetic, and moral discourse. In the final analysis, the underlying foundation of this ideal personality is determined by the Confucian philosophy of humanity or benevolence (*ren xue*). The ultimate objective is pointed either to the achievement of the ideal society that enjoys "good and efficient government and harmonious human relations" or to the capacity of "keeping the country at peace and its people at ease" (*guo tai min an*).

---

[26] Confucius, *The Confucian Analects* (trans. James Legge), 11:16, p. 159; also see Confucius, *The Analects* (trans. D. C. Lau), XI:16, p. 108. D. C. Lau's rendering follows: "There is little to choose between overshooting the mark and falling short."

[27] "Yuan er bu nu." Cf. Zhu Xi, *Lun yü ji zhu* [The Confucian Analects Annotated], in *Si shu wu jing* [The Four Books and Five Classics], Vol. 1, p. 74.

CHAPTER 11

A Debate on the Function of Music

In ancient China, the culture of rites and music (*li yue wen hua*) would occupy the most important position for centuries due to its service in political, moral, pedagogical, and recreational arenas. With respect to music proper, it was a trinity of arts at that time. It was mingled with poetry and dance, including pantomime and singing on formal occasions. It would be performed not simply as part of ceremonial rites to worship ancestors and divinities, but also as a kind of entertainment at banquets in sumptuous surroundings to honor the powerful.

As a rule, the pattern of musical performance was determined according to social hierarchy, ranging from 64 performers for the Emperor, 48 performers for lords down to 32 performers for ministers, as specified by institutionalized rites. These rites were understood as laws and rules as well as codes of conduct. Such specifications, however, were frequently violated by local powers and eminent figures, who ventured to overstep their entitlement by having musical performances on a larger scale than they were allowed to have.[1] This overreaching was largely due to their

---

[1] Evidence can be found in Book III of *The Analects*. Confucius said of the Ji Family in his home State of Lu: "They use eight rows of eight dancers each to perform in their courtyard. If this can be tolerated, what else cannot be tolerated?" (*Lun yü*, 3:1). According to the rites concerned, the use of eight rows of eight dancers each that involve 64 performers

personal vanity or political ambition, especially with the decline of the central authority of the Zhou Dynasty from the late sixth century B.C. Hence, there arose much discussion of music among ancient thinkers, discussion that was basically carried out in terms of morality and society. The moral aspect was principally intended to promote personal cultivation and individual moral conduct, whereas the social dimension aimed to promote harmony or reconciliation of human relations and social cooperation. Throughout this line of thought, the discussion expressed a preoccupation with rites-music culture in general, yet, as shown in the recorded historical documents, differing voices emerged one after another. *The Book of Mozi* and *The Book of Xunzi*, in particular, represent opposite views constituting an acute polarity. These views are focally expressed in "Against Music" (*Fei yue*) by Mozi (c. 479–381 B.C.), an opponent of Confucius, and in the "Discourse on Music" (*Yue lun*) by Xunzi (c. 298–238 B.C.), a realistic representative of Confucianism. They came into being as a consequence of two opposing kinds of value judgment and teleological pursuit.

Mozi judged music in terms of a negative utilitarianism that was anti-aesthetic in principle. In his view, the entire process of composing, performing, and appreciating music is useless. It is conducive to wastefulness and deprives social production of time and energy. All these negative functions can do nothing to resolve the problems of satisfying such basic public needs as clothing, food, and shelter.

In contrast, Xunzi argued in terms of a positive utilitarianism that explicitly favors music and is pro-aesthetic. For Xunzi, music is a composite art that encompasses a full range of positive functions. Music is effective not merely morally for personal cultivation and socially for harmonizing human relations, but also politically in enhancing communal morale and cohesion for national defense. What for Mozi seems to be useless and wasteful, for Xunzi turns out to be useful and necessary. This critique tackles the polar opposition of their conceptions of music through a comparative intellectual anatomy.

---

is a prerogative of the Emperor. The head of the Ji Family, as a minister of the State of Lu, is entitled to use no more than four rows of four dancers each that involve 32 performers. It is because of this violation of the rites that Confucius was condemning the head of the Ji Family. Cf. Yang Bojun, *Lun yü yi zhu* [The Analects Paraphrased and Annotated] (Beijing: Zhonghua Book Company, 1988), p. 23; also see Ren Jiyu, *Zhongguo zhexueshi* [A History of Chinese Philosophy] (Beijing: Renmin Press, 1990), Vol. 1, pp. 64–66; Confucius, *The Analects* (trans. D. C. Lau, London: Penguin Books, 1983), III:6, p. 67.

11.1 Against Music: Mozi's Negative Utilitarianism

Among ancient Chinese thinkers, Mozi stood out as the first opponent of Confucius. Mozi developed a different way of thought regarding the human condition and the status quo of his contemporary society. He attacked Confucianism as a whole and asserted that Confucian principles would ruin China in four ways: First, Confucian denial of the existence of God and the spirits would displease these beings and make them ready to punish Chinese society. Second, Confucian insistence on elaborate funerals and a three-year period of mourning on the death of a parent would waste the wealth and energy of the people. Third, Confucian emphasis on the practice of music would also waste the wealth and energy of the people. Fourth, Confucian belief in predetermined fate would lead people to laziness and passive resignation.[2]

To correct these Confucian errors, Mozi told his disciple Wei Yue that he proposed five principles to govern the state. He would recommend to the lord of a state in chaos the principle of honoring the worthy and identifying with the superior. He would advise the lord of a state in plight to recognize the principle of frugality and moderation in funerals. He would propose to the lord of a state obsessed with musical entertainments the principle of negating music and rejecting fatalism. He would persuade the lord of a state in cultural wildness to accept the principle of respecting the will of Heaven and the spirits. He would convince the lord of a state with aggressive ambitions to adopt the principle of exercising universal love and denouncing offensive warfare.[3]

Mozi, who sharply condemned music for being harmful, held that it must be prohibited. In the surviving fragment of his essay "Against

---

[2] Mozi, "Gong Meng" [Gong Meng Zi], in Wang Huanbiao (ed.), *Mozi ji gu* [Collected Annotations to The Book of Mozi] (Shanghai: Shanghai Guji Press, 2005), Ch. 48, pp. 1101–1102; also see Sun Yirang (ed.), *Mozi xiangu* [The Book of Mozi with Annotations] (Beijing: Zhonghua Book Company, 2001), Vol. 2, p. 459. The original remark on the Confucianist promotion of music is that "*xian ge gu wu, xiwei sheng yue, ci zu yi sang tianxia,*" It means that "The promotion of stringed music, songs, drums, and dances and the practice of singing and music performance for entertainment will suffice to ruin the whole world." Also see Fung Yu-lan, *A Short History of Chinese Philosophy*, in Selected Philosophical Writings (Beijing: Foreign Languages Press, 1991), pp. 248–249.

[3] Mozi, "Lu wen" [The Lord of State Lu], in Wang Huanbiao (ed.), *Mozi ji gu* [Collected Annotations to The Book of Mozi], Ch. 49, pp. 1125–1176; also see Sun Yirang (ed.), *Mozi xiangu* [The Book of Mozi with Annotations], Vol. 2, pp. 475–476.

Music," he argued that the harmfulness of music stemmed from its negative functions.[4] This being the case, making music is wrong because it is useless in at least three ways. First, music provides no welfare to the people, in contrast to the boats and carts that help gentlemen rest their feet and laborers spare their shoulders. Consequently, music offers no material benefits to the community and does not reduce in any way "the three great worries of the people" relating to food, clothing, and shelter. Mozi argued, "Let us try sounding the huge bells, striking the rolling drums, strumming the zithers, blowing the pipes, and waving the shields and axes in the martial dance. Does this do anything to provide food and clothing for the people? I hardly think so."[5] Second, music can do nothing to "rescue the world from chaos and restore it to order" in circumstances where "the great states attack the small ones; the great families molest the small ones; the strong oppress the weak; the many tyrannize the few; the cunning deceive the stupid; the eminent lord it over the humble; and the bandits and thieves rise up on all sides and cannot be suppressed."[6] Third, and worse still, music becomes loathsome as it "deprives the people of the wealth needed for their food and clothing (*kui duo min yi shi zhi cai*)." For when the rulers and ministers want musical instruments, such as bells, drums, zithers, and pipes, to be used in their government activities, they will lay heavy taxes upon the common people in order to let them make musical performances available. By so doing, the ruling class is amused with pleasure and comfort while the ruled are plunged into plight and poverty.[7]

Mozi also held that performing music is wrong because it is wasteful in two ways. First, it is a waste of human resources because musical performance "must have young people in their prime, whose eyes and ears are keen and whose arms are so strong that they can make the sounds

---

[4] Mozi, "Fei yue" [Against Music], in Wang Huanbiao (ed.), *Mozi ji gu* [Collected Annotations to The Book of Mozi], Chs. 33–34. His essay "Against Music" is said to have three parts. What is left in *The Book of Mozi* are two incomplete parts from which we see the key arguments relevant to his whole system of thought in this domain. Cf. Sun Yirang (ed.), *Mozi xian gu* [The Book of Mozi with Annotations] (Beijing: Zhonghua Book Company, 2001), Vol. 1, pp. 251–263.

[5] Mozi, "Against Music," in Mo Tzu, *Basic Writings* (trans. Burton Watson, New York and London: Columbia University Press, 1966), p. 111.

[6] Ibid., pp. 111–112.

[7] Ibid.

harmonious and see to strike the bells front and back." Young men who are employed in performing music will be taken away from plowing and planting, and young women from weaving and spinning. Performing music therefore interferes with the people's efforts to produce food and clothing. Second, performing music is a waste of material resources. Dancers cannot wear robes of cheap cloth or eat coarse food. Instead, they must dress themselves in beautiful robes of patterned and embroidered silk in order to make their figures and movements worth watching, and they must have the finest food and drink, such as millet and meat, in order to keep their faces and complexions fit to look at. But they themselves produce neither food nor clothing at all, but live like parasites on the provisions of others.[8]

Accordingly in Mozi, listening to music leads society astray in at least two ways. First, it appeals to sense perception of the rulers and ministers who are fond of musical performance, but if they sit quietly all alone and listen to music, they can hardly gain delight from it. Rather, they must listen in the company of others, either gentlemen or humble men. When listening in the company of gentlemen, they will keep their companions from attending to the affairs of state. When listening in the company of humble men, they will keep their companions from their farm work. Listening to music, therefore, is most likely to end up with the abuse of governing power and the bungling of social production. Second, listening to music, by consuming both energy and time, causes the people to neglect their duties, missions, or tasks. For example, if rulers and ministers spend their time listening to music, they will lack time and attention to look after government administration. If gentlemen spend their time listening to music, they will be unable to exhaust their strength and wisdom in directing bureaus within the state and abroad. If farmers spend their time listening to music, they will be unable to do more farm work and produce more food. If women spend their time listening to music, they will be unable to do more house chores and make more clothing. Eventually, the state will fall into disorder, the people will become poor, and the community will be in danger in the face of an external offensive attack. Mozi described this in detail:

[8] Ibid., pp. 112–113.

> Now if those who occupy the position of rulers and ministers are fond of music and spend their time listening to it, then they will not be able to appear at court early and retire late, or hear lawsuits and attend to affairs of government, and as a result the state will fall in disorder and its altars of soil and grain will be danger. If those who occupy the position of gentlemen are fond of music and spend their time listening to it, then they will be unable to exhaust the strength of their limbs and employ to the fullest the wisdom of their minds in directing bureaus within government and abroad, collecting taxes on the barriers and markets and on the resources of the hills, forests, lakes, and fish weirs, in order to fill the granaries and treasuries, and as a result the granaries and treasuries will not be filled. If those who occupy the position of farmers are fond of music and spend their time listening to it, then they will be unable to leave home early and return late, sowing seed, planting trees, and gathering large crops of vegetables and grain. If women are fond of music and spend their time listening to it, then they will be unable to rise early and go to bed late, spinning, weaving, producing large quantities of hemp, silk, and other fibers, and preparing cloth, and as a result, there will not be enough cloth.[9]

Obviously, Mozi tried to conclude that listening to music is a waste of time and energy and an interference with state affairs and social production. Those who are keen on music are most likely to enjoy themselves at the cost of their duty and work. If they get attached to musical entertainments, they will deviate from what they are expected to do and even become lazy or slack. All this tends to plunge the whole country and the good of the community into jeopardy.

As far as I can see, Mozi's perception of music as useless, wasteful, and misleading corresponds not only to his underlying rejection of music, but also to his utilitarian preoccupation with usefulness in material life. As announced at the outset of "Against Music" (*Fei yue*), it is the business of the human-hearted man to promote what is beneficial to the world and to eliminate what is harmful. In planning for the benefit of the world, the benevolent man does not consider merely what will please the eye, delight the ear, gratify the mouth, and give ease to the body.[10] For this reason, Mozi looked to usefulness as the test for policy and applied this test as the one and only measure to all practices, including music. What underlies all this seems to me to be a kind of radical

---

[9] Mo Tzu, *Basic Writings* (trans. Burton Watson), pp. 114–115.
[10] Ibid., p. 110.

negative utilitarianism that is sustained by Mozi's deep concern with the life of the common people in view of their three great worries about the supply of food, clothing, and shelter. This concern drove Mozi toward giving absolutely first priority to meeting the practical needs of the people. In giving this priority to the satisfaction of basic needs, he held that the process of making, performing, and appreciating music is detrimental to the welfare of the world, particularly to the development of social production and to the administration of state affairs.

We should note that his treatment of music per se does not necessarily mean that Mozi was unable to realize the aesthetic effect of music and other beautiful things. In fact, he deliberately follows this path of rejecting music for noble purpose:

> Mozi condemns music not because the sound of the huge bells and rolling drums, the zithers and pipes, is not delightful; not because the sight of the carvings and ornaments is not beautiful; not because the taste of the fried and broiled meats is not delicious; and not because lofty towers, broad pavilions, and secluded halls are not comfortable to live in. But though the body finds comfort, the mouth gratification, the eye pleasure, and the ear delight, yet, if we examine the matter, we will find that such things are not in accord with the ways of the sage kings, and if we consider the welfare of the world, we will find that they bring no benefit to the common people.[11]

Quite ostensibly, Mozi was conscious of the aesthetic pleasure contained in the delightful sound, beautiful dress, delicious food, and comfortable dwelling that everyone loves, but he suspended the aesthetic pursuit of the beautiful, delightful, and comfortable altogether for the sake of fulfilling his noble purpose. This purpose was to follow the ways of the sage kings (*sheng wang zhi shi*) and attend to the welfare of the populace (*wan min zhi li*). That is why he attached top priority on the gratification of the basic needs of the common folks and took this requirement as the premise for judging the enjoyment of the aesthetic in both art and life. This observation can be justified by what Mozi claims in another textual fragment.[12] "Only when you have enough to eat, then you seek after delicious food. Only when you have enough to keep yourself warm, then

---

[11] Ibid., pp. 110–111.
[12] Mozi, "Yi wen" [Fragments in the Appendix], in Sun Yirang (ed.), *Mozi xian gu* [The Book of Mozi with Annotations], pp. 653–659.

you seek after beautiful dress. Only when you have a safe shelter to live under, then you seek after an enjoyable dwelling."[13]

Nevertheless, the negative utilitarianism embodied in Mozi's thought led him to pay so much heed to the usefulness of things that he failed to gain a fuller insight into human nature. Paradoxically, Mozi showed a constant and great concern about the welfare of the common people, but he concentrated on the basic human needs of daily necessities while ignoring other higher needs, such as the need for the aesthetic or the beautiful. His consistent concern about "the three great worries of the common people" assumes that the common people care for nothing else but things such as food, clothing, and shelter. As a consequence, he confines his planning for humankind to the pursuit of these lower needs only. This is against human nature as a whole, however.

11.2 For Music: Xunzi's Positive Utilitarianism

As a representative of Confucianism, Xunzi continued to justify and develop the best of the tradition of rites and music. He held this tradition to be all the more necessary and helpful in both education of the populace and communal welfare. In his "Discourse on Music" (*Yue lun*), he formulated a strong counterargument to Mozi's claims against music. Compared with Mozi's account, his discussion of music as a special genre of art has greater eloquence, persuasiveness, integrity, and profundity in its argumentation and exposition. His discourse covers a wider scope, involving not only the essence and usage of music, but also human nature and higher human needs for self-expression and aesthetic enjoyment.

According to Xunzi, as the expression of joy, music is originally joyful. Joy is an essential part of man's emotional nature, and its expression is aesthetically significant, indicating a necessity that goes beyond the basic needs of physical existence. When artistically expressed in musical form, joy can be shared by other people and excite further joyful feelings among those who listen to it. For music is pleasing and appealing not only to the senses but also to the soul. Music thus becomes the means of guiding joy and the enjoyment of joy. It helps different people to meet their respective pursuits. That is to say, if the gentleman takes

---

[13] Ibid., p. 656.

joy in carrying out the *Dao* and the petty man takes joy in gratifying his desires, music can help the gentleman retain the *Dao* and help the petty man curb his desires in accordance with the *Dao*. In this way, both the gentleman and the petty man will stick to the *Dao* and remain joyful and happy, instead of falling into delusion and joylessness. Hence, joy expressed in music has the character of both aesthetic experience and moral feeling.

This interrelationship between music and joy helps explain why the same Chinese character is used for *yue* (music) and for *le* (joy), although with different pronunciations. As Xunzi confirmed, this coincidence seems to capture the essence of music.

> Music is joy (*fu yue zhe, le ye*). Being an essential part of man's emotional nature, the expression of joy is, by necessity, inescapable. Where there is joy, it will issue forth in the sounds of the voice and be manifest in the movement of the body. And it is the Way of Man that singing and movement, which are excitations of man's emotional states according to the rules of inborn nature, are fully expressed in music. Hence, since it is impossible for men not to be joyful, where there is joy, it is impossible that it should not be given perceptible form. But if its form is not properly conducted, then it is impossible that disorder should not arise.[14]

Music is defined here as originating from the expression of the joy as an emotion that man must sometimes feel. This necessary and inescapable aspect of man's emotional nature is expressed through vocal sounds and body movements in accord with the regulations for music-making established by the Ancient Kings. As a result, the musical forms of the *Odes* and the *Hymns* were available to offer guidance for the expression of joy. Following this guidance, human feelings of joy would be fully expressed without becoming wild and abandoned, and the form would be well ordered without being unduly restrictive. All this serves to make it possible for the intricacy or directness of melody, the elaboration or simplification of instrumentation, the purity or richness of sound, and the rhythm and meter of music to be adequate to stir and move the good in men's hearts, while keeping evil and base sentiments from finding a foothold

---

[14] Xunzi, "Discourse on Music," in the bilingual version *Xunzi* (trans. John Knoblock, Beijing: Foreign Languages Press, 2003), Vol. 2, pp. 648–649. Also see Hsün Tzu, "A Discussion of Music," in Hsün Tzu, *Basic Writings* (trans. Burton Watson, New York and London: Columbia University Press, 1963), p. 112.

there. Such are the principles according to which the Ancient Kings created music, and the main reason why Xunzi found Mozi's condemnation of music intolerable.

According to Xunzi, the best music is useful for political and social life in several ways.

> When music is performed within the ancestral temple, lord and subject, high and low, listen to it together and are united in feelings of reverence (*he jing*). When music is played in the private quarters of the home, father and son, elder and younger brother, listen to it together and are united in feelings of close kinship (*he qin*). When music is played in village meetings or clan halls, old and young listen to it together and are joined in obedience (*he shun*).[15]

On this account, the social order can be secured and human relations harmonized so long as government officials are united in feelings of reverence, family members are united in feelings of close kinship, and citizens of the community are united in obedience. In addition to these three consequences, the inclusion of martial dance as an integral part of musical performance can provide an even more important service to the safety of the state. Our demeanor and bearing acquire dignity from watching the way shields and battle-axes are brandished in the dance and from attending to the repetitive pattern of the dancers gazing down and lifting their faces up, bending and straightening their bodies. Through observing their ranks move within the borders of fixed areas in coordination with the rhythm and meter of the music, the arrangement of our ranks is corrected and our advances and withdrawals are made uniform.

How is that possible? It is because music at its best is sufficient to bring conformity with the single *Dao* and to bring order to the myriad transformations. Take the idea of the dance for example. According to the relevant rules,

> the eyes of the dancers do not see it and the ears do not hear it. Rather, it happens only when the order of every episode of gazing down and lifting up the face, of bending and straightening, of advancing and retreating, and of retardation and acceleration is executed with proper, restrained control; when the strength of bone and flesh has been so thoroughly trained that

---

[15] *Xunzi* (trans. John Knoblock), pp. 652–653.

every movement with the rhythm of the drums, bells, and ensemble that there is never an awkward or wayward motion; and when these, through constant practice, are combined into an ideal that is realized again and again with great concentration and endeavor.[16]

Moreover, music with its martial dance rehearsal and performance teaches men how to march forward to punish offenders and how to behave at home with courtesy and humility. If one marches forward to punish offenders in accordance with the way that is learned from music, then all will follow and submit. If one behaves at home with courtesy and humility, then all will follow and obey. It is in this sense that music is regarded as the great arbiter of the world, the key to the central harmony, and a necessary requirement of human emotion. According to Xunzi, all this leads to the action of the people in a uniform manner against disorder, strengthening societal cohesion and public morale to defend the sovereignty of the state. As a result, the army stays powerful and the cities are securely guarded so that their enemy states will not dare try to surround and attack them.

For Xunzi, music is required to have a morally proper character to realize this purpose. It must be moderate and tranquil so that the people will become harmonious and shun excess, and it must be solemn and majestic so that the people will become well behaved and shun disorder. If music is seductive and depraved, the people will become dissipated, indolent, mean-spirited, and base. They will fall into disorder and conflict with a collapse of community cohesion and morale. As a result, their army will be weakened, their city walls will be broken through, and the existence of their state will be threatened by foreign enemies. For this reason, any evil music must be banned and any licentious music must be abolished.

On the contrary, good music is both psychologically affective and morally constructive. When a man listens to singing like that of the *Odes* and the *Hymns*, his mind will be broadened, his aspiration will gain breadth, his manner will be refined, his heart will be made good, and his practical conduct will be perfected. Hence, Xunzi proclaimed the magical effect of music as follows:

---

[16] Ibid., pp. 662–663.

The influence of music and sound on man is very profound, and the transformation in him can be very rapid. Thus, the Ancient Kings were assiduous in creating proper forms. If music accords exactly with the Golden Mean and is evenly balanced, the people will be harmonious and not given to dissipation. If it is solemn and dignified, then the people will behave in a uniform manner and will not be inclined to disorder ... [For example] The broad sash, straight gown, and formal cap with the Peace Music of Shao and the Martial Dance of Wu cause the hearts of men to be filled with dignity. Thus, the gentleman will not let his ear hear lewd sounds, or his eye gaze on the female body, or his mouth utter evil words...He therefore uses the bell and drum to guide the inner mind and the se and qin zithers to gladden the heart...[Furthermore,] the music's purity and clarity [of melody] are in the image of Heaven; its breadth and greatness [of its rhythmic beat] are in the image of Earth; the dancers' poses and positions, their revolutions and movements, generally resemble the four seasons. Hence, when music is performed, the inner mind becomes pure; and when ritual is cultivated, conduct is perfected. The ears become acute and the eyes clear-sighted; the temper becomes harmonious and calm, manners are altered and customs changed. The entire world is made peaceful, and enjoys together beauty and goodness.[17]

Music works in this way because it has the power and charm to improve the souls of human beings morally, to influence them deeply, and to facilitate the reform of their customs and ways. At the same time, music provides a channel for men to release their feelings and emotions, including joy and anger, in a psychical catharsis. If these emotions are suppressed for too long without finding a means of expression, they grow into destructive impulses beyond normal human control. Thus, Xunzi asserted that "If the people have the emotions of love and hatred but have no means of responding with joy and anger, then there will be disorder (*fu min you hao wu zhi qing, er wu xi nu zhi ying, ze luan*)."[18]

In order to ensure that music is morally constructive, Xunzi argued that a correct form of music is indispensable. He considered the *Peace Music of Shao* and the *Martial Dance of Wu*, like the *Odes* and the *Hymns*, to be exemplary in form and style. These works can fill gentlemen with dignity and keep them from indecent behavior and other

---

[17] *Xunzi* (trans. John Knoblock), pp. 658–661. Also see Hsün Tzu, *Basic Writings* (trans. Burton Watson), pp. 116–117.

[18] *Xunzi* (trans. John Knoblock), pp. 656–657.

wrongdoing. By contrast, the seductive looks and decadent songs of Zheng and Wei should be banished as morally corrupting; they cause the hearts of men to grow licentious and dissipated.

As for musical instruments, bells and drums and the *se* and *qin* zithers should be played together in concord to have the performance symbolize harmony. Musical purity, musical breadth, and the dancers' movements are identified respectively with [the will of] Heaven, [the virtue of] Earth, and [the cycle of] the four seasons. In ancient Chinese thought, Heaven and Earth stand for nature as a whole, which begets all beings and things, and the four seasons refer to the passage of time, which shows the process of begetting and its results over the course of a year. By such allegorical description, the ethos of music, based on the unity of Heaven and man, is displayed in musical performance. In this way, Xunzi held that music in its correct form could be employed to guide human emotions, cultivate moral personalities, and above all, keep the world in peace.

We may perceive that Xunzi's ideal expectations of music and rites are hidden in this assertion: "When music is performed, the inner mind becomes pure; and when rites are cultivated, conduct is perfected. The ears become acute and the eyes clear-sighted; the temper becomes harmonious and calm, manners are altered and customs changed. The entire world is made peaceful, and enjoys together beauty and goodness."[19] Music works from within, and rites work from without. They join together to shape both the inward and outward aspects of men, thus turning them into refined moral beings and eventually making the entire world peaceful. Elsewhere, Xunzi further clarified the interaction between music and rites in more straightforward terms: "Music embodies the unchanging harmony, while rites represent unalterable reason. Music joins together what is common to all, while rites distinguish what is different; and through the combination of rites and music the human heart is governed."[20] From this argument can be inferred a necessary unity between music and rites. Music is originally joy as an essential part of human emotion, and rites are laws and codes in connection with practical reason. They are functionally exercised in distinct ways. Music should be appreciated and enjoyed freely and willingly, whereas rites

---

[19] *Xunzi* (trans. John Knoblock), pp. 660–661. Also see Hsün Tzu, *Basic Writings* (trans. Burton Watson), p. 117.

[20] Ibid.

should be imposed and operated forcefully. Because human nature is half emotional and half rational, a bridge is needed to cross the gap between these two hemispheres. Music plays this role, guiding the emotional side of the self to meet the rational side of the self and making the whole self into an integrated being. All Confucians tend to give much credit to musical education as the means to achieve this end.

In sum, Xunzi conceived human nature to be perfected by human culture, of which music is a fundamental component. Accordingly, human needs are not confined to basic needs, such as food, clothing, and shelter, for sheer existence, but extend to higher needs for emotional expression, aesthetic enjoyment, and moral development. Music, for Xunzi, bears multiple functions: It is originally joyful, aesthetically effective, sociopolitically useful, psychologically affective, and morally constructive. In acknowledging these virtues, Xunzi approaches music in a way that strikingly contrasts to the approach of Mozi. Although both evaluate music in utilitarian terms, Xunzi has a positive assessment, while Mozi has a negative one.

11.3 A Reconsideration of the Opposing Views

If both Mozi and Xunzi are primarily utilitarians as regards with music, how come they differed so much in their views? If we reconsider the matter, we will discover some main explanatory factors. As the first opponent of Confucius, Mozi was skeptical concerning all Confucian values. He sought to reverse Confucian arguments and their conclusions, thus upsetting the line of thought that Confucius initially posited. He developed a different value system to reflect his criticism that the principles of Confucianism would ruin the world. As a representative of Confucianism, Xunzi adhered to Confucius' preoccupation with the rites-music tradition, although he modified some Confucian doctrines put forth by his predecessors, especially Mencius. Thus, he sought to preserve the rites-music tradition by providing counterarguments to Mozi's position. In rejecting Mozi's preoccupation with the negative functions of music and condemnation of music as useless, wasteful, and misleading in our practical life, Xunzi attended instead to the positive functions of music and actively promoted music as useful, constructive, joyful, and affective.

Some leading commentators have held that Mozi and Xunzi differed in their views of music because of their differing social backgrounds.[21] Mozi expressed the point of view of the lower classes who were poor, less educated, and socially deprived. They had no access to music and other cultural entertainments because they lacked resources to rise above a daily struggle for existence. Confronted with the harsh reality of ordinary life, Mozi spoke on behalf of the poor and attacked the rich and powerful for their obsession with musical performance and other luxurious entertainments involved in the practice of rites. Xunzi, alike Confucius, spoke for the highly educated and socially and economically advantaged in society, people who apprehended the aesthetic value of art and also knew the significance of artistic activities in human life. Xunzi recognized their higher needs of such people and argued for the benefits that musical appreciation and education could bring to the people in general.

Mozi confined human needs to daily necessities, such as food, clothing, and shelter. He argued that, in order to satisfy these basic needs, the whole community should focus on social production and should avoid merely enjoyable recreational events, including musical performances. He saw these as a waste of time and energy and advised people to embrace a kind of asceticism that rejected any alleged aesthetic needs for the beautiful. One can imagine that his narrow-mindedness began with a naïvely innocent concern for the populace, but that it came to violate a natural development of human need for a more civilized and livable life. Conversely, Xunzi was highly aware of higher human needs and of the hard fact that "man cannot live by bread alone." He stressed the need for cultural literacy through musical education. He held that music, as an expression of joy, could work with rites to help people properly release and guide their emotions, satisfy their higher needs for the aesthetic and the spiritual, refine their moral conduct, and harmonize human relations. He held that music is beneficial and favorable to personal cultivation and

---

[21] Fung Yu-lan, *A Short History of Chinese Philosophy*, in *Selected Philosophical Writings of Fung Yu-lan* (Beijing: Foreign Languages Press, 1991), pp. 246–249. Also see Ren Jiyu, *Zhongguo zhexueshi* [A History of Chinese Philosophy] (Beijing: Renmin Press, 1990), Vol. 1, pp. 103–104, p. 218; Feng Qi, *Zhongguo gudai zhexue de luoji fazhan* [A Logical Development of Ancient Chinese Philosophy] (Shanghai: Shanghai Renmin Press, 1983), Vol. 1, pp. 96–102; Li Zehou and Liu Gangji (eds.), *Zhongguo meixueshi* [A History of Chinese Aesthetics] (Beijing: China Social Sciences Press, 1984), Vol. 1, pp. 168–170; Zheng Jiewen, *Zhongguo Moxue tongshi* [A History of Mohist Studies in China] (Beijing: Renmin Press, 2006), pp. 7–8.

communal good. That is why Xunzi accused Mozi of being one-sided in his judgment by saying that he "knew the dimension of practical usefulness only, but failed to understand the system of rites and music in human life" (*bi yu yong bu zhi wen*).[22]

Both Mozi and Xunzi placed their accounts of music in the context of their differing proposals to reduce poverty and enrich the state. According to Mozi, state poverty and disorder result from a fondness for musical performances and elaborate rites that lead to interference with both government affairs and social production. Because he was deeply concerned to satisfy basic needs for the populace, he demanded frugality while sharply criticizing extravagance. In particular, he tried to justify the elimination of music.

Xunzi also held that frugality was needed to make a state self-sufficient, but he also endorsed letting the people make a generous living and store up the harvest surplus (*jie yong yu min, er shan cang qi yu*).[23] He argued that this objective could be fulfilled only through the proper exercise of rites and government. In his view, human beings need to form a society with class divisions (*qun er you fen*), because if they form a society without class divisions (*qun er wu fen*), social disorder and state poverty will certainly follow. "In order to ensure human living, it is impossible for human beings not to form a society. If they form a society in which there are no class divisions, strife will develop. If there is strife, then there will be social disorder; if there is social disorder, there will be hardship and poverty for all."[24]

What should be done to secure a society with suitable class divisions? For Xunzi, it is nothing but the complementary practice of relevant rites and music. A society must be harmonized in terms of human relations, and class divisions must be stratified by means of an established hierarchy. Because music serves to harmonize what is common to people, and rites operate to distinguish what is different among them,

---

[22] Xunzi, "Jie bi" [Dispelling Blindness], in Jiang Nanhua et al. (eds.), *Xunzi quan yi* [The Book of Xunzi Annotated and Paraphrased] (Guiyang: Guizhou Renmin Press, 1995), pp. 442–446. Also see Xunzi, "Dispelling Blindness," in the *Xunzi* (trans. John Knoblock, Beijing: Foreign Languages Press, 2003), pp. 676–677. The English translation in this version follows: "Mo Di [Mozi] was blinded by utility and was insensible to the value of good form."

[23] Xunzi, "On Enriching the State," in the *Xunzi* (trans. John Knoblock), pp. 266–267.

[24] Ibid., pp. 272–273.

both can be deployed and performed to help create a harmonious society with class divisions. In this fashion, incentives will work, penalties will inspire awe, the worthy will be promoted, the unworthy will be sacked, the myriad things will have their appropriate function, affairs as they undergo changes will attain a suitable response, and moreover in Xunzi's poetic description, "above the natural sequence of the seasons is obtained from Heaven (*shang de tian shi*), below the benefits of earth are gained (*xia de di li*), and in the middle the concord of humanity is obtained (*zhong de ren he*), then goods and commodities will come as easily as water bubbling up from the inexhaustible spring, will flow forth in abundance like rivers and oceans."[25] Xunzi went on to claim that the teachings of Mozi worry too narrowly about the problems of a world suffering from the hardship of inadequate supplies. This "inadequacy" is not in fact a misfortune common to the world, but merely a hardship peculiar to Mozi's one-sided reckoning. For Xunzi, "It is Mozi who with his 'Condemnation of Music' (*Fei yue*) produces social anarchy throughout the world and who with his 'Moderation in Expenditures' (*Jie yong*) causes poverty throughout the world. My intention is not to depreciate Mozi himself, but the effect of his teachings makes this unavoidable."[26]

Finally, it is worth pointing out that the polar opposition between the views of music of Mozi and Xunzi is also related to their different personal assumptions about the function of music. In their arguments, they both exaggerate what they believe music will bring about. The more they argue for their own positions, the further their exaggerations move them apart.

---

[25] Ibid., pp. 288–289.
[26] Ibid., pp. 282–285.

CHAPTER 12

A Critical Illumination of Poetic Styles

People are born with sentiments,
Sentiments are conveyed in poetry.
Poetry appeared in the glorious antiquity,
And flourished with 'The Book of Poetry.'
Liu Xie (Ch. 6, Illuminating Poetry)

As a result of the Confucian promotion of poetry education for personal cultivation, literary criticism is claimed to play a significant role in this field. Meanwhile, it is bestowed with an important position in Chinese culture of intelligence, because it is conducted in light of artistic values and philosophical perspectives derived from the leading schools of thought. All this leads to a rich and fruitful production of poetic critiques in the long history.

Comparatively speaking, what marks a milestone in Chinese literary criticism is the *Dragon-Carving and the Literary Mind (Wenxin diaolong)* by Liu Xie (c. 465–532).[1] As noted in Chapter 6 on "Illuminating Poetry"

---

[1] It is controversial about the year of Liu Xie's death. For instance, there are typically three assumptions. Fan Wenlan assumed that Liu was born in 465 and died around 520–521. Li Qingjia concluded that Liu died in 532 after examining the records about Liu Xie in the Buddhist documents written in the Song Regime during the South and North Dynasties. Yang Mingzhao reckoned that Liu died around 538–539. The second edition of *Zhongguo wenxue baike* [The Encyclopedia of Chinese Literature] (1988) adopts Yang's view. I hereby follow the conclusion presented in the *Ci hai* [The Encyclopedia Dictionary in Chinese] (Shanghai: Shanghai Cishu Press, 1980), p. 1540.

© Foreign Language Teaching and Research Publishing Co., Ltd. 2019
K. Wang, *Chinese Culture of Intelligence*,
https://doi.org/10.1007/978-981-13-3173-2_12

(*Ming shi*), the focus is placed on a tangle of historical and formal issues in Chinese poetry dating from the antiquity to the fifth century. Even though it conducts a brief survey, it bears much significance to the development of Chinese poetics in general and its poetic styles in particular.

In order to reveal the implications of "Illuminating Poetry," it is necessary to pinpoint its hidden structure of formulation with a special reference to the "Postscript" (*Xu zhi*) for it serves as a methodological guideline. Therein Liu Xie proclaimed, "When I discussed verse and prose writing, I distinguished various genres. I traced their origins to demonstrate their developments, defined terms to clarify their meanings, listed exemplary pieces to illustrate my points, and looked into the general characteristics of each genre."[2] According to this statement, there arise a number of basic requirements. First and foremost, when it comes to evaluating each poetic genre or form, its origin and historical development should be tracked down; secondly, its designation should be explained with a clear-cut conceptual denotation; thirdly, the works that stand up for each genre should be selected out for attribution, analysis, and evaluation; and lastly, a theory of each poetic style should be based upon these interpretive efforts and then elaborated while due highlight to its substance and artistic features is given.

As for "Illuminating Poetry" itself, it follows up closely what it claims for such a structure of poetics. It sets out initially to present the connotation of *shi* (poetry) in a historical panorama by "seeking wide reference in the six classics," obviously an example of the methodology of "explaining the categorical term in order to reveal meaning." Then, it is immediately followed by an account of the origin and evolution of poetry, enumerating representative poets and their works that belong to different ages, and making a critical judgment in the description of their merits or flaws, i.e., the procedure of "selection of sample works for evaluation." Finally, in starting a linear search of poetry in different times and examining closely the classical genres and new trends, the chapter goes to draw its theoretical conclusion with regard to poetic style, its

---

[2] Liu Xie, "Postscript," in *Dragon-Carving and the Literary Mind* (trans. Yang Guobin, Beijing: Foreign Languages Press, 2003), Vol. 2, pp. 716–717.

function and effect, and the craft of poetic writing. This is no other than what Liu Xie justified for his poetic ideal in "unfolding the basic pattern and its requisites in the description of each style." In my initial reading, I have felt that the chapter in question, though with a striking note of stylistics, actually allows itself to operate a study of the history of poetics, for it largely devotes itself to an exploration of where poetry originally arises, thus demonstrating how poetry attains different styles in its historical development and change. What is more, Liu Xie's key conceptions of "*zhe zhong*" (correct inclusiveness) and "*qiu tong*" (holistic vision), together with other thought-provoking ideas in "Illuminating Poetry," have exerted great influence on artistic creativity, aesthetic ideal and stylistic characters, etc. This investigation only deals with three aspects among others, namely the development of literary style, artistic making, and stylistic paradigm.

12.1 The Literary Development: Form and Style

The so-called poetic style contains at least two levels of meaning: One is *ti shi*, which includes the formal types like what we find as requisites in the *si yan* (four-character) verse or the *wu yan* (five-character) verse the number of characters, syntax, rhyme, and rhythm; the other is style, i.e., the distinguishing feature that is achieved through the integrity of content and form or "mutual conquering" of each other.[3] Style is not only the way in which an artist carries himself toward his ideas, feelings, aesthetic tastes, pursuit of ideal, and personality, but also a manifestation of his individuality in artistic creation, his unique command over genres, his tailoring of subject matter, his use of language, and his way of image-making in particular.

One part of "Illuminating Poetry" that deals with "literary style" mainly relies on two modes, i.e., the diachronic mode of "tracing out the origin and historical development" and its synchronic counterpart of "selecting out the labeling works for attribution and analysis." Even though both of them pertain to the issue of style, the former places emphasis on the historical evolution of poetic form while the latter shifts to the diverse characteristics of different styles.

---

[3] Tong Qingbing (ed.), *Xiandai xinli meixue* [Modern Psychological Aesthetics] (Beijing: Zhongguo Shehui Kexue Press, 1993), pp. 463–524.

Generally speaking, Liu Xie's overview of the development of poetic paradigm is quite inclusive. It goes back as early as to the ballads in remote antiquity down to the verses in the early fifth century. This extensive review constantly mentions as its reference frame the key notions of *sishi* (four classics) and *liuyi* (six styles) in The *Book of Poetry* (*Shi jing*), and it is therefore able to identify the two poetic forms that achieve their tentative maturity during Liu Xie's time, that is, the *siyan* as four-character verse and the *wuyan* as five-character verse. Historically, these two forms used to be common in *The Book of Poetry*. However, they have gone through stages of evolution before they can stand as independent ones. As a matter of fact, it is not until the Han Dynasty around early 200 B.C. that the *siyan* verse first appeared in Wei Meng's *Poem of Fengjian*, a satirical persuasion to the Duke Mao of Chu Kingdom. Despite its attempts at formal innovation, the main content is largely composed of criticism and persuasion, with a view to rectify the lord's misconduct. Obviously, it has picked up the traditional allegory widely used in the Zhou Dynasty from the ninth to the fifth centuries B.C., which serves as evidence of the practice of cultivation through poetry. As for the *wuyan* verse, Li Ling's three poems *Dedicated to Su Wu* and Ban Jieyu's *Ode to Sorrow* are said to be the first efforts. Since there existed a widespread suspicion of the origin of the *wuyan* verse, Liu Xie, cautious not to rush to any assertion, turned for proof to the folk songs of "*Xing lu*" in *The Book of Poetry*, "*Cang lang*" in the *Mengzi* (The Book of Mencius), "*Xia yu*" (Happy and Leisurely) by You Shi in the Spring and Autumn Period (722–481 B.C.), and the children's rhyme "*Xie jing*" (The Crooked Path) which was popular in the time of Emperor Hancheng (32–8 B.C.), and eventually justified the factual existence of the *wuyan* verse in history. In addition, Liu Xie went on to enumerate it via Mei Cheng and Fu Yi (e.g., the "*Gu zhu*" as "Lone-growing Bamboo"), and then reached a positive conclusion that there were high-quality *wuyan* compositions as early as in the West Han Dynasty (206–8 B.C.). And thanks to "Wang Can, Xu Gan, Ying Yang, and Liu Zhen followed the lead of Cao Pi and Cao Zhi in their active literary production," the flourishing of the *wuyan* verse could come along in the early phase of the Jian'an period (196–220). Generally speaking, the evolution from the *siyan* verse to its *wuyan* counterpart is a diachronic process, which takes place by stages. This seems to show that each age will ensure the birth of a new style it needs conducive to its artistic production and development.

Here I venture to put forward a conjecture that there are at least three factors contributing to the rise of the siyan and wuyan forms. These factors seem to be related to the institutional, fashion, and political domains.

12.1.1   The Institutional Factor

During the Qin and Han Dynasties, the authorities set up the institution of Yuefu (the Music Bureau), sent officials everywhere to collect folk songs, and had literati compose song or score, in order to supply music for ritual performance or entertainment. This official establishment made great contribution to the development of music and poetry in that time, even though it is considered to have led to "the rampancy of the indecent music of Zheng and the peerlessness of the classical music of Shao." The distinguishing features of the *siyan* and *wuyan* modes lie in its much strengthened musicality and enhanced artfulness in the process of reciting. This adaptation in poetic pattern is evidently a result of both the social demand that poetry be accompanied by music, and of the technical innovation of singing. The advent, popularity, and maturity of the *siyan* and the *wuyan* verses are closely leagued with official or institutionalized promotion. A similar view is shared by Huang Kan as he assumes that "Ever since the Jian'an period, literati had vied to produce the *wuyan* verse, and as a result there appeared a large number of them. But the style of the ballads among folk songs remained as it had been in the Han Dynasty. Whenever we take into consideration the tone, music and lyrics carried within, we find that the *wuyan* style accounted for the vast majority. The expression sounded as an echo of Yuefu, the Music Bureau in the Han Dynasty."[4]

12.1.2   The Fashion Impact

This impact is closely associated with the institutional factor. During the Han Dynasty when the unified China realized its totalitarian ruling, whatever was promoted by the Yuefu (i.e., the Department of Music) as the official and mainstream paradigm of poetry, the general public would soon follow its lead. In the case of poetry, for example, when the writing

---

[4] Huang Kan, *Wenxin diaolong zhaji* [Notes on the Dragon-Carving and the Literary Mind] (Shanghai: Shanghai Guji Press, 2000), pp. 28–29.

in the *siyan* and the *wuyan* forms turned out to be a fashion owing to the governmental promotion, the literati and gentry would surely strive to imitate by all means. Therefore, from the historical and cultural context concerned, the prosperity and thriving of these poetic forms can be reasonably anticipated.

12.1.3 The Political Element

In the traditional Chinese society, the influence of the emperor and the aristocracy extended to the field of art and literature. Their taste and preference took the lead among literati and occasionally developed into a style or paradigm of great concern. The reason why the *wuyan* verse flourished during the Jian'an period was that the Cao brothers, emperor and prince, galloped ahead in producing poems of the new form and thus pushed the writing of the *wuyan* verse up to its high tide. This political influence varied in different times. As a matter of fact, the Cao brothers' accomplishment in poetry is also supposed to be owing to their coincidence with the prime time of the *wuyan* verse. By contrast, "Emperor Wu of the Han Dynasty loved literature and summoned his courtiers to improvise poetry on the Tower of Boliang,"[5] but their production of the *qiyan* as seven-character verse was of much less significance, because the new form was still in its infancy and had to wait for about 700 years to become mature and popularized later in the Tang Dynasty.

With respect of style, Liu Xie's expository description is rendered both diachronically and synchronically. On the one hand, he summarized on the grounds of works by different authors the overall historical development of poetry in its chronological order; on the other hand, his criticism of poetry varied with each individual poet, drawing a comparison between the generality and individuality of different poets that belonged to the same period. In Liu Xie's opinion, the *siyan* verse, first produced by Wei Meng, "followed the poetic tradition of the Zhou Dynasty with an intention to remonstrate"; the *Poem of Lament* by Zhang Heng was pure, elegant, and full of aftertaste; the *wuyan* pieces attributed to Mei Cheng and Fu Yi were "straight but not crude, with

---

[5] Liu Xie, "Illuminating Poetry," in *Dragon-Carving and the Literary Mind* (trans. Yang Guobin), pp. 64–65.

plaintive and moving description"⁶; the style of the Jian'an period was "generous of spirit, open in displaying talent, not caring for ingenious minuteness in description, and striving only for clarity in expression"⁷; down to the Zhengshi period (240–249), its poets began to attach themselves to *xuanxue* (neo-Daoism that integrates *The Book of Changes* and the works by Laozi and Zhuangzi), among whom He Yan was very "shallow," "Ji Kang stood out with his austere purity and Ruan Ji with his depth"; "writers of the Jin Dynasty leaned towards the frivolous and the ornate…, their works were more ornate than those of the Zhengshi period and not as forceful as those of the Jian'an period when some sought ingenuity in embellishment and some others indulged in smooth cadences"⁸; "poetic styles continued to change in the South and North Dynasties and early years of the Song era, because with Daoism receding into the background, nature poems came to the fore, parallelisms were sustained as long as a hundred characters, and great pains were taken to produce one striking line. Descriptions were meant to be imaginatively exhaustive; language was for all purposes made to be newly expressive."⁹

As is discerned in Liu Xie's commentary, it involves at least three causes of the change in style, say, group dynamic, historico-cultural context, and artistic individuality of each poet, which in turn facilitates the flourish and development of literature in general, and poetry in particular.

12.1.4 Group Dynamics

Literature in the Jian'an period stood out for its generous and robust spirit. Although specific social factors (war and peace) and political enhancement (the Cao brothers' relationship with poetry and rhymed writing) were accountable for its unique and unparalleled literary style, the Jian'an school of seven writers (*Jian'an qizi*), who joined together in their parallel pursuit of similar artistic ideal, was also an important element that deserves more attention. As a group, those writers "loved wind and moon, frequented ponds and parks, gloried in honors and

---

⁶Ibid.
⁷Ibid., pp. 66–67.
⁸Ibid.
⁹Ibid., pp. 68–69.

made merry at parties,"[10] enjoying much in common in lifestyles and subject matter of poetry. Meanwhile, they benefited much from mutual inspiration and group dynamic, breathing into their own style what they communicated with each other through poetry. As a result, their poems could excel for their generosity and unrelenting outpouring of talents, all of which are rarely found in the literary output by their contemporaries or their following generations. They played down the novelty in overly elaborate expression or description and turned to conciseness with much concern about the theme. In history, any poetic school or style that sustains time as a model for posterity has never outgrown the influence of its specific group dynamic.

12.1.5 Historico-Cultural Context

So far as the historico-cultural context is concerned, it varied in accord with the popularity of Laozi's and Zhuangzi's ideas in the Zhengshi period, the indulgence in neo-Daoism and *qingtan* (pure talk in philosophically speculative terms) in the West Jin Dynasty, and the downfall of *xuanyan* (Daoism-themed verse) along with the recession of Daoist philosophy as well as the rising of nature poetry. This being the case, it had different kinds of influence upon the alteration in literary styles. With both compliment and disapproval in his criticism of poetic composition in the East Jin Dynasty, Liu Xie did not hold a high opinion of the overall poetic accomplishment of that time. According to his observation, except Guo Pu's extraordinary *Roaming in Fairyland*, which stood out among its mediocre contemporaries, the works by Yuan Hong, Sun Chuo, and others, although each blessed with its own ornate style, were invariably impaired by their efforts to seek both diction and purport from neo-Daoism because of the lack of freshness and sincerity in their eloquent but monotonous abstraction. Such condition seemed unfavorable for the sake of the "verse inspired by emotion" (*wei qing er zao wen*). For it was associated with the fact that the notion of "sit to talk about the Dao" was running so rampant that the literati and gentry flocked after it and competed with one another in order to produce a singular and striking line. In Liu Xie's own words, it was entangled in a rather engaging trend that the people "submerged in the Daoist

---

[10] Ibid., pp. 66–67.

atmosphere, ridiculed worldly ambitions and indulged in metaphysical conversations."[11] Of course, the historico-cultural context of this kind is bound to have a multi-dimensional impact upon literary production, but here we just want to throw highlight upon the negative role it played in that specific period of time.

12.1.6 Artistic Individuality

To a great extent, the artistic individuality of an artist is well justified in its claiming authorship of a given style, although it is true that the style can also be attributed to a certain literary group or school. The Western notion of *principium individuationis* fits well in the study of artistic style. What makes a Tom cannot make a Peter because of the former's distinguishing individual features such as complexion, height, name, voice, look, facial expression, the way he carries himself. Similarly, a given style is recognized merely by its distinguishable individual character (the author's spirit, taste, artistic ideal, mastery of language, the special way to treat subject matter, and artistic traits of his works). For example, although He Yan, Ji Kang, Ruan Ji, and others were contemporaries in the Zhengshi period, they developed different styles from their distinct forms of disposition, erudition, pursuit, experience, and value judgment. According to Liu Xie, the depth of thinking was absent in He Yan's works because of his shallowness, the ideal profundity and purity found in Ji Kang's works were due to his stern and unyielding character, and the deep thoughts in Ruan Ji's works were firmly established upon his quiet and speculative disposition. As we know, the extraordinary artistic individuality is taken to be one of the essential elements for developing a unique style.

It should be pointed out that Liu Xie's description of the evolution of poetic paradigms that spans several thousand years is a bit too brief for it uses merely about 600 words in all. This is inevitably conducive to negligence, especially when it comes to the selection of representative works, which is no less than "one citation leaves out ten thousand other possibilities (*gua yi lou wan*)." For example, in his comments on the *siyan* verse and the Jian'an poets, Cao Cao was not mentioned; in his comments on the *wuyan* verse and the poets in the Eastern Jin period,

---

[11] Ibid., pp. 68–69.

Tao Qian was not reviewed. Huang Kan, a renowned annotator of the *Dragon-Carving and the Literary Mind*, rightly points out that "With an abundance of poetic styles and their complicated origins, it is not advisable to sum them up with too short a survey."[12]

Liu Xie was alleged to be "orthodox" and live up to the ideal of modeling on the classics (*zongjing*), capable of resting his judgment upon the objective fact and succeeded in drawing a correct conclusion that the *wuyan* verse originated from ballad. This finality is well backed up in the *Shipin Jiangshu* (Explanation and Annotation of Poetry) as it says that "The *wuyan* verse turned up mostly as ballad and *yuefu*-style poem in the West Han Dynasty when the literati were still unwilling to imitate it as a model. Li Duwei, a soldier, and Ban Jieyu, a concubine, still identified it with folk song and believed it to have emerged from singing for a sentimental expression excited by things. However, the *wuyan* verse achieved predominance later on, and since then it has been looked upon and deployed as a handy model. The reason is no other than its origin as folk song.... Ever since the Jian'an period, the literati turned to the *wuyan* verse and competed among themselves to produce this renewed poetic paradigm in great number. The folk song still held fast to the style of the Han Dynasty. With the *wuyan* verse, when we take into consideration the tone, music and lyrics carried within, its style accounted for the vast majority. The import and expression sounded as an echo of *Yuefu*-style poem in the Han Dynasty. All this should be able to convince us that the form of the *wuyan* verse derives from ballad."[13]

12.2 Artistic Creation: Proper Inclusiveness and Holistic Vision

The theory of artistic creation can be witnessed in "Illuminating Poetry," where "expression arises when emotions stir" stood out among other exemplary illustrations in the chapter. Tong Qingbing holds that this conception of the origin of poetry should be conceived as "the central category of Chinese poetics." His paper on "Expression Arises when Emotions Stir in the *Dragon-Carving and the Literary Mind*" presents a

---

[12] Huang Kan, *Wenxi diaolong zhaji* [Notes on the Dragon-Carving and the Literary Mind], p. 25.

[13] Ibid., pp. 27–29.

precise observation among the existent literature about Liu Xie's system of literary criticism.[14]

In sooth, "Illuminating Poetry" commences with the introduction of such classical definitions as "poetry carries sentiments in words," "poetry as the discipline of human nature," "evil thoughts are absent in poetry," and "the exegesis of poetry as discipline."[15] All of them are intended to explain the content and meaning of poetry, its basic functions, and primary role in moral cultivation related to other Confucian expectations. Then, this opening turns to define the character of poetic production, asserting that "human beings are blessed with seven types of emotion, which stir in response to the environment, and it is natural that people express themselves when emotions stir."[16] With respect to the nature of art, this assertion is both reasonable and refreshing, but it does not quite go in tune with the aforementioned classical ideal of poetry, where the notion of "to discipline" predominates as a means for the bridling of emotion. By contrast, Liu Xie hereby upheld the ideal of "natural rendering," and stressed the necessity of "emotional expression." Thus, a morality-based theory of emotional restraint and that of spontaneous outflow of emotion come into being as a pair of contradictory categories in his poetics.

Now questions arise about what on earth Liu Xie wanted to promote when he mentioned simultaneously the pair of contradictory categories. Did he intend to persuade people to follow the "Golden Mean," a principle of poetic cultivation to "discipline human nature"? Or did he approve of the essence of poetry as "expression arising from response to things" and speak up for the rule of artistic making that art should go the way it is? This follows a subsequent question about how Liu Xie treated the relationship between the classical doctrines and the new voices. With these two questions in mind, Tong Qingbing reached a conclusion that throughout "Illuminating Poetry," Liu Xie kept swaying between the inheritance of "the classical doctrine" and the acceptance of "the new voices." As for the relevant significance of the former,

---

[14] Tong Qingbing, "Wenxin diaolong ganwu yinzhi shuo" [Expression Arises When Emotions Stir in the Dragon-Carving and the Literary Mind], in *Wenyi yanjiu* [Journal of Literary Studies], No. 5, 1998, p. 19.

[15] Liu Xie, "Illuminating Poetry," in *Dragon-Carving and the Literary Mind* (trans. Yang Guobin), Vol. 1, pp. 60–61.

[16] Ibid., pp. 62–63.

Liu Xie readily offered his affirmative praise. However, he did not confine himself to this alone, for he was fully aware that questions around the creation of poetry could not be solved simply through the classical definition which was then in need of being renovated by virtue of some new elements to be added. That is how the notion of "poetic expression arising from the response to things" was proposed as a complement, correction, and renovation of the traditional conception of poetry. The relation of poetry to emotion and to the correspondence between human beings and their surroundings is believed to be the outcome of "the new voices" in his poetics that deserves more attention.[17] Tong's interpretation appears convincing in that it exclusively coincides with what Liu Xie intended in his hypothesis. In a similar light, we can go on to examine the idea of correct inclusiveness (*zhe zhong*) and the methodology of holistic vision (*qiu tong*), both of which run through Liu Xie's horizon of poetics for the most appropriate and unbiased judgments.

Liu Xie declared in the "Postscript (*Xu zhi*)" his own conception of correct inclusiveness:

> To evaluate one piece of work is easy; to give an overview of so many is hard.... If some of the ideas here coincide with past opinion, it does not mean that I have copied them but that they are irrefutable. If they differ, it does not mean that I deliberately set out to contradict past opinion but that I have no reason to accept them as true. Whether my views differ or not from other people's has nothing to do with whether these people are ancients or moderns. My foremost concern is to combine close analysis with unbiased judgments.[18]

As is noticed from the statement above, Liu Xie should be regarded as a practical literary critic although he advocated from the very outset of his book the two fundamental principles of *zhengsheng* (relying on the sages) and *zongjing* (modeling on the classics). Regarding those conventional theories that allow no different interpretation, he readily took them in only if he considered them to be irrefutable and still making sense; as for

---

[17] Tong Qingbing, "Wenxin diaolong ganwu yinzhi shuo" [Expression Arises When Emotions Stir in the Dragon-Carving and the Literary Mind], in *Wenyi yanjiu* [Journal of Literary Studies], No. 5, 1998, p. 21.

[18] Liu Xie, "Postscript," in *Dragon-Carving and the Literary Mind* (trans. Yang Guobin), Vol. 2, pp. 718–719.

the new voices that do not welcome the same interpretation, he encouraged those that worked through and did not mechanically return to the beaten track, nor did he indulge himself in any sheer novelty or fanciful invention. What he had in view was to take over the old with the new, or the different with the similar, placing them onto the platform of deep analysis, and finally coming up with a sound, unbiased, and appropriate assessment. This shows how the principle of *zhezhong* as correct inclusiveness works for his poetics refined through an integrated tactic. This tactic basically "lies in its recognition and integration of different and even contradictory aspects without putting overemphasis on each."[19] As is seen in the text on "An Appreciative Critic" (*Zhi yin*), Liu Xie imputed the failure in achieving correct inclusiveness to the attempt at "apprehending constant change of the world from a household angle," depicting it as "looking into the east to find out the west wall." In addition, the meaning of so-called *yuangai* or *yuanzhao* (panoramic viewing and observation) comes very close as synonyms to that of correct inclusiveness (*zhezhong*).

However, the principle of correct inclusiveness was intended only as an approach to arriving at the holistic vision (*qiu tong*) as the ultimate end. The notion of *tong* was frequently mentioned in *Dragon-Carving and the Literary Mind*. In this context concerned, *tong* is meant as a comprehensive correspondence in one sense, and in the other, as a virtue of incorporating things of different nature. In "The Treatise and the Speech" (*Lun shuo*) Liu Xie claimed, it is a must to "investigate subtle problems and penetrate mysterious depths" in order to "attain a sound and intelligible thesis" that could be comprehended by all without being distorted.[20] When talking about "Choosing the Style or Natural Tendency" (*Ding shi*), he affirmed that a truly great writer "can manipulate styles as different as the fanciful and the orthodox," because "if one loves the elegant style but despises the ornate, there is no versatility or compatibility to speak of."[21] Elsewhere, he insisted that "Only a gentleman know what human beings under the sky think and feel, and

---

[19] Li Zehou and Liu Gangji (eds.), *Zhongguo meixueshi* [A History of Chinese Aesthetics] (Beijing: China Social Sciences Press, 1987), Vol. 2, p. 609.

[20] Liu Xie, "The Treatise and the Speech," in *Dragon-Carving and the Literary Mind* (trans. Yang Guobin), Vol. 1, pp. 248–249.

[21] Liu Xie, "Choosing the Style or Natural Tendency," in *Dragon-Carving and the Literary Mind* (trans. Yang Guobin), Vol. 2, pp. 424–425.

therefore resort to no crooked arguments."[22] Noticeably, he was mission-bound to arrive at a disinterested, appropriate, and inclusive conclusion, which was free from distortion, and left no misleading guidance to the posterity. For this sake, he also devoted another chapter under the heading of "Continuity and Change" (*Tong bian*), where he discussed the interrelationship between inheritance and renovation in view of tradition. Therein he borrowed from *The Book of Changes* the dialectic interaction between change and continuity, that is, "Wherever there is no room for further development changes arises; change results in continuity, and continuity leads to constancy." Accordingly, he argued that "The genres of writing are constant; the art of writing is changeable…. Language and thought will retain lasting appeal only when they are constantly renewed: This is the art of change."[23] This naturally conduces to his logical conclusion that "Constant change produces lasting appeal, and continuity prevents the impoverishment of the source."[24] That is why he actively recommended that the alteration of inheritance via imitation and renovation via transformation constitutes the laws of change and continuity; for it is according to such laws that a poet or writer *par excellence* will be able to strike a balance between substance and form and between the classical and the popular.

In the final analysis, Liu Xie's schema of correct inclusiveness and holistic vision is very similar to the way of *yinge* (inheriting and renovating). In principle, *yin* is to cling to tradition, while *ge* is to reform or erase the defect or bias. Although the pair occasionally contradicts each other, they are the key links in the continuance and development of poetic legacy. The self-evident interaction and mutual completion of *yin* and *ge* run consistently throughout Liu Xie's poetics. In light of the principle of sage-guided reference, "Illuminating Poetry" starts in the first place from the reiteration of the poetic significance in its ancient phase and its conventional definition. This approach comes as a result of "allowing no different exegesis (*zi bu ke yi*)." When discontented with the lack of inclusiveness in the old theory, Liu Xie turned to the praxis of poetic writing for the root of potential renovation and consequently

---

[22] Liu Xie, "The Treatise and the Speech," in *Dragon-Carving and the Literary Mind* (trans. Yang Guobin), Vol. 1, pp. 248–249.

[23] Liu Xie, "Continuity and Change," in *Dragon-Carving and the Literary Mind* (trans. Yang Guobin), Vol. 2, pp. 408–409.

[24] Ibid., pp. 418–419.

offered new hypothesis that conforms to the law of artistic production. This fresh tone is said to be the result of "never permitting the same exegesis (*zi bu ke tong*)." Thanks to the theoretical configuration going under the law of *yinge*, Liu Xie did not only fulfill his mission as a gentleman that the apprehension of one's ideal relies on his sound and unwarped judgment, but also leave as legacy in poetics his thought of "inspiration from things and expression of feelings."

In Tong Qingbing's analysis, the notion of "inspiration from things and expression of feelings" in fact covers the four elements sufficient for an unbroken process of poetic production. Specifically, "things" is used as a general term for the object, "inspiration" as an emotional activity on the part of the subject, "expression" as the formal impression of internal stirring, and "feelings" as the meaningful substance of artwork. Since the four elements help actualize an integral poetic production, they are considered to be of great theoretical value. The notion of "things" refers not merely to the external and natural beings, but to what the subject beholds, speaks about, thinks and feels, in one word, the things tinged with subjective hue. Likewise, "inspiration" amounts to the imagination triggered by the things, and the emotional response to the things and empathy with the things as well. This being the case, it can be said that the oneness (psychological correspondence) between emotion and scenery, and the unity of subject and object, can hardly be attained and maintained without emotion as an indispensable precondition. "Expression" is as much accented as vocal or verbal treatment of "feelings," which can be identified with the process of writing or "elaboration." The "feelings" largely overlap with the range of *qingzhi*, say, what is harbored at heart and expressed out as poetry. On the whole, there are four points in connection with the idea of "inspiration from things and expression of feelings" in terms of artistic creation:

> Firstly, poetry arises from the correspondence between the feelings within and the things without. With the absence of the feelings, the things and their mutual relation, poetry can never spring up. Hence the feelings and the things are necessary for the emergence of poetry. Secondly, the correspondence is critical to the feelings carried through poetry. Due to the correspondence as a psychological agent, the natural feelings in the poet will be charged with poetic meaning in its relation to the things. Thirdly, the feelings carried through poetry need to go through artistic treatment so as to become aesthetic feelings, and expression is therefore the necessary

access as the second agent in the production of poetry. Fourthly, poetry is by nature the feelings, which has endured from the bud of natural feelings a dual psychological forge of inspiration and expression.[25]

It is worthy to be pointed out that the doctrine of "inspiration from things and expression of feelings" is in fact not Liu Xie's original invention. It arises as a result of his effort to extend and renovate old theories of poetry. It has been agreed in much scholarship that he drew his inspiration from in the *Yue ji* (Record of Music)[26] or the *Yue lun* (Discourse on Music).[27] More specifically, it is stemmed from the interpretation of music qua sound that appears as the echo of human heart; for when the heart is inspired by things, it will be released in the form of sound. Such an interactive process is prone to pump up sort of inspiration from things and expression of feelings. Liu Xie continued along this line of thought. He thereby seized upon the old theory of the origin of music and then reshaped it into a fitting vehicle for poetry. In my opinion, this act of reshaping or transformation is far from being the whole story. Instead, a complete analysis should be extended to the influence of the *Wen fu* (Literary Criticism) by Lu Ji. Actually, it is Lu Ji who first came out to claim that poetry was "arising from feelings (and becoming gorgeous)" in defiance of the traditional theory of poetry as "expressing aspirations in words (*yan zhi*)." Liu Xie held with the idea of "expressing aspirations in words" on the one hand in his attempt to follow up the tradition, while on the other hand, he promoted the novel assumption of poetry as "arising from feelings (*yuan qing*)" in an effort to improve the old conception. He even pushed further by affirming that "Humankind possesses seven types of emotion, and they come alive when inspired by things." This serves as a logical foundation to meet with what he spoke up for in "writing verse for the expression of feelings (*wei qing er zao wen*)" and what he spoke up against in "arousing feelings by means of verse-writing (*wei wen er zao qing*)." Such relationship cannot be treated in great detail on this occasion.

---

[25] Tong Qingbing, "Wenxin diaolong ganwu yinzhi shuo" [Expression Arises When Emotions Stir in the Dragon-Carving and the Literary Mind], in *Wenyi yanjiu* [Journal of Literary Studies], No. 5, 1998, p. 26.

[26] One of the Confucian classics. It is available as part of *The Book of Rites (Li ji)*.

[27] An essay by Xunzi in *The Book of Xunzi*.

12.3 Stylistic Paradigms: Naturalness, Gracefulness, and Elegance

What is noteworthy in the text of "Illuminating Poetry" are three eye-catching styles that need further exploration, namely naturalness, gracefulness, and elegance. With their different characteristics, "naturalness" is a never-ending theme in the history of Chinese poetry while "gracefulness" is concerned with the proper paradigm of the *siyan* as four-character verse, and "elegance" with the popular style of the *wuyan* as five-character verse.

12.3.1 Naturalness as Beauty

When Liu Xie said that "it is all natural for people to get inspired from things and express their feelings" through poems, the inspiration and expression in their usage here are believed to stand for the critical elements in the art of poetic production, and naturalness is intended to set up a stylistic model. If we take a closer look at Liu Xie's critical illumination of poetry from a historical and comparative perspective, we are bound to discover that naturalness in this context has two layers of meaning. In the first place, the inspiration through things and the ensuing expression of feelings are concerned with the objective laws of poetic production, which would barely promise a good poem in the case of deviance. In the second place, it sets up standards for poetic writing and artistic treatment, allowing no other means than a spontaneous expression of feeling and sentiments as the way to acquire a fair style. The first layer of meaning seemingly corresponds to "lawfulness" while the second one to "purposiveness" in view of artistic creation. The unity of the two makes up the so-called *ziran* as naturalness in Chinese poetics.

Naturalness as beauty (*zi ran wei mei*) is an ideal principle that evidently predominates all over the history of Chinese poetic style. Although the conception of *ziran* as naturalness originated from Daoism, Laozi never identified it with our modern concept of nature because it equals the way of Heaven and Earth in his philosophizing. Practically, the idea of *ziran* is apprehended by Laozi as the spontaneous and lawful standing that coincides with the *Dao*. In his conception of that "the *Dao* follows *ziran*," which is the cornerstone of Daoism and its aesthetics alike, the *Dao* in this context is no more than the way of naturalness or spontaneity. For Laozi, only when everything between

Heaven and Earth, including human society, abides by the universal law of "being natural," they can live in harmony and the order can be maintained. Zhuangzi then picked up this notion and developed it into that of the "natural" *Dao*. Accordingly, "naturalness" is interpreted by Zhuangzi from a manifold dimension, say, as the universal law in his lecture of the *Dao*, as the aesthetic object in his observation of beauty, as the follow-up of *tian* (Heaven) in his commentary on life, and as the sincerity in his remark about human disposition. He believed that a sincere person appeals to others only by his trueness. Since the "sincerity" is "subject to Heaven" and "naturally irreversible," it is obliged to follow the law of *ziran* as "naturalness." Zhuangzi argued in the text of the "Fisherman" (*Yu fu*) that "Trueness is the height of sincerity. Without sincerity, no one else is to be touched. Affected crying is sadness without grief; affected rage is severity without awe; affected intimacy is a smile without empathy. In contrast, genuine sadness is grief without tears; real anger is awe before its explosion; real intimacy is vicarious sympathy before any smile. Trueness comes from within and appears in one's look, therefore trueness should be cherished.... The trueness or sincerity, which is subject to Heaven, remains natural and irreversible. Therefore, the saint follows Heaven and respects trueness."[28] Obviously, men cannot pretend to be expressive of their temperaments, which would otherwise turn out to be repulsive "ostentation" or "false feeling" in disguise. Men are tied to following the way of "naturalness," staying sincere and natural, because only true feeling, which "holds within and flows outward," can reach out to the bottom of human heart and thus acquires its aesthetic value when embodied in art. This is the cause for the natural to become aesthetically appealing and artistically engaging.

It is ever since Laozi and Zhuangzi that "naturalness" as an ideal stylistic paradigm has been prominent and influential throughout the history of Chinese literature and art. During the Wei, Jin, South and North Dynasties, Tao Qian's poetry came out as its typical example. It was not until the Tang Dynasty that Sikong Tu dedicated a chapter on naturalness in his *Ershisi Shipin* (Twenty-four Poetic Styles), strongly recommending the natural poetic style for being not ornate and pretentious at all. The poet Li Bai also contributed lines to describe the natural poetic scenery and literary mind, for instance, "The lotus flower blooming out

---

[28] Chen Guying (ed.), *Zhuangzi jinzhu jinyi* [The Works of Zhuangzi Annotated and Paraphrased] (Beijing: Zhonghua Book Company, 1983), pp. 823–824.

of the pure water, its beauty appears natural without carved ornament." Similarly, Su Shi in the Song Dynasty put forth the naturalness as "floating cloud and flowing water" or "pure naturalness"; and Li Zhi in the Ming Dynasty compared natural charm to an infant-like innocence, etc. Practically, naturalness as beauty has been promoted alike in horticulture where the highest principle of design is termed as "being made by man, but appearing natural as if it was so arranged by Heaven" (*sui you ren zuo, wan zi tian kai*). All this is related to the idealization of naturalness as beauty, so to speak.

12.3.2 Gracefulness and Elegance

These two aspects came out as two distinctive styles in Liu Xie's examination of the accomplishments of the *siyan* and the *wuyan* verse forms. Just as he concluded, "The spirit of the *siyan* (four-character) verse, the classical genre, is elegance and grace. The nature of the *wuyan* (five-character) verse, a later development, is purity and beauty. Talent alone determines to what degree a poet can achieve one or another of these qualities. Zhang Heng achieved elegance, Ji Kang grace, Zhang Hua purity, and Zhang Xie beauty. Cao Zhi and Wang Can combined all the qualities; Zuo Si and Liu Zhen excelled in one of them."[29] Apparently, Liu Xie distinguished between the *siyan* verse as the classical genre (*zheng ti*) and the *wuyan* verse as the popular style (*liu diao*). Some Liu Xie scholars tend to hang on the literal meaning and therefore have considered the classical genre as orthodox and the popular style as vulgar. They thus assume that the former takes its root in the *jing* (classics) whereas the latter gives up to the *bujing* (non-classics). Correspondingly, they often criticize Liu Xie for speaking in favor of the *siyan* verse, a discrimination that originates from his piety toward classics. So far as I can see, this criticism is a result from misunderstanding the annotation. In the original text, it can be found out that "the *siyan* verse, the classical genre" is meant to be a standard paradigm, and its spirit of "elegance and grace" is meant to be a stylistic characteristic. Then, "the *wuyan* verse, a later development" is meant to point out the historical fact that the five-character verse came into fashion much later, and its nature of "purity and beauty" is meant to be a stylistic feature.

---

[29] Liu Xie, "Illuminating Poetry," in *Dragon-Carving and the Literary Mind* (trans. Yang Guobin), Vol. 1, pp. 70–71.

Specifically, Liu Xie went on with the argument that "Talent alone determines to what degree a poet can achieve one or another of these qualities," thus declaring his unbiased stand when different styles are concerned.

Liu Xie might have a very clear vision of what elegance and gracefulness possibly mean, thus citing several poets as supporting evidence. Yet, his comment is too general as he only mentioned poets but not their poems at all. To my mind, it turns out to be as ambiguous and confusing as "looking at a flower through fog." How should we understand the two aspects as they are? A common understanding is that *yarun* (gracefulness) is identified with being graceful and decent like a moist breeze, and *qingli* (elegance) with being refreshing and elegant. Some other scholars have made further analysis and came out with such a paraphrase as follows: "In Liu Xie's poetics *ya* is meant to be gracefulness, i.e., what a poem suggests should conform to Confucian philosophy of being gentle, honest and sincere; *run* is meant to modify and polish a poem in order to make it 'resplendent with grace'; ... *qing* is what the later generation thought as 'a poem revives with an original theme'; *li* requires that a poem be overflowing with flowery expression and sweet melody; ... *ya* with its orthodox overtone goes in tune with the thought of *zongjing* (modeling on the classics) in Liu Xie's literary criticism while *run* as an attempt to refine is a poetic commitment to literature. *Qing*, originality in theme, corresponds to 'the law of poetic evolution' while *li* is what arises in accordance with the fashion in its time."[30] This is a carefully worked-out interpretation, but we need to read more relevant works before we are able to realize the keynote in Liu Xie's commentary. Since Liu Xie recommended that we "select out representative works to carry out evaluation," we can only apprehend his theories by reading between the lines the works referred to in the particular context and see to what level his hypothesis can be justified.

According to Liu Xie, Zhang Heng's verse is more of elegance; Ji Kang's is more of grace; Zhang Hua's is more of purity; and Zhang Xie's is more of beauty. Cao Zhi's and Wang Can's combine all the abovementioned qualities, while Zuo Si's and Liu Zhen's just excel in one of them. Although Liu Xie did not go on to explore in greater depth these poets' works, we can rely on them for a more clarified vision of what *yarun* as

---

[30] Zu Baoquan, *Wenxin diaolong xuanxi* [Analysis of Selected Texts from Dragon-Carving and the Literary Mind] (Hefei: Anhui Education Press, 1985), p. 119.

gracefulness and *qingli* as elegance actually hold in different cases. Take, for example, a *siyan* verse by Zhang Heng, *Poem of Lament*, which won Liu Xie's loud critical acclaim. The poem follows:

> What a special orchid in autumn!
> Among grass it grows into blossom.
> With its yellowish flower
> Full of fragrance and charm.
> It is solitary in a deep valley,
> And spreading afar its beauty.
> My situation is quite the same,
> But what could I do about it?

Apparently, it is a piece that integrates personal discontent through its description of orchid as a wildflower with a noble character. The description of the orchid includes its living environment (deep valley), color, shape, and fragrance as well as the poet's admiration for its unique disinterestedness and serenity. The poem ends up with an analogy between the orchid and the poet himself, with a hidden intention to express his discontentment with his embarrassment of being socially neglected. Even though the poem carries with it a tone of self-relief from grievance and anxiety, it is by no means an outrageous outcry. It therefore bears no violation of the Confucian principle of "complaining (about the social *status quo*) without being desperately angry with it (*yuan er bu nu*)." Owing to such a subtle treatment of the theme, it is capable of retaining the "gentle, honest and sincere (*wen rou dun hou*)" look of a Confucianized type. The style of *yarun* as gracefulness is therefore more likely to be experienced in this poem. Liu Xie also agreed that this poem by Zhang Heng could justifiably claim its retention of elegance and gracefulness and suggestive richness of aftertaste (*qing dian ke wei*).

In order to expose further the usage of the two poetic forms (*siyan* and *wuyan*) and the two styles (*yarun* and *qingli*), Liu Xie specified the apprehension of the difference in their application, saying "simplicity and floridity applies differently" as do flower and fruit (*hua shi yi yong*). Accordingly, a poet should never give himself up to the popular taste, nor should he allow himself to seek after what another poet has made a name with. If any poet wants to develop an individual style and does well with one of the poetic paradigms, he probably has nothing to do except "leaving himself to his own talent (*weicai suo'an*)," which is preceded by the recognition of one's natural gift and born disposition as well. This insight amounts to a truth-seeking attitude and bears fruit with a dialectic theory that enlivens the relationship between the style of simplicity and that of floridity. As a matter of fact, the poetry is rather an outburst of emotion than an all-around accommodation of each paradigm. In reality, "poetry has unchanging forms, thinking follows no fixed rule. Each writes according to his natural gift; few can be all-round masters."[31] This observation is quite faithful to the experience of poem writing. In one sense, it testifies the truth in what "simplicity or floridity depends on one's natural talent (*huashi weicai*)" contains; and in the other sense, it also sets a poet free to some extent from the influence of "established poetic paradigms (*heng cai*)." When a poet is blessed with distinctive faculties and rests with his exceptional tastes, a given poetic paradigm is invariably built up with static components. If a poet alive ever attempts to stretch his neck into a "dead cocoon," he will undoubtedly be "stifled in the cocoon spun by himself (*zuo jian zi fu*)." Holding fast to convention and imitating others, a poet is doomed to fail in bringing his talents into full play, neither can he develop any individual style. He is sure not capable of producing anything that holds sway in the domain of poetry.

Furthermore, Liu Xie examined the issue of difficulty in poem production and came up with a fairly comprehensive argument. He warned that, without a deep understanding of the difficulty in composing a poem, anyone who is longing for a good piece is most likely to run into entanglement because of their negligence; on the contrary, the recognition of where the *impasse* stands will likely help the poet get over obstacles. Apparently, poem writing will probably gear in a process where the difficult could be reversed to a certain extent. As a rule, difficulty exists as it does anywhere, but it can be overcome through painstaking efforts and consequently changed into its opposite counterpart. Of course, the transformation of difficulty relies on untiring exertion and perseverant pursuit, but the key element lies in *miaoshi*, the profound and subtle insight into the nature of an object concerned. It can lead a poet to take effective steps in his practice. Liu Xie's conception of difficulty in poem writing can be named as the theory of apprehending the difficult and the easy (*miaoshi nanyi*). In fact, this theory also applies to other

---

[31] Liu Xie, "Illuminating Poetry," in *Dragon-Carving and the Literary Mind* (trans. Yang Guobin), Vol. 1, pp. 70–71.

kinds of practice as well. For example, we can have the theory of *miaoshi* unfolded in a different perspective like what we can find in the teachings of Laozi, that is, "The most difficult things begin with the easy, and the largest things arise from the minute. Hence, tackle the difficult while it is still easy; achieve the large while it is still minute."[32] Whenever we start with the easy and minute, through constant endeavors, it will be most liable for us to end up with a successful transformation according to the golden rule proposed above.

All in all, the whole argument in "Illuminating Poetry" deals with three aspects of history, style, and production. Some of its remarks are brief but significant, touching upon some important issues in poetics. It deserves more attention and study. The theory of inspiration from things and expression of feelings (*ganwu yinzhi*) has invited widely acclaimed analysis, while those of "being natural above all in style (*mofei ziran*)," "being graceful and elegant in style (*yarun qingli*)," "style of simplicity or floridity agrees with the poet's talents (*huashi weicai*)," and "writing poems according to one's natural gift (*suixing shifen*)," among others, still need further investigation. This discussion bears no more than an intention to raise our awareness of them and expects more fruitful research to come up in the wake.

---

[32] Laozi, *Dao de jing* [The Book of Laozi], Ch. 63. Cf. Wang Keping, *The Classic of the Dao: A New Investigation* (Beijing: Foreign Languages Press, 1998), p. 249.

CHAPTER 13

A Moralistic View of Poetry

The Confucian view of poetry education is morality-based at large. It is handed down from one generation to another with marginal progression but more explicit exposition. It is especially so when it comes to Neo-Confucianism in the Song Dynasty. As a leading figure of the Neo-Confucianists, Zhu Xi (1130–1200) is said to have spent four decades on the scrutiny of the *Book of Poetry* (*Shi jing*). Accordingly, he has made an impressive contribution to its reinterpretation by clarifying some ambiguous comments related to Confucius himself.

As evinced in his moral consideration, Zhu Xi is chiefly preoccupied with heavenly principles that he identifies with *tianli*. As he argues, "Whatever the sagely predecessors teach is not but to help people obtain a clear vision of *tianli* and meanwhile get rid of *renyu*. Any form of teaching and education is found needless so long as *tianli* are clarified in full sense."[1] This shows that *tianli* are conceived of as both the key

---

[1] Zhu Xi, *Zhuzi yu lei* [The Sayings of Zhuzi] (Beijing: Zhonghua Book Company, 1986), Vol. 12. In Chinese, *tianli* can be seen as a collective term, including "the three cardinal guides and the five constant virtues" (*san gang wu chang* among others. The "three cardinal guides" are known as "Ruler guides subject, father guides son, and husband guides wife," and the "five constant virtues" are known as "reciprocal humanity, righteousness, propriety, wisdom and trustworthiness." They are all specified in the feudal system of ethical code. In Zhu Xi's mind, they are definitely right and proper, as perfectly justified as heavenly that are ultimately directed toward the One as the highest good (*zhi shun*). The highest good is based on the "four beginnings" (*si duan*) in Mencius' terminology, including *ceyin zhi xin* as the feeling of commiseration, *xiuwu zhi xin* as the feeling of shame

content and ultimate objective of teaching and education. *Tianli* as heavenly principles are opposite to *renyu* as human desires, thus forming a binary pair in Neo-Confucianism. The former is taken as constant virtues to be nourished and cherished whereas the latter as base vices to be reduced and shed away. In Zhu Xi's mind, *tianli* are distinguished between the one and the many. The one refers to the universal principle behind all, abstract and metaphysical. The many refer to the particular principles embodied in all things, concrete and physical. Analogically, the one is like the moon in the sky while the many are like the multiplied imagery of the moon reflected in all the rivers and lakes (*yue yin wan chuan*). Hence the one is essential and original while the many are extensional and derivative. This line of thought remains dominant and decisive not merely in Zhu Xi's philosophizing, but also in his literary criticism as well.

13.1 Conformity to the Moral Principle a Priori

Approaching *The Book of Poetry* (*Shi jing*), for instance, Zhu Xi sets up and sticks to a moral principle a priori. This principle is largely originated from the Confucian conception of poetry education (*shijiao*). According to Confucius, poetry education is intended to help people develop "a temperate, refined, courteous and frugal personality" (*wenliang gongjian*). In this regard, poetry is vital in a sense that it "stimulates" [people's good conscience and moral awareness] (*xing yu shi*). Under such circumstances, people will be motivated to observe and nurture their virtues in order to accomplish their humanity-based personality.

---

and dislike, *cirang zhi xin* as the feeling modesty and complaisance, and *shifei zhi xin* as the feeling of approving and disapproving) (Cf. *The Works of Mencius* 3:6). The four beginnings are the premises of developing the four virtues of reciprocal humanity, righteousness, propriety, and wisdom. Anyone who follows these heavenly principles is bound to have a just and righteous mind and able to retain his good nature in all cases. In contrast, *renyu* as human desires are negative and misleading. They reflect the selfish, morbid and even evil aspects of human mind which is confused and covered up with "material desires" (*wu yu*) or "insatiable greed" (*shi yu*). Such a confused mind is usually indifferent to "the four beginnings" and "the four virtues" as well. One who has this kind of mind is inclined to act against the constant virtues and accordingly against the heavenly principles. Hence, Zhu Xi encourages people to get "the heavenly principles purified" (*tianli chun*) in order to have "the human desires completely abandoned" (*renyu jin*).

Zhu Xi agrees with Confucius and maintains that "poetry is the expression of feelings and emotions that can be categorized into the *xie* (unconventional and vicious) and the *zheng* (serious and virtuous). The verbal descriptions in poetry are easy to understand. But reading and reciting them enable people to experience the musical rhythms and melodic effects, which then move them to their heart's content and remold their personalities. At the very beginning, poetry stirs up people's awareness of the good and the evil. It gets them engrossed in the poetic experience as if they have lost themselves in it. It is on this point that they have enriched their spiritual nourishment."[2] Elsewhere, he continues to advocate the idea that "the Dao of human morality is completely available in *The Book of Poetry (ren lun zhi dao, shi wu bu bei)*."[3]

When it comes to the *Guo feng* as an anthology of lyrical songs in *The Book of Poetry*, Zhu Xi persistently adheres to the moral principle a priori derived from Confucius' two conclusive remarks on music as part of poetry: One denies the educational merits of the *Zhengfeng* anthology, announcing that "The *Zhengfeng* tunes are excessively wanton (*zheng sheng yin*)" and thus Confucius "detests them for corrupting the *ya* music (*wu zheng sheng zhi luan ya yue ye*)."[4] In this context, the *ya* music denotes an ancient and classical type, identified with the music of peace (*Shao*) and of war (*Wu*), and characterized with simplicity in style and solemnity in tone. By contrast, the *Zhengfeng* tunes demonstrate a folk and popular type seeming rather sophisticated and sensuously pleasing or tantalizing. Seeing people become more pleasure-seeking than ever before, Confucius condemns the *Zhengfeng* tunes and even attempts to banish them (*fang zheng sheng*) as their growing popularity poses a threat to the position of the *ya* music.[5]

The other remark Confucius makes is to affirm the pedagogical value of the *Zhounan* and the *Shaonan* anthologies, claiming that "To be a man

---

[2] Zhu Xi, *Lun yü ji zhu* [The Commentary on the Confucian Analects], in *Sishu zhangju jizhu* [The Four Books with Annotations] (Beijing: Zhonghua Book Company, 1983), pp. 104–105.

[3] Ibid., p. 178.

[4] Confucius, *The Analects* (trans. D. C. Lau, London: Penguin Books, 1979), XV:11, p. 134; XVII:18, p. 146.

[5] Confucius, *The Analects* (trans. D. C. Lau), XV:11, p. 133.

who does not study these two anthologies is like standing with one's face directly towards the wall."⁶ This means such study is necessary to help one widen his scope of perspective and become well qualified to communicate with others, for in antiquity poetry was utilized as a special genre of political discourse to hint at their foreign or interstate policies on many social occasions. Scholars and officials must be well equipped with the capacity of citing and singing the songs from *The Book of Poetry* as freely and properly as they could when talking with or entertaining their guests as diplomats or envoys from other states. It was a highly delicate and demanding enterprise such that one could not afford to make any errors by using a wrong song in response to another. Otherwise, the guests would feel offended, and the two states involved might go into conflict and even warfare sometimes. This practical use of poetry is subtle and frequent as is recorded in the historical documents like the *Zuo zhuan*.⁷

Confucius's condemnation of the *Zhengfeng* tunes for their being excessively wanton and harmful to the *ya* music ends up in a negative guideline, while his praise of the *Zhounan* and *Shaonan* anthologies in a positive counterpart. Both of them provide a direct impact on Zhu Xi's conceptual conformity to Confucius' viewpoint and consequently conduce to the binary dimension of the moral principle a priori Zhu Xi accepts and applies to his poetics. That is why his commentary is found less fair and convincing enough in certain cases. His treatment of the lyric "A Deer Hunter and a Jade-like Maiden" (*Ye you si jun*), for example, discloses not merely his preset misconception, but his hypocritical attitude. Depicted in this poem is a more daring and even erotic clandestine love affair:

> An antelope is killed
> And wrapped in white afield,
> A maid for love does long,
> Tempted by a hunter so strong.
> He cuts down trees amain
> And kills a deer again.
> He sees the white-drest maid
> As beautiful as jade.
> "O soft and slow, sweetheart,

---

⁶ Ibid., XVII:10, p. 145.

⁷ Wang Keping, "Confucius' Expectations of Poetry," in *The Social Sciences in China* (English), Vol. 4, Winter 1996, pp. 134–146.

Don't tear my sash apart!"
The jade-like maid said, "Hark!
Do not let the dog bark!"⁸

Believe or not, the depiction above is most explicit in the expression of the secret love affair among all the lyrical songs. The hunter, deer, and jade-like maiden are bound together to form a symbolic interaction. The hunter is not simply a hunter of animals, but also a hunter of women. He has killed a deer, wrapped it in white rushes, and then presented it as a gift to his beloved. The killed deer as the hunter's prey easily reminds the reader of the hidden destiny of the young girl. The phrase of "jade-like maid" signifies the female beauty whose charming innocence and naked body represent a sexual prey of tremendous temptation. The two lovers are now trysting alone in a tranquil grove outside the village. The hunter tries every means to please the maid with an intention to satisfy his lust. The last stanza literally shows their lovemaking during which whispers are uttered, requesting the man to be gentle and quiet instead of being too harsh and noisy. The atmosphere here implies the man's eagerness and sexual thirst and the girl's willingness but cautiousness. The whole scene appears so natural, real, and human.

Yet, since this poem is collected in the *Shaonan* anthology instead of the *Zhengfeng* anthology, Zhu Xi pretends not to see the reality but offers a ridiculous defense via his commentary. As is noticed in his statement, "The Southern State was civilized through the rites under the leadership of the King Wen of Zhou. The beautiful maiden was purely chaste and morally dignified, defending herself against a sexual seduction and attack as is seen in the hunter's way to treat her. The poet admired her self-defensive deed and wrote to eulogize it. The sexual seduction continues through the poem until the maiden holds her back with dignity and pushes away the hunter who is touching her all about."⁹ Few people could accept this far-fetched interpretation as it is obviously branched off the sheer logic of a secret love affair the song as such sets forth.

---

⁸ *The Book of Poetry* (trans. Xu Yuanchong, Changsha: Hunan Press, 1993), pp. 38–41. A minor modification is made in the English version.

⁹ Zhu Xi, *Shi jing ji zhuan* [Annotations and Comments on The Book of Poetry], in *Sishu wujing* [The Four Books and Five Classics] (Tianjin: Guji Bookshop, 1984), Vol. 2, p. 9.

Comparatively, when it comes to the poem "Cadet My Dear" (*Qiang zhong zi*) from the *Zhengfeng* anthology, Zhu Xi goes so far as to label it a love poem full of lustful and flirting expressions (*yin ben zhi ci*). But reading the first stanza of the poem:

> Cadet my dear,
> Don't leap into my hamlet, please,
> Nor break my willow trees!
> Not that I care for these;
> It is my parents that I fear.
> Much as I love you, dear,
> How can I not be afraid
> Of what my parents might have said!....[10]

we can easily discern the secret romance involved in a dilemma and find nothing licentious and morally problematic on the part of the maiden. Instead, we may have the feeling that the maiden is timid, fragile, and self-defensive because she confines herself to her parents' advice or patriarchic power. Such an interaction between the girl and her parents actually unfolds a bilateral awareness of moral conduct as a result of adhering to the rigid rites. Noticeably, the two lovers have met each other before as the man is indicated to steal his way into her dwelling. But now she advises him not to come along this way any more. This implies her face-consciousness and moral rationality mixed up with psychical ambivalence.

Through comparative illustrations, Zhu Xi's bi-polarized treatment of the lyrics is found restricted to a designated sphere contained in the moral principle a priori. This principle is composed of two dimensions: positive and negative in accord with the two categories of poems in his perception. The positive is applied to the so-called serious and virtuous category (*zheng*) mainly from the *Zhounan* and *Shaonan* anthologies, while the negative is applied to the so-called vicious and wanton category (*xie*) mainly from the *Zhengfeng* and *Weifeng* anthologies. What he does in this regard is like what the old saying suggests: He draws a circle on the ground to serve as a prison to detain himself within (*huadi weilao*). That is why some amount of his commentary turns out to be far-fetched, lopsided, and even misconceived. No one knows whether Zhu Xi speaks out what he really feels and experiences in the love poems. But, in order

---

[10] *The Book of Poetry* (trans. Xu Yuanchong), pp. 142–145.

to secure his position as a moralist teacher, he seems obliged to do whatever possible to defend the *tianli* or the rites as a foundation stone for moral education.

In spite of his preoccupation with the moral principle a priori, Zhu Xi's treatment of the "Cadet My Dear," among many others, reveals his individual and sharp observation if compared with the conventional interpretation provided by Mao Heng in the Han Dynasty. As is read in the *Mao shi zheng yi* (Mao Heng's Commentary on *The Book of Poetry*), the thematic line of all the *feng* lyrics is overshadowed by sheer political allegory that is used "to educate the ruled by the ruling" (*shang yi feng hua xia*) and "to satirize the ruling by the ruled" (*xia yi feng ci shang*), aiming to rectify their morals and manners altogether.[11] Regarding the case of the "Cadet My Dear," Mao Heng repeats a sort of intentional fallacy by linking it with a historical story in the *Zuo zhuan* and asserts that the lyric itself signals a moral lesson and political teaching concerning the dramatic interrelationship in a power game between the two brothers, Zhuang Gong and Shuduan.[12] In a word, Mao Heng paraphrases

---

[11] Mao Heng, *Mao shi zheng yi* [Mao Heng's Commentary on The Book of Poetry] (Beijing: Peking University Press, 1999), Vol. 1, p. 13. The original remark runs: "*Shang yi feng hua xia, xia yi feng ci shang, zhu wen er jue jian, yan zhi zhe wu zui, wen zhi zhe zu yi jie, gu yue feng.*" Its English rendering runs: "The ruling use the *feng* lyrics to educate the ruled; the ruled use the *feng* lyrics to satirize the ruling. This recommends literary and diplomatic satire or analogy. Those who make such satirical utterances are freed from any blame; and those who hear about them ought to mind their conduct. So named are the *feng* lyrics."

[12] This historical story is read in the *Zuo zhuan*, and used by Mao Heng to interpret the political overtones as are assumingly attached to the poem "Cadet My Dear" (*Jiang zhong zi*). It is documented in what happens in the first year of the Lord Yin of Lu State as briefly follows: Lord Wu of Zheng State married Lady Wu Jiang who gave birth to Zhuanggong first and to Shuduan second. As she had a hard time when having her first delivery, the Lady loved Shuduan so much more than Zhuanggong that she persuaded her husband, Lord Wu, to allow Shuduan to take the throne but did not succeed. When Zhuanggong became the Lord of the Zheng State, he accepted his mother's request and offered his young brother Shuduan an important position in the capital. Zhai Zhong, a minister, advises Zhuanggong to restrain the power and stop the misbehavior of Shuduan for the safety of the state power, but Zhuanggong rejected due to his mother's preference. In turn, he told Zhai Zhong that Shuduan would be doomed if he continued his wrongdoings. As a result, Shuduan was so spoiled and corrupted that he ventured to usurp the state power from Zhuanggong. Eventually, Shuduan failed and got killed after a chaotic and warring period. Cf. *Zuo zhuan* [Zuo Qiuming's Commentary on The Spring and Autumn Annals] (Beijing: Peking University Press, 1999), Vol. 1, pp. 50–54.

it as a satire against Zhuang Gong for his failure to prevent his younger brother Shuduan from being spoiled and corrupted to his doomed end. Quite some readers, both Chinese and Western, are induced into this far-fetched interpretation and tend to parrot back what Mao Heng says.[13] Instead, it is Zhu Xi who first breaks away from this beaten track and grounds his explanation on the subject matter represented. He concludes that it is merely a love poem intensified by the daring expression of private experiences. All this seems to me justifiable in terms of textual and contextual anatomy. As is noticed in the three stanzas of the poem, the maiden exhorts her lover not to break the willows, mulberries, and sandal trees when he sneaks through the surroundings and "leaps into her garden." This is not because she cares about the trees themselves. Rather, the only thing she cares or fears about is what her parents, brothers, and neighbors might say about their trysting adventures. In fact, she herself enjoys such adventures even though she appears highly alert against the noises and traces that might be made and left behind during the process. She therefore announces repeatedly "Much as I love you, dear" (*zhong ke huai ye*) with passionate affection and heartfelt delight. The poetic ambiance as a whole impresses me as if the female persona unwillingly suppresses her passion due to the social pressure while implicitly complaining about the family supervision and moral discourse not in her favor.

Zhu Xi is renown to have spent over 40 years on the study of *The Book of Poetry*. He has scrutinized each text and grounds most of his interpretations on textual investigation by reading all the poems numerous times for an aesthetic contemplation and insightful understanding. Hence, he has come out to define poetry as "the artistic expression of feelings

---

[13] Some Western scholars have noticed the political overtones in these poems as a result of making a particular reference to Mao Heng's interpretation in the *Mao shi zheng yi* [Mao Heng's Commentary on The Book of Poetry], Vol. 1, pp. 279–280. Cf. Francois Julien, *Detour and Access: Strategies of Meaning in China and Greece* (New York: Zone Books, 2000). Mao Heng's statement follows: "*Jiang zhong zi, ci Zhuang Gong ye. Bu sheng qi mu, yi hai qi di. Di Shu shi dao er Gong fu zhi, Zhai Zhong jian er Gong fu ting, xiao bu ren yi zhi da luan yan.*" It means basically as such: The poem of the "Cadet My Dear" is satirical against Lord Zhuang Gong of Zheng State. The Lord takes no measures as his mother spoils his younger brother Shuduan. Thus Shuduan misbehaves more brutally, but the Lord Zhuang Gong lets him become what he wants to. Zhai Zhong, a minister, advises the Lord to stop Shuduan behave as such, but the Lord refuses to do anything. Consequently, Shuduan goes so far as to launch a political coup and causes great disorder in the state.

inspired by things or events" (*ganwu daoqing*) rather than the documentary representation of political overtones. Thus confidently he knocks down the conventional approach to promoting overstrained explications and far-fetched analogies and criticizes Mao Heng's doctrine of literary satirization (*meici shuo*) as being in many cases a "fantasized conjecture" (*wangyi tuixiang*) and "originally absent of truth" (*chuwu qishi*).[14] Specifically, regarding the "Cadet My Dear," he says it is "simply about a male-and-female romance, and therefore has noting to do with [any political overtones or moral teachings relating to such historical figures as] Zhuang Gong and Shuduan at all."[15]

13.2 A Bi-polarized Treatment of the *Guofeng*

The moral principle a priori as is presented above can be further justified with reference to Zhu Xi's preoccupied stance toward the lyrics of the *Guofeng* anthology. The anthology is the first part of *The Book of Poetry* (*Shi jing*), comprising 160 lyrical songs most of which are allegedly composed from the eighth to the sixth century B.C. and collected by royal musicians from 15 states in ancient China. Since Confucian traditionalists persist in rigid prevention of private interactions between man and woman, they tend to decline the recognition of the romances presented in quite a number of the lyrical songs. Instead, they take them arbitrarily for political pieces in a documentary sense, deal with them from a sociohistorical perspective and even distort the poetic imports in such mechanical terms as direct narrative (*fu*), analogy (*bi*), and inspiring means (*xing*). Zhu Xi, however, goes off the beaten track by pointing out the authentic sources of the *Guofeng* as is proclaimed in the "Preface" to the *Shi jing jizhuan*:

> Most of the entries in the Guofeng anthology come from the folk songs, sung by men and women when they are meeting together and expressing their romantic sentiments. Among these poems both the Zhounan and the Shaonan anthologies are refined [in both wording and accompanied

[14] Zhu Xi, *Zhuzi yu lei* [The Sayings of Zhuzi], Vol. 80, p. 2077.

[15] Ibid., Vol. 81, p. 2108. His Chinese statement follows: "*Ru Jiang zhongzi, zi shi nan nü xiang yu zhi ci, que yu Zhai Zhong Gong Shuduan shen shi?*" It implies that "Take the 'Cadet My Dear' for example. It is just about a romance between a male and a female. And it has nothing to do with Zhai Zhong and Shuduan at all, doesn't it?"

music] by King Wen of Zhou so as to help people accomplish virtues. Those who are inspired by these refined poems are most likely to nourish just and moral temperament or disposition. Hence, what is expressed in them bears such features as being joyful without conducing licentiousness, and being sorrowful without causing excessive grief. Accordingly, the two anthologies are respectively considered belonging to the serious and virtuous category (zhengjing). By contrast, the songs collected from other 13 states [ranging from Bei, Yong, Wei, Zheng, Qi, Tang, Qin, Chen, Gui, Cao to Bin, etc.] are varied from one another for being either serious or popular, virtuous or vicious, right or wrong (zhengxie shifei). This is corresponding to the fact that the 13 states involved are varied from one another in degree of being either well-governed or ill-governed along with good or bad citizenship. Consequently, the songs therein are revealing altered characteristics (bian) if compared with those in the Zhounan and the Shaonan anthologies refined by King Wen of Zhou.[16]

Noticeably, Zhu Xi views the *Guofeng* as a collection of folk songs popular among the populace or the so-called grass roots in the society. These songs are not perceived as historical documents of any specific events. Instead, most of them are poetic expressions of romantic sentiments attributed to the young boys and girls in particular, reflecting the emotional and intellectual life of the Zhou people through poetic expression. In a feudal society shrouded in the omnipresent moralization of human conduct and ideology during Zhu Xi's days, any recognition of the above fact is by no means easy. It requires not merely relevant observation but also enough courage to speak out the truth. This may seem absurd to the contemporaries but understandable in the past when the moralistic Neo-Confucianism was running rampant and dominant then. Apparently, Zhu Xi steps over the restrictive boundary and comes out with a breakthrough.

However, when credits are given to the breakthrough as such regarding the substance of the *Guofeng* lyrics, what cannot be neglected is Zhu Xi's distinguishing between such binary categories as the *zheng* and the *xie*. The Chinese notion of *zheng* signifies what is conventional, serious, virtuous, or non-depraved. Rather, the notion of *xie* as its counterpart means what is unconventional, popular, vicious, or depraved. As a result of moral judgment, the former is identified with the *shi* (right

---

[16] Zhu Xi, "Shi jing zhuan xu" [Preface to the Annotations and Comments on The Book of Poetry], in *Sishu wujing* [The Four Books and Five Classics] (Tianjin: Guji Bookshop, 1984), Vol. 2, p. i. The English translation is mine.

and proper) whereas the latter with the *fei* (wrong and improper). Both of them relate to the subject matter and stylistic aspects of the *Guofeng* songs, and meanwhile represent at least two moral aspects aforementioned. They all work to influence and even moralize Zhu Xi's general stance and approach to poetry. As is discerned in the *Shi jing jizhuan*, his treatment of the verses in the *Zhounan* and the *Shaonan* anthologies is extremely positive while his treatment of the verses in the *Zheng* and the *Wei* anthologies is extremely negative. All this demonstrates a bi-polarized tendency merely in a moral rather than an aesthetic sense.

With respect to the basic themes and values of the verses, for instance, Zhu Xi insists that the *Zhounan* and the *Shaonan* anthologies belong to the *zheng*, the serious and non-depraved category while the *Zhengfeng* and *Weifeng* anthologies belong to the *xie*, the popular and depraved category. Let us first look at his generalization of the *zheng* category.

Historically, the *Zhounan* and *Shaonan* anthologies were initially collected and refined by King Wen of Zhou who used them to cultivate and educate the populace by means of the moral messages contained. When the King Cheng of Zhou came into the throne, he was assisted by the prime minister Duke Dan of Zhou who launched the program of making rites and music as rules of governance and codes of conduct. The music thus produced was partly based on the verses in the *Zhounan* anthology handed down from the preceding King Wen.

Teleologically, Duke Dan of Zhou managed to accompany the verses with music firstly for chamber performance. Then, he promoted the music to the villages all over the country to show the flourishing prospects of enculturation and moralization. Meanwhile, he aimed to set up artistic paradigms and hereby to guide people to cultivate themselves, regulate families, run the country in order, and bring peace to all under the sky.

Thematically, the first five poems in the *Zhounan* anthology are singing praises of the moral virtues of Lady Si, King Wen's wife. *The Wooing and Wedding* (*Guan ju*) expresses her virtuous personality as a whole in one sense, and in the other, eulogizes her gentleness and kindness serving to benefit other people around. It seems to be a representation of King Wen's wife, but actually it is a manifestation of the effects of the King's personal cultivation and family regulation. As for other poems like *The Newly-wed* (*Tao yao*), *The Rabbit Catcher* (*Tu ju*), and the *Plantain Gathering* (*Fu yi*), they are all describing the effects of how a family is harmoniously regulated and how a state is kept in good order. In addition, they are exposing the spread of peace under the sky.

The Good Unicorn (*Lin zhi zhi*) exemplifies the human-hearted nature of King Wen's wife, attempting to explain why her children were born with the same nature. It is the last piece in this anthology, and supposed to correspond to *The Wooing and Wedding* (*Guan ju*) as the first piece. With respect to the *Shaonan* anthology ranging from *The Magpie's Nest* (*Que chao*) to the *Sacrifice before Wedding* (*Cai ping*), we read between the lines the depiction of personal cultivation and family regulation. Then, the rest of the anthology ranging from *The Duke of Zhao* (*Gan tang*) to *A Hunter* (*Zou yu*) implicitly indicate King Wen's personal influence via his modeling behavior, and accordingly his outstanding achievement in terms of moral education, civilized citizenship, effective governance, and social order.

Controversially, most of the critics assume that the *Zhounan* anthology is solely devoted to the exposure of King Wen's virtuous wife. Zhu Xi argues that a women's personality cannot be well established and accomplished alone. That is to say, King Wen plays an important and decisive role in this regard. It is therefore misleading if King Wen's role is ignored, and his wife's accomplishment overestimated.[17]

In striking contrast to the foregoing remarks about the *zheng* category, we will see another side of the story when turning to the so-called *xie* category that is considered popular and depraved. It is in this case that Zhu Xi's commentary provides a morally bleak picture as follows:

1. Morally, the music in both the Zheng and Wei states is prevailingly popular among the masses due to its licentious touch. Correspondingly, the poems in the *Zhengfeng* and *Weifeng* anthologies are subject to the musical impact. As a consequence, a fourth of the 39 *Weifeng* lyrics are about romantic encounters between man and women who violate the proper rites as moral codes; over two-thirds of the 21 *Zhengfeng* lyrics turn out to be concerned with such undisciplined and boorish conduct.[18]

---

[17] Zhu Xi, *Shi jing ji zhuan* [Annotations and Comments on The Book of Poetry], in *Sishu wujing* [The Four Books and Five Classics], Vol. 2, pp. 1–10.

[18] Zhu Xi, *Shi jing ji zhuan* [Annotations and Comments on The Book of Poetry], in *Sishu wujing* [The Four Books and Five Classics], Vol. 2, p. 38. Here, Zhu Xi says that the *Weifeng* anthology consist of 39 pieces in total number. But, there are only 10 pieces recorded in *The Book of Poetry*. In addition, Zhu Xi makes little distinction between the lyrical songs and their accompanied music or tunes. This differs from what Confucius does. Confucius attacks the licentious touch of the *Weifeng* music and the *Zhengfeng* music, but never the lyrical songs concerned. Otherwise, he would have cancelled them altogether when rearranging *The Book of Poetry*.

2. Comparatively, the *Weifeng* anthology features more description of how the male please the female, whereas the *Zhengfeng* anthology is saturated with the expressions about how the female seduce the male. The Wei people tend to produce satires and mockeries with a hidden intention to criticize and punish the debauched behavior and licentious acts. But, the people from the Zheng State remain shameless and show no sign of regret for their debaucheries. Hence, the music in the Zheng State is even more vicious and licentious than its counterpart in the Wei State. It is for this reason that Confucius advises people to keep alert against the latter in particular.
3. Geographically and psychologically, Zhu Xi reiterates Zhang Zai's personal assumption in order to reinforce his own comment. Zhang claims that the Wei State (modern Henan) is located close to a big river (the Yellow River). Those who live in this area with infertile land would be subject to frivolous social atmosphere; those who live in a flat and lower region will become pliant and weak in temper; those who live in a rich land and get good bumper harvests so easily are apt to grow slack and pleasure-seeking. Such being their disposition and mentality by nature, their songs are most liable to be licentious and lavishly vulgar. On hearing their music, the audiences are most likely to become sluggish and yield to depraved fantasies. This is seemingly reflected in the poetry of the *Zhengfeng* anthology.
4. Consequently, Zhu Xi picks out 10 poems from the *Zhengfeng* anthology and labels them as morally problematic and improper. In other words, he holds that these poems are representations of demoralized interactions between male and female. From a moralistic perspective, he bitterly attacks these writings filled with dissolute sentiments and dissipated inwardness, for he suspects that they may appeal to the base desires and hedonistic passions of the youth in particular. This is of course detrimental not only to the moral being of the youth, but also to the moral codes and social order sustained via the rites.[19]

Zhu Xi's distinction between the highbrow category of the *zheng* and its lowbrow counterpart of the *xie* is grounded on two binary orientations

---

[19] Ibid., pp. 29–39.

aforementioned. His commentary is in accord with his moral and pedagogical preoccupations. He deliberately plays up one category from a positive viewpoint while hammering down the other from a negative one. This bi-polarized treatment can be further illustrated through his critique of two poems, namely, *The Wooing and Wedding* (*Guan ju*) from the *Zhounan* anthology and *To a Scholar* (*Zi jin*) from the *Zhengfeng* anthology.

The Wooing and Wedding has five stanzas in all, describing the process of how a young couple fall in love before marriage. With an oral and lucid style, the poem begins with a depiction of two cooing birds that allegorically lead to a human romance:

> By riverside a pair
> Of turtledoves are cooing;
>   There's a good maiden fair
>   Whom a young man is wooing.
>
> Water flows left and right
>   Of cress long here, short there;
> The youth yearns day and night
>   For the good maiden fair.
>
> His yearning grows so strong
>   He cannot fall asleep,
> But tosses all night long,
>   So deep in love, so deep!....[20]

As has been noted in these lines, the romance is simple and straightforward. On the part of the young man, his passion is strong, his mentality is natural, and his behavior is normal. On the part of the maiden, her beauty seems to be redoubled by means of the goodness or moral virtue she is claimed to possess. Without reading through the whole text, we may predict and wish the two young folks would make a good match and an ideal couple in the end. What impresses us most is the symbolism of the birds used as a device to spur up the romantic sentiments. Incidentally, Zhu Xi defines it as a poetic technique of *xing*,

---

[20] *The Book of Poetry* (trans. Xu Yuanchong), p. 3. The last two stanzas in English version follow: "Now gather left and right/Cress long or short and tender!/O lute, play music light/For the fiancée so slender!/Feast friends at left and right/on Cresses cooked tender!/o bells and drums, delight/The bride so sweet and slender!"

meaning to "say some other kind of thing first in order to conduce what is intended to be said" (*xing zhe, xian yan tawu yi yinqi suo song zhi ci ye*). In this context, the cooing birds are employed as a form of *xing* to inspire human emotions and feelings associated with the courting couple and their romantic experience. The symbolism derived from the birds is peculiar of Chinese poetry owing to its moral suggestiveness. As is traditionally perceived, the turtledoves themselves live a special way of life and enjoy a "stable and fixed" relationship. They stay as lifelong partners from birth to death. Neither of them will mate again with an outsider even if one of them happens to be missing or dead. They move around together as if they treat each other with mutual care and respect in a dignified manner. Hence, they are often personified and likened to a fine model for everlasting love, bilateral loyalty, and unconditional devotion.

Notwithstanding the above perception, Zhu Xi's commentary goes further as follows: "King Wen of Zhou has sagely virtues. He is married with Lady Si. When all the attendants in his palace have first observed her virtues of being easy-going, chaste and calm, they are so impressed that they have composed this song in praise of her personality. The cooing turtledoves make a good match, and so do the fair maiden and the wooing young man accordingly. The turtledoves represent a loving couple with mutual respect and loyalty, and so do King Wen and Lady Si.... In the Han Dynasty Kuang Heng as a classicist claims that the portrayal of the fair good maiden and the wooing young man indicates the ability to retain such virtues of chastity, kindness, loyalty and devotion to love, apart from proper sentiments and proprieties without being predetermined by mere physical appearances, manners and actions. Such ability shows the maiden's moral adequacy to be an ideal wife of King Wen in that she can help him promote the moral education of the masses then. This observation justifies its relevance and Kuang Heng's competence in poetic criticism."[21] Judging from the text as it is, the young couple can be looked upon either as two beings without specific identity each, or as representatives of any man and woman who go through the process of courting experience anywhere. But quite arbitrarily, Zhu Xi steps into the shoes of his predecessors by specifying the two persons as King Wen and his wife Lady Si. Regarding the young man's yearning for love and his tossing on bed sleepless, Zhu Xi does not look into his psychology

---

[21] Zhu Xi, *Shi jing jizhuan* [Annotations and Comments on The Book of Poetry], in *Sishu wujing* [The Four Books and Five Classics], Vol. 2, p. 1.

of anxiety and love-sickness. Instead, he goes so far as to turn the man's natural desire into political morality or sense of mission. As he says in such a far-fetched tune, "Why the man cannot fall asleep and tosses all night long? Because he yearns so much to win the maiden's love even when he is supposed to repose at night. He feels sleepless as he misses the maiden with such virtues and finds her a rare being. He longs to marry her as he seeks after her assistance to accomplish the good governance and social order under his regime. It is for this reason that he cares and worries to such an extent."[22]

In the poem *To a Scholar* (*Zi jin*) from the *Zhengfeng* anthology, we will detect similar sentiments:

> Scholar with a collar blue,
> How much I long for you!
> Though to see you I am not free,
> O why not send a word to me?
>
> Scholar with a belt-stone blue,
> How long I think of you!
> Though to see you I am not free,
> O why not come and see me?
>
> I'm pacing up and down
> On the wall of the town.
> When to see you I am not free,
> One day seems like three months to me.[23]

Compared with *The Wooing and Wedding*, this above scene witnesses another romance in which the maiden is the persona and emotionally active. Instead of describing a young man's yearning for love, it is bringing out a young maiden's sorrows stemmed from love-sickness. As the male scholar is away from home and the girl is left behind alone for a long time, she misses him as much as she worries about what has become of him because she has never heard of him ever since his departure. All this intensifies the loneliness she can no longer bear. Hence, she is murmuring to herself a heartfelt complaint with mixed feelings, which strikes the reader as both pathetic and sympathetic. Apparently, she is growing

---

[22] Ibid., p. 2.
[23] *The Book of Poetry* (trans. Xu Yuanchong), pp. 165–167.

anxious and restless, which is observed in her "pacing up and down on the wall of the town." The image of the wall is meaningful in this case. For in an ancient town, it usually stands for the highest place from where people can see afar and await their beloved or family members returning home, etc. Evidently, the maiden is overwhelmed with her longing, and her conception of time has dramatically changed in a relativistic mode. She thus feels that one-day short seems to be three-month long, which in turn renders her solitariness and grievance more impressive and stirring.

Then, what does Zhu Xi say about it? After explaining some expressions like *youyou* (think of) and *woxin* (the maiden herself), he concludes that this poem is one of *yinben zhishi*, a poetic depiction of licentious or immoral act against the social norms. Regarding the last stanza, for instance, Zhu Xi sharply criticizes the frivolous passion and wanton behavior of the yearning maiden, for they are, from his viewpoint, all violating and damaging the proper rites as moral codes. Accordingly, it is scandalous and intolerable to have a woman play an active role in any romantic event because it will not only seduce the male, but also corrupt the female. Bias of such kind is surely leagued with the dominance of male chauvinism. This being the case, Zhu Xi tends to denounce most of the love lyrics in which the female persona happens to play an emotionally initiative and courageous part in romantic affairs. It is particularly the case with the *Zhengfeng* anthology. Actually, he censures many other poems because of his moralized intention. In the *Lady Jiang* (*Younü tongju*), for example,

> A lady in the cab with me
> Looks like a flower from a hedge-tree.
> She goes about as if in flight;
> Her girdle-pendants look so bright.
> O Lady Jiang with a pretty face,
> So elegant and full of grace....[24]

What is perceived in these lines is a description and admiration of the flowery beauty and graceful manners of the lady in the cab. But what Zhu Xi sees is quite different. He suspects the two persons therein are undergoing a clandestine love affair, if not a secret elopement.

---

[24] Ibid., pp. 156–157.

His critique of this kind runs through the *Zhengfeng* anthology so long as there is the poetic characterization of female appearance and romantic sentiment.

As is aforementioned, Zhu Xi is the first to see the *Guofeng* as a collection of folk songs many of which are popular among men and women in their prime age. This is to prove the fact that *The Book of Poetry* in its entirety reflects the social, political, and emotional aspects of life in the Zhou Dynasty. Typically represented thereby are the ideas, sentiments, social interactions, and personal experiences of the populace in a variety of tones and styles. Nevertheless, Zhu Xi embraces a bi-polarized stance that leads to arbitrary and biased findings with reference to the two categories illustrated above. Hence, one may find it less authentic but rather confusing with regard to his lopsided commentary.

13.3 Second Reflection on "Having no Depraved Thoughts"

The school of canonic studies (*jingxue*)[25] undergoes a substantial development in Zhu Xi's era. The methodology he exercises manifests certain hermeneutic features. It can be broadly classified into two interrelated modes: One is textual as is based on the sentence patterns (*ju fa*), and the other is empirical as is based on personal apprehension (*xin fa*). In Western terminology, the textual mode is essentially objective while the empirical mode is subjective. These two modes are interactive and even interwoven instead of being clear-cut and monadically self-closed. That means personal apprehension or empirical explanation can penetrate into the textual interpretation in the praxis of literary criticism.

With respect to the textual mode, Zhu Xi retains that any textual interpretation should be preconditioned by the fundamental theme of the text concerned. The theme as such serves as an indispensable premise

---

[25] The school of canonic studies (*jingxue*) in China is basically devoted to the interpretation of Chinese canons or classics. It can be traced back to Confucius' compilation and treatment of the five classics, including the *Shi jing* (*The Book of Poetry*), *Shu jing* (*The Book of History*), *Li jing* (*The Book of Rites*), *Yue jing* (*The Book of Music*), *Yi jing* (*The Book of Changes*), and *Chun qiu* (*The Spring and Autumn Annals*). Ever since the Han Dynasty or from the second century B.C. onward, the school of canonic studies is developed into an orthodox in favor of Confucianism. In the Song Dynasty, it reached its acme to which Zhu Xi is acknowledged as the most outstanding and comprehensive contributor.

or master key to clarify the meaning of the phrases and sentences used in the text. From his viewpoint, "*The Book of Changes* (*Yi jing*) is thematically about the *Yin* and the *Yang*; *The Book of Poetry* (*Shi jing*) is thematically about the *xie* (depraved) and the *zheng* (non-depraved); and *The Book of History* (*Shu jing*) is thematically about the *zhi* (social order) and the *luan* (social chaos)."[26] A good command of their respective themes can secure a relevant orientation to understand and explicate the text. This being the case, the use of philological devices can help pinpoint what the phrases and sentences really mean, which then goes further to locate and clarify the meaning of the text as a whole. As there arise doubted points with ambiguous implications in the text, it is necessary to interpret and reinterpret them in order to clear away the possible ambiguities and misunderstandings.

Then what on earth the interpretation aims at? According to Zhu Xi, it aims to find out three things: The first is the original meaning of the canonic text; the second is the intention of the author; and the third is the message of the enlightened reader.[27] To my mind, the first objective depends on the intended meaning of the text that can be largely specified by virtue of textual analysis; the second objective is subject to variables and mostly based on extended significance of the text, and so is the third objective. The extended significance often deviates from the textual meaning because of its implicitness and suggestiveness. To fulfill these three objectives, the textual mode is not adequate enough. It therefore requires the assistance from its counterpart of the empirical mode as a complementary dimension. The latter is closely associated with fore understandings, personal observations, cultural literacy, moral cultivation, intelligible capacity, and cognitive familiarity with the past undertakings in canonic studies and interpretations, etc. It encourages the reader to feel into the text along with all his schematic resources available. By so doing can the hidden meaning be exposed and the significance be extended.

As an outcome of this methodological drive, Zhu Xi has brought into light many ambiguous arguments even though he has also distorted the pictures of some lyrical poems in terms of the moral principle a priori.

---

[26] Zhu Xi, *Zhuzi yu lei* [The Sayings of Zhuzi], Vol. 11.

[27] Pan Derong, "Jingdian yu quanshi: lun Zhu Xi de quanshi sixiang" [Classic Cannons and Interpretations: On Zhu Xi's Hermeneutic Ideas], in *Social Sciences in China* (Chinese), 2002, No. 1, pp. 60–63.

A typical example lies in his second reflection on Confucius' conclusive remark: "In *The Book of Poetry* are three hundred pieces in number. They can be summed up in one sentence—'Have no depraved thoughts (*si wu xie*)'."[28] This overgeneralization is conducive to misconception, for it is often taken for a moralized summary of the general theme or subject matter of the three hundred poems or so. People tend to get confused when reading the love songs that represent, implicitly or explicitly, the romantic sentiments and erotic deeds between the young lovers. They find quite a number of the love songs falling short of the expectation of "having no depraved thoughts" if viewed from a moralized perspective. So they cannot help but wonder what Confucius really means by this line ("Having no depraved thoughts") cited from a hymn of Lu entitled the "Horses" (*Jiong*).

Zhu Xi firstly points out that "The Confucius' remark bears a profound implication. For what is expressed in the poetry can be either good-natured or evil-natured in content. The former stimulates the good conscience of people, whereas the latter warn them of their sensuous pursuits and unhealthy fantasies. Eventually, both of them are intended to help people develop a decent and moral personality. Since the poetic discourse is indirect and suggestive, it is not easy to exhaust its meaning in clarity."[29] This given comment does not work to justify what Confucius means by the phrase-based summary even though Zhu Xi quotes Cheng Yi's vague interpretation in terms of "sincerity" (*cheng*). Later on, Zhu Xi offers a more elaborate and individual explanation of this ambiguous point when he rereads the love poem of the "Trysts" (*Sang zhong*) from the *Yongfeng* anthology:

> By claiming that all the poems [in The Book of Poetry] "have no depraved thoughts (si wu xie)", Confucius means to use the three hundred pieces to promote the good while punishing the evil. Although its basic intention is good-natured and directed to the right path, it is not completely and justly understood yet. As a matter of fact, it does not suggest that all the poets be freed from depraved thoughts. Now there arise two interpretations: One argues that the poets do describe the love romances but

---

[28] Confucius, *The Analects* (trans. D. C. Lau), II:2. The translation is modified with reference to the Chinese original. One may well go to check James Legge's version.

[29] Zhu Xi, *Lun yü ji zhu* [The Commentary on the Confucian Analects], Vol. 1, in *Sishu zhangju jizhu* [The Four Books with Annotations], pp. 53–54.

they themselves have no depraved thoughts. They do so to denote a moral message with both a sense of sympathy and that of punishment relating to the victims. The other argues that the poets write about these poems when they have depraved thoughts, but readers are expected to rid themselves of any depraved thoughts when reading the pieces. They can learn moral lessons from the ugly in the poetic representations and keep alert against such wrong doings. These sayings are varied from one another. In my mind, it would be better to look into oneself rather than into others from the light of non-depravedness. Likewise, it would be even better to banish the vice of depravedness on one's own rather than attributing the virtue of non-depravedness to others.[30]

This interpretation is highly instructive as a consequence of its moralized intention and requirement. It is a consequence not merely of empirical analysis pointed to the merits of cultural literacy and personal sensibility, but also of second reflection in pursuit of the general objective of Confucius himself regarding the use of the poems in all. With the objective identified and the attitude rectified, whether or not to have depraved or non-depraved thoughts is found far less decisive when it comes to reading the love poems in particular, for what really counts in this experience is the reader's aesthetic attention, normal attitude, and moral conscience. Just as the old saying runs, you should not bother so much about your slanting shadow on the ground so long as you yourself are walking straight ahead. That is, whatever types of depraving and seducing depiction in poetry matter too little provided you can manage to keep yourself in a decent and innocent state of mind. Such a state of mind is sustained by at least two essential characteristics: one is the inward transcendence and the other is aesthetic detachment. All this is not adequately heeded and reconsidered, however. It is Xiong Shili, a modern Chinese philosopher, who perceives the message and pushes it further in plain language as follows:

> Reading through each piece in The Book of Poetry, we find it groundless to conclude that they all have no depraved thoughts (si wu xie). Subsequent Confucian scholars insist that Confucius says this to let people draw moral lessons from both the good and bad contents. This is not against the possible intention but narrows down what Confucius means.

---

[30] Kang Xiaocheng, *Xianqin rujia shijiao sixiang yanjiu* [A Study of the Pre-Qin Confucian Ideas of Poetry Education] (Taipei: Wenshizhe Press, 1988), pp. 159–160.

> In fact, Confucius applies this idea to The Book of Poetry as a whole, calling for a complete and thorough understanding of literature. Originally, literature expresses the human life or condition. Though saturated with the exposure of the bright and dark or the good and bad aspects, it enlightens people to think of moving from the dark toward the bright, and to explore the nature of human freedom. It is for this reason that Confucius talks about having no depraved thoughts in the case of the poems.... From antiquity up till now, "The Wooing and Wedding" (Guan ju) has been widely read. But how many people have ever experienced the spiritual state of "being joyful without causing licentiousness and being sorrowful without excessive grief."... As human beings are enslaved by the instrumental values and corrupted by material wants, they are so wanton and licentious that they have lost their original nature of innocence. They tend to delight in the licentious life and suffer from excessive grief to the extent that they have confined themselves to the small and selfish "I," transformed themselves along with things and desires, and consequently lost their real essence to be integrated with the great universe. This is so tragic of human existence.[31]

Apparently what Xiong Shili tries to say is reconfirm what Zhu Xi, among others, have done before by approving the moral purpose of the poems in terms of "having no depraved thoughts." Corresponding to Zhu Xi and the like, Xiong Shili encourages people to look inward, instead of looking outward in view of personal cultivation and spiritual sublimation. But he ventures further with a critique of the narrower preoccupation with merely moralized intention and attitude concerning the subject matter of the poems proper. He, in fact, announces the hidden function of literature as an expression of the human condition and advocates the nature of human freedom for value judgment. This largely broadens the scope and perspective of literary criticism. According to Xiong Shili's observation, the human condition is rendered so harsh by instrumental confinement, material corruption, pleasure-seeking greed, small-minded selfishness, etc. Worse still, many people appear self-obsessed in this plight and even self-deprived of their sense of justice, not to speak of their real knowledge and courage to face the tragic aspect of

---

[31] Xiong Shili, "Shi jing lüe shuo" [A Rambling Talk on The Book of Poetry], in *Du jing shi yao* [A Basic Approach to Reading the Chinese Classics], quoted from Huang Kejian (ed.), *Xiong Shili ji* [Selected Writings by Xiong Shili] (Beijing: Qunyan Press, 1993), p. 269.

their being. This being the circumstance, Xiong Shili assumes and possibly expects literature to play an important role and enlighten the victims at loss. As is seen in the genre of poetry, literature exposes and typifies both the positive and negative respects of the reality. Once "a complete and thorough understanding of literature" is attained, people are supposed to be enlightened to the extent that they will act to go beyond the negative toward the positive. In other words, they will be enabled to get back the nature of human freedom, confront with the harsh reality and become conscious of changing their existing condition. All this requires such traits as moral awareness, personal responsibility, psychical equanimity, and courageous spirit, in addition to poetic sensibility in particular. Such poetic sensibility is, in Xiong's opinion, rather crucial and even determinate in a way as it stirs up people's aspirations and facilitates the possibility of all the other virtuous traits above mentioned. Further more, the product of literature, like *The Book of Poetry*, "is difficult to read. Without sufficient wisdom, that it is read makes no difference from that it is unread"[32] because any literal reading cannot easily secure an insightful apprehension or relevant understanding. Xiong seems to make so big a story of literature in general and *The Book of Poetry* in particular at a time when he grows much worried about the human condition and corruption. He therefore attempts to advise people to mirror themselves through the poetic imagery, in order to wake up from their illusions, realize their downfalls, and hopefully mend their ways in the end.

Now let us turn back again to the notion of "having no depraved thoughts" with reference to Zhu Xi and Xiong Shili who open up a new horizon in contrast to the traditional and narrower interpretations concerned. Quietly noticeably, the second reflection as they have operated sheds considerable light on what Confucius says about the predominant theme of the three hundred poems or so. It seems to me, for instance, that "having no depraved thoughts" can be taken as a threefold principle to guide the reading and treatment of the *feng* lyrics in particular.

First and foremost, it is often applied as a moralized guideline to poetic criticism. By so doing, the moral values and practical usages are apt to be overstressed. Accordingly, the critique of poetry tends to be mechanical and conformistic without respect to specific contexts, say, the ancients used to live and love according to the "old" rites as moral codes

---

[32] Ibid., p. 268.

of their times. Judging from the "new" rites as the Neo-Confucianists granted, the ancients appeared as if they were so laissez-faire and dissipated. As is shown in his commentary on the love poems, Zhu Xi is inclined to impose the current moral codes onto the departed ancients and make his judgment according to the value systems of his time. This is similar to the case of "cutting the feet to fit the shoes."

Secondly, the notion of "having no depraved thoughts" can be seen as a realistic principle for literary creation. Cheng Yi, Zhu Xi's master, once identifies this notion with the Chinese conception of *cheng*. In this context, *cheng* signifies sincere instead of pretentious, genuine instead of fake, true instead of false, natural instead of artificial, etc. It is hereby assumed that the poems "have no depraved thoughts" because they are authentic expressions of the natural flow of human emotions and feelings along with their experiences of lifestyle. Both Cheng Yi and his brother Cheng Hao champion "the sincerity and authenticity of verbal expression (*xiu ci li qi cheng*)" as a guiding rope for all literary writings. When reading the *feng* lyrics and especially the love songs, we feel strongly and value highly the sincerity, authenticity, and simplicity in the descriptions of romantic adventures and clandestine love affairs. This does not mean we don't care about morals. In fact, we ponder over them from an artistic viewpoint and find the way of love so natural among the ancients who were not subject to the moral codes or taboos as were the later descendants, say, centuries later in the Song Dynasty. In other words, the interaction between man and women enjoyed an unconceivable latitude in accordance with their free will and less restricted norms in antiquity. Even nowadays, among certain minority ethnic groups in China, the similar trysts as we read about in the love songs are still common according to their folklores, for instance, the Li people in Hainan, the Suoluo people in Lijiang, and the Yi people in Guizhou.

Thirdly, the notion of "having no depraved thoughts" can be identified with an aesthetic attitude of detachment. This attitude features a "serene contemplation" (*jing guan*) as Cheng Zi recommends. It is free or detached from any practical needs. Idealistically speaking, it is intended to nurture a transcendental outlook in order to make life both artistic and moralistic, integrating emotionality (aesthetic sensation) with rationality (moral reason) in harmony. To clarify it in Kantian terms, this aesthetic attitude is supposed to be characterized with kind of disinterestedness and purposelessness in a pragmatic sense. With the help of this attitude, even the love songs can be appreciated without being morally upset or corrupted. In this case, personal cultivation and moral conscious are all the more important and determinant just as Zhu Xi perceives and claims.

All in all, Zhu Xi's critique of poetry is somewhat moralized against a preset or a priori imperative subject to his preoccupation with *tianli* (heavenly principles) in terms of the cardinal virtues and feudal rites as codes of conduct *par excellence.* Moreover, it is somewhat preconditioned by his conceptual conformity to Confucius' overgeneralized observations, and practically pushed forward by his methodology of interpretation. His justification of "having no depraved thoughts" is noteworthy as it opens a new horizon for poetic criticism despite of its moral finality. His poetics places more emphasis on the Dao of morality rather than the literary value as is noticed in his commentary on the poetry. This can be well justified by his renowned statement that "The Dao is the root of literature while literature is the bough and leaf of the Dao (*dao zhe wen zhi gen ben, wen zhe dao zhi zhi ye*)."[33] Nevertheless, Zhu Xi treats the *feng* lyrics as love poems expressing the male-and-female romances instead of far-fetched political overtones in many cases. This shows that he gets much closer to the nature of poetry as a literary genre. Hence, his moralistic view implies a tendency to break away from the earlier conventionalized mode of literary criticism shaped in the Han Dynasty. It is just in such a historical and comparative sense that his moralistic view is acknowledged as a step forward anyway.

---

[33] Zhu Xi, *Zhuzi yu lei* [The Sayings of Zhuzi], Sect. 139. Also see Peking University Philosophy Department (ed.), *Zhongguo meixueshi ziliao xuanbian* [Selected Materials of the History of Chinese Aesthetics] (Beijing: Zhonghua Book Company, 1981), p. 59.

CHAPTER 14

Between Chinese and Western Aesthetics

The advent of modern Chinese aesthetics came along with the collision between Chinese and Western cultures around the turn of twentieth century. It went parallel to a continuous interaction between the two heritages and envisaged an influx of Western ideas in Chinese context. With regard to its content and methodology, it was initially leagued with a theoretical shift from the old into the new due to the assimilation of Western paradigms. Moreover, it was bestowed with a crucial role of performing a spiritual enlightenment against the sociopolitical background of China then.

Incidentally, the path to modern Chinese aesthetics was not smooth at its outset. For the early introduction of Western learning (*xixue*) into China met with strong resistance for a period of time. Native conservatists held on to an obstinate position, decried the criticisms of their rival reformists, launched a radical protest against any kind of exotic ideology, and waived unconditionally any program of Westernization in a country with long history. However, what occurred to their mindset was passive rectification and gradual self-adjustment that came into effect with the passage of time. This change helped clarify the worth of Western learning and reduce the intensity of cultural bias after all.

For instance, when facing the opposition and contention between "old learning" (Chinese) and "new learning" (Western), Wang Guowei stepped out of the beaten track and championed a truth-seeking and bias-free stance. As read in the preface he wrote in 1911 for the *Journal of Chinese Studies*, he called for "a wider cultural vision to balance the prejudiced distinction between the old and the new learning."[1] When reflecting on cultural eclecticism, some scholars voiced their negative comments and skeptical criticisms. Zong Baihua, for instance, contributed to the *Magazine of Current Issues* an article on Chinese academics engaged in the study of communication and mediation (1919).[2] Thereby, he expressed his objection against the trend of looking exclusively for "similarities" between Chinese and other cultures for the sake of single-minded mediation. Meanwhile, he advised his contemporaries to shrug off the fantasy of easygoing communication and eclecticism in their investigation of Chinese and Western thoughts, and assured them that there was only one way out to hanker after truth only for truth's sake. When encountered with the crying demand for "complete Westernization" and active permeation in terms of heterogeneous cultures, ten professors gathered together in Shanghai and published a joint "Manifestation of Reconstructing Chinese Culture" in 1935, holding high the "banner of endogenous culture" in a resolute manner.[3]

Looking into the cultural consciousness of the opposing orientations given, Zhang Dainian and other intellectuals brought forth a constructive proposal on "synthetic creation." According to them, equal attention should be paid to what was the best and most worthy both in Chinese culture and its Western counterpart at the time when all the related issues were taken into consideration. By the same token, what should be cherished and carried forward are the positive aspects of Chinese cultural legacy. Such legacy should get renewed and revived

---

[1] Wang Guowei, "Guoxue congkan xu" [Preface to the Journal on Chinese Studies], in *Wang Guowei Wenji* [Collected Works of Wang Guowei] (Beijing: Zhongguo Wenshi Press, 1997), Vol. 4, pp. 366–367.

[2] Zong Baihua, "*Zhongguo xue wen jia—gou tong—tiao he*" [Chinese Scholars: Communication and Reconciliation], in *Shishi ri bao* [Current Events Daily], Nov 27, 1919.

[3] Zhang Dainian, et al., "Zhongguo benwei wenhua jianshe xuanyan" [Declaration on the Construction of Chinese Indigenous Culture], in *Zhang Dainian wenji* [Collected Works of Zhang Dainian] (Beijing: Tsinghua University Press, 1989), Vol. 1, p. 265; also see Fu Changzhen, "Wenhua yu zhexue de zhenghe: lun Zhang Dainian xiansheng zaoqi de wenhua zhexueguan" [A Synthesis Between Culture and Philosophy: The Early Philosophic View of Mr. Zhang Dainian], in *Xuehai* [The Journal for Scholars], No. 1, 2001, pp. 136–137.

in a long run by virtue of assimilating the valuable accomplishments in Western culture. Then, what was of great need for China was the initiative and corresponding capacity of creative synthesis rather than mediocre mediation. The agenda of "creative synthesis" required adequate endeavors to fulfill a many-fold mission, as it was deployed to oppose the lopsided practice by cultural conservatives and eclecticists, terminate the obsolete and outworn folklores of the endogenous kind, absorb new vitality from other cultures, speed up the digestion of the heterogenous heritages, and finally bring up a new transformation of Chinese culture that should be propitious to metabolism and renaissance. Later on, Zhang proceeded to advocate "cultural creationism" and uplifted the significance of "synthetic creation" to the level of facilitating as well as actualizing cultural and national rejuvenation. What he expected from all this was no other than cultural innovation and modernization. Many Chinese intellectuals followed suit as they were deeply concerned with the possibility of China reform and claimed a sense of responsibility to find out a better future for their country and people altogether. What they thought and did procured a consistent impact upon the Chinese philosophical community, and thus inspired some philosophers of different generations to upgrade modern Chinese aesthetics at any rate.

As discerned in the historical process of development, modern Chinese aesthetics commenced with particular reference to the basic categories of its Western counterpart. Yet, it was by no means simple imitation or mechanical reduplication in this case. Rather, its selective use of subject matter from the West was made according to the principle of suitability for maximal elaboration and reconsideration. It eventually fostered favorable conditions for transformational creation and mature rethinking. Say, the conditions were fitting not merely for the meeting of Chinese and Western aesthetics, but also for the theoretical incorporation and innovation from a transcultural horizon. What was done in this domain owed to the guiding rope of Western aesthetic structure as much as to the treasure house of Chinese art and literature.

In the final analysis, there have emerged five principal models during the progression of modern Chinese aesthetics from infancy to maturity over a span of 100 years up till now. Each model has its own focus of concern and interest, notwithstanding that one serves as a ladder for the other to climb up in a chronological sequence. More specifically, what can be drawn from the five models is a linear sketch of different but interrelated stages, namely, the fragmentary elaboration based on translation and introduction, systematic disciplinary construction through relevant transplantation, theoretical incorporation via creative reformation due to the East-West interaction, interdisciplinary and comprehensive art education, and cross-cultural probe into distinctive cultural origins.

14.1 Fragmentary Elaboration of Western Aesthetics

The confrontation with the imperialist powers from overseas and their repeated invasions plunged China into a chain of political turmoil around the turn of twentieth century. A lot of conscientious, aspiring, and patriotic intellectuals grew more worried than ever before about the destiny of the nation at stake. They tried every possible means to seek for a right road of reform in order to tackle the fatal crisis of national survival. At that time, the introduction of Western science and technology worked hand in hand with the pursuit of cultural transformation. It shifted the public attention from one area to another, encompassing the instrumental dimension (modern technology-equipped gunboat), institutional dimension (political system and educational model), and conceptual dimension (natural science, philosophy, aesthetics, literature, and arts). Although the debate between "old learning" (Chinese) and "new learning" (Western) still lingered on, the former gradually withdrew to obscurity while the latter forced its way into prominence. Against this background, Wang Guowei advocated his stance to "go beyond the distinction between Chinese and Western learning" (*xue wu zhong xi*); Lu Xun recommended his strategy of "looking for new voices in foreign cultures" (*bie qiu xinsheng yu yibang*). Those views turned out to be so prevailing that all sorts of Western theories and ideologies flooded into China through translated versions. As noted in the arena of modern Chinese art and literature ranging from 1920s to 1930s, translators and thinkers made joint efforts to promote cultural change and social reform, followed one another to attack conservative mindset, and took an active part in importing Western theories. With respect to aesthetics, they assumed that Western theories could be employed to facilitate spiritual enlightenment and resolve the negative symptoms in conventional Chinese ideology and lifestyle.

This marked the rudimentary stage of modern Chinese aesthetics as a discipline. Historically, it turned out at a time subject to social unstability and political disorder. It was therefore not possible for the pro-reform scholars to conduct a systematic study of the complete asset of Western aesthetics. Instead, they selected some fundamental theories from it according to the prevailing needs, public concerns, and artistic ideals associated with the status quo of China. They incorporated them with relevant elements drawn from Chinese tradition and proposed on revised theories of their own. Among those leading theses were Kant's critique of "disinterestedness," "the beautiful and the sublime," Schiller's exposure of "free play" and "aesthetic education," Schopenhauer's hypothesis of the "will to live" and "serene contemplation," and Nietzsche's analysis of the "genius," "over-man" and "tragedy of Appollonian and Dionysian types," so on and so forth.

Accordingly, it gave rise to some issues in their practice of fragmentary elaboration, such as surface comprehension, mechanical imitation, deliberate exaggeration, far-fetched argumentation, textual misinterpretation and misappropriation, contextual misplacement, and deformation. As reviewed in light of academic etiquettes, the kernel substance of their revised theories appeared quite loose, sloppy, and lack of solid scholarship. Having double-checked in terms of disciplinary requirements, all these defects could be seen as unavoidable consequences of fragmentary selection, lopsided introduction, and inadequacy of systematic research. They seemed to be inevitable at an elementary stage under harsh conditions for academics during that historical phase.

In spite of the gaps and holes resulting from a modest understanding of Western tradition at large, the pioneering period of modern Chinese aesthetics underwent some intriguing cases after all. Namely, it fruitfully accommodated the arrival of Western theorizing modes, produced a number of insightful observations, invented a set of new categories, made a sensible choice of concepts, and attained a creative synthesis of cross-cultural ponderings. What are often considered as exemplary samples in this sphere are Wang Guowei's theory of the poetic state par excellence (*yijing*) and the refined [classical grace] (*gu-ya*). All this owed to his original thinking, sharp observation, profound erudition, transcultural innovation, and self-consciousness of theoretical reformation. As noted in the existent writings then, variation and modification occurred when Western aesthetic concepts and theoretical arguments were rendered into Chinese expression.

As a rule, culture transmits itself through language; and in return, it forms and enriches language. It operates so subtly in the coinage of new terminology and vocabulary as well as the variation of syntax et al.

Language proceeds to take in such coinage and variation especially in a dynamic setting of cultural exchange. It is particularly so in bilingual translations prone to creative misunderstanding or overinterpretation. Regarding the interrelationship between language and culture, Edward Sapir claims that language is capable not only of enumerating what constitutes our environmental background, but also of living up to its role as a real imposing force. The reason why language can define our experiences lies in that it possesses some kind of completeness in its own form. Meanwhile, it is leagued with the fact that we always subconsciously project into the realm of our experiences the ideas expected to be fully articulated by language.[4]

For example, the Chinese equivalent of aesthetics was *mei-xue* that could be literally retranslated into beauty studies or beautology. It was coined in Japan first and adopted in China later. Its implication does not correspond to the original term stemmed from ancient Greek αισθητικος. Aesthetics (αισθητικος) is usually referred to the perceptual faculty or sense perception. It is just in opposition to its antonym anaesthesia (anaesthetos) that means the lack of sensation or an insensitive state. Now aesthetics as a discipline mainly studies the sense of beauty, artistic creation, and aesthetic judgment in the main. Westerners can easily recognize the logical connection between the term and the discipline in question. By contrast, the Chinese character *mei* as beauty can be traced back to its etymological formation of two elements known as "goat" (*yang*) and "big" (*da*), and its semantic indication of a pleasant taste of mutton. Very often than not, the visual outlook of *mei* as a pictographic symbol easily dissolves the logical interlink between the parts and the whole as aesthetics suggests. Moreover, as noticed in Chinese culture and particularly in classical Confucianism, the notion of *mei* as beauty bears not only aesthetic or artistic value, but also moral or ethical significance. For it is used interchangeably with the conception of *shan* as goodness. After all, the translation of aesthetics into *mei-xue* confines the discipline to a narrow scope according to its Chinese meaning. Hence vulnerable misunderstanding and linguistic variation would be bound to affect the commencement of modern Chinese aesthetics to some degree.

---

[4] Edward Sapir, "Conceptual Categories in Premiere Languages," in *Science*, No. 74, 1931, p. 578; also see Carol R. Ember and Melvin Ember, *Cultural Anthropology* (New Jersey: Prentice Hall, 1985); see Chinese version, 1988, pp. 136–137.

14.2 Systematic Construction of Aesthetics as a Discipline

The outbreak of the New Culture Movement in 1919 propelled Chinese aesthetic inquiry onto a higher plane. In particular, the widespread practice of aesthetic education attempted to incorporate aesthetics with art and literature on the one hand, and to substitute the peculiar role of religion in Chinese society on the other hand. It was applied to the enlightenment of the general populace and the reconstruction of national identity in many schools and colleges across China. This motivated some scholars to build up a systematic discipline of aesthetics that in turn elicited a systematic paradigm of further inquiry. The key principle of this paradigm was to make the most of Western scientific methods, absorb the valid components of Chinese tradition, and clarify the historical course of development with reference to cultural backgrounds, philosophical contexts, theoretical categories, aesthetic objects, etc. It was carried forward to remode and improve its disciplinary structure and system on such basis. It proved helpful not only to remove the disequilibrium in fragmentary investigation (e.g., the mode of argument with focus on one specific point but with no heed to the others involved), but also to enhance art and aesthetic criticism from a systematic perspective. Additionally, it aroused a strong interest in an all-round rediscovery of Chinese aesthetic thoughts and art theories. This can be seen as a logical necessity of developing modern Chinese aesthetics.

The most leading aesthetician who initiated systematic probe and aesthetic education was Cai Yuanpei. He himself received philosophical training with focus on aesthetics at Leipzig and other universities in Europe. After his return to China, he took an active part by distributing *The Approaches to Aesthetics* (1921), lecturing on Western aesthetics at many colleges, and drafting the outlines for a coursebook *On Aesthetics* (in fact he drafted out two chapters on "The Tendency of Aesthetics" and "The Object of Aesthetics"). Since he became the Rector of Peking University, his proposed curriculum of aesthetic education exerted nationwide impact, laid a solid foundation for extensive implementation, evoked much interest in scholarly research, and stimulated more active exploration in this realm.

Another major factor related to the systematic inquiry of aesthetics was offered in a large number of works translated from Western languages into Chinese versions. The first translator was Liu Renhang whose Chinese translation of *Modern Aesthetics* was published in 1920. Later on, Zhu Guangqian and others continued to translate more Western classics. Between 1980s and 1990s, for instance, it was advised d by Li Zehou that the large-scaled "Translation Series of Aesthetic Works" were rendered into Chinese one after another. The series provided the Chinese reader not merely with much-needed theoretical findings from the Western sources, but with many alternative frames for a systematic reflection on the substance of modern Chinese aesthetics.

Incidentally, modern Chinese aesthetics made substantial progress from 1930s to 1950s. Such aestheticians as Lü Cheng, Chen Wangdao, Li Anzhai, Fan Shoukang, Zhu Guangqian, Cai Yi, and Fu Tong followed one another to produce successive publications on general Western aesthetics, covering descriptive conspectus, thematic survey, historical map, appreciating art, psychological anatomy, and so on. Some of them chose to define the characteristics of aesthetics as a discipline in accordance with the triple division of truth, goodness, and beauty. They tried to address the nature of aesthetics in view of relevant scholarship, value, spirit, cause and effect; reorganized the main structure of aesthetics with focus on the sense of beauty; and set up a new system in contrast with its old counterpart according to the shifted orientations of art creation and criticism.

As a consequence, there arose a bundle of so-called theories. Some of them were inclined to simplify a complicated schema, totter around at a superficial and overgeneralized level, distort what was subjectively appropriated, retell similar theses with minor modifications or restate existent arguments through eye-catching expressions. However, many others succeeded in defining the essential features, principles, and methods in a more logical and cohesive fashion. At the same time, a holistic paradigm was put into effect as a result of systematic ponderings over Chinese art theories. All this laid a solid foundation for a fruitful rediscovery of Chinese aesthetic thoughts in a chronological sequence. In this respect, significant achievements were displayed through Zhu Guangqian's theory of poetry, Feng Zikai's theory of painting, Deng Yizhe's theory of calligraphy, and so forth.

Quite distinctively, a most flourishing period came up from 1980s forward and witnessed some remarkable writings on the history of Chinese aesthetics in particular. An offhanded list of the renowned authors includes Li Zehou, Liu Gangji, Ye Lang, and Min Ze, among others. With regard to the argumental strategy and the structural formulation in use, they have left behind some traces of theoretical reflection, conceptual recreation, philosophical reconsideration, and semantic transformation in certain cases. Moreover, they have made tremendous endeavors not only to embed the arguments into Chinese sociocultural context and traditional thinking sphere, but also to map out the history of Chinese aesthetics along with its unique properties and values from either a vertical or a horizontal standpoint.

14.3 Theoretical Incorporation Through East-West Interaction

Since modern Chinese aesthetics owes much to the interaction between Chinese and Western cultures and related ideas, it is always escorted by either explicit or implicit comparison between Chinese and Western aesthetics. Grounded on the exercise of deduction and inferring, this comparison requires an expanded vision of cross-cultural studies, a self-consciousness of dialogue based on equal footing, erudite knowledge of both Chinese and Western heritages, and the capacity to assimilate different ideas and methods. Only by so doing is it possible to activate integration, transformation and innovation in a most creative manner.

As luck would have it, there are a number of high achievers in the field of modern Chinese aesthetics. Among them are Zhu Guangqian, Feng Zikai, Deng Yizhe, Zong Baihua, and so on. What is common to them all happens to be their reception of philosophical training in Western universities, their acceptance of scientific thinking of Western aesthetics, and their acquaintance with the indispensable approaches to academic research. On the other hand, it involved the background of historical scholarship, insight into Chinese tradition, knowledge of Chinese philosophy, wisdom of Chinese intuition, and a sense of mission dedicated to rejuvenating Chinese culture, among many others.

As observed in the *Psychology of Literature and Art*,[5] *On Beauty*[6] and other early works, Zhu Guangqian linked his arguments and analyses with influential theories of modern Western aesthetics. He managed to soften the exotic appearance of Western ideas by virtue of semantic

---

[5] Zhu Guangqian, *Wenyi xinlixue* [Psychology of Literature and Art] (Shanghai: Kaiming Bookshop, 1936).

[6] Zhu Guangqian, *Tan mei* [Letters on Beauty] (Shanghai: Kaiming Bookshop, 1932).

transfer, conceptual comparison, and illustrative device drawn from traditional Chinese art and literary theories. Such points, for instance, as "fusion of emotion and scene" (*qing jing jiao rong*) and "identifying oneself with the object contemplated" (*chao ran wu biao*) were utilized to interpret Theodor Lipps' doctrine of "*Einfühlung*" and Bullough's) principle of "psychical distance." Similarly, when handling Kant's assumption of "disinterested contemplation" and Schiller's promotion of "free play" in terms of Daoism, he moved on to elaborate a theory of "artistic or articized life." As read in his treatise *On Poetry*,[7] he assimilated the old and the new learning in general and incorporated Chinese and Western poetics in particular. Through detailed analysis and comparative study of rhythm, rhyme, imagery, taste, grammar, figurative craft, and so forth, he exposed authentically and essentially the art of poetry from a transcultural angle. His lucid style, sound reasoning, solid justification, and well-grounded argumentation marked a new milestone for modern Chinese aesthetics and comparative poetics. Zhu himself once confessed that he had in his lifetime published many books but written this single work only. He therefore treated it as an authorized representative of his own scholarship. As for Feng Zikai, Deng Yizhe, Zong Baihua, and others, they started their probe into Chinese and Western aesthetics with focus on the genres of calligraphy and painting. When dealing with the aesthetic ideals, artistic values, creative rules, constitutive elements and other factors in Chinese and Western arts, they opened up a new area of comparative study among their community. They came out with theoretical generalizations and predicted a promising development of comparison between different cultures and art forms. Their success in practical application set a fine example for upcoming art critics and aestheticians.

It must be pointed out that the meeting of Chinese and Western aesthetics does not simply mean a cross-cultural transplantation of concepts and theories. Instead, it is directed to a careful reinvestigation of the differences in learning and thinking. It therefore crops up a good harvest of new findings in related areas. In practice, it applies Western methodology and scientific spirit to rediscovering the essential components of Chinese aesthetics with particular reference to traditional art theories. It does so in order to clarify the implicit, ambiguous, and

---

[7] Zhu Guangqian, *Shi lun* [A Study of Chinese Poetics] (Chongqing: Guomin Books Press, 1943); revised version (Beijing: Zhonghua Book Company, 1948).

vague conceptions and actualize a creative synthesis in view of interrelated textual and contextual backgrounds.

As affirmed in his analysis of the meeting of Chinese and Western philosophies, for instance, Mou Zongsan argues that such meeting aims to "dissolve antinomy," say, to admit both entities with universality and particularity in one sense, and in the other, to seek for general truth rather than integrating the two systems in the process of interaction and assimilation.[8] On the contrary, the two systems retain their respective characteristics; Chinese philosophy keeps to its own traits, and so does its Western counterpart. They should not identify with one another. This being the case, the universal does not exclude the particular, and the particular does not negate the universal. Accordingly, what becomes possible is not merely the meeting of the two systems, but also the preservation of their diversities. This is the same with the meeting of Chinese and Western aesthetics. A typical example herein is the theory of art as sedimentation due to its speculative originality and transformational creativity. The theory is developed by Li Zehou in 1980s, collected into the new edition of *Norton Anthology of Literary Criticism*, and acknowledge as a keystone of Li's practical aesthetics and a milestone of modern Chinese aesthetics in its maturity. Its detailed discussion is to be given later in this volume.

In brief, Li's exposition of art as sedimentation exemplifies the logic of his anthropo-historical ontology. It is largely based on the practical philosophy associated with Karl Marx, verified by Clive Bell's hypothesis of "the significant form," and consolidated by Carl Jung's conception of "the collective unconscious," and justified by Jean Piaget's theory of cognitive development. At the same time, it is attributed to the historical consciousness as a crucial feature of Confucian pragmatic reason, and the practical service of Chinese thoughtway, the thoughtway that is partly reflected in this old saying—"What is perceived through faculties cannot be expressed by words." According to the doctrine of art as sedimentation, the appreciation of artworks involves historical consciousness and sense perception in addition to rich imagination extended, for instance, downward to the primordial archetypes and upward to the cultural-psychological formation. In short, it entails a dynamic process

---

[8] Mou Zongsan, *Zhongxi zhexue zhi huitong shisi jiang* [Fourteen Lectures on the Transformation Between Chinese and Western Philosophies] (Shanghai: Shanghai Guji Press, 1998), pp. 5–6.

of aesthetic contemplation, a contemplation that leads human beings to restore their remembrance of the past events, rediscover the hidden symbolism in the significant form, explore the unknown in disguise of the known, and eventually hanker after enlightened pleasure and spiritual sublimation. Naturally, the process can serve to activate more insightful pondering over what can be done in art making and theorizing.

14.4 Cross-Disciplinary and Comprehensive Practice of Art Education

In the early twentieth century, many Chinese thinkers like Wang Guowei were haunted with cares and worries about the decaying society plagued with opium and other problems. It was part of the terrible aftermath left behind by the Opium War during which the British invaders forced the drug as a commodity into China. It afflicted the victimized country in many sectors ever since 1848. Envisaging the fatal abuse and national crisis, Wang devoted himself, like many other contemporaries, to searching for possible solutions. Soon afterward, he issued his emphasis on a substantial reform of educational enterprise and a critical necessity of art education. His contemporary Liang Qichao shared deep concern with the same matter. Liang was the first to propose "education by taste," and perceived the role of art education as a must in human life. However, being constrained by the social environment and historical obstacles, the two thinkers did not do much in putting their ideas into practice even though they had done what they could with regard to theoretical feasibility. By contrast, their successor Cai Yuanpei made a breakthrough. Working as the Rector of Peking University, he committed himself to save the country through education. His outstanding contribution is renowned even today for his theory of "replacing religion with aesthetic education." Actually, he conducted the first course of aesthetic education at the university. His pioneering practice opened up a new page and laid a sound foundation for other practitioners.

It is not until late 1990s that the practitioners of art education in China have taken a new step forward at a nationwide scale. What they have done turns out to be fairly fruitful regarding the outcome of theories and praxes. Among many others in this domain, the most noteworthy is the eco-model of art education that outshines the conventional "spoon-feeding model" that is teacher-based and heedless of students' initiative as well as creativity. Moreover, it is distinguished from the "gardener-centered model" with overemphasis on students' self-representation instead of artistic inspiration.

In brief, the eco-model is designed to develop the intuitive and creative capacity on the part of students through a synthesis of diverse but interrelated disciplines apart from artworks and living experiences. Just as Teng Shouyao depicts in the *Art and Generative Wisdom*, the "ecological system" of nature in its most proper configuration involves all kinds of things living in an interdependent, inter-complementary, vigorous, and sustainable relationship. Art education needs to fully manifest ecological wisdom and constantly puts it into practice in a suitable and effective way. For instance, it should work to level down the walls separating aesthetics, art history, art criticism, artistic creation, art psychology, art sociology, and cultural anthropology, only to establish and retain an ecological relationship among these subjects. Stress should therefore be laid on mutual assimilation and infiltration between art appreciation and art making, through which it is qualified to set up a potentially close link between the aesthetic sensitivity and artistic creativity. All this is grounded on the perception and analysis of artistic and organic forms in diversity, hence encouraging an exploration of the ecological interaction between discrepant and even paradoxical components in artworks, say, the clear versus the murky, the large versus the small, the short versus the long, the fast versus the slow, the sad versus the joyful, the strong versus the tender, the high versus the low, the outward versus the inward, the thick versus the thin, the abstract versus the real, etc. Such a training to be conducted in the form of art education features a gradual nurturing process and will in the long run enable human psychic structure to grow as much open as that of great works of art.[9]

As detected in its theoretical setting, the eco-model of art education has an interdisciplinary nature. It attempts to introduce as a guiding principle the integration of several disciplines into classroom teaching and students' performance in a democratically interactive atmosphere. This seems inspired by the hypothesis of "discipline-based art education" proposed in early 1990s in the New World. According to Ralph Smith as a leading theorist in this field, the discipline-based art education is literally an approach to teaching visual arts more effectively through the incorporation of concepts and activities from a number of interrelated

---

[9] Teng Shouyao, *Yishu yu chuangshen* [Art and Generative Wisdom] (Xi'an: Shaanxi shifan daxue chubanshe, 2002), pp. 47, 50, 337–338.

disciplines, namely, artistic creation, art history, art criticism, and aesthetics. However, it does not mandate that the four disciplines be taught separately without reference to one another. Instead, it employs them to provide sufficient justification, suitable subject matter, pragmatic methods, and appropriate attitudes, which are relevant to the cultivation of percipience in art matters. This is mainly because they offer different analytical contexts to enhance our understanding and aesthetic enjoyment, the contexts that facilitate the making of unique objects of visual interest (artistic creation), the apprehension of art in the aspects of time, tradition and style (art history), the reasoned judgment of artistic merit (art criticism), and the critical analysis of basic aesthetic concepts and puzzling issues (aesthetics).

In a word, the discipline-based art education assumes that an ability to engage intelligently in artworks consists in a number of factors, such as the intention to produce artworks, the awareness of experiencing the mysteries and difficulties of artistic creation in the process, the familiarity with the history of art, the sensibility of aesthetic judgment, and so forth. All this is prerequisite to building a sense of art in the young, which is the overarching objective aesthetic learning.[10] This statement is verifiable to the extent that the meaning and significance of many artworks are by no means easy to be apprehended, because they are lying in the bygone contexts of specific history, culture, society, etc. Hence, what is highly desirable and helpful in this scope will be relevant description, analysis, interpretation, and comparative study in terms of time, tradition, style, and even ethos. They could be supplied and clarified by such professionals as art historians, art critics, and art philosophers or aestheticians. Accordingly, "we may say that a well-developed understanding and enjoyment of art presupposes some familiarity with the arts of creation (the making of artworks), the arts of communication (works of art as artistic statements), the arts of continuity (the understanding of artworks in historical context), and the arts of criticism (criticism that interprets artistic statements as well as philosophically analyzes aesthetic concepts)."[11]

In sum, the discipline-based art education is comprehensive *par excellence* owing to its dynamic synthesis of four interrelated disciplines. It is meanwhile systematic in nurturing a sense of art according to the general

---

[10] Albert W. Levi and Ralph A. Smith, *Art Education: A Critical Necessity* (Urbana and Chicago: University of Illinois Press, 1991), p. xi.

[11] Ibid., pp. xiv–xv.

curriculum divided into five phases of aesthetic learning as follows: simple exposure to artworks, familiarity and perceptual training, historical awareness, exemplar appreciation, and critical analysis.

By contrast, the eco-model of art education appears to be more ambitious. It is schemed to go beyond the discipline-based approach. Apart from the more disciplines required, it demonstrates a kind of intercultural dimension, a dimension that aims to adopt certain positive elements from Chinese doctrines of music-poetry education and to readapt some involving principles taken from environmental ecology and post-modern culture of design. For example, it argues that eco-environmental protection is not merely a technical notion that copes with natural objects rather than human beings. Instead, it should be based on the traditional ethics of "loving people and then treasuring things" (*ren min er ai wu*), and the present-day expectation of sustainable development for the common good. Naturally, it should be applied to upbringing a double-fold awareness, an awareness that is demanded not only to protect the external eco-environment of the physical world, but also to adjust the internal eco-environment of the psychical world. Ultimately, it should lead people to rediscover and secure the harmony between Nature and humankind, the material and the spiritual, the individual and the collective, the emotional and the reasonable ….

Appealing and thought-provoking as it is, the eco-model itself requires further questioning and investigation as it still leaves some room for theoretical clarification and practical justification. This being the case, an intercultural approach is highly desirable to find out more insights and alternatives.

14.5 Transcultural Pondering in View of Cultural Origins

Modern Chinese aesthetics continues to develop along with a comparative study of aesthetic cultures. Such study focuses more on cultural pattern, social ethos, artistic spirit, and aesthetic quality, among others. It requires vertical survey and horizontal analysis. Meanwhile, it advises the researcher to be capable of assimilating the historical and the modern, reconsidering the native and the foreign, and incorporating his knowledge of literature, history, and philosophy into a productive whole. In this respect, the achievements made by Thomé Fang (Fang Dongmei), Tang Junyi, and Xu Fuguan deserve much of our attention.

As noted in many of his works, such as the *Three Kinds of Wisdom of Philosophy*, *The Mood of Life and Sense of Beauty*, the *Poetry and Life*, the *Boundless and Harmonious Spirit of Life*, *On Human Beings and Nature in Chinese Culture in the Perspective of Comparative Philosophy*, and the *Artistic Spirit of Chinese People*,[12] Thomé Fang tried to probe into distinctive cultural origins from a transcultural perspective, and demonstrated respective cultural ideals and aesthetic qualities by means of comparison. He adopted a holistic viewpoint and looked into three kinds of wisdom related to ancient Greece, modern Europe, and traditional China. He came to reveal the thoughtways, lifestyles, cultural ideals, national identities, and artistic tastes each.

According to his description, the ancient Greeks were well equipped with the faculties of intelligence that conduced to the wisdom of reality and produced the culture of rationality. They were therefore liable to pursue and justify truth with the power of reason. Their lifestyle was characterized with three forms of spirit in connection with Dionysus, Apollo, and Olympus symbolizing passion, reason, and lack of emotion. Among them the Apollonian spirit was regarded as the main stream. The modern Europeans would dedicate themselves to seeking after beneficial momentum that led to the wisdom of convenience and nourished industrial craftiness. They therefore developed the culture of worshipping might as right, thus driving emotion and feeling into illusion complex. Their lifestyle featured such three types of ethos as were reflected in the Renaissance, the Baroque, and the Rococo. The Renaissance was attributed to artistic enthusiasm, the Baroque to the scientific enlightenment, and the Rococo to the contradiction between emotion and reason. They could be integrated into the Faustian spirit. The traditional Chinese would be obsessed with taking delight in a subtle understanding of nature and change. They would rely on the wisdom of reality, make use of the wisdom of convenience, and accomplish the wisdom of equality. They therefore developed a culture of subtleness and naturalness, attempting mainly to control the illusive and return to the sincere. As a result, the traits of their lifestyle may be exemplified by three historical thinkers known as Laozi (Laotzu), Confucius, and Mozi (Motzu).

---

[12] Fang Dongmei, *Fang Dongmei xinruxue lunzhu jiyao* [Thomé Fang's Selected Writings on Modern Confucianism] (eds. Jiang Baoguo and Zhou Yazhou, Beijing: Zhongguo Guangbo Dianshi Press, 1993).

As what Thomé Fang believed, the respective features of the three cultures had impact on their corresponding forms of artistic expression and aesthetic quality. In addition, Fang, a philosophical poet, asserted that culture was a complete manifestation of the human soul and presented a sophisticated picture of human life, feeling, and reasoning. In order to understand the sense of beauty and aesthetic characteristics pertaining to a national identity, one should bear in mind the particular aspects of a national lifestyle and considerate duely the cosmic view of a nation as a whole. Relatively speaking, the ancient Greeks and modern Europeans tend to approach the cosmos from a scientific perspective whereas the traditional Chinese tend to approach it from an artistic perspective. Hence, there arise different tastes, judgments, and expressions, which might be thematically displayed on a well-lighted platform as follows (Table 14.1).

This condensed illustration does not transpose every factor onto the succinct table given. It just offers a sketch of some most perceivable and ostensible features of the three heritages concerned. Nevertheless, it

Table 14.1 Features of the three heritages to highlight their cultural origins

Cast	Ancient Greek	Modern European	Traditional Chinese
Background	Limited cosmos	Boundless cosmos	Deserted wildness
Setting	The Pantheon in Athens	Gothic church	Ancient temples in remote mountains
Accessory scene	Sculpture of naked body	Oil painting and musical instrument	Landscape painting and flowers
Subject matter	Imitating nature and its objects	Governing nature and its objects	Following the *Dao* and being unconscious of the object and the self
Hero	Apollo	Faust	Poet
Acting	Singing eulogy	Dancing	Composing poetry
Music	The seven-stringed lyre and the harp	The violin and the piano	The bamboo flute and the inverted bell
Situation	A sunny day after rainfall	Lightening in a sunny day	The sound of the flute in the moonlight
Scene	Lifelike	Real illusion	Illusionary reality
Season	A clear autumn day	Hot summer and cold winter	Warm spring
Mood	Outward expression of simplicity and elegance	Struck by thunder, shocked and stirred up	Flower into dream and relaxation of mind

goes down to the fundamental roots each so as to highlight their cultural origins for the sake of contrast. Quite interestingly, it lays bare the cardinal discrepancies and hidden resemblances between the three cultures. Take each "hero" on the table for example. "Apollo" is often viewed as a symbol of Greek mythology from which Greek art, ideal beauty, and even philosophical spirit are originated during the Hellenic Age. "Faust" is usually conceived as an image of European mentality that is aligned not only with persistent probe into the unknown, but also with non-stop curiosity about creating something novel. "Poet" is normally seen as a figure of spiritual freedom and rich imagination who is sensitive to the living environment and human condition; he enjoys contemplating the outer universe and speaking for the inner world, ready to identify himself with the object while roaming through visible and invisible landscapes. As regards the "music" performance, "the lyre and the harp" are played to produce the lyrical tone and unique harmony of Ionic and Doric types. "The violin and the piano" are played to demonstrate the grand style and profound theme of symphony through orchestra. "The flute and the bell" are played to describe the pastoral ambiance of the poetic and the picturesque in particular. In brief, all the listed factors in each heritage are interrelated and interactive at large as a consequence of historical inheritance and innovation.

Teleologically, Fang's study of the three cultures attempts to sort out the characteristics of their typical origins in one sense and strives to facilitate a possible transcendence through transformational creation in the other sense. It is thus pointed to a noble motive to fulfill the mission of upgrading cultural innovation and bettering human life. According to Fang in this regard, Nietzsche's ideal of the Overman (*Übermensch*) was empty by nature. If it could take up a reasonable stance to assimilate all virtues of valuable cultures, say, to synthesize the cognitive and aesthetic wisdom of the three sources, it would be able to go beyond their limits and enrich their values. Under such circumstances, it would ask for open-mindedness, honesty, sincerity, integrity, creativity, and so forth. The so-called Overman in this case should be an ideal personality who would get over the defects of ancient Greeks, modern Europeans, and traditional Chinese in all. He would be adept at pursuing human perfection by absorbing their merits of excellences each. To my mind, this assumption is obviously romantic and idealistic; it is far from being attainable because it usually resides in mere imagination, if not wishful thinking. Notwithstanding that, it may shed some light on the context of cultural globalization and glocalization.

To conclude, the five models briefed above denote a logical and historical development of modern Chinese aesthetics in the past ten decades or so. They are one way or another related to the spiritual enlightenment even though they focus more on Sino-Western aesthetic inquiries. Relatively speaking, the first two models stand for an elementary exploration with tremendous enthusiasm, and the next three models mark a more mature progression with a fruitful output. According to my understanding, the theoretical incorporation conducted in later stages represents both the transformational creation of Western aesthetics in the Chinese context and the active advancement of modern Chinese aesthetics in connection with its own heritage. Above all, the transcultural approach is proved to be somewhat rewarding, forward-looking and constructive, because it is directed to the future of Chinese aesthetics in spite of its idealistic touch, spiritual orientation, and over-loaded mission.

CHAPTER 15

Aesthetic Criticism of Transculturality

Around the turn of the twentieth century, China opened the door to the influx of Western ideas for sociopolitical reasons. It was during this ideologically hectic period that Wang Guowei (1877–1927) established himself as one of the pioneering thinkers in such fields as diverse as philosophy, aesthetics, literary criticism, Chinese history, epigraphy, and ancient geography. He was also highly celebrated as a poet in the classical form of *ci* lyrics that had flourished in the Song Dynasty (960–1279).

In his early preoccupation with aesthetic and literary criticism, Wang was inspired in part by German idealism and in part by Chinese literature. As noted in his enterprise of scholarship, his engagement in philosophizing was largely influenced by Kant, Schiller, Schopenhauer, and Nietzsche; his revaluation of Chinese literature was characterized by a preference for *ci* poetry; and his aesthetic criticism gave a central role to the value of art. In his view, pure art is crucially worthy and significant in terms of enlightenment in spite of its being instrumentally useless. This is precisely because artworks express philosophical, aesthetic, spiritual, and ethical values. More specifically, the philosophical aspect of art exposes the truth of human existence in both a universal and a particular sense through artistic imagery and form. Wang's observation on this account is connected with Schopenhauer's idea as the object of knowledge or the origin of art. The aesthetic dimension of art lies in a kind of disinterestedness that goes beyond the will to live and secular desires as it facilitates an aesthetic state or serene contemplation. From this viewpoint, one is prone to experience a kind of infinite delight and pleasure. The spiritual spectrum of art as a genre of free play expresses and releases the suppressed feelings and emotions that beget pain and depression. By virtue of procuring consolation and exoneration, art reduces the amount of suffering and boredness encountered in human life. As regards its ethical function, art is like a boat that helps humans sail across the bitter sea and frees them from the worldly cares and anxieties. Art aims not only to expose the misery of the human world, but also to provide an alternative paradigm for self-enlightenment that in turn assists the victimized in extricating themselves from the abyss of predicament.

These four aspects of art are essential components threading their way, explicitly or implicitly, through the entire course of Wang's philosophical ponderings. To his mind, they parallel six cardinal doctrines about aesthetic education (*meiyu shuo*), spiritual detachment (*jietuo shuo*), art as free play (*youxi shuo*), artist as genius (*tiancai shuo*), category of the refined (*gu-ya shuo*), and the poetic state *par excellence* (*jingjie shuo*). In his theoretical speculations, Wang hovered over the vast territory of Chinese culture with conceptual wings borrowed from the West. His aesthetic scholarship was grounded in his native heritage, but greatly benefited from his ability to stand astride both Eastern and Western heritages.

15.1 Beyond East and West: A Transcultural Transformation

Wang Guowei's positive attitude toward both native and foreign cultures is noticeable throughout his early writings. It can be attributed to his insight into the universal property of all forms of learning. This property is oriented toward truth due to scientific analysis and factual justification. He himself sought a transcultural standpoint that would disentangle him from any one-sided perception. His chief motive for this strategy derived partially from his intention to reconstruct the Chinese cultural legacy and partially from his conviction that flourishing academic studies in a global sense must rely on the further progress through honest and unbiased investigations within significant existing cultures. Thus, he affirmed the necessity of "going beyond any prejudiced preference or distinction between the Chinese and Western learning (*xue wu zhong xi*) in sincere multicultural explorations." For he was well in a position to recognize the intellectual diversity in the history of ideas.[1] He therefore put forth a more detailed argument as follows:

> The nature of learning has nothing to do with the so-called discrepancy between the modern and the classical, the Chinese and Western, or the useless and the useful. Why is this so? The investigation of things in the world leads to different conclusions if considered from the perspectives of science or history. However, it all aims to seek truth from facts.... Human knowledge the world over is basically contained in such disciplines as science, history and literary studies which categorically exist in both China and Western nations. They only vary in their degree of width, roughness, superficiality or elaboration. In plain words, any biased discrimination between the two cultures is definitely groundless, for it originated in senseless worries that the imagined aftermath of the flourishing of Western culture in China would prevent and impede the evolution of Chinese culture or vice versa. China is, as it were, exempt from such worries, but lacks real and substantial scholarship. Thus in Beijing, the capital and cultural centre of the country, there are no more than ten scholars of great learning in the field of Chinese classical studies. As for those who are engaged in the study of Western culture, most tend to scratch the surface and hardly master either its profound spirit or broad scope. We cannot name even one or two figures for their devotion to the target subject and compare them with those who devote their lifetime to the learning of the Chinese classics.... I personally maintain that Chinese and Western studies par excellence can interact on and promote each other to the extent that they thrive and decline in a synchronous fashion. That is to say, one cannot do without the other in terms of their respective rise and fall. This is especially so in the case of the contemporary world and learning.[2]

Wang's cultural openness and tolerance seem to be based on observation in essence. For instance, the Chinese language strikes him as ambiguous in meaning. As a consequence, Chinese mode of thought appears logically weaker than the mode of thought fostered by Western

---

[1] Wang Guowei, "Lun jin nian zhi xue shu jie" [About the Academic Society in Recent Years], 1905. Note: All the citations, if not specified, are translated into English by myself. The Chinese essays by Wang Guowei are available in his collected works. Cf. Wang Guo, *Wang Guowei wen ji* [Collected Works of Wang Guowei] (Beijing: Zhonguo Wenshi Press, 1997), Vols. 1–4.

[2] Wang Guowei, "Guoxue congkan xu" [Foreword to *Journal of Chinese Studies*], 1911.

languages. As Western cultural identity places greater emphasis on scientific speculation, it has a greater capacity for abstraction and classification. Accordingly, generalization and specification are two strategies that are widely applied in the West to both visible and invisible substances. They are, in Wang's opinion, well manifested in Kant's analyses of reason and Schopenhauer's formulation of sufficient reason. Quite the contrary, Chinese cultural identity lies in a cluster of pragmatic circumstances or instrumental conditions. When it comes to theoretical pursuits, it tends to be easily contented with common factual knowledge and stays reluctant to get down to the bottom of things and issues in question. As usual, the theoretical specification of things is rarely exercised unless it is driven by practical needs.[3]

To verify his observation, he attempted to employ a strategy of transcultural transformation to handle three basic issues in Chinese philosophy, namely the questions of human nature (*xing*), principle (*li*), and fate (*ming*). He used Kantian epistemology as distinguished between a priori and a posteriori to explore the possibility of escaping a dualistic trap that results from dichotomizing human nature in terms of good and evil. According to his statement in an essay "On Human Nature" (*Lun xing*), the knowledge a priori is based on theoretical hypotheses while its counterpart a posteriori is based on empirical observations and relevant cases. In Chinese considerations and doctrines of human nature, the perspective a priori gives rise to two opposite views: One maintains that all humans are innately good, and it is the environment and learning a posteriori that makes the difference between the evil and the good among people. The other confirms that all humans are innately evil, and it is through education and enculturation that make them become good. The former is represented by Confucius whereas the latter by Xunzi. Similarly, the perspective a posteriori also leads to two reverse positions regarding human nature in light of good and evil. They are all, when compared with one another, dramatically contradictory both a priori and a posteriori in one sense, and in the other, "beyond human knowledge" owing to the agnostic characteristic of human nature. This agnosticism drives at such a conclusive remark: "Good-naturedness and evil-naturedness are antithetical to each other as they are empirically revealed in human deeds. Both of them could be tenable only if they happen to

---

[3]Wang Guowei, "Lun xin xueyu zhi shuru" [On the New Terminology Imported from the West], 1905.

coincide with their corresponding evidences. But, it is not reliable to infer human nature in general from sheer experience (for experience does not reflect the origin of human nature). When human nature is talked out of human nature alone, there arises a kind of absolute monism in terms of either good or evil. It could be tenable only if it is conceived of as something non-empirical, for contradictions and paradoxes would come up once it is applied to justifying experiences or personality cultivation pertaining to the dichotomy of good and evil. Hence, I have deliberately pointed out this fact in the hope that young scholars in China will save up their breath and energy by not engaging themselves in such fruitless discussion of human nature."[4]

By the same token, Wang also examined the Neo-Confucian principle (*li*) with reference to the Schopenhauerian articulation of "sufficient reason" and the Kantian distinction between "pure reason" and "practical reason." He thereby assumed that the principle (*li*) in its narrow sense means causal reason (*li you*) and, in its wider sense, means intellectual reason (*li xing*). Of the two primary meanings, "the former suggests the universal form of human knowledge while the latter denotes the function of the relationship between the fabricating of ideas and the defining of ideas. It is a kind of intellectual power.... " Furthermore, li as an object of knowledge, it contains both metaphysical values (i.e., *zhen* as truth) and ethical values (i.e., *shan* as goodness), for *zhen* as truth and *shan* as goodness remained undifferentiated in ancient Chinese thought. This is self-evident in Zhu Xi's conception of heavenly principle (*tianli*).[5]

In addition, Wang compared the conventional Chinese interpretation of fate (*ming*) with the Western concepts of fatalism and causality, even though he rejected the assumptions underlying the problem of free will and determinism. At this point, he accepted Zhu Xi's explication of the interconnection between fate (*ming*), human nature (*xing*), and truth or principle of multi-values (*li*), and eventually drew a practically moral responsibility or sense of mission from it.[6]

Here, there are a number of things worth mentioning. First and foremost, Wang's transcultural perspective never failed him to detect some of the fundamentally dissimilar traits of Chinese and Western cultures.

---

[4] Wang Guowei, "Lun Xing" [On Human Nature], 1904.
[5] Wang Guowei. "Shi li" [Interpreting the Notion of "Rites"], 1904.
[6] Wang Guowei, "Yuan ming" [The Original Fate], 1906.

The Chinese culture places more stress on personal cultivation and moral virtues that are expected to harmonize human relations and sustain social stability, while the Western counterpart emphasizes might and right that are deployed to win an upper hand in the conquest of both nature and other nations. From his transcultural standpoint, Wang claimed that all these features could be gathered together to establish a complementary relationship of great significance.

Secondly, although he insisted on the critical necessity of learning from the West, he was neither a social activist nor a revolutionary at all. He remained a single-minded academic and an earnest advocate of transculturalism throughout his life. He succeeded in avoiding the relatively superficial debates about cultural preference and the political instrumentalism of his time and served as a cultural bridge between the first wave of Westernization that was launched by the generation preceding him and the New Culture Movement that was unleashed by a group of radical intellectuals around the time of May Fourth Movement in 1919.

Thirdly, his new approach to historical studies, however, also embodied transcultural features and was termed "a methodology of double proof" (*er chong zheng ju fa*). It benefited from his previous commitments both to German idealism and to his unique inheritance of the Chinese philological tradition that flourished in the Qing Dynasty. In practice, it was derived from the three interrelated features as aforementioned, say, mutual interpretation and attestation by comparing unearthed relics with relevant historical records, reciprocal supplementation, and correction by comparing old books of other ethnic groups with existing classics in China, and bilateral consultation and justification by using Western concepts and sources available from Chinese literature.[7] Take his etymological study of the Chinese character *xun* for example. He applied his double-proof approach by "searching through all the oracle records available" (*bian sou bu ci*) and meanwhile double checking such classics as the *Yi jing* (*The Book of Changes*) and the *Shuo Wen* (*The Dictionary of Ancient Chinese Characters*). When conducting reciprocal interpretation and attestation between the former as new historical documents unearthed and the latter as old historical literature existent, he went so far as to seek authentic evidences in antique sacrificial vessels and their inscriptions to identify the contextual usage of the

---

[7] Chen Yinque, "Wang Jingan yishu xu" [Preface to Wang Guowei's Posthumous Works], 1934.

character concerned, and re-justify the possible interpretations attained. So convincingly he concluded that "a ten-day period" (*xun*) related to The Heavenly Stems (*tian gan*) could be traced back to the Yin or Shang Dynasty (around 1300 BC) when it was utilized to tell fortunes.[8]

Finally, Wang's concern for Western culture as a whole was marked by a passionate desire to introduce and promote German idealism, emphasizing its account of life (ethics) and art (aesthetics) in particular. This led him to select more relevant doctrines in accord with his observation and apprehension. Of course, his formulation of them was subject to modification and reinterpretation as an outcome of his Chinese sensibility and expression. In his critique of Chinese literary texts, for example, he adopted and extended such idealist concepts and categories as "disinterested contemplation," "aesthetic play," "will to live," "genius," "the beautiful," "the sublime," "the pure subject of knowledge," and "serene contemplation," among others. He also resorted to the distinctive features of and evident differences between realism and idealism. As a result, he brought forth his reflection on the six cardinal theories that not simply comprise the structure of his philosophy of aesthetic criticism, but exemplify his capacity for transcultural transformation, if not creative misinterpretation.

15.2 Aesthetic Education as a Critical Necessity (*Meiyu Shuo*)

The Western notion of aesthetic education (*meiyu*) was first introduced to China by Wang Guowei and then more effectively promoted by Cai Yuanpei (1868–1940). Both were convinced that the declining institutions of old China could be reconstructed and revived by means of modern education. They emphasized the integral wholeness of education in its physical, intellectual, moral, and aesthetic dimensions. They enthusiastically advocated the importance of the aesthetic dimension, drawing their inspiration from German idealism and especially from Friedrich Schiller. However, Wang Guowei's impact was restricted to the circle of academic research whereas Cai Yuanpei's influence reached the operation of institutions and even spilt over into the society at large. Cai Yuanpei took advantage of his role as a frontline administrator and

---

[8] Wang Guowei, "Shi xun" [Interpreting *Xun* as a Ten-Day Period], 1918.

renowned educator who led the administrative renovation of Peking University to spread his ideas. He was especially known for his slogan of "replacing religion with aesthetic education." In light of Chinese conditions at the time, Wang Guowei and Cai Yuanpei intended aesthetic education to reshape the obsolete educational paradigm in China and to remold national identity. More precisely, they sought to plant the seeds of spiritual freedom in the soil of superstition and misery, to cultivate creativity and wholeness by minimizing the excessive emphasis on rote memory work and one-sided learning, and to nourish a popular concern for good taste and human dignity in order to combat social ills such as opium addiction and wanton pleasure-seeking.

As early as 1903, Wang Guowei wrote:

> What is the philosophy of education? It is to develop the whole personality. What could such a personality be? It is the outcome of the all-round and harmonious development of human capabilities. These capabilities can be divided into two basic categories: One is physical, and the other is spiritual. One cannot become a whole being if his physical powers are strengthened whereas his spiritual counterpart weakened, or vice versa. Human wholeness must be well and harmoniously developed in both physical and spiritual aspects. In respect of the latter, it can be subdivided into three elements, namely, the cognitive, the emotional and the volitional, which in turn correspond to the ideals of the true, the good and the beautiful. The true is the ideal target of cognitive pursuit, the beautiful is that of the emotional pursuit, and the good is that of the volitional pursuit. A whole personality cannot do without these three virtues of truth, beauty and goodness. Such an actualization inevitably depends on education. Therefore, the enterprise of education in its entirety consists of three such components: the intellectual, the moral (i.e., volitional) and the aesthetic.... With these three subdivisions proceeding in parallel and moving step by step towards the fulfillment of the three ideals, and with physical education added, there surely arises the feasibility of developing whole personalities and accomplishing all educational functions.[9]

Being so committed to the underlying benefits of aesthetic education, Wang strongly recommended its importance in many of his publications. In his critical comments on an influential proposal for a nationwide

---

[9] Wang Guowe, "Jiaoyu zhi zongzhi" [About the General Objectives of Education], 1903.

educational program in 1906, he urged that aesthetics as a discipline be offered to students in both humanities and engineering.[10] He proceeded to argue that aesthetics could help develop a sound cognitive structure and broad academic perspective in addition to enhancing aesthetic judgment and personal cultivation. In his discussion of how to deal with the mental torture of endless boredom and opium addiction, he again gave priority to the aesthetic contemplation of works of art, such as sculpture, painting, music, and literature.

As a matter of fact, Wang gave three main reasons for the value of aesthetic contemplation in dealing with addiction. He warned that opium addiction was caused not only by political failure, low education, and national poverty, but more fundamentally by frustration, hopelessness, and lives devoid of meaning. In this respect, he considered it to be an emotional disease that could subjugate a nation. It could be cured neither by dry science nor by rigid morality. Instead, a cure had to work by emotional means. The solution to opium addiction lay in treating the emotions through religion and art as well as in sound civic politics and universal cognitive and moral education. Both religion and art could provide catharsis and mental consolation. While religion offered what is idealistic and pointed to the future, art offered what is realistic and related to the present. Among all the genres of art, literature touched human emotion and the human condition most powerfully. Accordingly, a sincere love of literature could provide many benefits. It could help appease the pain of boredom by giving some meaning to life, and it could prevent one from sinking into base activities by spiritually enriching one's inner world.[11]

The second reason to employ aesthetic contemplation in dealing with drug addiction can be found in Wang's examination of human activities.[12] In this discussion, he distinguished between positive and negative pain. Positive pain is generally experienced in necessary activities like daily work. Negative pain arises from too much leisure or the pursuit of unnecessary pastimes (*xiao qian*). In order to divert themselves from the negative pain of boredom, people seek activities to "kill time."

---

[10] Wang Guowei, "Zouding jingxueke daxue wenxueke daxue zhangcheng shu hou" [Critique of the Proposed Program and Curriculum for Advanced Education in China], 1906.

[11] Wang Guowei, "Qu du pian" [On Getting Rid of the Opium Problem], 1907.

[12] Wang Guowei, "Renjian shihao zhi yanjiu" [A Study of Human Hobbies], 1907.

Different persons pursue different activities. Some activities may be healthy and noble, such as the pursuit of truth through reading or the enjoyment of beauty and grace in calligraphy, painting, and antiques. Some activities may be pretentious and vain, such as the acquisition and ostentatious display of artworks that are possessed merely as symbols of private wealth. Other activities may be vulgar and base, such as taking opium or the pursuit of sensuous pleasure in brothels. The love of art and literature provides the basis for the most decent activities and is highly recommended because of its special value. As he claims,

> The psychical drive goes in either this direction or that one. If it is not guided toward noble hobbies, it will be unavoidably attached to other despicable ones. In the provision of spiritual consolation and emotional release, nothing can be more relevant and efficacious than a real taste of arts such as sculpture, painting, music and literature, etc.[13]

Finally, Wang promoted aesthetic education in the specific historical and social context of China. The school curriculum paid little attention to aesthetic education through literature and art. Rather, it focused on political instrumentalism or ideological orthodoxy under the guise of moral teaching. As a result, Chinese literature, according to Wang Guowei, could not match Western literature, and public taste was inadequately developed due to these inadequacies. As a result, the mass of the population had a morbid state of mind that turned them to addiction to the base pleasures of opium, gambling, food, or sex. Aesthetic education could be supported as a critical necessity for refining and uplifting the national spirit.[14]

Characteristically, Wang advised that aesthetic education could be effective in improving human life:

> With the human mind unexceptionally fettered by self-interests, the beautiful alone enables humans to forget personal gains or losses and enter a meaningful kingdom of great purity as well as happiness.... In the final analysis, aesthetic education as such assists humans to enhance their emotions and to realize their wish for self-perfection. Meanwhile, it serves as

---

[13] Wang Guowei, "Qu du pian" [On Getting Rid of the Opium Problem], 1907.

[14] Wang Guowei, "Jiaoyu ougan size" [Four Random Thoughts on Education in China], 1904.

a means for both moral and intellectual education.... For the cognitive, emotional and volitional dimensions of mind are not separated but interrelated.... These three aspects work in parallel and gradually move toward the actualization of ideals such as truth, goodness and beauty.[15]

This point was linked to his acceptance of Kant's analyses of the cognitive, emotional, and volitional trinity of human mind. Yet, he extended the analyses with due consideration of the interrelationship between modern education and philosophy. In addition, he did so with reference to Schiller's notion of the aesthetic state (*dem asthetischen Zustand*), "a middle disposition in which sense and reason are both active at the same time." In other words, "This middle disposition, in which the psyche is subject neither to physical nor to moral constraint, and yet is active in both these ways, pre-eminently deserves to be called a free disposition."[16] Schiller elaborated his account of the aesthetic state in the 24th letter *On the Aesthetic Education of Man* as an indispensable link between physical and moral state. According to Schiller, "Man in his physical state merely suffers the dominion of nature; he emancipates himself from the dominion in the aesthetic state, and he acquires mastery over it in the moral."[17] A similar expression was available in the 27th letter where the aesthetic state (*dem asthetische Staat*) was seen to be the bridge between the dynamic state of rights (*dem dynamischen Staat der Rechte*) and the ethical state of duties (*dem ethische Staat der Pflichten*).[18] Schiller proclaimed that when a man attains the aesthetic state:

> Beauty alone can confer upon him a social character. Taste alone brings harmony into society, because it fosters harmony in the individual. All other forms of perception divide man, because they are founded exclusively either upon the sensuous or upon the spiritual part of his being; only the aesthetic mode of perception makes of him a whole, because both his natures must be in harmony if he is to achieve it.[19]

---

[15] Wang Guowei, "Shu jiaoshi jiaoyu sixiang yu zhexue zhi guanxi" [Of the Interrelations Between Modern Thoughts on Education and Philosophy], 1906.

[16] F. Schiller, *On the Aesthetic Education of Man* (trans. E. M. Wilkinson and L. A. Willoughby, Oxford: Oxford University Press, 1967).

[17] Ibid., p. 172.

[18] Ibid., pp. 213–219.

[19] Ibid., p. 215.

Virtually in all of his writings on aesthetic education, Wang cited Schiller now and then as he was inspired to conduct his own explanation. He moved on thereby to treat Confucianism as the keystone of Chinese cultural legacy. With a specific reference to the remarks of Confucius on poetry, rites, music, and landscapes of mountains and waters, Wang was the first among contemporary Chinese thinkers to assert:

> The Confucian way of teaching starts and ends in aesthetic education. It thus leads to the personality of the gentleman (junzi renge), amounting to either "the beautiful soul" (Schiller) or "the pure subject of knowledge." (Schopenhauer) The state of mind at this level is free from expectations, fears, inner struggle, interestedness and egoism. It therefore self-conscientiously conforms to moral imperatives without any feeling of being coerced by any rules.... Hence whoever is concerned about education must put this aspect into full consideration.[20]

This assertion is backed by relevant quotations from *The Confucian Analects* (*Lun yu*). For instance, "[The personal cultivation of *junzi* as the superior man] is evoked by poetry, made firm by rites and completed by music."[21] On this account of Confucian teaching, Wang suggested that music, both vocal and non-vocal, be taught in primary schools, with materials selected from the rich resources of classical Chinese poetry. He attributed to such kind of education three major functions: harmonizing the emotions, molding the temperament and the will, and ameliorating the faculty of hearing as well as the vocal organs.[22]

Like Prometheus, Wang Guowei "stole the flame" of German idealism and tried to use it to ignite a fire of aesthetic education in China. He seemed to be highly motivated in this regard, for he embraced a strong belief that aesthetic education could be used as a means of enlightenment to solve the social problems and spiritual crises of his age. In order to justify this, he took up psychoanalysis of Chinese people and an anatomy of their morbid pastimes. He displayed many insights in this field with respect to their unreasonable pursuit of temporary enjoyment

---

[20] Wang Guowei, "Kongzi zhi meiyu zhuyi" [Confucius' Aesthetic Educationism], 1904.

[21] Confucius, *The Analects* (trans. D. C. Lau), VIII:8: *The Confucian Analects* (trans. James Legge), 8:8.

[22] Wang Guowei, "Lun xiaoxuexiao changgeke zhi cailiao" [On the Subject Matter of Vocal Music in Primary Schools], 1907.

and short-term interest. Apart from reconsidering the relevance of the Confucian approach to poetry education, he recommended aesthetic education as a remedy for the social ills. However, what he attempted to do was no other than wishful thinking because of the harsh and chaotic environment of China at that time. And what he said about the practical benefits of aesthetic education turned out to be rather arbitrary and exaggerative. All this proved that he held up to a romantic vision, and thus piled up great hopes on aesthetic education. Such hopes were in no way to be fulfilled under unfavorable conditions in China of the past.

15.3 Art as a Refuge from Suffering (*Jietuo Shuo*)

Chinese philosophy of life assumes the truth of aphorisms, say, "human existence confronts with endless hardships and miseries" (*han xin ru ku*), "human life is troubled with a short flow of time" (*ren sheng ku duan*). Early Daoists like Laozi warned that "Man's biggest trouble is no more than having a body," because the body is the inborn stimulus of desires and passions for self-preservation. Similarly, Zhuangzi regarded "the situation of men enslaved by external things" (*ren wei wu yi*) to be the original cause of the miserable condition. This enslavement would result in greed-ridden acquisitiveness and possessiveness with regard to the material objects and physical pleasures that lie outside the real meaning of human life. For the sake of extricating men from suffering, Laozi advised that people should "live in detachment" (*yan chu chao ran*) either by "reducing selfishness and desires" (*shao si gua yu*) or by "acting instead of competing for gains" (*wei er bu zheng*). For the same reason, Zhuangzi encouraged people to "be spring with all things" (*yu wu wei chun*) through "free and easy wandering" (*xiao yao you*) for spiritual emancipation and personal independence. This advice fostered among Chinese literati a spiritual inclination to take refuge in the silent beauty of landscape as well as in the engaging beauty of art and encouraged the naturalistic Quietism that has enjoyed a long tradition in China. Like Zhuangzi, who compared life to a tumor and death to the breaking of the tumor, Sakyamuni, the Buddha, saw life as the fountainhead of all cares and worries because it was full of insatiable desires. The Buddha instructed victims of such a life to sail a boat of wisdom from this word to the realm of nirvana. In a nihilistic manner, the Buddha sought to persuade us to see life as an illusion and the human world as the veil of Maya. This doctrine led to the mysteries of meditation as an exercise to assure mental purity or renunciation of an egoism that is filled with greed and worldly cares.

These ideas were all too familiar to Wang Guowei as a consequence of his bitter experience, his poor health, and his philosophical concern with the human condition.[23] He portrayed life in terms of care and toil. He presented it in a dark and bleak form that was shrouded in absolute despair. This despair grew from his own retrospection and experience, but also reflected the impact of Schopenhauer's negative pessimism as well as the influence of Daoism and Buddhism.

> Care and toil accompany life all along. Nevertheless, everyone wants to live even though he hates both care and toil.... In the process of living, one has a drive to self-preservation: when hungry, he wants food; when thirsty, he wants drink; when cold, he wants clothes; when living in the open air, he wants a shelter.... Sometimes he has sexual desire and therefore gets married and takes up household chores and family duties.... The nature of life lies deep in desire. Desire comes from insufficiency. The case of insufficiency leads to pain or suffering. A desire vanishes when fulfilled. Yet, a fulfilled desire is usually one out of ten or a hundred unfulfilled desires. Worse still, a satisfied desire gives rise to another unsatisfied one in a successive chain. Hence, consolation in the end is in no way attainable. Even when all desires are satisfied and there are no more objects to be desired, boredom and weariness naturally arises.... In this case, human life is made to swing like a pendulum between pain and boredom. Boredom in its actuality is looked upon as another type of pain. What can help get rid of these two negative feelings is so-called happiness. In order to pursue happiness, one has to make painstaking efforts, which are again in turn reduced to pain. Furthermore, the sense of pain is frequently intensified after a momentary experience of happiness. There are pains that remain as what they are without reverting to the lived experience of happiness, but there is hardly any happiness that is not preceded or followed by suffering pain. The degree of pain increases rather than decreases as world civilization progresses. Why is this so? As civilization progresses, the range of knowledge widens, the number of desires multiplies and the sense of pain deepens. On this account, the nature of life is none other than pain: desire, life and pain can be taken as a trinity.... Nevertheless, there is something that can lift us above utilitarian interests and make us oblivious of subject-object relations. On these occasions, the mind is freed from any expectations or fears because the person is no longer the subject of desire

---

[23] Wang Guowei, "Zi xu" [A Brief Autobiography], 1907.

but is the pure subject of knowledge.... Now he is free and at ease. He is like a boat that is floating near its homeport after escaping a rough sea, ... like a fish that has slipped alive through a net or like a bird that has flown out of its cage. It is as though he were starting to enjoy a happy excursion in beautiful mountains and forests, along picturesque rivers or over blue oceans. This something that enables him to be detached from interests is presupposed by its disinterested connection with him. In plain language, this is possible only when we consider art instead of anything practically material or physical.... Those who are desire-ridden cannot contemplate a work of art, and, conversely, those who can contemplate it are free from desires. The beautiful in art is therefore superior to its counterpart in nature because it enables the viewer easily to forget subject-object relations.... So Goethe poetically uttered: "What in life doth only grieve us; that in art we gladly see." Here gladness lies in oblivion to the subject-object ties of utility.[24]

Noticeably, Wang reinterpreted Schopenhauer's account of "the will to live," "the vanity and suffering of life" and "the pure subject of knowledge" against the hidden background of China then. He therefore carried out some modifications in Chinese expression. Schopenhauer's view of art as a means of spiritual freedom derived from the capacity of an artwork to facilitate the becoming of "the pure subject of knowledge." The artwork is a perceivable object that "exists entirely outside the province of things which are capable of having a relation to the will, because it is nothing real, but a mere picture." It can be either poetic or picturesque, involving an event of actual life that is rendered artistic, such as the scene of a blithe morning, a beautiful evening or a still and moonlighted night. Its effect is "conditioned by indifference, will-less, and thereby a purely objective apprehension" or "the complete silence of the will, which leaves the man simply the pure subject of knowledge." The will vanishes from consciousness, the peace of heart enters, and the intuitive apprehension of ideas is attained, and so is aesthetic satisfaction. Finally, "individuality also, with it its suffering and misery, is really abolished."[25]

Again along Schopenhauer's line of thought, Wang Guowei made great demands on art as such. Schopenhauer announced that the fine

---

[24] Wang Guowei, "Hong lou meng pinglun" [A Review of *A Dream of Red Mansions*], 1904.

[25] A. Schopenhauer, *The World as Will and Idea* (trans. R. B. Haldane and J. Kemp, London: Routledge & Kegan Paul, 1883, rep. 1964), Vol. 3, pp. 126–137.

arts were fundamental to resolving the problems of human existence, and every artwork aimed to show life and things as they are in truth.[26] Wang reaffirmed that fine arts aimed to illustrate the suffering of life and the Dao of extricating humans from this suffering; artworks were thus intended to save humans from the spiritual shackles of this world, and to free them from conflict with the desire to live in order to achieve temporary peace.[27] Nevertheless, Wang did not derive his individual observations from skeptical thought, but developed them by exposing both the aesthetic and ethical values of art. For Wang himself, these values become significant only through living in the troubled situation in an imperfect world, for they serve to free people from the desire to live and to allow them to enter the realm of pure knowledge. In a word, they are interconnected in their orientation toward exoneration, or intended to free people from the burden of sufferings in living experiences.

Taking *A Dream of Red Mansions* as a culturally central example, Wang Guowei asserted that the novel was a tragedy in which every character is tied to the desire to live and is deeply entangled in the mire of suffering. It is authentic in its description of daily events, profound in its exposure of the human condition, and completely different from all the other works of Chinese romance, which, without exception, lead to a happy ending. Furthermore, its style is antagonistic to the inclination to joy in the mentality of the Chinese people; the entire progression of the story is saturated with an explicit or hidden tragic atmosphere. It enacts the claim that all the misery of life springs from the drive of egoism and that the solution to the problems of life has to be sought in the self. This solution is a spiritual exoneration from the burdens of misery and lies in abstaining from the secular world rather than in ending life through suicide. One who renounces the world rejects all the cravings of life because he knows that life as such cannot escape from misery. Factually, a suicide complexity still abides by the cravings and ends his life as he is crushed down by despair.[28]

A Dream of Red Mansions displays two possibilities in the process of spiritual exoneration. The first is realized by contemplating the suffering of others, and the second is through an awareness of one's own suffering.

---

[26] Ibid., pp. 176–177.
[27] Wang Guowei, "Hong lou meng pinglun" [A Review of *A Dream of Red Mansions*], 1904.
[28] Ibid.

Both ways awaken people to the truth of life: The former is possible for those who have extraordinary powers of understanding, while the latter is available to those who are ordinary in this regard. Through their unusual perception and wisdom, the extraordinary obtain insight into the universality of life afflicted with suffering and in their search for spiritual emancipation break away from their desire to live. The ordinary are subject to a succession of miserable encounters that stem from a repeated circle of intensified but unsatisfied desires and are consequently trapped in hopeless circumstances. Nevertheless, they gradually realize the truth in the universality of life and come to long for spiritual extrication. With their dispositions changed and their desires abandoned, they transcend both the hell of suffering and the paradise of joy.

The extraordinary way of spiritual exoneration may still be confronted from time to time by the will to live, and this confrontation produces illusions or visions. The ordinary way of exoneration is like a bronze cooking vessel that is forged in the furnace of life over the fire of suffering. It is the outcome of becoming tired of life and therefore is freed forever from the will to live and its related illusions. In Wang Guowei's terminology, "The former type of exoneration is supernatural and mysterious whereas the latter is natural and human. Furthermore, one is religious and peaceful, and the other artistic, tragic and sublime."[29]

In Jia Baoyu, the hero of *A Dream of Red Mansions*, Wang Guowei found the symbolic embodiment of the ordinary way of seeking spiritual freedom from one's troubled life. He idealized this way as the ultimate solution to the problem of human existence, without regard to the ambit between literary invention and living reality or to subsequent questions about the validity of this solution. Quite paradoxically, his argument for human salvation through art was upset by his skeptical pondering over the following aspects. First, the spiritual exoneration of an individual does not necessarily mean the spiritual exoneration of mankind as a whole, even though individuals and mankind as a whole are supposed to share by nature a similar will to live. Secondly, ever since Sakyamuni, who demonstrated how to gain access to nirvana, and Christ, who sacrificed himself for the salvation of mankind, the desire to live has never vanished for a moment among human beings or any other species.[30]

[29] Ibid.
[30] Ibid.

Finally, Wang Guowei followed Schopenhauer in glorifying the value of art as an object of pure knowledge and thus cut art off from any practical relations. Even though he was conscious of Zhuangzi's proposed "usefulness of the useless" (*wu yong zhi yong*), there was a contradiction between the claimed disinterested quality of art and the social expectation of art as a therapy for social ills. Further on, there was a paradox between Wang's word and deed, as shown in his tragic decision to drown himself in spite of his firm rejection of suicide as a way of spiritual exoneration and his treatment of art as an alternative device to free oneself from the miseries in life.

15.4 Art as Aesthetic Play for Freedom (*Youxi Shuo*)

As revealed in modern literary studies, the theory of play occupies a notable position. It is most obviously indicated by the catchphrase in the art world, that is, play with brush and ink (*bi mo you xi*). Wang Guowei was the first to advocate the theory aesthetic play in China. In 1906, he claimed:

> Literature is nothing but an enterprise of play. When a man has more energy than he uses in the struggle for survival, he will apply the surplus to joyous play…. When growing into adulthood, he is no longer content with the form of play he rejoiced in during childhood and is liable to describe and express what he observes and feels in order to release the exuberant energy stored up within him. That is why the culture of any nation cannot do without literature during its progression at a certain level. Naturally, he who is merely plunged into the struggle for survival is by no means qualified to become a man of letters.[31]

Such a person is too exhausted and engaged in struggle, to have either any surplus energy or any impulse to play as the underlying motivation for artistic creation. In 1907, Wang restated this view in an analysis of human activities.[32] He therein employed the thesis of play as a new key to the nature of art. The origin of this account can be traced back to two major sources. The first was Kant's "division of the beautiful arts,"

---

[31] Wang Guowei, "Wenxue xiaoyan" [Notes on Literature], 1906.
[32] Wang Guowei, "Renjian shihao zhi yanjiu" [A Study of Human Hobbies], 1907.

through which the third category of art (music) was broadly defined as "the art of the beautiful play of sensations" or as a "free play of sensations" that "proceeds from bodily sensations to aesthetic ideas."[33] The second was Schiller's further elaboration of "aesthetic surplus" (*asthetische Zugabe*) and "aesthetic play" (*asthetischen Spiele*) to exalt the human spirit and freedom.[34]

Wang Guowei simplified Schiller's conception of play, but contributed little to it in a theoretical sense. The significance of what he did in this area is embodied via his purpose of "fetching a stone from other mountains for its toughness to tackle jade," that means to use Schiller's theory to throw light on the issues in Chinese literature. Because of his concern for the freedom of aesthetic play, he condemned political interference as a handicap to literary development in China. Such interference came into effect, for example, when literature was required to beautify reality or to publicize a governmental program for the communal good. In these cases, literature would be deprived of its independent judgment and degenerated into a sort of propaganda. In addition, Wang attacked the dominance of moral didacticism over the creative organism of art itself. He cried out that the ideological instrumentalism of such political and moral demands on art would ruin not only the imagination and creativity of the artist, but also the taste of the public. In addition, it would tender much advantage and bate to the utilitarian-minded writers who were ready to produce works only for cash or other benefits. In this context, Wang introduced the theory of play in order to fulfill three intentions. First, art as free and aesthetic play should become independent of any form of political instrumentalism. Secondly, art as such should perform effectively as a means of "hidden education in an appealing form" (*yu jiao yu le*) by disentangling itself from sheer moral teaching. Thirdly, a genuine artist must embrace a non-utilitarian conception of art in order to free himself from any external compulsion or boundary. If these intentions were not fulfilled, creativity would be strangled, Chinese literature would be spoiled, and full development of art would be nowhere to search for.

---

[33] I. Kant, *Critique of Judgment* (trans. J. B. Bernard, New York: Hafner Press, 1951), pp. 168–181.

[34] F. Schiller, *On the Aesthetic Education of Man*, pp. 205–209.

15.5 THE ARTIST AS CREATIVE GENIUS (TIANCAI SHUO)

Wang Guowei realized that pure philosophy was rare and the fine arts were underdeveloped in Chinese culture, because of the priority given to political ideology and the dominance of moral orthodoxy. He became disillusioned with the persistent tendency to force philosophy and art onto the political and moral track.

> The most sacred and noble of all that is in the world are philosophy and art. Even though they are considered "useless" in a practical sense, their values are not decreased at all.... For they aim at everlasting instead of temporary truth. In this regard, a philosopher strives to discover truth, and an artist to express it via symbols, thus making historically permanent achievements.... Therefore, as a result of years of study, they will be much happier than the king the moment that they either capture a sudden understanding of the truth of the universe and life or obtain a wonderful expression of an elusive image in literature, painting or sculpture. All this shows the development of their natural gifts.[35]

In this context, "natural gifts" are the talents that are most likely innate in genius (*tiancai*). Sympathetic with Schopenhauer and Nietzsche, Wang spoke of genius in terms of intellect, sensibility, understanding, spirit, tolerance, and creativity altogether. He maintained that a genius and an ordinary man may look and live alike, but they would differ not only quantitatively in their capacities, but also qualitatively in their thinking and feeling. In similar environments, the genius would distinguish himself from the ordinary man by an individual and insightful outlook of life and the world. When subject to the same pressures and predicaments, the genius would know what the ordinary man did not know, and demand what the ordinary man would not demand. The level of genius could be in direct proportion to intellectual wisdom, volitional power, and miserable intensity in his living experience of the surroundings. A genius was alleged to be more sensitive and observant regarding the challenges and problems of human existence. He would be apt to suffer more from pain and strive harder for the way of consolation. He may look upon himself as a lord and looked down on humble or small men. He would sing the

---

[35] Wang Guowei, "Lun zhexuejia yu meishujia zhi tianzhi" [On the Bounden Duties of Philosophers and Artists], 1905.

song of free will and laugh at all tragedies.³⁶ This vision of genius as an intellectual and creative aristocracy was drawn from Schopenhauer's picture of genius³⁷ and Nietzsche's distinction between "the Overman" and "the small man."³⁸

It followed that Wang placed great emphasis on the role of genius in the production of art. He there asserted:

> Literature consists in at least two key elements: one is jing (scene, event) and the other qing (feeling, affection). The former mainly describes the facts of nature and life whereas the latter concerns human attitudes toward the spirit of the facts. Therefore, the former is objective and cognitive while the latter is subjective and emotional. One who has a broad and purified mind is able to contemplate and experience things deeply.... In short, literature is the fruit of cognitive and emotional communication. One cannot succeed in literature unless he enjoys sharp observation and profound feeling. Hence, he cannot be taught via other ways to be a writer precisely because literary creation is nothing but the consequence of the play of genius.³⁹

Elsewhere, Wang echoed Kant in arguing that "beautiful art is only possible as a production of genius" and subsequently asserted this claim as "the established rule of art in the past century or so ever since Kant."⁴⁰ He rejected the craft of imitation and endorsed Kant's view that originality and exemplariness are the most important properties of genius. At this point, Wang's thought was directly linked to Kant's elucidation of genius in *The Critique of Judgment*.⁴¹ He thus applied his account of genius to Chinese literature:

---

³⁶Wang Guowei, "Shubenhua yu Nicai" [Of Schopenhauer and Nietzsche], 1904.

³⁷A. Schopenhauer, "On Genius," in A. Schopenhauer (ed.), *The Art of Literature* (trans. T. Bailey Saunders, London et al.: Swan Sonnensche In. and The MacMillan Press, 1897), pp. 129–149.

³⁸F. Nietzsche, *Thus Spake Zarathustra*, in *The Portable Nietzsche* (trans. and ed. Walter Kaufmann, London: Penguin Books, 1976), pp. 279–284.

³⁹Wang Guowei. "Wenxue xiaoyan" [Notes on Literature], 1906.

⁴⁰Wang Guowei, "Gu-ya zhi zai meixue shang zhi weizhi" [The Position of Classical Gracefulness in Aesthetics], 1907.

⁴¹I. Kant, *Critique of Judgment* (trans. J. B. Bernard), pp. 151–161.

The most outstanding of all Chinese poets are Qu Yuan, Tao Qian, Du Fu and Su Shi. They are not only bestowed with poetic talents, but also have lofty personalities to be cherished in history. A writer without noble and great personality cannot produce any noble and great works. It is often the case that a literary genius is so rare that he emerges once in decades or several centuries, and hereby ought to be nourished via cultivation and guided by virtues in order to produce really great literature.[42]

As noticed in the above statement, Wang's conception of genius differed somewhat from both the Kantian and the Schopenhauerian views. He gave greater emphasis to moral and cultural cultivation. This is very likely due to the Chinese educational tradition, according to which genius is accomplished through constant cultivation of personality and frequent praxis of judgment. The moral aspect of personality is embodied in the actualization of virtues such as sincerity, humanity, righteousness, grace, intellect, honesty, loyalty, devotion, and courage. The cultural dimension of judgment is then perfected through a process of continuous learning. Using examples from poetry, Wang divided the process into three stages:

> Throughout the ages all those who have been highly successful in great ventures and in the pursuit of great learning must have successfully undergone three stages. The lines which read "Last night the west wind shriveled the green-clad trees; alone I climb the high tower, to gaze at the road stretching to the horizon" represent the first stage. The lines which read "I have no regrets as my girdle grows looser on my waist; with everlasting love I pine for you" represent the second stage. The lines which read "I have sought her in the crowd a hundred, a thousand times; suddenly turning back my head, I see her under the dimming lanterns" represent the third stage. It is impossible to skip over to the last stage without experiencing the first two. It is also the case with literature. Hence, a literary genius ought to have an incredible amount of cultural cultivation.[43]

A similar remark is available in Wang's *Ren jian ci hua*, a selection of his critical remarks on Chinese poetics. Although his use of the renowned lines from Song Dynasty *ci* lyrics was startling, we can examine their implications in his thinking context. The whole depiction denotes a process of personal development. The first stage suggests painstaking endeavors to

---

[42] Wang Guowei, "Wenxue xiaoyan" [Notes on Literature], 1906.
[43] Ibid.

learn and to broaden one's perspective; the second stage shows the perseverance in practice for further improvement; and the last stage expresses the joy of complete enlightenment and the attainment of real creativity in literary ventures. Together, they remind us of the two sources from which Wang kept drawing his inspiration. The first source was Schopenhauer's stratification of authors into three classes.[44] The numerous authors of the first class write without thinking, but produce their work from a full memory or base them on the books of other people. Authors of the second class think while writing or think in order to write. There is no lack of them. Rarely, there are authors of the third class, who think before they begin to write. Wang Guowei's second source was Nietzsche's description of the metamorphoses of the spirit from a camel via a lion to a child.[45] Symbolically, "the camel" signifies the stage of learning, tolerance, and hard work; "the lion" signifies the stage of conquest, mastery, and rediscovery of existent values; and "the child" signifies a new beginning and the creation of new values. For Schopenhauer, Nietzsche, and Wang Guowei, the ultimate stage of their schemes reflected genius in its aspects of creativity, uniqueness, originality, and exemplariness.

15.6 THE REFINED AS THE SECOND FORM (GU-YA SHUO)

Although taking literary invention as the enterprise of genius alone,[46] Wang Guowei had wider encounters with creative works. Among the men of letters, he found that only a few of them were naturally gifted with genius. Yet, he did not neglect the fact that some works by others who were not inborn genius could be equally appealing and aesthetically significant. The haunting question about how it was possible in this case led to his hypothesis of *gu-ya* as the secondary form of artistic creation.

> There are certain objects in the world that are neither original artworks nor practically useful stuff. Their producer is by no means a genius. However, works of this kind seem to have little difference from what is created by a genius. It can be called gu-ya since there is no ready name for it.[47]

---

[44] A. Schopenhauer, "On Authorship," in *The Art of Literature*, p. 45.

[45] F. Nietzsche, *Thus Spake Zarathustra*, in *The Portable Nietzsche* (trans. and ed. Walter Kaufmann).

[46] Wang Guowei, *Wenxue xiaoyan* [Notes on Literature], 1906.

[47] Wang Guowei, "Gu-ya zhi zai meixue shang zhi weizhi" [The Position of Classical Gracefulness in Aesthetics], 1907.

The term *gu-ya* combines two Chinese characters: *gu* (ancient or age-old) and *ya* (grace or elegance). Wang Guowei took the term as a whole, and according to context, he used it mainly for a kind of classical gracefulness or refined elegance in art. We may render *gu-ya* as the refined. Wang perceived the refined as a kind of creativity in contrast to genius in one sense, and as an aesthetic category in contrast to the beautiful and the sublime in the other sense. He characterized the refined in terms of its basic traits: As a kind of artistic creation, the refined is produced not by a genius, but by learned person of high personality. Hence, its production depends on personal effort rather than natural talent. As a kind of artistic form, the refined is found solely in art, distinguished from the beautiful and the sublime in nature and art as well. As a kind of aesthetic value, the refined is independent to the extent that it does not possess the properties of the beautiful and the sublime. As a kind of technique, the refined brings refinement or elegance into what is not beautiful in nature, for example, in landscape painting. As a kind of aesthetic object, the refined is subject to a posteriori judgment that is based on experience, in contrast to the universal and a priori judgment of the transcendental categories of the beautiful and the sublime.[48]

To facilitate the understanding of the refined (*gu-ya*) as a new category, it requires further clarification. As Wang Guowei understood form in a broad sense, he asserted that all beauty was by definition formal and contained in symmetry, variety, and harmony. For example, the hero and his situation provide the subject matter of a drama, but this subject matter can arouse aesthetic feelings only through adequate form. Only this form that is differentiated from the subject matter can be turned into an aesthetic object. There are generally two types of form at this point: the primary and the secondary. In the former, what is expressed perfectly will produce an aesthetic object of either the beautiful (*youmei*) or the sublime (*zhuangmei*), whereas in the latter, what is skillfully represented will produce an aesthetic object of the refined (*gu-ya*). On this account, the form can transform something into an aesthetic object by provoking aesthetic feelings, but it must employ the subject matter as its content at any rate.

Subsequently, the refined is identified with the secondary form and often taken as a counterpart to the primary form aligned with both the beautiful and the sublime. The subdivisions of the first form, as

---

[48] Ibid.

formulated by Burke and Kant, exclusively represent the creative output of genius and provide other artists with exemplary models for mimesis. By contrast, an artwork of the refined is produced by an artist who is not a genius, but who has a highly cultivated aesthetic taste along with adequate creativity. This taste emerges naturally from learning, imitating, and refining. An artist who produces the refined can be identified with artists of the first caliber in respect of what he makes. Nevertheless, his works are generally fashioned and refined far more by his effort than by his innate talent.

Thirdly, the refined is thought to have an independent value. It helps increase the beauty of the beautiful even though it lacks the properties inherent in either the beautiful or the sublime. By being "a special mode of formal beauty," the refined serves as an indispensable element in the first form of the beautiful and the sublime. In this context, the refined is the necessary method, skill, or technique without which beautiful or sublime artworks cannot be produced.

Finally, we must approach the concept of the refined with reference to the concept of genius (*tiancai*). In aesthetic creation, there is a complementary relation between the two. So rare is the artistic genius who offers works of originality and exemplariness. To fill the gaps between artists of genius, there are artists who can produce the refined as excellent works of paramount aesthetic value that supplement the output of genius. As supplementary works of art, the refined does not negate the worth of works produced on the model of the original and exemplary products of genius. Rather, the refined confirms the need for learning, experience, taste, and endeavor in the process of artistic creation. It is in this connection that the refined has its independent value.

In spite of such explanations, the refined still seems perplexing and, in some cases, self-defeating. Take for example the distinction between the primary form and the secondary form. The former is held to comprise the beautiful and the sublime in both nature and art and thus has two varieties: the natural and the artistic. It (the primary form) in its artistic variety is supplemented by the secondary form the refined, which is available only in art and is hence only an artistic form. On this account, the beauty of all things is formal and should thus be capable of being increased when expressed through the second form, but this contradicts the claim that the refined is available solely in art and not in nature. Wang Guowei needs an explanation of why this restriction is not arbitrary. His essay on the refined in aesthetics finds a blend of different ingredients. His recipe for the refined stays thought-provoking and especially encouraging to artists who lack genius. From a hermeneutic standpoint, however, the Westernized delineation of his theory of the refined hinders its reception and popularity in China.

Some Chinese critics treated the refined (*gu-ya*) so literally that they separated the term into *gu* and *ya* for interpretation. They saw *gu* (ancient, age-old) as the antonym of *jin* (present-day, modern) and saw *ya* (elegant, cultivated) the antonym of *su* (vulgar, popular). Accordingly, works of *gu* and *ya* were assumed to belong exclusively to classical or high art, which is appreciated by a cultivated minority and has nothing to do with present-day reality. Works of *jin* and *su* were seen to be typical of mass or popular art, which was appreciated by the vulgar majority and reflected present-day circumstances. On this basis, Wang Guowei was labeled as a conservative or elitist, and his doctrine of the refined (*gu-ya*) was condemned for being estranged from reality and life and for being antagonistic to both the social aspect and the mass appreciation of the beautiful.[49] This critique ignored the contextual implications that I have mentioned and thus failed to answer Wang Guowei's actual views. The criticism was also arbitrary in light of Wang's stance toward high and popular art. In a historical review of Chinese drama, he provided an initiative study of the art genre that scholars previously considered unrefined and unworthy of serious consideration. In an opening remark for this study, he showed his appreciation of both high art and this popular genre:

> Each era has its own literature; just like the shi poetry (in the Tang Dynasty, the ci lyrics in the Song Dynasty, and the qu songs or drama in the Yuan Dynasty, literature of a specific kind only flourishes during its own phase and cannot be revived continuously in later ages.[50]

Noticeably, Wang's evolutionary view of literary development was free from any restriction to the classical or any bias against the popular. Some critique of his elitist stance in this regard sounds out of place or far-fetched at least.

---

[49] Chen Yuanhui, *Lun Wang Guowei* [A Study of Wang Guowei] (Changchun: Northeast Normal University Press, 1989), pp. 71–75.

[50] Wang Guowei, *Song-Yuan xiqu kao* [A Historical Study of Drama in the Song and Yuan Dynasties], 1912.

15.7 The Theory of Poetic State par Excellence (Jingjie Shuo)

Compared with his other essays on art and literature, Wang Guowei's *Ren jian ci hua* (Poetic Remarks in the Human World) has a special importance. The notion of *jingjie* (the poetic state) that it formulated was an aesthetic touchstone on his path of thought.

Ren jian ci hua is made up of 64 small sections. Its structure can be divided into two major parts: theoretical pondering and practical criticism. Sections 1–9 are devoted to a theoretical discussion of *jingjie*, and the remaining sections give examples of creating and appreciating *jingjie* in literary praxis through sample texts.[51] *Jingjie* is conventionally taken to be a Chinese rendering of the Sanskrit word *Visaya*, which was used in Buddhist sutras to mean the scope of sense perception or the characteristic of sense experience. This original meaning has become extended in complex ways, with implications, such as boundary (*jiangjie*), academic or artistic attainment (*zaoyi*), scene or site (*jingxiang*), and mood, state, or significance of an artwork (*yijing*).

Against this background, Wang used *jingjie* as a term in literary criticism for the essential quality of art. On some occasions, he used *jingjie* interchangeably with *yijing*, and they are taken as equivalents by many Chinese scholars. In my observation, *jingjie* can be rendered as the poetic state *par excellence*. It is seen as "the most important element in a consideration of *ci* lyrics" in Wang's leading argument.

> If a ci lyric has jingjie,, it will naturally achieve a lofty form and naturally possess eminent lines. The unique excellence of ci lyrics of the Five Dynasties and Northern Song periods rests precisely on this point.... The poetic state is not limited to scenery and objects alone. Pleasure and anger, sorrow and joy are also a sort of jingjie in men's hearts. Therefore, those poems that describe true scenes and objects (zhen jingwu), true emotions and feelings (zhen ganqing), can be said to possess jingjie. Otherwise, they may be said to lack jingjie. "Red apricot blossoms along the branch, spring feelings stir." With that one word "stir" (nao), the jingjie of the poem is

---

[51] Ye Jiaying, *Wang Guowei jiqi wenxue piping* [Wang Guowei and His Literary Criticism] (Shijiazhuang: Hebei Education Press, 1997), pp. 186–188.

completely expressed. "As the moon breaks through the clouds, flowers play with their shadows." With that one word "play" (nong), the jingjie of the poem is fully expressed.[52]

Elsewhere coping with Chinese drama, Wang Guowei used *yijing* instead of *jingjie*:

> The subtlety of literary works can be summed up in one phrase: having yijing. Then what is yijing? It is in the expression of qing (feelings) that is heart-stirring and mind-freshening, in the description of jing (scenes) that is vivid and engaging, and also in the narrative of shi (events) that is lucid and authentic as though coming straight from the mouth [of a good story teller]. It is unexceptionally true of all the best pieces among the ancient shi and ci poems. It is also the case with the qu songs of the Yuan Dynasty.[53]

According to the first quotation, *jingjie* or *yijing* must have two sorts of components: true or authentic scenes and objects (*zhen jing wu*) and true or sincere emotions and feelings (*zhen gan qing*). In the second quotation, we notice similar things—feelings (*qing*) as the shortened form of feelings and emotions (*ganqing*), scenes (*jing* as the shortened form of scenes and objects (*jingwu*), and events (*shi*) as the shortened form of events and matters (*shijian*). All of these elements, when woven together and expressed in an artwork, should be true and sincere, vivid and touching, natural and suggestive; their presence without these merits would not make sense in terms of the poetic state *par excellence* (*jingjie*). Feelings are subjective; scenes and events are objective. Hence, the poetic state can be seen as a fusion of the subjective and objective aspects of experience. According to some theorists, the poetic state is like "an artistic integration of *yi* and *jing*," where *yi* stands for feelings and affections (*qingyi*) and *jing* stands for scenes and objects

---

[52] Wang Guowei, *Wang Kuo-wei's Jen-Chien Tzi-hua: A Study in Chinese Literary Criticism* (trans. Adele Austin Rickett, Hong Kong: Hong Kong University Press, 1977), p. 42.

[53] Wang Guowei, *Song-Yuan xiqu kao* [A Historical Study of the Drama in the Song and Yuan Dynasties], 1912, p. 389.

(*jingwu*).⁵⁴ According to Chen Yong, the poetic state (*jingjie*) is "the distinctive imagery in art" that involves "the emotional substance" and "the specific atmosphere." It stems from an artistic expression of how an objective scene or event is reflected and contemplated in the mind or aesthetic sensibility of the poet.⁵⁵ For Ye Jiaying, the poetic state (*jingjie*) is a special term in literary criticism that emphasizes "the characteristic of genuine feelings and lively expressions. Feelings of this kind incorporate both inner and outer affective dimensions." The poetic state of this kind may well signify either a real scene of sensory perception or a poetic vision of imaginative association.⁵⁶ The most frequently discussed definition of the poetic state (*jingjie*) was proposed by Li Zehou: "As shown in Wang Guowei's usage, *jingjie* can be called *yijing*.... It is a higher category than image (*xingxiang*) and feelings (*qinggan*) in aesthetics, for it conjoins both image and feelings." Serving as the basis for *yijing*, image (*xingxiang*) signals not only resemblance in form (*xingsi*) but also likeliness in spirit (*shensi*). Feelings (*ganqing*) not only refer to the emotional aspect, but also imply the intellectual aspect concerning truth, concepts, and intrinsic laws or norms. The emotional aspect would become extremely wild without the mediation of the intellectual aspect. The poetic state *par excellence* can be therefore defined as the unity of a twofold fusion, the fusion of the emotional aspect with the intellectual aspect, and the fusion of resemblance in form with likeliness in spirit. In other words, the poetic state is the bearing of uniting artistically objective scenes or events with subjective feelings and interest.

In spite of all these efforts at interpretation, we cannot easily locate *yijing* and *jingjie* by means of a single definition. The mist of its subtlety and ambiguity can be lifted to some extent by examining Wang Guowei's following illustrations of the poetic state as the poetic state *par excellence*.

⁵⁴Li Zehou, "Yijing qian tan" [An Initial Enquiry into the Theory of *Yijing*], in Yao Kefu (ed.), *Renjian cihua ji pinglun hui bian* [Renjian Poetic Remarks and Selected Essays on Wang Guowei's Poetics] (Beijing: Shumu Wenxian Press, 1983), pp. 161–174.

⁵⁵Chen Yong, "Lue tan jingjie shuo" [A Note on the Theory of *Jingjie*], in Yao Kefu (ed.), *Renjian cihua ji pinglun hui bian* [Renjian Poetic Remarks and Selected Essays on Wang Guowei's Poetics], pp. 210–214.

⁵⁶Ye Jiaying, "Dui Renjian cihua zhong jingjie yici zhi yijie de tantao" [About the Definitions of Jingjie as a Term in Wang Guowei's Renjian Poetic Remarks], in Yao Kefu (ed.), *Renjian cihua ji pinglun hui bian* [Renjian Poetic Remarks and Selected Essays on Wang Guowei's Poetics], pp. 147–159.

15.7.1 The Creative Sate Versus the Descriptive State

In poetry, there are both the creative state (*zao jing*) and the descriptive state (*xie jing*). This is the basis of the distinction between idealists and realists. However, it is difficult to make a differentiation between the two because the state (*jing*) which the great poets create must accord with what is natural (*zi ran*), and the state which they simply describe must approach the ideal.[57]

This distinction is made from the perspective of producing artworks. The creative state, which is usually embodied in the works of idealists or romantics, employs mechanisms such as imagination, invention, exaggeration, and the grotesque to express subjective feelings and to characterize ideal models of society or romantic fantasies. The descriptive state, which is often reflected in the works of realists, represents and exposes a picture of the reality or actuality of the human condition. Yet, both the creative state and the descriptive state naturally share the common pursuit of the poetic state *par excellence* (*jingjie*).

15.7.2 The State of Self-Involvement Versus the State of Self-Detachment

In poetry, there are both the state of self-involvement (*you wo zhi jing*) and the state of self-detachment (*wu wo zhi jing*). Self-involvement is present in the lines: "With tear-filled eyes I ask the flowers, but they do not speak. Red petals swirl past and swing away." By contrast, self-detachment is implied in the lines: "I pluck chrysanthemums by the eastern fence, far distant appear the southern mountains." In a state of self-involvement, the poet views objects in terms of himself or egoism, and everything therefore takes on his own coloring. In a state of self-detachment, the poet views objects per se, and one cannot tell what should be ascribed to the poet himself and what to the object. The state of self-detachment can be attained only in complete quietude. The state of self-involvement is attained in the quiet that follows a conscious act. The former is beautiful, and the latter is sublime.[58]

---

[57] Wang Guowei, *Wang Kuo-wei's Jen-Chien Tzi-hua: A Study in Chinese Literary Criticism* (trans. Adele Austin Rickett), p. 40.

[58] Ibid., pp. 41–42.

Wang Guowei drew a parallel between these two seemingly distinct states in light of aesthetic appreciation. The state of self-involvement (*you wo zhi jing*) employs a self-identification with the object that is subjective and emotional and appears highly personified. It bears some analogy to the condition of empathy that Lipps depicts in his *Spatial Aesthetics*. In the state of self-detachment (*wu wo zhi jing*), the self is so deeply lost in the object that it seems to disappear. The state of self-detachment is therefore more poetically subtle, natural, harmonious, and suggestive than the state of self-involvement. However, the difference between the two states is quantitative rather than qualitative. The state of self-involvement tends more to be "a state with an explicit self" (*xian*) whereas the state of self-detachment is a more "a state with an implicit self" (*yin*).[59]

The state of self-detachment can be further explored in terms of the *chan* (*Zen*) Buddhist concept of being desire free (*wu nian*) or Schopenhauer's concept of the pure subject of knowledge. A person in the state of self-detachment would detach himself from any differentiation between subject and object and contemplate things in a purely objective manner. There seems to be a hidden connection in this regard. Specifically, the key to the distinction between self-involvement and self-detachment lies nowhere but in the Schopenhauerian notion of the desire-ridden will to live on the part of the subject. When confronted with the beautiful, the subject is freed from the disturbance by the will and thus obsessed in the serene contemplation of the idea itself. In this case, the subject is reduced to the pure subject of knowledge and consequently goes into the state of self-detachment as if the subject is naturally identified with the object. Instead, when coming up with the sublime, the subject is disturbed and shocked by the will and thus filled with desire for self-preservation, etc. But, it moves on to transcend the disturbance and returns to inner peace or mental tranquility by means of which it can still appreciate the aesthetic values in the object of sublimity even though it undergoes something painful and terrible. All this reveals two kinds of aesthetic experience and mental states relating to the distinctive features of the two categories: the beautiful and the sublime.

---

[59] Zhu Guangqian, "Shi de yin yu xian" [Of the Implicit and Explicit State in Poetry], in Yao Kefu (ed.), *Renjian cihua ji pinglun hui bian* [Renjian Poetic Remarks and Selected Essays on Wang Guowei's Poetics], pp. 87–89.

15.7.3 The Great Poetic State and the Minor Poetic State

The idea of the poetic state may be either large or small, but one cannot use this as a basis for determining the excellence or inferiority of a poem. Why cannot [the poetic state] in lines such as "Little fish jump in the fine rain; swallows dip their wings in the faint breeze" stand in comparison with that in the lines "The large banners glow in the setting sun; horses neigh in the rustling wind"? Why is not [the poetic state] in lines such as "The pearled curtain idly hangs on the little silver hook" as impressive as that in the lines "Mist enfolds the tower and pavilion; the moon shines dimly on the ferry"?[60]

In the first example, the fish and swallows are small in size, and the rain and breeze are pleasingly gentle. These images suggest not only smallness and gentleness, but also playfulness, delight, delicacy, and peace. According to Wang Guowei, the lines contain a small poetic state, notwithstanding the description that the banners and horses are large in size, and the sun and wind are dynamically powerful. These images imply greatness, power, a grand battlefield, excitement, motivating drive, pressure, and even terror. According to Wang Guowei, the lines contain a great poetic state. Both sets of lines are aesthetically appealing and equally expressive, no matter what kinds of objects or scenes are presented in the poems. With reference to Edmund Burke's *Philosophical Enquiry into the Origin of Our Ideas of the Sublime and Beautiful*, we can say that the small type of poetic state shares certain features with the category of the beautiful and that the great type of the poetic state shares certain features with the category of the sublime.

15.7.4 The Veiled and the Non-veiled

We can also distinguish between the poetic state as veiled (*ge*) and as non-veiled (*bu ge*). According to Wang Guowei, the veiled poetic state is weak in scenic description and leads us to approach some poems as if we were viewing flowers through a mist. Rather, the artistic excellence of lines such as "Spring grasses come to life beside the pond" and

---

[60] Wang Guowei, *Wang Kuo-wei's Jen-Chien Tzi-hua: A Study in Chinese Literary Criticism* (trans. Adele Austin Rickett), pp. 42–43; also see Wang Kuo-wei, *Poetic Remarks in the Human World* (trans. Ching-I Tu, Taiwan: Chung Hwa Book Company, 1970), p. 5.

"Swallows drop bits of mud from the desolate beams" lies in their not being obstructed by a veil. In *ci* lyrics, it is just the same. For example, the first stanza of Ouyang Xiu's *ci* poem "A Youth's Wandering" (*Shao nian you*) contains these lines below:

> Against the twelve zig-zag railings I lean along in spring,
> The clear azure stretches far to the clouds.
> A thousand miles, ten thousand miles,
> The second month, the third month,
> To think of travel distresses the heart.

Each image is direct therein, and not obstructed by a veil. When we come to other lines in the same poem, such as: "Beside the pond of Xie Lingyun, on the river-bank of Jiang Yan," we find that we are looking through a veil.[61] The reason why the last two lines are veiled is the use of two allusions. One refers us to Xie Lingyun's description in the line: "Spring grasses come to life beside the pond." The other is related to Jiang Yan's sentimental reflection *On Parting* (*Bie fu*):

> The spring grasses blue-green in hue,
> Spring water all waves of green.
> As I see you off on the southern shore,
> What hurt, ah, what pain!

The original lines are direct and vivid, while the lines alluding to them are indirect and bewildering, as if they were veiled. The first stanza cited demonstrates an intuitively natural style with elements from sensory experience and immediate perception. The other two lines that Wang Guowei saw as veiled reveal a contemplative style with allusions for rational and associative inference.

For Wang Guowei, veiled poetry mainly embodied a pedantic use of allusions, overdecorative phrases, and a pretentious style that deprives the reader of sincere feelings and vicarious experience. Non-veiled poetry is available through the natural expression of real feelings and scenes that enables the reader to attain intuitive apprehension and profound

---

[61] Wang Guowei, *Wang Kuo-wei's Jen-Chien Tzi-hua: A Study in Chinese Literary Criticism* (trans. Adele Austin Rickett), 1977, pp. 56–57; also see Wang Kuo-wei, *Poetic Remarks in the Human World* (trans. Ching-I Tu), pp. 26–27.

appreciation.[62] This capacity is in accord with the chief qualities of the poetic state par excellence that rest on the representation of both sincere feelings and emotions (*zhen qinggan*) and true scenes and objects (*zhen jingwu*). "Only when 'sincere feelings and emotions' as the soul are blown into the fine imagery of 'true scenes and objects' as the body, can the unique charm of the poetic state be fully displayed. Hence 'sincere feelings and emotions' can be conceived of as the life of the poetic state while 'true scenes and objects' [can be conceived of] as the manifestation and symbolization of this life."[63]

It is on this occasion that Wang quoted Nietzsche for emphasis: "If all that is written, I love only what a man has written with his blood. [Write with blood, and you will experience that blood is spirit.]"[64] This metaphorically denotes that the successful making of the poetic state is by no means an easy task because it calls for painstaking efforts along with creative power and heartfelt sincerity, etc.

The final analysis of the poetic state *par excellence a*s a special aesthetic category can be viewed holistically through the complex distinctions that I have suggested. The poetic state is concerned with style, imagery, mechanism, aesthetic value, significant form, truth-content, criteria of judgment, and the creative activity of poetry, but all for the sake of "the investigation of the nature of art in general."[65]

Wang's doctrine of the poetic state was deeply rooted in the rich soil of Chinese philosophy of criticism and blossomed in that context. His views can be traced back to Zhuangzi's speculation of words (*yan*) and meanings (*yi*) and then down to Wang Changling, Yan Yu, Wang Shizhen, Liu Xizai, and others who have thought about the poetic realm (*shijing*) or the significant state (*yijing*). Wang's debt to this tradition is self-evident, for instance, in his comment:

> In his Canglang shi hua (Canglang's Poetic Discourse), Yan Yu said: "The poets of the Golden Tang period were concerned only about inspiration and

---

[62] Ye Jiaying, *Wang Guowei jiqi wenxue piping* [Wang Guowei and His Literary Criticism], p. 220.

[63] Zhang Bennan, *Wang Guowei meixue sixiang yanjiu* [A Study of Wang Guowei's Aesthetics] (Taiwan: Wenjin Press, 1992), pp. 231–232.

[64] F. Nietzsche, *Thus Spake Zarathustra*, Part I, 1976.

[65] Nie Zhenbin, *Wang Guowei meixue sixiang pingshu* [Critique of Wang Guowei's Aesthetic Ideas] (Shenyang: Liaoning University Press, 1997), p. 139.

interest (xing qu). Like the antelope that hangs by its horns leaving no discernible traces on the ground, their excellence lay in their crystal-like transparency, no more to be grasped than a sound in empty space, the changing color in a face, the moon in the water or an image in a mirror. The words had a limit, but the meaning went on forever." However, what Yan Yu called inspiration and interest and what Wang Shizhen called spirit and tone (shen yun) only seem to touch the surface, while the term of two characters, jingjie, which I have chosen really probe the fundamentals of poetry.[66]

This interconnection with Chinese aesthetic tradition is strong as Wang himself stood on the shoulders of the preceding critics. In reality, he was mainly inspired by the insights of Yan Yu's theory of "inspiration and interest" (*xing qu*) and Wang Shizhen's theory of "spirit and tone" (*shen yun*). Yet, he played them down because he considered the poetic state to be the most essential of poetic creation and its aesthetic values. Thus in his mind, the poetic state accommodates within itself both an aesthetically touching or enlightening effect (*xing qu*) and a stylistic outcome or magic power of imagery (*shen yun*). Moreover, the touching effect implies a subtle enlightenment in connection with the mystic *Zen* whereas the magic power indicates an obscure contemplation of the poetic style in terms of exquisiteness and far-reachingness. Therefore, neither of them could be specifically formulated owing to their vagueness and ambiguity. Relatively, the poetic state can be described, as Wang believed, in more tangible terms such as "authentic scenes" and "sincere feelings," for instance. It is therefore treated by some readers as a so-called unity of the subjective and the objective, the ideal and the real, the emotional and the natural.

In addition, Wang Guowei enlarged the scope of the poetic state both through his writing and aesthetic judgment and through his capacity to absorb relevant elements from Western sources. His account of the poetic state has reminded many Chinese scholars of its possible association with Schiller's concept of "the aesthetic state" as elaborated in his 27th letter. But, in the specific context of Schiller's thought, the concept was intended to idealize things such as aesthetic culture, aesthetic man, and the cultivated taste involved in "the aesthetic state." It was related

[66]Wang Guowei, *Wang Kuo-wei's Jen-Chien Tzi-hua: A Study in Chinese Literary Criticism* (trans. Adele Austin Rickett), p. 43.

primarily to a concern for the advantages of aesthetic education rather than to a concern for the principles of artistic creation and appreciation.

Schiller's impact on Wang Guowei extended more to his other theories concerning aesthetic education (*meiyu shuo*), spiritual detachment (*jietuo shuo*), and art as play (*youxi shuo*) than to his doctrine of the poetic state (*jingjie shuo*). Rather, there is a more direct link between *jingjie* and *Geist* (spirit or mind) as presented in Kant's *Critique of Judgement*:

> Of certain products which are expected, partly at least, to appear as beautiful art, we say that they are without spirit; and this, although we find nothing to censure in them as far as taste goes. A poem may be very pretty and elegant, but is without spirit.... Even of a woman, we well say, she is pretty, affable and refined, but without spirit. What then do we mean by spirit? "Spirit" (Geist) in an aesthetic sense, signifies the animating principle in the mind. But that whereby this principle animates the psychic substance (Seele)—the material which it employs for that purpose that which sets the mental powers into a purposively swing, i.e., into a play which is self-maintaining and which strengthens those powers for such activity. Now my proposition is that this principle is nothing else than the faculty of presenting aesthetic ideas.[67]

Whatever differences they may have, both the poetic state and *Geist* are chiefly concerned with the essence, vitality, and significance of art. In short, Wang developed his theory of *jingjie* not only as an ultimate measure of literary value, but also as an ideal of artistic creation. However, his account fails to offer any easily intelligible definition or systematically coherent clarification. The poetic state is like an eel that the reader may assume to have caught, only to find that it has slipped through his fingers. Hence, a contextual reading is required to gain greater confidence in understanding and assessing the poetic state *par excellence*.

To sum up, we see that the structure of Wang Guowei's philosophy of literary criticism is largely built upon six doctrines. The first four doctrines are concerned with aesthetic education, spiritual exoneration, aesthetic play, and the artist as genius. Although they were all borrowed or transplanted from the West with minor modifications, the enlightenment that they brought to China remains a significant feature of Chinese

---

[67] I. Kant, *Critique of Judgment* (trans. J. B. Bernard), pp. 156–157.

intellectual and aesthetic culture. In striking contrast is the light that has flowed from his theoretical consideration of the refined (*gu-ya*) and the poetic state (*jingjie*). His individual contribution is best exemplified in his investigation of the poetic state, which at the beginning of the twentieth century marked the end of classical Chinese literary criticism and the beginning of modern Chinese aesthetic thought. His theory of the poetic state *par excellence* can be also seen as an inviting fruit on the upgrowing tree of transcultural transformation, which stays alive and appealing to reconsideration and reflection up till today.

CHAPTER 16

A Sublime Poetics of *Māratic* Type

The first quarter of the twentieth century witnessed drastic changes in the ideological sphere of China. As a historical milestone during this span of time, the New Culture Movement broke out as a strong tendency of Westernization, which stimulated a long-term endeavor to speed up all-round modernization and procured a persistent impact on social development. Such endeavor was largely attributed to the forward-looking intellectuals, progressive writers, and other elites who were so preoccupied with the enlightenment of the populace then.

Among this group, Lu Xun (1881–1936) is widely acknowledged as the foremost leading figure in literary and cultural criticism. As a prolific writer, his main publications provide the Chinese reader with food of thought. *The Theories of Māratic Poetic Power* (*Moluo shili shuo*, 1907), for example, is a lengthy essay, representing his early concern with the Romantic poets, and his ultimate intention to explore the possibility of ideological enlightenment amid all walks of life. It discloses not merely a proclamation full of enthusiasm for democratic revolution, but also a humanistic ideal to facilitate a fundamental change in Chinese mentality, thus promoting what the Romantic poetry extols as "intending to revolt by action" and calling for the "initiative and spirited kind of soldiers." In other words, it comes out as a blend of Lu Xun's strong passion for Chinese enlightenment with his expectation of artistic creation.

It is at this point seen as having realized the integrity of lawfulness with purposiveness in view of poetic writing and its sociopolitical effect. Accordingly, it is highly celebrated for its historic contribution to breaking up the old and setting up the new. For its publication caught the focus immediately at the time when the transformational process of Chinese poetics was underway from the classical pattern of illusory harmony toward the modern paradigm of *māratic* sublimity.

16.1 Historical Significance in Perspective

No sooner had Lu Xun given up his study of medicine[1] and returned to Tokyo in 1906 than he began to take part in the contentions between the revolutionist and the reformist. In the following year, he wrote in classical

---

[1] In his early years when Lu Xun was directly influenced by social ideology, he made "three drops – out and three takes – up" as to choose what to study in school and what to pursue for his career. This remarkable experience was partly owing to his initial aspirations held in his youth. First, it is out of his interest in "warship and artillery," which were commonly believed as powerful weapons to defend and fortify the declining China. The May of 1898 witnessed his registration in Nanjing Jiangnan Navy School to study military science. Later, deeply disappointed by the unqualified faculty and their teaching among others, he dropped the major and transferred in January 1899 to Nanjing Mining Affairs and Railway School to learn natural sciences and technology. There he graduated with a diploma in January 1902. Not long afterwards, he was determined to quit his pursuit of natural science and turned to medical science in order to become a doctor and cure patients like his own father whose treatment had been delayed by pseudo doctors (Cf. Lu Xun, "Nahan xu" [Preface to The Streaming], 1923). In Lin Yusheng's analysis, there were literally several factors that led Lu Xun to taking up medical science: one of them was his distrust in Chinese theory of medicine, which started since an unhappy "incident of toothache" in his childhood. "When he was between fourteen and fifteen years old, he once suffered toothache. The ailing was not cured through traditional Chinese therapy, and his pain became more acute when Lu Xun felt himself humiliated in the treatment. According to the traditional theory of Chinese medicine, tooth is related to kidney which is held as part of reproductive system of a male; toothache is believed to result from "insufficiency of the *yin*," i.e., "lack of physical contact with the female." For this unreasonable reason at that time, it was shameful of a person to tell about his own toothache. Therefore, Lu Xun never mentioned it on any another occasion. Lu himself once told Sun Fuyuan that it was one of the reasons why he decided to take up medical science." (Cf. Sun Fuyuan, "Lu Xun xiansheng ersan shi" [Some Anecdotes of Lu Xun], pp. 66–67; also see Lin Yusheng, "Lu Xun de fuza yishi" [Lu Xun's Complex Mentality], in Yue Daiyun (ed.), *Guowai Lu Xun yanjiu lunji* [Anthology of Overseas Study of Lu Xun] (Beijing: Peking University Press, 1981), p. 44.) In fact, another important contributing factor was that Lu Xun learnt that Japan's successful Reformation mainly started with Western medicine, which he thought would be very

helpful to strengthen his fellow people's belief in new thoughts. (Cf. Tang Tao, *Lu Xun de meixue sixiang* [Lu Xun's Aesthetic Thought] (Beijing: Renmin Wenxue Press, 1984), pp. 260–261). In addition, the social factor was that Lu Xun believed his study of Western medicine would help treat Chinese women's deformed feet and help them out of this malpractice. (Cf. Xu Shaoshang, *Wo suo zhidao de Lu Xun* [Lu Xun: the Person I Know]).

In 1902, Lu Xun went to Japan, first learning Japanese for two years in Tokyo Hirohumi Gakkou (1902–1904) and then moving to Sendai Medical School to study Western medicine for nearly three years (1904–1906). In 1906 when he was inwardly hurt by the "slideshow incident" (Cf. Lu Xun, "Nahan xu" [Preface to The Screaming], 1923), he finally decided to give up medicine and turned to literature. In the same year, he returned to Tokyo and joined in the contention between the revolutionist and reformist. It took him three years (1906–1909) before he returned to China (1909). The motivation that drove him to focus on literature was widely interpreted as "being saddened by their misfortune and being inflamed by their submission," the evidence of which can be found in his "Nahan xu" [Preface to The Screaming]. Both the slideshow about the Russian–Japanese War (1904–1905) and the pitiable Chinese "culture of passersby (a muscular body, an insensitive look, and habitual on–looking)" greatly upset the young and patriotic Lu Xun. Since then, as he said, he "felt that the study of medicine did not appear urgent any more, for the stupefied and vulnerable people, no matter how strong and sound they were built, could be nothing more than meaningless stuff for public displaying or on–looking. Therefore, their death from illness was not worth our mourning. The first thing for us to do was to enlighten their spirit then; for my part, the most potential medium for this cause was surely literature and art. So, I wanted to push ahead literature and art movement." (Cf. Lu Xun, "Nahan xu" [Preface to The Screaming].) As a matter of fact, Lu Xun's resuming of literature was not an overnight and whimsical decision. As early as in his childhood, he had developed a strong interest in literature and art, becoming particularly sensitive to the enlightenment of humanity. All this could be justified by the facts as follows: (1) Life-long attachment to engraving art. When he was a little boy and later a teenager, he began to take to copying down works of wooden cutting and books written on slate; at 17, he produced *Ga Jiansheng zaji* [The Anecdotes of Ga Jiansheng]; between 19 and 20, he wrote Bie zhu di [The Farewell to My Brothers] and Xi hua [The Pity with Flower] among other verses and prose writings. (Cf. Zhou Zuoren, *Lu Xun de gushi* [Stories of Lu Xun]). (2) Extraordinary preference of literature. In 1903, he translated Around the World in Eighty Days and All Around the Moon, science fictions by French novelist Verne (published by Tokyo Evolutionism Society, and included in the first volume of Anthology of Lu Xun's Translation Works). (3) Deep concern with politics and national character. Xu Shoushang recalled that, when he became acquaintance in 1902 with Lu Xun in Tokyo Hirohumi Gakkou, he found Lu Xun was primarily concerned about such issues as what the perfect humanity was, what was missing in Chinese character, and where the root of defect in national character was to be found. In their discussion, Lu Xun said that he had pinned down the mostly needed and the most undesirable in Chinese national character, i.e., the lack of "honesty and love." "In another word, it is the evil of fraud, disguise, shamelessness, suspicion, and mutual attacking." (Cf. Xu Shaoshang, *Wo suo zhidao de Lu Xun* [Lu Xun: the Person I Know]). (4) The influence of domestic scholars. Particularly, Lu Xun had been under the influence of Yan Fu's translation of the theory of evolution promoted in The Origin of Species and the thought of "revolution in the field of novel" held up in Liang Qichao's essay on "Lun xiaoshuo yu qunzhi zhi guanxi"

Chinese a sequence of four essays,[2] and had them consecutively published in the *Henan Magazine*, a monthly sponsored by the Henan-born students in Japan. The longest of the four essays is *The Theories of Māratic Poetic Power* (*The Poetic Power* as its shortened title to be used onward) that appeared successively under the pen name of Ling Fei in the January and February issues, and turned out to be a representative work of Lu's sublime poetics with particular reference to the Western Romanticism.

The Poetic Power draws on the evolutionism as its theoretic ground, exploits literary revolution as its means, and aims to provide a driving impetus for spiritual enlightenment and social reform in the chaotic China then. It features an in-depth analysis of those highly developed civilizations and the main causes of "their decline from past prosperity." Then,

---

[The Relationship between Novel and Democracy]. (5) Inspiration from overseas scholars, especially from the conception of literary and artistic reform put forward by Japanese counterparts. For example, Kimura Takatarou, a Japanese biographical writer of Byron, thought that Japan at that time was characterized by a great number of weakened and defenseless literati and charlatan scholars who claimed to be genius; there went rampant the flattery, blarney, hypocrisy, jealousy, and slander; the whole society had come to a standstill with humanity being deteriorated; Byronic heroism was urgently needed to restore to order and promote healthy growth of literature and art (Cf. Kitaoka Masako, *Moluo shili shuo caiyuan kao* [Investigation of Source Materials for The Theories of Māratic Poetic Power] (Beijing: Beijing Normal Uiversity Press, 1983), p. 5). In my own opinion, that Lu Xun dropped the study of medical science and took up literary career appeared occidental but was actually an inevitable choice; for this choice was based on the above-listed factors.

[2] The four papers follow: (1) "The Human History" (*Ren de li shi*). This paper was first published in the first issue of the monthly Henan in December, 1907. In 1926 Lu Xun added it to his prose collection The Grave (*Fen*). It was his earliest paper that introduced the theory of biological evolution through a systematic account of monistic genealogy by Ernst Haeckel (1834–1919), and a brief overview of biological evolutionism by Jean de Lamarck (1744–1829), and Charles Darwin (1809–1882) among others. The theoretical ground of Lu Xun's early thought can be traced out in this paper. (2) "Education in the History of Science" (*Kexue shi jiao pian*). It was written in 1907 under the penname of Ling Fei and first came out in June, 1908 in the fifth issue of Henan. In this important paper written in his early years about the history of Western natural sciences, Lu Xun attributed to scientists a progressive role in human history, illustrated the role of a stimulus science has been playing in modern and contemporary civilization, and dealt with the relationship between basic theory and applied science, with a purpose to expose for condemnation those countrymen who stubbornly resisted reform, adhered to outdated customs, and backed up restoration of the archaism and even regression. (3) "On Ideological Error in Culture" (*Wenhua pian zhi lun*). It was written under the penname of Xun Xing in 1907 and first appeared in August 1908 in the seventh issue of Henan. The gist of this reconsideration was for the purpose of "curbing the material development, spurring spiritual enlightenment, appointing the trustworthy and

it glorifies a critical conception of cultural transformation and decries the conservative world outlook held by the old-fashioned advocates of cultural restoration, the advocates that remained too stubborn to accept the keynote of national salvation via Westernization Campaign. This Campaign is by nature a radical downplay of the spiritual strength in the indigenous culture and a severe condemnation of the Confucian notion of moral cultivation through non-depraved poetry. To Lu Xun's mind, it is accountable not merely for the suppression of genius-based individuality, but also for the stagnant development of Chinese literature and art. On the other hand, it tones up the significance of education through new art and attributes it an indispensable role in aesthetic welfare. Consequently, it proceeds to affirm that the Romantic poets are outstanding for its vigorous pursuit, unbending spirit, and genuine expression, etc. In addition, the role of their poetry is able to break up the "filthy mess of stillness" and strike a challenging note of rebellion. Lu thereby cried out his enthusiastic applause of Byron's *māratic* spirit and romantic style, intending to collect new opinions from foreign states, for he believed that the transference would be likely to give birth to Chinese Byron and Shelley as "spirited kind of soldiers" who would be the awakening prophecy for literary revolution. These soldiers would be those whom the new type of Chinese culture and even the whole nation could rely on, because they would be able to help Chinese nationals to put an end to the status quo of stagnation and open up a new path for literary revolution.

Historically, from 1906 to his death in 1936, Lu Xun strived more than 30 years for the revival of Chinese literature and art in order to enlighten the Chinese people and reconstruct the national character. It has been widely recognized that his later accomplishments in such domains as

---

competent individual, and unyielding to the stupid masses." In this way, Lu Xun was trying to drive forward spiritual freedom, build up individuality, lay bare the partiality of bourgeoisie culture, and accuse the Westernization advocates of their barren-grounded showiness, hypocrisy, deception, and big talk about military affairs. He therefore called them "a flock with a tint of ability and petty wit." As for those people who once studied abroad and worshiped the Westernization Campaign as the only way out, Lu Xun slashed with unsparing criticism for their shallowness and self-deception, pointing out that they "do not know Chinese reality, neither do they truly understand European and American cultures. Whatever dust they could pick up, they would present it as a sharp weapon, which they hold up as top priority of a country. They introduce language of modern civilization in order to put on as ornament." (4) "The Theories of Māratic Poetic Power" (*Moluo shili shuo*).

poetics, aesthetic pursuit, literary output, art criticism, political ideal of democratic revolution, and humanistic philosophy largely owed to this critical essay in question. A Japanese scholar, for example, observes that:

> The Poetic Power can be taken for a faithful and comprehensive statement of Lu Xun's idea of literature. It outweighs the introduction and criticism of a certain poetic style in that it has found out among Russian poets and the suppressed East European poets the genealogy of Byron, a so-called devil in England and a māratic poet in Lu's terminology. In this critical essay Lu spoke out his observation and criticism in order to explore from the perspective of spiritual development the way out of national crisis. Therefore, it can be considered the starting point where Lu went on to build his architecture of literature.[3]

Similarly, a Chinese scholar states that:

> The Poetic Power is a war proclamation calling on an ideological revolution in the old China. With a clear-cut stand and passionate tone, it reflects the most advanced level of democratic revolution before the Revolution of 1911. What is most noticeable therein is Lu Xun's skeptic view, that is, "searching all over China, where could we find out our spirited soldiers?" Tentatively taken as the ideal form of expressing his aspirations, poetics literally turned out to be the object of his study through which he carried on with his idealistic pursuit. He also protested, "Is anyone striking a most sincere note to convert us to be kind-hearted, beautiful, and robust people? Is anyone striking a warming note to lift us out of chilly desolation?" For this, we have no reason to suspect Lu's political enthusiasm and readiness to fight for his idealism. As a matter of fact, the underlying theme of social reform is always well incorporated into his artistic creation.[4]

When we take into due consideration the history of change and development of Chinese literary criticism in the first half of the twentieth century, the significance and historic import of *The Poetic Power* can be perceived in its dramatic part in developing the new culture along with

---

[3] Kitaoka Masako, *Moluo shili shuo caiyuan kao* [Investigation of Source Materials for the Theories of Māratic Poetic Power] (Beijing: Beijing Normal University Press, 1983), p. 1. Here, the English translation is based on the Chinese version and offered by the author of the paper.

[4] Tang Tao, *Lu Xun de meixue sixiang* [Lu Xun's Aesthetic Thought] (Beijing: Renmin Wenxue Press, 1984), p. 67.

a parallel action to dismantle the old one. Lu Xun's groundbreaking achievement includes such efforts as encouraging individuality, promoting Romantic poetry, building up anti-traditional personality, championing a sublime poetics of *māratic* type, pushing forward the literary enlightenment to fish out "the second reformation," sticking to the aesthetic principle of relative integration of lawfulness with purposiveness, and finally "resorting to foreign lands for new voices" so as to realize the communication between Western and Eastern thinking. In a word, what cannot be underestimated is the dynamic organism of *The Poetic Power*, as it is performed either in Lu's own poetics and artistic production or in the transformation of Chinese poetics, aesthetics, and literary criticism in twentieth century. For this reason, further illustration is plainly needed.

16.2 The *Māratic* School and the *Māra* Allegory

The *Māratic* School refers to the Romantic poetry that once spread all over Europe. "*Māra*" is originally a mythological figure in Indian Buddhism, but herein stands for what the Europeans call "devil" or "demon" that allegedly resides in the Heaven. When the English public used the term "devil" to address Byron, a deviant poet of radical Romanticism, Lu Xun characterized Byron with the *Māra* allegory instead and accordingly looked upon other Romantic poets as natural components of the so-called *Māratic* School, involving Shelley from England, Pushkin and Lermontov from Russia, Adam Mickiewicz et al. from Poland, and Petöfi Sándor from Hungary. Personally speaking, I assume that Lu, in order to break down cultural barriers, introduced the exotic term *Māra* and came up with a symbolic coinage of the *Māratic* School for its future popularity. For this, he kept Byron as their mouthpiece who was full of defiant spirit, revolutionary passion, and heroic devotion.

16.2.1 The Basic Features of the Māratic School

As mentioned above, the *Māratic* School refers to the Romantics or Romantic Movement. The word *romantic* is originated from old French *romant*, which means legendary story (*roman*) written in Romance languages derived from Latin. Since *roman* is mainly about the fantasies and adventures of medieval knights, it is eventually used to denote fantastic novelty. In modern French, *roman*, *romance*, and *romanticisme* stand, respectively, for legendary or long novel, lyrical song, romantic music, and Romantic Movement. In the history of literature and art, the period spanning from the eighteenth century to the first half of nineteenth century is claimed to be the time when the Romantic Movement occurred, but, its influence actually persisted until the end of the nineteenth century.

Romanticism appears not only as a new style in the development of artistic creation, but also as a new prevailing trend of thought in the intellectual history. From a philosophical perspective, it goes strongly against the foregoing rationalism initiated by the enlightenment and equally rejects the rampant materialism that came up as a result of industrialization. The influence of French thinker Rousseau and the French Revolution once held a strong sway among most Romantic poets who invariably returned to emotion as their resource, relied on individuality and imagination for artistic creation, and preferred to exposing truth in a unique way. In addition to their common love for Nature, the Romantic poets appeared to share such characteristics as fundamental and appealing to the Chinese men of letters. These characteristics follow:

1. They do not yield to rigid rules but bring their imagination into full play in the process of art creation; with a self-commitment of their lives to infinite fluidity, they engage themselves in a free exploration of the way to express their unrestrained feelings.
2. They emphasize the value of individuality, liberty, inner feeling, and spiritual life, and show a remarkable tendency to express themselves through soliloquy.
3. They prefer passionate expression, fantasy, and exaggeration in the creation of artistic image.
4. As idealists, they tend to idealize social reality or criticize it from an idealistic point of view. They therefore hold a favorable opinion of individual revolt against society.
5. They love Nature, folklore, and exotic atmosphere, and remain curious about oriental or remote countries.
6. They are interested in exploring the idea of "infinity" and think highly of the knighthood in the Middle Ages.[5]

---

[5] Tang Tao, *Lu Xun de meixue sixiang* [Lu Xun's Aesthetic Thought], p. 67. Also see "Romanticism," in Wang Shide (ed.), *Meixue cidian* [A Dictionary of Aesthetics] (Beijing: Knowledge Press, 1986), pp. 429–430.

In England, a landmark of English Romanticism was the *Lyrical Ballads* (1798) by William Wordsworth and Samuel Coleridge. Later on, Byron, Shelley, and Keats, among many others, joined up to follow the lead. As far as the paramount theme is concerned, English Romanticism is closely associated with English Radicalism, with Byron responding to John Locke, and Shelley to William Godwin. Locke's political philosophy went so far as to champion the idea of liberty, civil rights, and civil society while attacking at the religious orthodoxy, divine right of the kings, and other forms of supreme authorities. Godwin was even notable for his extreme anarchism and utilitarianism, through which he advocated political justice, political ideal of equality, and natural rights of humans while opposing the corruption and policy executors by governmental institution. As a matter of fact, the source of Romanticism and Radicalism could be traced back to Rousseau's philosophy of liberty and democracy as well as the ideal pursuit of French Revolution. It is for this reason that Rousseau has always been enshrined in history as the father of Romanticism and philosopher of French Revolution.[6]

Lu Xun believed that the Romantic or *māratic* poets in Europe as a whole should be an abundant source of inspiration, for they could strike the greatest and masculine note that was in their language and bore in their thought. In his view, those poets shared the common goal in spite of being different from one another in their backgrounds. In contrast to the soft-toned and oversentimental compositions by other submissive poets, the *māratic* poetry rose out as a powerful weapon for its vicariously excited readers to challenge the privilege of divinity and defy the structure of social establishments. Its rebellious spirit even found their way to later generations and met no end of its influence. Despite the differences that occurred among them, either in character, nationality, social climate, speech, action, or theory, the *māratic* poets manifested in their literary output the same poetic style, which excelled with truthfulness, sincerity, and unyielding fortitude, etc. In particular, they never kowtowed to the vulgar; instead, by contributing vigorous lines, they kept their people awakened and made the whole nation strengthened. For example, their spokesman, the lonely, brave, defiant, and brooding Byron, was always ready to step ahead, allowed nobody left behind, and

---

[6] Sally Scholz, *On Rousseau* (USA: Wadsworth/Thompson Learning, Inc., 2001), pp. 3–5.

sacrificed his life on the battlefield. He clapped his hands for Napoleon's subversion of the world and Washington's fight for freedom; he longed for the piratical adventures and stood out to combat against Turks for Greek independence. Both suppression and rebellion were bound up to reside in Byron himself. Lu highly appreciated and recommended such a *māratic* character singing hymn to the mighty and hence posed a question to all whether a Chinese Byron had ever been born.

It is noteworthy that Lu Xun fashioned the *Māratic* School with a purpose to express his admiration of idealized character and artistic genius. When it comes to their character as above mentioned, the *māratic* poets are worshiped as spiritual soldiers; when it comes to their artistic accomplishments, they are renowned for spiritual strength, forceful language, and new viewpoint. In Lu's terms, this strength is "so powerful to spur up others," thus specifying the soul-stirring artistic charm and the far-reaching impact of its artistic rendering and infinite creativity; this language is "so profound and appealing," thus referring to their stimulating literary language or the depth of thought; and this voice is of "beautiful majesty and macho," thus representing a new voice from foreign land that is deafening and thought-provoking enough to overturn the old and stale. All this could lead people to be aroused and enlightened as Lu expected. Actually, it is mainly due to this possibility that he regarded the Romantic poetry as one of the new voices and likened it to an alarming drum to dispel the bleak desolation out of China under harsh conditions.

16.2.2 The Multi-implications of Māra

The Chinese transliteration of *Māra* is *moluo*, which bears the resemblance of devil or identity with Satan in Christianity. Lu Xun once confessed that he "borrowed an Indian word '*Māra*' and made it into '*moluo*' to signify a devil in Heaven which Europeans call 'Satan'." Contextually by *Māra* is meant disturbing, destructive, or obstructive. In Buddhism, it is held to upset body and mind, spoil good things, and prevent the practice of good code. According to Indian mythology, Pāpīyas as the king of the sixth kingdom of desire often headed a band of devils to prevent good deeds and indulged in subjecting people either under their control or to their vicious will. Buddhism picked up this legend and identified *Māra* with anxiety, perplexity, attachment, and all the other mental activities that would cut down Buddhist's observance.

In the fifth volume of *The Sutra on Greatest Wisdom*, *Māra* is defined to be no other than a dark force of killing monks and destroying morality, charity, piety, beneficence, and classics.[7] The Buddhist *Māra* is said to have infinite power and wisdom, apart from being a great source of temptation. Allegedly, when Shakyamuni was about to achieve the highest enlightenment, *Māra* attempted to seduce him with a female beauty in order to upset his state of mind, outdo his *dhyana* of tranquility, and stop him from becoming the Buddha. Naturally, this attempt ended up in failure.

What Lu Xun reckoned as being *māratic* in *The Poetic Power* is referred to the *Māratic* School headed by Byron. However, it has multiple implications in its sociohistorical context. It implies, for instance, a number of heroic images vividly portrayed in the Romantic poetry, say, the unconventional Don Juan who "fought against Satan, challenged God, and exclaimed what others dare not say"; the iron-willed pirate Corsair who put law and morality to his sword; the dignified Lara who defied destiny and sacrificed life for self-respect; the courageous Manfred who resisted temptation and oppression from any kind of authority; the deviant Cain who modeled himself on Satan to revolt against both the divine and the public; and also the "national enemy" who acquired this posthumous title because they held fast to truth and rejected stupidity and mediocrity. All of them seem to be as much *māratic* as what the Romantic poets adored as the mighty who remained indignant of earthly pursuits, cherished chivalry and righteousness, and embodied the Byronic pride and freedom from any restraints, so to speak.

From the perspective of artistic creation, *Māra* signifies a kind of genius. He is neither an ambitious emperor who only seeks to secure his own ruling and eternal crowning of his descendents nor a common person who, contented with being well-off, would rather crouch and yield than rising to revolt. The birth of a genius is therefore in danger of being stifled by others. However, these *māratic* poets were indeed loudly protesting on behalf of the populace. They were so sensitive to and sympathetic of what their fellow men were suffering that they were able to render a faithful and heart-swelling description of their misfortunes. They did not compose poems merely for their own sake; they wrote lines

---

[7] "Māra" and "mo" in *Ci hai* [An Encyclopaedic Dictionary] (Shanghai: Shanghai Cishu Press, 1980).

that reached the soul of all men alike. Just as Lu Xun proclaimed, "The *māratic* poets have expressed what people are able to feel but unable to let out. The moment these poets have struck the first key, people will immediately respond to it. The sound is just so pure that the compassionate will lift their eyes as if they have caught the sight of sunlight. When enlightened, people will become increasingly good, strong, and elevated, and accordingly the filthy mess of stillness will fall apart. Only then will humanity rise."[8]

Subsequently, from the perspective of spiritual revolution, *Māra* is symbolic of "spirited soldiers" that Lu Xun frequently praised. In his opinion, soldiers of this kind are bestowed with strenuous and endless efforts that could "bring to an end the desolation in China" and push forward "the second reformation." They are no other than those who fought for liberty and democracy, i.e., those who "intend to revolt and aim to take action." After the publication of *The Poetic Power*, Lu Xun also contributed another essay titled "The Ideological Error in Culture" (*Wen hua pian zhi lun*, 1908) in the seventh issue of *Henan Magazine*. Thereby, he criticized not merely the Western materialism, but the political partiality and the superficiality of those Chinese who embarked upon exclusive pursuit of advantages and material gains in the process of Westernization. By so doing, he intended to throw light onto the notion of "curbing the material development, spurring spiritual enlightenment, and appointing the trustworthy and competent individual while unyielding to the stupid mobs." The so-called "individual" here is meant both as individual liberation and self-dignity in a humanistic sense, and as a prophetic "fighter" of democratic and liberal ideal. This corresponds to Lu's conviction that "to encourage individuality is the primary principle of life"; for he believed that the individuality as a virtue means to be extraordinary and outstanding in that those who have unparalleled willpower are ready to express what they feel and wish, and brave to fight for what they pursue and expect. Although they may have failed from time to time in such cases, they will be able to accomplish their ideals in the end. All this speaks out their noble characters.[9]

---

[8] Lu Xun, *Moluo shili shuo* [The Theories of Māratic Poetic Power], 2nd section.
[9] Lu Xun, "Wenhua pian zhi lun" [The Ideological Error in Culture].

As is noted in his argument "About Anti-Hypocritical Language" (*Po e sheng lun*, 1908), Lu Xun went on to explicate the significance of "individuality" he held in high esteem:

> As a result, what we value and rely on is the personage [of individuality] that does not go along with plebeian opinions and is capable of independent thinking as well as keen insight into the hidden. In judging the flaws and merits of any civilization, he does not agree to those absurd and confusing ideas. Instead, he only sticks to what he thinks true, never allowing himself overwhelmed by popular compliment or general condemnation. He allows followers, whom he turns to for satire, and is never afraid to be left in isolation. He takes painstaking efforts to enlighten his people with his dim candlelight. If everyone commits to this individuality and denies general trend, then China will rise above the world.[10]

In modern scholarship, this heroic personality has been interpreted as the courage in taking up the responsibility of social reform, the ability to think unconventionally and reject naïve conformity, the possession of firm belief and fighting spirit, the disregard for personal interests and infamy, and the accommodation of followers and tolerance of temporary isolation, etc. Such an individual is actually qualified to be an anti-imperialist and anti-feudalist fighter that Lu was anticipating.[11]

When holding up "an individual" as a model, Lu Xun intended for the enlightenment of Chinese people, the reformation of their national character, and finally the salvation of China as a nation-state. Thus, he developed such a thesis as that the survival and prosperity of a nation should begin from the character building of its people. For this, he strongly insisted that "in the competition with other nations we Chinese are plunged into a life-and-death struggle. The first thing we must do is to build up a new form of national character. When this is done by any chance, the rest of other enterprises will be well on the way to thrive and develop. The best solution in this case is to hold individuality in high regard and to encourage spiritual growth."[12] This is essentially different

---

[10] Lu Xun, "Po e sheng lun" [On Anti Hypocritical Language].

[11] Zeng Qingrui, "Dui zhongguo jindai sixiang qimeng yundong de xingongxian" [A New Contribution to Modern Intellectual Enlightenment Movement in China], in *Lu Xun yanjiu* [The Journal of Lu Xun Studies] (Beijing: China Social Sciences Press, 1981), Vol. 2, p. 212.

[12] Lu Xun, *Wen hua pian zhi lun* [On Ideological Error in Culture].

from what was sought after in the Westernization Campaign. With his recognition of bitter historical lessons and stern social reality, Lu fully understood that China would definitely lose the competition if it were still contented with its inferior position and its unconditional observance of perverse customs. In other words, if China still kept to the beaten track in striking contrast with a rapidly changing world, any form of tearful crying and mourning could do nothing to prevent it from decline and collapse. Hence, he always maintained that the one and only key to the national crisis was held in the hands of Chinese people themselves provided they became competent, dignified, wise, and individual. In addition, they ought to have an insight into the world affairs, an ability to scrutinize and apply to China what they came up with in their comparative study of different cultures, and the wisdom to do away with the partiality in order to catch up with the world trend of thought while preserving their good heritage. Only by so doing, new thought would be nourished and individual spirit be evoked. Consequently, the once sandcast country like China would turn into a civilized and humane one.[13]

Critical and observant as he may be, Lu Xun was still at a distance to see through the social crisis of China in light of the problematic political system. Say, if he had gone further to track down to its most fundamental causes in view of institutional drawbacks, he would have come out with a more adequate diagnosis of "knocking down the old world in order to set up a new one." In spite of all this, Lu was the first to be aware of the urgency of cultural enlightenment and the reconstruction of national character. Accordingly, the depth in his thought is still of practical importance and plays a mind-broadening role even today.

16.3 Dismantling the Old While Establishing the New

Active in the New Culture Movement in China in the early twentieth century, Lu Xun championed a strategy of cultural borrowing. Actually, he once gave an account of certain attitudes toward borrowing, strongly asserting that "without borrowing from others, man cannot renew himself; without borrowing from abroad, literature and culture cannot renew themselves."[14] In this regard, *The Poetic Power* can be also seen as the

---

[13] Ibid.
[14] Lu Xun, *Nalai zhuyi* [On Borrowing Strategy].

precursor of cultural borrowing, with its idea of looking for new voices in heterogeneous cultures as an early declaration and its introduction of Romantic poetry as the demonstrative evidence. Ostensibly, the purpose to borrow lies in the dismantlement of the old (i.e., old mentality, outlook, and tradition) and the establishment of the new (i.e., new national character, worldview, literature, and art). On this occasion, *The Poetic Power* offers a keynote and even a guiding rope about how to set up the new while breaking up the old, which covers at least four aspects in a thematic sense.

16.3.1 A New Notion of Culture

Right at the outset of *The Poetic Power* is a quoted remark from Nietzsche, saying that the man who has exhausted his exploration of an ancient well is destined to seek successively after another new source for future, and likewise the man will exclaim to his fellows that it will not be long before the coming of a new birth and the exploding of a new spring from under the abyss.[15] The quotation comes from the 25th section "On Old and New Tablets" in *Thus Spoke Zarathustra*. But there is a slight discrepancy between Chinese and English renderings of the same statement. According to Walter Kaufmann, for instance, Nietzsche actually meant that whoever obtained the wisdom of ancient origin is bound to explore future wells and new origins, and it would not be long before we witnessed the birth of new people and the flooding of fresh spring into new abyss.[16]

In my observation, Lu Xun seemed to take an exceptional approach by introducing Nietzsche's comment at the beginning of *The Poetic Power*. He thereby employed it to illuminate the theme of turning to other cultures for new values, and to express his disappointment with national character and old-fashioned literature. Teleologically he looked forward to an earnest anticipation and an all-round reform. He thus

---

[15] Wang Shijing, *Lu Xun Zaoqi wupian lunwen zhushi* [Annotations of Lu Xun's Early Five Essays] (Tianjin: Tianjin People's Press, 1978), p. 198.

[16] The English translation follows: "Whoever has gained wisdom concerning ancient origins will eventually look for wells of the future and for new origins. O my brothers, it will not be overlong before new peoples originate and new wells roar down into new depths." Cf. Walter Kaufmann (ed. and trans.), *The Portable Nietzsche* (New York: Penguin Books USA Inc., 1976), p. 323.

went on to account for the distressing ebb tide of both Chinese culture and its poetry as follows:

> Whoever studies the history of civilization of ancient nations is certain to perceive, if following a chronological order, the gloom that pervades his reading of the last chapter. It is as if he has been plunged from spring warmth into autumn chill, with every sprout removed and each token of life faded. I am overwhelmed by the vision of the withered that I feel at a loss as to how to describe it, so I have to stop here with the word depression. The strength of heritage each ancient civilization leaves alive is no more than a spiritual language. Blessed with intuitive power, our ancestors reached so far into the fathomless and ageless, and cried out what the mind's eye could see. That was how the inspired poetry came into being. Their poetic sound went far and wide and survived each passing generation, echoed in the alive and from the deceased. It overtopped its people. In turn, when literature began to decline, so did its national destiny. People gave up their high-spirited music, and consequently, the halo above their civilization would immediately die out. Upon this, the reader of history would burst out with the feeling of being deprived. And it must be the time he finished the last pages of the recorded civilization. No ancient country, once glorious at the dawn of history for the light it brought to civilization, could escape the fate of disappearing into an obscure shadow.[17]

Apparently with keen awareness of the social reality, Lu Xun identified the prosperity of culture and poetry with the food for thought, the spiritual nutrition for the soul, and the decisive factor in national revival and character rebuilding. In this sense, the adherence to outdated thoughts and the lack of aspiration would inevitably conduce to the decline of culture and poetry. This being the case, the Chinese nation would be doomed to extinction, and the whole nation would become mere history. Ancient India, Egypt as well as China, all of which were once highly developed civilizations, were then unexceptionally desolate. For this reason, Lu ridiculed the vanity of those from declining families who were still obsessed in nostalgia of the past and kept mentioning the glory of their ancestors. By the same token, he bitterly attacked the advocates of Westernization Campaign and their indiscreet behaviors, such as lopsided boasting, blind optimism, self-conceit, or self-deception by repeatedly singing "army songs" for self-encouragement and

---

[17] Lu Xun, *Moluo shili shuo* [The Theories of Māratic Poetic Power], 1st section.

indiscriminating the reprobation of Indian and Polish slavishness. In China of Lu Xun's times, the self-complimentary note was so popular that it became close to a kind of national anthem, and the mass affectation went so excessive that no match could be found out in the existent history.

Nevertheless, Lu Xun did not mean he rejected all the attempts at cultural restoration. Instead, he advised that the nostalgia of the past be backed up by the efforts to renew the old. "It should be admitted that the prospect of the country owes to our study of history, provided that we remain critical of and clear-sighted about the past, taking it as a mirror where we can learn many lessons from the historical reflection. Since we keep moving ahead along a promising journey, the innovation will continually go on; since we hold dear to our prosperous past, the renovation of the old will last likewise."[18] Evidently, to cherish the old and to establish the new were believed to help realize their dialectical unity in the case of cultural reform. In practice, the retrospective efforts were believed to draw historical lessons and thus serve as a stimulus to wake people up; the journey to bright future was believed capable of getting the old renewed and the new thrived. Therefore, efforts should be directed toward getting rid of the depressive pessimism, overcoming obstinacy and stupidity, recognizing the infinity of civilization, and engaging oneself in the endless pursuit of social and cultural progress. In the case of China, leave alone what and how we should do to the past, the priority should be given to resorting to the new voices from other countries, that is to say, what to be borrowed from abroad was to lay a new foundation. Specifically speaking, the voice and spirit drawn from the Romantic poetry would be applied as a vigorous and driving force to initiating the creation of a new culture, especially new literature and art.

Incidentally, evolutionism is the bulk as the theoretical ground upon which Lu Xun developed his idea of new culture.[19] As early as in his

---

[18] Ibid.

[19] Undoubtedly, Lu Xun's thought is rich with its theoretical sources relating to humanitarianism, democracy, the Enlightenment, and new idealism, etc. He personally devoted himself to promoting the ideas of freedom of thought, equality, fraternity, individuality, initiative spirit, and human dignity, in hope that people would think in accordance with the latest trends. His pursuits were in sharp contrast to those pragmatists (chong shi lun zhe) or those who either daydreamed cultural restoration, held fast to the quintessence of national legacy, or relied solely on Westernization for national revival. Here, this difference is left for future discussion.

school years in Nanjing (Nanking), he was deeply influenced by this biological breakthrough. Later on, he began to study Western thinkers, among whom Darwin and Huxley were the most leading ones. As stated in the *Collection of Miscellanea* (*Zhao hua xi shi*), Lu Xun took great interest in *The Origin of Species* whose first Chinese translator is Yan Fu, a well-known scholar in favor of the Reformation Movement at that time. When hearing the news that the Chinese version of the book had come out in print, Lu Xun "hurried downtown on Sunday for it," and then "quickly read it through," just to have discovered a new world where only "the fittest will survive." He did not simply catch glimpses of the book; instead, he scrutinized it to the extent that he could still remember and recite its main passages even many years thereafter.[20] In two of his essays, "The Human History" (*Ren de li shi*) and "Observations on the History of Science" (*Ke xue shi jiao pian*), he gave a detailed and faithful account of the theory of evolution, declaring that "the new is promised to get over the old and the evolutionary theorem is the natural law." Meanwhile, he predicated that evolutionism could be applied as a solution to many problems and able to contribute to the cultural renewal and artistic renovation, national revitalization, and even social progress. His belief in the evolutionary hypothesis can be attested by his admiration of the *Māratic* School and their new voices, while his predication can be justified by his own commentary in 1918 when he said, "I think the survival of a race, that is, the continuance of life, deserves to be the main enterprise in the bio-kingdom. But why is there such persistence? Of course, it is for the sake of evolution. On the way of evolution, there is metabolism, with which the newborn things are bound to make further progress while the old things are to linger on. For the former, the continuance means growth while for the latter it means death. Everyone moves along to its own destiny, and that is the road of evolution."[21] It seems that, although he drew on the theory for his rethinking of a new culture, he was also subject to its limitation and therefore arrived at an

---

[20] As Xu Shoushan recalled, "One day, when the book was mentioned during a conversation between Lu Xun and me, he immediately recited several chapters of it." Cf. Li Zehou, "Lüe lun Lu Xun sixiang de fazhan" [A Brief Review of the Development of Lu Xun's Thought], in *Lu Xun yanjiu jikan* [The Anthology of Lu Xun Study] (Shanghai: Shanghai Literature and Art Press, 1979), Vol. 1, p. 33, Note 4.

[21] Lu Xun, *Lu Xun quan ji* [The Complete Works of Lu Xun] (Beijing: Renmin Wenxue Press, 1958), Vol. 1, p. 412.

arbitrary but a simplified conclusion. Yet, all his endeavors to promote the construction of new culture and the necessity of social reform owed to his accommodation and application of this introduced theory.

16.3.2 A New Conception of Literature and Art

In *The Poetic Power*, Lu Xun passionately depicted the lives, works, and poetics of the *Māratic* School including Byron, Shelley, Pushkin, Lermontov, Mickiewicz, Slowacki, Kraszewski, and Petőfi. From his heartfelt appreciation of their revolting temperaments and persistent pursuits, we can tell that Lu Xun was quite sympathetic over the radical spirit of these poets. As a matter of fact, he was greatly inspired by the ethos of Romanticism even before he commenced his literary career. As a result, he went on to develop his Romanticism-oriented theory in which the seed of literary reform was simultaneously implanted.

First and foremost, Lu Xun expected a real poet to be a revolution-spirited legislator just as those "spiritual fighters" of the Romantics or the *Māratic* School in his terminology. Through writing poems, they resisted against malpractice in old conventions that got in the way of the development of poetry. These *māratic* poets sacrificed their lives for the ideal of justice, and their efforts did swell the "tide of reform"; they fought alone against outdated customs and even encouraged the destruction of the old without any compromise. All of them were blessed with intuitive power, engaged themselves in endless pursuit and exploration, and moved headlong without any retreating at all. People in the street can never understand their deep and complex thoughts. If someone happened to recognize their outstanding characters, he would probably see these poets as those who came from the lofty realm, for they were so passionate, sincere, and high-spirited that nothing could frustrate them or prevent them from advancing into the imaginative world. It is in this world that the beautiful substance exists.[22] This argument reflects Shelley's impact on Lu who even accepted the corresponding ideas presented in *A Defense of Poetry*. Therein, we read such catchphrases in a similar tone as follows:

> The most unfailing herald, companion, and follower of the awakening of a great people to work a beneficial change in opinion or institution, is

---

[22] Lu Xun, *Moluo shili shuo* [The Theories of Māratic Poetic Power], 6th section.

poetry.... Poets are the hierophants of an unapprehended inspiration; the mirrors of the gigantic shadows which futurity casts upon the present; the words which express what they understand not; the trumpets which sing to battle, and feel not what they inspire; the influence which is moved not, but moves. Poets are the unacknowledged legislators of the world.[23]

It followed that Lu Xun equally held in esteem both genius (*xingjie*) and individuality, just like most Romantic poets who admitted the importance of genius in artistic creation and intellectual reform. In his perception, the most leading of all gifted poets were no other than Byron and Shelley belonging to the *Māratic* School. By contrast, Qu Yuan, a most talented Chinese poet, "produced marvelous pieces describing grievance and sorrow. When confronted with the flood of secular torrents, he remained brave to lash out the dirty aspects of the world while eulogizing the virtues and talents of his own.... His fearless and carefree lines cried out what his predecessors dare not. However, with the intertwined flowery notes of painful sadness and the absence of a resisting and challenging tone, his poetry was not powerful enough to inspire the posterity."[24] Therefore, Lu thought Qu Yuan's poetry did not live up to what was composed by the *māratic* poets. As for the personality of genius, Lu Xun considered it mainly reflected in such things as the creative efforts, the pursuit of ideal and trueness, the resistance against outdated customs, and the struggle for freedom and liberation. Its inborn unyielding spirit was most liable to meet strong resistance from those who were contented with being comfortably off, and rejecting any aspiring efforts. In his critical essay "The Ideological Error in Culture," Lu sighed again not only for the misery a genius came upon in China, but also the unbearable weight of historical consequence that worked to suppress individuality. Thus to his mind, China used to seek after material comforts but loathe genius. With the heritage from ancient sage-kings vanishing day after day and foreign invasion already at the doorway, it found itself nowhere to retreat and exist for itself. Some self-arrogant fellows with a tint of ability and petty wit rose up for the

---

[23] Percey Bysshe Shelley, "A Defense of Poetry," in Hazard Adams (ed.), *Critical Theory Since Plato* (New York: Harcourt Brace Jovanoich, 1971), pp. 512–513. Also see Percey Bysshe Shelley, "A Defense of Poetry," in Wang Peiji et al. (trans.), *Yingguo zuojia lun wenxue* [English Writers on Literature] (Beijing: Sanlian Bookshop, 1985), pp. 122–123.

[24] Lu Xun, *Moluo shili shuo* [The Theories of Māratic Poetic Power], 2nd section.

sake of self-redemption. Since they resorted merely to material force and conformed to the blind majority, they were utterly deprived of their individuality. Apparently, this cynical criticism under Lu's pen expresses his eagerness to call on the birth of genius and persuade the whole society to be conscious of their special role.

In Lu Xun's conception, genius is identified with individuality, and essentially different from a stereotype. In literature and art, for instance, a poet is normally held up as a genius because of his bestowed talents. Such talents are so rare that they are only possessed by the very few. However, Lu deduced from a different viewpoint and seminated that "Every man is born a poet and blessed with the same poetic power," and "deep in everyone's heart there dances a poem; poetry does not exclusively belong to a poet. Hence, anyone who can apprehend poetry is unexceptionally capable of poem-writing; otherwise, how could he understand other's poetry?"[25] This insight into the nature of poetic genius is an outcome of the influence from Shelley who defined poetry as "the expression of the imagination." Furthermore, Shelley was convinced that "Poetry connate with the origin of man…there is a principle within the human being, and perhaps within all sentient beings, which acts otherwise than in the lyre, and produces not melody alone, but harmony, by an internal adjustment of the sounds or motions thus excited to the impressions which excite them. It is as if the lyre could accommodate its chords to the motions of that which strikes them, in a determined proportion of sound; even as the musician can accommodate his voice to the sound of lyre. A child at play by itself will express its delight by its voice and motions, and every inflection of tone and every gesture will bear exact relation to a corresponding antitype in the pleasurable impressions which awakened it;…Man in society, with all his passions and his pleasures, next becomes the object of the passions and pleasures of man; an additional class of emotions produces an augmented treasure of expressions;…."[26] What Lu and Shelley said, respectively, above appear to be fairly commensurable with regard to the nature and advent of poetry. The discrepancy between them lies in nowhere but the degree of elaboration and analogical depiction.

[25] Ibid.
[26] Percey Bysshe Shelley, *A Defense of Poetry*, in Hazard Adams (ed.), *Critical Theory since Plato*, p. 499. Also see Wang Peiji, et al. (trans.), *Yingguo zuojia lun wenxue* [English Writers on Literature], pp. 90–91.

Thirdly, Lu Xun actively circulated the artistic principle that the true is beautiful, or the law of truth conforms to the law of art. The so-called trueness means both genuine feeling and sincerity in artistic expression. The feeling conveyed is supposed to arise from the heart of the artist, who is "really aroused without a single pretence"; and the sincere expression in artistic creation is supposed to be the freedom of speech and expression, which springs from the disarming of the typecasting ideology. To live up to this principle, an artist is expected to "transcend the classical model and stay candid about his belief," that is to be a "sincere" or *māratic* "spokesperson of truth." Hereby, unrelentingly denied is such conception of literature as a mouthpiece of the ruling, as a means to indulge in breeze and moon, or as an instrument to obscure the truth and mislead the public. Accordingly, the poems that "are intended to praise and please the ruling power" are of no value, and even unworthy of mentioning; the verses that "are empathetic with insect, bird, wood and spring" are mostly kept in between heaven and earth, thus unable to discover real beauty therein; the literature or art that comes out as "obscurity and deception because of the fear to confront with the reality" is next to the source that poisons and pollutes the mentality of the people as a whole. Lu Xun was so indignant about the abuse of literature and art that he reinforced this point in his satirical article "On Keeping Eyes Wide Open" (*Lun zheng le yan kan*, 1925), claiming that "Chinese people are prone to evading the confrontation with the reality and are left nothing else but deceive and keep truth in the dark. This mentality has given rise to misleading and foggy literature and art, because of which the Chinese have fallen into an entangling confusion, plainly unaware of how they have been deceived and kept from the truth." At the same time, he earnestly cried out that with an ever-changing world, it is the time for our writers to have removed their masks, wholeheartedly, deeply, and bravely facing up to the reality, and to have written out their own blood and flesh; we should have had a new literary world along with devoted and fierce fighters. As is seen from this statement, the artistic truth Lu Xun advocated cannot do without the spirit of realism and enlightenment. In practice, this twofold implication goes hand in hand with his conception of literature and art as "blaze shining from national spirit" and as "beacon light that leads the voyage of national spiritual development." As is so proved, the claim for artistic truth as part of Lu Xun's poetics does not only involve artistic lawfulness (artistic creation), but also concern with artistic purposiveness (social effect).

Last but not least, Lu Xun well recognized the complementary relationship between science and art. This vision even survives those partisan, radical or short-sighted notions held among many contemporaries in China. As is known in his early years, he took up natural science in school because he thought it could help remedy the diseased culture. So he was fully aware of the importance of science and technology in terms of national economy and social welfare, maintaining that literature and art, whose pursuits are charged with humanistic spirit, are equally important and cannot be replaced by science when it comes to the representation and perception of life and the enlightenment of people. He thus affirmed that great literature is capable of exposing us to the secret of life and blessing us with a faithful account of its truth and legislation, of which science is far beyond the reach.[27] Regarding the education in the history of science elsewhere, he continued to elaborate in depth the same idea, proclaiming that science is capable of promising a strong nation and affluent people, but it is not advisable to let its exaggerated role slant toward extremes. Otherwise, social development would go astray and run into a dead end, humanistic spirit would die out, and the nation would perish eventually. In his terms, if "science were exclusively promoted, life would end up in exhaustion and deadly silence. If this went on for long, refined feelings would be diluted, illumination and intelligence would be lost, and even the so-called science would die away."[28] Therefore, the development of wholeness will not do without the complementarity between science and art, that is to say, it calls for both revolutionary scientists and philosophers, like Newton, Boyle, and Kant, and ingenious artists like Shakespeare, Raphaelo, and Beethoven.

16.3.3 A New Type of Aesthetics

Preoccupied with the artistic ideal ascribed to Romanticism and Realism, and with the mission to enlighten the Chinese citizens and save the homeland in jeopardy, Lu Xun struck the strongest key to idolize the

---

[27] Lu Xun, *Moluo shili shuo* [The Theories of Māratic Poetic Power], 3rd section.
[28] Lu Xun, "Kexue shi jiao pian" [Education in the History of Science], 1907.

Māratic School, in hope that the citizens would be eventually awakened, and change into self-committed spiritual fighters who would abound to lift themselves from deserted desolation and do away with the depression in China, providing they were able to produce grand and sublime poems, compose independent and free melody, make a robust, resisting, and subduing voice over the classical mode, get enlightened by great artworks, and thus transform themselves into the good, the beautiful, and the courageous.

Everywhere between the lines in *The Poetic Power* permeates the passionate, virile, and stalwart solemnity, ranging from its biographical recount of the Romantic poets in terms of their heroic deeds and poetic images to its ideal of breaking apart the old and setting up the new. This aesthetic quality is attributed to Lu Xun's admiration of the sublime as the supreme beauty that is differing essentially from the classical paradigm of illusory harmony in Chinese traditional poetics. In his notion, the sublime, as a new aesthetic category, was above all characterized not simply by the Romantic poets themselves, but also by the heroes created in their poetry. It is therefore considered to be of *māratic* type, in sharp contrast both to the mode of illusory harmony that could only be imagined through roaming about ancient land, cowardly secluding from the harsh reality, and yielding to the fantasy of happy ending that is often witnessed in "the performance of *ya* as grand finale." Well equipped with such a critical weapon, Lu Xun looked into the cause of upgrading the modern or tragic form of conflict-based sublimity, triggering the transformation of Chinese literature and art, and thus bringing them out of the classical paradigm of illusory harmony.

During their lifetime, most poets of the *Māratic* School behaved themselves as heroes, notable for their defiant spirit, heroic deed, free speech, and playful ridicule of any tragedy. For example, Byron was a sincere, straightforward, and rebellious romantic personage. He was described in *The Poetic Power* as a hero of all virtues, say, full of self-respect, deep in concern for the enslaved, striking the first blow to get over his opponent, ready to assist the subdued to win independence, aggressive and might-worshiping, merciless to crush his enemy but sympathetic for the suffering of the imprisoned. Could anyone else be so *māratic* as Byron himself?[29] Comparatively, Shelley was portrayed as being upright

---

[29] Lu Xun, *Moluo shili shuo* [The Theories of Māratic Poetic Power], 5th section.

and honest, opposing out-fashioned customs and unyieldingly advocating revolution. As a genius of rich imagination, he "engaged himself in lifelong pursuit and exploration, and moved headlong resolutely without retreating. His personality was prominent and outstanding. He was so enthusiastic and resolute that nothing could frustrate him or stop him from marching forward. He devoted his whole life to invigorate the humanistic spirit of sympathy, and defend the freedom of thought he cherished. Being such a heterodox figure, he was commonly despised and shunned away by all others, and consequently ostracized in southern Italy until his unexpected death at a prime age. His short span of life turned out to be an actualization of tragedy."[30] Lermontov was a Byronic character, saturated with self-esteem and even self-conceit. He was exiled for addressing defiantly to the Tsar an elegy protesting the death of Pushkin on the one hand, and on the other, charging the tyrant for suppressing freedom and art. Although he could not stop what was to occur, he could be proud of himself for his unusual bravery when his fate was at stake. Each of his poems was not but an impetuous and rough outcry.[31] As for the three Polish laureate poets whose passionate pursuit of liberty and independence bound them up with the struggle for patriotism and national revenge as their ultimate target, they were fighting a lifelong combat against the Tsar's tyranny. The crystallized music of their poetry was so uproarious and discordant that it aroused complex feelings and reached far and wide to every corner of Poland. For so long a time, their unexhausted and boundless influence was still alive and echoed in the heart of by every Polish.[32] Then, there came along Petöfi who loved the poetic output by Byron and Shelley, and his character was quite similar to that of those two *māratic* beings. His own works were declaration of freedom at large. Unconstrained and filled with his sensibility toward nature, the artistry of his poetry became unparalleled and immortal. Eventually, he gave up his literary career, enrolled in the army, and died in a battle. Short as his life was, he sang his ode to love and sacrificed his life for his country.[33]

With respect to the heroes presented in the works by the *Māratic* School, most of them are vividly remembered as men of iron will,

---

[30] Ibid., 6th section.
[31] Ibid., 7th section.
[32] Ibid., 8th section.
[33] Ibid., 9th section.

bravery, chivalry, masculinity, and tragic ending. Ill-fated as they are, they defy death and try every means to realize their ideals. For example, the heroes in Byron's works are endowed with powerful brains and unconventional actions; either embittered by unequal reality, they shun the human world and associate themselves with Heaven and Earth for companionship, as does Harold; or being extremely weary of earthly world and bitterly desperate, as is Manfred; or being greatly afflicted and poisoned to the bone, the only thing left for them to do is to seek ruin of and revenge upon the foe, as does Corsair; or being libertine and dissipated, they entertain themselves in cynical mocking of society, as does unrepentant Don Juan. By contrast, other Byronic heroes hold fast to chivalry and integrity, aid the needy and poor, and make complaints against injustice. In their endeavor to trample down the overwhelming stupidity, they are fearless of stubborn resistance from the outraged public.[34] Although these heroes are modeled upon Byron himself, they are outdone with the Byronic scorn of desperation, sighing, sorrow and escapism, for Byron distinguished himself in that he often exploded in a way of slamming grievances or defying criticisms. In addition, he was arrogant and self-indulgent, fearing nothing and ready to destroy and revenge. It is as though his noble chivalry took root in a kind of wildfire. He loved both independence and freedom; with a slave standing before him, he would feel heartbroken while looking a hateful look because of being saddened by the slave's suffering while inflamed by the slave's submission. In the end, Byron dedicated his life when he was fighting for Greek independence from Turks.[35]

Most of the abovementioned poets died as tragic heroes filled with courage and generosity. In Lu Xun's observation, different nationalities as they were and different countries as they came from, they resembled one another in character and action. Blessed with strong volition and unyielding spirit, and equipped with utopian ideal, they did not make up to the plebeian, nor did they go along with the eroding customs. Instead, they made an explosive voice in order to wake up their fellow citizens. Eager to build a prosperous and powerful country, each of them defied death and fought in war to defend their motherlands and justice. The main idols thus invented under their pen all appeared as chivalrous

---

[34] Ibid., 5th section.
[35] Ibid.

men tinged with wild Romantic spirit, and meanwhile manifested in mirror the reflections of the poets themselves. These Romantic figures and their mirror images finally became identical and thus reinforced the *māratic* sublimity imbued with blood and fire. This sublimity is an integrated attraction of *māratic* individuality and poetic power, including the excellence of vigorously macho character, the appeal in brave rebellion, the beauty of sincere art, and the shutter of any heart-swelling tragedy. The attraction was of such power that Lu was fervent to give highlight to its forcefulness, for he firmly believed that "once charged with this power, man is bound to rise, regenerate, spread, aspire, and attain where he can reach.[36]

Lu Xun himself was a fearless fighter in his pursuit of an uprooting change in Chinese mentality. He put into action what he had spared no efforts to advocate, with his admiration of *māratic* sublimity and its poetics being realized in his own artistic practice. For example, he rejected eulogistic literature that was intended to flatter one's master or man in power; he turned a cold shoulder to those who contented themselves with rhymed writing and heavily ornate poetry; he showed contempt for those "unworthy lines of lamentation" that "soured by reality and sighed for olden days"; he criticized the malpractices of "completing with ten scenic spots"; he put an end to "grand finale" treatment of happy ending. These efforts produced most of his stirring works in the genre of novella, including the *Diary of A Mad Man* (*Kuang ren ri ji*), a portrayal of national tragedy; *The True Story of Ah Q* (*Ah Q Zhengzhuan*), an account of the tragedy of an impoverished Chinese peasant; *The Blessed* (*Zhu fu*), a narration of an ill-fortuned woman servant; *The Drinker* (*Kong Yiji*) and the *Lamenting the Passed* (*Shang shi*), profiles of Chinese literati from lower class; and *The Medicine* (*Yao*), a story of tragic ending associated with the old democratic revolution.[37] These original works of tragedy, arising from Lu's voluntary endeavors to incorporate Chinese literature with the transplantation of foreign voice, induced an earthquake in the Chinese literary arena and greatly stimulated his readers of his time and even aftermath, thus pushing forward the renewal process of old Chinese literature and transforming the

---

[36] Ibid., 2nd section.

[37] Liu Zaifu, *Lu Xun meixue sixiang lungao* [On Lu Xun's Aesthetic Ideas] (Beijing: China Social Sciences Press, 1981), p. 97.

classical paradigm of illusory harmony into its modern counterpart of *māratic* sublimity.

As a matter of fact, Lu Xun's poetics was a further development of what he initially eulogized in *The Poetic Power*. One of the influences upon his theorization in this regard lied in his notion of the role of tragedy as "a display of destroying the valued in humanity."[38] In his literary praxis, he watched closely the *status quo* of China, faced up to the social reality as the origin of tragedy, and created his tragic works as the strongest evidence and justification of his conception of tragedy. On many occasions, he employed the genre of tragedy as a weapon and applied it as much to the spiritual enlightenment of Chinese readers as to the struggle against both imperialism and feudalism; and at the same time, he brought it up as a blood-and-tear indictment of what foreign imperialism did to bully and exploit China as a nation-state apart from what feudalism did to wreck the country and ruined its people. Accordingly, the most distinguishable accomplishment of his novel writing is drawn from his production of a series of tragic stories that are considered the most down-to-earth and thought-evoking in modern China. These stories rendered in a matter-of-fact manner the miseries and sufferings of Chinese peasants, women, and men of letters, who lived, as it were, in the semi-colonial and feudal society then.[39]

16.3.4 *A New Mode of Literary Criticism and Poetic Cultivation*

The Chinese tradition of poetic discourse (*shihua*) or literary criticism (*cihua*), which was intended exclusively for masters and literati alone, largely relied on a verbal pattern that sought enlightenment with a minimum of words. More often than not, its argument was formulated via a series of exemplary authors and their works, which were mostly arranged in a parallel structure with a poetic touch.

However, the introduction of Western thinking into China then broke up the once conventional reading circle and posed a threat to the traditional mode of poetic discourse. Literary criticism as an increasingly important medium that bore and spread cultural information could no

---

[38] Lu Xun, "Zailun leifengta de daodiao" [A Second Review of the Fallen Leifeng Tower], 1925.

[39] Liu Zaifu, *Lu Xun meixue sixiang lungao* [On Lu Xun's Aesthetic Ideas], pp. 96–97.

longer go on with its stereotyped approach. As a result, it began to seek as its aim a systemized mode capable of offering a luminous and theoretical interpretation.[40] Historically, Liang Qichao's "Comments on the Relationship between Novel and Democracy" (*Lun xiao shuo yu qun zhi zhi guan xi*, 1902) featured a pioneering experiment that opened up a new style of literary criticism, whereas Wang Guowei's "Critique of *A Dream of Red Mansions*" (*Hong lou meng ping lun*, 1904) was another unique case that attempted by borrowing Western critical methodology to save Chinese literary criticism from deteriorating stagnancy. In this context, *The Poetic Power* by Lu Xun was regarded as a further progression of the newborn tendency of literary criticism that was credited with a well-balanced and all-around observation. As is observed in *The Poetic Power*, aside from the introduction and commentary concerned, the new paradigm contained both analysis and inductive reasoning, emphasizing both spreading of information and interpretation through factual evidence, and accommodating both the recount of an author's biography and his personality and that of his heroes' thought, action, and related episode. Furthermore, the narration and critique, detailed or sketchy, were mutually mixed up and faithfully presented with genuine feelings. The invigorating, vivid and sublime style amounted to a spur that was stimulating and enlivening the static mode of thought and criticism that had been overshadowing the literary arena in the old China for too long a time.

As noticed in *The Poetic Power*, Lu Xun also criticized the orthodox theory of education through non-depraved poetry and explicitly rejected the dehumanized practice of disciplining human emotions. He went so far as to compare it to letting go freedom under whipping and curbing.[41] This censure was followed by his emphasis upon the usefulness of the useless art in intellectual enlightenment and spiritual nourishment, and thus it stood for his theory of poetic cultivation. In spite of the inseparable role attributed to art, he was quite objective in arguing that art is neither so practical nor systematic as science, and neither is it directly linked with individual survival nor national salvation. Accordingly, neither literature nor art can be so much effective in doing good service to intelligence as history, so much capable of admonishing people as moral motto, so much

---

[40]Wen Rumin, *Zhongguo xiandai wenxue pipingshi* [A Critical History of Modern Chinese Literature] (Beijing: Peking University Press, 2000), p. 3.

[41]Lu Xun, *Moluo shili shuo* [The Theories of *Māratic* Poetic Power], 2nd section.

adequate for money-making as industry and commerce, or so much fruitful in gaining prestige as the passport to officialdom, etc. Nevertheless, both literature and art may well nurture our intuitive power, inspire and delight the reader or the audience. This is because literature and art, as a carrier of life truth, exert an imperceptible impact upon us in cognitive and affective scopes such that we become spiritually enlightened and come to apprehend the truth of life. All this is quite like the swim in the sea where we are being infused in a vast expanse of water and surfing with the waves. After the swim naturally, we could undergo changes in our mind and body. When we come across the great poets ever since Homer, we do not simply have access to poetry, but also contact with the essence of human existence. With a clearer awareness of our own merits and demerits, we can move faster and closer to perfection. This effect is derived from educational implication and thus contributive to our life fulfillment. Art or literary education is so extraordinary in that it leads us to be more initiative, courageous, and ready to pursue excellence and progress. Hence, any nation that has been going downhill or dejected cannot restart without relevant cultivation of cultural literacy.[42] As is noted above, Lu Xun was basically under Liang Qichao's influence, but he exaggerated the social function of art education to a much larger extent owing to his anxiety over the enlightenment of the public and the salvation of the nation.

16.4 A Tentative Observation

As is mentioned above, *The Poetic Power* was written at the time when the cultural context of Chinese society was rather complicated. It therefore bears a multi-dimensional import. It rounds out thematically "an intention to revolt and an aim to take action" against the foreign imperialist invasion, feudalist political culture, and perverse conventions. Meanwhile, it promotes the necessity of democratic revolution, intellectual reform, liberation of individuality, and reconstruction of national identity. All this is attributed to what the purposiveness is presumed to cover in a social sense. On the other hand, if seen from a theoretical perspective, it calls deliberately for a cultural innovation and recreation by breaking up the old and setting up the new. In this case, the old largely refers to the outdated literary tradition, content, form, device, structure

---

[42] Lu Xun, *Moluo shili shuo* [The Theories of *Māratic* Poetic Power], 3rd section.

and aesthetic ideal, whereas the new calls for a modern conception of culture, literature and art, aesthetic style, paradigm of literary criticism, and art enlightenment, etc. These aspects can be classified under the category of lawfulness in art creation. This being true, *The Poetic Power* seems to have realized the integrity of purposiveness with lawfulness in a given historical context. As far as its primary value and impact are concerned, the most fundamental dimension of *The Poetic Power*, as exemplified in Lu Xun's literary practice, marks not merely the turning point of Chinese literary criticism in the early twentieth century, but the transformational process of the classical mode of illusory harmony into its modern counterpart of *māratic* sublimity.

When looking into the past in comparison with the present, Lu Xun's pioneering spirit and transforming effort are perceived as signposts at the turning point of China modernity. As articulated in the preceding chapters in this book, Confucius assumes at least seven functions of poetry. Among them, there are basically four aspects more significant, including the poetic *xing*, *guan*, *qun*, and *yuan*, which means to inspire, reflect, communicate and admonish. They are mainly concerned with the expression and communication of feelings, ideals and events that comprise a threefold form of social, aesthetic and ethical discourse in Confucius' poetics. Confucius applies his conception of poetry to music when looking into its essential values and uses. This is because of the fact that the two genres of art are closely interconnected and share in principle some similar features. Even though Mozi and Xunzi hold different attitudes toward music, they still see eye to eye with each other regarding the aesthetic and artistic characteristics of music proper. What really makes them differ from each other is nothing but the economic and political conditions on which music is performed.

Liu Xie continues the conventional notion of poetry on the one hand and makes a breakthrough on the other. He therefore argues that poetry is a medium not merely to describe lofty aspirations (*shi yan zhi*), but also to express emotions and feelings (*shi yuan qing*). Proceeding partly from this line of thought, Zhu Xi revives the Confucian preoccupation with moral education. He attempts to reconsider the nature of poetry with a particular reference to *The Book of Poetry*, and comes up with a fundamental principle of trinity, involving such three elements as being emotionally aroused by things (*ganwu*), expressing feelings (*daoqing*), and cultivating the personality (*huaren*).

By means of a second reflection on what is said about the art of poetry and music, we may arrive at a conclusion that it bears two most determinate dimensions: moral and aesthetic. The former is allied with political and social orientations, whereas the latter is related to the emotional and psychological directions. This tradition undergoes a transcultural transformation and creative synthesis with the help of Wang Guowei's poetic discourse and Lu Xun's sublime poetics. Both of them place more emphasis on the importance of autonomy even though they have different expectations of art and literature. As is discerned, for instance, Wang's theory of the poetic state *par excellence* advocates a more classical taste with stress on the poetic sensibility and picturesque significance (*shiqing huayi*) as well as spiritual transcendence (*jingshen chaoyue*), while Lu's promotion of Romanticism champions a political and revolutionary objective for the sake of cultural redemption and national salvation (*jiuwang tucun*) as well as ideological enlightenment (*sixiang qimeng*). These two tracks appear parallel to each other, never to meet at any point ahead. However, they create a dramatic tension to spur the development of Chinese art and literature as is exemplified in the process of the twentieth century. Their legacy in this domain stays alive even in the new millennium, for it is continuously rediscovered and reconsidered now and then when it comes to transcultural studies in China et al.

CHAPTER 17

An Escalated Experience of Appreciating Nature

> Men go abroad to wonder at the height of mountains, at the huge waves of the sea, at the long course of rivers, at the vast compass of ocean, at the circular motion of the stars, and they pass by themselves without wondering. (St. Augustine)

Nowadays, more and more people go out to travel around, thus making the tourism or hospitality sector prevailing all over the world. This sector in China occupies a lion's share of the tertiary industry in recent years. For millions of Chinese tourists venture into the regions and countries across the five continents. Regarding the major attractions in their eyes, many of them are basically natural landscapes dotted with such culturescapes as historical sites of various kinds. (All this does not play down the great potential of the deluxe shopping malls available here and there to satisfy the material needs of the visitors.) They are so appealing to those who love to return to nature for sightseeing as an aesthetic activity or social therapy against the suffocating overcivilization and endless urbanization. Consequently, aesthetics in tourism has got somewhat revived by virtue of "stepping into the open" for natural beauty as Theodor W. Adorno once put it.

Being back to nature, most travelers tend to be feeling in different degrees when engaged in aesthetic contemplation. But they may encounter something in common: It is like what Tao Yuanming describes as follows: "Long being shut inside a sophisticated cage, now feeling released upon return to nature." This indicates that they are personally freed from the life pressure and invisible imprisonment when moving out of crowded cities and social nets, and mingling themselves up with beautiful natural environment. In addition, it implies that those who are able to discover and appreciate natural beauty seem to enjoy a "fine soul" in a Kantian sense and then capable of restoring one's "real self" in Emerson's vision. This chapter attempts to probe sightseeing from the perspective of an escalated experience of aesthetic engagement attributed to practical aesthetics in principle. The experience is trifold per se, ranging from visual pleasure via emotional delight to spiritual joy. As for practical aesthetics, it was initiated by Li Zehou in 1950s and further developed from 1980s onward through relevant modifications and in-depth critiques. Its key substance is condensed in the Four Essays on Aesthetics (*Meixue sijiang*) published in 1989.[1] It is primarily based on the sources of Chinese thought with reference to Western philosophy and considered as a conspectus of practical aesthetics in its own.

17.1 Three Levels of Aesthetic Experience

There are at least three levels of aesthetic experience with regard to the appreciation and contemplation of natural landscape. In the case of the travelers as aesthetic subjects who go sightseeing in the world of nature, they tend to be simultaneously delighted with the beautiful scenery of high mountains and running rivers, splashing waterfalls and moonlit lakes, green trees and colorful flowers, singing birds and flying butterflies, etc. Right on the spot with a first glance, they are most likely to be obsessed with the colors, shapes, sounds, and spatial images that please such faculties as the ear and the eye. The ear is the organ of hearing and the eye the organ of sight. As primary aesthetic faculties, they

---

[1] Li Zehou. *Meixue sijiang* [Four Essays on Aesthetics] (Beijing: Sanlian Bookshop, 1989). The Chinese version of this book is reprinted by other publishers in China. It is already translated in Korean and Japanese. Its English version is rendered by Professor Jane Cauvel and has come in print in 2006 (Cf. Li Zehou and Jane Cauvel, *Four Essays on Aesthetics*, Lanham et al.: Lexington Books, 2006). This is one of the few writings on aesthetics in China that features an individual, philosophical, and transcultural view as a result of transformational creation by virtue of Chinese sources and Western methodology.

are working to perceive the beautiful in appearance. That is to say, they enable the travelers to observe and enjoy firstly a kind of sensual pleasure drawn from the external aspects of the object looked at. This is usually seen as the initial stage of aesthetic experience that features the pleasing of the ear and the eye (*yue er yue mu*).[2] Yet, it does not mean the aesthetic experience on this occasion is exclusively attributed to these two organs. The matter of fact is that the appreciation of natural landscape is usually an all-sensory perception, involving all the fives senses (sight, hearing, smelling, taste, and touch) and even ESP (extrasensory perception) as well. We human beings are so sensitive that we can hardly enjoy any apparently good-looking environment that bothers us with an unpleasant smell, for instance. Being an elementary level of aesthetic experience, it is immediate, intuitive, and momentary, chiefly characterized by physical beauty, sensory pleasure, joyful feelings and emotions, or a delightful state of mind. In practice, travelers have an easy access to this kind of aesthetic experience as is available to all those whose sense organs are in normal condition. At this stage, some people are satisfied enough, but some others are not yet. So they explore further and detect more.

---

[2] Liu Xiang (c. 77–6 B.C.) is the first to put forth the idea when talking about the beauty of voice and that of dressing, etc. His statement concerned can be rendered as follows: "Those who are properly dressed and have good manners please the eye. Those who have a nice voice and respond well in conversations please the ear. Those who like to develop good hobbies and abandon bad ones please the mind. People find it pleasing to the eye when seeing the superior man [or lord] properly dressed with good manners. People find it pleasing to the ear when hearing the superior man [or lord] speaking properly and responding timely. People find it pleasing to the mind when observing the superior man [or lord] exercising the virtue of human-heartedness while abandoning the vice of non-human-heartedness. The above three aspects are kept in the mind, circulated through the body, and demonstrated in the action and non-action." Cf. Liu Xiang, "*Xiuwen*" [Cultivating Culture], in *Shuo yuan* [Selected Essays from Schools of Thought in the Han Dynasty], Vol. 19. Li Zehou, a contemporary philosopher of distinction in China, develops this idea in view of aesthetic activity and corresponding experience of common practice. Li continues to argue that "Aesthetic experience has different levels. The most common of them is associated with the pleasing of the ear and the eye (*yue er yue mu*). The above state is associated with the pleasing of the mind and the mood (*yue xin yue yi*). The highest state is associated with the pleasing of the will and the spirit (*yue zhi yue shen*). Yet, the pleasing of the ear and the eye is not equal to sheer pleasure, and the pleasing of the will and the spirit is not equal to religiously mystical experience." Cf. Li Zehou, "Zhongguo meixue ji qi ta" [Chinese Aesthetics and Other Matters], in *Meixue shulin* [Journal of Aesthetic Criticism] (Wuhan: Wuhan University Press, 1983), Vol. 1, p. 27. These ideas are subsequently elaborated in Li Zehou's *Four Essays on Aesthetics*.

As they contemplate the landscape longer and deeper, there would reach the second stage of aesthetic experience. It is depicted to be pleasing to the mind and the mood (*yue xin yue yi*) in Li Zehou's terminology. During this process, faculties of understanding and imagination come into play, enabling the contemplators to go beyond the external aspects of the object and venture into its internal aspects in a cognitive sense. Outwardly, they draw from the physical *Schein* or form something meaningful in connection with aesthetic value judgment. Inwardly, they gaze at the object through a mind's eye and subsequently nurture an agreeable mood along with a poetic impulse. Thus, they tend to feel themselves into the beautiful as such and even transform it into a picture or poem so as to express their appreciation and gratitude. This is why a beautiful landscape is often depicted as picturesque in its allegorical sense.

Compared with the preceding level of an immediate and transient kind, the second level of aesthetic experience is of more profundity and longer duration. For it stays in the memory due to its involvement of some insights into an imagined vision out of an existent image (*xiang wai zhi xiang*) and an idealized scene out of a visual landscape (*jing wai zhi jing*). Here at this moment, "the language of the scene is transfigured into the language of emotion" (*yi qie jing yu jie qing yu*) according to Wang Guowei's observation. The language of this kind is assumed to contain certain amount of magic power, helping the travelers to get released to varied degrees from worldly cares, pressures, tensions, depressions, and other negative sentiments by substituting them with aesthetic detachment or enjoyment. For instance, they are liable to feel relaxed as they are counting the wildflowers in blossom instead of the fallen leafs on the ground, and become enlightened when they come to realize the associated significance of natural freedom as is manifested through the free motion of a bird flying among trees or a fish swimming in waters. Talking about a fish, we are easily reminded of a relevant fable in *The Book of Zhuangzi* as follows: When strolling along a river with his friend Shi Hui, Zhuangzi happens to see a fish jump out of the water and then dive into it again. He is delighted to assume that the little creature is so happy to move like that. On hearing this, Shi Hui denies this assumption with a counterargument. Logically, Shi Hui maintains that Zhuangzi cannot know whether the fish is happy or not simply because he himself is not the fish, and therefore cannot feel what the fish really feels. Empirically, Zhuangzi defends himself by means of his personal observation of an empathic kind. Neither of them can convince the other by words, but their dispute leaves a larger space of imagination about the harmonious interaction between natural and human beings. The fable itself is highly metaphorical and suggestive, constantly posing a subject matter for poetry, painting, and even gardening. An offhanded example is found in the Garden of Harmony located inside the Summer Palace. There you see a small stone bridge over a water pond that is called "The Bridge of Knowing the Fish" (*Zhi yu qiao*) with a particular reference to Zhuangzi's story. In order to figure out its hidden message, we need to trace back to the fact that Zhuangzi always attempts to equalize all things in the universe (*qi wu*). He therefore treats all beings alike, including humankind. He himself is not the fish, but he can feel what the fish feels according to his emotional projection or empirical inference. Apparently, he finds the fish happy as a result of his self-identifying contemplation and psychical response. Actually, he himself becomes happy when seeing the fish move around so freely. The fish stirs up his happy mood and he, in turn, projects his happy feeling into the fish. Such an interaction between Zhuangzi and the fish seems to be inter-subjective by principle and aesthetic in kind. And the experience of this kind reflects the essential traits of what pleases the mind and the mood (*yue xin yue yi*), in which the aesthetic transposition or empathy exerts an important part.

The appreciation of nature is undoubtedly open to further findings from an aesthetic perspective. It is therefore assumed that above the second level of aesthetic experience is the third one in sequence. For in some cases you would make the utmost use of such psycho-aesthetic functions as sensuous perception, imagination, understanding, and feeling altogether when contemplating the landscape you are obsessed with. If by any chance you happen to come up with a sudden enlightenment, you will be liable to approach the third level of aesthetic experience that is said to please the will and the spirit (*yue zhi yue shen*). At this stage, you are supposed to be completely enlightened all of a sudden of your real being in an ontological sense. Your personal perception of space and time appears exceptionally enlarged to the extent that it can accommodate all things under the sky. One the one hand, you are well in the position to move out of your small "I" and into the big "We" by identifying yourself with the whole world of nature or the entire universe; and on the other, you have become highly aware of the eternal from the momentary and of the infinite from the finite. In a word, you are feeling yourself into the oneness between you and the universe as a whole.

Your will (*zhi*) and spirit (*shen*) are thus exalted or sublimated up to a super-morally transcendent realm. Hypothetically under such circumstances, you have not only attained a kind of absolute spiritual freedom and independent personality, but also go beyond the moral values in pursuit of super-moral ones. In the former case, according to Zhuangzi, you would "interact only with the spirit of Heaven and Earth" for a happy excursion, which enables you to "accompany all things to rove about with a free and easy mind" in one sense, and in the other, to "step onto the clouds, ride on the sun and moon, and wander around out of the four oceans."[3] In the latter case, according to Confucianism in the main, you would strive for self-perfection by assimilating the Heaven and the Earth in the following modes: The Heaven moves eternally and energetically; therefore, the superior man must model himself upon it in order to make himself stronger and more resolute. The Earth begets and carries all things on itself, and the superior man must learn from this example in order to develop his full virtue and offer selfless service to others.[4] So long as the spiritual and moral dimensions aforementioned were fulfilled, the superior man would have become a free and universal being who claims the virtue of "loving all people and treasuring all things" (*ren min ai wu*) with neither discrimination nor reservation.

Regarding the three levels of aesthetic experience described above, it is noticeable that the initial level is commonplace and easily attained to those who go sightseeing in nature either for leisure or for relaxation. As for the second and the third levels of aesthetic experience, there arise some requirements on the landscape contemplator. What is indispensable above all is definitely a special affinity for nature. This affinity is structurally sustained by such merits as adequate cultural literacy, aesthetic taste, and spiritual pursuit. And functionally, it is claimed to reinforce human interaction with and appreciation of nature in general and natural beauty of landscape in particular. Comparatively, the intermediate level of experience in appreciating Nature implies an aesthetic transposition and even a personification of the object from a psycho-cultural viewpoint. Its effect is inclined to stay with the subject for a long period of time. The third level of experience in this regard is characteristic of the sublime with some mystical features from a moralistic and even religious

---

[3] Zhuang Zhou, *Zhuangzi nei pian* [The Inner Chapters in The Book of Zhuangzi].
[4] *Yi jing* [The Book of Changes].

perspective. Its effect at its best helps remold and perhaps transform the mentality, the spirit, and even the personality of the subject.

17.2 Aesthetic Effects of Heaven-Human Oneness

In Chinese culture, the affinity between human and his surroundings is closely associated with the conception of *tian ren he yi* that threads throughout the entire history of Chinese thought. The conception itself consists of four basic characters or elements: *tian, ren, he,* and *yi*. According to one of the two main interpretations,[5] *tian* refers to heaven or sky that is metaphorically used for the world of nature composed of heaven or sky, earth, and the myriad things; *ren* refers to humankind; *he*

---

[5] One leading interpretation is briefed above. Now, it goes through a rediscovery and revaluation by virtue of instrumental rationality and pragmatic reasoning in face of ecological crises and environmental problems. This trend has been prevailing ever since the 1990s among quite a number of Chinese scholars and Western sinologists who tend to read modern messages into this old doctrine. It is therefore claimed to be conceptually significant and valid in reconstructing a more healthy relationship between humans and nature for the sake of environmental protection and ecological balance. The other leading explication is different, according to which the concept of *tian* is said to denote heaven in a symbolic sense. In other words, it is symbolic of a system of feudal morality or ethical codes. This system is also called the *Dao* that is grounded on the five constant virtues known as human-heartedness, righteousness, propriety, reasonability, and trustworthiness (*ren yi li zhi xin*). The *Dao* is considered one as a whole and remains the same in both cases. That is to say, it can be called the Heavenly *Dao* (*tiandao*) when it is up to identify with the Heaven, and likewise, it can be the Human *Dao* (*rendao*) when it is down to identify with the human. Accordingly, *tian ren he yi* (heaven-human oneness) can be replaced by *tianren hede* (heaven-human oneness in morality). This morality-based oneness is intended to perform a twofold service at least. First, it is to identify the Heavenly *Dao* with the Human *Dao*. This works not only to make them equally important, but moralize the interaction between heaven and human in spite of its mystical features. Second, such oneness is supposed to lift the moral system up to the sky so as to ennoble and divinize it. This helps to emphasize and reinforce the objective necessity and eternal characteristic of the moral system. Such being the case, *tian* as heaven is above *ren* as human. The former is legitimated with a metaphysical priority to determine the human conduct, while the latter is deprived of its individual subjectivity and thus expected to be a devoted follower. All this bears a hidden purpose, both ethical and political, to make people comply with this oneness under all circumstances in order to coordinate human relations and secure social order as well as stability. In a word, what the doctrine of heaven-human oneness in this regard emphasizes is the divinity and eternality of feudal morality rather than the unity between nature and humankind. This interpretation is inclusively peculiar of Confucianism proper due to its moral orientation and political commitment.

means the act of integrating; and *yi* means oneness as a kind of inseparable and harmonious interrelationship. A literal translation of *tian ren he yi* could be "heaven and humankind integrated into oneness." As a result of economical wording, it is usually termed heaven-human oneness in accord with my personal preference. As heaven in this case stands for nature, the translation can be altered as nature-and-human oneness if in need. Logically, such oneness is inferred on the basis of the conventional belief that humankind is the product and part of nature even though being the highest of all species in existence. When talking about this oneness, it does not mean nature and humankind are radically identical. Instead, they differ from and even oppose to one another on many occasions. However, what is meant by such oneness is to stress their possible unity and interdependence rather than their difference and opposition. By so doing, it is intended to create a harmonized coexistence rather than a hostile conflict between the human race and nature. It is right in this sense that the idea of heaven-human oneness is being rediscovered and transvaluated by virtue of an instrumental rationality or pragmatic reasoning against the background of ecological crises and environmental problems confronted nowadays.

What I am trying to say here is about how to appreciate nature from the perspective of heaven-human oneness. Based on what it implies as is aforementioned, I would rather look upon the notion of such oneness as a meta-aesthetic *Geist* that helps to shape one's aesthetic attitude and also as the highest state of spiritual cultivation that helps to develop one's aesthetic sensibility. When it is applied to the appreciation of nature or contemplation of landscape as an aesthetic activity in particular, it is thought to enrich and enlighten one's aesthetic experience from the initial stage of sensory pleasure and satisfaction up to the third level of spiritual enlightenment and sublimation. All this is facilitated by the conception of heaven-human oneness as it is conducive to three interactive modes at least.

First and foremost, the conception itself features the oneness between nature and humankind in a holistic sense. Ontologically, nature is believed to be eternal and beget all beings and things alike; accordingly, humankind is part of nature and one species only instead of the so-called measure of all things. This outlook is fundamentally influential in the psychology of Chinese people and conducive to a harmonized synthesis between nature and humankind. Accordingly, each individual is usually compared to the small "I" along with an inner world, and the entire nature or universe is likened to the big "We" along with an outer world. The former is limited and finite, whereas the latter is unlimited and infinite. When the two are harmonized into one, the small "I" is then located into the big "We," the inner world synthesized with the outer world, the limited and finite transformed into the unlimited and infinite. In other words, when you as an individual identify yourself with the boundless nature or universe, your mind can be expanded enough to understand and accommodate all things under the sky. You are then no longer confined to your isolated self and narrow vision. Instead, you are freed from all these confinements and narrowness as you have become part of the whole. From this viewpoint, you make no distinction between things and simply see others as part of your being.

In *The Book of Zhuangzi,* for instance, we read an interesting story about a dream of a butterfly. Right in the dream, Zhuangzi identifies himself with the butterfly. He is feeling so happy that he even forgets himself. When awakened, he is still feeling lost in the dream, unable to realize whether he has dreamed of the butterfly or vice versa a moment before. Hence, he cannot distinguish himself from the butterfly even though he has the intention to differentiate the two sides involved. He then calls this experience as a "transformation of things" (*wu hua*). Metaphorically, the story reveals an important message in that it exposes the true meaning of the oneness between humankind represented by the dreamer and natural beauty exemplified by the butterfly. Such oneness makes no distinction among things but features a transformation of things. That is to say, things are not distinguished from but transformed into each other. This being the case, the dreamer not only feels himself into but also identifies himself with the butterfly. Symbolically, the human spirit and the natural phenomenon are integrated into one; aesthetically, the subject and the object are synthesized into one; ontologically, the small "I" and the big "We" are harmonized into one. All this kind of oneness embodies a free interaction and harmonious union between humankind and nature. It is particularly so at the third level of aesthetic experience in the contemplation of natural beauty or landscape as is presented above.

Second, the appreciation of nature is largely determined by two factors: One is the emotional and the other is the scenic. The aesthetic experience in this case is deepened and enriched by virtue of an interfusion between the two factors. The emotional factor comes from the moved traveler as an aesthetic subject, while the scenic factor from the beautiful landscape as an aesthetic object. This interfusion is only possible when the former projects his emotion and even vital force into the latter. In Chinese aesthetics, such interfusion between emotion and scene (*qing jing jiao rong*) is assumed to be the most essential drive for both aesthetic experience and artistic creation. By means of this interfusion, a lifeless rock can be transfigured into a living being, and likewise, a wildflower can be personified as a maiden image, and a huge tree can be transformed into a rising giant, etc.

Originally, the theory of such interfusion is derived from and based upon the notion of heaven-human oneness. In other words, it is the harmony between humankind and nature that makes the interfusion possible, for the harmony of this kind works to humanize the scene via the emotion on the one hand and objectify the human emotion through the scene on the other. Consequently, in this case, the emotional factor is neither purely subjective nor a psychological phenomenon because it is mixed up with and concretized by the scene. Correspondingly, the scenic factor is neither purely objective nor a natural landscape because it is fused with and humanized by the emotion. It is at this moment that the language of the scene has turned out to be the language of the emotion as is mentioned with a particular reference to the second level of aesthetic experience. Incidentally, the projection of the emotion into the scene is not enough in the pure sense of heaven-human oneness as an aesthetic attitude. It usually requires a twofold process of projection in an interactive way, that is, the aesthetic subject can project his emotion, wish, and ideal into the aesthetic object, and meanwhile, the aesthetic object can project its image, vitality, and natural spirit into the aesthetic subject. Such reciprocal interaction can be all the more inspiring, dynamic, and even creative. It is thus adept to please not merely the mind and mood (*yue xin yue yi*), but also the will and spirit (*yue zhi yue shen*). In addition, it would lead to a sudden enlightenment and illumination of what things are and what you can become.

Third, according to Daoism *par excellence*, one of the key aspects of heaven-human oneness is often characterized by a "free and happy excursion" (*xiao yao you*). Specifically, it assists you to "let your mind rove with things" (*shen yu wu you*), "ride on things to travel with a free and easy mind" (*cheng wu yi you xin*), and "interact alone with the spirit of Heaven and Earth" (*du yu tian di jing shen xiang wang lai*). Such excursion is certainly not realistic. It is by nature spiritual, imaginative, and nothing more than a wishful thinking. Nevertheless, it would serve to extend the imaginative power and nourish higher ideals. Apart from being appealing to artistic creation, it would offer an imagined compensation for what is lacking in reality and an idealized fulfillment of what is impossible but wishful in life. Accordingly, you may employ such imagination to make your excursion more idealistic and enjoyable as you expect.

All in all, the notion of heaven-an-human oneness can help to nurture a strong affinity for nature and possibly develop a more positive attitude toward beautiful landscape. When putting this notion into practice, you would "take the specific aspects of the universe and life for an object of contemplation. You appreciate and play with its color, order, rhythm and harmony, and thereby you may perceive what reflects the deepest dimension of your soul. Then you will become capable of transfiguring a physical scene into an imagined one, transforming a visual image into a symbolic one, and turning the highest human soul into an objectified or corporal one. This is what is called 'the artistic realm' (*yi shu jing jie*)."[6] Ostensibly, this poetic depiction goes hand in hand with the poetic wisdom originated from the conception of heaven-human oneness. Yet, the artistic realm in this regard is not merely relating to aesthetic value judgment and creative possibility. It is in fact recommending an artistization of human existence par excellence. Such artistization corresponds to the spirit of Chinese philosophy and aesthetics as a whole. It could be deployed as a walking stick not only to appreciate nature and other things in all, but also to enjoy life as such even by drawing some pleasure from bitter and harsh conditions (*ku zhong zuo le*).

---

[6] Zong Baihua, *Meixue yu yijing* [The Aesthetics and the Artistic Realm] (Beijing: Renmin Press, 1987), p. 210.

CHAPTER 18

Art as Sedimentation

For so long a time, it has been getting increasingly formidable, if not possible, to define art in general ever since the advent of the so-called found art or ready-mades of Marcel Duchamp and Andy Warhol, among other avant-garde or pop artists. But this does not have too much constraint over some philosophers who have made persistent attempts in this regard. What have turned out to be considerably influential are the art world framed by Arthur C. Danto and the institutional theory proposed by George Dickie. Nevertheless, Li Zehou, a contemporary Chinese philosopher, argues that the two theories aforementioned are not self-sufficient and convincing enough. For they could not well explicate the distinction between art and non-art, not to speak of the difference between artworks as artifacts and those as aesthetic objects. He then continues to treat art as sedimentation from an anthropo-historical viewpoint peculiar of his practical aesthetics (*shijian meixue*). His argument is underlined by a transcultural approach that is deployed to expand the intellectual horizon and bear the theoretical fruit.

18.1 Art as Sedimentation

As is formulated in the *Four Essays on Aesthetics (Meixue si jiang)*, art is defined as the sum total of various artworks relating to human aesthetic psychology. Artworks manifest themselves in varied media and exist as aesthetic objects. They are so considered because they can directly incite an aesthetic contemplation or experience in spite of whether they are produced for appreciative, practical or spiritual purposes. It is often the case with music as is felt by someone with a "musical ear." Moreover, art by nature is the product of history based on human practice and symbolic creation. It involves a long process of sedimentation in the stratification of its form, image, and significance. Accordingly, a work of art is reckoned to consist in at least three interrelated stratifications and sedimentations, namely the stratification of form along with primitive sedimentation, the stratification of image along with artistic sedimentation, and the stratification of significance along with life sedimentation.

The stratification of form along with primitive sedimentation undertook a gradual progression of material and social labor. Its early stage emerged with the employment of certain aspects of natural order and form by primitives. Later on, it underwent the evolution of objective lawfulness and subjective purposiveness into a new unity. This unity conduced to the crudest forms of beauty and aesthetic experience. In other words, through labor humans endowed the material world with such forms that originally discovered in nature itself, but grew independent through the application of humans' abstract faculty. Eventually, it is through social labor and material production that humans created the forms of beauty. As humans lived with subjective emotions and sensations, they became more and more sensitive to the visible orders and apparent shapes, and also capable of detecting an isomorphic correspondence with the external objects at the time when they commenced to utilize the laws of nature to produce the objects of beauty for either decoration or enjoyment. The awareness of the isomorphic correspondence was by no means an inborn mentality or capacity, but an outcome of the human activities of making and using tools for social production. It was therefore imbued with sociality and humanity as well. As the awareness continued to evolve along with the human practice, there arose the dynamic structure of isomorphic correspondence that would be extended and enriched through successive and diverse social activities. As a consequence, when a person achieved certain goals in the process of such activities as part of reforming the objective world, the regularity and purposiveness of the process would be linked up with the human sensuous construction to arouse feelings of pleasure. Although aesthetic experience features vague understandings, imaginations, and intentions, it is sensation that dominates in any case. All this could be regarded as the pre-historical mode of humans' spiritual world or the process of primitive sedimentation.[1]

The formal stratification of artworks commences from primitive sedimentation, but develops and extends itself in at least two directions: One is the naturalization of humanity embodied not merely in such physical activities as Chinese *qigong* (breathing system for health condition and spiritual nourishment), *taiji quan* (a kind of martial art for bodybuilding and mind cultivation), and *yangsheng shu* (practical expertise for longevity), but also in the formal stratification of artworks, including *qi* (life force) and *guqi* (noble vitality). It takes considerable efforts to get the formal stratification of artworks to tally with the rhythm of the universe and thereby to form an isomorphic structure. That is, why the key principle of garden designing in Chinese tradition emphasizes the value of naturalness, for it suggests that a fine garden appear "as if it were created by nature itself even though made by man" (*sui you ren zuo, wan zi tian kai*). In regard to the other direction, it refers to the *Zeitgeist* and sociality, say, the ever-changing objects, events, and relationships that embody the tendencies of different times and societies which would cause formal variations and aesthetic trends. Hence, there are diversified styles or formal transformations in literary movements and different genres of art. Briefly, the formal stratification involves three forces as such: primitive sedimentation, naturalization of humanity, and social life underlined by ideology in religious, political, ethical, and cultural scopes. These forces are intermingling and interplaying in intricate patterns; and by so doing will they turn out to inspire a succession of impressive aesthetic objects. The joint endeavors of them constitute the root of art as the objective existence of the materialized substance of human mind and emotion.[2]

Subsequently, the stratification of image along with artistic sedimentation would have a person's emotion and desire as are humanized and

---

[1] Li Zehou and Jane Cauvel, *Four Essays on Aesthetics* (Lanham et al.: Lexington Books, 2006), p. 134.

[2] Li Zehou and Jane Cauvel, *Four Essays on Aesthetics*, p. 144. Also see Li Zehou, *Meixue si jiang* [Four Essays on Aesthetics] (Beijing: Sanlian Bookshop, 1989), p. 205.

expressed through symbols. These symbols, such as the Chinese *taiji*, the Christian cross, and the Buddhist *mandala*, constitute the subject matters, themes, and even contents of mimetic arts in particular. In both China and the West, Li Zehou assumes, art originated from ancient witchcraft practices through its rituals, whereas aesthetic experience originated from human labor. As the rituals developed, they divided into three branches: The first branch recognized and reflected natural things, which gave rise to science; the second controlled and organized the masses into group activities, which gave rise to religions, political systems, and ethical norms; the third imitated the production and phenomena in real life to form lively images, demonstrating the formal aspect of witchcraft. This formal aspect is related to gestures, languages, costumes, and performances, leading to the making of art. For the key preoccupation in this process is the phenomenal imitation and simulation of life, and production in reality, thus bearing the fruit of various images.[3] The trinity of poetry, song, and dance in China, for example, used to be artistic forms of primitive witchcraft activities. In later times, they developed into an integral part of *li* (rites) in Chinese history and served in antiquity as the earliest means of constituting human nature and enculturating human temperament. As they were performed over and over again during the magical services or ritual etiquettes with practical utility, they came up to function like fairy tales that are as much to children today as they were to people in ancient periods, molding their minds and cultivating their emotions and desires. This way of repetition nurtured a new sensuousness, which transcended the stratification of sensory forms and entered into the realm of mind relating to emotions and desires.

Progressively and eventually, the natural functions of psychology and the social functions of history would be combined and interwoven one with another, and then constitute the emotional stratification of images in artworks, which is far deeper than the sensuous stratification of form. This stratifying process of images tends not simply to enculturate human instincts and human nature, but also to interweave organically among desires and conceptions alike. As is detected in the psychoanalysis, animal instincts, and emotional desires on the part of human beings involve the issue of the unconscious. It demonstrates itself in the stratification of image in complex and intricate relationships between the

---

[3] Li Zehou and Jane Cauvel, *Four Essays on Aesthetics*, p. 144.

unconscious and the conscious in the act of either creation or appreciation. For example, figures in artworks that are similar but not identical to those in dreams are apt to transfigure, overlap, and condense in various ways and shapes. This renders the illusory world in the stratification of images more diverse, obscure, extensive, indefinite, and even unspeakable beyond logical reasoning and interpretation. Thus, the task of aesthetic experience is to explore the complex character, function, and pattern of this construction through the materialized but invented world of art. Incidentally, the *"dianxing"* (typical models) in the stratification of images are, just like the *"goujia"* (frames) in science, the generalized expressions of real life itself. Historically, the process of image stratification goes along with change. It circulates from representation (imitation) to expression (abstraction), from expression to decoration, from decoration back to representation and expression. This can be seen in the gradual abstraction and symbolization of living animals into geometrical patterns as is shown in the different styles of paintings ranging from primitive to classical and modern.[4]

With respect to the stratification of significance along with life sedimentation, the significance that is suggested in the image gives rise to significant form. It is therefore inseparable from the sensuous forms and images of artworks. Yet, it transcends them in a manner that means more than the humanization of sense organs and the emotional desires in addition to the realization of such emotional desires in art illusions. It in fact humanizes the psychological condition of humans and accounts for the endurance of artworks as it enables them to provide continuing satisfaction of aesthetic experience instead of momentary effect like fireworks. Saturated with such great significance, the artworks are appealing not merely to the pleasures of the ear and the eye (*yue er yue mu*), but to the pleasures of the heart and mind (*yue xin yue yi*) as well as those of lofty aspiration and moral integrity (*yue zhi yue shen*). As a rule, the fine artworks thus created as emotional symbols are rich in and characteristic of significance and life sedimentation. From the viewpoint of philosophical aesthetics, they bear both endurance and eternality not merely due to the subtle significance and aesthetic value, but also due to the fact that their expressional power goes beyond the physiological existence of human species, and helps construct the psycho-emotional substance (*qinggan*

---

[4]Li Zehou, *Mei de licheng* [The Path of Beauty] (Beijing: Wenwu Press, 1981), pp. 17–20.

benti) of pure humanity. In a word, it is in the stratification of significance that the degree of fulfilling human nature is embodied.[5] Now the significance in artworks specifically refers to the deepest meaning of human life and condition as well. In theological terms, as Li Zehou claims, it implies an ontological world as it centers around and touches upon the implications from the absolute spirit or the divine being. This being the case, the highest truth in art does not consist in the accurate imitation of things via its representational form at all, but in the communication of the subtle significance that appeals not to rational cognition but to aesthetic taste.

Moreover, the stratification of significance in artworks cannot be divorced from life itself. The significance in this case can be considered to be the significance of life. Although its expression is sometimes mystical and even religious, it is still felt to be related to life in reality. In many cases, art serves in its own way to preserve the significance of human life and often demonstrates itself as the materialized confirmation of the incessant expansion of a person's spiritual life and substance. Sometimes it goes so far as to stir up the whole psychology of humankind, awaken people from their numbness, and even lead them to reflect on the fate of human existence. Correspondingly in artworks, people sense their own existence, condition, and growth and come thereby to understand and cultivate their own lives. Take Chinese art for example; the most important aspect of the significance is to express the value of life. It transcends the emotional image and sensual form as it is enhanced by the experience of the integrity of nature and humanity or the oneness between heaven and human (*tian ren he yi*), exemplifying a human's isomorphic emotional response to the cosmic order. It is the interactive communion between life's significance and the isomorphic structure expressed in artworks that reveals the sense of destiny, the sense of historical mission, and the sense of life's meaning, and meanwhile attributes to them great mystical power. Here on this occasion, the individual is general and universal, and the abstract is concrete and particular. That is, why Chinese artistic abstraction is neither transformed abstraction of real things nor formal abstraction of emotional expression, but comprehensive abstraction of the rational-emotional intercourse and interfusion between the cosmic order and human life.[6]

---

[5] Li Zehou, *Meixue si jiang* [Four Essays on Aesthetics], pp. 237–238.
[6] Li Zehou and Jane Cauvel, *Four Essays on Aesthetics*, p. 163.

In short, art is the product of history. Its creation and development involve the stratification of form, image, and significance parallel to primitive, artistic, and life sedimentation. The three stratifications are interrelated to the extent that we cannot draw a hard and fast line between them. For they interweave and interpenetrate one another along with the three sedimentations, which conduces to the organic unity of the structure in a great artwork. The above discussion of art as sedimentation is intended to denote that form and image are analogous to sensation and desire. They mutually penetrate, blend, and often overlap in the same object, aesthetic or artistic. They also exist in very complicated and crisscross patterns. For example, the stratification of form that appeals to sensation in literary work is vague. A novel appears to us through paper and words but the sensations of a novel are not sensations of the paper and printed characters; instead, they are manifested in an imaginative presentation. Even the stratification of significance cannot exist by itself because it exists only in the stratification of form-sensation and in the stratification of image-desire but simultaneously transcends them after all.[7] Regarding the three sedimentations, we may arrive a tentative conclusion that primitive sedimentation results in aesthetic, artistic sedimentation in form, and the life sedimentation in art. All this makes up a dynamic and changing process in close association with the daily experience of humankind as a whole.

18.2 A Critical Pondering

The 1980s in China witnessed an extensive attention to Li Zehou's theory of art as sedimentation in view of the cultural-psychological formation. For this theory stimulated much rethinking among philosophers, anthropologists, critics, psychologists, and the like across the country. From then on the newly coined term of *jidian* as sedimentation has been used as a catchphrase of high frequency to expose the essential characteristics of aesthetic experience in art. It has naturally spurred up a heated discussion and criticism, especially among Chinese academics and some overseas sinologists since *The Path of Beauty* (*Mei de licheng*) is made accessible in a number of languages including English, German, and Korean.

---

[7] Ibid., p. 133.

According to some critical observations, the notion of art as sedimentation often comes under trenchant attack for it seems to be something static instead of dynamic, completed instead of uncompleted. As it is placed in the context of his anthropo-historical ontology, it appears to be enclosed within the past and the existent, and therefore leaves no room for further alteration and progression. For on this point, it tends to neglect the fact of constant change and openness in art movements and plays down the potential power of creativity and originality of art that often breaks through the history of establishment. This is often the case with the artworks produced by genius in particular, which are liable to set up not only new paradigms and styles but to shape or remold the audiences' aesthetic mentality and sense of art altogether.

In the face of this criticism, Li Zehou defends for himself by explicating his notion of sedimentation in two senses. In a broad sense, sedimentation refers to the constitution of human minds from rationality to sensuousness, from sociality to individuality, and from history to psychology, possibly including the rational internalization (intellectual structure) and the rational condensation (volitional structure). In a narrow sense, sedimentation refers to the constitution of aesthetic sensibility and feeling. His theory of art as sedimentation looks into the second aspect only. Apart from this explication, he proceeds to emphasize the dynamic process and open nature of sedimentation in connection with daily activities and living experiences, and deliberately affirms the fact that sedimentation, art, experience, and aesthetic appreciation are all subject to constant renewal and development due to the freshness, objectiveness, and pioneeringness of everyday life and human practice. Here is a citation of what he claims,

> Sedimentation flows from history into psychology, from rationality into sensuousness, from sociality into individuality. Therefore, sedimentation changes when the general, common sedimentation is realized through the unique, sensuous existence of each individual and when each individual displays the common sedimentation in herself or himself. These changes are displayed by differences in personality, ideals, experiences, and aesthetic faculties (including creation and appreciation). These individual sedimentations have ontological significance for individuals, who are thrown into this world by chance and vested with no significance, but who make a great effort to attain significance in their own lives. A person's own emotional psychology brings forth significance because logic cannot do so. This means that each person must pursue, discover, create, and constitute

a unique life...Therefore, a person should never be a tool or means, for persons are ends in themselves...Let us return to persons, to individuality, to sensuousness, and to fortuity. Come back to everyday life! Throw away any shackles of metaphysical ideas and actively greet, constitute, and break up the sedimentations. Art is nothing but the psychological homologue to our sensuous existence; it lies in our living experience, say, our psychological-emotional substance.[8]

Hence, we must learn to contemplate disinterestedly our surroundings, to purify our emotions and desires alike, to sustain our living experiences always with something new, and to keep our sensation, understanding, imagination, and emotion in a state of ongoing variation and combination. "If we develop these consistently, we will change art from an artistic product designed for only a few elites to an art that is self-fulfilling, expression of every individual. If this occurs, all persons will be able to realize their individual existence by themselves. Their inborn potentialities, talents, and qualities of individuality will come into full play, simultaneously embracing and shattering the mental sedimentations to make room for newer processes."[9]

Incidentally, it is in the late 1990s that Li deliberately modified his notion of *jidian* "sedimentation" into "sedimenting." He shifted the noun form into its gerund in order to denote a continuing act or ongoing process, attempting to ascribe to it a dynamic feature on the one hand, and on the other, to decrease the probability of misconception against the static implications of "sedimentation." This is also true of his conception of *wenhua xinli jiegou* as cultural-psychological structure, which invites the similar criticism owing to its seemingly fixed and static character as is often conceived. In like manner, Li has clarified the hidden features of "cultural psychological structure" as a changing process and thereby altered the previously used term "structure" into "formation" so as to get rid of any possible misinterpretation.

It is worth pointing out that Li often announces his stubborn adhering to his early arguments as a whole. But we can observe his way of modification if not patchwork. It is true that he manages to keep the consistency and coherence of his system in principle. However, his

---

[8] Li Zehou and Jane Cauvel, *Four Essays on Aesthetics*, p. 167.
[9] Ibid., p. 167. Also see Li Zehou, *Meixue si jiang* [Four Essays on Aesthetics], pp. 250–251.

constant re-explications betray his announcement as they reveal his attempt for further improvement. It is for this reason that his system can be seen as one open to modest modification instead of drastic change.

Now let us turn to his notion of cultural-psychological formation, it takes in a main component of *shenmei xinli jiegou* qua aesthetic psychological construction that goes along with primitive, artistic, and life sedimentations in connection with the stratifications of form, image, and significance altogether. According to Li's argumentation, an insight into the aesthetic psychological construction can be illustrated through aesthetic experience. This experience is a subtle and complex activity, comprising at least four basic factors, namely aesthetic sensation, understanding, imagination, and feeling.

Respectively speaking, aesthetic sensation is based on the senses like sight and hearing as the outcome of humanization of the inner nature. Even though it seems to be entirely sensuous, it is in practice supra-sensuous as it contains many elements, especially cognitive perception and social conventions that could be traced back to the process of primitive sedimentation in connection with the unconscious world. In a word, aesthetic sensation is the product of both psychology and sociality, marking the progression of human sensuousness.

Aesthetic understanding has at least four implications. Firstly, it implies that the subject is always conscious of the context, and inclined to differentiate it from the experience of daily life as if he keeps a "psychical distance" in terms of what is articulated by Edward Bullough. Secondly, it calls for a relevant knowledge of the object contemplated, particularly in representational art. Thirdly, it requires an intellectual cognition of the technical aspects of the object. Fourthly, it demands a profound but indefinite cognition that permeates sensation, imagination, and emotion, and blends with them to form an organic unity. This process is characteristic of thinking-in-images. It could hardly be explicated in common expressions because "It can be sensed, but cannot be expressed in words" (*zhi ke yi hui bu ke yan chuan*) as the old saying claims. On this point, Li stresses again the distinction between two types of aesthetic understanding: *yin* and *xiu*. *Yin* suggests that in the process of appreciation the faculty of understanding integrate so completely with other psychical factors that it functions unconsciously. The meaning of the object lies beyond its literal forms and words. *Xiu* refers to a sudden realization of the meaning of the object, as if it had already been known. At the moment when we approach the comic, for example, we are fully aware of the role of understanding in aesthetic experience. Nevertheless, the importance of complexity, indefiniteness, and non-conceptual cognition of aesthetic understanding remains.[10]

Aesthetic imagination works as a kind of perceptual activity of synthesis and unification because it recalls certain events experienced or comprehended in the past, and associates them with other ideas, which enriches aesthetic experience in the end. The free play of imagination is an indispensable medium through which aesthetic sensation and understanding come to effect. The triangle interaction among them runs like this: "Sensation in physiology and understanding in cognitive processes are constraints. Imagination transforms both into variables and links them up with the emotion and desire in aesthetic experience. Imagination leads sensation to go beyond itself, prevents understanding from turning into conception, and facilitates emotion in the creation of an illusory world."[11]

Last but not the least, aesthetic emotion as a primary part of aesthetic psychological construction differs from ordinary emotion. For it is transformed by virtue of understanding and imagination into an emotional expression according to R. Collingwood's observation, or into a logical form of emotion in terms of S. Langer's proposal. It is self-evidently demonstrated in aesthetic pleasure. As is often discerned in an aesthetic activity, such emotion, whether mixed up with the state of mind, will and desire, or expressed in an artistic object, sets imagination free, heightens sensation, increases understanding, and develops a pattern of aesthetic experience, so to speak.

At this stage, aesthetic experience can be construed as a dynamic synthesis of the functions of sensation, understanding, imagination, and emotion. It is owing to such variables as individual differences, artistic expressions, and values that aesthetic experience can be divided into three levels from a morphological viewpoint, ranging from the surface to the depth, from the simple to the complex, or from the formal to the significant. In Li's terminology, it commences with pleasures of the ear and eye. These pleasures are physiological by nature, but arise from different conditions of social life and culture, from different personal

---

[10] Li Zehou and Jane Cauvel, *Four Essays on Aesthetics*, p. 105. Also see Li Zehou, *Meixue si jiang* [Four Essays on Aesthetics], p. 140.

[11] Li Zehou and Jane Cauvel, *Four Essays on Aesthetics*, p. 106. Also see Li Zehou, *Meixue si jiang* [Four Essays on Aesthetics], pp. 140–141.

experiences and cultivation. They can help free human ears and eyes from purely physiological demands and domination by social volition, thus working to build up a new sensuousness and upgrade the human psychological-emotional construction.

The second level of aesthetic experience refers to pleasures of the mind and heart. Stemmed from the sense of beauty through the ear and eye, these pleasures permeate the inner world. They practically derive from the unification of sensual desire and reason and that of sociality and nature. They may remove the repression of instincts and desires and yield the delight and satisfaction of other mental activities including emotions of nostalgia, patriotism, and friendship. For instance, "When appreciating a poem, a painting, or a piece of symphony, we can often unconsciously experience something more lasting and deeper through those limited images in sensation, and comprehend the interior, infinite significance of daily life from the limited, casual concrete images appealing originally to visual and aural organs, thus increasingly raising the level of spiritual life."[12]

Just as Li himself asserts, pleasures of lofty aspiration and moral integrity stand not only for the highest realm of aesthetic experience but the supreme form of aesthetic capacity. These pleasures tend to effect simultaneously in two domains. On the one hand, they are apt to pursue and find satisfaction in certain purposive ideas of morality, mold, and cultivate human will, fortitude, and ambition. On the other hand, they are supposed to facilitate the integrity of a finite "I" with its infinite counterpart such that it is analogical to the oneness between human and universe. That is to say, they may bring forth a mental experience of supra-morality that is identical with the experience of infinity. Yet, this supra-morality doe not negate morality but refers to an experience freed from all moral principles and natural laws. For this reason, the pleasures of lofty aspiration and moral integrity relate mainly to the contemplation of the sublime rather than the beautiful.[13]

According to Li Zehou, pleasures of lofty aspiration and moral integrity stand not only for the highest realm of aesthetic experience, but the supreme form of aesthetic capacity. These pleasures tend to effect simultaneously in two domains. On the one hand, they are apt to pursue and

---

[12] Li Zehou and Jane Cauvel, *Four Essays on Aesthetics*, p. 118. Also see Li Zehou, *Meixue si jiang* [Four Essays on Aesthetics], p. 324.

[13] Li Zehou and Jane Cauvel, *Four Essays on Aesthetics*, p. 120. Also see Li Zehou, *Meixue si jiang* [Four Essays on Aesthetics], pp. 197–225.

find satisfaction in certain purposive ideas of morality, mold, and cultivate human will, fortitude, and ambition. On the other hand, they are supposed to facilitate the integrity of a finite "I" with its infinite counterpart such that it is analogical to the oneness between human and universe. That is to say, they may bring forth a mental experience of supra-morality that is identical with the experience of infinity. Yet, this supra-morality doe not negate morality but refers to an experience freed from all moral principles and natural laws. For this reason, the pleasures of lofty aspiration and moral integrity relate mainly to the contemplation of the sublime rather than the beautiful.[14]

Under ideal conditions, pleasures of the ear and eye are basically physiological and sociocultural, serving to cultivate human sensations. Pleasures experienced by the mind and heart are coordinated with such faculties as understanding and imagination, working to cultivate human desires, emotions, and intentions as well. Pleasures experienced from lofty aspiration and moral integrity assist humans in transcending moral constraints and attaining a higher state of supra-moral existence characterized with aesthetic and spiritual freedom.

There is some truth in such a hypothesis of aesthetic psychological construction given above. But it strikes me as if the mystical dimension of aesthetic experience still remains as it is especially in the pleasures of lofty aspiration and moral integrity. Elsewhere Li identifies this aspect with something as mysterious as religious enlightenment in a loose manner without further investigation, not to speak of any authentic justification. The matter of fact is that he is highly conscious of the difficulty and problem in this case. He therefore grounds his argument and judgment on empirical inferring, but this inferring is semi-transcendental in that it is largely dependent upon a kind of *sensus communis a priori*. For this reason, he has no minimum of vacillation to recognize its lack of sufficiency and often makes a metaphorical use of Watson-Crick's Double Helix to suggest the complicated and variable aspects of aesthetic psychological construction. He also expects a real solution from the further development of brain science and psychology in the future. By then, as he assumes, the issues in question could be properly addressed in a more valid and convincing way. It follows that his theoretical hypothesis

---

[14]Li Zehou and Jane Cauvel, *Four Essays on Aesthetics*, p. 120. Also see Li Zehou, "Guanyu chonggao yu huaji" [On the Sublime and the Comic], in Li Zehou, *Meixue lunji* [Selected Essays on Aesthetics] (Shanghai: Shanghai Wenyi Press, 1980), pp. 197–225.

is just provided as a conjecture only, and it should be left open to further verification in a more scientific mode.

18.3 A Methodological Reflection

When looking into Li Zehou's philosophizing about art as sedimentation along with cultural and aesthetic psychology, we find it more stimulating in a methodological sense as it straddles two cultural domains, Chinese and Western. It can be conceived of as a transcultural approach by and large. For it proceeds from a fundamental basis on such constituents as Chinese traditional thoughts in the mainstream of Confucianism, Marx's practical philosophy in view of historical materialism, Kant's critical aesthetics of judgment, Bell's hypothesis of significant form, Freud's psychoanalysis of the unconscious, and Jung's probing into the archetype. It is especially so in respect to Li's aesthetic ponderings about art. Interestingly, he appropriates some suggestions and even concepts from Marx, Kant, Freud, and Bell, but reconstruct them in new shapes and implications in his own system, which they seem to fit fairly well as if they were salt dissolved in water. All this comes out from a critical transformation and creative synthesis in a Chinese context of glocalization and consequently leads him to widen his thinking scope and venture across some theoretical boundaries encountered in his speculative pursuits.

For instance, in order to illustrate the primitive sedimentation of content, imagination, and concept into form in art, Li makes a particular reference to some archeological findings in China with a more elaborate description and analysis. Thus reads a passage from *The Path of Beauty* published in 1981,

> Some of the geometric patterns of Yangshao and Majiayao clearly evolved from realistic animal images into abstract symbols. The direction of development, in form and content, was from simple imitation to stylized abstraction, from realism to symbolism. This was the primary process in the development of the concept of beauty as "significant form." Thus the geometric patterns that to later generations seemed to be only ornamentation, with no specific meaning or content, actually possessed much of both in earlier times—they had serious totemic implications. Those seemingly pure forms were far more than mere visually balanced, symmetrical stimuli; they possessed a highly complicated conceptual significance. Though totemic images gradually became simplified and abstracted into

pure geometric patterns—turned into symbols—their totemic implications did not disappear. Indeed, these implications could be said to have been enhanced by virtue of the fact that geometric patterns covered the whole surface of a vessel more often than animal images did. Thus abstract geometric patterns were not merely formed beauty, for there was content in the abstract form and concept in what was perceived by the senses. This is a characteristic that beauty and aesthetics have in common.[15]

Incidentally, beauty lies in "significant form" instead of ordinary form. The significant form is natural form that possesses a socially defined content or sociality. As is noticed in the hypothesis proposed by Clive Bell in the *Art*, "significant form" and "aesthetic emotion" are interpreting each other in a repeated circle. Having discerned this problem, Li attempts to break away from it by resorting to his theory of aesthetic sedimentation (*shenmei jidian*) and its explication given above. He therefore maintains that the pure geometric lines evolved from realistic images and sedimented within some amount of social content and significance. They turn out to be "significant form" because human feelings toward them incorporated special conceptual and imaginative elements concerned. In this context, they tend to elicit a special kind of "aesthetic emotion" because they are different from ordinary emotions, perceptions, and experiences as well. In many cases, such feelings in primitive rituals and magic services would be passionate and mystical but confused and ambiguous, containing ideas and imagination that could not be explained via reasoning, logic, or conception. They therefore stir up some deep emotional reaction that is unspeakable in words. Some psychoanalysts like Jung tried to expose this unspeakability by virtue of "archetype" as part of the mysterious "collective unconscious." However, Li gives it a second reflection in light of historical sedimentation and arrives at the conclusion that it is actually not mystical in this regard providing we understand the particular social content and feelings (meaning and significance) sedimented and dissolved into the form itself and the emotional response to it. "It should be noted that," he proceeds, "as time passed, what was originally significant form gradually lost its significance through repetition and imitation." It became

---

[15] Li Zehou, *Mei de licheng* [The Path of Beauty] (Beijing: Wenwu Press, 1981), pp. 18–19; also see Li Zehou, *The Path of Beauty* (trans. Gong Lizeng, Oxford: Oxford University Press, 1994), p. 16.

ordinary, standardized, formal beauty, reducing aesthetic emotion into a general sense of form for its own sake. Thus, these geometric patterns became in time the earliest models and specimens of decorative and formal beauty.[16] All this can be evinced in some of the geometric patterns of Yangshao and Majiayao as is depicted in the foregoing citation.

Moreover, when it comes to his aesthetic considerations, Li undertakes to make the most of the implications of such Kantian concepts as "aesthetic judgment" (*ästhetischen Urteilskraft*) and "teleological judgment" (*teleologischen Urteilskraft*) in an interactive and complementary mode. The former involves the free play of faculties like understanding and imagination, while the latter regards freedom as the final purpose for man as man. He thereby draws from them the key point of freedom (*Freiheit*) that is grounded principally on reason and moral law, and then applies it to the three interrelated aspects of human mind, say, "free intuition" (*ziyou zhiguan*) that appeals to cognitive power in pursuit of true knowledge of lawfulness and nature, "free will" (*ziyou yizhi*) that appeals to volitional power of desire in connection with a high awareness of obligation and morality, and "free feeling" (*ziyou ganshou*) that appeals to pleasure and displeasure in connection with purposiveness and art.[17] This being the case, he ascribes to beauty and sublimity two more properties aside from its aesthetic experience and enjoyment. One is cognitive and the other is moral as they are expressed in his terms: *yi mei qi zhen* meaning to enlighten the knowing of truth with beauty, and *yi mei chu shan* meaning to assist the cultivating of goodness with beauty. As beauty penetrates into artistic expression, art is then acclaimed to perform the similar function because of its twofold quality. That is, it presents itself in a material form that corresponds to the cultural-psychological construction of humankind, and meanwhile, it indicates a materialized confirmation of the incessant expansion of a person's spiritual and emotional life. Under such circumstances, art is alleged to throw light upon truth with beauty through its stratification of sensation that has a potential intelligibility; and furthermore, it is assumed to store goodness through its stratification of desire that has a potential action. Altogether it works directly

---

[16] Li Zehou, *Mei de licheng* [The Path of Beauty], p. 27; also see Li Zehou, *The Path of Beauty*, p. 21.

[17] Li Zehou, *Pipan zhexue de pipan* [Crique of Kant's Critical Philosophy] (Beijing: Renmin Press, 1984), pp. 422–437.

to nourish and educate human nature in terms of the cultural-psychological construction peculiar of human race.[18]

Li is known as one of the leading founders of practical aesthetics in China. This can be naturally traced back to Marx's observation on the role of labor in the developmental process of civilization as a result of the humanization of nature. Along this line of thought, he develops his practical aesthetics with a constant emphasis on the determinate part of labor that is specifically conducted by tool-making and tool-using. From the perspective of his anthropo-historical ontology, he argues that the long history of tool-making and tool-using as the most primary and important form of human practice has made possible a good command of *du* as proper-measure *par excellence*. This *du* as proper-measure features operational capability that derives from historical accumulation and rational internalization relating to human existence and pragmatic reason in one sense; and in the other, it generates dialectic wisdom that reveals itself at two levels: the operational and the existential. At the operational level, the act of knowing-how is to some degree identical to that of doing-what, whereas at the existential level the relationship between them is rather indirect. The former has mathematical quality and pays attention to the unlimited possibility of logic while the latter has dialectic character and pays attention to the limited possibility of reality.[19]

Additionally, *du* as proper-measure is closely leagued with individual creation that results in the sense of form and then of beauty. Such a sense is actually fostered and evolved from the long history of tool-making and tool-using. For the repetition of tool-making and tool-using has brought forth a kind of rhythmic and regular operation that not only makes the manual work easier, but also allows people to feel the pleasure from their applying formal forces to the external objects and artifacts. This leads them to grow more and more conscious of such elements as rhythm, sequence, symmetry, equivalence, proportion, order, and harmony. In spite of all this, it is by means of *du* that a person is enabled to freely employ such formal forces to create things in accordance with his sense of form and beauty as well. Nevertheless, *du* is not equal to beauty in that the former ends up in craft while the latter in

---

[18] Li Zehou, *Meixue si jiang* [Four Essays on Aesthetics], p. 242; also see Li Zehou and Jane Cauvel, *Four Essays on Aesthetics,* p. 162.

[19] Li Zehou, *Shiyong lixing yu legan wenhua* [Pragmatic reason and a Culture of Optimism] (Beijing: Sanlian Bookshop, 2005), p. 21.

art. Only by a free play or use of the craft can one enjoy the pleasure from it, and even go further to produce forms of beauty. On this point, Li acknowledges that a command of *du* is dependent upon the integration of subjective purposiveness with the objective lawfulness, and *du* itself is an active creation in light of right timing, suitable setting, and material quality. When *du* as proper-measure is established and applied to human conduct, material activity, and living behavior altogether, beauty is made available in them. By making beauty according to *du* as proper-measure (*yi du li mei*) is meant not merely to turn out some objects of beauty, but also to build up the sense of beauty. It can be identified, in classical terms, with "the unity of lawfulness and purposiveness in action," which then gives rise to a sense of freedom and pleasure in all cases. This sense of freedom is in fact the origin of aesthetic consciousness or sense of beauty, which will then continue to develop, create, and renew the proper-measure and the beautiful with the passage of time.[20] Meanwhile, Li maintains that the sense of beauty originates from the humanization of internal nature within humans as is distinguished from external nature in the physical world. In this regard "musical ear" is a self-evident example. Since mankind is endowed to make through his labor "according to the law of beauty" (Karl Marx), his awareness of beauty in varied manifestations would be awakened in this historical process, and gradually developed along with the increasing discovery of the order and form intricate in natural objects. Then it follows that art came into being when artworks were originally made as practical and aesthetic objects owning to their purposiveness for witchcraft services and sensuous pleasures. Accordingly, Li also accepts the Marxist outlook of historical materialism, but he transforms it critically and synthetically into his historical ontology, where he asserts that history bears at least two senses. "In one sense, it refers to relativity and particularity by which history is the outcome (occurrence and emergence) of things and events in specific time, space, environment and condition. In the other sense; it refers to absoluteness and accumulativeness in the context of which things and events are incessantly inherited and becoming as the result of human practical experience, consciousness and thinking altogether. Traditional Marxism puts more emphasis on the first aspect while I place more stress on the second aspect because it concerns with the ontological being of

---

[20] Li Zehou, *Lishi bentilun* [Historical Ontology] (Beijing: Sanlian Bookshop, 2003), pp. 8–11.

humankind."[21] This argument about history in terms of accumulativeness strikes me as being somewhat related to his historical view of art as a sedimentational process to be explicated subsequently.

As is observed from what has been discussed so far, Li Zehou tends to engage himself in his philosophical and aesthetic preoccupations in a way like some of his predecessors such as Wang Guowei among others, all rejecting any rigid divide between the Chinese learning and its Western counterpart. Li never confines himself to a single lane of thinking; instead, he makes a reflective use of the essential components and implications of a variety of working theories by either reading new messages into them in a different cultural context or by transforming them creatively to fit his system. Regarding the apparent and hidden structure and functions of art as the product of history, he once again experiments with the transcultural approach aforementioned. Thus, he goes further to articulate his doctrine of sedimentation in a more detailed and systematic fashion as is sketched at the outset of this discussion. Now his transcultural approach, together with his conception of art as sedimentation and his practical aesthetics as a whole, still appeal to critical reconsiderations and rediscoveries, thus showing the theoretical liveliness or vitality apart from a room for further improvement.

Up till now there still arises a question as regards whether or not the theory of art as sedimentation has overcome the difficulty in defining art as such. The answer could be "yes" and "no." By "yes" is meant that the theory itself helps expose and explain the essential aspects of significant form and its developmental process in art from a cultural and historical perspective. Consequently, the experience of the aesthetic value in significant form is not that mystical but becomes somewhat intelligible instead. By "no" is meant that the definition of art as sedimentation in terms of form, image, and significance is considerably exclusive because it can be applicable only to the artworks in a traditional sense. That is to say, it excludes the ready-mades or found art promoted by the avant-garde artists. Off-handed examples could be Marcel Duchamp's urinal, Robert Rauschenberg's bed, and even Andy Warhol's boxes. As a matter of fact, Li Zehou is more less like John Dewey, both turning a blind eye to the art movements and changes of their own times. For instance, Dewey did not care about the post-impressionists then, while Li simply denies the

---

[21] Ibid., p. 42.

art identity to the contemporary avant-garde production such as "The Heavenly Book" (*Tianshu*) by Xu Bing. For he holds up to his conception of art as sedimentation of form, image, and significance and retains his personal preference for the aesthetic values, cultural properties, and moral messages all exemplified in artworks to his mind. He therefore finds the avant-garde pieces failing to meet the requirements on art in his conception. Quite ironically, Li follows Dewey to stress the necessity and importance of daily life and intends to propose a broad scope and view of art as experience, but both of them stay in their individual tastes and senses of art that seem to be more traditional and classical than modern, more moral than sensual, more serious than playful, more elite than popular. It is noticeable that both of them are somewhat confined to their theoretical constraints over art, even though they pretend not to be so.

Chinese Materials

Cai, Yuanpei, *Cai Yuanpei meixue wenxuan* 蔡元培美学文选 [Selected Essays of Cai Yuanpei on Aesthetics], Beijing: Peking University Press, 1983.
Chan, Hongxiang, *Wang Guowei zhuan* 王国维传 [A Biography of Wang Guowei], Beijing: Tuanjie Press, 1998.
Chen, Guying, *Laozi zhuyi ji pingjie* 老子注释及评介 [An Annotated and Paraphrased Version of Laozi's *Dao De Jing* with Commentary], Beijing: Zhonghua Book Company, 1992.
Chen, Guying (ed.), *Zhuangzi jinzhu jinyi* 庄子今注今译 [The Works of Zhuangzi Annotated and Paraphrased], Beijing: Zhonghua Book Company, 1983.
Chen, Yinque, "*Wang Jing'an yishu xu*" 王静安遗文序 [Preface to Wang Guowei's Posthumous Works], Beijing: Commercial Press, 1934, reprinted in 1940.
Chen, Yong, "*Luetan jingjie shuo*" 略谈境界说 [A Note on the Theory of *Jingjie*], in Yao Kefu (ed.), *Renjian cihua ji pinglun huibian* 人间词话及评论汇编 [Renjian Poetic Remarks and Selected Essays on Wang Guowei's Poetics], Beijing: Shumu Wenxian Press, 1983, pp. 210–214.
Chen, Yuanhui, *Lun Wang Guowei* 论王国维 [A Study of Wang Guowei], Changchun: Dongbei Normal University Press, 1989.
Chinese Academy of Social Sciences Institute of Philosophy (ed.), *Zhongguo zhexueshi ziliao xuanji* 中国哲学史资料选辑 [Selected Sources of the History of Chinese Philosophy], Beijing: Zhonghua Book Company, 1982.

Confucius, *Kongzi jiayü* 孔子家语 [The Sayings of Confucius], Beijing: Beijing Yanshan Press, 1995.

Cui, Dahua. *Zhuang xue yan jiu* 庄学研究 [A Study of Zhuangzi's Thought], Beijing: Renmin Press, 1992.

Dong, Zhongshu, *Chunqiu fanlu* 春秋繁露 [Exuberant Dew of Spring and Autumn], Shanghai: Shanghai Guji Press, 1989.

Fang, Thomé & Fang, Dongmei, *Fang Dongmei xinruxue lunzhu jiyao* 方东美新儒学论著辑要 [Thomé Fang's Selected Writings on Modern Confucianism], eds. Jiang Baoguo and Zhou Yazhou, Beijing: Zhongguo Guangbo Dianshi Press, 1993.

Fan, Wenlan (ed.), *Wenxin diaolong zhu* 文心雕龙注 [Dragon-Carving and Literary Mind with Annotations], Beijing: Renmin Wenxue Press, 2000.

Feng, Qi, *Zhongguo gudai zhexue de luoji fazhan* 中国古代哲学的逻辑发展 [A Logical Development of Ancient Chinese Philosophy], Shanghai: Shanghai Renmin Press, 1983.

Feng, Youlan (Fung, Yu-lan), *Zhongguo zhexueshi xinbian* 中国哲学史新编 [A New Edition of the History of Chinese Philosophy], Beijing: Renmin Press, 1992.

Fo, Chu, *Wang Guowei shixue yanjiu* 王国维诗学研究 [A Study of Wang Guowei's Poetics], Beijing: Peking University Press, 1987.

Fudan University History Department (ed.), *Rujia sixiang yu weilai shehui* 儒家思想与未来社会 [Confucianist Ideas and the Future Society], Shanghai: Shanghai Renmin Press, 1991.

Fung, Yu-lan (Feng, Youlan), *Zhongguo zhexueshi xinbian* 中国哲学史新编 [The History of Chinese Philosophy: A New Edition], Vol. 1, Beijing: Renmin Press, 1992.

Fung, Yu-lan, *Zhenyuan liushu* 贞元六书 [Consistency and Fundamentality: Six Books], Shanghai: East China Normal University Press, 1996.

Gao, Boyuan, *Zhuangzi neiqipian sixiang yanjiu* 庄子内七篇思想研究 [A Study of the Seven Inner Chapters in the Book of Zhuangtzi], Taipei: Wenjin Press, 1992.

Gao, Heng, *Laozi zhenggu* 老子正诂 [A Revised Annotation of Laozi's Da.o De Jing], Beijing: Zhonghua Book Company, 1988.

Guo, Xiang & Cheng, Xuanying (eds.), *Zhuangzi zhu shu* 庄子注疏 [The Works of Zhuangzi Annotated and Explained], Beijing: Zhonghua Book Company, reprinted in 2013.

Gu, Di & Zhou, Ying, *Laozi tong* 老子通 [A Complete Study of Laozi's Dao De Jing], Changchun: Jilin Renmin Press, 1991.

Huang, Kan, *Wenxi diaolong zhaji* 文心雕龙札记 [Notes on the Dragon-carving and the Literary Mind], Shanghai: Shanghai Guji Press, 2000.

Huang, Kejian (ed.), *Xiong Shili ji* 熊十力集 [Selected Writings of Xiong Shili], Beijing: Qunyan Press, 1993.

Hu, Jingzhi (ed.), *Zhongguo xiandai meixue congbian* 中国现代美学丛编 [Collected Essays on Modern Chinese Aesthetics], Beijing: Peking University Press, 1987.

Hu, Jingzhi (ed.), *Zhongguo gudian meixue congbian* 中国古典美学丛编 [Selected Writings of Classical Chinese Aesthetics], Vols. 1-3, Beijing: Zhonghua Book Company, 1988.
Jiang, Nanhua, et al. (ed.), *Xunzi quanyi* 荀子全译 [The Book of Xunzi Completely Annotated], Guiyang: Guizhou Renmin Press, 1995.
Jin, Jingfang, et al. *Kongzi xinzhuan* 孔子新传 [A New Biography of Confucius], Changsha: Hunan Press, 1991.
Kang, Xiaocheng, *Xianqin rujia shijiao sixiang yanjiu* 先秦儒家诗教思想研究 [A Study of the Pre-Qin Confucian Ideas of Poetry Education], Taipei: Wenshizhe Press, 1988.
Kitaoka, Masako, *Moluo shili shuo caiyuan kao* 摩罗诗力说材源考 [Investigation of Source Materials for the Theories of *Maratic* Poetic Power], Beijing: Beijing Normal University Press, 1983.
Li, Zehou & Liu, Gangji (eds.), *Zhongguo meixueshi* 中国美学史 [A History of Chinese Aesthetics], Vol. 1, Beijing: China Social Sciences Press, 1984.
Li, Zehou, *Lishi bentilun/Jimao wushuo* 历史本体论/己卯五说 [Historical Ontology/Five Essays from 1999], Beijing: Sanlian Bookshop, 2003.
Li, Zehou, *Zhongguo gudai sixiang shilun* 中国古代思想史论 [Essays on Traditional Chinese Thoughts], Beijing: Renmin Press, 1985.
Li, Zehou, *Zhongguo jindai sixiang shilun* 中国近代思想史论 [Essays on Modern Chinese Thoughts], Beijing: Renmin Press, 1986.
Li, Zehou, *Zou wo ziji de lu* 走我自己的路 [Along My Own Path], Beijing: Sanlian Bookshop, 1986.
Li, Zehou, "*Yijing qian tan*" 意境浅谈 [An Initial Enquiry into the Theory of *Yijing*], in Yao Kefu (ed.), *Renjian cihua ji pinglun huibian* 人间词话及评论汇编 [Renjian Poetic Remarks and Selected Essays on Wang Guowei's Poetics], Beijing: Shumu Wenxian Press, 1983, pp. 160–178.
Li, Zehou, "*Lüe lun Lu Xun sixiang de fazhan*" 略论鲁迅思想的发展 [A Brief Review of the Development of Lu Xun's Thought], in *Lu Xun yanjiu jikan* 鲁迅研究集刊 [An Anthology of Lu Xun Studies], Shanghai: Shanghai Wenyi Press, 1979.
Li, Zehou, *Meixue lunji* 美学论集 [Selected Essays on Aesthetics], Shanghai: Shanghai Wenyi Press, 1980.
Li, Zehou, *Shiyong lixing and legan wenhua* 实用理性与乐感文化 [Pragmatic Reason and a Cultural of Optimism], Beijing: Sanlian Bookshop, 2005.
Li, Zehou, "*Shuo tianren xinyi*" 说天人新义 [On the Humanization of Nature], in *Jimao wushuo* 己卯五说 [Five Essays from 1999], Beijing: Sanlian Bookshop, 2006.
Li, Zehou, *Pipan zhexue de pipan* 批判哲学的批判 [Kant in a New Key], Beijing: Renmin Press, 1984.
Li, Zehou, *Meixue si jiang* 美学四讲 [Four Essays on Aesthetics], Beijing: Sanlian Bookshop, 1989.

Li, Zehou, *Mei de licheng* 美的历程 [A History of Beauty], Beijing: Wenwu Press, 1981.

Li, Zehou, *Lunli xue gang yao* 伦理学纲要 [Ethics], Beijing: Renmin Press, 2010.

Liang, Qichao, "*Lun xiaoshuo yu qunzhi zhi guanxi*" 论小说与群治之关系 [Comments on the Relationship Between Novel and Democracy], 1902.

Liang, Shuming, *Zhongguo wenhua yaoyi* 中国文化要义 [Essentials of Chinese Culture], Beijing: Xuelin Press, 1987.

Lin, Guoliang (ed.), *Fodian xuandu* 佛典选读 [Selected Readings of Buddhist Sutras], Guilin: Guangxi Normal University Press, 2006.

Liu, Kesu, *Shihang gu-yan: Wang Guowei biezhuan* 失行孤雁：王国维别传 [A Solitary Wild Goose: A Separate Biography of Wang Guowei], Beijing: Huaxia Press, 1999.

Liu, Shuxian, *Rujia sixiang yu xiandaihua* 儒家思想与现代化 [Confucianist Ideas and Modernization], Beijing: Zhongguo Guangbo Dianshi Press, 1993.

Liu, Xie, *Wenxin diaolong* 文心雕龙 [Dragon-Carving and the Literary Mind], Beijing: Zhonghua Book Company, 2012.

Liu, Xuan, *Wang Guowei pingzhuan* 王国维评传 [A Critical Biography of Wang Guowei], Nanchang: Baihuazhou Wenyi Press, 1996.

Liu, Zaifu, *Lu Xun meixue sixiang lungao* 鲁迅美学思想论稿 [On Lu Xun's Aesthetic Ideas], Beijing: China Social Sciences Press, 1981.

Lu, Shanqing, *Wang Guowei wenyi meixue guan* 王国维文艺美学观 [Wang Guowei's Artistic and Aesthetic Views], Guiyang: Guizhou Renmin Press, 1988.

Lu, Xun, *Lu Xun quanji* 鲁迅全集 [The Complete Works of Lu Xun], Beijing: Renmin Wenxue Press, 1958.

Lü, Buwei, *Lüshi chunqiu* 呂氏春秋 [Spring and Autumn Annals of Lü Buwei], Shanghai: Shanghai Guji Press, 1989.

Mao, Heng, *Mao shi zheng yi* 毛诗正义 [Mao Heng's Commentary on The Book of Poetry], Beijing: Peking University Press, 1999.

Mencius, *Mengzi* 孟子 [The Book of Mencius], Beijing: Zhonghua Book Company, 1988.

Min, Ze, *Zhongguo meixue sixiangshi* 中国美学思想史 [A History of Chinese Aesthetic Ideas], Vol. 1, Jinan: Qilu Bookshop, 1989.

Mou, Zongsan, *Caixing yu xuanli* 才性与玄理 [Genius and Metaphysical Principles], Taipei: Xuesheng Book Company, 1975.

Mou, Zongsan, *Zhong xi zhexue zhi huitong shisijiang* 中西哲学之会通十四讲 [Fourteen Lectures on the Transformation Between Chinese and Western Philosophies], Shanghai: Shanghai Guji Press, 1998.

Mou, Zongsan, *Zhongguo zhexue de tezhi* 中国哲学的特质 [The Characteristics of Chinese Philosophy], Shanghai: Shanghai Guji Press, 1997.

Nakamura, Moto, *Bijiao sixianglun* 比较思想论 [A Comparative Study of Ideas], trans. Wu Zhen, Hangzhou: Zhejiang Renmin Press, 1987.

Nie, Zhenbin, *Wang Guowei meixue sixiang pingshu* 王国维美学思想评述 [Critique of Wang Guowei's Aesthetic Ideas], Shenyang: Liaoning University Press, 1997.

Qian, Mu, *Xiandai zhongguo xueshu lunheng* 现代中国学术思想论衡 [Essays on Modern Academic Thoughts of China], Beiing: Sanlian Bookshop, 2006.

Qian, Mu, *Zhongguo sixiang tongsu jianghua* 中国思想通俗讲话 [Lectures on Chinese Thought], Beijing: Sanlian Bookshop, 2006.

Qian, Mu, *Kongzi yu lunyu* 孔子与论语 [Confucius and the Analects], Taipei: Lianjing Publishing Company, 1985.

Peking University Philosophy Department (ed.), *Zhongguo zhexueshi* 中国哲学思想史 [A History of Chinese Philosophy], Beijing: Zhonghua Book Company, 1980.

Peking University Philosophy Department (ed.), *Zhongguo meixueshi ziliao xuanbian* 中国美学史资料选编 [Selected Sources of the History of Chinese Aesthetics], Beijing: Zhonghua Book Company, 1981.

Pu, Ji (ed.), *Wu deng hui yuna* 五灯会元 [A Collection of Ko-an in Zen Buddhism], Beijing: Zhonghua Book Company, 2002.

Ren, Jiyu, *Zhongguo zhexueshi* 中国哲学史 [A History of Chinese Philosophy], Beijing: Renmin Press, 1990.

Sima, Qian, *Shi ji* 史记 [The Historical Records], Changsha: Yuelu Press, 1992.

Sun, Wu, *Sunzi bingfa* 孙子兵法 [The Art of War], Beijing: Military Science Press, 1993.

Sun, Xingyan (ed.), *Kongzi jiyü* 孔子集语 [The Quotations of Confucius], Shanghai: Shanghai Guji Press, 1993.

Sun, Yirang (ed.), *Mozi xian gu* 墨子闲诂 [The Book of Mozi with Annotations], Beijing: Zhonghua Book Company, 2001.

Tang, Junyi, *Zhongguo zhexue yuanlun* 中国哲学原论 [Principles of Chinese Philosophy], Taipei: Taiwan Xuesheng Book Company, 1978.

Tang, Junyi, Tang Junyi *xinruxue lunzhu jiyao* 唐君毅新儒学论著辑要 [Tang Junyi's Selected Writings on Modern Confucianism], ed. Zhang Xianghao, Beijing: Zhongguo Guangbo Dianshi Press, 1993.

Tang, Tao, *Lu Xun de meixue sixiang* 鲁迅的美学思想 [Lu Xun's Aesthetic Thoughts], Beijing: Renmin Wenxue Press, 1984.

Teng, Shouyao, *Yishu yu chuangshen* 艺术与创生 [Art and Generative Wisdom], Xi'an: Shaanxi Normal University Press, 2002.

Tong, Qingbing, "*Wenxin diaolong ganwu yinzhi shuo*" 文心雕龙感物吟志说 [Expression Arises When Emotions Stir in the "Dragon-Carving and the Literary Mind"], in *Wenyi yanjiu* [Journal of Literary Studies], No. 5, 1998.

Tong, Qingbing (ed.), *Xiandai xinli meixue* 现代心理美学 [Modern Psychological Aesthetics], Beijing: China Social Sciences Press, 1993.

Wang, Bangxiong, *Zhongguo zhexue lunji* 中国哲学论集 [Collected Essays on Chinese Philosophy], Taipei: Taiwan Xuesheng Book Company, 1983.

Wang, Fuzhi, *Zhuangzi jie* 庄子解 [The Book of Zhuangzi Interpreted] Beijing: Zhonghua Book Company, 1976.

Wang, Fuzhi, *Zhangzi zhengmeng zhu* 张子正蒙注 [*Zhang Zai's Works* Annotated], Beijing: Zhonghua Book Company, 1975.

Wang, Guowei, *Wang Guowei wenji* 王国维文集 [Collected Works of Wang Guowei], Vols. 1–4, eds. Yao Ganming & Wang Yan, Beijing: Zhongguo Wenshi Press, 1997.

Wang, Guowei, *Wang Guowei wenxue meixue lunzhuji* 王国维文学美学论著集 [Wang Guowei's Anthology on Literature and Aesthetics], ed. Zhou Xishan, Taiyuan: Beiyue Wenyi Press, 1987.

Wang, Guowei, *Wang Guowei meilun wenxuan* 王国维美论文选 [Wang Guowei's Selected Essays on Beauty], ed. Liu Gangqiang, Changsha: Hunan Renmin Press, 1987.

Wang, Guowei, *Wang Guowei xueshu wenhua suibi* 王国维学术文化随笔 [Selected Essays of Wang Guowei], ed. Fo Chu, Beijing: China Youth Press, 1996.

Wang, Huanbiao (ed.), *Mozi jigu* 墨子集诂 [Collected Annotations to The Book of Mozi], Shanghai: Shanghai Guji Press, 2005.

Wang, Keping, *Zouxiang kuawenhua meixue* 走向跨文化美学 [Towards a Transcultural Aesthetics], Beijing: Zhonghua Book Company, 2002.

Wang, Zhimin & Fang Shan, *Fojiao yu meixue* 佛教与美学 [Buddhism and Aesthetics], Shenyang: Liaoning Renmin Press, 1989.

Wang, Peiji (ed.), *Yingguo zuojia lun wenxue* 英国作家论文学 [British Writers on Literature], Beijing: Sanlian Bookshop, 1985.

Wang, Shijing, *Lu Xun zaoqi wupian lunwen zhushi* 鲁迅早期五篇论文注释 [Annotations to Five Early Essays by Lu Xun], Tianjin: Tianjin Renmin Press, 1978.

Wang, Ming, *Daojia yu Daojiao sixiang yanjiu* 道家与道教思想研究 [Studies of Daoism as a Philosophy and a Religion], Beijing: China Sciences Press, 1987.

Wang, Wenjin (ed.), *Li ji yi jie* 礼记译解 [The Book of Rites Paraphrased and Annotated], Beijing: Zhonghua Book Company, 2001.

Wang, Xiaoyu, *Zhuangzi neipian xinjie* 庄子内篇新解 [New Interpretations of the Inner Chapters in The Book of Zhuangzi], Changsha: Yuelu Bookshop, 1983.

Wen, Rumin, *Zhongguo xiandai wenxue piping shi* 中国现代文学批评史 [A Critical History of Modern Chinese Literature], Beijing: Peking University Press, 2000.

Xu, Fuguan, *Zhongguo yishu jingshen* 中国艺术精神 [The Spirit of Chinese Art], Shenyang: Chunfeng Wenyi Press, 1987.

Xunzi, *Xunzi* 荀子 [The Book of Xunzi], Guiyang: Guizhou Renmin Press, 1995.

Yan, Yu, *Canglang shi hua* 沧浪诗话 [Canglang's Poetic Discourse], Beijing: Renmin Wenxue Press, 1983.

Yang, Anlun, *Zhongguo gudai jingshen xiangxiangxue--Zhuangzi sixiang yu zhongguo yishu* 中国古代精神现象学: 庄子思想与中国艺术 [The Phenomenology of Spirit in Ancient China: Zhuangzi's Thought and Chinese Art], Changchun: Northeast Normal University Press, 1993.

Yang, Bojun (ed.), *Lun yü yizhu* 论语译注 [The Confucian Analects Paraphrased and Annotated], Beijing: Zhonghua Book Company, 1988.

Yao, Kefu (ed.), *Renjian cihua ji pinglun huibian* 人间词话及评论汇编 [Renjian Poetic Remarks and Selected Essays on Wang Guowei's Poetics], Beijing: Shumu Wenxian Press, 1983.

Ye, Jiaying, "*Dui Renjian cihua zhong jingjie yici zhi yijie de tantao*" 对人间词话中境界一词之义界的探讨 [About the Definitions of "*Jingjie*" as a Term in Wang Guowei's Renjian Poetic Remarks], in Yao Kefu (ed.), *Renjian cihua ji pinglun huibian* 人间词话及评论汇编 [Renjian Poetic Remarks and Selected Essays on Wang Guowei's Poetics], Beijing: Shumu Wenxian Press, 1983, pp. 147–159.

Ye, Jiaying, *Wang Guowei jiqi wenxue piping* 王国维及其文学批评 [Wang Guowei and His Literary Criticism], Shijiazhuang: Hebei Jiaoyu Press, 1997.

Ye, Lang, *Zhongguo meixueshi dagang* 中国美学史大纲 [An Outlined History of Chinese Aesthetics], Shanghai: Shanghai Renmin Press, 1987.

Yin, Xieli (ed.), *Baihua Jingang jing and Tan jing* 白话金刚经与坛经 [The Diamond Sutra and The Sutra of Hui Neng Paraphrased in Modern Chinese], Shijiazhuang: Hebei Renmin Press, 1992.

Zeng, Qingrui, "*Dui zhongguo jindai sixiang qimeng yundong de xingongxian*" 对中国近代思想启蒙运动的新贡献 [A New Contribution to Modern Intellectual Enlightenment Movement in China], in *Lu Xun yanjiu* 鲁迅研究 [Lu Xun Studies], Vol. 1, Beijing: China Social Sciences Press, 1981.

Zeng, Zuyin, *Zhongguo fojiao yu meixue* 中国佛教与美学 [Chinese Buddhism and Aesthetics], Wuhan: Central China Normal University Press, 1991.

Zhang, Bennan, *Wang Guowei meixue sixiang yanjiu* 王国维美学思想研究 [A Study of Wang Guowei's Aesthetics], Taiwan: Wenjin Press, 1992.

Zhang Dainian wenji 张岱年文集 [Collected Works of Zhang Dainian], Beijing: Tsinghua University Press, 1989.

Zhang, Dainian, *Zhongguo zhexue dagang* 中国哲学大纲 [An Outline of Chinese Philosophy], Beijing: China Social Sciences Press, 1982.

Zheng, Jiewen, *Zhongguo Moxue tongshi* 中国墨学通史 [A General History of Mohist Studies in China], Beijing: Renmin Press, 2006.

Zhong, Zhaopeng, *Kongzi yanjiu* 孔子研究 [A Study of Confucius], Beijing: China Social Sciences Press, 1983.

Zhou, Manjiang (ed.), *Shi jing* 诗经 [The Book of Poetry], Shanghai: Shanghai Guji Press, 1980.

Zhou, Zhenfu (ed.), *Wenxin diaolong jinyi* 文心雕龙今译 [A New Paraphrased Version of the Dragon-Carving and the Literary Mind], Beijing: Zhonghua Book Company, 1986.

Zhu, Guangqian, *Zhu Guangqian meixue wenji* 朱光潜美学文集 [Collected Works of Zhu Guangqian on Aesthetics], Vol. II, Shanghai: Shanghai Wenyi Press, 1982.

Zhu, Guangqian, *Wenyi xinlixue* 文艺心理学 [Psychology of Literature and Art], Shanghai: Kaiming Bookshop, 1936.

Zhu, Guangqian, *Tan mei* 谈美 [Letters on Beauty], Shanghai: Kaiming Bookshop, 1932.

Zhu, Guangqian, *Shi lun* 诗论 [A Study of Chinese Poetics], Chongqing: Guomin Books Press, 1943; revised version, Beijing: Zhonghua Book Company, 1948.

Zhu, Xi, *Sishu zhangju jizhu* 四书章句集注 [Annotations of the Four Books], Beijing: Zhonghua Book Company, 1983.

Zhu, Xi (ed.), *Shi jing jizhuan* 诗经集传 [Annotations and Comments on The Book of Poetry], in *Sishu wujing* 四书五经 [The Four Books and Five Classics], Vols. 1–3, Tianjin: Guji Bookshop, 1990.

Zhu, Xi, *Zhuzi yulei* 朱子语类 [The Sayings of Zhuzi], Beijing: Zhonghua Book Company, 1986.

Zu, Baoquan, *Wenxin diaolong xuan*xi 文心雕龙选析 [Analysis of Selected Texts from Dragon-Carving and the Literary Mind], Hefei: Anhui Education Press, 1985.

Zuo, Qiuming, *Zuo zhuan* 左传 [Zuo Qiuming's Commentary on the Spring and Autumn Annals], see Yang Bojun (ed.), *Chun qiu Zuo zhuan zhu* 春秋左传注 [Zuo Qiuming's Commentary on the Spring and Autumn Annals Annotated], Beijing: Zhonghua Book Company, 1984.

English Materials

Adorno, Theodor W., *Aesthetic Theory*, trans. Robert Hullot-Kentor, Minneapolis: University of Minnesota Press, 1997.

Anderson, Albert, et al. (ed.), *Mythos and Logos*, Amsterdam and New York: Rodopi, 2004.

Arnold, Matthew, *Essays in Criticism*, London: Dent, 1964.

Bargeliotes, L. C., et al. (eds.), *Religion, Politics and Suffering: Intercultural Dimensions of Challenges for Philosophy*, Hellas: Ennoia Books, 2004.

Bell, Clive, *Art*, London: Chatto & WIndus, 1947.

Benitez, Eugenio (ed.), *Before Pangaea: New Essays in Transcultural Aesthetics*, Sydney: University of Sydney Press, 2005.

Burke, Edmund, *A Philosophical Enquiry into the Origin of Our Ideas of the Sublime and Beautiful*, London: Routledge & Kegan Paul, 1958.

Cassirer, Ernest, *An Essay on Man*, New Haven and London: Yale University Press, reprinted in 1975.

Chan, Wing-tsit, *A Source Book in Chinese Philosophy*, Princeton, NJ: Princeton University Press, 1973.
Chen, Jingpan, *Confucius as a Teacher*, Beijing: Foreign Languages Press, 1990.
Cheng, Chung-Ying & Nicholas Bunnin (eds.), *Contemporary Chinese Philosophy*, Oxford: Blackwell, 2002.
Confucius, *The Analects*, trans. D. C. Lau, London: Penguin Books, 1983.
Confucius, *Analects of Confucius*, trans. Lai Bo & Xia Yuhe, Beijing: Sinolingua Press, 1994.
Chuang-tzu, *A Taoist Classic: Chuang-tzu*, trans. Fung Yu-lan, Beijing: Foreign Languages Press, 1989.
Creel, Herrlee G., *What Is Taoism?* Chicago and London: The University of Chicago Press, 1970.
Danto, Arthur C., "The Artworld," in *The Journal of Philosophy*, 1964, pp. 571–584.
Danto, Arthur C., *After the End of Art: Contemporary Art and the Pale of History*, Princeton: Princeton University Press, 1997.
Dewey, John, *Art as Experience*, New York: Milton Balch, 1934.
Ducaase, C. J. *The Philosophy of Art*, New York: The Dial Press, 1929.
Eagleton, Terry, *The Idea of Culture*, Oxford: Blackwel, 2004.
Einstein, Albert, 'Principles of Research', in *Ideas and Opinions*, ed. Carl Seelig, trans. Sonja Barmann, New York: WINGS Books, 1954.
Ember, Carol R. & Ember, Melvin, *Cultural Anthropology*, Upper Saddle River, New Jersey: Prentice Hall, 1985.
Emerson, Ralph Waldo, *Emerson: Essays*, Tianjin: Tianjin Education Press, 2004; Also See *The Collected Works of Ralph Waldo Emerson*, Oxford: Oxford University Press, 1971.
Ficinus, Marsilius, *De Amore: Commentarium in Convivium Platonis*, trans. Liang Zhonghe & Li Yang, Shanghai: East China Normal University Press, 2012.
Fung, Yu-lan, *Selected Philosophical Writings of Fung Yu-lan*, Beijing: Foreign Languages Press, 1991.
Graham, A. C., *Disputers of Tao*, La Salle, Illinois: Open Court, 1991.
Guthrie, W. K. C., *A History of Greek Philosophy*, Vol. IV, London: Cambridge University Press, 1975.
Han Fei Tzu, *Basic Writings*, trans. Burton Watson, New York and London: Columbia University Press, 1966.
He, Zhaowu, et al., *An Intellectual History of China*, Beijing: Foreign Languages Press, 1991.
Hong, Yingming, *Caigen tan* (Tending the Roots of Wisdom), trans. Paul White, Beijing: New World Press, 2001.
Huang, Maolin (tr.), *The Sutra of Hui Neng*, Changsha: Hunan Press, 1996.

Hussain, Mazhar & Wilkinson, Robert (eds.), *The Pursuit of Comparative Aesthetics*, Farnham: Ashgate, 2006.
Hsün, Tzu, *Basic Writings*, trans. Burton Watson, New York and London: Columbia University Press, 1963.
Jaspers, Karl, *The Origin and Goal of History*, London: Routledge & Kegan Paul, 1953.
Jung, Carl, *The Collected Works of C. G. Jung*, ed. F. F. C. Hull, Princeton, New Jersey: Princeton University Press, 1969.
Kant, Immanuel, *Critique of Pure Reason*, trans. Norman Kempt Smith, London: Macmillan Press, 1933.
Kant, Immanuel, *Critique of Judgment*, trans. J. B. Bernard, New York: Hafner Press, 1951.
Kaufman, Walter (ed. & tr.), *The Portable Nietzsche*, New York: Penguin Books USA Inc., 1976.
Krieger, Silke & Trauzettel, Rolf (ed.), *Confucianism and the Modernization of China*. Mainz: v. Hase & Koehler Verlang, 1991.
Lao Zi, *Dao De Jing*, trans. Wang Keping, Beijing: Foreign Languages Press, 2008.
Legge, James (tr.), *The Four Books*, Changsha: Hunan Press, 1995.
Legge, James (tr.), Record of Music, in *The Sacred Books of China* (The Li Ki, Book xvii. Yo Ki), Delhi et al.: Motilal Banarsidass, reprinted in 1976.
Levi, Albert W. & Smith, Ralph A. *Art Education: A Critical Necessity*, Urbana and Chicago: University of Illinois Press, 1991.
Li, Zehou, *The Path of Beauty*, trans. Gong Lizeng, Oxford: Oxford University Press, 1994.
Li, Zehou & Jane Cauvel, *Four Essays on Aesthetics*, Lanham et al.: Lexington Books, 2006.
Li, Zehou, *The Chinese Aesthetic Tradition*, trans. M. B. Samei, Honollulu: University of Hawaii Press, 2010.
Liu, Xie, *Dragon-Carving and the Literary Mind*, trans. Yang Guobin, Beijing: Foreign Languages Press, 2003.
Liu, Xiaogan, *Classifying the Zhuangzi Chapters*, trans. William E. Savage, Michigan: The University of Michigan Press, 1994.
Lynn, Richard John (tr.), *The Classic of Changes*, New York: Columbia University Press, 1994.
Marx, Karl, *Economic and Philosophic Manuscripts of 1844*, trans. Martin Mulligan, Moscow: Progress Publishers, 1959.
McCready, Stuart (ed.), *The Discovery of Happiness*, London: MQ Publications Limited, 2001.
Mo, Tzu, *Basic Writings*, trans. Burton Watson, New York and London: Columbia University Press, 1966.

Mote, Frederick W., *Intellectual Foundations of China*, New York: Alfred A. Knopf, 1971.
Nietzsche, Friedrich, *Aurore*, Paris: Gallimard, 1980.
Nietzsche, F., *The Portable Nietzsche*, trans. & ed. Walter Kaufmann, London: Penguin Books, 1976.
Northrop, F. S. C., *The Meeting of East and West*, New York: MacMillan Company, 1960, 1st ed., 1946.
Pascal, *Pensées*, Paris: Librairie Générals Française, 1962.
Plato, *Symposium*, trans. W. R. M. Lamb, Cambridge and London: Harvard University Press, 1996.
Plato, *Republic*, trans. Paul Shorey, Cambridge and London: Harvard University Press, 1994.
Plotinus, *The Enneads*, trans. Stephen MacKenna, London: Penguin Books, 1991.
Rosen, Stanley, *Plato's Symposium*, New Haven: Yale University Press, 1987.
Ross, Stephen David (ed.), *Art and Its Significance*, Albany: State University of New York Press, 1994.
Schellekens, Elisabeth, *Aesthetics and Morality*, London: Continuum, 2007.
Schiller, Friedrich, *On the Aesthetic Education of Man*, trans. E. M. Wilkinson & L. A. Willoughby, Oxford: Oxford University Press, 1967.
Schilpp, P. A. (ed.), *The Philosophy of John Dewey*, New York: Tudor, 1951.
Schopenhauer, Arthur, *The World as Will and Idea*, trans. R. B. Haldane & J. Kemp, London: Routledge & Kegan Paul, 1883, reprinted in 1964.
Schopenhauer, Arthur, *The Art of Literature*, trans. T. Bailey Saunders, London & New York: Swan Sonnensche & The MacMillan Press, 1897.
Schwartz, Benjamin I., *The World of Thought in Ancient China*, Cambridge and London: Harvard University Press, 1985.
Shelley, Percey Bysshe, "A Defense of Poetry," in Hazard Adams (ed.), *Critical Theory Since Plato*, New York: Harcourt Brace Jovanoich, 1971.
Shusterman, Richard, *Pragmatist Aesthetics: Living Beauty, Rethinking Art*, Rowman & Littlefield, 2000.
Sparshott, P. E., *The Structure of Aesthetics*, Toronto: University of Toronto Press, 1963.
Toynbee, Arnold, *Mankind and Mother Earth: A Narrative History of the World*, Oxford: Oxford University Press, 1976.
Toynbee, Arnold & Daisaku Ikeda, *Choose Life: A Dialogue*, Oxford: Oxford University Press, 1977.
Voegelin, Eric, *The Ecumenical Age*, Columbia: University of Missouri Press, 2000.
Volpe, Galvano Della, *Critique of Taste*, London: Western Printing Service Ltd., 1978.

Wang, Guowei, *Wang Kuo-wei's Jen-Chien Tzi-Hua: A Study in Chinese Literary Criticism*, trans. Rickett, Adele Austin, Hong Kong: Hong Kong University Press, 1977.
Wang, Keping, *The Classic of the Dao: A New Investigation*, Beijing: Foreign Languages Press, 1998, reprinted in 2004.
Wang, Keping, *Reading the Dao: A Thematic Inquiry*, London: Continuum, 2011.
Wang, Keping, "Confucius' Expectations of Poetry," in *The Social Sciences in China* (English), Vol. 4, Winter 1996, pp. 134–146.
Wang, Kuo-wei, *Poetic Remarks in the Human World*, trans. Ching-I Tu, Taiwan: Chung Hwa Book Company, 1970.
Wasten, Burton (tr.), *The Lotus Sutra*, New York: Columbia University Press, 1993.
Whitehead, Alfred N., *The Aims of Education*, New York: Mentor Books, 1960.
Whitehead, Alfred N., *Modes of Thought*, Cambridge: Cambridge University Press, 1956.
Whitehead, Alfred N., *Adventures of Ideas*, New York: Mentor Books, 1932.
Xu, Yuanchong (tr.), *The Book of Poetry*, Changsha: Hunan Press, 1994.
Xunzi, *Xunzi*, trans. John Knoblock, Beijing: Foreign Languages Press, 2003.
Zhang, Dainian, *Key Concepts in Chinese Philosophy*, trans. & ed. Edmund Ryden, Beijing: Foreign Languages Press, 2002.
Zhuangzi, *The Taoist Classic: Chuang-tzu*, trans. Fung Yu-lan, Beijing: Foreign Languages Press, 1989.
Zhuangzi, *The Zhuangzi*, trans. Wang Rongpei, Beijing: Foreign Languages Press, 1999.

Author Index

A
Adorno, Theodor W. (阿多诺), 393
Aristotle (亚里士多德), 111, 184

B
Ban Jieyu (班婕妤), 256, 262
Bell, Clive (贝尔), 313, 418, 419
Bullough, Edward (布洛), 312, 414
Burke, Edmund (博克), 347, 354
Byron, George Gordon (拜伦), 364–367, 369–371, 379, 380, 384–386

C
Cai Yi (蔡仪), 310
Cai Yuanpei (蔡元培), 309, 314, 329
Cao Cao (曹操), 261
Cao Pi (曹丕), 256
Cao Zhi (曹植), 256, 271, 272
Cheng Hao (程颢), 8, 147, 300
Chen Guying (陈鼓应), 3, 74, 75, 87, 94, 103, 104, 270

Cheng Yi (程颐), 8, 12, 296, 300
Chen Jingpan (陈景磐), 219
Chen Wangdao (陈望道), 4, 310
Coleridge, Samuel T. (柯勒律治), 369
Confucius (Kongzi 孔子), 10, 35, 39, 43, 45, 52–56, 66, 169, 178, 217–223, 229–234, 235–237, 248, 249, 277–280, 288, 289, 294, 296, 297, 301, 318, 326, 334, 391

D
Danto, Arthur C. (丹托), 141–144, 405
Deng Yizhe (邓以蛰), 310–312
Dewey, John (杜威), 64, 187, 191, 211, 423
Dickie, George (迪基), 405
Dong Zhongshu (董仲舒), 2–5, 70
Duchamp, Michel (杜尚), 141
Du Fu (杜甫), 344

E

Einstein, Albert (爱因斯坦), 185, 213, 214
Emerson, Ralph Waldo (爱默生), 1, 137, 394

F

Fan Shoukang (范寿康), 310
Feng Zikai (丰子恺), 310–312
Ficinus, Marsilius (斐奇诺), 111, 114
Freud, Sigmund (弗洛伊德), 211, 418
Fung Yu-lan (Feng Youlan 冯友兰), 3, 20, 66, 70, 88, 89, 93, 96, 100, 103, 146, 231, 232, 237, 249
Fu Tong (傅统), 310
Fu Yi (傅毅), 256, 258, 287

G

Gao Heng (高亨), 74
Godwin, William (葛德文), 369
Goethe, Johann Wolfgang von (歌德), 15
Guo Pu (郭璞), 260

H

Hayek, Friedrich A. (哈耶克), 211
Hegel, G.W.F. (黑格尔), 184, 196, 211
Heidegger, Martin (海德格尔), 123, 194, 211
He Yan (何晏), 259, 261
Hong Ren (弘忍), 149, 151, 152
Huang Kan (黄侃), 257, 262
Hui Neng (惠能), 136, 138, 149, 151–156

J

Jaspers, Karl (雅思贝尔斯), 29, 108

Jia Baoyu (贾宝玉), 339
Jian'an (建安), 256–259, 261, 262
Jiang Yan (江淹), 355
Ji Kang (嵇康), 259, 261, 271, 272
Jung, Carl (荣格), 313, 418, 419

K

Kant, Immanuel (康德), 186, 191, 193, 199, 209, 211, 307, 312, 323, 326, 333, 340, 343, 347, 358, 383, 418
Keats, John (济慈), 369
Kong Anguo (孔安国), 224, 228, 229
Kong Yiji (孔乙己), 387
Kuang Heng (匡衡), 291

L

Laozi/Laotzu (老子), 66–81, 83, 86, 123, 126, 127, 169, 259, 260, 269, 270, 275, 318, 335
Legge, James (理雅各), 5–8, 10, 11, 39, 54–56, 75, 85, 176, 177, 221, 222, 231, 232, 234, 296, 334
Lermontov, Mikhail (莱蒙托夫), 367, 379, 385
Liang Qichao (梁启超), 314, 363, 389, 390
Liang Shanbo (梁山泊), 105
Li Anzhai (李安宅), 310
Li Bai (李白), 270
Li Duwei (李都尉), 262
Liezi (列子), 94, 96
Li Ling (李陵), 256
Ling Fei (令飞), 364
Lipps, Theodor (里普斯), 312, 353
Liu Bang (刘邦), 25, 26, 31
Liu Che (刘彻), 27, 34
Liu Gangji (刘纲纪), 233, 249, 265, 310

Liu Renhang (刘仁航), 309
Liu Xie (刘勰), 253–256, 258–269, 271–274, 391
Liu Xizai (刘熙载), 356
Liu Zhen (刘祯), 256, 271, 272
Li Zehou (李泽厚), 14–18, 159, 183–186, 189–195, 197–199, 201, 202, 204, 206–208, 210, 212, 213, 233, 265, 310, 313, 351, 378, 394–396, 405, 407–413, 415–423
Li Zhi (李贽), 223, 271
Locke, John (洛克), 369
Lü Cheng (吕澂), 310
Lu Ji (陆机), 268
Lu Xun (鲁迅), 306, 361–384, 386–392

M

Mao Heng (毛亨), 283–285
Marx, Karl (马克思), 17, 194, 211, 313, 418, 421, 422
Mei Cheng (枚乘), 256, 258
Mencius (Mengzi 孟子), 2, 5–7, 20, 35, 70, 150, 177, 248, 256, 278
Mickiewicz, Adam (密茨凯维支), 367, 379
Min Ze (敏泽), 310
Mou Zongsan (牟宗三), 9, 313
Mozi/Motzu (墨子), 169, 236–242, 244, 248–251, 318, 391

N

Nietzsche, Friedrich (尼采), 82, 132, 211, 212, 307, 320, 323, 342, 343, 345, 356, 375
Northrop, F.S.C. (诺思罗普), 48–52, 64

O

Ouyang Xiu (欧阳修), 355

P

Pascal (帕斯卡尔), 107, 133
Piaget, Jean (皮亚杰), 211, 313
Plato (柏拉图), 107–112, 114, 124–126, 129–131, 380, 381
Pushkin, Alexander (普希金), 367, 379, 385

Q

Qian Mu (钱穆), 178
Qu Yuan (屈原), 344, 380

R

Rauschenberg Robert (劳森伯格), 141, 423
Rawls, John (罗尔斯), 211
Rosen, Stanley (罗森), 125
Rousseau, Jean-Jacques (卢梭), 368, 369
Ruan Ji (阮籍), 259, 261

S

Sándor, Petöfi (裴多菲), 367, 379, 385
Schiller, Friedrich (席勒), 307, 312, 323, 329, 333, 334, 341, 357, 358
Schopenhauer, Arthur (叔本华), 120, 213, 307, 323, 326, 334, 336, 337, 340, 342, 343, 345, 353
Shelley, Percey Bysshe (雪莱), 365, 367, 369, 379–381, 384, 385
Shen Xiu (神秀), 149–153

Shuduan (叔段), 283–285
Shusterman, Richard (舒斯特曼), 64
Sikong Tu (司空图), 270
Sima Qian (司马迁), 26–28, 34, 100
Smith, Ralph A. (史密斯), 315, 316
Song Rongzi (宋荣子), 93, 94
Su Shi (苏轼), 271, 344

T
Tang Junyi (唐君毅), 317
Tao Qian (陶潜), 270, 344
Tao Yuanming (陶渊明), 146, 394
Teng Shouyao (滕守尧), 315
Thomé Fang/Fang Dongmei (方东美), 163–166, 169–171, 173, 176, 179, 317–319
Tong Qingbing (童庆炳), 255, 262–264, 267, 268
Toynbee, Arnold (汤因比), 13, 25, 26, 29–31, 33, 35, 46

V
Voegelin, Eric (沃格林), 13, 32

W
Wang Changling (王昌龄), 356
Wang Fuzhi (王夫之), 8, 40, 61, 87, 88, 103, 230
Wang Guowei (王国维), 303, 304, 306, 307, 314, 323–325, 327–332, 334, 336–358, 389, 392, 396, 423
Wang Shizhen (王士祯), 356, 357
Warhol, Andy (沃霍尔), 141, 405, 423
Wasten, Burton (沃森), 145
Weber, Max (韦伯), 211
Wei Meng (韦孟), 256, 258

Whitehead, Alfred N. (怀特海), 164, 167, 168, 180, 181
Wittgenstein, Ludwig (维特根斯坦), 161
Wordsworth, William (华兹华斯), 369

X
Xie Lingyun (谢灵运), 355
Xiong Shili (熊十力), 297–299
Xuan Zi (宣子), 218, 219
Xu Fuguan (徐复观), 317
Xu Gan (徐幹), 256
Xunzi/Hsün Tzu (荀子), 99, 236, 242–251, 326, 391

Y
Yan Yu (严羽), 356, 357
Ye Jiaying (叶嘉莹), 349, 351, 356
Ye Lang (叶朗), 310
You Shi (优施), 256

Z
Zhang Dainian (张岱年), 304
Zhang Heng (张衡), 258, 271–273
Zhang Hua (张华), 271, 272
Zhang Xie (张协), 271, 272
Zhang Zai (张载), 8, 22, 40, 61, 289
Zheng Xuan (郑玄), 226
Zhuanggong (庄公), 283
Zhuang Zhou (庄周), 102–105, 398
Zhuangzi/Chuang Tzu (庄子), 2–5, 79–81, 86–88, 90–101, 103–107, 115–122, 124, 126–130, 138, 150, 175, 259, 260, 270, 335, 340, 356, 396–398, 401
Zhu Guangqian (朱光潜), 310–312, 353

Zhu Xi (朱熹), 193, 224, 225, 227, 228, 234, 277–291, 293–296, 298–301, 327, 391
Zhu Yingtai (祝英台), 105
Zi Gong (子贡), 10, 220
Zi Xia (子夏), 220
Zong Baihua (宗白华), 304, 311, 312, 403
Zuo Si (左思), 271, 272

Subject Index

A

abandoning knowledge (*qu zhi* 去知), 99
admonish [through poetry] (*yuan* 怨), 222, 223, 230
aesthetic component, 51, 52
aesthetic education *(mei yu* 美育), 222, 229, 307, 309, 314, 324, 329, 330, 332–335, 341, 358
aesthetic exaltation of intellectual intuition and spiritual freedom (*yue zhi yue shen* 悦志悦神), 207
aesthetic experience pleasant to the ear and the eye (*yue er yue mu* 悦耳悦目), 206
aesthetic feeling pleasant to mind and mood (*yue xin yue yi* 悦心悦意), 207
aesthetic metaphysics, 185, 198, 199, 208–212
aesthetic wisdom, 112, 208, 211, 320
all things/myriad things *(wan wu* 万物), 2, 3, 5, 20–22, 36, 56, 61, 66, 68, 69, 85, 87, 88, 90, 94, 98, 100–102, 104, 127, 136, 145, 153, 155–158, 169, 170, 175, 176, 206, 251, 278, 347, 397–401
all under/below heaven (*xian-xia* 天下), 2, 11–13, 22, 25, 26, 30–32, 118, 287
appropriate measure (*du* 度), 132, 185, 193, 195–197, 202, 203, 205, 207, 211, 212
the artistic realm' (*yi shu jing jie* 艺术境界), 167, 173, 403
attachedness (*youdai* 有待), 102

B

the beautiful (*yo mei* 优美), 17, 77, 104, 109, 110, 112–114, 136, 147, 160, 161, 167, 196, 197, 204–207, 209, 211, 241, 242, 249, 281, 307, 329, 330, 332, 334, 337, 340, 341, 346–348,

353, 354, 379, 384, 394–396, 401, 416, 417, 422
beauty *(mei* 美), 3, 4, 6, 14, 104–106, 108–114, 124–126, 128–132, 135–139, 157, 160, 170, 175, 181, 196, 197, 206, 219, 220, 226, 233, 246, 247, 270–273, 281, 290, 293, 308, 310, 311, 318–320, 330, 332, 333, 335, 346, 347, 371, 382, 384, 387, 393–395, 398, 401, 406, 409, 411, 416, 418–422
beauty in itself, 109, 114, 115, 124–126, 129, 197
beauty ladder, 107–111, 124–126, 128, 129
be spring with all things *(yu wu wei chun* 与物为春), 335
beyond the distinction between Chinese and Western learning *(xue wu zhong xi* 学无中西), 306
breathing system *(qigong* 气功), 128, 407

C

ci poetry *(ci* 词), 323
cognitive development, 107, 108, 124, 129, 313
collective unconscious, 313, 419
communicate [through poetry] *(qun* 群), 223, 230
compassion *(ceyin* 恻隐), 26, 31, 33, 35, 37, 51, 198
complain without being angry with it *(yuan er bu nu* 怨而不怒), 234, 273
complete detachedness *(wudai* 无待), 102
conflict is to be harmonized and resolved *(chou bi hé er jie* 仇必和而解), 40

Confucianism *(ru jia* 儒家), 2, 5, 8, 9, 11, 23, 36, 38, 52, 53, 70, 71, 82, 150, 164–166, 169, 170, 173, 176, 178, 179, 183, 184, 186, 187, 189, 190, 198, 199, 209, 211, 217, 236, 237, 242, 248, 277, 278, 286, 294, 308, 318, 334, 398, 399, 418
contemplate things in view of what they are *(yi wu guan wu* 以物观物), 145
contemplative life, 114, 130, 131
correct inclusiveness *(zhezhong* 折衷), 255, 264–266
cosmic state of being *(tian di jing jie* 天地境界), 175
create the beautiful by means of the measure *(yi du li mei* 依度立美), 205
the creative state *(zao jing* 造境), 352
cultivation of the personality *(xiu shen* 修身), 11, 12
cultural-psychological formation *(wenhua xinli jiegou* 文化心理结构), 16, 18, 19, 190, 198, 203, 204, 207, 208, 211, 212, 313, 411, 414
culture *(wen hua* 文化), 2, 15, 17, 18, 26, 28, 31, 33, 35, 38, 48, 50–52, 59–64, 71, 72, 79, 106, 135, 142, 164–166, 168–173, 177, 180, 185, 186, 189, 191, 192, 195, 197–199, 201, 204, 206, 207, 212, 214, 236, 248, 253, 304, 305, 307, 308, 311, 316–319, 324, 325, 328, 329, 340, 342, 357, 359, 363–366, 372–380, 383, 390, 391, 395, 399, 415, 421
culture of rites and music *(li yue wen hua* 礼乐文化), 37, 235

D

Daoism as a philosophy (*Dao Xue* 道学), 66, 79, 135
Daoism as a religion (*Dao Jiao* 道教), 66, 135
Daoism/Taoism (*dao jia* 道家), 2, 3, 11, 46, 47, 65, 66, 71, 80, 108, 119, 127, 130, 131, 137, 150, 178, 211, 259, 260, 269, 312, 336, 402
Dao of Heaven (*tian zhi dao* 天之道), 4, 67–69, 72–74
Dao of man (*ren zhi dao* 人之道), 67–69, 73, 83
Dao of the sage (*sheng ren zhi dao* 圣人之道), 69, 70, 72, 73, 83, 116
Dao/Tao (*dao* 道), 2, 66, 86, 225, 261, 287, 363, 366, 368
describe lofty aspirations (*shi yan zhi* 诗言志), 391
the descriptive state (*xie jing* 写境), 352
dharma (*fa* 法), 135, 140, 148, 151, 153, 156, 158, 160
dhyāna (*channa* 禅那), 136, 138, 143, 145–147, 157
dhyāna of "Thus Come One" (*rulai chan* 如来禅), 145
dhyāna (Zen/*Chan* 禅), 137, 140, 141, 144, 145, 158, 160
divine wisdom, 72, 73, 114
divinus amore, 111, 114
drawing pleasure from bitter and harsh conditions (*ku zhong zuo le* 苦中作乐), 403

E

ecumenism (*xianxian zhuyi* 天下主义), 13, 25, 26, 29, 31–38, 45, 46
elegance (*qingli* 清丽), 269, 271–273, 346
emotional root (*qing benti* 情本体), 36, 185, 197–199, 205–207, 209–212
emotion/feeling (*qing* 情), 17, 18, 36, 67, 82, 90, 92, 95, 124, 128, 133, 137, 159, 169–171, 180, 185, 188, 189, 191, 196, 198, 199, 206–208, 232, 243, 245, 247, 260, 263, 264, 267–270, 274, 282, 318, 319, 331, 334, 342, 343, 368, 376, 382, 393, 394, 396, 397, 401, 402, 407, 412–415, 419, 420
emotio-reasonable inseparableness (*qingli bufen* 情理不分), 184, 188
the empirical changes into the transcendental (*jingyan bian xianyan* 经验变先验), 184, 193
enhance the good through the beautiful (*yimei chushan* 以美储善), 18
enlighten…by virtue of education (*ren wen jiao hua* 人文教化), vi
enslaved by things (*ren wei wu yi* 人为物役), 119, 120, 335
epistemic agency, 114
equalize all things in the universe (*qi wu* 齐物), 397
Eros, 16, 113, 198, 209
erotic agency, 111
ethicalness (*lunli xing* 伦理性), 184, 186, 191
events (*shi* 事), 22, 29, 31, 189, 190, 197, 199, 202, 210, 214, 218, 249, 285, 286, 304, 314, 338, 350, 351, 391, 407, 415, 422
excursion (*you* 游), 3, 86–88, 91–100, 106, 121, 337, 398, 402, 403
express emotions and feelings (*shi yuan qing* 诗缘情), 391
expressing aspirations in words (*yan zhi* 言志), 268

extension of knowledge (*zhi zhi* 致知), 11, 12
external things (*wai wu* 外物), 61, 99, 115, 119, 120, 124, 128, 143, 151, 335

F

fate (*ming* 命), 82, 199, 237, 326, 327, 376, 385, 410
feeling and reason (*qing li* 情理), 168
feeling modesty and complaisance (*cirang zhi xin* 辞让之心), 278
feeling of approving and disapproving (*shifei zhi xin* 是非之心), 278
feeling of commiseration (*ceyin zhi xin* 恻隐之心), 278
feeling of shame and dislike (*xiuwu zhi xin* 羞恶之心), 278
feelings (*ganqing* 感情), 19, 22, 74, 109, 138, 194, 198, 219, 222, 225, 230, 242–244, 246, 255, 267–269, 275, 279, 284, 291, 292, 300, 324, 336, 346, 349–352, 355–357, 368, 383, 385, 389, 391, 395, 407, 419
ferinus amore, 111, 114
following the spontaneity in nature (*shunying ziran* 顺应自然), 137
form a ternion with Heaven and Earth (*yu tiandi can* 与天地参), 176
free appreciating of beauty (*ziyou shenmei* 自由审美), 201
free intuition of the world (*ziyou zhiguan* 自由直观), 201
fusion of emotion and scene (*qing jing jiao rong* 情景交融), 312

G

gatha (ji偈), 135, 136, 148–152, 156

gentle and kind character training (*wen rou dun hou* 温柔敦厚), 218
gentleman (*jun zi* 君子), 41, 43–45, 54–56, 222, 224, 230, 231, 234, 242, 243, 246, 265, 267, 334
gentlemanship (*jun zi ren ge* 君子人格), 44, 55
golden mean (*zhong yong* 中庸), 52, 188, 189, 233, 246, 263
good life, 5, 107, 108, 113, 115, 116, 124, 126, 128, 130, 133
goodness (*shan* 善), 112, 113, 129, 155, 196, 246, 247, 290, 308, 310, 327, 330, 333, 420
gracefulness (*yarun* 雅润), 269, 271–273, 343, 345, 346
great harmony (*tai he* 太和), 53, 61

H

harmonism (*hé qia lun* 和洽论), 35, 37, 38, 41, 44–46, 163, 172
harmonization without being patternized, 43, 44, 48, 60, 62–64
harmony (*hé* 和), 3, 4, 26, 32, 37–45, 52–59, 72, 118, 169, 171, 189, 196, 197, 203, 228, 231, 236, 245, 247, 270, 300, 317, 320, 333, 346, 362, 381, 384, 388, 391, 397, 402, 403, 421
harmony without uniformity (*he er bu tong* 和而不同), 48, 64
having knowledge (*you zhi* 有知), 99, 131
heaven (*tian* 天), 1, 2, 4–14, 20, 22, 23, 25, 26, 30–32, 36, 67, 70–72, 105, 117, 120–122, 125, 127, 136, 159, 167, 170, 171, 176–178, 189, 219, 237, 246, 247, 251, 270, 271, 367, 370, 398–400, 403, 410

Heaven and Earth (*tiandi* 天地), 2, 3, 6–8, 13, 31, 69, 70, 101, 176, 178, 247, 269, 382, 386, 398, 402

heaven-human oneness (*tian ren he yi* 天人合一), 1, 2, 4–9, 13, 14, 17–20, 23, 70, 72, 170, 175, 185, 204, 205, 207, 210, 211, 399, 400, 402, 403

heavenly citizen (*tianmin* 天民), 20

Heavenly Dao/Heavely Way (*tiandao* 天道), 171, 176, 187, 193, 399

heavenly principles (*tian li* 天理), 277, 278, 301

hexagram (*gua* 卦), 6, 7, 53, 85

"hidden education in an appealing form" (*yu jiao yu le* 寓教于乐), 341

historical consciousness (*lishi yishi* 历史意识), 184, 188, 313

historical ontology (*lishi bentilun* 历史本体论), 14–16, 18, 19, 184, 192–199, 201, 202, 206–209, 212, 213, 313, 412, 421, 422

history constitutes rationality (*lishi jian lixing* 历史建理性), 184, 192

holistic vision (*qiu tong* 求同), 255, 262, 264–266

human desires (*ren yu* 人欲), 16, 20, 23, 41, 243, 278, 335, 417

humaneness/benevolence/love (*ren* 仁), 4, 9, 10, 12, 16, 18, 21, 23, 26, 35–37, 44, 52, 53, 55, 59, 69, 76, 80, 103, 105, 106, 108–114, 125, 129, 131, 132, 139, 140, 169, 171, 187, 198, 206, 209, 218, 222, 226, 228, 232, 234, 237, 246, 280–282, 284, 290–293, 296, 297, 299–301, 331, 332, 344, 356, 363, 368, 385, 393

humanization of Nature (*ziran renhua* 自然人化), 14–18, 199, 211, 212, 421

human/man (*ren* 人), 1–10, 13–23, 29–33, 35–37, 41, 43–47, 50, 51, 53–56, 61, 62, 64–74, 76, 78, 80–83, 85–87, 93–97, 99, 100, 102, 104, 107, 109–112, 115, 117, 119–121, 125–127, 129, 131, 136–139, 144, 147, 150, 151, 153, 158–160, 164–166, 167, 168, 170, 171, 173, 175–178, 183–189, 191–215, 218, 220–223, 226, 228–230, 232–234, 236–238, 240, 242–250, 263–265, 268, 270, 271, 278, 279, 281, 282, 285, 286, 288, 290–292, 298–300, 307, 314, 315, 317–320, 323–328, 330–343, 349, 352, 354–357, 364, 374, 375, 377, 378, 381, 386, 387, 389, 390, 395, 397–403, 406–410, 412, 414, 416, 417, 419–422

human mind/heart-mind (*ren xin* 人心), 119, 140, 148, 150, 153, 178, 185, 278, 332, 333, 407, 420

human relations (*ren lun* 人伦), 4, 6, 14, 15, 33, 37, 45, 53–56, 61, 72–74, 78, 188, 189, 191, 198, 223, 228, 230, 234, 236, 244, 249, 250

humanus amore, 111, 114

I

identify oneself with the object contemplated (*chao ran wu biao* 超然物表), 312

illuminate the true with the beautiful (*yimei qizhen* 以美启真), 18

imagined vision out of an existent image (*xiang wai zhi xiang* 象外之象), 396
immanent (*neizai* 内在), 9, 152, 153, 156
inheriting and renovating (*yin ge* 因革), 266
inspiration and interest, 356, 357
inspire [through poetry](*xing* 兴), 222
interfusion between emotion and scene (*qing jing jiao rong* 情景交融), 402
internal nature (*nei zai zi ran* 内在自然), 14, 16, 18, 422
intuition (*zhijue* 直觉), 19, 53, 127, 136, 168, 169, 201, 204, 205, 208, 311, 420
investigation of things (*ge wu* 格物), 11, 12, 325

J

Jixia Literati Palace (Jixia Xuegong 稷下学宫), 108
joy-conscious culture (*legan wenhua* 乐感文化), 185, 186, 194, 195, 197, 198, 212

K

kalokagathia, 112
keeping the world in peace (*ping tianxia* 平天下), 11, 12
kingliness without (*wai wang* 外王), 12, 170
ko-an (公案), 142–144, 146, 148

L

light of reason (*yi ming* 以明), 90
looking for new voices in foreign cultures (*bie qiu xinsheng yu yibang* 别求新声于异邦), 306

Love (Eros), 113, 198, 209
love of beauty, 4, 105, 110, 113
loving people (*renmin* 仁民), 5, 20, 21, 23, 198, 317

M

makes use of the mind as a mirror (*yong xin ruo jing* 用心若镜), 150
Māra (*moluo* 摩罗), 367, 370–372
mean-directed harmonization (*zhong hé* 中和), 171
mind-heart excursion (*youxin* 游心), 107, 115, 116, 118, 119, 123, 126, 128–131
modeling on the classics (*zongjing* 宗经), 262, 264, 272
the moon reflected in all the rivers and lakes (*yue yin wan chuan* 月印万川), 278
moral wisdom, 113
music (*yue* 乐), 16, 19, 33, 37–39, 41, 42, 52–54, 57, 196, 197, 217, 218, 222, 227, 228, 233–251, 257, 262, 268, 279, 280, 285, 287–290, 294, 317, 320, 331, 332, 334, 341, 367, 376, 385, 391, 392, 406

N

naturalization of humankind (*ren ziranhua* 人自然化), 14
naturalness as beauty (*zi ran wei mei* 自然为美), 269, 271
natural spontaneity (*ziran er ran* 自然而然), 140, 145, 146, 150, 154, 160
New Culture Movement (*xin wen hua yun dong* 新文化运动), 163, 190, 309, 328, 361, 374
nirvana (*niepan* 涅槃), 148, 151, 158, 335, 339

no depraved thought (*si wu xie* 思无邪), 231, 294, 296–301
noetic agency, 114
nomophylaktic agency, 113

O

openness (*kaifang xing* 开放性), 184, 186, 190, 325, 412
opposites stand in opposition to what they do (dui bi fǎn qi wei 对必反其为), 40, 61
opposites within forms of things (*yǒu xiang si yǒu dui* 有象斯有对), 40
opposition leads to conflict (*yǒu fan si yǒu chou* 有反斯有仇), 40, 61
Overman (*chaoren* 超人), 168, 172, 179, 320, 343

P

panoramic viewing and observation (*yuanzhao* 圆照), 265
perceiving things from an egoist vision (*yi wo guan wu* 以我观物), 144
perfect happiness (*zhi le* 至乐), 88
the perfect man without self (*zhiren wuji* 至人无己), 95, 98
personal apprehension (*xin fa* 心法), 294
petty man (*xiao ren* 小人), 43–45, 54–56, 243
philikos agency, 111
philologos, 131, 132
philopraxis, 132
philosophical life, 131
poetic sensibility and picturesque significance (*shiqing huayi* 诗情画意), 392
poetic state par excellence (*jing jie* 境界), 307, 324, 349–352, 356, 358, 359, 392

poetry (*shi* 诗), 16, 19, 136, 217–235, 253–260, 262–264, 266–271, 274, 275, 277–299, 301, 310, 312, 317, 318, 334, 335, 344, 348, 352, 353, 355–357, 361, 365, 367, 369–371, 375–377, 379–381, 384, 385, 387, 389–392, 397, 408
poetry education (*shi jiao* 诗教), 218, 253, 277, 278, 297, 317, 335
political wisdom, 113
Power/Virtue (*De/Te* 德), 2, 4–9, 11, 16–18, 21, 26, 27, 29–37, 40, 41, 44, 48–50, 52, 53, 60–63, 68, 72, 74, 77, 87, 89, 93–97, 101, 109, 114, 115, 118, 119, 125, 127, 129–131, 137, 141, 142, 149, 151, 166, 167, 169, 170, 172, 175–178, 184, 185, 188, 192–194, 196–198, 201, 204–206, 208, 209, 211, 212, 214, 220, 223, 224, 239, 246, 247, 264, 265, 282, 283, 290, 295, 297, 305, 311, 318, 327, 342, 354, 356, 357, 361, 364–367, 371, 372, 374–376, 379–384, 387–391, 393–396, 398–402, 409, 410, 412, 415, 419, 420
practical aesthetics, 204, 205, 207–209, 313, 394, 405, 421, 423
practical philosophy, 199, 201, 313, 418
practical wisdom, 31, 51, 65, 72, 73, 78, 83, 139, 183
pragmatic reason (*shiyong lixing* 实用理性), 14, 38, 154, 183–195, 197–201, 204, 206, 207, 209, 211, 212, 313, 421
prajñā (*boruo* 般若), 136, 140, 160
prajñā pāramitā (*boruo boluomi* 般若波罗蜜), 136, 160

primordial Dao (*yuan dao*原道), 169
proper governance of the state (*zhi guo* 治国), 12
psychical agency, 138
psychology turns into substratum (*xinli cheng benti*心理成本体), 184, 194

Q

the *qian* hexagram (*qian gua*乾卦), 53
quasi-religiousness (*zhunzongjiao xing* 准宗教性), 184, 186, 190, 191

R

rectification of the mind (*zheng xin* 正心), 12
the refined (*gu-ya* 古雅), 307, 324, 345–348, 359
reflect [through poetry] (qun 观), 222
regulation of the family (*qi jia* 齐家), 12
rites *(li* 礼), 38–41, 52–54, 57, 154, 156, 160, 187, 217, 218, 220, 222, 229, 231, 233–236, 242, 247–250, 268, 281–283, 287–289, 293, 294, 299–301, 327, 334, 408

S

sage *(sheng ren*圣人), 3, 12, 39, 41, 54, 57, 67, 69, 72, 73, 88, 101, 102, 115–117, 146, 150, 159, 167, 170, 177, 224, 241, 266, 380
sageliness within *(nei sheng*內圣), 9, 12, 76, 155, 170
samadhi (定/三昧), 144, 146, 154, 156
scenes (*jing* 景), 16, 19, 136, 137, 158, 160, 350, 351, 354, 355, 357
sedimentation (*ji dian* 积淀), 17–19, 186, 199, 204, 205, 208, 212, 313, 405–407, 409, 411–414, 418, 419, 423, 424
self-awakening and self-liberating of his original nature (*zi xing zi du* 自性自渡), 156
serene contemplation (*jing guan* 静观), 120, 122, 126, 131, 136, 145, 300, 307, 324, 329, 353
significant form, 313, 314, 356, 409, 418, 419, 423
sincerity *(cheng* 诚), 7, 8, 12, 21, 23, 146, 176, 178, 229, 231, 260, 270, 296, 300, 320, 344, 356, 369, 382
sincerity of the thoughts (*cheng yi* 诚意), 12
sitting in self-forgetfulness (*zuowang* 坐忘), 129
Six arts/six classics (*liu yi* 六艺), 217, 254
somatic aesthetics, 112, 126
spirit/Geist (*jingshen* 精神), 31, 50, 52, 60, 82, 97, 98, 105, 109, 110, 113, 126, 128, 132, 169, 175–178, 189, 192, 204, 224, 225, 229, 231, 259, 261, 271, 299, 310, 312, 317, 318, 320, 325, 332, 341–343, 345, 351, 356–358, 363, 365, 367, 369, 373, 374, 377, 379, 380, 382–387, 391, 395, 397–403, 410
the spiritual man without achievement (*shenren wugong* 神人无功), 95, 98
state of self-detachment (*wu wo zhi jing* 无我之境), 352, 353
state of self-involvement (*you wo zhi jing* 有我之境), 352, 353
the sublime (*zhuangmei*壮美), 170, 307, 329, 346, 347, 353, 354, 384, 398, 416, 417
Subtle Light (*wei ming* 微明), 74

the Sudden School (*dunwu zong*顿悟宗), 136, 149, 152, 154, 157
sūnyatā/void/emptiness (*kong* 空), 61, 116, 120, 136, 151–153, 155, 157–160, 185
Supreme Ultimate (*Taiji* 太极), 75

T
take-no-action (*wu wei* 无为), 127
theoretical component, 51
theoretical wisdom, 114, 139
transcendent (*chaoyue* 超越), 9, 22, 46, 88, 137, 140, 150, 166–168, 186, 192, 398
transcultural pursuit (*kua wen hua tan suo* 跨文化探索), 163, 168
transformational creation (*zhuan huan xing chuang zao* 转换性创造), 42, 48, 58–61, 132, 180, 184, 190, 192, 199, 211, 212, 305, 320, 321, 394
"transformation of things" (*wu hua* 物化), 102–104, 401
treasuring things (*aiwu* 爱物), 5, 20, 21, 23, 198, 317
the true sage without name (*shengren wuming* 真人无名), 95, 98
true scenes and objects (*zhen jingwu* 真景物), 349, 356
truth (*zhen* 真), 9, 10, 66, 107, 108, 113, 114, 124, 125, 129, 139, 145, 157, 166–168, 170, 171, 173, 187, 191, 229, 274, 285, 286, 304, 310, 313, 318, 323, 325, 327, 330, 332, 333, 335, 338, 339, 342, 351, 356, 368, 371, 382, 383, 390, 410, 417, 420

U
Ultimate Void (*taixu* 太虚), 61, 185
uniformity without harmony (*tong er bu he* 同而不和), 40–42, 44, 48, 52, 55, 56, 58, 59, 63, 64
usefulness (*you yong xing* 有用性), 184, 186, 187, 191, 195, 200, 240, 242, 250, 340, 389
usefulness of the useless (*wu yong zhi yong* 无用之用), 340, 389

V
vital energy/material force (*qi* 气), 61, 62, 120–122, 128, 166, 210, 381

W
Way (*Dao/Tao*道), 2–10, 13, 29, 31, 36, 37, 44, 52, 55, 59–61, 64, 66, 70, 72, 76, 79–81, 86, 88, 90, 96–99, 104, 105, 115, 120, 122, 125, 127, 128, 131–133, 135, 137, 139–141, 145–147, 150, 151, 154, 160, 161, 166, 172, 175–178, 191, 192, 194, 197, 199, 206, 210, 211, 218–221, 223, 224, 228, 237, 238, 243–248, 255, 261, 263, 266, 269, 270, 281, 282, 291, 299, 300, 304, 306, 315, 321, 324, 334–336, 339, 340, 342, 365, 368, 369, 373, 378, 379, 386, 402, 408, 410, 413, 417, 423
Weltbild, 185, 213, 214
Western learning (*xi xue* 西学), 303, 324
worthy man (*xian ren* 贤人), 93

Y

the Yan*g (yang* 阳), 61, 295
the Yin (yin 阴), 61, 94, 295, 329, 362

Z

zazen/zen meditation *(zua zen* 坐禅), 140

zen/*dhyana (chan*禅), 135–137, 139–153, 155–161, 211, 353, 357, 371
zendo (chan tang 禅堂), 140

Lightning Source UK Ltd.
Milton Keynes UK
UKHW012017120219
337112UK00003B/169/P